The Illustrated Encyclopedia of Active New Religions, Sects, and Cults

Benjamin Beit-Hallahmi

The Rosen Publishing Group, Inc.
New York

Published in 1993, 1998 by The Rosen Publishing Group, Inc.
29 East 21st Street, New York, NY 10010

Revised Edition, 1998

Manufactured in the United States of America

Library of Congress Cataloging-in-Publication Data

Beit-Hallahmi, Benjamin
The illustrated encyclopedia of active new religions, sects, and
cults / Benjamin Beit-Hallahmi
   p.   cm.
   Includes bibliographical references and index
   ISBN 0-8239-2586-2
   1. Religions—Encyclopedias   1. Title
BL80.2.B385   1993
291.9'03-dc20   93-18928
                       CIP

Photographs courtesy: The Bettmann Archive, Inc., The Associated Press, United Press
International, Reuters News Service, and Impact Visuals (Bill Biggart)
Photo research by Vera Ahmadzadeh.

ABOUT THE AUTHOR

BENJAMIN BEIT-HALLAHMI received a Ph.D. in clinical psychology from Michigan State University in 1970. Since then he has held full-time appointments at the University of Michigan and the University of Haifa and visiting appointments at the Hebrew University, Tel-Aviv University, the Israel Institute of Technology, the University of Pennsylvania, Michigan State University, Central Michigan University, Vassar College, Columbia University, New York University, King's College London, and the Centre National de la Recherche Scientifique in Paris.

Beit-Hallahmi is the author of *Psychoanalysis and Religion*: *A Bibliography* (1978), *Prolegomena to the Psychological Study of Religion* (1989), *Despair and Deliverance*: *Private Salvation in Contemporary Israel* (1992), and *The Psychoanalytic Study of Religion*: *Critical Assessment and Annotated Bibliography* (1996). He is the coauthor of *The Social Psychology of Religion* (with Michael Argyle, 1975), *Twenty Years Later*: *Kibbutz Children Grown Up* (with A. I. Rabin, 1982), *The Kibbutz Bibliography* (with S. Shur, J. R. Blasi & A. I. Rabin, 1981), and *Belief, Experience, and Behaviour: The Psychology of Religiosity* (with Michael Argyle, 1996). He edited *Research in Religious Behavior* (1973) and coedited *Tradition, Conflict, and Continuity*: *Judaism in Israel* (1992) and *Religion, Coping, and Pathology* (1996). His publications also include seventy-five articles and book chapters. In addition to his publications in psychology, Beit-Hallahmi has written widely about political affairs, including his books *The Israeli Connection* (1987) and *Original Sins* (1992, 1993).

ACKNOWLEDGMENTS

Several organizations, and many individuals, have made this work possible. I would like to mention the help and facilities provided by the University of Haifa library, the Elmer Holmes Bobst Library at New York University, the New York Public Library and the Columbia University libraries, the University of Haifa Research Authority, CETSAP–CNRS (Paris), King's College Centre for New Religious Movements, King's College Embankment Library, INFORM (London), the Bahai Office of Public Information, Bahai National Center, the First Church of Christ, Scientist, and the Liberal Studies Program at New York University.

Among the individuals whose help was vital, I would like to mention Shlomo Abramovitch, Hanni Amit-Kochavi, Jim Andrea, Yigal Arens, Robert Balch, Eileen Barker, Avner Ben-Ner, Yoram Bilu, Alan Black, Lisa Cohen, Simon N. Coleman, Thadeusz Doktor, Ronald Enroth, Daniele Friedlander, Daniel Friedmann, Maxine Gold, Yvonne Haddad, Michael Hill, Edna H. Hunt, Bill Johnston, Judy Klein, Rachael L. E. Kohn, Elizabeth S. Landis, Nicole Lapierre, Yolanda Lazo, Burton Levine, Efrat Levy, Shqipe Malushi, Jean-François Mayer, Susan J. Palmer, Leonard Prager, Ronald B. Precht, Roger Rosen, Roy A. Rosenberg, John A. Saliba, Ulysses Santamaria, Joanna Savory, Richard Schuster, Israel Shahak, Nira Shamir, Michal Sherbak, Stanley Stark, Shanee Stepakoff, Robert H. Stockman, James D. Tabor, Madeleine Tress, Michael Valenti, Anthony van Fossen, Cynthia L. Ward, M. Victor Westberg, and Leonard Zeskind.

Errors, ambiguities, redundancies, and omissions are unavoidable accompaniments of any attempt to gather such an enormous quantity of facts and names, many of which are controversial, and few beyond dispute. I alone am responsible for all errors and omissions, and will appreciate corrections.

HOW TO USE THIS ENCYCLOPEDIA

The listings in this Encyclopedia include:

Group names, with information about them; *e.g.*, JEHOVAH'S WITNESSES;

Major ideas or concepts, often related to numerous movements; *e.g.*, FUNDA-MENTALISM;

Cross references to related entries appear within the text rendered in small caps or right after the entry as *see* references.

In addition, there are four indices in the back of this volume that will allow you to find religious groups classified by alternative and former names, geographical locations, important figures, and common attributes.

Please note that unattributed quotations that appear in the entries originate from the actual publications of the group in question: pamphlets, posters, and advertisements of all kinds. Bibliographic sources listed in entries include only books based on scholarly research, not publications representing the group itself.

INTRODUCTION

This book is designed to provide basic information about modern religious movements and to be accessible to a wide variety of users, from students at all levels, to media professionals and scholars.

In writing the entries (more than 1,800 in number) in this Encyclopedia, we have tried to be both concise and accurate. The numerous photographs serve to remind us that we are not dealing with abstract "movements," but with human faces, endeavors, imagination, and emotions.

To be included in the book, a group has to espouse a religious belief system; that is, belief in an invisible, supernatural world inhabited by a deity or deities, the souls of the dead and the unborn, and sometimes other entities (angels, devils). That is the minimal basis for inclusion.

To be classified as a new religious movement, a group has to demonstrate novelty in both organization and beliefs. The listed groups demonstrate some organizational and doctrinal discontinuity with their environment; there is a clear intention, demonstrated in action, to start a new body based on a new set of beliefs. There must be, and there always is, a clear distinction from established religious groups in terms of a new leadership and new claims to divine truth. Most of the groups listed are currently active and likely to be encountered, if not directly then through media reports or published references. Some defunct groups have been included when their activities have played an important role in recent history or when they provide contextual information for active groups.

To be classified as "modern," a group must have started its existence over the last 200 years. The entries include groups that one is most likely to encounter in academic literature and the media when modern religious movements are discussed. Some of the groups are clearly small and eccentric; our reason for giving them attention is that most groups start this way, and there is no way of predicting which will succeed and grow.

The information about the groups covered in this Encyclopedia has been gathered by first relying on scholarly literature, from specialized research monographs to standard reference works. In addition, writings produced by the groups themselves were consulted, and such writings are often cited to present most faithfully their beliefs. Media reports were followed in some cases, although these are less reliable than scholarly sources. Last but not least, direct contact with numerous groups and their members has been a constant source of knowledge. We are grateful to countless members of new religious movements, and to the official group leadership in many cases, for their readiness to offer information and insights.

A

Aaronic Order

Also known as the Levites, or the Utah Levites, this U.S. dissident MORMON group was founded in the 1930s in Utah by Maurice Lerrie Glendenning, who became a Mormon in 1929 but was excommunicated a few years later for publishing dissident ideas. The group attempts to revive Mormon communalism. Group scriptures include traditional Mormon publications, together with the writings of its founder. The organization is based in Salt Lake City, Utah.

Source:
Baer, H. A. *Recreating Utopia in the Desert: A Sectarian Challenge to Modern Mormonism.* Albany: SUNY Press, 1988.

Abilitism

Known also as the Institute of Ability and as the Santana Dharma Foundation, this U.S. group is an offshoot of SCIENTOLOGY founded by H. Charles Berner (1929–) in California in 1965. Its doctrine combines Scientology with Hindu concepts. Meditation, *tai chi*, vegetarianism, and physical exercises are used. Headquarters are in Lucerne Valley, California.

Abode of the Message, The

Also known as the Abode community, this U.S. Sufi Order commune is made up of nuclear families. It was founded by Pir Vilayat Inayat Khan in 1975 in an old SHAKER village in New Lebanon, New York. It operates AEgis, a school for "Spirituality in Our Time," and the "Alchemical Retreat Process," developed by its founder. [*See also* SUFI ORDER IN THE WEST.]

Abyssinian Methodist Holy Church of Christ

South African independent ETHIOPIAN church, started in the 1920s.

Acts of Apostles Christ Church, Nigeria

African indigenous PENTECOSTAL group, founded in 1957 in Lagos by former members of the Roman Catholic Church.

Actualism

NEW THOUGHT healing group founded in 1960 in Los Angeles, California, by Russell Paul Schofield, whose declared goal is "to enlighten awareness to the interdependence and interaction of body, mind, identity, and spirit. This results in a continuously renewing force which brings about the transformation of the personality to the point of wholeness." The group offers "life-energy" and "abundance" courses. It claims that its meditation technique is "related to AGNI YOGA (an Eastern discipline based on spiritual alchemy)."

Advanced Ability Center (AAC)

Also known as the Church of the New Civilization, this is an international SCIENTOLOGY splinter group based in California. It was formed in the early 1980s by David Mayo, a former

Scientology leader. The group was sued by Scientology for using the latter's ideas. The case was won by the AAC after a legal struggle. Branches have operated in Europe. [*See also* ABILITISM; *and* DUGA (ABILITY).]

Advent Christian Church

U.S. ADVENTIST group created following the Great Disappointment of 1844. William Miller, founder of the Second Adventists, predicted that the Second Coming of Jesus Christ would occur by 1844. Failure of the Apocalypse to happen was termed the Great Disappointment. Various groups tried to maintain and revise Millerite predictions about the impending Second Coming. One group believed that Miller was mistaken in his calculations by ten years and thus the Second Coming would occur in 1854. In 1855 the Advent Christian Church was formed in Worcester, Massachusetts, by a group under the leadership of Jonathan Cummins. Members still follow the Millerite notion of an imminent Coming. They do not believe in the immortality of the soul but in a conditional immortality dependent on individual salvation. The wicked do not enjoy immortality and would not share in the final resurrection of the dead. [*See also* CHURCH OF GOD (ABRAHAMIC FAITH); PRIMITIVE ADVENT CHRISTIAN CHURCH; *and* ADVENTISTS, SECOND.]

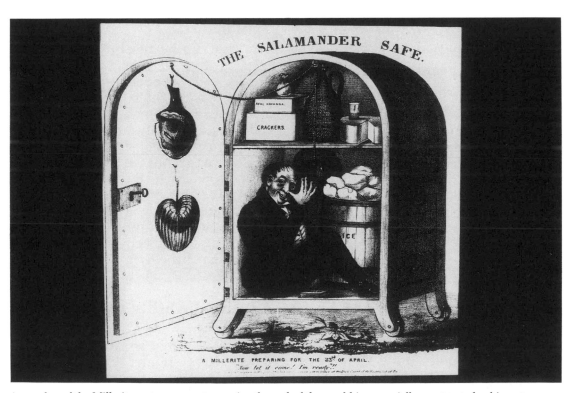

A member of the Millerite sect prepares to survive the end of the world in a specially constructed refrigerator.

Adventists

Sometimes known as Second Adventists, these are Christian groups that proclaim the imminent Second Coming of Jesus Christ. Examples are the SEVENTH-DAY ADVENTISTS CHURCH and JEHOVAH'S WITNESSES. [*See also* ADVENTISTS, SECOND.]

Adventists, Second

U.S. 19th-century movement started by William Miller (1781–1849). Miller announced that the Second Coming of Jesus Christ would occur in 1831; the Second Coming was then expected to happen between March 21, 1843, and March 21, 1844. Miller based his calculations on a literal reading of apocalyptic Bible passages. He started with Daniel, 8:14: "Unto two thousand and three hundred days; then shall the sanctuary be cleansed." He found the exact meaning of this number in Ezekiel 4:6: "I have appointed thee each day for a year." The starting point for this period of 2,300 years was determined, with the help of Ezra 7:12–26 and Daniel 9:22–27, to be 457 BCE. With a few more calculations, he fixed 1843–1844 as the year of the Second Advent.

When the end did not come, Miller admitted his error in May 1844. One of his followers, Samuel S. Snow, did not give up and announced that the date was set for October 22, 1844. This date is now known as the "Great Disappointment."

The Millerite version of the movement died out when the prophecy failed to materialize, but at least one hundred religious movements in the United States can be traced back to the Great Disappointment. Some Adventists still kept hoping and reformulating their prophecies. In 1858 the American Millenial Association was organized, and a few years later the name Evangelical Adventists was chosen. The Great Disappointment led eventually to the formation of several well-known religious movements, such as the SEVENTH-DAY ADVENTIST CHURCH and JEHOVAH'S WITNESSES.

Sources:

Cohen, D. *Waiting for the Apocalypse*. Buffalo: Prometheus Books, 1983.

Cross, W. *The Burned-Over District*. New York: Harper & Row, 1965.

Gaustad, E. S. *The Rise of Adventism*. New York: Harper & Row, 1974.

Harrison, J. F. C. *The Second Coming, Popular Millenarianism 1780–1850*. London: Routledge & Kegan Paul, 1979.

Numbers, R. L., and Butler, J. M., eds. *The Disappointed: Millerism and Millenarianism in the Nineteenth Century*. Knoxville: University of Tennessee Press, 1993.

Advent Sabbath Church

African American, ADVENTIST, Sabbath-keeping congregation founded in 1941 in New York City by Thomas I. C. Hughes, a former SEVENTH-DAY ADVENTIST. In 1956 it joined with other groups to form THE UNIFICATION ASSOCIATION OF CHRISTIAN SABBATH KEEPERS.

Aetherius Society

International UFO-Christian group founded in 1954 in England by George King (1919–), known to followers as His Eminence Sir George King. King is a second-generation spiritual medium and

George A. Stallings sings as he celebrates mass at the African American Catholic Congregation, a breakaway Roman Catholic group in Washington, D.C.

occultist. In March 1954, King reported hearing a voice saying, "Prepare yourself. You are to become the voice of the Interplanetary Parliament." King stated that he was to be the "primary terrestrial channel" for the Interplanetary Parliament, which, he was also told, meets on Saturn. Later he claimed to have been contacted by "Master Aetherius" from the planet Venus and to have received messages from Aetherius, as well as from "Master Jesus." Jesus Christ is reported to be alive and well and living on Venus or Mars. Group members claim to communicate with Space Masters, who give help, advice, and love to the faithful. The solar system is believed to be fully inhabited (except for Mercury). Visits by spaceships and movements of cosmic energies are reported and celebrated. Group branches, and a College of Spiritual Science, have operated in Great Britain and the United States.

Source:
Evans, C. *Cults of Unreason*. London: Harrap, 1973.

Africa Church

South African separatist church founded in 1889 by Khanyane Napo, former Anglican evangelist.

Africa Gospel Unity Church (AGUC)

African independent HOLINESS church, founded in Kenya in 1964.

African American Catholic Congregation

Originally known as the Imani Temple, and sometimes as the Afro-American Imani Temple (*Imani* means "faith" in Swahili), this is a breakaway Roman Catholic group. It was founded in July 1989 in Washington, D.C., by George Augustus Stallings Jr., a former Roman Catholic priest who was excommunicated in 1990. In the same year Stallings was ordained by Archbishop Richard Bridges of the INDEPENDENT OLD CATHOLIC CHURCH. The group seeks to express African-American cultural traditions through doctrines and practices. It rejects Roman Catholic doctrine on abortion, remarriage following divorce, and the ordination of women or married men. In September 1991, the group ordained a woman, Rose Vernell, as its first female priest. Since founding the Temple, Stallings has been accused of sexual and financial offenses.

African Apostolic Catholic Church in Zion

South African independent ZIONIST church founded in the 1920s.

African Apostolic Church of Johane Maranke (AACJM)

Known sometimes as African Apostles, the Apostolic Church of Johane Maranke, the Church of John Maranke, and also as VaPostori, this syncretistic, nativist African movement was started in 1932 in Southern Rhodesia (now Zimbabwe) by Muchabaya Momberume, later known by his religious name of Johane Maranke (1912–1963). It then spread to Zambia. The group's doctrine is based on the founder's revelations, received after a period of illness, seclusion, and symbolic "death." After becoming a "prophet of God," he had visions that included messages connecting the Bible to African traditions. Members are supposed to avoid both Western medicine and traditional healing methods, and to rely solely on faith healing. They take part in public ceremonies for the confession of sins, followed by the judgment of the group's prophets. These ceremonies include trances, glossolalia (speaking in tongues), and visions. Physical illness is considered to be the result of witchcraft, and deviant, sinful behavior is sometimes judged to be the result of spirit possession, which is treated by exorcism. The membership is divided into four ranks (pastors, healers, evangelists, and prophets), each of which has three internal grades. Both males and females can be priests and healers but only men may be evangelists and prophets. In recent years, the movement has had its strongest followings in Zaire, Zambia, and Zimbabwe.

Source:
Jules-Rosette, B. *African Apostles: Ritual and Conversion in the Church of John Maranke.* Ithaca: Cornell University Press, 1975.

African Apostolic Church St. Simon and St. Johane

African indigenous Christian PENTECOSTAL church founded in Zimbabwe in 1963 in a schism from the AFRICAN APOSTOLIC CHURCH OF JOHANE MARANKE (AACJM), following the death of Johane Maranke.

African Assemblies of God (Back to God)

African indigenous Christian PENTECOSTAL church founded in South Africa in 1959 by Nicholas Bhengu in a schism from the local branch of the U.S.-based ASSEMBLIES OF GOD.

African Brotherhood Church (ABC)

African nativist, independent Protestant church in Kenya, started in 1945.

African Church Mission

Nativist, independent Protestant church in Kenya started in 1941 in secession from the NOMIYA LUO CHURCH. It allows members to practice polygyny, which is strongly opposed by other Christian churches.

African Church of the Holy Spirit

Kenyan nativist, independent Protestant church started in the 1920s. It joined the World Council of Churches in the 1970s.

African Congregational Church

South African independent church founded by Gardiner Mvuyana in 1917 and officially recognized by the government in 1937.

African Divine Church

African independent Protestant PENTECOSTAL church in Kenya, started in 1949.

African Faith Healing Mission

South African separatist ETHIOPIAN church that seceded from the AFRICAN NATIVE MISSION CHURCH in 1919.

African Free Presbyterian Church of South Africa

South African independent nativist church created by a secession from the Presbyterian Church.

African Gospel Church

South African indigenous independent church, founded near Durban in 1942 in dissent from the white-led Full Gospel Church of God (South Africa) by Job Chiliza (1886–1963). The founder came from a family whose members were affiliated with the American Board Mission. In 1922 he was "baptized by the Holy Spirit." In 1949 the group was recognized by the South African government.

African Greek Orthodox Church

East African syncretistic movement, founded in the 1930s by Reuben Spartas, which has been influenced by the ZIONISTS movements in South Africa. It emphasizes faith healing, speaking in tongues, and traditional African purification rites, as well as the central role of its founder-prophet.

African Holy Zionist Church

Kenyan indigenous independent church founded in 1949.

African Independent Church of Kenya

Nativist, independent Protestant church in Kenya started in 1943 among the Kamba, in secession from the Anglican mission organization.

African Independent Pentecostal Church (AIPC)

Nativist, independent Protestant PENTECOSTAL church in Kenya, started in 1925 among the Kikuyu. Its members suffered persecution by British colonial authorities between 1930 and 1957.

African Israel Church Nineveh (AICN)

Nativist, independent PENTECOSTAL church in central Kenya, started in 1942. Members dress in white robes for their charismatic mass services and follow strict rules about sexuality. Group's headquarters are located in the holy city of Nineveh. The church joined the World Council of Churches in the 1970s. A branch operated in Uganda until it was banned by authorities in 1977.

African Methodist Episcopal Church

South African indigenous separatist group that grew out of the AFRICAN METHODIST EPISCOPAL CHURCH (AME) mission in South Africa. It was founded in 1904 in Makosini.

Source:
Sundkler, B. G. M. *Bantu Prophets in South Africa.* London: Oxford University Press, 1961.

African Methodist Episcopal Church (AME)

African American Christian church, founded in 1816 in Philadelphia by Richard Allen (1760–1831), who in 1787 left the Methodist Church because of its racial segregation policy. In 1801 Allen published the first collection of African American spirituals. The AME started mission work in Liberia in 1820 and then established missions in west and southern Africa. It has had much influence on the development of independent native churches in Africa, especially in South Africa.

African Methodist Episcopal Zion Church (American Zion Church)

African American Christian group, incorporated in New York City in 1800.

African Mission of Holy Ghost Church (AMHGC)

African independent Christian PENTECOSTAL church, formed among the Kikuyu of Kenya in 1930 out of the Watu wa Mungu (People of God) movement. It forms part of the WAKORINO group of churches.

African Native Mission Church

South African separatist ETHIOPIAN church, founded in the Transkei by Nehemiah Tile in 1884 as the Tembu Church ("Thembu Church"), or National Tembu Church. Ngangelizwe, the chief of the Tembu people, was its official head, but his appointed successor, Jonas Goduka, withdrew support. After Tile died in 1892, Goduka reorganized the church and gave it its current name. [*See also* ETHIOPIAN CATHOLIC CHURCH OF SOUTH AFRICA.]

Source:
Sundkler, B. G. M. *Bantu Prophets in South Africa*. London: Oxford University Press, 1961.

African Orthodox Church

U.S. Eastern Orthodox church with an African American membership. It was founded in 1921 by George Alexander McGuire (1866–1934), who first founded the Independent Episcopal Church to serve African Americans and then left the Episcopal fold when thwarted in his aspirations for promotion.

African Orthodox Church (AOC)

African independent Christian church based in Kenya, founded in the 1920s among the Kikuyu. In 1946 it was accepted into communion by the Greek Orthodox patriarch of Alexandria, Egypt.

African Orthodox Church (AOC)

South African independent Christian church, started in the 1920s and based in Alexandra, near Johannesburg. It is connected with the group of the same name in Kenya.

African Presbyterian Church

South African independent indigenous church, founded in 1898 by A. P. J. Mzimba, who seceded from the United Free Church of Scotland. Membership has been mainly of the Fingo people.

African Reform Coptic Church of God in Christ, the First Fruit of Prayer, God's Army Camp

RASTAFARIAN group founded by Claudius Henry in the 1950s in Jamaica.

Marcus Garvey in 1922. He led the back-to-Africa movement in the early 20th century, which influenced the Afro-Athlican Constructive Gaathly.

In December 1959 Henry urged his followers to sell their possessions and prepare for a move to Ethiopia. In 1960 the group was arming itself for violent action and was involved in several lethal incidents. Most of the group leaders were imprisoned.

African Seventh-Day Adventists

South African independent Adventist church, formed by secession from the official SEVENTH-DAY ADVENTIST CHURCH.

African Universal Church

African American PENTECOSTAL group founded in 1927 in Jacksonville, Florida, by Clarence C. Addison. It was inspired by Abibipim, a nativist African movement started in the early twentieth century in Ghana. The group advocated black nationalism and a black nation in Africa and opposed integration. It has also operated a commercial insurance company.

Afro-Athlican Constructive Gaathly

South African independent indigenous ETHIOPIAN church, founded in the 1930s in Kimberley. It has a strong African nationalist ideology, influenced by Ethiopian myth and by the back-to-Africa movement led by Marcus Garvey in the early twentieth century.

Source:
Sundkler, B. G. M. *Bantu Prophets in South Africa.* London: Oxford University Press, 1961.

Agama Islam Desjati ("True Islamic Religion")

Indonesian Islamic syncretistic movement, started in 1950, with a strong anti-Arab emphasis.

Agama Jawa

Syncretistic Indonesian belief system containing elements of Islamic, Hindu, Buddhist, and traditional Javanese beliefs, characteristic of the populations on the island of Jawa (Java).

Agama Jawa-Sunda

Syncretistic Indonesian belief system containing elements of Hindu, Buddhist, and traditional Javanese beliefs, characteristic of the Sundanese in West Jawa (Java).

Agape Center of Religious Science

U.S. NEW THOUGHT group founded by Michael Beckwith in 1987 and based in Los Angeles, California. It focuses on the practice of daily meditation. [*See also* RELIGIOUS SCIENCE INTERNATIONAL; *and* UNITED CHURCH OF RELIGIOUS SCIENCE.]

Agasha Temple of Wisdom

U.S. spiritualist group founded in the 1930s by Richard Zenor (1911–1978). Zenor is thought to be the medium of Agasha, an ancient Egyptian master. After the founder's death, the work continued through new mediums and different ancient masters.

Agni Yoga Society

International Theosophical group started in the 1920s by Nicholas Roerich (1874–1947). The founder, a painter from Eastern European origins, published messages received from Master Morya, one of the Ascended Masters discussed by Helena Petrovna Blavatsky, founder of THEOSOPHY. This group later inspired the WELT-SPIRALE movement in Europe. Followers practice yoga and meditation. In 1993 one of its leaders was sued for sexually exploiting women followers.

Agon Kyo

Japanese religion started in the 1980s.

Ahimsa Community

Hindu-inspired commune founded in 1965 in Parsons, Kansas.

Ahmadiyya Anjuman Isha'at Islam Lahore (AAIIL) (Ahmadiyya Society for the Propagation of Islam)

International heterodox Muslim sect that formed within the AHMADIYYA MOVEMENT in 1914 after a schism that followed the death of the founder. The dispute arose because of differing beliefs about the true nature of the Ahmadiyya Movement's founder. The majority views him as a true prophet, while the Ahmadiyya Anjuman Isha'at Islam Lahore regards him as a "fourteenth-century reformer." The group "seeks to revive the original liberal, tolerant and rational spirit of Islam. It presents Islam as a great spiritual force for bringing about the moral reform of mankind, and shows that this religion has never advocated coercion, the use of physical force or the pursuit of political power, in its support." World headquarters of this group are in Lahore, Pakistan, with branches in other countries.

Members of this sect have been subject to persecution in Pakistan. By Pakistani law, they are forbidden to call themselves Muslims or practice their faith. Amnesty International reported in May 1994 that two Ahmadis were killed and thirteen seriously wounded in attacks by armed Islamist groups in Lahore.

Ahmadiyya Movement

Popularly known as Ahmadis, Quadianis, or Mirzais, and officially known as the Ahmadiyyat Movement in Islam, this schismatic Islamic Shia movement was founded by Ghulam Ahmad (1835–1908) of Qadian in Punjab, India. Known as el-Qadiani, in 1889 he said he had received a divine revelation and later claimed to be the Messiah expected by various traditions, including, among others, the Mahdi of Islam, Jesus of Christianity, and an avatar of Krishna, as well as the fulfillment of Zoroastrian and Buddhist traditions. Such claims naturally led to negative, sometimes violent, reactions on the part of orthodox Muslims. When Ahmad died in 1908, a disciple was chosen as the *khalifa*, and when that *khalifa* died in 1914, a split ensued, with the majority of believers following the founder's son, Mirza Bashir-ud-Din Mahmud Ahmad. The group's center is in Rabwah, Pakistan, and it has engaged in missionary activities in Africa, Asia, and America. It has spread to many parts of the world, with branches in the United States, West Africa (Nigeria, Liberia, Ghana, and Sierra Leone), East Africa (Kenya, Uganda, and Tanzania), Europe, and Israel, in addition to Pakistan and India.

This group presents itself as the "Renaissance of Islam," and its doctrine is a sectarian version of Sunni Islam, claiming that divine revelation was not ended with Muhammad and the Quran, and that Ghulam Ahmad was either a prophet or a major reformer. The group's doctrine is sometimes considered a reconciliation of Christianity and Islam. Christian ideas are influential, and the myth of Jesus Christ plays a role. According to Ahmadiyya doctrine, Jesus prophesied the coming of the movement. He did not die on the cross, but was taken alive to India and preached in Kashmir until he died at age 120. Otherwise, Islamic doctrine is followed with few changes (tobacco is banned). Ahmadis believe, according to their founder's prophecies, that a major apocalypse will soon take place on earth, and only they will survive. There is an emphasis on pacifism, but aggressiveness in missionary work is advocated. The movement is led by a *khalifa*, usually a descendant of the prophet. A minority of the membership formed the AHMADIYYA ANJUMAN ISHA'AT ISLAM LAHORE.

Members of the Ahmadiyya have been subject to persecution in Pakistan. In 1984 it became an offense, under Pakistani law, for Ahmadis to call themselves Muslims and to do anything "to injure the feelings of a Moslem." Such offenses are punishable by up to thirteen years in prison. In 1994, 2,432 Ahmadis were charged with such offenses in Pakistan.

Sources:
Fisher, H. J. *Ahmadiyyah: A Study of Islam on the West Africa Coast.* London: Oxford University Press, 1963.

Friedmann, Y. *Prophecy Continues: Aspects of Ahmadi Religious Thought and Its Medieval Background.* Berkeley: University of California Press, 1988.

Ai Zion Elected Church, The

South African independent ZIONIST church founded in the 1920s.

Akhanananda Saraswati, Swami

Hindu leader and holy man, born July 25, 1911, to a Brahmin family in Northern India as Shantanu Behari. His ashram in Vrindaban has attracted both Indian and foreign followers since the 1940s. Several founders of new religious groups have claimed him as a teacher.

Aladura

Nativist Christian PENTECOSTAL movement in Nigeria that developed into a large number of churches. It was started in 1918 by Josiah O. Oshitelu, then expanded in the 1930s under Joseph Babalola.

Aladura in Yoruba means "prayer people," and the movement gained this name because of its emphasis on prayer and faith healing. It advocates a modest lifestyle and responsible work habits. Smoking and drinking alcohol are forbidden. The doctrine is syncretistic, with Christian practices and ideas of salvation combined with African traditions. Thus, polygyny in marriage is the rule, and traditional divination methods and amulets are used.

The movement operates schools, factories, food stores, health centers, and other essential services. The Nigeria Association of Aladura Churches had fifty-five member groups in 1982, and the movement has spread all over West Africa and to Great Britain. [*See also* CE-LESTIAL CHURCH OF CHRIST; CHERUBIM AND SERAPHIM (ETERNAL SACRED ORDER OF); CHRIST APOSTOLIC CHURCH; CHURCH OF THE LORD (ALADURA); *and* TWER NYAME CHURCH.]

Sources:

Peel, J. D. Y. *Aladura: A Religious Movement among the Yoruba.* London: Oxford University Press, 1968.

Turner, H. W. *History of an Independent African Church.* Oxford: Clarendon Press, 1967.

Aladura International Church

British branch of the ALADURA nativist African PENTECOSTAL movement, started in London in 1970. [*See also* CELESTIAL CHURCH OF CHRIST; CHERUBIM AND SERAPHIM (ETERNAL SACRED ORDER OF); CHRIST APOSTOLIC CHURCH; *and* CHURCH OF THE LORD (ALADURA).]

Alamo Christian Foundation

Sometimes known as the Holy Alamo Christian Churches, Consecrated, the Alamo Christian Church, the Tony and Susan Alamo Foundation, or the Alamo Foundation/Music Square Church, this is a U.S. conservative Christian group, part of the JESUS MOVEMENT of the late 1960s–early 1970s. The group was started in the late 1960s by Tony and Susan Alamo. Susan Alamo, who was born in the late 1920s in Arkansas as Edith Opal Horn, came from a Christian background. Tony Alamo, who was born Bernard Lazar Hoffman in Missouri, was

Tony Alamo leaves Federal Court in Florida after his arrest on charges of child abuse.

nominally Jewish. They met in a bible class that Susan was teaching. The two went to Southern California in search of success in the entertainment industry. Both converted to evangelical Christianity in the early 1960s.

The group is Christian fundamentalist and anti-Communist; it takes an active anti-abortion stand. Group members often live together, and most of them are employed by the Foundation, which operates several businesses.

In 1969 the Alamos incorporated their group, known officially as the Christian Foundation, in Los Angeles, California. Then in 1970 the group moved to Saugus, California. Its headquarters were moved to Dyer, Arkansas. Susan

Alamo died in 1982. The group was sued by the U.S. government for not paying wages to worker members, and in 1983 the Foundation was ordered by the U.S. government to pay minimum wages to its member employees. In 1985 this order was upheld by the U.S. Supreme Court.

In 1986 the Alamo Christian Foundation was reorganized as the Alamo Christian Church, headed by Tony Alamo, and based in Alma, Arkansas. Alamo is also the president of the American Association of Non-Denominational Christian Schools. He has presented himself as an "Israelite" and a Hebrew Christian, and he preaches vehemently against Catholics. The group has operated several successful corporations. In the late 1980s, it was involved in serious legal troubles, and Tony Alamo was a fugitive wanted by the FBI. The group still has an active membership. [*See also* JESUS MOVEMENT.]

Alaph Catolico Filipino

Philippine indigenous Christian church founded in secession from the Roman Catholic Church in Sagay in the 1950s.

Al-Arqam

Officially known as Dar Al-Arqam, this international messianic Muslim group of Sufi origin was started in 1968 by Ashaari Muhammad (1937–). The founder, who claims prophetic visions and revelations, is considered the messiah. Members live in communes, and the group operates schools and businesses, enjoying great economic success. It has gained visibility in South Asia since the 1980s.

The group is considered subversive by several governments. Al-Arqam was declared illegal by the Malaysian government in August 1994. Anyone wearing its symbols or badges was subject to arrest. Later it was banned in Indonesia and Brunei. Its leader was expelled from Thailand and arrested in September 1994.

Aleph: Alliance for Jewish Renewal

Known until 1984 as P'nai Or Religious Fellowship, and originally known as B'nai Or, this U.S. Jewish group was started in the 1960s in Philadelphia by Zalman Schachter-Shalomi. Its doctrine combines Jewish beliefs and practices with Hindu-style meditation, pacifism, and social concerns. The name B'nai Or, which means "Sons of Light," was dropped because of its gender bias. Aleph was created in 1994 through the merger of P'nai or Religious Fellowship with the SHALOM CENTER, headed by Arthur Waskow. Group branches have operated in the United States and Europe.

Aletheia Psycho-Physical Foundation

U.S. occultist group founded in 1969 in California by Jack Schwartz. Practices include meditation, diagnosing the human "aura," Tarot reading, and *I Ching* readings. The group is based in Grant's Pass, Oregon.

All Faiths Church/Science of Mind

U.S. NEW THOUGHT group based in El Monte, California, founded by David Thompson in the 1950s.

Alpha and Omega Christian Church

U.S. PENTECOSTAL group based in Hawaii, founded in 1962 by Alezandro B. Faquaragon. Membership is drawn from the Filipino community, with connection to similar groups in the Philippines.

Alpha and Omega Pentecostal Church of God of America, Inc.

African American PENTECOSTAL group, initially known as the Alpha and Omega Church of God Tabernacles. Based in Baltimore, it was founded in 1944 by Magdalen Mabel Phillips, who withdrew from the UNITED HOLY CHURCH OF AMERICA. A schism in the Alpha and Omega Pentecostal Church of God of America, Inc. in 1964 created the TRUE FELLOWSHIP PENTECOSTAL CHURCH OF GOD OF AMERICA.

Amana Church Society

Sometimes known as Amana (Faithfulness) Church Society, or the Church of True Inspiration, this is a U.S. Protestant group originally founded in Germany in 1714 as the Community of True Inspiration. A large section of the membership moved to the United States in 1842 and settled near Buffalo, New York, organized as the Ebenezer Society. The settlements were communes in which all property was held collectively. In 1854 the Society started moving to eastern Iowa, where the villages of Amana, East Amana, South Amana, Middle Amana, High Amana, West Amana, and Homestead were founded between 1854 and 1861. Here again, the settlements were completely communal, and life was tightly controlled by the *brudderrath*, the Council of Elders. Mandatory church services were held eleven times per week, and contact with outsiders was limited. The Amana Church Society was reorganized in 1932 as a cooperative corporation, producing well-known electrical appliances, furniture, beer, and wine under the Amana name. The group doctrine is pietistic, with members admitted at age fifteen and no ordained ministry.

Source:
Barthel, D. L. *Amana, From Pietist Sect to American Community*. Lincoln: University of Nebraska Press, 1984.

Amen Church

Japanese indigenous Christian church founded in the 1950s.

American Catholic Church

U.S. group, part of the OLD CATHOLICS movement, which follows Roman Catholic traditions but rejects papal authority and infallibility. It was founded in 1915 by Joseph Rene Vilatte. The church has several branches in the United States and Canada. It follows a THEOSOPHICAL Christianity, which makes it similar in beliefs and practices to the LIBERAL CATHOLIC CHURCH (LCC).

American Catholic Church (Syro-Antiochean)

U.S. OLD CATHOLIC group created through a secession by Herbert F. Wilkie from the AMERICAN CATHOLIC CHURCH in the 1950s.

American Catholic Church Archdiocese, The

North American Eastern Orthodox church with an African American membership, founded in 1927 by James F. A. Lashley as an outgrowth of the AFRICAN ORTHODOX CHURCH.

American Conference of Undenominated Churches

U.S. conference of FUNDAMENTALIST churches founded in 1922 by R. Lee Kirkland and others, which was superseded in 1930 by the INDEPENDENT FUNDAMENTAL CHURCHES OF AMERICA (IFCA).

American Evangelical Christian Churches

U.S. association of FUNDAMENTALIST ministers that offers doctrinal freedom in regard to questions of predestination, within a strictly Fundamentalist framework. It was founded in 1944 and is based in Pineland, Florida.

American Evangelistic Association, The

PENTECOSTAL group founded in 1954 in Baltimore by John E. Douglas. It licenses ministers and operates overseas missions, mainly in Asia.

American Indian Evangelical Church

U.S. PENTECOSTAL group with Native American membership, first organized in 1945. The current name was adopted in 1956. Based in Minneapolis, Minnesota.

American Messianic Fellowship

Formerly known as the Chicago Hebrew Mission, this is a U.S. HEBREW CHRISTIAN group founded in the 1940s.

American Orthodox Catholic Church

U.S. OLD CATHOLIC group founded in 1962 by Robert S. Zeiger, with parishes all over the United States. The clergy work full time in secular occupations.

American Rescue Workers

U.S. conservative Protestant group, formed in 1882 as the result of a secession from the SALVATION ARMY, and incorporated in 1896. The cause for secession was the wish of American members in the Salvation Army for more national independence. The group follows the Salvation Army in practice and doctrine, with few exceptions, and engages in offering emergency aid, but also functions as a church. The doctrine is Protestant FUNDAMENTALIST. The military organizational structure is retained.

American Teilhard Association

U.S. Christian group committed to the teachings of Pierre Teilhard de Chardin, a Jesuit who attempted an interpretation of evolution within a Christian framework.

American Universalist Temple of Divine Wisdom

U.S. Christian-THEOSOPHICAL group founded in 1966 in Escondido, California.

Amis de la Croix Glorieuse de Dozulé

French Christian group founded in 1982 in Saint-Quentin by Albert Delbauche. The founder has predicted the occurrence of various catastrophes and claimed witnessing many apparitions. In 1981 he announced that he would have a son who would liberate France. When a daughter was born, he declared that she would reestablish the French monarchy.

Amis de L'Homme

French MILLENARIAN group started after a schism in the CHURCH OF THE KINGDOM OF GOD, PHILANTHROPIC ASSEMBLY around 1950. It was founded by Lydie Sartre (1898–1963), known as "dear mother" to her followers. Based in Lot-et-Garonne, it draws its adherents mostly from Southern France. Members live communally and follow a tightly regimented life. [See also JEHOVAH'S WITNESSES.]

Ammal's Garden

U.S. religious commune based in Tucson, Arizona, and founded in the early 1970s. Its doctrine and practices combine Western and Hindu traditions, including meditation.

AMORC Rosicrucian Order

Known officially as the Ancient and Mystical Order Rosae Crucis, this international occultist group was founded in 1909 in New York by Harvey Spencer Lewis (1883–1939), who combined traditional European occultism with turn-of-the-century enthusiasm for ancient Egyptian civilization. AMORC teachings include belief in black magic and "mental poisoning," reincarnation, and auras. Christianity plays a special role in Lewis's teachings, as he claimed to know the true messages contained in the New Testament and offered a new version of the events described there, supposedly based on ancient documents from India, from Egypt, and from the "Great White Fraternity" in Tibet. In his interpretation, Lewis connected early Christianity with ancient Egyptian traditions. Joachim, the grandfather of Jesus, is a priest in a secret temple in Heliopolis, while Mary is a consecrated virgin in the same temple. The Essenes and their traditions are also involved in this story. In keeping with ROSICRUCIAN ideals, Jesus travels to India, Tibet, and Greece. His final initiation takes place in the Great Pyramid of Egypt. He does not die on the cross, but is revived by his comrades and retires to a Mount Carmel monastery.

AMORC headquarters were moved to San Jose, California, before World War I. After the founder's death, the group was led by his son, Ralph Maxwell Lewis (1904–) and in recent years by Gary Stewart. The group does most of its work by mail, offering correspondence courses to members around the world. [See also EMIN SOCIETY; and THEOSOPHY.]

Amuri Free Church

Polynesian independent Christian church started in the Cook Islands around 1940, in secession from European missionary groups.

Ananaikyo

Japanese MILLENARIAN new religion started in the late 1940s, growing out of the OMOTOKYO (OMOTO) movement. [*See also* SEICHO-NO-IE; *and* SEKAI KYUSEI KYO (SKK–WORLD MESSIANIC ASSOCIATION).]

Ananda Ashrama

U.S. Hindu group that was originally the Boston branch of the VEDANTA SOCIETY. It was founded in 1909 as the Boston Vedanta Center by Swami Paramananda (1884–1940), a disciple of Swami Vivekananda who followed him from India to the United States. In 1923 Paramananda started a monastic community in California. Swami Paramananda was succeeded by Srimata (Reverend Mother) Gayati Devi (1906–) in 1940. The group follows the teachings of Sri Ramakrishna. [*See also* RAMAKRISHNA MATH AND MISSION.]

Ananda Ashrama

U.S. Hindu group founded in 1964 by Guru Shri Brahmananda Sarasvati Udasina (Ramamurti Mishra, M.D.) and based in Monroe, New York. The group teaches meditation and Hindu scriptures.

Ananda Cooperative Village (ACV)

Also known as Ananda World Brotherhood Village, this eclectic Hindu-Christian community was founded in 1968 by James Donald Walters (1926–), also known as Swami Kriyananda. It is based in North San Juan, California. The founder was active in the SELF-REALIZATION FELLOWSHIP until 1962, when he decided to start the Village. Members are followers of Paramahansa Yogananda, who was the founder of

the Self-Realization Fellowship and the teacher of Swami Kriyananda, and practice Yogananda's technique of kriya yoga. Their doctrine is syncretistic and combines Hindu, Christian, and occultist traditions, such as astrology. The founder, Swami Kriyananda, is regarded as the absolute authority in all matters. The group is not a commune, but a cooperative community, where members are expected to provide for their welfare by working. Ananda Cooperative Village operates the Expanding Light, which offers programs to nonmembers. Community branches operate in Italy and the western United States.

Ananda Marga

Officially known in the West as the Ananda Marga Yoga Society, this is a Hindu revival movement founded in India in 1955 by Prabhat Ranjan (P. R.) Sarkar (1921–1990), a former railway employee. The founder is known to his followers as Shrii Anandamurti, Anandamurtiji, or "Baba." The scripture is the *Ananda Sutra*, written by the founder. It prescribes the group's practices, which include meditation several times a day. Sexual intercourse is permitted only for procreation in marriage, but devout members practice celibacy. Ananda Marga promotes a two-pronged program of individual salvation through meditation, and social reform through the total restructuring of human institutions. The group claims a "monist" philosophy, in which absolute peace can be the ultimate reality but will be achieved through "God's surgery" in the form of violence and disasters.

Sarkar had developed a radical political ideology, in addition to his religious teachings, and this caused friction with the Indian government and other governments as well. His followers say, "The movements he founded—Ananda Marga, Prout, and Neo-Humanism—have championed the removal of caste, racial, nationalistic, and religious barriers between people while supporting the preservation of cultural expression and unity of all animate and inanimate beings." Sarkar advocated a world government, a world language, and a world army, and his social vision is known as PROUT, which stands for Progressive (pro) Utilization (u) Theory (t).

The movement's political arm, the Proutist movement, took part in Indian elections in 1967 and 1969 but failed to achieve representation. Ananda Marga has been accused of violence toward members and nonmembers. Two members were convicted of political assassination in Australia. Sarkar was accused of a conspiracy to commit murder in 1971, together with other members of his movement. He was sentenced to life imprisonment in 1976 but was released in 1978. Ananda Marga was declared an illegal organization by the Indian government in 1975, but this ruling was rescinded in 1977. As protest against their treatment by government authorities, eight adherents committed self-immolation in the 1960s and 1970s. In 1982, seventeen members of Ananda Marga were killed by a mob in Calcutta. In 1987 a U.S. member of the group, Ravi Batra (1943–), published the best-selling *The Great Depression of 1990* (New York: Simon & Schuster) in which he predicted a major economic depression in accordance with Sarkar's "law of social cycles." In 1989 Batra published a book on "economic cycles" entitled *Regular Economic Cycles* (New York: St. Martin's Press), again based on insights

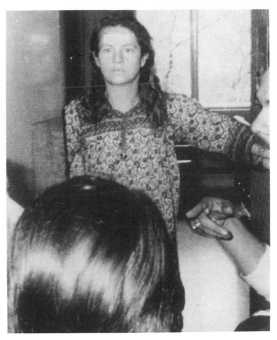

In Calcutta, a member of Ananda Marga in police custody in a hospital because of her connection with the secretive group.

gained from Sarkar, who is identified in the work only as an "Indian philosopher."

Anandamayee Charitable Society

British branch of the SRI MA ANANDAMAYI ASHRAMS, a twentieth-century Hindu movement focused on the personality of Sri Ma Anandamayi. The first ashram was founded in 1932 in Dehra Dun, India.

Anchor Bay Evangelistic Association

U.S. PENTECOSTAL group that is an offshoot of the FOURSQUARE GOSPEL

CHURCH. Formally incorporated in 1940, it was founded by Roy John Turner, who joined Pentecostalism in 1916 and worked with Aimee Semple McPherson in the 1930s. The group is based in New Baltimore, Michigan, and is a member of the PENTECOSTAL FELLOWSHIP OF NORTH AMERICA.

Ancient Mayans, Order of

U.S. offshoot of AMORC ROSICRUCIAN ORDER, founded by Rose Dawn and claiming to reveal secrets of Mayan esoteric traditions. The group's doctrine combines belief in reincarnation with NEW THOUGHT ideas about the power of positive thinking.

Ancient Order of Druids

British neo-pagan group, started in London in 1781, which claimed to revive ancient Druid customs and celebrations. Members met to celebrate the summer solstice at Stonehenge, starting a modern British tradition.

Andromeda, the Chapel of the Open Door

U.S. Christian-occultist group founded in 1969 in Long Lake, Minnesota. It is connected with the CONGREGATIONAL CHURCH OF PRACTICAL THEOLOGY.

Ange Albert

Spiritualist healing group started in Luxembourg in the 1980s. Practices include seances in which mediums speak for angels, belief in the legendary island of Atlantis, and healing through the use of holy water.

Anglican Catholic Church in North America

U.S. Anglican group started in 1976 in secession from the Episcopal Church in the United States in protest over the ordination of women.

Anglo-Saxon Federation of America

U.S. BRITISH-ISRAELIST group founded by Howard B. Rand of Haverhill, Massachusetts, in 1928. In 1930 W. J. Cameron became president of the Federation. This group was most active in the 1930s and the 1940s, disseminating literature containing the BRITISH-ISRAELISM message.

Anthroposophical Society

Western occultist movement founded through the defection of Rudolf Steiner (1861–1925), an Austrian, from the THEOSOPHICAL SOCIETY. Steiner had joined the Society in 1902 and became the secretary of its German branch, but in 1912 he withdrew in protest against the formation by Annie Besant of the Order of the Star in the East. He founded the Anthroposophical Society. All German members and some Swiss members followed him in defecting from THEOSOPHY.

Steiner regarded his theory as Christian occultism and regarded Jesus Christ as the "central happening of all history." According to Steiner, the Christian Trinity is the ultimate reality, and the Second Coming of Jesus Christ will lead to the "respiritualization of the cosmos." Steiner created an eclectic system based on Theosophy, other occult traditions,

Rudolf Steiner, founder of the Anthroposophical Society, with Marie von Sivers.

especially ROSICRUCIANISM, and Christianity. According to his teachings, the universe, including humankind, has evolved through three stages. The early stages were dominated by intuitive and "clairvoyant" forms of consciousness (and matter). These were "astral" or "etheric" stages of development. These forms of consciousness can be recovered by following Steiner's techniques of meditation. Steiner had his own theory of evolution through reincarnation, and his own theories of Atlantis, "Lemuria," and Egyptian mythology. Thus, the New Testament figure of Jesus Christ was the result of numerous incarnations that pre-

pared the incarnation as Christ. He has been manifested in Zoroaster, Buddha, and Krishna.

Steiner was a prolific writer, and his books contain information on nutrition (vegetarianism is recommended), organic farming, known as biodynamic agriculture, child care, education, and cures for cancer, among other diseases. Steiner's book *Atlantis and Lemuria* (1913) claimed occult knowledge from the Akashic record (a hypothetical bank of all events, ideas, and emotions that have ever occurred, said by some occultists to be preserved in the "astral plane") to describe Atlantean history. According to Steiner, the Atlanteans used the energy latent in plants to drive airships, while the Lemurians were unable to reason or calculate, living chiefly by instinct and communicating by telepathy. They lifted enormous weights by exercising great willpower.

The movement has been known for its educational work, especially with the mentally handicapped. The world center of Anthroposophy is in Dornach, Switzerland. [*See also* CAMPHILL MOVEMENT; *and* CHRISTIAN COMMUNITY CHURCH (CHRISTENGEMEINSCHAFT).]

Anthroposophische Vereinigung in der Schweiz

Swiss splinter group of the ANTHROPOSOPHICAL SOCIETY started in 1949.

Antioch Baptist Church

International, independent Protestant group, founded in 1962 by Afro-Americans of the Caribbean.

Antioch Church

Korean independent PENTECOSTAL group founded in the 1960s.

Antoinisme

Officially incorporated as the *Société des Antoinistes,* and named for its founder, Louis Antoine (1845–1912), known as *le Guérisseur* ("the Healer"), this healing-spiritualist group has about sixty branches in France and Belgium. Antoine was born to a poor Catholic family and worked as a miner and metalworker. His reputation as a healer kept growing during his lifetime. Like the principles of other nineteenth-century healing cults (*see* CHRISTIAN SCIENCE), *Antoiniste* doctrine denied the existence of evil, or even the existence of matter, and assumed the existence of "fluids" that control the world and the human body. Evil, suffering, and death exist only in human imagination and are based on fallible human perceptions. Antoine founded the "New Spiritualism" in 1906 and died in 1912. Healing practitioners today dress in black, lay their hands on the locus of pain, and pray.

Apocalypse Society, Inc., The

Monotheistic group founded in the 1980s in New York City by Romiche Henry. Its doctrine is based on the "Virgin Life Principle of God which is a catalyst to achieve the individual highest level of spiritual awareness." It is opposed to any kind of sexuality.

Apostelmat Jesu Christi (AJC)

German Protestant splinter group that grew out of the NEW APOSTOLIC CHURCH in 1923.

Apostelmat Juda

German Protestant splinter group that grew out of the NEW APOSTOLIC CHURCH in 1902.

Apostles in Zion Church

African indigenous ZIONIST, PENTECOSTAL church that started in South Africa in the early twentieth century and spread to other countries in the region, such as Zambia.

Apostles of Infinite Love

Originally known as the Order of the Mother of God, this Roman Catholic traditionalist splinter group was founded in 1952 in Canada by Jean Grégoire de la Trinité. In 1968 he declared himself Pope Gregory XVII, reported divine revelations (especially apparitions of the Virgin Mary), and spoke against reforms in the official Church. The movement is based in Québec, where it has established several monasteries and centers. Branches have operated in the United States and in the Caribbean, especially in Guadeloupe and Puerto Rico. The group doctrine denounces reforms in the Roman Catholic Church since 1960.

In the 1960s and 1970s this group collaborated with the RENOVATED CHURCH OF CHRIST THE KING. Later, the group was linked to the PALMARIAN CATHOLIC CHURCH. In North America, the group is sometimes known as the Catholic Church of the Apostles of the Latter Times.

Apostolic Christian Church (Nazarean), The

U.S. conservative Protestant group founded around 1850 by Samuel H.

Froehlich with a membership of Swiss and German immigrants. Members "are converted to Christ, born again and baptized, and must live in accord with the New Testament."

Apostolic Christian Church of America, The

U.S. Protestant group started around 1850 by Benedict Weyeneth, with a membership of Swiss and German immigrants.

Apostolic Church

INTERNATIONAL PENTECOSTAL group with branches in North America and in Great Britain, founded by Daniel Powell Williams in 1916 in Wales after a split in the APOSTOLIC FAITH CHURCH.

Apostolic Church of Ghana

African PENTECOSTAL group founded in the early twentieth century in the then British colony of Gold Coast. Splinters in this group have led to the creation of the GHANA APOSTOLIC CHURCH and the DIVINE HEALER'S CHURCH.

Apostolic Church of God

British PENTECOSTAL group started in 1973 by Jamaican immigrants in London.

Apostolic Church of God

U.S. Sabbath-keeping, ADVENTIST group formed in 1949 by Dewey E. Skagg, who dissented from the doctrine of the CHURCH OF GOD (SEVENTH-DAY, SALEM,

WEST VIRGINIA). It is based in Edgewater, Florida. [See also GENERAL CONFERENCE OF THE CHURCH OF GOD (SEVENTH-DAY); and SEVENTH-DAY ADVENTIST CHURCH (SDA OR S.D.A.).]

Apostolic Church of God Christians

Philippine indigenous PENTECOSTAL church founded in 1964.

Apostolic Church of Great Britain

British PENTECOSTAL church founded in 1904 in Wales.

Apostolic Church of Jesus

PENTECOSTAL group founded by Raymond P. Virgil and based in Pueblo, Colorado. Membership is drawn from Hispanic communities.

Apostolic Church of Jesus Christ

British PENTECOSTAL group started around 1960 by Jamaican immigrants in London. Tithing, glossolalia (speaking in tongues), and faith healing are practiced.

Apostolic Church of Jesus Christ

U.S. PENTECOSTAL group with African American membership, based in Indianapolis. It was formed in 1924 after the white members of the PENTECOSTAL ASSEMBLIES OF THE WORLD left the originally integrated group.

Apostolic Divine Church of Ghana

African indigenous PENTECOSTAL church founded in Ghana in 1957.

Apostolic Door of Faith

Philippine indigenous PENTECOSTAL church founded in 1965.

Apostolic Faith

U.S. PENTECOSTAL group founded by Charles and Ada Lochbaum in 1923 and based in Hawaii. Doctrine emphasizes healing, tithing, and the coming of the millennium.

Apostolic Faith (Born Again) Church

African indigenous PENTECOSTAL group founded in the 1960s in Zambia.

Apostolic Faith and Acts Church

African indigenous PENTECOSTAL group founded in 1965 in Bulawayo, Zimbabwe.

Apostolic Faith Church

British PENTECOSTAL group founded by W. O. Hutchinson in 1908. In 1916 a split led to the creation of the APOSTOLIC CHURCH.

Apostolic Faith Church (Kansas)

PENTECOSTAL group founded by Charles Parham in Topeka, Kansas. Parham founded the Bethel Healing Home in 1898 and the Bethel Bible College in 1900. Twentieth-century PENTECOSTALism is said to have started in the winter of 1900 in the Bethel Bible College. Later on, Parham spent his time traveling around the southern United States, and in 1905 he established a Bible school in Houston. The group's doctrine emphasizes healing and tithing. A schism during the late 1940s resulted in the formation of the FULL GOSPEL EVANGELICAL ASSOCIATION.

Apostolic Faith Holy Gospel Church

African indigenous PENTECOSTAL group. Founded in 1947 in Bulawayo, Zimbabwe, it spread to Zambia.

Apostolic Faith Mission (AFM)

U.S. PENTECOSTAL group started by Minnie Hanson in Topeka, Kansas, in 1907. It emphasizes faith healing and speaking in tongues.

Apostolic Faith Mission of Portland, Oregon, U.S.A.

Known also as the Apostolic Faith, this PENTECOSTAL evangelical group was founded in 1907 by Florence L. Crawford. A "born again" experience is required for membership, and worldly amusements are banned.

Apostolic Faith of Africa

African independent PENTECOSTAL group. Founded in 1959 among the Kikuyu of Kenya, it later spread to Uganda.

Apostolic Faith Star Church

African indigenous PENTECOSTAL group founded in 1971 in Zambia.

Apostolic Fellowship Tabernacle

Indian independent PENTECOSTAL group started in the 1950s.

Apostolic Gospel Faith of Jesus Christ, The

PENTECOSTAL group founded in 1963 in California by Donald Abernathy. In 1968, the founder had a vision predicting the destruction of the West Coast by an earthquake. As a result, the members moved to cities on the East Coast. The group's doctrine emphasizes faith healing and pacifism. A strict dress code is followed.

Apostolic Hierarchy Church

Formerly known as the African God Worshippers Fellowship Society, this African independent Catholic group was founded in 1940 among the Kikuyu of Kenya, in a secession from the Roman Catholic Church.

Apostolic Holy Zion Mission of South Africa

Independent PENTECOSTAL group founded in 1932 in South Africa, with a strong emphasis on faith healing.

Apostolic Overcoming Holy Church of God (AOH Church of God)

Formerly known as the Ethiopian Overcoming Holy Church of God, this U.S. PENTECOSTAL group was founded by William Thomas Phillips (1893–1973) in 1919 in Birmingham, Alabama. Membership has been made up mostly of African Americans. Worship includes faith healing and speaking in tongues. The group's doctrine is influenced by "black-Jewish" ideas, in which Ethiopia plays a special role.

Apostolic Reformed Church of Ghana

African indigenous PENTECOSTAL church founded in Ghana in 1958.

Apostolic United Order

Known also as Apostolic United Brethren, this is a MORMON splinter group committed to the practice of polygyny. Founded by Joseph Musser in the early 1950s. It was lead by Rolon C. Allred until he was killed by members of the CHURCH OF THE LAMB OF GOD in 1977. Since then the group has been led by members of the Allred family. [*See also* THE CHURCH OF THE FIRST BORN OF THE FULLNESS OF TIMES; CONFEDERATE NATIONS OF ISRAEL; REORGANIZED CHURCH OF JESUS CHRIST OF LATTER-DAY SAINTS; *and* UNITED ORDER EFFORT.]

Source:
Bradlee, B., Jr., and Van Atta, D. *Prophet of Blood.* New York: G. P. Putnam's Sons, 1981.

Apostolowo fe Dedefia Habobo (Apostolic Revelation Society— ARS)

African PENTECOSTAL independent church in Ghana. It was founded in 1945

25

by Charles Kobla Nutonuti Wovenu (1918–), known as the Prophet.

Apres

French spiritualist group founded in the 1950s by Maguy Lebrun. It has branches in several European countries.

Aquarian Brotherhood of Christ, The

U.S. spiritualist group founded in 1925 and headed by Caroline Duke, former president of the Independent Associated Spiritualists, the short-lived organization that included both the SPIRITUAL SCIENCE CHURCH and the Aquarian Brotherhood of Christ.

Aquarian Educational Foundation

THEOSOPHICAL-occultist group founded in California in 1963. It follows the teachings of the Arcane School started by Alice B. Bailey, augmented by the teachings of the group's founder, Haroutiun Saraydarian. The message of Christianity also plays some role in its teachings. [See also LUCIS TRUST.]

Aquarian Foundation

Spiritualist-Theosophical group founded in 1955 in Seattle, Washington, by Keith Milton Rhinehart. Its doctrine includes many elements familiar from THEOSOPHY, such as the Great White Brotherhood, which is a group that believes it has attained a higher plane of spirituality and reincarnation. Masters of the Great White Brotherhood are said to communicate with the group. The founder has also claimed to have the Christian stigmata (marks resembling the crucifixion wounds of Jesus) on his body.

Aquarian Minyan of Berkeley

Jewish revival group started in the 1970s in Berkeley, California. It has combined traditional Jewish ideas with Eastern practices such as meditation. In the 1980s it became affiliated with the P'nai Or Religious Fellowship (ALEPH).

Aquarian Spiritual Center and College of Black Gnostic Studies

NEW THOUGHT group started in the 1980s in Los Angeles, California, by Alfred Ligon. It claims that the word *black* in its name is Sufi for "wise" or "hidden" in the context of "Islamic mystical teachings." It offers "a system of education (especially in the black community) which encompasses both mental and spiritual development," including "mystery teachings, alchemy, the tarot and the kabala."

Arcana Workshops

U.S. occultist group in the Alice Bailey tradition, based in Southern California; it operates mainly through correspondence. [See also LUCIS TRUST.]

Archdiocese of the Old Catholic Church in America

OLD CATHOLIC group, founded in 1941 by Francis X. Resch, a former priest in the

NORTH AMERICAN OLD ROMAN CATHOLIC CHURCH, with headquarters in Milwaukee, Wisconsin.

Arco Iris

European occultist group started in the 1970s in Spain.

Arica Institute

U.S. occultist group that started in the 1960s in Arica, Chile, and was formally founded by Oscar Ichazo in 1971 in New York City. It is a system of religious psychotherapy, combining Christian concepts, Eastern religious concepts taken from Hindu traditions and Sufism, GURDJIEFF ideas, and secular psychotherapy techniques.

Ariel Ministries

HEBREW CHRISTIAN group with headquarters in California, founded in the 1980s by Arnold Fruchtenbaum.

Arising Sun IFO (Identified Flying Objects)

UFO-Christian group based in Milwaukee and founded around 1970 by June Young, known as Bright Star. Messages are reportedly received from Jesus Christ, the Virgin Mary, and Elvis Presley.

Arizona Metaphysical Society, The

U.S. NEW THOUGHT group founded by Frank Alper in the 1970s. Beliefs include traditional Western occultism, spiritualism, and Hindu ideas. Meditation, spiritual healing, and channeling (communicating with the spirits of the dead) are practiced. The group is affiliated with the CHURCH OF TZADDI.

Armageddon Time Ark Base (ATA Base)

U.S. Christian-UFO group, founded in the 1970s in Texas by O. T. Nodrog. Group members predict the coming of an apocalyptic S-Day, when only they will be saved by spaceships.

Arunachala Ashrama Bhagavan Sri Ramana Maharshi Center, Inc.

North American Hindu group devoted to the teachings of Sri Bhagavan Ramana Maharshi (1879–1950). The group's North American ashramas follow in their practices the schedule of activities in the original RAMANA MAHARSHI ashrama on the sacred hill Arunachala in Tiruvannamalai, India. The group's doctrine of "Self-abidance" is based on "the wholehearted practice of Self-Enquiry and submission and surrender to the supreme Self as taught by Sri Bhagavan Ramana Maharshi."

Arya Maitreya Mandala

International Tibetan Buddhist order founded in 1933 in Darjeeling, India, by Lama Angarika Govinda (1898–), a German-born disciple of Tulku Lama Geshe Ngawang Kalzang. Doctrine calls for living out the Buddha's message in one's life. Govinda was especially active in spreading the group's message to the West and founded Western branches. [*See also* HOME OF THE DHARMA.]

Arya Samaj

This name, which means Noble Society, denotes a reform group within Hinduism, founded on April 10, 1875, in Bombay by Dayananda Sarasvati (1824–1883). He was a Hindu follower of Siva who, after becoming disillusioned at the age of fourteen, became a wandering religious mendicant in India between the ages of twenty-one and thirty-nine. The last twenty years of his life were spent on preaching tours throughout India.

Both Hindus and Sikhs eventually joined the group, which was strongly anti-Muslim and anti-Christian. The doctrine was unitarian, egalitarian, and nationalistic, with the slogan, "Back to the Vedas!" It interpreted Hinduism in a strictly monotheistic way, claiming a return to the purity of early Vedic tradition. The founder preached that the Vedas, properly interpreted (*i.e.*, by himself) were sufficient for achieving salvation. He denounced the Hindu traditions of caste, image worship, and child marriage. In 1878 the Arya Samaj established a short-lived alliance with the THEOSOPHICAL SOCIETY and became known for four years as the Theosophical Society of the Arya Samaj. After the founder's death in 1883, a schism occurred, but the group is still active today in education and charity.

Source:

Farquhar, J. N. *Modern Religious Movements in India*. New York: Macmillan, 1919.

Asatru

Icelandic revival movement of ancient Nordic traditions that started in the 1960s and was active until the 1980s. Branches of the group operated in Great Britain and the United States.

Assemblies (Jehova Shammah)

Indian Christian indigenous church founded by Brother Bakht Singh. Based in Hyderabad, India, it operates branches in Asia, Africa, and Oceania.

Assemblies of God (A/G)

U.S. PENTECOSTAL group with branches in more than 100 countries, started in April 1914 by E. N. Bell and J. Roswell Flowers in Hot Springs, Arkansas, and now based in Springfield, Missouri. It has been one of the most active Pentecostal churches, operating eleven colleges, an active publishing outfit, and a large missionary organization. Out of the group came many splinter groups and independent movements, such as the LATTER RAIN MOVEMENT, the MANIFEST SONS OF GOD, and the CHRISTIAN GROWTH MINISTRIES. Some well-known televangelists in the United States, such as Jim Bakker of the NEW COVENANT CHURCH and Jimmy Swaggart, were ordained by A/G.

Sources:

Blumhofer, E. L. *Restoring the Faith: The Assemblies of God, Pentecostalism, and American Culture*. Urbana: University of Illinois Press, 1993.

Poloma, M. M. *The Assemblies of God at the Crossroads: Charisma and Institutional

A huge crowd gathers at an Assembly of God annual rally in Winter Park, Florida, to hear Christian celebrities give testimony to their faith.

Dilemmas. Knoxville: University of Tennessee Press, 1989.

Assemblies of God in Great Britain and Ireland

British PENTECOSTAL body founded in 1924 following a Pentecostal revival movement that started in Britain in 1907. Speaking in tongues and faith healing are main parts of its tradition.

Assemblies of Jesus Christ

Indian Christian indigenous church founded in the 1950s.

Assemblies of the First-Born

Jamaican indigenous PENTECOSTAL Christian church founded in 1950 and based in Kingston, Jamaica. It is related to the CHURCH OF THE FIRST-BORN.

Assemblies of the Lord Jesus Christ, Inc.

U.S. PENTECOSTAL group formed in 1952 through the merger of the Assemblies of the Church of Jesus Christ, the Jesus Only Apostolic Church of God, and the Church of the Lord Jesus Christ. It is based in Memphis, Tennessee.

29

Assemblies of Yahweh

ADVENTIST group founded in 1966 in Baltimore by Jacob O. Meyer. The group is totally Old Testament-oriented, keeping all its commandments and being non-Trinitarian. Tithing, nonviolence, and conscientious objection to military service are also advocated. The "Sacred Name Broadcast," a radio ministry, is a major part of the group's activities. It is headquartered in Bethel, Pennsylvania. [*See also* SACRED NAME MOVEMENT.]

Assemblies of Yahweh (Michigan)

ADVENTIST-Sabbatarian group founded in 1939 in Holt, Michigan, that ascribes special importance to the sacred name of Yahweh. Members believe that the sacred names of the Bible have been corrupted and neglected and should be put back into daily use. In addition, they advocate the Old Testament dietary laws, the Jewish festivals, tithing, and divine healing. [*See also* SACRED NAME MOVEMENT.]

Assembly, The

U.S. evangelical group founded by George Gustafson in the 1970s and operating in small "Assemblies" or "Gatherings of God's People." There are no formal organizational structures, and members meet in private homes. All Christian churches and church organizations are considered perversions of true Christianity.

Assembly of Christian Churches, Inc., The

U.S. Spanish-speaking PENTECOSTAL group founded in New York City in 1939 when, as BETHEL CHRISTIAN TEMPLE, it joined other Spanish-speaking groups to form The Assembly of Christian Churches, Inc. The group engages in missionary activities all over the world. [*See also* CONCILIO OLAZABAL DE IGLESIAS LATINO AMERICANO.]

Assembly of Christian Soldiers

U.S. Christian group affiliated with the Ku Klux Klan and committed to white supremacy and racial segregation. [*See also* IDENTITY MOVEMENT.]

Assembly of Yahvah

U.S. ADVENTIST group, started in 1949 in Emory, Texas, by Lorenzo Dow Snow (1913–) and E. B. Adam. Snow was a member of the ASSEMBLIES OF YAHWEH (MICHIGAN), but disagreed with that group over the spelling of the sacred name. In 1968 Wilburn Stricklin became the group leader. Doctrines include adherence to Old Testament dietary laws, tithing, and faith healing. The group operates Missionary Dispensary Bible Research, which produced the *Restoration of Original Sacred Name Bible*; the book uses Yahvah, Elohim, and Yashua as sacred names in its text. [*See also* SACRED NAME MOVEMENT.]

Associated Brotherhood of Christians

U.S. PENTECOSTAL group founded in 1933.

Associated Churches of God

Founded in 1974 by former members of the WORLDWIDE CHURCH OF GOD who disagreed with church policies. Specifically, the dissenters rejected tithing in favor of free-will offerings and the theocratic government maintained by Herbert W. Armstrong in favor of a congregational governing structure.

Associated Gospel Churches

U.S. FUNDAMENTALIST group founded by W. O. H. Garman. Its membership came from former Methodist Protestant congregations that refused to enter the Methodist merger of 1939. The group believes in DISPENSATIONALISM. Group headquarters are in Pittsbugh, Pennsylvania, and its missions operate all over the world.

Associated Spiritualists

U.S. spiritualist group started in the 1940s that is very similar in doctrine and practices to the SPIRITUAL SCIENCE CHURCH.

Association for Research and Enlightenment, Inc., The (ARE)

Occultist organization with a strong Christian bent, headquartered in Virginia Beach, Virginia, and devoted to the teachings of Edgar Cayce, known to his followers as the "sleeping prophet." Cayce (1877–1947) became famous among U.S. occultists for his "readings" given in a trance state, during which he made "medical diagnoses" as well as prophecies about future events. The Association was founded in 1931.

Cayce had no medical qualifications of any kind and left school after seventh grade. His method of diagnosis was to enter a self-hypnotic trance lying on his back facing south (or later north). Most of Cayce's early trances were given with the aid of an osteopath who asked him questions while he was asleep and later helped to explain the readings. The origin of Cayce's readings can be ascribed to associations with osteopaths and FUNDAMENTALIST Christians. The remedies included spinal massage, herbal concoctions, special diets, tonics, electrical treatments, and such unusual prescriptions as "oil of smoke" for leg sores and almonds for cancer. Cayce was a kind man by all accounts, with a charming manner and a willingness to listen to those interested in THEOSOPHY, pyramidology, and the fabled island of Atlantis. He said he believed that Atlantis would rise again around 1968–1969. Cayce also taught that Arcturus is the next abode of souls leaving the solar system and stated that throughout his life he had been able to diagnose a patient's health and character from the "coloured aura" that he could see surrounding everybody's head and shoulders.

The Association describes itself as "made up of individuals interested in spiritual growth, parapsychological research, and the work of Edgar Cayce. . . . Central to the philosophy of these [Cayce's] readings is the premise that man is a spiritual being whose purpose on earth is to reawaken and apply this knowledge. Meditation as well as other principles of physical, mental and spiritual attunement are studied and practiced." The ARE doctrine combines belief in reincarnation, auras, Christianity, astrology, and a variety of "psychic discoveries."

In the 1950s, the Association was headed by Hugh Lynn Cayce (1906–

31

Edgar Cayce, of The Association for Research and Enlightenment, Inc. known as the "sleeping prophet."

1983), the son of the founder, and afterward by Charles Thomas Cayce, his grandson. [*See also* LOGOS WORLD UNIVERSITY CHURCH.]

Association for the Understanding of Man, The

U.S. spiritualist-Christian organization, founded by Ray Stanford in the 1960s. Stanford's "readings," which have been published in several volumes, deal with illness and healing, meditation, psychic communications, marriage, death, and the supraphysical functions of endocrine glands.

Association Francaise des Libres Étudiants de la Bible

French offshoot of JEHOVAH'S WITNESSES, started in 1956.

Association Internationale des Clubs Archedia Sciences et Traditions

Also known as "Clubs Archedia," this international occultist movement was founded in Geneva, Switzerland, in 1984 by Luc Jouret (1947–). The group is devoted to natural healing, as well as to reviving the medieval Templar Order. Branches have operated in Europe and North America.

Association of Covenant People

Canadian BRITISH-ISRAELIST organization based in Vancouver.

Association of International Gospel Assemblies, Inc.

U.S. PENTECOSTAL organization that is a loose grouping of independent Pentecostal churches.

Association of Sananda and Sanat Kumara

U.S. Christian-occultist group founded by Dorothy Martin (known as Sister Thedra). Her early group became famous under the name Lake City Group after being portrayed in a well-known psychological study by Leon Festinger and Henry W. Reicken, *When Prophecy Fails* (1956). The group leader, Mrs. Martin, named Marian Keech in the study, claimed to have received messages from a space being named Sananda warning her about a flood that would destroy most of North America at a later date. This date was announced (December 1953), and group members expected the end of the world and their own salvation. After the prophecy failed, some of the group members maintained their faith. Mrs. Martin claimed that the world was saved by the group's faith. She made additional predictions about various disasters that also failed to materialize. These prognostications were made in Chicago in late 1953, but the leader continued her extraterrestrial contacts later on. She joined the Brotherhood of the Seven Rays for several years. In 1965 she founded the Association, which distributes her communications from various masters, mainly Sananda, otherwise known as Jesus Christ.

Source:

Festinger, L.; Riecken, H. W.; and Schachter, S. *When Prophecy Fails*. New York: Harper & Row, 1956.

Association of Seventh-Day Pentecostal Assemblies

International PENTECOSTAL group with branches in the United States, Canada, Ghana, and Nigeria, founded in 1967 by members of several Sabbatarian churches. Members follow Old Testament commandments and practice faith healing.

Associazione Pitagorica

Italian occultist group founded by Arturo Reghini (1878–1946) that claims an affiliation with ancient Pythagorian traditions.

Astara Foundation

U.S. spiritualist, THEOSOPHICAL, Christian group founded in 1951 in Santa Monica, California, by Robert and Earlyne Chaney, with the goal of being "a center of all religions and philosophies, a school of the ancient mysteries and an institute of psychic research." The group also promotes healing.

Earlier, Robert Chaney was a founder of the Spiritualist Episcopal Church and had been a prominent medium at Camp Chesterfield, near Anderson, Indiana, one of the most important centers of spiritualism in the United States. The group has had branches in Europe and Africa.

Source:
Judah, J. S. *The History and Philosophy of the Metaphysical Movements in America.* Philadelphia: Westminster, 1967.

Astrological, Metaphysical, Occult, Revelatory, Enlightenment Church (AMORE)

Christian-occultist group founded in 1972 in Meriden, Connecticut, by Charles Robert Gordon, a former minister of the AFRICAN METHODIST EPISCOPAL ZION CHURCH. The group's doctrine combined FUNDAMENTALIST Christianity with occultism and belief in a coming Aquarian Age. It ceased to exist in the late 1970s.

Athanor Fellowship

Neo-pagan group founded in the 1970s in Boston by Andras Corban Arthen and Deirdre Pulgram Arthen. It describes itself as ". . . a family of traditional magical groups which follow the practice of the GLAINN SIDHR ORDER." The Fellowship is affiliated with the COVENANT OF THE GODDESS. [*See also* EARTHSPIRIT COMMUNITY.]

Atitso Gaxie Habobo

Officially known as the White Cross Society, this is an African Christian PENTECOSTAL healing group founded in Ghana in 1941.

Atlanteans

British spiritualist-occultist group founded in 1957 in London and led by Jacqueline Murray. Members of the group believe in the existence of the ancient island of Atlantis, which they believe was populated by earthmen with Venusian souls. Messages are reported from Helio-Aracnophus, the high priestess of Atlantis. Spiritual healing is practiced, and occult traditions, such as astrology and palmistry, are taught.

Source:
Evans, C. *Cults of Unreason.* London: Harrap, 1973.

Atmaniketan Ashram

U.S. Hindu monastic residence. Founded in 1971 by Sadhu Loncontirth and based in Pomona, California, it is devoted to the teachings of SRI AUROBINDO. [*See also* CULTURAL INTEGRATION FELLOWSHIP; *and* MATAGIRI.]

Atom Foundation

Christian-occultist group founded by Michael Francis in Anchorage, Alaska, in the early 1980s. It is loosely affiliated with the LOGOS WORLD UNIVERSITY CHURCH.

Aum Center for Self-Realization

U.S. religious commune founded by Ken and Mona Piller around 1970 and located in Kalispell, Montana. It is devoted to Eastern yoga and meditation as well as natural healing.

Aum Shinrikyo (Aum Supreme Truth)

International Buddhist, Hinduist–inspired group with branches in Japan, South Korea, Sri Lanka, Germany, Russia, and the United States. It was founded in 1987 and led by Shoko Asahara (1955–), whose real name is Chizuo Matsumoto. After visiting the Himalayas, Asahara claimed he had reached the highest stage of enlightenment and was ready to offer it to others.

The group offers its members "Real Initiation," "Astral Initiation," and "Causal Initiation." The goal is spiritual enlightenment. According to its publications, "after passing through Earthly Initiation which purifies one's consciousness, Astral Initiation which purifies one's subconsciousness, over 2,000 members in Japan have promoted their spiritual growth remarkably, and experienced astral projection and feelings of supreme bliss within half a year." Those who reach spiritual enlightenment will survive the coming global apocalypse.

Members are encouraged to leave their families and adopt a monastic life. They are also expected to sign over their worldly possessions to the group. The founder ran unsuccessfully in the elections for the Japanese parliament in 1990. In the 1980s the group's doctrine predicted the end of the world in 1997.

In 1989, according to investigations by the Japanese Diet, Tsutsumi Sakamoto, an attorney who was involved in suing the group, was murdered, along with his wife and son, on Asahara's orders. In June 1994, seven individuals were killed in Matsumoto, Japan, as a result of a sarin nerve gas attack widely held to have been carried out by the group. Then, on March 20, 1995, thirteen persons died in Tokyo following another sarin nerve gas attack in the subway, an assault attributed to Aum.

Huge quantities of dangerous chemicals were later found at group facilities. Scores of Aum members were arrested. Asahara claimed that his followers were attacked by the U.S. military using biological weapons, and that the huge chemical stores found at one of the

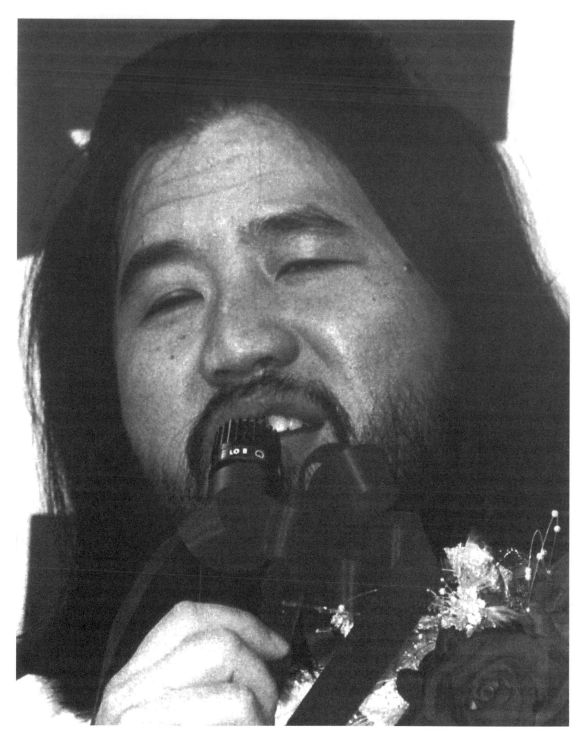

Shoko Asahara is the founder and leader of Aum Shinrikyo, the group believed to have carried out sarin nerve gas attacks in Japan.

36

group's compounds were used to make "plastics, fertilizers, and pottery."

On May 16, 1995, Asahara was arrested, and the group's many centers were raided. In April 1995 Hideo Murai, the group's "science department" chief, announced that the group's property holdings were worth $1 billion. He was then mysteriously killed two weeks later. Fumihiro Joyu was appointed group leader following Asahara's arrest, but he himself was arrested in October 1995.

Ausar Auset Society

ROSICRUCIAN group founded in New York around 1975 by R. A. Straughn, also known as Ra Un Nefer Amen. The name is derived from the supposed ancient alternate names of the Egyptian gods Isis and Osiris. Straughn was a member of the ROSICRUCIAN ANTHROPOSOPHIC LEAGUE in the 1970s; he formed the Society specifically to serve African Americans. The group, based in New York City, operates on the East Coast of the United States.

Ayie Remb Yesu

Officially known as Children of God Regeneration Church, this is a Kenyan independent Protestant group founded in 1947 among the Luo of Kenya.

B

Baba League, The

U.S. Sufi-oriented syncretistic group in existence since the 1960s, devoted to the teachings of MEHER BABA and based in Berkeley, California. [*See also* SUFISM REORIENTED, INC.]

Babism

MILLENARIAN group of Islamic origins that developed out of the messianic Shiite tradition and was founded by Ali-Muhammad (1819–1850), known as the Bab, of Shiraz, Iran. In 1844, Ali-Muhammad proclaimed himself to be the Bab (Gate) to the twelfth Imam, who had disappeared a thousand years before. At first, Muhammad's claim was welcomed, but when he started deviating from the Islamic tradition, the reaction was violent. In 1848 the Babis declared publicly their secession from Islam, and two years later Muhammad was executed by a firing squad.

The leadership was then assumed by two half-brothers, Yahia Nuri (1830–1912), known as Subh-i Azal, and Husayn Ali Nuri (1817–1892), known as Baha Allah (or Bahá'u' lláh). Later, a split in the movement occurred when the former insisted that he was the appointed successor and the latter claimed to be the prophet foretold by the Bab. Followers of Baha Allah started a new movement, Bahaism. The followers of Sabh-i Azal, known as Azalis, continued the tradition of Babism.

The sacred book of Babism is *al-Bayan*, written by Ali-Muhammad. According to this book, some elements of traditional Islamic law are abolished, and a promise is made of a prophet to come. The number nineteen has central significance in Babism. A calendar of nineteen months, having nineteen days each, was created.

Another splinter group, the Bayanis, rejects Subh-i Azal and claims to follow the Bab alone. [*See also* BAHAIS.]

Source:

Smith, P. *The Babi and the Bahai Religions: From Messianic Shiism to a World Religion.* Cambridge: Cambridge University Press, 1987.

Back to the Bible Way

U.S. offshoot of JEHOVAH'S WITNESSES started in 1952 by Roy D. Goodrich (?–1977), who was excommunicated by the Witnesses in 1944. Goodrich dissented from the original teachings of Charles Taze Russell, founder of the Witnesses. He disagreed with Russell's views about the signficance of events that occurred in 1914 and with the status of Russell himself. This group was dissolved following the founder's death.

Bahais

International movement started in the late nineteenth century as a heterodox Muslim sect, developed from the BABISM movement in nineteenth-century Iran. It has proselytized successfully in the West, and Bahaism is a global religion with followers on all continents.

The founder, Husayn Ali Nuri (1817–1892), known as Baha Allah or Baha'u' llah ("Glory of God"), was a follower of the Bab who, while in exile and in prison, became convinced that he himself was the prophet or the Messenger of

Abdu'l-Baha (Courtesy U.S. Baha'i Office of Public Information)

A Bahai house of worship in Wilmette, Illinois, one of seven in the world.

God whose coming was announced by the Bab. He wrote the group's scripture, *Kitab-i-Aqdas*, detailing the laws of the faith. In 1863 he announced that he was the promised "Manifestation of God." After his death, his son, Abbas Effendi (1844–1891), known as Abd-ul-Baha (also Abdu'l-Bahá, meaning "Servant of Baha"), was recognized as the leader. In 1908, when he was released from prison after political changes in the Ottoman Empire, he undertook successful missionary work, especially in English-speaking countries. In 1921, the leadership passed to the founder's great-grandson, Shogi Effendi (1897–1957), after whose death the movement was reorganized. It is currently being run by a nine-member body, the Universal House of Justice, elected in 1963.

The holy places and world center of Bahaism are in Israel. Bahaism's holiest shrines are concentrated in the Haifa area, where the founder worked and died. The Shrine of the Bab, with its golden dome, is one of Haifa's best-known landmarks. The Bahai organization in the United States, among the largest in the world, is known as the National Spiritual Assembly of Bahais in the United States. A National Spiritual Assembly (NSA) exists in more than 100 countries. Having distanced itself from Islam, Bahaism claims to be a universalist religion, preaching human equality and the religious unity of humankind. The religious prophecies of all past religions are supposedly being fulfilled through Bahaism. Baha'u'llah is described as the messianic figure expected by Judaism, Christianity, Islam, Zoroastrianism, Hinduism, and Buddhism. Earlier prophets are recognized, but with the coming of Baha'u'llah, the "Manifestation of God," a new era has begun, expected to last 1,000 years. It will lead to the Bahai Cycle, lasting 100,000 years. However, this will happen only after a global "calamity," interpreted variously as a natural disaster, environmental decline, nuclear war, or moral decline.

In Bahaism there are rules covering prayers, fasting, marriage, divorce, and burial, and prohibitions against political activities, homosexuality, and the use of drugs. Alcohol and pork are avoided. Prayers are said five times a day. In addition there are blessings for many everyday occasions. The numbers nineteen and nine are considered sacred to the Bahais. Members are expected to pay 19 percent of their earnings to the group. According to the Bahais calendar, which was started in 1844, a year has nineteen months composed of nineteen days, and members meet on the first day of each month. The first day of the year is March 21, following the Zoroastrian calendar, and the nineteen days preceding it are fast days till sundown. Local congregations are tightly knit. Regular meetings are devoted to scripture readings. While there is no involvement in politics, Bahais support the ideal of a world government and the activities of the United Nations. Bahais have suffered persecution in various Islamic countries, especially Iran. According to Amnesty International, about 200 Bahais were executed between 1979 and 1992 in Iran. [*See also* BABISM; *and* NEW HISTORY SOCIETY.]

Sources:

Hatcher, W., and Martin, D. *The Bahai Faith: The Emerging Global Religion.* New York: Harper & Row, 1985.

Smith, P. *The Babi and the Bahai Religions: From Messianic Shiism to a World Religion.* Cambridge: Cambridge University Press, 1987.

Bahais Under the Hereditary Guardianship

Known also as Orthodox Bahais or Remeyites, this international BAHAI splinter group was founded in 1960 by Charles Mason Remey (1873–1974). By 1957 he had become one of the twenty-seven members of the Bahai collective leadership, known as Hands of the Cause, and also of the nine Chief Stewards, following the death of Shoghi Effendi. In 1960 Remey proclaimed himself to be the Second Guardian of the Faith and was excommunicated as a Covenant-Breaker by the other members of the leadership.

According to the group's doctrine of a great global catastrophe, major changes in the earth's crust would lead to the rise of the seas and the death of two-thirds of humanity. Remey predicted in 1960 that a catastrophic flood would inundate most of the United States and urged his followers to move to the Rocky Mountains. This catastrophe was initially prophesied to occur in 1963 and later was prophesied to occur in 1995.

Source:

Smith, P. *The Babi and Bahai Religions: From Messianic Shiism to a World Reli-*

41

gion. Cambridge: Cambridge University Press, 1987.

Bahais Under the Provisions of the Covenant (BUPC)

U.S. schismatic Bahai group founded in 1971 by Leland ("Doc") Jensen (1913–), a chiropractor. Jensen left the official United States Bahai organization in 1960 and joined the BAHAIS UNDER THE HEREDITARY GUARDIANSHIP. Noting the predictions of Charles Mason Remey about the impending flood that would cover the low-lying areas of the United States in 1963, Jensen moved to Missoula, Montana, where he opened a chiropractic office in 1964. He then dropped out of the Bahai faith altogether. In 1969 he was convicted of sex offenses and sentenced to twenty years in prison. In jail, Jensen reported having a series of revelations and claimed several identities mentioned in the Bible.

To create the BUPC credo, Jensen combined Bahai teachings, occult ideas, and Christian eschatology. He predicted a nuclear holocaust in 1980, followed by a thousand years of peace for those who would join BUPC and save themselves from destruction. He was paroled in 1973 and started recruiting followers immediately. Jensen predicted that on April 29, 1980, at 5:55 p.m. a nuclear war would destroy one-third of humanity. This devastation would be followed by twenty years of added upheavals, starvation, revolutions, and natural disasters. In the year 2000, God's Kingdom would be established and 1,000 years of peace would follow.

About 150 followers made preparations for the nuclear holocaust. When this did not take place, revised predictions were issued. The group entered a period of crisis and decline, but managed to survive.

Bahai World Federation

BAHAI dissident organization uniting various groups in opposition to the official leadership of Bahais by Shoghi Effendi. It was founded in 1950 in Acre, Israel, by Amin Effendi, the grandson of Husayn Ali Nuri, the founder of the Bahais.

Bahai World Union

Known also as the World Union of Universal Religion and Universal Peace, this international BAHAI dissident group was founded in 1930 by followers of American Ruth White and German Wilhelm Herrigel. Based mainly in Germany, it was in existence until May 1937, when all Bahai activities in Germany were stopped by the Nazis. In 1948 it was revived by Hermann Zimmer in Stuttgart, Germany. [*See also* NEW HISTORY SOCIETY.]

Balokole ("The Saved Ones")

Also known as the East African Revival, this separatist Protestant movement started in the 1920s as a PENTECOSTAL trend within the offical Protestant mission churches of the colonies of Uganda, Kenya, Tanzania, and Ruanda-Urundi. By 1935 it had become independent. Its doctrine and practices emphasize proselytizing and ecstatic testimony.

Bana Ba Mutimu

Known also as the Followers of Emilyo, or the Catholic Church of the Sacred Heart, this is a Zambian independent

Catholic church, created among the Bemba in 1955 in secession from the Roman Catholic Church. It was banned by the Zambian government in 1960 but has continued to grow.

Bangemela

Known also as the Last Church of God and His Christ, this is an African syncretistic communal group that allows polygyny while following Christian ritual. It is based in Zambia.

Bantu Bethlehem Church of Zion in South Africa

South African independent PENTECOSTAL "healing" church founded around 1940.

Bantu Methodist Church

South African independent indigenous ETHIOPIAN church, known also as the "Donkey Church," founded in the Witwatersrand region in 1932 by J. Mdelwa Hlongwane. This church was created through a secession, led by whites, from the Transvaal Methodist Church. T. M. Ramushu led a secession a year later, creating the Bantu Methodist Church of South Africa. Additional secessions from the two bodies occurred during the following ten years, leading to many legal battles.

Source:
Sundkler, B. G. M. *Bantu Prophets in South Africa.* London: Oxford University Press, 1961.

Bantu New Christian Catholic Apostolic Church

South African independent nativist church founded in 1917 through a secession from the Roman Catholic Church.

Baptist Church of God

British PENTECOSTAL, multiracial group founded in London in the 1970s. This group is made up of West Indian Pentecostals and Free British Baptists.

Baptist Movement of Divine Healing-Mediation, The

U.S. Christian, spiritualist group founded in 1953 in Jacksonville, Florida. The group believes that the Bible gives proof of reincarnation.

Basic Bible Churches of America

U.S. Protestant organization that offers ministry ordination by mail.

Basilio Scientific School

International spiritualist group founded in Argentina in 1917 by Blanca Aubreton and Eugenio Portal. Its branches have operated in Latin America and Italy.

Bathalismo

Philippine indigenous Christian nationalist movement started in 1948.

Batuque

Syncretistic Brazilian spiritualist movement started in the early twentieth century, combining elements of African religions, Catholicism, and Indian shamanism. In recent decades it has been influenced by UMBANDA.

43

Source:
Simpson, G. E. *Black Religions in the New World*. New York: Columbia University Press, 1978.

Bayudaya

Ugandan syncretistic movement started in 1923. Inspired by Christianity, its doctrine regards members as the true successors to the Jews described in the Bible.

Beacon Light Ministry

U.S. British-Israelist occultist group founded by William Kullgren (1887–) in Atascadero, California, in 1933. In addition to BRITISH ISRAELISM, Kullgren promoted astrology, spiritualism, and health foods.

Source:
Roy, J. L. *Apostles of Discord*. Boston: Beacon Press, 1953.

Bear Tribe, The

U.S. commune that promotes Native American traditions, founded in Spokane, Washington, in the late 1970s by Sun Bear, a Chippewa medicine man from Minnesota. Sun Bear "teaches people how to find and follow their own Path of Power, and to live in balance and harmony with the Earth Mother."

Bedwardism

Also known as Spirit Baptist or Native Baptist, this is a Caribbean syncretistic African-Christian movement started in 1889 by Alexander Bedward, who claimed to be the Christian Jesus Christ and predicted his own "ascension to heaven and second coming." Bedward's movement grew out of the ETHIOPIAN Baptist movement, started in Jamaica in 1784 by George Liele, an escaped African American slave. Out of the nineteenth-century Bedwardism movement grew the Jamaica Native Baptist Free Church (Bedwardites). [*See also* SHOUTERS (SPIRITUAL BAPTISTS).]

Behais

International BAHAI splinter movement started following the death of Abdul-Baha in 1891. It has remained in existence in various countries around the world.

Beit Assaph

Israeli Messianic Judaism group founded in the early 1980s in Netanya by David Loden. Its doctrine and practices are PENTECOSTAL.

Beit Immanuel

Israeli HEBREW CHRISTIAN charismatic group established in the 1970s in Tel Aviv by Henry Knight, who came to Israel as an Anglican missionary. A branch known as HaMa'ayan was founded in the 1980s in Kfar Saba, twenty miles north of Tel Aviv.

Bensu

African nativist movement started in Ghana (then the Gold Coast) in the late 1920s by the prophet Appiah. In November 1932 the group clashed with local police, with some loss of life.

Berean Bible Fellowship

FUNDAMENTALIST, DISPENSATIONALIST group, centered in the U.S. Pacific Southwest.

Berean Bible Fellowship (Chicago)

U.S. FUNDAMENTALIST, DISPENSATIONALIST group founded in 1970 by Cornelius Stam as a result of a schism with the GRACE GOSPEL FELLOWSHIP.

Berean Bible Institute

Australian offshoot of JEHOVAH'S WITNESSES, started in Melbourne in 1918 by R. E. B. Nickolson.

Berean Bible Students Church

U.S. offshoot of JEHOVAH'S WITNESSES, started in Cicero, Illinois, in the 1960s.

Berean Fundamental Churches

U.S. FUNDAMENTALIST, evangelical organization started in 1936 by Ivan E. Olsen. The headquarters are located in North Platte, Nebraska.

Beshara Trust

Western Sufi school founded in 1971 in Great Britain by Bulent Rauf (?–1987) in cooperation with J. G. Bennett. It is devoted to the teachings of Muhyiddin Ibn Arabi (1165–1240), a Sufi from Andalusia. The group teaches the practices of meditation and *Zikr*, or "Rememoration," the classical Sufi ceremony described as "the naming and rememoration of God in His singleness and in His aspects of universality." Branches have operated in the United States, Europe, Australia, and Israel. [*See also* SUFI ORDER IN THE WEST.]

Bethany Bible Church and Related Independent Bible Churches

U.S. FUNDAMENTALIST, DISPENSATIONALIST group started in the 1950s in the Phoenix, Arizona, area. It continues to operate in the Phoenix area.

Bethany Church Mission

African independent PENTECOSTAL church, founded in Ghana in 1962 in secession from HOLY TRINITY HEALING CHURCH.

Beth Bnai Abraham (BBA)

U.S. African American Jewish group founded in 1924 in New York City by Arnold Josiah Ford. Ford was an associate of Marcus Garvey, the renowned proponent of Black Nationalism, and had earlier headed a similar organization known as the Moorish Zionist Church. The BBA disbanded after Ford left the United States and disappeared in 1931. It was succeeded by the COMMANDMENT KEEPERS CONGREGATION OF THE LIVING GOD.

Source:
Brotz, H. M. *The Black Jews of Harlem.* New York: Schocken Books, 1970.

Bethel Apostolic (Shilo) Church

Jamaican indigenous PENTECOSTAL movement, started in the 1930s. It is connected with the British FIRST UNITED CHURCH OF JESUS CHRIST (APOSTOLIC).

Bethel Christian Temple

U.S. Spanish-speaking PENTECOSTAL group founded in 1931 in New York City by Francisco Olazabal. In 1939 it joined other Spanish-speaking groups to form the ASSEMBLY OF CHRISTIAN CHURCHES, INC. [See also CONCILIO OLAZABAL DE IGLESIAS LATINO AMERICANO.]

Bethel Ministerial Association

Formerly known as the Evangelistic Missionary Alliance, Bethel Assembly, and Bethel Baptist Assembly, this U.S. PENTECOSTAL group was founded in 1934 by A. F. Varnell in Evansville, Indiana. The group doctrine emphasizes faith healing, placing less emphasis on speaking in tongues.

Bethel Temple

PENTECOSTAL group formed in 1914, based in the northwestern United States.

Bethesda

Israeli Hebrew Christian congregation founded in Haifa in the 1970s by foreign missionaries.

Bethesda Church Mission

African independent PENTECOSTAL church founded in Ghana in 1965 in secession from the DIVINE HEALER'S CHURCH.

Bethlehem of Judea Apostolic Church in Zion, South Africa

South African independent ZIONIST church founded in the 1940s.

Beth Messiah

U.S. MESSIANIC JUDAISM group based in Cincinnati, Ohio. This group was founded by Martin Chernoff in 1970.

Beth Messiah

U.S. MESSIANIC JUDAISM group based in New Hanover, New Jersey. This group was founded by Larry Feldman in the 1970s.

Beth Messiah

U.S. MESSIANIC JUDAISM group based in Virginia Beach, Virginia. This group was founded by Joseph Rosenfarb in the 1970s.

Beth Messiah Congregation

U.S. MESSIANIC JUDAISM group that serves as the headquarters of the UNION OF MESSIANIC JEWISH CONGREGATIONS. This group was founded in the 1970s by Daniel C. Juster in Gaithersburg, Maryland. [See also HEBREW CHRISTIANS.]

Beth Yeshua

U.S. HEBREW CHRISTIAN group founded in 1972 by Raymond Cohen, a former associate of the American Board of Missions to the Jews Inc. Beth Yeshua has branches in New York City, Philadelphia, and Florida. It is operated and financed by American Messianic Missions, Inc. [See also CHOSEN PEOPLE MINISTRIES.]

Bible Churches (Classics Expositor)

U.S. independent FUNDAMENTALIST, DISPENSATIONALIST group in Oklahoma, founded by C. E. McLain in the 1940s. It publishes *The Classics Expositor*.

Bible Fellowship Union

British offshoot of JEHOVAH'S WITNESSES, founded in 1945 by A. D. Hudson. Hudson claims to follow the original teachings of Charles Taze Russell (1852–1916), founder of Jehovah's Witnesses. It is similar in doctrine to the U.S.-based PASTORAL BIBLE INSTITUTE.

Bible Holiness Movement

North American conservative Protestant group with headquarters in Vancouver, British Columbia. It was originally organized in 1949 as the Bible Holiness Mission by Wesley H. Wakefield. Like the SALVATION ARMY, from which it grew, the Bible Holiness Movement engages in social welfare activities. It also promotes interracial cooperation and integration.

Bible Missionary Church

U.S. conservative Protestant group founded in 1955 by Glenn Griffith, a former minister in the Church of the Nazarene. Doctrine emphasizes strict adherence to a simple lifestyle, which includes avoiding television.

Bible Pattern Church Fellowship

International Christian, FUNDAMENTALIST, PENTECOSTAL, and BRITISH-ISRAELIST group founded in 1940 by George Jeffreys. The group, which practices healing and speaking in tongues, announces the imminent arrival of Jesus Christ, beginning the thousand-years reign. Some branches operate under the name Union for Revival. [*See also* ELIM FOURSQUARE GOSPEL.]

Bible Presbyterian Church

U.S. FUNDAMENTALIST group founded by Carl McIntire (1906–) in 1937 in dissent from the ORTHODOX PRESBYTERIAN CHURCH, which McIntire and his followers considered too liberal. The group became known for its militant conservative stance and its anti-Communist crusades. To unite churches with similar conservative views, McIntire formed the American Council of Christian Churches (ACCC) in 1941 and the International Council of Christian Churches (ICCC) in 1948. In 1956 the majority of the members left to form the Evangelical Presbyterian Church in protest against McIntire's policies. In 1969 McIntire was removed from the leadership of the ACCC and formed the American Christian Action Council (ACAC). Another group of members left the Bible Presbyterian Church to form the WESTMINSTER BIBLICAL FELLOWSHIP.

Bible Speaks

U.S. FUNDAMENTALIST church founded in 1973 by Carl H. Stevens, Jr., in Lenox, Massachusetts. By the mid-1980s it had its own radio and television programs and sent missionaries to twenty-one countries. In 1986 the church was sued by a former member for fraud; it lost the case and filed for bankruptcy. Next, Stevens founded a group called Greater Grace World Outreach in Baltimore, Maryland.

Dr. Carl McIntire (left center), founder of the Bible Presbyterian Church, leads a parade in Chicago in 1975, urging America to resist further Communist takeovers in Southeast Asia and elsewhere.

Bible Student Examiner, The

U.S. offshoot of JEHOVAH'S WITNESSES, started in 1939 by Olin Moyle (?–1959). Later, Moyle joined the UNITED ISRAEL WORLD UNION.

Bible Temple

U.S. PENTECOSTAL, FUNDAMENTALIST group founded in the 1980s in Portland, Oregon. It has been one of the centers of the Restoration Movement in North America.

Bible Way Church of Our Lord Jesus Christ World Wide

U.S. PENTECOSTAL group with African American membership, founded in 1957 by Smallwood E. Williams and other former members of the CHURCH OF OUR LORD JESUS CHRIST OF THE APOSTOLIC FAITH.

Biosophical Institute (Biosophy)

U.S. NEW THOUGHT group founded in 1923 in New York City by Frederick Kettner.

Birmingham Church of Christ

Local British branch of the BOSTON CHURCH OF CHRIST, founded in the 1980s. [See also BODY OF CHRIST; CHRISTIAN

GROWTH MINISTRIES; CHRISTIAN RE-
STORATION MINISTRIES; *and* CROSSROADS
CHURCHES OF CHRIST.]

Black Hebrews (The Kingdom of God Nation)

Known also as the Hebrew Israelites or
the Original Hebrew Israelite Nation,
this is an African American Jewish
group founded in Chicago in the 1960s.
Its leader, Ben-Ami Carter, sometimes
known as Ben-Ami Ben-Israel, was born
in Chicago in 1940 with the birth name
Gerson Parker. In the 1960s he became
a storefront preacher for the Abeita
Culture Center, an evangelical church
on Chicago's South Side. There he
developed his theology of Black Hebrews. The basis for the Black Hebrews'
faith is the claim that the original
Israelites, written about in the Old Testament and exiled from Israel 4,000 years
ago, were black. The Black Hebrews
believe that descendants of those
blacks should now go back to this land
and reclaim it. The faith states that the
real heirs to ancient Judaism are not contemporary Jews but contemporary
blacks.

The Black Hebrews' faith includes a
belief in immortality. Their leader is
quoted as saying, "We are phasing out
death and are on the path toward solving
the mysteries of everlasting life. The
Bible shows that some of the prophets
lived to be 900 years old. I am positive
that, following the way of righteousness,
some of our people will live to be 600."
The group practices a holistic lifestyle,
and members do not consume meat,
dairy products, tobacco, sugar, or alcohol. Purity is also kept through the use of
clothes according to "natural" rules; that
is, they wear only natural fibers such as
cotton.

Members fast every Saturday. They do
not watch movies or television. They
change their names, most of which were
given by slave owners and traders, to
Hebrew names and practice polygyny.
There is a priestly caste, and twelve ministers serve under the spiritual leader,
Carter. He prophesied 1977 as the year of
the final battle of Armageddon, after
which his sect would dominate the
world.

In the late 1960s, Carter led his followers first to Liberia and then to Israel. The
first Black Hebrew families arrived in Israel by late 1969. The Israeli government
and the Israeli public have objected to
the arrival of the Black Hebrews, and
most remained in Israel as illegal immigrants. The government has tried to keep
other Black Hebrews from entering the

Ben-Ami Carter, founder and leader of the Kingdom of
God Nation (Black Hebrews).

49

Ben-Ami Carter of the Black Hebrews holds a press conference on Mount Zion after Israeli authorities had ordered him and his followers to leave the country.

country and joining their group there. In the past many have been denied entry, but in the 1990s most have been granted permanent resident status in Israel. In Israel group members sell organic foods and are in demand as musical performers.

Source:

Lounds, M., Jr. *Israel's Black Hebrews: Black Americans in Search of Identity.* Washington, DC: University Press of America, 1981.

Black Israelites

Jamaican indigenous syncretistic group started around 1900. Its doctrine combines Christian ideas with African traditions.

Blue Rose Ministry

U.S. occultist group founded in Arizona in the 1970s. It claims to receive messages from extraterrestrials.

B'nai Noach ("Children of Noach")

Also known as the Noachide movement, and officially known as Agudat Keren B'nai No'ach, this U.S. Jewish-oriented group was started in the 1970s by Vendyl Jones, a former Baptist minister, in Fort Worth, Texas. Members are "Gentiles who follow the Laws of Noah, and practice Torah faith for non-Jews as defined by orthodox Judaism."

The group proclaims the value and superiority of Judaism, as it believes all Christians should do. Members call upon gentiles to keep the "Seven Laws of Noah," according to Jewish traditions. A special Jewish liturgy, including a marriage ceremony and a prayerbook, are being prepared. The movement has been recognized and encouraged by Orthodox Jewish organizations in the United States and Israel. Branches have been started in Europe and West Africa. [*See also* EMMANUEL; *and* FRAZIER CHAPEL.]

B'nai Yeshua

U.S. HEBREW-CHRISTIAN group founded in the 1970s.

B'nei Avraham

British HEBREW-CHRISTIAN group founded in London in 1813.

Body of Christ

International Protestant FUNDAMENTALIST organization founded in Argentina in 1970 by Juan Carlos Ortiz, former ASSEMBLY OF GOD minister. The organization is structured according to the SHEPHERDING principle, which provides for an authoritarian leadership style and close supervision of members. This style has been the basis of what has been called the SHEPHERDING movement, which includes, in addition to the Body of Christ, CHRISTIAN GROWTH MINISTRIES *and* CHRISTIAN RESTORATION MINISTRIES.

Body of Christ, The

Known officially as the Endtime Body-Christian Ministries, Inc., and also as the End Times Ministry, The Movement, or The Body, this is a U.S. PENTECOSTAL, ADVENTIST group founded in the late 1960s by Sam Fife (1925–1979), a minister from Miami, and C. E. ("Buddy") Cobb, an airline pilot. Fife has referred to himself as "the light of the world" and has called on followers to separate themselves from their communities and families in preparation for the "fullness of time." To separate its members from the world in preparation for the Second Coming, the group opened "wilderness" farms in Mississipi, South America, Canada, and Alaska. Local chapters functioned with great autonomy and were known by different names. Thus, the chapter in Greentown, Ohio, has been known as Christian Ministries, and the one in Hollywood, Florida, as Word Mission. The doctrine included beliefs in possession by demons, as well as an imminent Second Coming. [*See also* MANIFEST SONS OF GOD.]

Bong-Nam Gyo

Korean indigenous religious movement started in the early twentieth century. By the late twentieth centrury, it had given rise to about fifteen new branches.

Boston Church of Christ (BCC)

U.S. FUNDAMENTALIST organization founded in Boston in 1980 by Kip McKean. A branch of the CROSSROADS CHURCHES OF CHRIST, BCC grew out of the Lexington Church of Christ and is structured according to the SHEPHERDING principle, which provides for an authoritarian leadership style and close supervision of members. This style has been the basis of what has been called the shepherding movement, or "discipleship," which includes the BODY OF CHRIST, CHRISTIAN GROWTH MINISTRIES, and CHRISTIAN RESTORATION MINISTRIES.

The group has operated branches and missions in the United States, Latin America, and Europe. [*See also* INTERNATIONAL CHURCHES OF CHRIST; LONDON CHURCH OF CHRIST; *and* NEW YORK CHURCH OF CHRIST.]

Bovar (Oric) Group

U.S. Christian group based in New York City, founded and led in the early 1970s by Oric Bovar (1918–1977), a former opera coach. Bovar claimed that he was Jesus Christ and that he could raise the dead. When one of his disciples died, he kept the body and was found by police praying over it. He was charged with a misdemeanor for keeping the body. On April 11, 1977, the day he was supposed to stand trial, Oric Bovar jumped out of a tenth-floor window, committing suicide.

Brahma Kumaris (Raja Yoga)

Officially known as the Brahma Kumaris World Spiritual University (BKWSU) or BK, and sometimes known as Raja Yoga or World Spiritual University, this is an international Hindu revival movement founded in 1937 in Karachi by Dada Lekh Raj (1877–1969). A wealthy diamond merchant, he started having visions at the age of sixty and adopted the name of Prajapita Brahma. In the early 1970s, the group opened a branch in London, its first outside of India, and since then it has spread to continental Europe, North and South America, Africa, and Australia. International headquarters are located in Mount Abu, Rajastan, India.

Brahma Kumaris teaches the practice of Raja Yoga meditation, which does not require the use of mantras, special postures, or breathing exercises, but focuses on visual contact with the founder's picture and with red lights representing the "supreme soul." It offers courses in "stress management and positive thinking" to nonmembers. Sexual activity is proscribed, and the sexes are strictly separated. Members are known as BKs or brahmins. Most active members of the group are celibate women, and the leadership is exclusively female. The Brahma Kumaris belief system is based on pacifism and love, but at the same time it predicted a nuclear war in 1996 that would wipe out all of the world's population except for the Brahma Kumaris membership. The group operates the Global Co-Operation for a Better World organization, which engages in charity work around the world. While the requirements for full membership include a strict vegetarian diet, celibacy, and daily meditation, "partial members" are also recognized.

Brahma Samaj

Also known as Brahmo Samaj (the God Society or the Fellowship of Believers of the One True God), the Theistic Church of India, and the Unitarian Union, this is a Hindu revitalization movement founded by Ram Mohan Roy (1774–1833) in 1828 in Calcutta. Roy was born into a wealthy Indian family and held a high position in the Indian civil service. After retiring at age forty-two, he devoted his life to religious writing, translations, and leadership. He is considered the initiator of the cultural movement known as the Bengali Renaissance. The Brahma Samaj developed out of the British India Unitarian Association, which Roy founded in 1827. He was first exposed to Islamic teachings and then studied Western languages and religions, which led him to founding the Unitarian Association, where followers of all theistic faiths met weekly for common prayers. He regarded contemporary Hinduism as a degeneration of earlier monotheism and promoted a return to the original unitarian doctrines.

After the founder's death, Debendranath Tagore (1817–1905) became leader. The movement suffered a split in 1865 when the majority of its members followed Kehsab Chandra Sen (1838–1884) in forming a new organization known as Brahma Samaj of India. Tagore represented more conservative Hindu views, since he was opposed to intercaste marriages and to the remarriage of widows. Unlike Roy, he was committed to a return to the ancient Vedas rather than to a rapprochement with Christianity. The group under the Tagore leadership, which became known as the Adi Brahma Samaj, concentrated on trying to reform Hinduism. Sen's followers represented less conservative views. The Brama Samaj of India later split into the Sadharan Brahmo Samaj (Universal Society of God) and THE CHURCH OF THE NEW DISPENSATION. [See also ARYA SAMAJ; and PRATHANA SAMAJ.]

Branch Seventh Day Adventists (Branch SDA)

Commonly referred to as Branch Davidians, this is a U.S. ADVENTIST group started in Texas in 1959. Members of the Branch, in its various organizational forms, have followed the teachings of Victor T. Houteff. Houteff deviated from established SEVENTH-DAY ADVENTIST CHURCH teachings in the 1930s by predicting the coming of a Davidian kingdom in Palestine, preceding the Second Coming of Christ. Most of Houteff's followers became members of the DAVIDIAN SEVENTH-DAY ADVENTIST ASSOCIATION. The Branch Seventh-Day Adventists refused to accept Houteff's wife, Florence, as leader of the group, especially after a failed prophecy for the arrival of the Davidian Kingdom. The group was based in Waco, Texas. Group beliefs include an expectation of an imminent Second Coming, preoccupation with Biblical prophecies, and keeping the Sabbath on Saturday.

In the 1960s, Ben Roden (?–1978) renamed the group Branch Davidians. He was succeeded by his wife, Lois (1915–1986). Their son George Roden (1938–) tried to become leader in the 1970s but was then ousted by a new leader, Vernon Wayne Howell. (Roden, after leaving the group, shot his roommate in 1989 and then cut the body to pieces. He was found innocent by reason of insanity by a court in Texas and hospitalized. In 1995 he escaped to New York but was caught and returned to Texas.)

Howell (1960–1993), known after 1990 as David Koresh, came from a Seventh-Day Adventist family and grew up in that movement. Howell joined the Branch Davidians in 1982, became the lover of Lois Roden, and became the group leader in 1987 after she died. In 1988 he stood trial for the attempted murder of George Roden, but the deliberations of the court ended in a hung jury.

Under Koresh's leadership, the group became known as the "Students of the Seven Seals." Koresh alleged that he had experienced a revelation showing that he was the seventh and final angel of God. He claimed to be the Messiah. In 1989 he

The Mount Carmel compound of the Branch Seventh Day Adventists, in 1993, during a stand-off with the FBI and the Bureau of Alcohol, Tobacco, and Firearms.

officially announced to the membership his right to all females in the group. Some followers left because of this proclamation. At age twelve, girls were moved to gender-segregated adult quarters, where they were made available to Koresh. By 1993 more than a dozen women in the group considered themselves wives of the leader. His legal wife, Rachel Howell (1970–1993), married him at age fourteen.

Koresh gathered an arsenal in the 1990s—350 guns and 2 million rounds of ammunition—thereby attracting the attention of federal officials. On February 28, 1993, the Davidian Compound, called Mount Carmel, was raided by more than 100 agents of the U.S. Bureau of Alcohol, Tobacco, and Firearms (ATF) searching for illegal weapons. The Branch Davidians opened fire and four agents, as well as four group members, died in the exchange of gunshots that followed. This led to a fifty-one-day siege by the FBI and the ATF, leading the Davidians to dub their compound Ranch Apocalypse.

On April 19, 1993, as millions around the world watched the events unfold on television, the Mount Carmel compound went up in flames. Eighty-six group members and their dependents died, including Koresh and seventeen children. Most of the adults who died in Mount Carmel were recruited to the group from among Seventh Day Adventists in Hawaii, England, and Australia.

Following the end of the siege, nine members of the group, who had left the compound before the fire, were sentenced to prison terms for their involvement, five of them for forty years.

Sources:

Reavis, D. J. *The Ashes of Waco: An Investigation.* New York: Simon & Schuster, 1995.

Wright, S. A., ed. *Armageddon in Waco: Critical Perspectives on the Branch Davidian Conflict.* Chicago: University of Chicago Press, 1995.

Branham Tabernacle

Known also as Branhamites, or End Time Believers, this U.S. PENTECOSTAL group was founded by William Marrion Branham (1909–1965) in Indiana in 1946. Branham became known during his lifetime for his claims of visions and angelic voices speaking to him. He also became known as a faith healer. His doctrine, as presented in many sermons, deviated from mainstream Christianity in rejecting trinitarianism (the divinity of the Trinity composed of Father, Son, and Holy Ghost) and emphasizing belief in Jesus Christ as God. Missions around the world have made his message internationally known, especially in Asia and Africa.

Sources:

Harrell, D. E., Jr. *All Things Are Possible.* Bloomington: Indiana University Press, 1975.

Weaver, C. D. *The Healer-Prophet, William Marrion Branham: A Study in the Prophetic in American Pentecostalism.* Macon, GA: Mercer University Press, 1987.

Brazil for Christ (OBPC)

Known also as Igreja Evangelica Pente O Brasil Para Cristo, this Protestant PENTECOSTAL group was founded in Rio de Janeiro in 1955 by Manoel de Mello Silva (1929–). It has become prominent because of its use of modern communications and its political involvements.

Bread of Life Ministries

Filipino independent FUNDAMENTALIST Christian group founded in 1983. It operates through small bible study groups that meet regularly.

Brethren in Christ

North American FUNDAMENTALIST group dating in its present form back to 1862, but having earlier European roots. Members practice faith healing.

Bridge Center for Spiritual Studies, The

U.S. Christian-Theosophical, New Age group founded in 1975 in Wheaton, Illinois, by Brent D. Ferre, and relocated in Arizona in 1985.

It is "devoted to facilitating Self-Awareness and Spiritual Empowerment through the Christian Philosophy." Its doctrine includes mostly Theosophical concepts, and the group operates mainly by mail.

Bridge Meditation Center, The

U.S. occultist group based in Georgia

and founded around 1970. Practices and beliefs combine "meditation, new thought principles, aquarian age living, Christ truth teaching, Zen and Tibetan Buddhist philosophy, and universal scriptures."

Bridge to Freedom, The

Known today as the New Age Church of the Christ, this U.S. THEOSOPHICAL group was founded in the 1950s in New York by Geraldine Innocente and other members of the "I AM" group. Teachings are based on messages received from the Ascended Masters. The Bridge to Freedom has inspired several similar groups around the world. [*See also* LICHTKREIS MICHAEL.]

British Israelism

Known also as Anglo-Israelism, this belief system, shared by numerous Christian groups and individuals, states that the modern Celto-Saxon nations, such as Great Britain and the United States, are the racial and true descendants of the biblical Children of Israel. This is related to the idea of the Ten Lost Tribes, which were said to have existed in the ancient Kingdom of Israel and were then dispersed. British Israelism asserts that some of these lost tribes reached Britain.

Such ideas were held by the seventeenth-century Levellers, but the movement really started in the nineteenth century, following the visions of Richard Brothers (1757–1824) and the writings of John Wilson (?–1870), F. R. A. Glover (1800–1881), and Edward Hine (1825–1891). In 1875 the Anglo-Israel Association was founded in London, and in 1919 the British Israel World Federation was established. These groups have promoted British Israelism through publications and lectures.

British Israelism represents a FUNDA-MENTALIST position, asserting the literal truth of the Bible. Some of the groups have adopted sabbatarianism, the practice of strictly observing the Sabbath. Numerous British-Israelism groups have operated in the United States, where the movement had its own seminary, the Dayton Theological Seminary, between 1947 and 1953.

The movement has attracted attention because of its prejudices and assertions in regard to all groups that are not considered Anglo-Saxon. British-Israelists in the United States have been the inspiration for the related IDENTITY MOVEMENT, which encompasses a number of small groups.

Source:
Roy, R. L. *Apostles of Discord.* Boston: Beacon Press, 1953.

British Israel World Federation

International group that is the central organization of BRITISH ISRAELISM in Great Britain and the British Commonwealth. It was started in 1890, officially organized in 1919, and is headquartered in London.

Brockwood

British school founded in 1969 in Brockwood, Hampshire, England. This school, for children over fourteen, is conducted according to the teachings of Krishnamurti.

Brotherhood of Light

U.S. occultist group dating back at least to 1876, when Emma Harding Britten presented the Brotherhood of Light to the public in her book *Art Magic*. The group was headed by "a scribe, an astrologer, and a seer," and astrology played a major role. Between the two World Wars, under the leadership of the astrologer Elbert Benjamine (1882–1951), also known as C. C. Zain, it developed into an international organization also known as the Church of Light (incorporated in 1932). The group states that "astrology is the science of finding and utilizing the natural potentialities as indicated in the planetary chart of birth. It becomes a religion when it shows the individual how these natural tendencies can and should be used for the benefit of mankind and the furtherance of the purposes of Deity." Branches operate across the United States and in Britain, Mexico, Canada, and Chile.

Brotherhood of the Cross and Star

Sometimes known as the Holy Apostles Community, this is a syncretistic African movement with strong Christian elements and some Hindu influences. It was started in 1954 by Offu Ebongo (1918–), known as the Father or Olumba Olumba Obu. The founder, believed to be an incarnation of Jesus Christ and a successor to Krishna, protects members from diseases and troubles. He is considered to be omnipotent, omniscient, and in possession of "spiritual X-rays," that his followers also share. The mere mention of his initials, O. O. O., is believed to save the person from any danger. According to Ebongo, "The Kingdom of God, which

our Lord Jesus Christ had promised, has now been established." Members are called upon to follow a modest lifestyle, and to avoid smoking, drinking, and having sex.

The Brotherhood founded the Aiyetoro ("happy city") socioreligious community in Western Nigeria. This community includes industry, hospitals, and schools, and provides its members with the highest living standards of any village in the country. The Brotherhood also operates plantations and trade organizations. It has had branches in the United States and Great Britain.

Brother Julius

U.S. Christian-inspired group founded and led by Julius Schacknow (1924–). During Schacknow's U.S. Navy service in World War II, he experienced considerable difficulties, resulting in visits to psychiatric wards. In 1947 he heard the "voice of God" and converted from Judaism to Christianity. He has said that he is Jesus Christ, back on earth for the Second Coming.

Brother Julius was established in 1968 in New York City and in 1971 moved to Meriden, Connecticut. It practices faith healing and since 1976 has operated several successful business enterprises, specializing in real estate and construction. The founder has been accused of having sexual relations with underaged female followers.

Bruderhof

Known officially as the Hutterian Brethren and also as the Hutterian Society of Brothers, or just the Society of Brothers, this is a neo-orthodox, Christian, communal, pacifist movement founded in 1920 in Germany by Eberhard Arnold (1883–1935). Arnold's Christian Anabaptist ideas led this group to merge temporarily with the Hutterites which lasted until 1956. Since their split, relations between the original Hutterite communities and the Bruderhof, which regards itself as neo-Hutterite, have been tense. Political and economic pressures have necessitated the Bruderhof's migration to Lichtenstein, Great Britain, Paraguay, and eventually the United States, where it has remained since 1954 in several communal settlements. A commune has been in existence in Britain since 1971, and one was started in Germany in the 1980s.

Sources:

Whitworth, J. *God's Blueprints: A Sociological Study of Three Utopian Sects.* London: Routledge & Kegan Paul, 1975.

Zablocki, B. *The Joyful Community*. Baltimore: Penguin, 1971.

Brunton (Paul) Philosophic Foundation

U.S. syncretistic group based in New York state and founded in the 1970s to "seek a practical philosophy that will embrace but not merge the distinctive contributions of each system of thought in order to create a living synthesis of timeless truths." It distributes the teachings of Paul Brunton (1898–1981), known to his followers as P. B., who claimed to be a disciple of RAMANA MAHARSHI. Brunton, born in Great Britain, lived for many years in Mysore, India, before coming to the United States.

Source:

Masson, J. M. *My Father's Guru: A Journey through Spirituality and Disillusion.* Reading, MA: Addison-Wesley, 1993.

Buchwezi Spirit Society

Traditional African group devoted to spirit possession and exorcism, started in Tanzania in the 1940s.

Builders, The

Also known as Sunburst Farms, this is a U.S. syncretistic commune founded as Brotherhood of the Sun by Norman Paulsen (known as Brother Norman) at Sunburst Ranch near Santa Barbara, California, in 1971. Paulsen had been a member of the SELF-REALIZATION FELLOWSHIP, and his beliefs combine Hindu ideas with Christianity. According to Paulsen, the Second Coming occurred on January 1, 1961, together with the coming of the Aquarian Age. "The Builders derives it name from the ancient ones referred to in Genesis as the Sons of God, who were on earth before the creation of man. These beings are Christ-conscious entities, responsible for the evolution of life forms in the expanding spheres of creation. The Builders of old and of present are the true Sons and Daughters of Divine Spirit." The group practices "the SUN meditation technique" and vegetarianism, and avoids drugs and alcohol.

Builders of the Adytum (BOTA)

U.S. occultist group inspired by the Hermetic Order of the Golden Dawn (OGD), which was founded in 1920 in New York by Paul Case (1894–1954).

Teachings, which are mostly transmitted by correspondence, instruct in tarot reading, healing, the Kabbalah, and alchemy. They also include messages from the Masters, in the tradition of THEOSOPHY.

Source:

Ellwood, R. S. *Religious and Spiritual Groups in Modern America.* Englewood Cliffs, NJ: Prentice-Hall, 1973.

Bungan

Indonesian nativist syncretistic movement with a strong Christian emphasis, started in Kalimantan and Sarawak in 1947.

Bussho Gohnen Kai

Started after World War II, this Japanese religion developed out of the Nichiren Shu tradition. It has been involved in politics since the 1960s and has taken a right-wing, nationalistic stance. In the 1970s it formed a right-wing religious group together with SEICHO-NO-IE and SEKAI KYUSEI KYO. [*See also* RISSHO KOSEI-KAI (INTEGRATIVE BECOMING, OR THE SOCIETY FOR THE ESTABLISHMENT OF RIGHTEOUSNESS AND FRIENDLY RELATIONS).]

Bwiti

Known also as mbueti, *Église des Banzie* (Church of the Initiates), or Religion d'Eboga, this is an African syncretistic movement combining Catholic beliefs and local ancestral cults. It was started around 1910 among members of the Fang group of Gabon, West Africa, and is especially strong in Gabon and Equatorial Guinea. Members are initiated through the use of the local drug known as *eboga*, or *iboga*, a hallucinogen that induces visions of the supernatural world. In the 1990s there were hopes that this drug could be used to cure drug addiction in the West.

Source:

Fernandez, J. W. *Bwiti: An Ethnography of the Religious Imagination in Africa.* Princeton: Princeton University Press, 1982.

Byakko Shinkokai (White Light Society)

Japanese religion founded by Masahisa Goi in the 1960s. Its doctrine emphasizes supernatural healing powers (attributed to the late founder) and worship of a "space god." Members pray for world peace by chanting the names of all the countries on Earth.

C

Cafh Spiritual Culture Society

International GURDJIEFF-inspired group devoted to "spiritual unfolding." According to official Cafh history, the group was founded in 1937 in Buenos Aires, Argentina, by Santiago Bovisio, known as Don Santiago. He has acquired a following in the Spanish-speaking world, in the United States, Australia, and Israel. Members study the writings of Jorge Waxemberg, an Argentine mystic who wrote the book *De la Mistica y los Estados de Conciencia* in Buenos Aires in 1971.

California Miracles Center

U.S. Christian, NEW THOUGHT group organized around the A COURSE IN MIRACLES belief system. Started in San Francisco, California, in 1978 by Tony Ponticello, it offers weekly services, ordination for ministers, classes, workshops, books, and other materials. [*See also* FOUNDATION FOR "A COURSE IN MIRACLES"; FOUNDATION FOR INNER PEACE; INTERFAITH FELLOWSHIP; *and* MIRACLE DISTRIBUTION CENTER (MDC).]

Calumet Pagan Temple

U.S. neo-pagan group founded by Richard Clarke in the 1960s, and based in Calumet City, Illinois. The group is a member of the MIDWEST PAGAN COUNCIL.

Calvary Chapel

U.S. FUNDAMENTALIST organization incorporating numerous independent congregations, especially on the West Coast. It was started by Chuck Smith in Costa Mesa, California, in 1965. Some members use glossolalia, or speaking in tongues. The group sponsors an active outreach ministry under the name The Word for Today. Overseas operations have been extensive, including branches in Latin America, Europe, and West Africa. [*See also* VINEYARD CHRISTIAN FELLOWSHIP.]

Calvary Fellowship, Inc.

U.S. FUNDAMENTALIST, PENTECOSTAL, BRITISH-ISRAELIST group founded by Clyde Edminster, and based in Tacoma, Washington.

Calvary Pentecostal Church

U.S. PENTECOSTAL group founded in 1931. It is active in the Northwestern United States, with headquarters in Bellingham, Washington.

Camp Farthest Out

U.S. FUNDAMENTALIST-NEW THOUGHT group devoted to prayer and faith healing. It was founded by Glenn Clark, a member of the Plymouth Congregational Church in Minneapolis, Minnesota, in 1930. The group has branches in Canada, Great Britain, and India.

Camphill Movement

International ANTHROPOSOPHICAL subsidiary movement devoted to taking care of mentally handicapped individuals through "curative education" in cooperative farming communities. Founded

Members of a Brazilian spiritualist movement called Candomblé perform a ceremony to honor their sea goddess. In a Catholic country, they combine elements of Catholicism with African and Indian traditions.

in Scotland in 1940 by Karl König, it had sixty communities in Europe, the Americas, South Africa, and Israel in 1990. The quality and results of its work with the retarded have been considered remarkable by experts in the field. Members farm through "byodynamic," or organic (using no chemicals), means and follow the idea of "nature cycles" advanced by Rudolf Steiner, the founder of the Anthroposophical Society. The Camphill Association of North America, founded in 1983, is made up of five communities.

Candomblé

Syncretistic neo-African movement in Brazil, started in the nineteenth century.

Its pantheon of saints and spirits, which combines figures drawn from African and Roman Catholic traditions, guides believers seeking answers to life's problems. A divination system based on sixteen shells is used, and public ceremonies attract large crowds.

Cao Dai

Vietnamese syncretistic, MILLENARIAN movement that started as a secret society and grew into a large-scale movement after World War I. It was begun in 1919 by Nguyen Van Chieu, a colonial civil servant, and officially founded in 1926 by Le Van Trung. Membership was drawn from the lower middle class around Saigon. Its doctrine is elaborate and its well-developed bureaucracy, modeled after the Roman Catholic Church, is headed by a pope. The group claims to represent the final manifestation of God, and combines Taoist, Buddhist, Confucian, and Christian traditions. Asian leaders, Europeans (e.g., Victor Hugo), and Vietnamese personages are numbered among its saints. Membership is divided into nine levels. Moving up the scale requires devotion and self-denial. Members are vegetarian, but their children are allowed meat several days a month.

Cao Dai, which was supported by church-owned corporations and members' contributions, operated a well-developed social welfare system. It was first tied to the French colonial administration. During the Japanese occupation, the group's second pope, Pham Long Tac, supported Japan against the French, and then supported the Bao Dai regime. The group had its own military force, fighting for the Japanese, and then the French. In the early 1950s it fought against the Viet-Minh. When Ngo Din Diem came to power in South Vietnam in 1954, the Cao Dai controlled a whole province. In April 1954 Ngo Din Diem defeated the Cao Dai militia, which was completely dissolved in 1956. Cao Dai was neutral during the years of U.S. involvement in Vietnam, and since 1975 has been free to operate, experiencing much growth. [*See also* HOA HAO.]

Cargo Cults

Collective term for a variety of nativist, syncretistic movements that have appeared most often in Oceania, which is a collective name for islands in the Pacific Ocean, usually including Australia and New Zealand. Promoting the belief in obtaining "cargo" (*i.e.*, manufactured goods and wealth) through spiritual means, these groups sometimes expect that ancestors will return, delivering the "cargo."

Sources:

Lanternari, V. *The Religions of the Oppressed*. New York: Knopf, 1963.

Maher, R. F. *New Men of Papua: A Study of Culture Change*. Madison, WI: University of Wisconsin Press, 1961.

Worsley, P. *The Trumpet Shall Sound*. New York: Schocken, 1968.

Carolina Evangelistic Association

U.S. PENTECOSTAL group founded in 1930 in Charlotte, North Carolina, by A. G. Garr (1874–1944), a traveling revival preacher and former missionary for the CHURCH OF GOD (CLEVELAND, TENNESSEE). This group is a member of the PENTECOSTAL FELLOWSHIP OF NORTH AMERICA.

Cathedral of Tomorrow

U.S. FUNDAMENTALIST congregation founded in 1958 by Rex Humbard, Jr. Humbard came from a family of radio preachers and became one himself at an early age. In 1953 he founded the Calvary Temple in Akron, Ohio, and in 1958 decided to build the Cathedral in the same place. The main activity of the Cathedral has been a television service, broadcast over hundreds of stations in the United States. In the 1970s the organization ran into serious financial difficulties but recovered later.

Catholic Apostolic Church

Officially known as the Holy Catholic Apostolic Church. Also known as the Irvingites, after Edward Irving (1792–1834), whose teachings inspired it. This is an international MILLENARIAN movement. In 1825 Irving, minister of the Caledonian Church in Hatton Garden, London, started preaching apocalyptic messages that proclaimed the impending Second Coming of Jesus Christ, fixed for 1864. In preparation he called for a restructuring of the Christian church. In 1829 a larger church, the Regent Square Presbyterian Church, was built for him, but his popularity was already in decline. In 1830 he was charged with heresy and in 1833 lost his pulpit. The Catholic Apostolic Church was actually organized in 1831, supported especially by Henry Drummond (1786–1860), a wealthy Member of the British Parliament whose estate became the center of the movement.

The group rejected the traditional Christian doctrine of apostolic succession, the presumed continuation of the authority created by the twelve apostles of Jesus Christ, in favor of living apostles. Twelve apostles were designated, and in 1835 they were sent to inform the world of the Second Coming, addressing the Pope, among others. Their message was not received with much enthusiasm. The Church attempted to revive the early practices of the Christian church by adopting the ritual and ornaments of the Roman Catholic Church as well as those of the Anglican and Greek churches. Practices included speaking in tongues and heal-

ing. During the nineteenth century, this group experienced some success in Great Britain, Holland, Germany, and the United States. The first U.S. branch was opened in 1851 in Potsdam, New York. In 1863 it experienced its worse schism, when German members who doubted the 1864 prediction defected to create the NEW APOSTOLIC CHURCH. [*See also* OLD APOSTOLIC CHURCH.]

Catholic Charismatic Renewal (CCR)

Sometimes called just Charismatic Renewal, it was a North American movement within the Roman Catholic Church, starting in California in 1958, and in Pennsylvania, Indiana, and Michigan in 1967. According to some reports, the first CCR prayer groups appeared on the campuses of Duquesne University in Pittsburgh and Notre Dame University in South Bend, Indiana. It involved introducing the historically Protestant traditions of PENTECOSTALism ("Baptism in the Spirit") into middle-class Catholic parishes. Glossolalia (speaking in tongues) is the most distinctive feature of the movement. Other features include beliefs in healing and prophecy as gifts of the Holy Spirit. This movement is sometimes referred to as Catholic Pentecostalism or neo-Pentecostalism.

Sources:

Bord, R. J., and Faulkner, J. E. *Catholic Charismatics: The Anatomy of a Modern Religious Movement*. University Park, PA: Penn State University Press, 1983.

McGuire, M. *Pentecostal Catholics: Power, Charisma, and Order in a Religious Movement*. Philadelphia: Temple University Press, 1982.

Neitz, M. J. *Charisma and Community: A Study of Religious Commitment within the Charismatic Movement.* New Brunswick, NJ: Transaction Books, 1988.

Celestial Church of Christ

Nativist Christian PENTECOSTAL church in Nigeria, part of the ALADURA group of churches. It was founded by S. B. J. Oschoffa (?–1985) in 1947. The group operates schools, factories, food stores, health centers, and other essential services. Branches have operated among Nigerian emigrants in Europe. [*See also* CHERUBIM AND SERAPHIM (ETERNAL SACRED ORDER OF); CHRIST APOSTOLIC CHURCH; *and* CHURCH OF THE LORD (ALADURA).]

Center for Consciousness

U.S. NEW THOUGHT group based in New York City and founded in the 1980s by Theodore Smith.

Center for Spiritual Awareness (CSA)

U.S. Hindu-inspired group created by a merger in 1962 between the CHURCH OF THE CHRISTIAN SPIRITUAL ALLIANCE (CSA) and NEW LIFE WORLDWIDE. The group is headed by Roy Eugene Davis, who was a disciple of Paramahansa Yogananda of the SELF-REALIZATION FELLOWSHIP in Los Angeles in the 1950s. It is based in northeast Georgia, with branches in the United States and Europe. CSA's official doctrine is based on "man's certain destiny to spiritually awaken and consciously live in harmony with natural laws. Transcending the boundaries of sectarianism, while honoring all useful traditions, it encourages sincere seekers to enter into a process of needed self-transformation and to experience the reality of God." The group practices Yogananda's technique of kriya yoga and collaborates with NEW THOUGHT groups, notably RELIGIOUS SCIENCE INTERNATIONAL, and Hindu-oriented groups. [*See also* ANANDA COOPERATIVE VILLAGE (ACV); *and* TEMPLE OF KRIYA YOGA.]

Center of Cosmic Brotherhood Studies

European group devoted to and "directed by extraterrestrials and their Vicars on Earth." The Center claims to have made such discoveries as the cure for cancer.

Center of First Light, The

New York City center founded by Anishinabe (translated as Turtle Heart) in the 1980s, devoted to the preservation and propagation of Native American religious traditions. It is affiliated with the XAT AMERICAN INDIAN MEDICINE SOCIETY.

Center of Light Community, The

U.S. occultist commune founded in Great Barrington, Massachusetts, in the late 1970s by Gene and Eva Graf. It is devoted to "healing" and growing herbal remedies. The commune is affiliated with the Church of Christ-Consciousness, "a healing church believing in the divinity of the entire human family."

Centre for Social Development, The

British ANTHROPOSOPHY organization founded in London in 1975.

Cherubim and Seraphim Church of Zion of Nigeria

Nigerian independent Christian PENTECOSTAL movement founded in 1948 in a secession from the CHERUBIM AND SERAPHIM (ETERNAL SACRED ORDER OF). [*See also* ALADURA.]

Cherubim and Seraphim (Eternal Sacred Order of)

Nigerian independent Christian PENTECOSTAL movement inaugurated by Moses Orimolade Tunolase (1867?–1932) around 1925. The founder was a member of the Anglican church who claimed to have been cured of paralysis through the power of prayer. This power is offered to believers, who wear white uniforms. Many branches have operated in west Africa and Western Europe, and it is estimated that more than 200 groups have claimed the original Cherubim and Seraphim legacy. [*See also* ALADURA.]

Chibarirwe

Known also as the African Congregational Church, this is an African independent Christian church founded in Zimbabwe (then Southern Rhodesia) in 1930 by members of the Ndau group.

Chiesa Cattolica Riformata d'Italia

Italian OLD CATHOLIC group founded in 1881 in Milan when twelve Roman Catholic priests left the Church.

Chiesa Cristiana Millenarista

Italian offshoot of JEHOVAH'S WITNESSES, started in Pescara in the 1960s. [*See also* CHRISTIAN MILLENIAL CHURCH.]

Chiesa Guirisdavidica

Known also as Giurisdavidici, this is an Italian schismatic MILLENARIAN Roman Catholic group founded in 1878 by the followers of David Lazzaretti (1834–1878). In the 1860s he started having visions and announced plans for a "Holy League" of Christian princes to rule the world until the Second Coming. Later he declared himself the returned Messiah. Starting in 1869, he gathered his followers on Monte Amiata, near his native village of Arcidosso in southern Tuscany. He was killed by government soldiers during a demonstration by his group in which they called for the "new order."

Chiesa Universale Guirisdavidica

Italian schismatic MILLENARIAN Roman Catholic group that split from the CHIESA GUIRISDAVIDICA and considers one of its leaders, Elvira Giro, to be an incarnation of the Holy Spirit. The group combines the ideas of David Lazzaretti, founder of Chiesa Guirisdavidica, with modern occultism.

Chiltern Yoga Foundation

International Hindu organization with branches in North America, Australia, and South Africa. Founded in the 1980s

65

by Swami Venkatesananda, this group is devoted to the teaching of "integral yoga." [*See also* SIVANANDA YOGA VEDANTA CENTERS.]

Chinmaya Mission

International Hindu revival movement founded by Swami Chinmayananda in India in the 1950s. Branches in the West developed in the 1960s in Europe and North America, but most followers are in India.

Chinook Community

U.S. syncretistic commune founded in the 1970s in Clinton, Washington, by Fritz Hull, a former Presbyterian minister, and Vivian Hull. It combines such themes as "Planetary Consciousness" with Christianity, but attempts to maintain connections with mainline churches. Practices include silent meditation and prayers.

Chirothesian Church of Faith

U.S. THEOSOPHICAL-Christian group founded in 1917 in Los Angeles by D. J. Bussell. The group does not proselytize, but some meetings are open to the public.

Ch'ondogyo

Korean MILLENARIAN, nativist, syncretistic movement started in the early 1860s as Tonghak ("Eastern Learning"). Its doctrine combines Buddhist, Confucian, shamanistic, and Christian elements. In 1894 followers started a peasant rebellion that led to the Sino-Japanese War. In 1905 it was renamed the Ch'ondogyo ("Religion of the Heavenly Way"), and it became a major element in the nationalist movement in the following decades.

Chondokwon (or Chondogwan)

Known also as the Olive Tree Church (Evangelical Church), the Preaching Tabernacle, or the Korean Christian Revival Society, this is a Korean syncretistic movement founded in 1955 by Pak T'aeson. The group emphasizes faith healing, which is performed through the "special powers" of the founder, who is referred to as the "Olive Tree."

Chosen Church of the Holy Spirit of Kenya

African independent Christian PENTECOSTAL group formed in 1930 from the Watu wa Mungu (People of God) movement by the Kikuyu people. It is part of the WAKORINO group of churches.

Chosen People Ministries

Also known as Beth Sar Shalom or Beth Sar Shalom Hebrew Christian Fellowship. This North American HEBREW-CHRISTIAN organization was founded in 1894 in Brooklyn, New York, by Leopold Cohn, a former Orthodox rabbi, as the American Board of Missions to the Jews. Branches have operated in the United States and Canada.

Christadelphians

Also known as Brethren of Christ, this MILLENARIAN group, whose name means Brothers in Christ, was founded in 1844 in London and Birmingham, England, by physician John Thomas. Thomas moved to the United States in 1832. It grew out of the DISCIPLES OF CHRIST. Thomas first taught that Jesus Christ would return in 1866–1868. The millennium will be inaugurated by a resurrection, as the elect gain everlasting life and the damned are annihilated in Hell. Christ will reign in Jerusalem, and the Biblical twelve tribes will be reunited there. The doctrine rejected Trinitarianism, and the group has no formal clergy. Members are pacifists and do not vote or hold political office. Branches have been operating in Great Britain as well as the United States.

Christananda Yoga Ashram

U.S. syncretistic group based in California and founded by Sri Yogi Raj Evangelos Alexandrou. The group's doctrine combines Hindu, Islamic, and Eastern Christianity traditions. Practices included "deep meditation techniques from Tantra Yoga, Tao, Zen, Sufi, dancing and singing in joyous celebration and Christian mysticism."

Christ Apostolic Church

Nativist Christian church in Nigeria founded in 1917 and initially known as the Faith Tabernacle. In the 1930s, it was expanded under the leadership of (later Sir) Issac Akinyele. Part of the ALADURA group of churches, Christ Apostolic Church is headquartered in Ibadan and operates branches in countries of West Africa and Western Europe. [See also CELESTIAL CHURCH OF CHRIST; CHERUBIM AND SERAPHIM (ETERNAL SACRED ORDER OF); and CHURCH OF THE LORD (ALADURA).]

Christ Apostolic Mission Church

Part of the ALADURA group of churches, this nativist Christian PENTECOSTAL church in Nigeria was founded in 1952 in Mushin, seceding from the CHRIST APOSTOLIC CHURCH.

Christ Apostolic Universal Church

Part of the ALADURA group of churches, this nativist Christian PENTECOSTAL church in Nigeria was founded in 1962 in Mushin, in a secession from the CHRIST APOSTOLIC CHURCH.

Christ Brotherhood

Known sometimes as the Messianic Brotherhood, this is a U.S. Christian commune founded in 1968 in Eugene, Oregon, by Thomas Paterson Brown (1939–). Known as "Paterson," Brown is reportedly a former philosophy professor. The commune members, never numbering more than fifty, moved around the United States, living in Santa Fe, New Mexico, Colorado, and Missoula, Montana, then returning to Eugene in 1981. There, in September 1981, the founder was convicted of third-degree rape and third-degree sodomy and sentenced to five years in prison. He broke his parole conditions in 1985 and disappeared. Group members have resurfaced in Europe and Israel.

Christ Brotherhood, Inc.

U.S. Christian UFO group founded by Wallace C. Halsey in 1956, it claimed to receive messages from extraterrestrials. Halsey died in a plane crash in 1963.

Christ Catholic Church (Diocese of Boston)

U.S. OLD CATHOLIC group, founded in

67

Boston in 1965 by Karl Pruter. In 1974 its center was moved to Phoenix, Arizona.

Christ Center for Positive Living

U.S. NEW THOUGHT group founded by John McClain in Mesa, Arizona, in the early 1980s. The group's doctrine states: "It is God's will that every individual on the face of the earth live a healthy, happy and prosperous life; life is within the reach of each one of us and the way to its attainment begins with the realization that the Kingdom of God is within us, waiting for us to bring it into expression; we can bring this kingdom forth by practicing the universal principles handed down through the ages by Jesus Christ; the basis for right thinking is Love."

Christ Faith Mission

U.S. PENTECOSTAL group founded by Finis E. Yoakum (?–1920) in Los Angeles in 1908 as the Old Pisgah Tabernacle. In 1914 Yoakum also established a model Christian commune named Pisgah Grande that existed until the 1920s. Christ Faith Mission emphasizes faith healing.

Christian and Missionary Alliance (CMA or C & MA)

U.S. evangelical HOLINESS group founded in 1887 by Albert Benjamin Simpson, a former Presbyterian minister in New York City. It emphasizes cooperation with other Christian groups and the practice of faith healing. It has operated missions around the world. [See also CHRISTIAN NATION CHURCH, U.S.A.]

Christian Apostolic Church in Zion (of South Africa)

Also known as Eqiniswenisweni or Mabilitsa's Zion, this is a South African independent ZIONIST church. It was founded in 1920 in the Johannesburg suburb of Alexandra by Paulo Mabilitsa (?–1942), who was converted by the Berlin Lutheran Society at the end of the nineteenth century. Branches have operated in all the nations of southern Africa.

Source:
Sundkler, B. G. M. *Bantu Prophets in South Africa*. London: Oxford University Press, 1961.

Christian Apostolic Faith Church in Zion

Known also as AmahlokoHloko, this is a South African independent indigenous ZIONIST church, founded in 1942.

Christian Assembly

U.S. Christian-NEW THOUGHT group founded by William Farwell in 1900 in San Jose, California, as a branch of the HOME OF TRUTH MOVEMENT. In 1920 it separated from that group, seeking a stronger Christian emphasis.

Christian Assembly

African Christian communal movement founded in Ghana in 1947.

Christian Bantu Apostolic Church in Zion

South African ZIONIST independent church founded in 1966.

Christian Believers Conference

Also known as the Christian Believers Assembly, this is a U.S. MILLENARIAN group. It was founded in 1910 in Chicago by a group who dissented from the teachings of Charles Taze Russell and the WATCH TOWER Bible and Tract Society. Led by H. C. Hennings, M. L. McPhail, and A. E. Williamson, the Christian Believers Conference objected to doctrine about the status of Russell himself and the meaning of the Lord's presence on earth since 1874. [See also JEHOVAH'S WITNESSES.]

Christian Brotherhood Church (CBC)

African independent Protestant group founded in 1952 in a secession from the Anglican mission organization.

Christian Catholic Apostolic Church in Zion

Earlier known as the Universal Christian Church, and sometimes as the Christian Apostolic Church, this is a MILLENARIAN U.S. group founded by John Alexander Dowie (1847–1907) in 1896. Dowie was born in Edinburgh, Scotland, and emigrated to Australia in 1860, becoming a Congregational minister in Sydney and then a spiritual healer in Melbourne. In 1890 he moved to Chicago, and in 1901 he founded Zion City on Lake Michigan, north of Chicago. The group's doctrine emphasized the imminent Second Coming, and the main practice was "divine healing." The government structure of the organization was a "theocracy."

Dowie called himself "Elijah the Restorer," considering John the Baptist the Second Elijah, and himself the third. Dowie was charged with polygyny and embezzlement in 1906 and died a year later, but the movement survived his death. For the next thirty years the community was ruled by Wilbur Glenn Voliva. For years he offered $5,000 to anyone who could prove to his satisfaction that the Earth is round, and he traveled the world lecturing on this theme and predicting the end of the world in 1923, then 1927, then 1930, then 1935, and then 1943. He died in 1942.

Missionary efforts by Dowie's disciples in South Africa around the turn of the century have led to the creation of the nativist ZIONIST movement and to the appearance of thousands of Zionist churches that follow the charismatic and healing aspects of the Church.

Christian Catholic Apostolic Holy Spirit Church in Zion

South African independent indigenous ZIONIST church that grew out of the native branch of the CHRISTIAN CATHOLIC APOSTOLIC CHURCH IN ZION. It was founded in 1917 in Charlestown by Daniel Nkonyane (?–1935), former member of the Dutch Reformed mission. The new name was adopted in 1922.

Source:

Sundkler, B. G. M. *Bantu Prophets in South Africa.* London: Oxford University Press, 1961.

Christian Church of North America, The

U.S. PENTECOSTAL group with membership of Italian Americans, created from a merger of the UNORGANIZED ITALIAN CHRISTIAN CHURCHES OF NORTH

AMERICA and ITALIAN PENTECOSTAL ASSEMBLIES OF GOD.

Christian Church of Salvation

Formerly known as Shou Shan Christian Church, this is an independent Chinese Christian church founded in Taiwan in 1958.

Christian Community

U.S. Christian commune founded in the 1930s in Vernon Parish, Louisiana, by Samuel W. Irvin.

Christian Community Church (Christengemeinschaft)

Known also as the Christian Community, this is an international Christian organization affiliated with ANTHROPOSOPHY and founded in 1922 by Rudolf Steiner (1861–1925) and Friedrich Rittelmeyer (1872–1938), a Lutheran pastor from Berlin. It expresses the connection between conventional Christianity and the occultist innovations of Anthroposophy. Worship services follow Protestant traditions, though clergy are known as "priests." Organizationally, this group is separate from the ANTHROPOSOPHICAL SOCIETY, but most priests are members of the Society. Branches operate throughout Western Europe and the English-speaking world.

Christian Community of Boston

U.S. Christian mystical commune founded around 1970. It is devoted to "Christianity as a vehicle for the expression of Light, Life, and Love" and to the teaching of "inner Christian mysteries and their application to one's daily living situation."

Christian Conservative Church of America

U.S. IDENTITY, white-supremacist, and militarist group founded by John R. Harrell in 1959. The founder has often been in trouble with the law, and the group is noted for its racist and anti-Semitic positions.

Christian Defense League

U.S. IDENTITY group founded in the Los Angeles area in the late 1950s by Wesley Swift and William (Bill) Potter Gale, a U.S. Army colonel in World War II. It is connected with the CHURCH OF JESUS CHRIST–CHRISTIAN and the NEW CHRISTIAN CRUSADE CHURCH.

Christian Fellowship International

Canadian offshoot of JEHOVAH'S WITNESSES founded in 1981 by M. James Penton in Alberta.

Christian Growth Ministries (CGM)

U.S. PENTECOSTAL group based in Fort Lauderdale, Florida. CGM is known for its SHEPHERDING, or "discipleship," doctrine, which creates a highly authoritarian structure of discipline in the group. Growing out of the Charismatic Renewal movement within mainline Protestant churches, it was founded in 1972 by Bob Mumford, and later led by Mumford, Charles Simpson, Derek Prince, Don Basham, and Ern Baxter. It was influenced by the BODY OF CHRIST, the FUNDAMENTALIST organization founded in Argentina in 1970 by Juan Carlos Ortiz. [*See also* CHRISTIAN RESTORATION MINISTRIES; *and* LATTER RAIN MOVEMENT.]

Christian Holy Ghost Church of East Africa (CHGC)

African independent Christian PENTECOSTAL group that was formed in 1934 among the Kikuyu people out of the conservative wing of the Aroti revival movement. It is part of the WAKORINO group of churches.

Christianisme Prophetique en Afrique

African independent PENTECOSTAL group founded around 1970 in the Central African Republic.

Christian Israelites

British MILLENARIAN group started by John Wroe (1782–1863) among the SOUTHCOTTITES, the disappointed followers of Joanna Southcott, who prophecied in 1814 that she would give birth to a divine child named Shiloh. Joanna, sixty-four at the time, was never pregnant, and died soon thereafter.

Before the establishment of the Christian Israelites, Wroe joined a Southcottites group led by John Turner, known as turnerites, and after Turner's death in 1821 claimed to be his successor. Wroe then announced that Shiloh, the divine child, was testing the people's faith and had disappeared, but would return. Followers had to observe Old Testament laws of purity to prove themselves. Males were circumcised, and all members abstained from tobacco and alcohol. Wroe traveled widely in the English-speaking world, gaining many converts. The Christian Israelites group was officially formed in 1830, as a result of a schism within the Southcotties.

The church exists today only in the American Midwest and in Australia. [*See also* NEW AND LATTER HOUSE OF ISREAL; *and* NEW HOUSE OF ISRAEL.]

Source:

Balleine, G. R. *Past Finding Out: The Tragic Story of Joanna Southcott and Her Successors*. New York: Macmillan, 1956.

Christianity Bible Church

Chinese indigenous Christian church founded in Taiwan in 1956.

Christian Messianic Fellowship

Canadian HEBREW CHRISTIAN group founded in the 1960s and based in Vancouver.

Christian Methodist Episcopal Church

U.S. African American Christian church founded in 1870, when the black members of the Methodist Episcopal Church sought to establish a separate organization known as the Colored Methodist Episcopal Church. The present name was adopted in 1956.

Christian Millenial Church

U.S. offshoot of JEHOVAH'S WITNESSES, started in the 1930s and active among Italian Americans.

Christian Mobilizers

U.S. religious-political group started in the 1930s. It combined FUNDAMENTALISM with right-wing, anti-Semitic, and pro-Nazi views.

Christian Nationalist Crusade

U.S. British-Israelist group started in 1947 by Gerald L. K. Smith. It became known for its anti-Semitic and anti-black propaganda, and Smith emerged as the most visible spokesman for BRITISH-ISRAELISM. This group published *The Cross and the Flag*, which campaigned against "Jewish Gestapo organizations" and for shipping blacks to Africa.

Sources:
Ribuffo, L. P. *The Old Christian Right: The Protestant Far Right from the Great Depression to the Cold War*. Philadelphia: Temple University Press, 1983.
Roy, R. L. *Apostles of Discord*. Boston: Beacon Press, 1953.

Christian Nation Church, U.S.A.

U.S. Protestant evangelical organization founded in 1895 in Marion, Ohio. Identical to the CHRISTIAN AND MISSIONARY ALLIANCE in doctrine, it advocates a strict behavior code.

Christian Patriots Defense League (CPDL)

U.S. IDENTITY group formed in the early 1980s in Flora, Illinois, by John Harrell. It advocated anti-Semitic and racist views and recruited members among Midwest farmers. Members predict a race war that will devastate the United States, and have supported the establishment of a "white America" in the Midwest.

Christian Research, Inc.

BRITISH-ISRAELIST group founded by Gerka Koch, and based in Arkansas after moving from Minneapolis. The group distributes British-Israelist literature and actively supports conservative political candidates. [*See also* LORD'S COVENANT CHURCH.]

Christian Restoration Ministries

Known also as the House Church Movement, Church of the Great Shepherd, or the Pyramid Church, this is an international PENTECOSTAL group founded in the 1970s and based in Wheaton, Maryland. It is known for its SHEPHERDING or "discipleship" doctrine, which creates a highly authoritarian structure of discipline in the group. The group was inspired by the BODY OF CHRIST, an international Protestant FUNDAMENTALIST organization founded in Argentina in 1970 by Juan Carlos Ortiz. The Restoration movement has been most visible in North America and in Great Britain. Its practices include glossolalia, or speaking in tongues, and healing. [*See also* CHRISTIAN GROWTH MINISTRIES.]

Source:
Walker, A. G. *Restoring the Kingdom: The Radical Christianity of the House Church Movement*. London: Hodder and Stoughton, 1985.

Christian Revolutionary Brotherhood

U.S. FUNDAMENTALIST group founded

by Barry I. Hyman in New York City in the 1980s. It advocates social revolution based on Christianity and communicates with the public via posters and leaflets. There are likely no members besides the founder.

Christian Science

Officially known as Church of Christ, Scientist, this is a healing movement founded in 1879 by Mary Baker Eddy (1821–1910). In 1881, the Massachusetts Metaphysical College was founded, but in 1889 the college and church were dissolved. In 1892 the Church of Christ, Scientist was reorganized in Boston under the First Church of Christ, Scientist, also called the Mother Church. All other Church of Christ, Scientist churches are considered branches of the Mother Church.

Eddy's belief in the healing power of prayer was partially influenced by Phineas Parkhurst Quimby (1702–1866) after he offered her temporary relief from a chronic illness in 1862. Quimby invented the term "Christian Science," used self-hypnosis, and invented the "science of health." Quimby originated the reliance on prayer for curing disease in the belief that physical disease is an illusion, and as such can be cured by the power of prayer. Eddy herself became convinced of the healing power of prayer when, in 1866, she was apparently healed of a serious injury while reading an account of one of Jesus' healings in the New Testament of the Bible. This led to her own understanding of what the group calls the Science of Christianity.

The group bases its belief in divine healing on examples and teachings of Jesus Christ in the New Testament. The doctrine of Christian Science holds that healing disease and all forms of inharmony can be achieved through an understanding of God and the relationship between God and humans. Humanity, they argue, is capable of perfection but is hampered by the illusion of reality. The body, sickness, and death are considered unreal and thus can be overcome through prayer. These ideas are outlined in the founder's book *Science and Health with Key to the Scripture* (1875). This book states, "There is no life, truth, intelligence, nor substance in matter. All is infinite Mind and its infinite manifestation, for God is All-in-all. Spirit is immortal Truth; matter is mortal error. Spirit is the real and eternal, matter is the unreal and temporal. Spirit is God, and man is His image and likeness. Therefore, man is not material; he is spiritual." Eddy taught also that "Malicious Animal Magnetism" is the only evil power that can overcome faith; she believed that this was responsible for the death of her third husband, Asa Gilbert Eddy, in 1882.

Church of Christ, Scientist doctrine differs from orthodox Christianity in regard to its understanding of the Trinity, which it considers to be "God the Father-Mother; Christ the spiritual idea of sonship; divine Science or the Holy Comforter." God alone is worshipped. Christ, as a title and spiritual concept representing truth, is differentiated from Jesus, who is considered a respected prophet and healer. These differences have been attacked by many Christian groups in the United States.

Members are known to reject medical care in favor of healing through prayer. They also avoid smoking and alcohol. Some studies have shown that many members are urban, middle-aged females, who suffer from physical or men-

Mary Baker Eddy, founder of the Christian Science movement, was a strong believer in the healing power of prayer.

Mary Baker Eddy (on balcony), founder of Christian Science, greets visitors to her home, Pleasant View, in New Hampshire in 1901.

tal difficulties and have turned to this group for healing.

Over the years some Church members have been involved in legal cases when their children died due to the avoidance of medical care. One such case in 1989, in Minnesota, involved an eleven-year-old child, Ian Lundman, who died of diabetes. His mother, stepfather, a Christian Science practitioner, and nurse were found guilty of negligence and ordered to pay $1.5 million in damages. Since 1908 the Church has published a daily newspaper, *The Christian Science Monitor*, which enjoys a solid reputation for its reporting on foreign affairs. The Church operates branches all over the world, mainly in English-speaking countries. [*See also* JEWISH SCIENCE; NEW THOUGHT MOVEMENT; *and* UNITED CHRISTIAN SCIENTISTS.]

Sources:

Bloom, H. *The American Religion: The Making of a Post-Christian Nation.* New York: Simon & Schuster, 1992.

Braden, C. S. *Christian Science Today.* Dallas: Southern Methodist University Press, 1958.

Gardner, M. *The Healing Revelations of Mary Baker Eddy: The Rise and Fall of Christian Science.* Buffalo: Prometheus, 1987.

Gottschalk, S. *The Emergence of Christian Science in American Religious Life.* Berkeley: University of California Press, 1973.

Peel, R. *Christian Science, Its Encounter with American Culture*. Garden City, NY: Doubleday, 1965.

Christian Theocratic Holy Church of God

African independent Protestant group founded among the Kikuyu group of Kenya in 1958.

Christian Truth Institute

Australian offshoot of JEHOVAH'S WITNESSES, founded by Frederick Lardent in the 1940s.

Christian Union

U.S. FUNDAMENTALIST group, founded in 1984 in Columbus, Ohio, and operating since then in the U.S. Midwest as well as in Africa, South America, and Japan.

Christian Way

U.S. group of former CHRISTIAN SCIENCE members in Lancaster, California, who have become evangelical Christians and oppose their former church.

Christian Witness to Israel

British branch of JEWS FOR JESUS.

Christian World Liberation Front

U.S. Christian FUNDAMENTALIST-MILLENARIAN group, founded in 1969 by Jack Sparks, Fred Dyson, and Pat Matrisciana, former employees of the Campus Crusade for Christ. It served as the informal headquarters of the JESUS MOVEMENT in the early 1970s in northern California. Located in Berkeley, it actively recruited young people on university campuses.

The group disbanded in 1975, and several of its members, headed by Jack Sparks, founded the NEW COVENANT APOSTOLIC ORDER. Others rejoined the Campus Crusade for Christ.

The Christian World Liberation Front was apocalyptic and predicted the imminent coming of an Antichrist, who would unite all false religions. The ecumenical movement among Christian churches, started in the mid-twentieth century, was regarded as a sign of this Antichrist.

Source:
Glock, C. Y., and Bellah, R. N., eds. *The New Religious Consciousness*. Berkeley, CA: University of California Press, 1976.

Christian Zion Church

African indigenous Christian PENTECOSTAL church founded in the 1960s in Zambia.

Christ Jesus Holy Church

Philippine indigenous church created by former Roman Catholics in 1958.

Christ Ministry Foundation

U.S. esoteric Christianity group founded in 1935 in Oakland, California, by Eleanore Mary Thedick (1883–1973). In 1970 the group merged with the SEEKER'S QUEST, but they separated in 1972, after the founder's retirement. Healing through "spiritual work" is a major practice, and the members believe in reincarnation.

Christohanon

Philippine indigenous MILLENARIAN group started in 1945.

Christ's Army Church

Nativist Christian PENTECOSTAL church in Nigeria, founded in 1915 by Garrick Sokari Braide in a secession from the Anglican mission. The founder claimed the name of Elijah II, and announced that he was offering salvation and health through prayer.

Christ's Gospel Fellowship

U.S. FUNDAMENTALIST, PENTECOSTAL group connected with BRITISH ISRAELISM. It is based in Spokane, Washington, where it was founded by Robert Thornton in the 1960s.

Christ's Sanctified Holy Church

U.S. African American PENTECOSTAL group started in 1892.

Christ Truth League

U.S. NEW THOUGHT group founded in the 1950s by Alden (?–1985) and Nell (?–1971) Truesdell and inspired by various New Thought and UNITY traditions. It is based in Fort Worth, Texas.

Chriszekial Elias

U.S. self-proclaimed pope, whose former name was Chester Olszewaski (1943–).

Olszewaski, a former Episcopal priest, proclaimed himself Pope in 1977 and was ordained by Bishop Edward M. Stahlik of Milwaukee. He has a small following in Pennsylvania.

Churches of Christ in Christian Union of Ohio, The

U.S. FUNDAMENTALIST group founded in 1909 in Marshall, Ohio.

Churches of God, Holiness

U.S. African American PENTECOSTAL group founded in 1920 in Atlanta by King Hezekiah Burrus (?–1963).

Churches of God in the British Isles and Overseas (Needed Truth)

Connected to the PLYMOUTH BRETHREN tradition, this British FUNDAMENTALIST Christian group started in 1889 with the founding of the periodical *Needed Truth*. Membership is concentrated in England, with some branches in North America. Members lead an ascetic lifestyle and marry within the group. They are also conscientious objectors.

Church of All Nations

U.S. PENTECOSTAL group in Scrabble Creek, West Virginia, noted for its use of snakes during services. Its members are popularly known as "snake handlers." Members follow a strict conduct code. Snake handling and the drinking of poison are regarded as signs of the Holy Spirit and as tests of faith. In practice, snake handling is only rarely accompa-

Morning Glory Zell, a member of the neo-pagan Church of All Worlds, performs a witchcraft ceremony to commemorate Halloween.

nied by drinking poison. [*See also* DOLLY POND CHURCH OF GOD WITH SIGNS FOLLOWING; *and* ORIGINAL PENTECOSTAL CHURCH OF GOD.]

Source:
La Barre, W. *They Shall Take Up Serpents.* New York: Schocken, 1969.

Church of All Worlds

Neo-pagan U.S. group founded in 1961 by Tim Zell, who in 1976 changed his name to Otter G'Zell following a vision. This group was for many years the best known of U.S. neo-pagan churches.

Church of Aphrodite

U.S. neo-pagan group founded in 1938 with the intention of resurrecting ancient pagan traditions.

Church of Apostolic Faith of Africa (AFA)

African Independent PENTECOSTAL group founded in 1962 in Thogoto, Kenya, by Willy "Nganga" Kago of the Kikuyu group. The founder was a former member of the Presbyterian Church of East Africa, as well as of the Mau-Mau and BALOKOLE. The group's focus has been on faith healing. In 1975, most members left the church.

Church of Basic Truth

U.S. occultist group founded in Phoenix, Arizona, in 1961 by George H. Hepker. The group teaches Hawaiian Huna and faith healing. [*See also* HUNA RESEARCH ASSOCIATES.]

Church of Bible Understanding (COBU)

Also known as We People, and formerly known as the Forever Family, this Christian FUNDAMENTALIST group was founded in 1971 by Stewart Traill (1936–), a former vacuum-cleaner salesman, in Allentown, Pennsylvania, as part of the JESUS MOVEMENT of that period. The group attracted hundreds of young Americans and established communes all over the eastern United States in its first five years of existence. It then declined, ending up by 1985 with only a center based in Philadelphia and residences in Arlington, Virginia, and Baltimore and Tacoma Park, Maryland, as well as several residences in New York City. Starting in 1984 the group encountered legal difficulties because of living conditions in the New York City residences, in which minors were housed. Since the late 1970s the group has operated the Christian Brothers Cleaning Company, a carpet cleaning service.

COBU's teachings are ADVENTIST and FUNDAMENTALIST, based on its own system of Bible interpretation. It believes that the Second Coming is imminent.

Church of Cherubim and Seraphim

British branch of the CHERUBIM AND SERAPHIM (ETERNAL SACRED ORDER OF), a nativist African movement started in Nigeria.

Church of Christ (Bible and Book of Mormon Teaching)

U.S. MORMON splinter group founded in 1946 by Pauline Hancock in

Independence, Missouri. Representing a return to orthodox Christianity among members of the CHURCH OF CHRIST (TEMPLE LOT), its doctrine rejects the Book of Mormon.

Source:
Sundkler, B. G. M. *Bantu Prophets in South Africa*. London: Oxford University Press, 1961.

Church of Christ (Fettingite)

U.S. MORMON splinter group that grew out of a schism in the CHURCH OF CHRIST (TEMPLE LOT) in 1930. Its founder, Otto Fetting (?–1933), in 1927 started claiming revelations, which eventually led to the schism. In 1947 a schism occurred in the new body, which led to the founding of the CHURCH OF CHRIST WITH THE ELIJAH MESSAGE.

Church of Christ (Holiness) U.S.A.

U.S. African American HOLINESS group, founded in 1894 in Jackson, Mississipi, by C. H. Mason. A schism in the group in 1908 led to the creation of the CHURCH OF GOD IN CHRIST.

Church of Christ (Temple Lot)

Founded in 1852, this U.S. MORMON splinter group opposed belief in polygyny and the baptism of the dead, as practiced then by a majority of MORMONS. This group still owns the Temple Lot in Independence, Missouri, designated by Joseph Smith, Jr., to be the future city of New Zion. [*See also* APOSTOLIC UNITED ORDER; THE CHURCH OF THE FIRST BORN OF THE FULLNESS OF TIMES; *and* UNITED ORDER EFFORT.]

Church of Christ at Halley's Bluff, The

U.S. MORMON splinter group that left the CHURCH OF CHRIST (TEMPLE LOT) in the 1950s.

Church of Christ for the Union of the Bantu

Officially named the Church of Christ for the Union of the Bantu and Protection of Bantu Customs, which is the Memorial of Ntsikana, this is a South African independent syncretistic native church founded by Edmund Sigcu in 1922. Among the Bantu customs Sigcu upheld was polygyny.

Church of Christian Liberty, The

U.S. FUNDAMENTALIST group founded in 1965 in Prospect Heights, Illinois, by Paul Lindstrom. It has been involved in right-wing political activities in the United States to an extent unusual for most religious groups. One of its declared goals is combating socialism and communism. Lindstrom has started such organizations as the Christian Defense League and the Douglas MacArthur Brigade, the latter of which was formed to free United States prisoners of war in Vietnam.

Church of Christ in Africa (CCA)

African indigenous Christian church started in Kenya first as an Anglican revival movement, becoming known as Johera in 1952, and then growing into a separate organization in 1957.

The Reverend Paul Lindstrom (right), founder of the Church of Christian Liberty, chats with families of crewmen shot down over North Korea in 1969.

Church of Christ, the Congregation of All Saints of South Africa

South African independent ZIONIST church founded by the Zulu prophet George Khambule (1884–1949), who started his activities in 1925, making claims of his divinity and appointing apostles. His visions were inspired by Christianity.

Sources:

Sundkler, B. G. M. *Bantu Prophets in South Africa.* London: Oxford University Press, 1961.

Sundkler, B. G. M. *Zulu Zion and Some Swazi Zionists.* London: Oxford University Press, 1976.

Church of Christ with the Elijah Message

Known also as Dravesites, this U.S. MORMON splinter group grew out of a schism in the CHURCH OF CHRIST (FETTINGITE) in 1947. Its founder, W. A. Draves, started in 1937 to claim various revelations, which eventually led to the schism.

Church of Daniel's Band

U.S. Protestant conservative group founded in 1893 in Marine City, Michigan. Doctrine advocates evangelism and a modest lifestyle. Practices include healing and the gift of the Holy Spirit.

81

Church of Divine Man

U.S. occultist group founded in 1972 by Lewis Bostwick (1918–) in Berkeley, California. Practices include healing, aura readings, and meditation.

Church of Emmanuel

German occultist group founded in the 1980s. Members claim to follow Caribbean voodoo practices and reportedly engage in exorcisms.

Church of God (Abrahamic Faith)

U.S. ADVENTIST group formed in the late 1880s in the United States by Adventists who continued to operate in small groups after the Great Disappointment of 1844. The Church is unitarian, denying the Christian trinity and the divinity of Jesus. It operates the Oregon Bible College in Oregon, Illinois, where church headquarters are located, and several overseas missions. [See also ADVENT CHRISTIAN CHURCH.]

Church of God (Apostolic)

Originally known as the Christian Faith Band, this U.S. PENTECOSTAL group was started in 1877 by Thomas J. Cox in Danville, Kentucky. The current name was adopted in 1919. The group is otherworldly and strict in standards.

Church of God (Black Jews)

U.S. African American Jewish group founded in the early twentieth century by F. S. Cherry, also known as Prophet Cherry. Group doctrine regards only blacks as true Jews, while Jews are regarded as usurpers of the legacy. Furthermore, all personages referred to in the early chapters of Genesis are believed to be black. According to this doctrine, blacks were chased out of ancient Palestine by the Romans to Africa and then sold into slavery. The year 2000 will bring about the millennium and the final victory of black Jews.

Source:
Fauset, A. H. *Black Gods of the Metropolis.* Philadelphia: University of Pennsylvania Press, 1944.

Church of God (Cleveland, Ohio)

U.S. FUNDAMENTALIST, ADVENTIST group started in 1974 by Carl O'Brien, a former WORLDWIDE CHURCH OF GOD minister who disagreed with the founder, Herbert W. Armstrong.

Church of God (Cleveland, Tennessee)

Originally known as the Christian Union, this U.S. PENTECOSTAL group was founded in 1886 by Richard G. Spurling in Monroe County, Tennessee. Later the name was changed to Holiness Church. The name Church of God was adopted in 1907 while A. J. Tomlinson was the leader. Since 1917, the group has operated three colleges. Schisms have led to the founding of the (ORIGINAL) CHURCH OF GOD, INC., THE CHURCH OF GOD OF PROPHECY, THE CHURCH OF GOD (WORLD HEADQUARTERS), THE CHURCH OF GOD (JERUSALEM ACRES), and THE CHURCH OF GOD, THE HOUSE OF PRAYER FOR ALL PEOPLE.

Church of God (Jerusalem)

Known also as Congregation of Elohim and Family of Elohim, it was founded in 1955 by A. N. Dugger (?–1975), a former SEVENTH-DAY ADVENTIST. Dugger's doctrinal emphasis was ADVENTIST. He was convinced that the founding of the State of Israel in 1948 had eschatological significance, and that after 1948 the Second Coming was imminent. Dugger's son, Charles Andy Dugger, established another group, WORKERS TOGETHER WITH ELOHIM.

Church of God (Jerusalem Acres), The

U.S. PENTECOSTAL organization created through dissension from THE CHURCH OF GOD OF PROPHECY. It was founded by Grady R. Kent in 1957. The church doctrine, known as "New Testament Judaism," ignores all traditional Christian holidays in favor of a calendar based on a newly created mythology. Headquarters are in Jerusalem Acres, Cleveland, Tennessee.

Church of God (Sabbatarian)

U.S. Sabbath-keeping ADVENTIST group that split off from the GENERAL CONFERENCE OF THE CHURCH OF GOD (SEVENTH DAY) in 1969. It was originally led by Roy Marrs of Los Angeles and R. F. Marrs of Denver. The Denver group became known as the REMNANT CHURCH OF GOD, and the Los Angeles group as the Church of God (Sabbatarian). [See also SEVENTH-DAY ADVENTIST CHURCH.]

Church of God (Seventh-Day, Salem, West Virginia)

U.S. ADVENTIST, Sabbath-keeping group formed in 1933 after a schism in the GENERAL CONFERENCE OF THE CHURCH OF GOD (SEVENTH DAY). [See also SEVENTH-DAY ADVENTIST CHURCH.]

Church of God (UK)

British PENTECOSTAL group founded in 1945, with membership drawn mostly from West Indian immigrants.

Church of God (World Headquarters), The

U.S. PENTECOSTAL group founded around 1945 in Queens Village, New York, by Homer Tomlinson (?–1968) after losing a leadership struggle with his brother Milton A. Tomlinson over the CHURCH OF GOD OF PROPHECY. The group has sponsored the Theocratic Party, which has taken part in U.S. elections as part of its program to create the Kingdom of God on Earth. Overseas, it has established branches in Europe, Asia, and Africa.

Church of God and Saints of Christ

South African independent indigenous ETHIOPIAN church that grew out of a U.S. mission of THE CHURCH OF GOD AND SAINTS OF CHRIST ("BLACK JEWS"). Members are known as "ISRAELITES," and their customs are said to come from the Old Testament. They keep the Saturday Sabbath and maintain a nonstandard schedule of time, beginning their daily

Homer A. Tomlinson, founder of the Church of God (World Headquarters), proclaims himself "King of Germany." The globe he holds symbolizes his claim to be king of twenty-seven nations.

routine six hours ahead of most people in the same time zone.

Source:
Sundkler, B. G. M. *Bantu Prophets in South Africa.* London: Oxford University Press, 1961.

Church of God and Saints of Christ ("Black Jews"), The

U.S. African American group whose doctrine combined Christianity, Judaism, and black nationalism. It was founded in 1896 by William S. Crowdy, who claimed that the mythological "lost tribes" are the present-day Africans. Practices included many of the prescriptions and proscriptions of the Old Testament and adherence to the ancient Hebrew calendar. The group operated a communal settlement in Belleville, Virginia.

Church of God, Body of Christ

U.S. Sabbath-keeping ADVENTIST group with headquarters in Mocksville, North Carolina. It combines a strong Old Testament orientation with beliefs in the gifts of the Holy Spirit and faith healing. Members abstain from pork and believe in the imminent return of Christ. [*See also* GENERAL CONFERENCE OF THE CHURCH OF GOD (SEVENTH DAY); *and* SEVENTH-DAY ADVENTIST CHURCH.]

Church of God by Faith

U.S. PENTECOSTAL group founded by John Bright in 1919 and based in Alachua, Florida.

Church of God Fellowship

British Christian multiracial group founded in the 1960s.

Church of God in Christ

British PENTECOSTAL church whose members come from the West Indian immigrant community. It was originally a branch of the U.S. group of the same name.

Church of God in Christ (COGIC)

U.S. African American PENTECOSTAL group founded in 1908 in Memphis, Tennessee, by Charles H. Mason, a former Baptist minister. The group came about as a result of schism in THE CHURCH OF CHRIST (HOLINESS) U.S.A. Initially, the group included white members, but they soon left to start what became the ASSEMBLIES OF GOD. COGIC emphasizes faith healing and is based in Memphis, Tennessee. [*See also* NEW BETHEL CHURCH OF GOD IN CHRIST (PENTECOSTAL).]

Church of God in Christ, Congregational

U.S. African American PENTECOSTAL group with branches in Great Britain and Mexico. It was founded in 1932 by J. Bowe, who departed from the CHURCH OF GOD IN CHRIST (COGIC). Members of the group are conscientious objectors.

Church of God in Christ, International, The

U.S. African American PENTECOSTAL group created in 1969 in Kansas City, Missouri, through a schism initiated by fourteen bishops in the CHURCH OF GOD IN CHRIST (COGIC). Group headquarters are in Brooklyn, New York.

Church of God in Christ (Pentecostal), The

U.S. PENTECOSTAL group founded in the early 1930s in Bluefield, West Virginia.

Church of God, International

Founded in 1978 by Garner Ted Armstrong, son of Herbert W. Armstrong, following his (second) suspension from his father's organization, the WORLDWIDE CHURCH OF GOD. Based on a radio ministry, its headquarters are in Tyler, Texas. It is similar in doctrine to the Worldwide Church of God.

Church of God of Prophecy

U.S. PENTECOSTAL group founded in 1921 by A. J. Tomlinson (1865–1943) following a leadership struggle in the CHURCH OF GOD (CLEVELAND, TENNESSEE). It was first known as the Tomlinson Church of God, and the present name was adopted in 1952. Following Tomlinson's death in 1943, his son Milton A. Tomlinson became the leader. A leadership struggle led to the founding of THE CHURCH OF GOD (WORLD HEADQUARTERS) by Milton's brother, Horner. Branches of the Church of God of Prophecy have operated in Africa and Europe.

Church of God of Prophecy

British PENTECOSTAL church similar in doctrine to the U.S. group of the same name. Membership is recruited among West Indian immigrant families.

Church of God of the Apostolic Faith

U.S. PENTECOSTAL group founded in 1914 near Ozark, Arkansas. It is now based in Tulsa, Oklahoma. Its doctrine is similar to that of the CHURCH OF GOD (CLEVELAND, TENNESSEE).

Church of God of the Mountain Assembly, The

U.S. PENTECOSTAL group founded in 1906 in Tennessee. Based in Jellico, Tennessee, it is active in the South and Midwest.

Church of God of the Original Mountain Assembly

Based in Kentucky, this U.S. PENTECOSTAL group resulted from a secession from THE CHURCH OF GOD OF THE MOUNTAIN ASSEMBLY in 1944.

Church of God of the Union Assembly

U.S. PENTECOSTAL group formed in 1920 after a schism in THE CHURCH OF GOD OF THE MOUNTAIN ASSEMBLY. Its center is in Dalton, Georgia. Members are permitted to seek medical treatment but are counseled to rely on the power of prayer in the case of illness. Since 1980 there have been several court cases involving church members and the right of children to medical treatment.

Church of God Seventh Era

U.S. ADVENTIST group founded by Larry Gilbert Johnson as a result of the schism in the WORLDWIDE CHURCH OF GOD in 1974.

Church of God, the Eternal

U.S. ADVENTIST group founded by Raymond C. Cole in 1975 because of disagreement with the WORLDWIDE CHURCH OF GOD. The church is based in Eugene, Oregon, where Worldwide Church of God founder Herbert W. Armstrong had started the Radio Church of God in 1934. Cole claimed that divine truth was revealed to Armstrong only in the years of the Radio Church. This divine truth is unchangeable, and the doctrinal changes instituted by Armstrong as the head of the Worldwide Church of God in 1974 were unacceptable. Branches of this group have operated in Western Europe.

Church of God, the House of Prayer

U.S. PENTECOSTAL group created as a result of a schism in the CHURCH OF GOD (CLEVELAND, TENNESSEE). It was founded in Cleveland, Tennessee, by Harrison W. Poteat in 1939.

Church of Grace

African independent Christian PENTECOSTAL church, founded in Ghana in 1949 in a secession from the European Methodist mission.

Church of Hanuman

U.S. syncretistic group founded in the late 1960s and based in Palo Alto, California. It combines Christian, occult, and Eastern traditions, including Hindu and Sufi ideas and practices.

Church of Holy Christ

U.S. African American PENTECOSTAL group, founded in the 1930s.

Church of Inner Wisdom

U.S. NEW THOUGHT group founded in 1968 in San Jose, California, by Joan Gibson, a former member of AMORC ROSICRUCIAN ORDER.

Church of Integral Living

U.S. NEW THOUGHT group based in New York City. It was founded in the 1980s by Valerie Seyffert.

Church of Israel, The

U.S. IDENTITY, white-supremacist group started in 1972 as a result of a split in the CHURCH OF CHRIST AT HALLEY'S BLUFF, a MORMON group based in Missouri. It was led by Daniel Gayman, a former pastor and self-declared bishop of the CHURCH OF CHRIST. Between 1974 and 1981 the new group was known as the Church of Christian Heritage. According to Gayman's teachings, humanity is descended from the Biblical Cain and Seth (Abel's brother and substitute), representing Satan and God, respectively. White gentiles are descended from Seth; blacks and Jews are descended from Cain. [See also CHURCH OF CHRIST (TEMPLE LOT).]

Church of Israel, The

U.S. BRITISH ISRAELIST group, based in Missouri and led by Gordon Winrod, son

of Gerald B. Winrod, founder of DEFEND-
ERS OF THE CHRISTIAN FAITH, INC.

Church of Jesus Christ, The

U.S. IDENTITY, white-suprematist group
based in Bass, Arkansas. It was founded
by Thomas Arthur Robb, a chaplain for
the Ku Klux Klan.

Church of Jesus Christ (Bickertonites), The

U.S. MORMON splinter group founded in
Greenock, Pennsylvania, in 1862 by William Bickerton. The group was opposed
to the practice of polygyny.

Church of Jesus Christ–Christian

U.S. BRITISH-ISRAELIST group founded in
1946 in Lancaster, California, by Wesley
Swift (?–1970), a member of the Ku Klux
Klan. He was joined by Bertrand L.
Comparet and Colonel William (Bill)
Potter Gale. By the founding of this
group Swift started the IDENTITY MOVE-
MENT. In addition to BRITISH ISRAELISM,
the group doctrine included beliefs in
Atlantis and Lemuria, positions typical
of THEOSOPHY and ANTHROPOSOPHY.
[See also CHURCH OF JESUS CHRIST
CHRISTIAN—ARYAN NATIONS.]

Church of Jesus Christ Christian—Aryan Nations

An outgrowth of CHURCH OF JESUS
CHRIST-CHRISTIAN, this group was
formed in 1974 as Richard Girnt Butler
inherited Wesley Swift's mantle and
moved the group headquarters to

Hayden Lake, Idaho. Butler was indicted
on conspiracy charges in 1988, together
with other members of the group. The
Church is connected to other IDENTITY
groups and has been linked to THE OR-
DER. It organized the Aryan Congress,
which in 1986 declared the five-state
area of Washington, Oregon, Idaho,
Wyoming, and Montana as the "white
homeland" in the United States. Notorious for his public activities, Butler has
become a major spokesperson for anti-
Semitism and white supremacy in the
United States in the 1990s. [See also
MOUNTAIN CHURCH OF JESUS CHRIST THE
SAVIOUR.]

Source:
Coates, J. *Armed and Dangerous.* New
York: Hill & Wang, 1987.

Church of Jesus Christ in Samoa

Samoan indigenous Christian church
that started in 1846 in a secession from
the Congregational Christian Church.

Church of Light

Known also as the Brotherhood of Light.
The doctrine of this U.S. occultist group
is based on astrology, alchemy, and the
Tarot. It was founded in 1932 in Los Angeles, California, by Elbert Benjamine
(?–1951), also known as C. C. Zain. The
group has operated mainly by mail.

Church of Mary Mystical Rose of Perpetual Help

U.S. OLD CATHOLIC group founded
in 1937 in Chicago and led by John
Skikiewicz. [See also AMERICAN CATHOLIC
CHURCH.]

Richard G. Butler founded the Church of Jesus Christ Christian–Aryan Nations, a neo-Nazi organization in Idaho.

Church of Mercavah

U.S. occultist group founded in 1982 in Louisiana by James A. Montandon.

Church of Messiah

African independent PENTECOSTAL healing church started in Ghana in 1965.

Church of Our Lord Jesus Christ of the Apostolic Faith

British PENTECOSTAL group started in London in 1964. The church is tied to the GREATER REFUGE TEMPLE of the United States.

Church of Our Lord Jesus Christ of the Apostolic Faith

U.S. African American PENTECOSTAL group founded in Columbus, Ohio, in 1919 by R. C. Lawson (?–1961). It is now based in New York City. Schisms in the group have created the CHURCH OF THE LORD JESUS CHRIST OF THE APOSTOLIC FAITH and the BIBLE WAY CHURCH OF OUR LORD JESUS CHRIST WORLD WIDE. Branches of this group have operated in the Caribbean.

Church of Peace and Healing

U.S. "alternative, holistic Christian ministry" founded in New York City in the 1980s.

Church of Religious Philosophy

U.S. THEOSOPHICAL, New Age group, founded by Jacob M. Sober and Miriam M. Sober in Arizona in the early 1980s.

It operates the New Age Learning Center.

Church of Te Kooti Rikirangi

Maori syncretistic movement started in the first decade of the twentieth century by Rua Kenana Hepetika (1869–1937). Hepetika claimed to be the heir to Te Kooti Rikirangi, the founder of RINGATU, and endorsed ideas similar to those of Ringatu. His followers were considered *Iharaira*, or "Israelites." He predicted the expulsion of all Europeans from New Zealand, with the help of King Edward VII.

Source:
Webster, P. *Rua and the Maori Millennium.* Wellington, New Zealand: Price Millburn, 1979.

Church of the Ancestors

Malawi independent syncretistic church combining African traditions with Christian practices.

Church of the Christian Crusade

Known also as the Christian Echoes Ministry, this is a U.S. FUNDAMENTALIST, evangelical group founded in 1948 in Tulsa, Oklahoma, by Billy James Hargis. The group and its leader became notorious for their militancy in right-wing causes. In the mid-1970s Hargis was accused of gross immorality and resigned from the movement, but he later returned. The Church has operated a number of outreach organizations, such as the David Livingstone Missionary Foundation and Evangelism in Action.

President Efraim Rios Montt, military dictator of Honduras, is a prominent member of the Church of the Complete Word. He is shown here during a 1983 visit by former president, Ronald Reagan.

Church of the Christian Spiritual Alliance (CSA)

U.S. Hindu-inspired group founded in the late 1950s by H. Edwin and Lois O'Neal and William Arnold Lapp. In 1962 it merged with the NEW LIFE WORLD-WIDE to form the CENTER FOR SPIRITUAL AWARENESS (CSA).

Church of the Complete Word

Known also as the Word Church, this was a U.S. FUNDAMENTALIST group founded in the early 1970s as the Lighthouse Ranch Commune in Eureka, California, by Jim Durkin. Later the group developed an active missionary program in Central America, especially in Guatemala. Efrain Rios Montt, military dictator in Guatemala between March 1982 and August 1983, is the best-known member of this group. Rios Montt, accused of murdering thousands of rebel peasants during his reign, was prevented from taking part in the presidential elections in January 1996. His candidate, Alfonso Portillo, lost, but Rios Montt remained quite powerful.

Church of the Covenants

U.S. FUNDAMENTALIST, PENTECOSTAL group, connected with BRITISH

ISRAELISM. It was founded by David Bruggman in 1940, with headquarters in River Forest, Illinois. In Dayton, Ohio, a branch was headed by Millard J. Flenner, operator of the Dayton Theological Seminary between 1947 and 1951.

Church of the Creator (COTC)

U.S. white-supremacist, anti-Christian group started by Bernard "Ben" Klassen (1918–) in 1973 in Otto, North Carolina. It has an active following in the Pacific Northwest region of the United States. In 1989, the Church gave an award to a white South African who had murdered several black Africans. [See also IDENTITY MOVEMENT.]

Church of the Eternal Source

U.S. neo-pagan group dedicated to the worship of ancient Egyptian gods. It is based in Burbank, California. [See also CHURCH OF ALL WORLDS; and COVENANT OF THE GODDESS.]

Church of the First-Born

West Indian indigenous PENTECOSTAL church based in Kingston, Jamaica. Members follow a strict code of behavior and are opposed to all medical treatment. Some members have gone to prison in the United States for failing to provide their children with proper medical care.

Church of the First Born of the Fullness of Times

U.S. MORMON group committed to polygyny. It was founded in 1955 by Joel LeBaron (murdered in 1972), who claimed to have had a visit by two divine messengers who appointed him a prophet. Before that he was a member of the APOSTOLIC UNITED ORDER. [See also THE CHURCH OF THE LAMB OF GOD; CONFEDERATE NATIONS OF ISRAEL; REORGANIZED CHURCH OF JESUS CHRIST OF LATTER-DAY SAINTS; and UNITED ORDER EFFORT.]

Church of the Fuller Concept

U.S. NEW THOUGHT group founded by Bernese Williamson in Washington, D.C., in the 1960s. It operated the Hisacres New Thought Center.

Church of the Gift of God

U.S. Christian-occultist group founded by James A. Dooling, III, in Magnolia, Massachusetts, during the 1970s. The group operates the New England Conservatory of Health. Practices include medical astrology, color therapy, and psychic healing.

Church of the Gospel, The

U.S. MILLENARIAN group founded in Pittsfield, Massachusetts, in 1911.

Church of the Healing Christ (Divine Science), The

New York City NEW THOUGHT group. It is officially part of Divine Science, which was founded by Albert C. Grier (who also founded CHURCH OF THE TRUTH). Starting in 1925, it was led by Emmet Fox (1886–1959). Fox was born in Ireland in a Roman Catholic family, studied engineering in England, and then joined the New Thought movement in the United

States. His version of New Thought was heavily Christian. He claimed that the Bible contained a hidden metaphysical message.

Church of the Holy Ghost/Spirit, The

Known also as the Church of the Canaanites. This is a South African nativist ZIONIST church founded in 1917 by Paulo Nzuza (1896–1959), in Himeville, near Durban. The church was founded after Nzuza experienced "the Holy Ghost" on May 9, 1916. Members believe this group is the third, and final, link in the sequence of three churches: the Church of the Jews, the Church of the Gentiles, and the Church of the Spirit. These were founded by Peter, Paul, and Paulo Nzuza, respectively.

Source:
Sundkler, B. G. M. *Zulu Zion and Some Swazi Zionists.* London: Oxford University Press, 1976.

Church of the Humanitarian God

U.S. Christian group founded in 1969, devoted to promoting nonviolence. It is based in Florida.

Church of the Kenya Family

African nativist Christian church founded in 1948 among the Embu group of Kenya. Doctrine and practice focus on spiritual healing.

Church of the Kingdom of God, Philanthropic Assembly, The

Known also as the Philanthropic Assembly of the Friends of Man, this is a FUNDAMENTALIST, MILLENARIAN group founded in 1921 by F. L. Alexander Freytag (1870–1947) in Switzerland. Freytag was the leader of the Swiss branch of the Watch Tower Tract and Bible Society (JEHOVAH'S WITNESSES), but started dissenting from the Witnesses' official teachings. The doctrine still follows some Jehovah's Witnesses ideas but states that Freytag was the "messenger of the eternal," chosen to announce the Second Coming. It also believes that two biblical days (which equal 2,000 years) have passed between the appearance of Jesus Christ and 1918. Since 1918 a new day (*i.e.*, millennium) has begun, in which a new earth will be created, on which eternal life will be achieved—partly through a special health diet. After the founder's death, the movement split into French (AMIS DE L'HOMME) and Swiss (Kirche des Reiches Gott/Menschenfreunde) branches. The Swiss branch, known today as the Assembly, has gained followers in Western Europe and the United States.

Church of the Lamb of God

U.S. MORMON splinter group formed in 1971 by Ervil LeBaron. LeBaron left the CHURCH OF THE FIRST BORN OF THE FULLNESS OF TIMES, claiming leadership over all polygynous groups and individuals. He resorted to murder in his war against other groups and leaders. On August 20, 1972, members of the Church of the Lamb of God killed Joel LeBaron, then the leader of The Church of the First Born in the Fullness of Times, on orders of his brother Ervil. On December 14, 1972, group members attacked the settlement of Los Molinos in Mexico where members of the Church of the First Born lived. Two individuals were killed. On May 10, 1977, members of the Church of the Lamb of God killed Rulon C. Allred, leader of the APOSTOLIC UNITED ORDER. Ervil LeBaron was sentenced to life imprisonment, and died in prison on August 16, 1981. The group no longer exists. [*See also* CONFEDERATE NATIONS OF ISRAEL; REORGANIZED CHURCH OF JESUS CHRIST OF LATTER-DAY SAINTS; *and* UNITED ORDER EFFORT.]

Source:
Bradlee, B., Jr., and Van Atta, D. *Prophet of Blood*. New York: G. P. Putnam's Sons, 1981.

Church of the Little Children

North American PENTECOSTAL group founded in 1916 by John Quincy Adams (1890–1951), former Baptist minister in Abbott, Texas. The group rejects various beliefs as pagan, including the Trinity, Sunday Sabbath, Christmas, Easter, neckties, and the names of the days of the week. Followers are conscientious objectors.

Church of the Living God

U.S. independent African American church led by the black "Messiah" St. John the Vine, whose birth name was John Hickerson. He was active in Baltimore, Maryland, and later in Harlem, New York City, in the early decades of the twentieth century. FATHER DIVINE is reported to have been among his followers, borrowing some of his teachings later on.

Church of the Living God, Christian Workers for Fellowship (CWFF)

U.S. African American PENTECOSTAL group founded in 1889 in Wrightsville, Arkansas, by former slave William Christian (1856–1928). The group claims that Biblical figures such as Jesus Christ were African and relies on revelations provided to its (hereditary) leadership. Tithing is required.

Church of the Living God, General Assembly

Originally known as Church of the Living God, Apostolic Church, this U.S. African American PENTECOSTAL group was founded in 1902 as a result of a schism in the CHURCH OF THE LIVING GOD, CHRISTIAN WORKERS FOR FELLOWSHIP (CWFF). In 1926 the group merged with the Church of the Living God, the Pillar and Ground of Truth, to form THE HOUSE OF GOD WHICH IS THE CHURCH OF THE LIVING GOD, THE PILLAR AND GROUND OF TRUTH.

Church of the Lord (Aladura)

Known sometimes as CLA, this nativist African Christian church is part of the ALADURA group of churches in Nigeria. [*See also* CELESTIAL CHURCH OF CHRIST; CHERUBIM AND SERAPHIM (ETERNAL SACRED ORDER OF); CHRIST APOSTOLIC CHURCH; *and* TWER NYAME CHURCH.]

Church of the Lord (Ghana)

Nativist African Christian church founded in Ghana in 1971 in a secession from the CHURCH OF THE LORD (ALADURA).

Church of the Lord Jesus Christ of the Apostolic Faith

U.S. PENTECOSTAL group founded in 1933 by A. C. Johnson, formerly of the Church of Our Lord Jesus Christ of the Apostolic Faith. The group views Christmas and Easter as pagan celebrations, and a strict dress code is enforced. The church is based in Philadelphia.

Church of the Lord Jesus Christ of the Apostolic Faith

British PENTECOSTAL group whose members come from the West Indian immigrant community. Originally part of the U.S. group of the same name, the London group seceded in the 1970s.

Church of the Loving Servant

U.S. "non-denominational church dedicated to service through healing," founded in the late 1970s by John Harvey Gray. The main practice is Reiki, which is described as "healing through energy."

Church of the Mystic Christ

Australian occultist-Christian church founded in the 1950s.

Church of the Nazarene

U.S. HOLINESS group founded in Pilot Point, Texas, in 1908 by Phineas Bresee. Its doctrine includes the notion of Perfectionism, according to which Christians become perfect through baptism of the Holy Spirit.

Church of the New Dispensation, The

Also known as Naba Bihan and Nava Vidhana, this is a Hindu-Unitarian group headed by Keshab Chandra Sen (1838–1884). It was formed in 1881 following a schism in the BRAHMA SAMAJ of India, which also resulted in the creation of the Sadharan Brahmo Samaj. Sen was strongly influenced by Christianity and by the Hindu revitalization attempts led by RAMAKRISHNA. His dream was of a unity of Hinduism, Islam, and Christianity into one world brotherhood. The Church rituals mixed Christian and Hindu practices. At the same time, he viewed Christianity as an Asian movement tied to Asian culture. In his later years, Sen became more mystical and claimed divine revelations. [*See also* ARYA SAMAJ.]

Church of the New Life

Brazilian PENTECOSTAL group founded in 1960 in Rio de Janeiro by Robert McAlister.

Church of the Redeemer Community

U.S. Christian commune founded by W. Graham Pulkingham in Houston, Texas, in the 1960s. Pulkingham was a Roman Catholic priest and a leader in the CATHOLIC CHARISMATIC RENEWAL movement.

Church of the Sacred Alpha, The

U.S. group, based in California and founded in the 1960s, whose rituals involved biofeedback and manipulation of

95

alpha electrical activity in the brain. [*See also* FEEDBACK CHURCH; *and* HOLY FEEDBACK CHURCH.]

Church of the Saviour

U.S. Christian communal group founded in 1946 in Washington, D.C., by Gordon Cosby. Church of the Saviour is a "nondenominational, interracial church. It requires a rigorous preliminary course of Christian studies for all potential members. Commitment to certain minimum spiritual disciplines is expected. Each person is considered a minister to the world and belongs to a mission group dedicated to Christian outreach. There is no church edifice."

The group is known as a "social action" congregation. Members express their religious commitment through service to the poor and the oppressed in their immediate vicinity.

Church of the Trinity (Invisible Ministry)

U.S. NEW THOUGHT group, founded in 1972 in California by Friend Stuart (A. Stuart Otto). Stuart started his activities in the New Thought movement in the 1950s following a religious awakening. The group's doctrine is specifically Christian, and faith healing is emphasized.

Church of the Truth

North American NEW THOUGHT group founded in 1913 in Spokane, Washington, by Albert C. Grier, a former Universalist minister.

Source:

Braden, C. S. *Spirits in Rebellion*. Dallas: Southern Methodist University Press, 1963.

Church of Time (Daku Community)

Known as Lotu ni Gauna, this is a Fiji nativist MILLENARIAN movement started in 1929. It was founded by Apolosi R. Nawai, also known as Ratu Emosi, in a secession from the European-led Methodist Church in Fiji. Its founder was a successful businessman turned prophet, who has been arrested and exiled several times for his anticolonialist activities. Its doctrine stresses a revival of Fijian traditions and liberation from European control.

Church of Tzaddi

U.S. occultist organization, self-described as a "non-denominational, metaphysical as well as spiritual church," founded in 1964 by Amy Kees (1914–) and her daughter Dorothe Jean Blackmere (1936–). Headquarters are located in Boulder, Colorado. Around 1940, Mrs. Kees reported hearing the voice and then seeing the figure of "Adonis, who had taught in a healing room—called Tzaddi—in King Solomon's Temple." Later she reported many contacts with other "Masters." In 1959, she joined the UNITY SCHOOL OF CHRISTIANITY, and then started her own group. The Church ministers offer "past life readings" and "Akashic records," as well as palmistry, handwriting analysis, and numerology. The Church has offered affiliation to similar groups. [*See also* ARIZONA METAPHYSICAL SOCIETY.]

Church of Universal Triumph / The Dominion of God

U.S. African American MILLENARIAN group started in 1938 in Detroit. The founder was James Francis Marion Jones (1908–1971), known as Prophet Jones, a former minister of the TRIUMPH OF THE CHURCH AND KINGDOM OF GOD IN CHRIST (INTERNATIONAL). Forbidden tobacco, tea, coffee, and alcohol, members are enjoined to follow a strict behavior code. Church doctrine predicts the coming of the millennium in the year 2000. All members alive then will become immortal.

The leader, Prophet Jones, was known in the 1940s and 1950s for his extravagant wealth. His personal charisma was compared to that of FATHER DIVINE and Daddy Grace.

Church Triumphant

U.S. CHRISTIAN SCIENCE schismatic group in New York City led by Augusta Stetson (1842–1928). It was started after the death of Mary Baker Eddy, the founder of Christian Science, in 1910.

Church Universal and Triumphant

Also known as Summit Lighthouse or Summit International. This U.S. occultist THEOSOPHICAL group was founded in 1958 in Washington, D.C., by Mark Prophet (1918–1973) and Elizabeth Clare (Wolf) Prophet (1940–), sometimes known as Guru Ma or Mother. Formerly members of THE BRIDGE TO FREEDOM, they claimed to be "on orders from The Ascended Master El Morya." The group proclaims a "Coming Revolution in Higher Consciousness." Its doctrine is based on the teachings of "I AM," combining Hindu ideas with Western occultist traditions such as the teachings of the Great White Brotherhood (White Light of the Aura) and of Master Saint-Germain, a figure that appeared to the founder of "I Am." The Bible and Christian traditions are also utilized. "The Summit Lighthouse publishes the teachings of the ascended masters of the Great White Brotherhood as taught by Elizabeth Clare Prophet. Study, meditation, and the science of the spoken Word in decrees and mantras are an essential part of their program to help the individual realize his God-potential and soul freedom and to assist people of every race and religion to live in harmony with cosmic law." In her public appearances, Mrs. Prophet has delivered "dictations from the Ascended Masters," including "Beloved Mother Mary" and Nicholas Roerich. In the 1980s, the group offered both faith healing and vegetarian diets designed to protect the body from AIDS and cancer. In 1982, the group acquired a 12,000-acre ranch in Paradise Valley, Montana. In the spring of 1990, many members moved there in anticipation of a global catastrophe predicted by Mrs. Prophet.

In the late 1980s, Summit Lighthouse was sued by Gregory Mull, a former member, who was awarded $1.56 million because the group had pressured him to give up his entire life's savings. The group has operated overseas branches in Latin America, Europe, and West Africa.

"Church Which Is Christ's Body," The

U.S. FUNDAMENTALIST group founded by Maurice M. Johnson in 1925 in Los Ange-

James Francis Marion Jones founded the Church of Universal Triumph/The Dominion of God, a group that predicts the coming of the millenium in the year 2000.

les. Members refuse to incorporate or use any formal designations, and are active evangelists.

Circle of Angels

Known also as the Metanoian Order, this is a U.S. GURDJIEFF GROUP commune founded in 1976 and based on the Walden Farm in East Hardwick, Vermont.

Circle of Light

U.S. Christian occultist group founded by Shirlee Dunlap in Lombard, Illinois, in the early 1980s. It is loosely affiliated with the LOGOS WORLD UNIVERSITY CHURCH.

Circle Sanctuary

Formerly known as the Church of Circle Wicca, this neo-pagan U.S. group, self-described as a Wiccan Church, was founded in 1974 in Wisconsin by Selena Fox (1949–) and Jim Alan. Headquartered in Mt. Horeb, Wisconsin, it holds a Pagan Spirit Gathering every summer, as well as other pagan festivals. The Church is committed to the worship of the Great Mother Goddess as well as a male consort and an additional pantheon of pagan deities. "The Wiccan religion is pantheistic in that the Divine is seen as everywhere and in everything. The Wiccan religion also is animistic in that every human, tree, animal, stream, rock, and other form of life is seen to have a Divine Spirit within. The Wiccan religion is monotheistic in that there is an honoring of Divine Unity. It also is polytheis-tic in that Wiccans honor the Divine through a variety of female and male deity forms—Goddesses and Gods which are aspects of the Divine Female and Divine Male and their Unity." The group has operated the Pagan Spirit Alliance (PSA), a network of self-declared pagans in North America and Great Britain. [*See also* CHURCH OF ALL WORLDS; *and* COVENANT OF THE GODDESS; *and* WICCA.]

Claymont Court

Formerly known as the Claymont Society for Continuous Education, Inc., this is a U.S. GURDJIEFF GROUP founded in 1975 and headquartered in Charles Town, West Virginia. It is devoted to "the principles and techniques of Spiritual Psychology, according to the ideas of Georgei I. Gurdjieff, and John G. Bennett." Claymont Court operates the American Society of Continuous Education. [*See also* INSTITUTE FOR THE COMPARATIVE STUDY OF HISTORY, PHILOSOPHY, AND THE SCIENCES.]

Coconut Palm Movement (Religion du Cocotier)

Syncretistic MILLENARIAN Vietnamese movement, started in the Mekong Delta in the 1950s. Nguyen Thanh Nam originated the Coconut Palm Movement in opposition to modernization and Western ideas.

Colony, The

U.S. Christian commune founded by Brother John in the 1970s. It is based in northern California.

Colorum

Filipino MILLENARIAN syncretistic movement started in the early twentieth

movement started in the early twentieth century.

Coming of Jesus

New Guinea syncretistic movement (CARGO CULTS) started in 1943 in the Markham Valley. The imminent arrival of Jesus Christ was announced, and this Second Coming was to be followed by the removal of white people. Two years later the claim was made that "cargo" destined for the people of New Guinea was being intercepted by white people. After the Second Coming, the blacks would become white and inherit all goods owned by the former whites.

Commandment Keepers Congregation of the Living God

Known also as ETHIOPIAN HEBREWS, this is a U.S. African American Jewish group founded in 1919 by Wentworth Arthur Matthew (1892–1973) in New York City. Group doctrine teaches that ancient Jews were black and that Orthodox Judaism is the true religion and culture of Africans. According to Commandment Keepers, present-day African Americans are the tribe of Judah, whereas the biblical lost tribes of I Kings, II Kings, and Esdras are the white people. Practices follow closely those of Orthodox Judaism. The group operates the Israelite Rabbinical Academy, which trains its rabbis.

Source:
Brotz, H. M. *The Black Jews of Harlem.* New York: Schocken Books, 1970.

Communion Phalangiste (La Phalange)

French traditionalist Roman Catholic group founded in 1970 by Georges de Nantes as the Ligue de la Contre Réforme Catholic (CRC). It assumed its current name in 1970. The group's doctrine regards the Roman Catholic Church as heretical, controlled by the Jews and the Masons. It opposes democracy and longs for a religious dictator who would establish Catholicism in France.

Community Chapel and Bible Training Center

U.S. FUNDAMENTALIST, PENTECOSTAL group founded by Donald Lee Barnett in Burien, Washington, in 1967. Born in Idaho in 1930, Barnett was an aerospace engineer at the Boeing company and a part-time ASSEMBLIES OF GOD preacher before starting his own church. He rejected the doctrine of the Trinity and promoted belief in demons, which he claimed to exorcise. Members were subject to a strict dress code. In March 1986, a group member killed her five-year-old daughter by drowning her in a motel swimming pool, claiming that a "hyperactivity demon" was possessing the child. In the same year, former members confronted Barnett with legal charges stemming from his authoritarian style and beliefs. In 1987 Barnett was disfellowshipped by church elders because of alleged sexual affairs he had with female members. In 1988 he was legally forced to give up his rights to group property.

Community of Jesus

First known as Bethany House, this is a U.S. charismatic Christian group based in Cape Cod, Massachusetts. It was started in 1969 by Cay Andersen and operates the 3D program—Discipleship, Discipline, and Diet—for overweight Christian women.

Community of the Many Names of God

Western Hindu-oriented group with headquarters in Wales. It was started in the 1970s.

Company at Kirkridge, The

U.S. Christian ecumenical group founded in 1976 in Pennsylvania by John Oliver Nelson. Members may keep their affiliation with other Christian groups and attend only four weekend meetings a year with the Company.

Concept-Therapy Institute

U.S. occultist THEOSOPHICAL group founded by Thurman Fleet in the 1970s. It is based at the Aum-Sat-Tat Ranch in San Antonio, Texas, and teaches Conceptology, "the laws of Life."

Concilio Latino-Americano de la Iglesia de Dios Pentecostal de New York, Incorporado

Also known as the Latin American Council of the Pentecostal Church of God of New York, this is a Spanish-speaking U.S. PENTECOSTAL group founded in 1957 in connection with the Puerto Rican IGLESIA DE DIOS PENTECOSTAL. Healing and tithing are emphasized in the group's doctrine.

Concilio Olazabal de Iglesias Latino Americano

U.S. Spanish-speaking PENTECOSTAL group with branches in Mexico. It was founded by Francisco Olazabal (1886–1937), a former Methodist minister, in Los Angeles in 1923.

Concordant Publishing Concern

International FUNDAMENTALIST, DISPENSATIONALIST group founded by Adolph Ernst Knoch (1874–1965). It is centered around a publishing project that offers new English and German versions of the Bible, aimed at correcting what Knoch and his disciples consider serious errors in translation and interpretation of inspired texts.

Confederate Nations of Israel

Originally known as The Church of Jesus Christ in Solemn Assembly. Committed to polygyny, this MORMON splinter group was founded by Alexander Joseph in 1974 after he left the APOSTOLIC UNITED ORDER. It is based in Big Water, Kane County, Utah, where most members live. [See also THE CHURCH OF THE FIRST BORN OF THE FULLNESS OF TIMES; REORGANIZED CHURCH OF JESUS CHRIST OF LATTER-DAY SAINTS; and UNITED ORDER EFFORT.]

Confraternity of Deists, Inc.

U.S. monotheistic group founded in 1967 in St. Petersburg, Florida, by Paul Englert. The group is opposed to established churches and accepted scriptures.

Congregacao Crista

Brazilian PENTECOSTAL movement founded in the 1960s and based in São Paolo.

Congregational Catholic Apostolic Church in Zion of South Africa

South African independent indigenous ZIONIST church founded in 1931 by Titus M. Msibi. It claims to follow the doctrines of the CHRISTIAN CATHOLIC APOSTOLIC CHURCH IN ZION, which in this Church means the avoidance of alcohol, gambling, pork, dancing, and medicine.

Source:
Sundkler, B. G. M. *Bantu Prophets in South Africa.* London: Oxford University Press, 1961.

Congregational Church of Practical Theology

U.S. Christian occultist group started in 1969 in Valley, Nebraska. The founder is E. Arthur Winkler, a former United Church of Christ and United Methodist minister. It operates the Eastern Nebraska Christian College and is connected with ANDROMEDA, THE CHAPEL OF THE OPEN DOOR. Practices include meditation and "success through thought."

Congregational Holiness Church

U.S. PENTECOSTAL group founded in 1920 in Georgia by Watson Sorrow following a dispute over healing in the Georgia Conference of the PENTECOSTAL HOLINESS CHURCH, INTERNATIONAL. The majority dismissed the need for human-made medicine and believed only in divine healing. The minority, led by Sorrow, recommended reliance on medicine. Later, Sorrow founded the FIRST INTERDENOMINATIONAL CHRISTIAN ASSOCIATION.

Congregation Beit Shechinah

Jewish NEW THOUGHT "spiritual renewal group" founded in the late 1980s in northern California by Leah Novick. Practices include guided visualizations and meditation.

Congregation of Mary the Immaculate Queen

U.S. traditionalist Catholic group started in 1971 in Idaho by Francis K. Schuckardt. It later moved its center to Spokane, Washington. This group believes that the Roman Catholic Church has been taken over by the Freemasons, who they believe murdered Pope Pius XII, and that reforms in the Church since 1965 reflect that takeover. The founder left the group in 1984, and the group has come under the guidance of George J. Musey of the SERVANTS OF THE SACRED HEART OF JESUS AND MARY.

Congregation of the Messiah

U.S. MESSIANIC JUDAISM group started in Philadelphia in the 1960s.

Conservative Judaism

U.S. Jewish renewal movement that has its origins among Jewish intellectuals in nineteenth-century Central Europe. Its real starting point can best be tied to the founding of the Jewish Theological Seminary in New York by Solomon Schechter (1847–1915) in 1887. The Rabbinical Assembly of America was founded at the same time. The United Synagogue of America was founded in 1913. Today this is the largest Jewish denomination in the United States, with more followers than either REFORM JUDAISM or the

The Jewish Theological Seminary, teaching center of the Conservative Jewish movement (courtesy Library of the Jewish Theological Seminary of America).

historical Orthodox Judaism. It is virtually unknown outside the United States.

In doctrine, this denomination stands midway between Orthodoxy, the complete adherence to traditional Jewish practices, and Reform Judaism, which initially rejected almost all practices and preserved only a few central beliefs. It started as a reaction to Reform Judaism, and refused to espouse modernity as the only ideal.

Source:

Sklare, M. *Conservative Judaism: An American Religious Movement*. Glencoe, IL: The Free Press, 1955.

Coptic Fellowship of America

U.S. esoteric Christianity group founded in 1927 in Los Angeles by Hamid Bey (?–1976), who claimed to have studied in hidden Christian temples in Egypt.

Cosmic Circle of Fellowship

U.S. UFO Christian group founded by William A. Ferguson (?–1962) in 1954 in Chicago. Ferguson reported his first extraterrestrial contact in 1938, when his soul reportedly traveled to Mars.

Cosmic Star Temple

U.S. UFO THEOSOPHICAL group founded in 1960 and based near Roseburg, Oregon. The founder, Violet Gilbert, claimed to have first contact with "space brothers" in 1937, and a first visit to Venus in 1939.

Cosmon Research Foundation

U.S. group devoted to communication with extraterrestrials. Founded in the 1950s, its central figure and medium for the messages from space was Gloria Lee (1925–1962). Lee published two books containing such messages, which were similar to previously published THEOSOPHICAL literature. In late 1962 she went to Washington, D.C., expecting to speak to government officials about her revelations. When she was ignored, she started a fast to protest government indifference and subsequently died. The group disbanded shortly thereafter. [*See also* HERALDS OF THE NEW AGE.]

A Course in Miracles (ACIM)

International NEW THOUGHT belief system transmitted by numerous teachers conducting many groups across the United States. The book *A Course In Miracles* was published in 1975 by Helen Schucman (?–1981), who claimed to have been the only medium for a divine revelation from Jesus Christ. According to other versions of the book, it is the joint work of Schucman and William Theiford (?–1988). ACIM has also been used by some Jewish groups.

The ACIM message is based on the notion that death is an illusion, sin unreal, and guilt to be avoided. Only the spirit is real. Thought is all-powerful, and through positive, nonjudgmental thinking, most human problems will be solved. Healing the mind is possible through universal forgiveness.

The book has been translated into German, Spanish, French, Portuguese, and Hebrew. [*See also* CALIFORNIA MIRACLES CENTER; FOUNDATION FOR "A COURSE IN MIRACLES" (FACIM); FOUNDATION FOR INNER PEACE; INTERFAITH FELLOWSHIP;

and MIRACLE DISTRIBUTION CENTER (MDC).]

Covenant Community Fellowship

U.S. FUNDAMENTALIST group started in the 1980s in Rennselaer, Indiana.

Covenant of the Goddess

International association of WICCAN (neo-pagan) groups dedicated to the worship of the Great Mother Goddess and her male consort. Members, known as witches, are organized in covens and celebrate solar festivals such as the Spring Equinox (March 21), Fall Equinox (September 21), Summer Solstice (June 21), and Winter Solstice (December 21). The Covenant was founded in 1975 in California, and headquarters are in Berkeley, California.

Covenant, the Sword, the Arm of the Lord, The

U.S. IDENTITY communal group established in 1976 by James D. Ellison in Zaraphath-Horeb, Arkansas. The founder was inspired by the Ku Klux Klan ideology of white supremacy, with an emphasis on military training. Ellison also believed in a world government plan, involving foreign troops occupying the United States. There was also the notion of survivalism, i.e., preparing for civil war and/or a major natural disaster that would destroy U.S. society. In 1980 the group started the Endtime Overcomers Survival School. In April of 1985 the group was raided by federal authorities and its firearms were seized. Ellison and two elders of the group were subse-

quently sentenced to twenty years in prison on racketeering and weapons charges. The group was dispersed in 1986, but active members remain. On April 19, 1995, Richard Wayne Snell, a sixty-four-year-old group member, was executed for the murder of a businessman who he thought was Jewish, and an African American police officer. Robert G. Millar, founder of ELOHIM CITY, served as spiritual adviser to both Ellison and Snell. [*See also* CHRISTIAN PATRIOTS DEFENSE LEAGUE (CPDL).]

Coven of Arianhu

U.S. witchcraft group founded by Louise and Loy Stone in Texas. It is associated with the church and school of WICCA.

Cross of Christ World Mission

Nativist Christian movement founded in the 1970s and based in Ibadan, Nigeria. The group has operated numerous social welfare and health programs.

Crossroads Churches of Christ

U.S. FUNDAMENTALIST organization, founded in 1973 by Chuck Lucas, at a congregation near the University of Florida in Gainesville, Florida.

The organization is structured according to the SHEPHERDING principle, which provides for an authoritarian leadership style and close supervision of members. This style has been the basis of what has been called the "shepherding movement," which includes the BODY OF CHRIST, CHRISTIAN GROWTH MINISTRIES, and CHRISTIAN RESTORATION MINISTRIES. Branches have operated all over the United States and the Western

Part of the cache of arms seized by police at a survivalist camp of the Covenant, the Sword, and the Arm of the Lord in a 1985 raid. Also found was the photograph of Adolf Hitler in the background. (see p. 105)

The Crystal Cathedral of television evangelist Robert Schuller in California.

hemisphere. [*See also* BOSTON CHURCH OF CHRIST; *and* NEW YORK CHURCH OF CIIRIST.]

Crusade for Christ and Country

U.S. IDENTITY group founded by Gordon "Jack" Mohr in the 1970s, and based in Mississippi.

Crystal Cathedral

U.S. Protestant NEW THOUGHT church founded in southern California in 1955 by Robert Schuller (1927–). The founder graduated from Hope College and Western Theological Seminary, in Holland, Michigan, and was ordained in 1950 as a

minister in the Reformed Church of America. In 1955 he moved to California and began his independent career. In 1980 the Crystal Cathedral, a huge glass and steel structure, was completed. The message of the church is one of positive thinking, making a connection between religious salvation and symbols of material success. It defines itself as a place where "positive attitudes are developed, good people become better, hurts are healed, lessons are learned, friendships are developed, marriages are strengthened, families are bonded, the restless find peace, love is alive, God is understood, Jesus is Lord." The Cathedral operates mostly through television programs and books.

Cultural Integration Fellowship

U.S. Hindu-oriented group devoted to the teachings of SRI AUROBINDO. It was founded in 1951 by Haridas Chaudhuri (1913–1975) in San Francisco and operates the California Institute of Integral Studies (formerly known as the California Institute of Asian Studies, founded 1968).

Cultural Minorities Spiritual Fraternization Church of the Philippines

Filipino healing group founded by Philip S. Malicdan in the 1960s. The founder has made claims to have powers of psychic surgery. Branches, known as healing centers, have operated in Europe, East Asia, and the United States.

D

Da'at

Israeli religion founded in 1987 by Shlomo Kalo (1922–), based on his personal vision of life and the universe. The group's name is an acronym of Da Et Atzmecha Tamid ("Always Know Thyself"). Kalo claims to be an entity from the star Sirius, created thirteen million years ago and now descended to Earth in human form to show humanity the road to enlightenment. His mission on Earth follows those of Moses of the Old Testament, Jesus of the New Testament, and Muhammad of the Koran. When his mission is over, Kalo will again assume the form of light radiation, nurtured by pure energy. He advocates celibacy; mandates the avoidance of meat, wine, anger, envy, and all sensual enjoyment; and encourages his followers to live communally in small groups. Kalo's writings, before his claims to being an emissary from Sirius, include about fifteen books devoted to explicating classical Buddhism and his interpretations of and additions to Buddhist beliefs.

Daheshism

Lebanese syncretistic group with Islamic origins, founded in the 1950s.

Dai-Hizen-Kyo (Great Sun Teaching)

Japanese religion with shamanistic features founded in the 1950s by Nami Orimo. The founder claimed to be possessed by gods.

Damanhur

Italian communal occultist movement founded in the 1960s in Baldissero Canavese (Turin). Its doctrine combines THEOSOPHICAL ideas with Eastern and Western occultism, and the movement claims to carry on ancient Egyptian traditions.

Damascus Christian Church

U.S. Spanish-speaking PENTECOSTAL group started in 1939 in New York City, with branches in the Caribbean.

Dangun

Also known as Dan-gun gyo, this is an indigenous Korean movement started in the mid-nineteenth century.

Davidian Seventh-Day Adventist Association

U.S. Adventist group founded by Victor T. Houteff (1885–1955), a dissenting SEVENTH-DAY ADVENTIST who was expelled from that organization in 1930. In the early 1930s he proclaimed himself a divine messenger charged with the task of gathering the 144,000 souls destined for salvation according to the New Testament Book of Revelation. In 1935 he moved with eleven followers to the Mount Carmel Center, started near Waco, Texas, to gather the 144,000. The next step would have been a move to Palestine, and the establishment of a Davidian kingdom, prior to the Second Coming of Christ.

When Houteff died in 1955 his wife took over the leadership. She later announced that the Davidian kingdom would arrive on April 22, 1959, when both Arabs and Israelis would disappear forever from the Holy Land. The faithful gathered at Mount Carmel to await this event, which did not transpire. In their disappointment, most left the group. One such group was the BRANCH SEVENTH DAY ADVENTISTS, more commonly known as Branch Davidians. In December 1961, Mrs. Houteff confessed her error and the error of the group's teachings. In March 1962 the association was officially dissolved. However, a few members were committed to reviving it, and in 1970 it was reestablished in Exter, Missouri.

Dawn Bible Students Association

U.S. outreach ministry organization started in the late 1920s in a secession from the JEHOVAH'S WITNESSES. It distributes the teachings of Charles Taze Russell (1852–1916), founder of Jehovah's Witnesses, through printed publications, radio, and television. Based in New York City, the group has members in the United States, Great Britain, Western Europe, and Oceania. [*See also* PASTORAL BIBLE INSTITUTE.]

Dawn Horse Communion

U.S. commune in existence in the early 1970s, led by Bubba Free John. [*See also* FREE DAIST AVATARIC COMMUNION.]

Dawn of Truth

North American Christian occultist group founded by Mikkel Dahl in Windsor, Ontario, in 1961. Teachings include the "power of the Great Pyramid" and "spiritual laws of successful living."

Death Angels

U.S. Islamic group started in the 1970s as a splinter group of the NATION OF ISLAM (NOI).

Defenders of the Christian Faith, Inc.

U.S. FUNDAMENTALIST group founded by Gerald B. Winrod (1898–1957) in 1925 as an interdenominational organization. It is politically conservative and anti-Semitic, with several publications, mainly *The Defender*, promoting its views. The group reached the height of its growth in the 1930s. After Winrod's death in 1957, the group declined, and then recovered somewhat in the 1960s under the leadership of G. H. Montgomery and Hunt Armstrong.

Sources:

Ribuffo, L. P. *The Old Christian Right: The Protestant Far Right from the Great Depression to the Cold War*. Philadelphia: Temple University Press, 1983.

Roy, J. L. *Apostles of Discord*. Boston: Beacon Press, 1953.

Defenders of the Faith (Iglesia Defensores de la Fe)

North American Spanish-speaking FUNDAMENTALIST group started in 1931 in Puerto Rico during a visit by Gerald B. Winrod, founder of the DEFENDERS OF THE CHRISTIAN FAITH, INC. In 1944, the group started recruiting members in the Spanish-speaking communities of the continental United States.

Deliverance Church

Kenyan independent Christian PENTE-COSTAL group founded in 1969.

Denver Area Wiccan Network (DAWN)

U.S. neo-pagan group based in Denver, Colorado, and founded in the 1980s. [*See also* WICCA.]

Destiny of America Foundation

U.S. BRITISH-ISRAELIST organization, founded by Conrad Gaard and based in his Christian Chapel Church in Tacoma, Washington. Gaard was an active author and radio speaker until his death in 1969.

Source:
Roy, R. L. *Apostles of Discord*. Boston: Beacon Press, 1953.

Deva Community

U.S. THEOSOPHICAL commune founded in the 1970s in Maryland.

Deva Foundation

International Western Hindu-oriented movement started in Sweden in the 1980s by Deva Maharaj (1948–). It is committed to the practice of "Tantric Yoga." Group branches have operated in Europe and North America.

Deva Samaj

Hindu reform movement ("The Divine Society") founded by Siva Narayana Agnihotri (1850–) in 1887 in Lahore, India (now Pakistan). The founder, a former leader of the ARYA SAMAJ, is worshiped as god. Spiritualism is practiced, but transmigration of souls is denied. Christian ideas are very influential.

Source:
Farquhar, J. N. *Modern Religious Movements in India*. New York: Macmillan, 1919.

Dianic Wicca

Originally known as the Susan B. Anthony Coven #1. This U.S. neo-pagan, witchcraft, feminist organization was founded by Zsuasznna Budapest in the early 1970s. The name change occurred in 1982. Based in California, it calls for lesbian separatism and prescribes all-female membership of covens. It practices the worship of a monotheistic goddess who represents the planet Earth. Through communication with nature, miracles are supposed to be produced. "Beyond nature there is only more nature. There is no other power but the planet." [*See also* COVENANT OF THE GODDESS; TEMPLE OF THE GODDESS WITHIN; *and* WICCA.]

Dianology and Eductivism

Also known as the Church of Eductivism, Church of Spiritual Science, the Association of International Dianologists, and the Personal Spiritual Freedoms Foundation. This U.S. offshoot of SCIENTOLOGY was founded in 1965 by Jack Horner (1927–), the first person to be awarded the "Doctor of Scientology" degree and one of L. Ron Hubbard's earliest associates.

Dini Ya Bapali

African indigenous syncretistic group founded in Uganda in 1924. It allows polygyny, while following Christian ritual. Branches operate in Tanzania.

Dini Ya Msambwa (DYM)

Officially known as the Religion of the Ancestral Spirits or the Israel Anglican Church, this is an African syncretistic group founded in Kenya in 1944 out of the Quaker movement. The group was banned by authorities in 1948 and 1968. A sister church has operated in Uganda.

Dini Ya Roho

Officially known as the Holy Spirit Church of East Africa, this is an African indigenous PENTECOSTAL group founded in Kenya in 1927. Members are noted for their white robes and turbans.

Disciples of Christ

Sometimes known as the Restoration Movement, or Campbellites, this is a Protestant MILLENARIAN denomination started in the United States in 1832 in Lexington, Kentucky. The founder, Alexander Campbell (1788–1866), was an Irish Presbyterian minister who moved to the United States in 1807. In 1812, he founded the Christian Association in Washington, Pennsylvania, which later became the Disciples of Christ. Preaching a return to "primitive Christianity" and the abolition of all formal creeds, Campbell predicted in 1829 that the "purification of the Sanctuary" would take place in 1847. Later he became convinced that the year 1866 would be decisive. Finally, in 1862, he determined that the millennium would occur between 1996 and 2996. In several English-speaking countries outside the United States, the movement is known as the Churches of Christ.

Disciples of Faith

U.S. NEW THOUGHT group based in Nashville, Tennessee. It operates strictly by mail and offers followers prayers that guarantee health and prosperity.

Discipulos de Santissima Trinidade, Sede

Brazilian Christian movement formed in the 1960s in a secession from the Roman Catholic Church.

Dispensationalism

The belief in seven dispensations, or ages, of history is found in many MILLENARIAN Protestant groups. According to the most common version, the seven dispensations are: innocence, conscience, government, promise, law, grace, and the personal reign of christ. [See also PLYMOUTH BRETHREN.]

Source:
Ehlert, A. D. *A Bibliographic History of Dispensationalism*. Grand Rapids, MI: Baker Book House, 1965.

Divine Filipino Catholic Church

Philippine independent Catholic group formed in 1954 from the PHILIPPINE INDEPENDENT CHURCH (PIC).

Divine Healer's Church

Also known as the Lord Is There Temple, an African independent PENTECOSTAL church founded in Ghana (then the Gold Coast) in 1954 by G. A. Lawson.

Divine Healing Church of Christ

African independent PENTECOSTAL church founded in Ghana in 1950.

Divine Healing Church of Israel

African independent PENTECOSTAL church founded in Ibadan, Nigeria, around 1960.

Divine Life Society (Divine Love Consciousness)

International Hindu group founded in 1936. It is devoted to the teachings of Swami Sivananda Saraswati (1887–1963), a noted twentieth-century Hindu guru who was the teacher of Swami Satchidananda and Swami Vishnu Devananda. Sivananda worked in a hospital for ten years before taking vows of holiness and renouncing the world. In 1924 he opened a small, free dispensary, which later became a hospital, and preached selfless service to humanity as the highest calling. In 1945 he founded an All World Religious Federation, and later on established the Yoga Vedanta Forest Academy, known as the Forest Academy. The Society is based in Shivanandanagar, Tehri-Garhwal, India. Its activities in the West started in 1954, when the European Divine Life Society was established in Switzerland. In 1959 branches were established in the United States following a visit by Swami Chidananda a disciple of Swami Sivananda Saraswati. [See also INTEGRAL YOGA INSTITUTE (IYA); and SIVANANDA YOGA VEDANTA.]

Divine Light Centrum

Swiss Hindu group founded in 1966 by Swami Omkarananda.

Divine Light Mission (DLM)

Also known as Dirya Sandesh Parishad, and more recently as Elan Vital. An international Hindu movement founded in 1960 in India, DLM became known worldwide in the 1970s under the leadership of Pratap Singh Rawat-Balyogeshwar, better known as Guru Maharaj Ji (the full title is Satguru Balyogeshwar Shri Sant Ji Maharaj), who was born in 1958 in India. He was the youngest of four sons born to Prem Nagar, also known as Shri Hans Maharaj Ji, who founded the Divine Light Mission in 1960. Shri Hans Maharaj Ji claimed to have reached enlightenment through the knowledge given to him by his guru Shri Sarupanand Ji in the 1920s. When his father, the founder, died in the summer of 1966, the eight-year-old Pretap stood up at the funeral to announce his ascent to the throne, thus becoming the movement's recognized leader. He went on a world tour in 1971, visiting Great Britain, France, Germany, Australia, South Africa, and the United States. His other three brothers were also active in the movement. Guru Maharaj Ji was considered the *satguru*, or the Perfect Master.

Members of the group, known as *premies* (devotees), were those who had received Knowledge from the Master that included four meditation procedures leading to ecstasy and perfection. The four procedures are known as Light, Music, Nectar, and Word, and two hours a day were devoted to them though continuous meditation on the Word was recommended. The recruitment of members occurred at meetings known as *satsang* held in local ashrams, or religious retreats. In addition to meditation and *satsang*, the *premies* were supposed to

Guru Maharaj Ji, leader of the Divine Light Mission, with his bride and former secretary, the former Karolyn Lois Johnson. At the time, in 1974, the Mission had thirty centers in the United States, with headquarters in Denver, Colorado.

spend their time at *darshans* (meetings with the *satguru*) and in service to the group. One form of *darshan* was *pranam*, in which the *premies* prostrated themselves on the ground in front of the *satguru*. Service activities included seeking donations and distributing group literature.

In the ashrams members of both sexes lived monastically and celibately. *Premies* living in ashrams gave all their material possessions to the *satguru* and obeyed strict discipline. They abstained from alcohol, meat, tobacco, other drugs, and food not provided by the ashram. Some members not living in ashrams lived communally, with less discipline, no hierarchy, and mutual support by members.

DLM's best-known recruit in the United States in the early 1970s was Rennie Davis, a cofounder of the radical Students for a Democratic Society (SDS) in the 1960s and a codefendant in the Chicago Seven trial in 1969. Davis became a DLM member in 1972. In November 1973 the DLM organized a gathering known as Millennium '73 in Houston's Astrodome, when Guru Maharaj Ji was crowned "Lord of the Universe." *Premies* expected the millennium to arrive and all the world's problems to be solved at the *darshan* given during the gathering, but the event was a failure even in terms of attendance and media attention. This disappointment started the group's decline. At the height of its lifecycle, in the mid-1970s, the Divine Light Mission had thirty ashrams in the United States, with headquarters in Denver, and a score of ashrams in Europe and Israel. In the late 1970s the organization was dismantled by Guru Maharaj Ji himself. He left his followers with the Knowledge, the four practices of meditation and ecstasy, which they could use and teach, but they no longer owed any allegiance to him or to the movement. DLM became the Knowledge, and the international movement, with headquarters in the United States and branches in many Western countries, became known as Elan Vital. It now communicates mostly through video presentations of appearances by the guru, and recruitment is extremely low-key. The guru has continued to travel and meet with students of the Knowledge.

Source:

Downton, J. V., Jr. *Sacred Journeys: The Conversion of Young Americans to Divine Light Mission*. New York: Columbia University Press, 1979.

Divine Prayer Society 1944

Also known also as the Church of the Family of God and of Jesus Christ, this African indigenous PENTECOSTAL group was founded in Accra, Ghana, in 1960. It has branches in Great Britain.

Divine Science Church

U.S. NEW THOUGHT group started by Malinda Cramer (?–1907), who chartered the Home College of Divine Science in 1888 in San Francisco. Her work was continued and expanded by Nona Brooks (1863–1945) and Fannie James, two sisters who founded the College of Divine Science in Denver, Colorado, in 1896. According to some accounts, the initiatives in San Francisco and Denver were independent and parallel though the three women met in Denver in 1889. The International Divine Science Association dates to 1892, and in 1957 the

Divine Science Federation International was organized. According to the group's doctrine, illness and poverty can be avoided by a return to oneness with the Divine Omnipresence.

Sources:

Braden, C. S. *Spirits in Rebellion*. Dallas: SMU Press, 1963.

Judah, J. S. *The History and Philosophy of the Metaphysical Movements in America*. Philadelphia: Westminster Press, 1967.

Divine Science of Light and Sound, The

U.S. syncretistic group founded in 1980 by Jerry Mulvin (1936–), a former leader of ECKANKAR in Marina del Rey, California. The doctrine and practices focus on "traveling into the inner world" and out-of-body travel.

Divine Trinity of Jesus Catholic Church

Philippine indigenous Catholic church founded in 1962 by former members of the Roman Catholic Church.

Doliasi Custom

Melanesian political-religious movement (CARGO CULT) that started in 1963 on Malaita in the Solomon Islands.

Source:

Cochrane, G. *Big Men and Cargo Cults*. Oxford: Clarendon Press, 1970.

Dolly Pond Church of God with Signs Following

U.S. PENTECOSTAL group noted for its use of snakes during services. It was founded in the 1930s by Thomas Harden. Members follow a strict conduct code and are popularly known as "snake handlers." Snake handling and the drinking of poison are regarded both as signs of the Holy Spirit and as tests of faith. However, in practice, snake handling is only rarely accompanied by drinking poison. There have been some deaths resulting from snakebites since the practice started, but bites are not a common occurrence. [*See also* CHURCH OF ALL NATIONS; *and* ORIGINAL PENTECOSTAL CHURCH OF GOD.]

Source:

La Barre, W. *They Shall Take Up Serpents*. New York: Schocken, 1969.

Donghak

Known also as Dong-hak gyo or Soo-un gyo, this is an indigenous Korean religion founded in the middle of the nineteenth century.

Door of Faith Churches of Hawaii

U.S. PENTECOSTAL group founded in 1940 by Mildred Brostek. It operates overseas missions in addition to its activities in Hawaii.

Dor Hashalom

U.S. Jewish NEW THOUGHT group based in New York City and founded in the 1980s by Burt Aaron Siegel. It later merged with the New Synagogue.

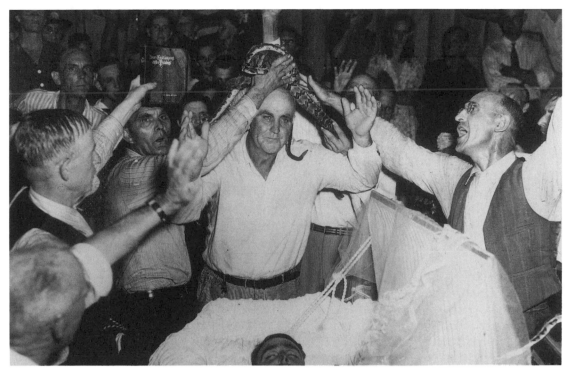

Members of a Pentecostal group Dolly Pond Church of God with Signs Following, popularly known as "snake handlers," performing a funeral ritual.

Dorje Khyung Dzong

U.S. Tibetan Buddhist retreat center founded in the 1970s in Colorado.

Doukhobors

The name, which means "spirit-wrestlers," refers to an anarchist religious group started in Russia at the end of the eighteenth century. Its doctrine opposes all civil authority and supports communal living. Members believe in reincarnation, and an early leader, Sergei Kapoustin, claimed to be an incarnation of Jesus Christ. Doukhobors are vegetarians committed to total nonviolence, refusing military service and even armed self-defense against wild animals.

Group members suffered persecution in Czarist Russia, and a migration to Canada occurred in 1898. Their leader changed the group's name to the Christian Community of Universal Brotherhood. Members still use the Russian language in their everyday lives. Since their settlement in Canada, they have been involved in many clashes with authorities in which they often use nudism as a form of protest. There have been several internal schisms, one of which created a group known as SONS OF FREEDOM.

Sources:

Maude, A. *A Peculiar People*. New York : Funk & Wagnalls, 1904.

117

Woodcock, G., and Abakumovic, I. *The Doukhobors*. Toronto: McClelland and Stewart, 1977.

Dreads, The

Nativist, African American nationalist movement based in Dominica and inspired by the RASTAFARIANS of Jamaica. The term "dread" is used by Rastafarians to mean "the power that lies within any man." The movement was subject to suppression by the government of Dominica in the 1970s.

Dromenon

U.S. syncretistic "nonresidential transformational community." Founded by Jean Houston and Robert Masters in the late 1970s, it is based in New York City. Doctrine combines Western and Eastern mythology.

Duck River (and Kindred) Association of Baptists (Baptist Church of Christ)

U.S. Conservative Protestant group founded in 1825 as the result of a split with the Elk River Baptist Association in the hill country of Tennessee and Alabama.

Duga (Ability)

Swedish splinter group of SCIENTOLOGY founded in December 1983 in Gothenburg. It is guided by the teachings of David Mayo, a former Scientology leader. [*See also* ABILITISM.]

Dzogchen Orygen Cho Ling

U.S. Tibetan Buddhist group connected with the XIV Dalai Lama and founded in the 1980s.

E

Earth People

African religion founded in Trinidad in the 1960s by Mother Earth (?–1984), following a psychotic episode. It uses Yoruba traditions and emphasizes female creativity. Members live communally and avoid the use of clothing. The group has been the target of government persecution and police raids but continues to survive.

Source:
Littlewood, R. *Pathology and Identity: The Work of Mother Earth in Trinidad.* Cambridge: Cambridge University Press, 1993.

Earthspirit Community

U.S. neo-pagan group founded in 1980 in Boston by Andras Corban Arthen and Deirdre Pulgram Arthen. The Arthens are members of the ATHANOR FELLOWSHIP, the inner circle of the group. The Earthspirit Community credo is that "all things in the Universe interact in both a physical and spiritual relationship." During its meetings and festivals, drumming, chanting, tarot, vision questing, healing, and dancing are practiced.

East-West Cultural Center

U.S. Hindu-oriented group devoted to the teachings of SRI AUROBINDO. It was founded in 1953 in Los Angeles by Judith M. Tyberg.

Eben Haezer

Dutch FUNDAMENTALIST Christian group founded by former members of JEHOVAH'S WITNESSES in 1987. It follows the CONCORDANT PUBLISHING CONCERN versions of the Bible.

Ecclesia

U.S. FUNDAMENTALIST group founded in the early 1980s by Eldrige Broussard, Jr.

Eckankar

U.S. occultist Sikh-inspired group founded in California in 1964 by John Paul Twitchell (1908–1971). Twitchell was a member of the SELF-REVELATION CHURCH OF ABSOLUTE MONISM between 1950 and 1955, and then joined RUHANI SATSANG and SCIENTOLOGY. The name Eckankar reportedly means "one god" in Punjabi. The group refers to itself as the Ancient Science of Soul Travel, and its teachings closely reflect the Sikh tradition of Kirpal Singh. Followers are expected to follow a Living Eck Master, who is able to deliver them from the wheel of reincarnation. The Living Eck Master is believed to be "the God man of the age . . . omnipotent, omniscient and omnipresent. He is all powerful, all wise, and is in all places simultaneously. . . . He has appeared as Krishna, Buddha, or Vishnu. . . . He is Zeus to the Greeks; Jupiter to the Romans; . . . Jehovah to the old Judean; . . . Jesus to the Christians; and Allah to the Mohammedans." The group teaches "spiritual travel of the soul body."

Église Adaiste

African indigenous Christian church

started in 1932 by the prophet Boto Adai in a secession from the Methodist Church.

Église Akeiste

African indigenous Christian church started in 1926 in West Africa in a secession from the HARRIS MOVEMENT.

Église Apostolique Unie en Afrique (EAUA)

African indigenous Christian PENTE-COSTAL church in Zaire and Congo, started in 1971.

Église Catholique Gallicane Autocephale

French OLD CATHOLIC group started in 1959 in a secession from the GALLICAN CHURCH (*Église Gallicane, Église Catholic Francaise*). It follows THEOSOPHICAL Christianity but also retains Roman Catholic traditions (though rejecting papal authority and infallibility).

Église Catholique Primitive

French Liberal Catholic group started in 1937 in Paris in a secession from the LIBERAL CATHOLIC CHURCH.

Église de Dieu de Nos Ancêtres

Zairian syncretistic church started in the 1950s among the Luba people in the then southwestern Belgian Congo. Its doctrine has combined Christian beliefs and rituals (praying to Mary, the mother of Jesus) with traditional beliefs in ancestral spirits (for example, magical serpents producing magical water).

Église Deimatiste

African syncretistic church started in 1922 among the Dida and Bere peoples of the Ivory Coast in a secession from the Methodist Church. Beliefs and practices combine Christianity with traditional beliefs and African nationalism. The founder, the prophet Marie Dahonon (?–1951), claimed to continue the work of William Wade Harris, a Liberian who started a religious movement in Ghana and the Ivory Coast, and his influence is evident in her message. [*See also* HARRIS MOVEMENT.]

Église de la Sainte Famille

French traditionalist Catholic group founded in 1974 by Pierre Poulain (1924–). The founder has announced the coming of great catastrophes as a divine punishment for the sins of the world. In 1979 he predicted the birth of his daughter, Marie. A son was born instead, and Poulain named him "Jésus-Pierre, the Savior and Redeemer of humanity." Coronation of a future king is predicted for 1999, with a golden crown being prepared.

Église des Noirs en Afrique Centrale (ENAC)

Also known as *Mission des Noirs*, Khakism, Ngunza-khaki, or Mpadism. This African nativist syncretistic movement in Zaire and Congo was started in 1941 by Simon-Pierre Mpadi in a secession from the SALVATION ARMY. ENAC doctrine identifies Africans as the contemporary suffering Israelites. The rituals and practices combine ancestor worship, magic, and divination with elements borrowed from Christianity, such as traditional church prayer. Influenced by the KIMBANGUIST MOVEMENT, ENAC regards Kimbangu as the Saviour of the Africans. Members wear khaki uniforms, similar to those of the Salvation Army, which is the source of one of the movement's names.

Église du Christianisme Celeste du Benin

African indigenous Christian church in Benin started in 1947 in a secession from the CHERUBIM AND SERAPHIM.

Église Evangelique Hinchiste

French independent Christian church founded in 1831 in Nîmes by Coraly Hinsch.

Église Neo-Apostolique

Founded in 1900, this Western European Christian gnostic group developed out of the CATHOLIC APOSTOLIC CHURCH. Branches have operated in France, Belgium, Italy, and Brazil.

Église Protestante Evangelique

French PENTECOSTAL group founded in 1945 in Lyons by a faith healer known as "Soeur" Gaillard.

Église Rosicrucienne Apostolique

European French-speaking ROSICRUCIAN group with branches in Belgium and France. [See also AMORC ROSICRUCIAN ORDER.]

Église Sanito (Saints)

Also known as Sanitos or Kanitos, this Polynesian syncretistic church in the Tuamotu archipelego of French Polynesia started with missionary activities by the REORGANIZED CHURCH OF JESUS CHRIST OF LATTER-DAY SAINTS (USA) in 1884. Later, the membership gained independence from the missionaries and adopted openly indigenous traditions, including ancestor worship and magic.

El Bethel Church (Mt Shiloh)

African Christian PENTECOSTAL group founded in 1926 in Nigeria. Its doctrines and practices have been greatly influenced by the CHERUBIM AND SERAPHIM.

Elijah Voice Society

U.S. offshoot of JEHOVAH'S WITNESSES that broke away from the Stand Fast Bible Students in 1923.

Elim Foursquare Gospel

Christian FUNDAMENTALIST, PENTECOSTAL group founded in 1915 in Belfast by George Jeffreys. The founder was very active preaching his message for twenty-five years throughout the British Isles, but left in 1940 to start the BIBLE PATTERN FELLOWSHIP, another fundamentalist group. Elim Foursquare Gospel practices speaking in tongues and healing. Members believe in spirit guidance and the rapidly approaching Second Coming. The group has operated branches in Southern Africa.

Source:
Wilson, B. R. *Sects and Society*. London: Heinemann, 1961.

Elim Missionary Assemblies

First known as the Elim Ministerial Fellowship, this U.S. PENTECOSTAL group was founded in 1932 and adopted its current name in 1947. The group operates the World Missionary Assistance Plan in foreign countries.

Elim Pentecostal Church

British FUNDAMENTALIST group founded in 1915. It operates branches in Southern Africa.

Elohim City

U.S. IDENTITY group founded in 1973 by Robert G. Millar (1926–) in Muldrow, Oklahoma. Millar was raised as a Mennonite in Canada, but in 1948 started having apocalyptic visions. Belief in the coming violent End is central to his teachings.

Elohists

U.S. syncretistic group founded in 1918 by Walter De Voe in Brookline, Massachusetts. In the early 1900s he was a student of NEW THOUGHT and started the Elohist Ministry, focused on healing. It "evolved into a ministry devoted to the rescue, education and revival of earthbound spirits through the assistance of mediums and angelic helpers." In the late 1930s De Voe discovered *OAHSPE: A New Bible*, published in 1882 by John Ballou Newbrough (1828–1891). The group then became closely connected to the UNIVERSAL FAITHISTS OF KOSMON (U.F.K.).

Source:
Goodspeed, E. J. *Modern Apocrypha*. Boston: Beacon Press, 1956.

El Shaddai

Philippine charismatic Catholic group founded by Mike Velarde (1940–) in 1985. Velarde, a real-estate investor, heard a "call" after suffering a minor stroke, and became a radio and television preacher. Practices include faith healing. The group operates among Filipino guest workers overseas. The group's name is one of God's names in the Hebrew Bible.

Embassy of the Gheez-Americans

U.S. Africanist, occultist group founded by the Empress Mysikiitta Fa Sennato, who runs the Mt. Helion Sanctuary in Long Eddy, New York. The Empress supposedly arrived from outer space and has reported many adventures there. She calls for the revival of the Gheez-Nation, the ancient people of Ethiopia, who she believes are truly the chosen people.

Emin Society, The

First known as the Eminent Way, the Faculty of Colour, and the Church of the Eminent Way, this is an international occultist-syncretist group founded in 1971 in London by Raymond Schertenlieb (1924–). Also known as Raymond John Armin, Schertenlieb is referred to by members of the Society as Leo. The group operates through "choirs, herbal groups, tarot groups, Bible study classes, poetry groups, mumming groups, theatrical groups, bands, vocal groups, music composition, dancing troupes, healers, astrology groups, palmistry, graphology, phrenology and other detection groups."

Many of the beliefs and practices of Emin are similar to those of other modern occult groups, especially the ROSICRUCIANS, GURDJIEFF, and ANTHROPOSOPHY. The practices of the Emin Society include reading auras and diagnosing individuals on the basis of aura colors. There is a rite of exorcism, which "arrests any hostile, degenerative or unreasonable essence, practice, mind or mental projection; which stands against anything which tries to prevent the given right of human life to become enhanced over its planetary station; . . . It is processed and dealt with entirely in the occult, electrical and electro-magnetic fields of human precincts, dwelling precincts, location precincts and all concentrated ground or dimensions." A major concern expressed in Emin writings is about becoming electrically polluted, and the means to avoid or rectify this pollution. "Electrical stumps travelling through the astral light can attach themselves, in the way of a barnacle or limpet, to the human aura. Understand that all sorts of electrical filth can be released by people which then moves through the astral light looking for a human host which is higher than itself upon whose aura it can attach itself, and from which it can electrically feed, and even grow. But there is worse to come, for at close quarters someone can stick upon you one of those electrical barnacles or limpets deliberately, through spite, malice, hatred, jealousy, sexual projection. . . . Now, this can become even more serious, in that once an electrical barnacle or limpet has attached itself to a person's

aura, it can then work like modern radar, acting as a beacon to that from which it came. . . . This indicates a very dangerous prospect should a 'branch office' be established on the very edge of your aura which is tranmitted on a long-term basis." The solution for this worrisome state, according to Emin writings, is cleansing your aura. For members of Emin, personal time is measured by Emin years, which are nine months long. "A normal seasonal life cycle is . . . seventy-two Emin years; which then translates into fifty-four calendar years, which is, interestingly enough, the age at which Mohammed is recorded to have become divine. Any more birthdays or cycles after this time are considered to be grace of extension." Standards of Behavior in the Society include rules about symbols and sexual behavior. "It is forbidden . . . to erect a pentagram or an aeneagram; and it is against God and creation to worship any symbol in an upside-down condition, or to practice a ceremony backwards. Any offender will be exorcised and excommunicated." This is, in part, because "the two symbols become portals or terminal points of the arrival and despatch of inter-galactic electrical form" causing death by "spontaneous combustion, petrification, lack of energy (wasting) and electrical gangrene." Regarding sex, "at no time will homosexuality, lesbianism, transvestism, nymphonic, or any other unnatural condition or freak practice . . . be permitted." Emin doctrine claims to be based on secret knowledge developed by ancient Egyptian culture.

The Society maintains branches in Israel, Canada, Australia, and the United States, in addition to the center in London. The Church of Emin Coils is the Florida branch of the Emin Society, organized in 1978 by Leo and his emissaries. Later on, the Emin Society of America was founded.

Emin has also operated the Ancient Egyptian School of Esoteric Arts and sciences in New York City. Later, the Emin University of Life operated in New York City as a branch of the Emin Society. It then became the Emin Foundation for Human Development.

Source:

Beit-Hallahmi, B. *Despair and Deliverance: Private Salvation in Contemporary Israel.* Albany, NY: SUNY Press, 1992.

Emissaries of Divine Light

Also known as the Ontological Society, Divine Light Emissaries, the Foundation of Universal Unity, the Universal Institute of Applied Ontology, and the Integrity Society. This international, esoteric, Christian-influenced group was founded in 1932 in Tennessee by Lloyd Arthur Meeker, also known as Uranda. He was succeeded as group leader by Martin Cecil (1909–1988), who has been responsible for formulating most of its official doctrine.

The belief system of the Emissaries contains a combination of modern occult ideas, like those of the GURDJIEFF GROUPS, together with some traditional Christianity. One of its tenets is the notion that humanity is undergoing a major change in consciousness, and that this change is occurring all around us, leading to revolutionary consequences. The main idea of the Emissaries is the centrality of consciousness and the unity of body and mind. The group promotes holistic healing. The International Emissary orga-nized the 10th International Human Unity Conference, held at Warwick University, England, in July 1983. It has been described as "part of a global, creative shift which transcends human beliefs, fears, ambitions, and differences." The group also promotes communal living, and members live in communes around the world.

The headquarters are at the Sunrise Farm in Loveland, Colorado, and the group has operated the Emissary Foundation International (EFI). Branches have operated in North America, Europe, Africa, and Israel.

Emmanuel

U.S. B'NAI NOACH congregation started in the 1980s in Athens, Tennessee, by J. David Davis, a former Baptist minister. [*See also* FRAZIER CHAPEL.]

Emmanuel Association

U.S. conservative Protestant group founded in 1937 by Ralph G. Finch (?– 1949). Group doctrine calls for a strict behavior code and extreme simplicity in lifestyle. Members are conscientious objectors.

Emmanuel Church of Christ Oneness Pentecostal

U.S. PENTECOSTAL group started in Dover, Tennessee, in the early 1930s. The church practices faith healing and glossolalia. It attracted much media attention when John David Terry (1944–), who had served as leader since 1969, was convicted of murder in 1988 and sentenced to death.

Emmanuel Holiness Church

PENTECOSTAL group with branches in the United States and Great Britain, formed in 1953 as a result of a schism in the PENTECOSTAL FIRE-BAPTIZED HOLINESS CHURCH. This, in turn, had been created by a schism in the PENTECOSTAL HOLINESS CHURCH. Disputes over dress standards (wearing neckties) led to the schism.

Emmanuel Messianic Congregation

Originally known as Emmanuel Presbyterian Hebrew Christian Congregation, this international HEBREW CHRISTIAN group based in Baltimore was founded in the first quarter of the twentieth century. It has been connected with LEDERER MESSIANIC MINISTRIES and with Christ Church, Jerusalem.

Emmanuel Movement

U.S. faith healing group influenced by CHRISTIAN SCIENCE and NEW THOUGHT. The Emmanuel Movement attempted to reconcile religious beliefs with medical views. It was started in Boston in 1904 at the Emmanuel Episcopal Church by Elwood Worcester, Samuel McComb, and Isador H. Coriat. The movement extended to other large cities in the Northeastern United States, and then to the Midwest. The group's doctrine claimed to offer "sound psychology, sound medicine, and sound religion."

End Time Ministries

U.S. ADVENTIST group started in Sioux Falls, South Dakota, in the late 1970s. It has preached reliance on faith healing and rejection of modern medicine.

"Envoy of the Messiah"

Founded by David Martins de Miranda in the 1950s, this Brazilian PENTECOSTAL group practices faith healing.

Epiphany Bible Students Association

U.S. ADVENTIST group formed by John J. Hoefle (1895–1984) as a result of a schism in the LAYMEN'S HOME MISSIONARY MOVEMENT. The dispute started after the death of Paul S. L. Johnson, the movement's founder, in 1955, and concerned accusations and counteraccusations between Hoefle and Raymond Jolly, Johnson's successor as leader. Hoefle was expelled in February 1956 and continued to express his dissenting view, claiming that other groups have distorted the original message of Charles Taze Russell, the founder of JEHOVAH'S WITNESSES.

Episcopal Church of Mexico

Mexican independent Christian movement that started in a secession from the Roman Catholic Church in 1857.

Epis Holy Temple and Tabernacle Mission

African indigenous Christian PENTECOSTAL church founded in 1920 among the Ashanti people of Ghana (then the Gold Coast).

Equifrilibricum World Religion

Sometimes known as the Equality-Fraternity-Liberty Church, or Moncadistas, this is an independent Protestant church started in 1925 among Filipinos in

125

the United States. It also has operated in the Philippines.

Erie Bible Truth Depot

A group of PLYMOUTH BRETHREN founded by A. E. Booth in Erie, Pennsylvania, around 1930.

Source:

Ehlert, A. D. *A Bibliographic History of Dispensationalism.* Grand Rapids, MI: Baker Book House, 1965.

Escuela Cientifica Basilio

Argentine spiritualist movement founded in the 1940s, with branches in Latin America and Italy.

ESP Picture Prayers

U.S. NEW THOUGHT group founded by Murcie P. Smith in Gary, Indiana, which has operated by offering its followers prayers and ESP readings by mail.

Essene Center

U.S. Christian group founded by Walter Hagen in Hot Springs, Arkansas, in 1972. Based on the claim of continuing ancient Essene traditions, Essene Center doctrine includes reincarnationism and belief in the imminent coming of the messiah, who will arise from among the Essenes.

Essene Network International

British Christian-THEOSOPHICAL group founded by Anne MacEwen in the 1980s. Beliefs center on the "Essene impulse which is re-emerging in our time." The group teaches "the basic Oneness of life" and "the Ageless Wisdom tradition that the Essene Brotherhood guarded for all humanity."

Etherian Religious Society of Universal Brotherhood

U.S. esoteric Christianity group founded in 1965 by E. A. Hurtienne in San Marcos, California. Practices include meditation and faith healing. It is affiliated with the LIVING CHRIST MOVEMENT.

Ethiopian Catholic Church in Zion

South African independent church founded in 1904 by S. J. Brander, when he seceded from the ETHIOPIAN CATHOLIC CHURCH OF SOUTH AFRICA.

Ethiopian Catholic Church of South Africa

Sometimes known simply as the Ethiopian Church, this is a South African independent indigenous church founded in 1892 in Johannesburg. The Ethiopian Church began in a secession from the AFRICAN NATIVE MISSION CHURCH by Mangena M. Mokone, who was joined by other indigenous leaders such as Khanyane Napo, James M. Dwane, and S. J. Brander. Membership was initially mostly non-Zulu. The group's doctrine emphasized African self-government and the revitalization of all African culture, regardless of group. For a while it was affiliated with the AFRICAN METHODIST EPISCOPAL CHURCH (AME), and in 1896 it won recognition from the South African government. In 1900, Dwane seceded, creating the ORDER OF ETHIOPIA.

Church branches have operated in the other nations of Southern Africa.

Source:

Sundkler, B. G. M. *Bantu Prophets in South Africa*. London: Oxford University Press, 1961.

Ethiopian Hebrews

U.S. "Black Jews" group started in Chicago in the 1940s by Abihu Reuben as an offshoot of the COMMANDMENT KEEPERS CONGREGATION OF THE LIVING GOD.

Ethiopian National Church, Nigeria

African independent PENTECOSTAL church founded in 1919 in Nigeria by Adeniran Oke.

Ethiopians

South African independent church movement created in a secession from European mission churches. "Africa for Africans" is the movement's slogan, but it otherwise follows the doctrines of mainline Protestantism. The special role of Ethiopia (Abyssinia) in black political consciousness factors greatly in the establishment of a separate, positive identity for Africans. Ethiopia is viewed as an African, Christian, and sovereign kingdom, a source of inspiration for all Africans. The other major church movement in South Africa is the ZIONISTS. [*See also* RASTAFARIANS.]

Ethiopian Star Church of God, The

South African independent ETHIOPIAN church founded after the Italian invasion of Ethiopia in 1935.

Ethiopian Zion Coptic Church

International RASTAFARIAN group incorporated in 1976 in White Horse, Jamaica, under the leadership of Keith Gordon, known as Nyah. Branches have operated in the United States, where members have run into legal trouble because of their use of marijuana, which Rastafarians smoke for sacramental purposes.

Etoism

Officially known as the Christian Fellowship Church, this syncretistic-PENTECOSTAL movement (CARGO CULT) started as an independent Melanesian church in the New Georgia group of the Solomon Islands in 1960 by Silas Eto (1905–). Eto was considered a messiah by his followers, who were former members of the Methodist Mission church. He was educated as a Methodist, but his dissatisfaction with the church organization led to the formation of an independent movement. The members of Etoism built the Holy Village of Paradise, which serves as its center. Church practices include faith healing and speaking in tongues.

Etzba Elohim (The Finger of God)

Israeli religion founded in 1981 by Rina Shani (1937–1983), whose given name is Rina Shomroni. Shani gained public attention in the 1960s as a poet and writer, and by 1970 she had three poetry books

127

to her credit. In 1981 she was again in the public eye, this time as a religious leader facing charges for the ritual use of marijuana. This metamorphosis, as she herself described it, started in 1970, when she first tasted cannabis. In 1973 Rina Shani had an illuminating experience in the form of an encounter with a schizophrenic artist whom she started treating through "awareness work," serving as a self-styled therapist until 1979. In January 1979, following her arrest on drug charges, she had another mystical experience: "I was dead, and then I was born again. On that day, and the following one, I experienced infinity, and on the third day I experienced God. I enjoyed Jehovah's presence and unity with him." After this revelation she changed her name to Rain Shine, moved to a new location, and started saving souls through her methods. By 1981 she had a score of devoted followers, some of whom were minors. In addition to marijuana, Rain Shine regarded LSD as a sacramental drug. Group members performed sacraments and had to choose new names as symbols of their personal transformations. According to some sources, Rain attempted to turn her followers against their families. She declared herself to be totally opposed to marriage, parenthood, and finally, sex. Rain Shine and members of her group were charged with illegal drug use on multiple occasions. Rain used her considerable charisma on Israeli judges and escaped punishment time and again. Rain left Israel and went to India. In November of 1983 she died of hepatitis on the banks of the Ganges River.

Eucharistic Catholic Church

U.S. Christian homosexual group founded in 1970 in New York City by Robert Clement.

Evadisme

An occultist-Christian group founded in Paris around 1830 by Caillaux. Known as Ganneau (?–1851), Caillaux called himself Le Mapah (a combination of *maman* and *papah*—mother and father) and proclaimed himself prophet and God. His teachings included the importance of the feminine in religion. He named his group after the androgynous Evadah (Eve + Adam) and also taught that Mary, of the New Testament, was the God-Mother, wife of the Man-God. Ganneau declared a new age that would start in 1838, the age of Evadah, in which all forms of oppression would be opposed.

Evangelical Bible Church

U.S. PENTECOSTAL group founded by Frederick B. Marine in 1947 in Baltimore. A strict conduct code is enforced and members are conscientious objectors.

Evangelical Catholic Church of New York

Founded by Samuel Durlin Benedict in 1921, in secession from the NORTH AMERICAN OLD ROMAN CATHOLIC CHURCH, this OLD CATHOLIC group disappeared after the death of its founder in 1945.

Evangelical Christian Science Church

Independent CHRISTIAN SCIENCE group that emerged after the death of Mary

Baker Eddy, the founder of Christian Science. The church was started in 1910 by Oliver C. Sabin, Jr.

Evangelical Church of Pentecost

African independent PENTECOSTAL church formed in 1936 in Gabon.

Evangelical Methodist Church, The

U.S. FUNDAMENTALIST group founded in 1946 in Memphis, Tennessee.

Evangelical Ministers and Churches, International, Inc.

An association founded in 1950 in Chicago for evangelical, FUNDAMENTALIST ministers in the United States.

Ewam Choden Tibetan Buddhist Center

U.S. Tibetan Buddhist group founded by Lama Kunga Thartse, Rinpoche, in 1971 and based in northern California. The founder is believed by his disciples to be "the designated reincarnation of Sevan Repa, Heart Disciple of Milarepa." Beliefs and practices include studies of the Tibetan Book of the Dead and meditation. [*See also* VAJRADHATU.]

Extra Terrestrial Communications Network

U.S. UFO group founded in the 1980s in Arizona by Michael El-Legion, who "works extensively with the Intergalactic Confederation and Ascended Masters of the Spiritual Hierarchy."

F

Factum Humanum

Also known as the White Order, this is a European occultist group founded in the 1970s.

Faith Assembly World Wide Church of Christ

Known initially as the Glory Barn Faith Assembly, and commonly known as the Faith Assembly. This evangelical, PENTECOSTAL group was founded in North Webster, Indiana, in 1963 by Hobart E. Freeman (1920–1984), a former professor at Grace Theological Seminary of Winona Lake, Indiana, and Melvin Greider (1937–). The Assembly had congregations in the U.S. Midwest and South. Freeman advocated the complete avoidance of modern medicine, relying instead on prayers: "Sickness and disease have been repeatedly defeated by maintaining a positive confession of faith in the face of all apparent evidence to the contrary. . . . When genuine faith is present it alone will be sufficient, for it will take the place of medicines and other aids." Since 1976, there have been at least 100 reported deaths among members and their children in Indiana, Illinois, Ohio, Kentucky, Michigan, and Missouri as a result of medical neglect. Legal action has been taken against members whose children died because of negligence, and in several cases parents were convicted of reckless homicide and sentenced to prison terms.

Faith Bible Chapel

U.S. FUNDAMENTALIST group founded in Denver, Colorado, in the 1960s by Bob Holly. The group's beliefs include the idea that the founding of the State of Israel in 1948 heralded the Second Coming.

Faith Mission

British evangelical group founded in Scotland in 1886 by John George Govan (1861–1927). Its work was aimed at rural communities in Great Britain and Ireland. Out of this movement grew the THE TWO-BY-TWO'S.

Faith Movement

North American FUNDAMENTALIST, PENTECOSTAL organization founded in the 1970s by Kenneth Hagin in Oklahoma. This is a loose association of congregations and media ministries. Its theological message emphasizes faith healing and the power of positive thinking. The group is connected with the Swedish WORD OF LIFE CHURCH.

Faith Tabernacle

U.S. PENTECOSTAL group founded in California in 1924.

Famile de Nazareth (Commune de Nazareth)

French Catholic schismatic, monastic group founded in 1980 in Paris by Daniel Blanchard, a former Benedictine monk.

David and Kathleen Bergmann, members of Faith Assembly, arrive at court for their trial on charges of reckless homicide and child neglect in the death of their infant daughter in 1984.

Members of the Children of God (now known as The Family), wearing sackcloth and a yoke around the neck, march in "warning and mourning." They believe that theirs is the last generation to survive on earth.

The Family

Formerly called Children of God (COG), and known officially since 1977 as the Family of Love and more recently as the Family, this is an international FUNDA-MENTALIST group. It was founded in California in 1968 by David Brandt Berg (1919–1994), who has adopted the name "Moses Berg," or Moses David, Father David, or "Mo." Berg started his religious leadership career as an evangelist for the CHRISTIAN AND MISSIONARY ALLI-ANCE. In 1964 he began work with radio and television evangelist Fred Jordan. In 1969 he led a group of followers, named Revolutionaries for Jesus, in Huntington Beach, California, and became visible as part of what was known around 1970 as the JESUS MOVEMENT or the Jesus Children. Until the end of 1971, Berg and his followers appeared regularly on television in a religious program, *Church in the Home*, run by Fred Jordan. They also operated an organization known as the American Soul Clinic, Inc.

In 1972, COG members started moving to Europe. In the mid-1970s, after finding himself in trouble with U.S. authorities and being charged with various offenses, Berg found refuge in Libya and praised the Libyan leader Muammar Khadafi as the "most remarkable voice of the Third World."

"In late 1977 Father David began receiving numerous reports that some leaders in the organization were misusing and abusing their authority. In a move that had the support of the grass-roots membership, he dismissed the entire leadership and subsequently dissolved The Children of God. He invited those who wished to remain in the fellowship with him to form a new group, *The Family of Love*, with a new organiza-tional structure. In recent years, we have become known simply as *The Family*."

Berg has communicated with his followers through the "MO letters," which supposedly contain divine revelations and secret knowledge. The group's teachings are contained in these letters issued by the leader, who is the sole authority over all matters. These teachings, though representative of evangelical Protestantism, are as critical of the religious establishment as they are of the political establishment. According to Berg, The Family constitutes the latter-day Israel, heirs to biblical promises to ancient Israel. Berg had been predicting a "Great Confusion and Tribulation" to take place soon (c.1993), after which Christ would rule on Earth. Since Berg's death, the group has been proclaiming "the Time of the End, God's soon-coming judgments upon an apostate world, and the ultimate establishment of His Kingdom on Earth." The family of the founder is considered the Royal Family, divinely inspired and appointed to rule. There is a Council of Ministers and twelve bishops. The world is divided into twelve areas, under the regional bishops. Berg believed that most of the world's resources and media are controlled by Jews, and that this world-wide conspiracy should, and would, be defeated.

In the 1970s and 1980s, The Family conducted an official campaign known as "flirty fishing," in which sexual seduction was used to attract new members. The group has been accused many times of child abuse and especially of child sexual abuse; in the 1990s members were arrested on these charges in France and Argentina. Such accusations have never been proven in court, though in October 1994 a teenage girl in Great Britain was

Followers of Father Divine parade in New York City, celebrating his accomplishments on their behalf.

awarded compensation of $8,000 by the British Criminal Injuries Compensation Board for abuse she suffered in the group.

Sources:

Davis, D. (Linda Berg) *The Children of God.* Grand Rapids: Zondervan, 1984.

Van Zandt, D. E. *Living in the Children of God.* Princeton: Princeton University Press, 1991.

Wallis, R. *The Elementary Forms of the New Religious Life.* London: Routledge & Kegan Paul, 1984.

Wangerin, R. *The Children of God: A Make-Believe Revolution.* Westport, CT: Bergin and Garvey, 1993.

Fanscifiaroan Church of Wicca

U.S. neo-pagan group started in the 1970s in Connecticut by Franklin Hedgecock. FANSCIFIAROAN stands for FANtasy, SCIence, FIction, ARt, and ROAN—the color reddish brown. The founder states that "Wicca is a religion of joy and love. . . . The goal of the craft is to live in harmony with nature and the spirit world on the other side. The other side, or the spirit world, has a leader who created all things." [*See also* WICCA.]

Farm, The

U.S. syncretistic commune located near Summerton, Tennessee, founded in 1971 by Stephen Gaskin (1936–) and his followers. The leader preaches "love, peace, telepathy, vibrations, meditation, honesty, truth and unity of human beings through spiritual enlightenment." The group's doctrine combines Christian and Buddhist ideas. Members are vegetarian. The use of marijuana to aid meditation has caused legal difficulties, and four members, including Gaskin, served prison terms in the early 1970s. Since then illegal drug use has been prohibited in the religion.

Source:

Hall, J. R. *The Ways Out: Utopian Communal Groups in an Age of Babylon.* London: Routledge & Kegan Paul, 1978.

Father Divine Movement

Officially known as the Universal Peace Mission Movement. Its founder, whose real name was George Baker, was known as the Messenger, as Major Morgan J. Devine, and later as Father Major Jealous Divine (1880?–1965). He is reported to

Father Divine (next to railing) and Mother Divine cheer as they inspect their newly acquired "Heaven," a donated estate near West Park, New York.

have been a follower and assistant of several African American "Messiahs" before branching out on his own. Comprised mostly of black members, the movement first became visible around 1914 and attracted more interest during the Great Depression of the 1930s because of its economic success. It experienced tremendous growth and gained much attention between the two World Wars. Father Divine initiated several profit-making businesses and was able to lift his followers out of poverty with his assistance and through his code of ideal conduct. While the group was based in New York City during its first thirty years, in 1942 the headquarters were moved to Philadel-

phia. Since the death of Father Divine, the movement has been led by Mother Divine, the former Edna Rose Ritchings of Montreal (1925–), who married Divine in 1946.

The movement's doctrine specifies that Father Divine and his wife, Mother Divine, are the personifications of God as father and mother, and that Father Divine has fulfilled all the Biblical prophecies about the Coming of the Messiah and the Second Coming of Christ. Members consider the present to be heaven and believe that the faithful are immortal. Followers are not supposed to mention time, since immortality also means timelessness. The movement prescribes communal living and the International Modesty Code prohibiting lust, smoking, drinking, gambling, obscenity, vulgarity, profanity, and the receiving of gifts and tips. Celibacy is expected of truly committed followers. If a married couple join the group, they become brother and sister.

Father Divine was active in the struggle for equality for U.S. African Americans. He preached and practiced integration and held up the U.S. Constitution as the basis for just government. The movement has operated several corporations that provide employment for members, and Father Divine exhorted his followers to pay only cash for expenses, so as not to incur debt.

In addition to U.S. branches on the East Coast and in California, the Movement has operated missions in Europe, Australia, and Africa.

Sources:

Burnham, K. E. *God Comes to America*. Boston: Lambeth, 1979.

Cantril, H. *The Psychology of Social Movements*. New York: Wiley, 1941.

Fauset, A. H. *Black Gods of the Metropolis*. Philadelphia: University of Pennsylvania Press, 1944.

Harris, S. *Father Divine*. New York: Macmillan, 1971.

Parker, R. A. *The Incredible Messiah*. Boston: Little, Brown, 1937.

Weisbrot, R. *Father Divine and the Struggle for Racial Equality*. Urbana: University of Illinois Press, 1983.

Father Jehovah (Father Jehovia)

Black Messiah whose real name was Samuel Morris. He was active in Baltimore, Maryland, in the late nineteenth century and the early decades of the twentieth century. FATHER DIVINE is reported to have been among his followers, later becoming his partner and equal.

F'eden Church

Officially known as the Eden Revival Church, this is an indigenous African PENTECOSTAL group founded in Accra, Ghana, in 1963. Branches have operated in Great Britain.

Federacao Espirita Brasileira (FEB)

Founded in 1884, this Brazilian spiritualist group follows the doctrine of KARDECISM. It has operated a large social welfare system that includes hospitals and schools.

Federation Universelle des Ordres et Sociétés Initiatques (FUDOSI)

Also known in Latin as Federatio Universalis Dirigens Ordines Societatesque Initiationis, this international organization of fourteen ROSICRUCIAN groups was founded in 1934.

Feedback Church

Founded in London in the late 1960s, this British group was devoted to biofeedback.

Fellowship in Prayer

U.S. syncretistic group founded in 1949 in New Jersey. Its main practice is ecumenical prayer.

Fellowship of Christian Believers

Also known as the Body of Christ Movement, this is a U.S. PENTECOSTAL group founded in the 1960s in Grand Rapids, Minnesota, by Charles P. and Dorothy Schmitt. The group's doctrine emphasizes the imminent coming of Jesus Christ, following the doctrines of LATTER RAIN awakening of the 1940s.

Fellowship of Christian Pilgrims

U.S. PENTECOSTAL and JESUS MOVEMENT group founded around 1970 in Hawaii. It collaborated with similar groups in California.

Fellowship of Crotona

British THEOSOPHICAL group founded in the early twentieth century.

Fellowship of Friends (FOF)

International GURDJIEFF GROUP founded in 1969 by Robert Burton in northern California. Unlike most Gurdjieff groups, this one recruits members by advertising in newspapers. It charges membership fees, which are 10 percent of gross monthly income. Branches operate worldwide. In French-speaking countries, the group is known as Rassemblement des Amis.

Fellowship of Independent Evangelical Churches

U.S. FUNDAMENTALIST group founded in 1949. Members believed in both Satanic forces and angels. [*See also* FUNDAMENTALISM.]

Fellowship of Isis (FOI)

International neo-pagan group founded in 1976 by Lawrence, Pamela, and Olivia Durdin-Robertson. It is devoted to the worship of the ancient Egyptian goddess Isis and other ancient goddesses. The founders are considered priests "from an hereditary line of the Robertson from Ancient Egypt." The group operates the College of Isis, which confers magi degrees.

Fellowship of the Followers of Jesus

Indian indigenous Christian movement founded by Kandiswamy Chetti in Madras in 1933.

Fellowship of the Inner Light

Also known as Inner Light Consciousness (ILC). This is a U.S. Christian-spiritualist group founded in 1974 in Virginia Beach, Virginia, by Paul Solomon, a former Baptist minister. Solomon offers readings, which include advice on illness and healing, past lives, information about the mythological places Atlantis and Lemuria, and prophecies about the fate of the world, all within a Christian framework. The content of the readings is similar to those offered by Edgar Cayce, an American occultist who was famous during the first half of the twentieth century. A related organization headed by Solomon is the Association of the Light Morning, and he has also founded the Carmel-in-the-Valley Cooperative Village. [*See also* ASSOCIATION FOR RESEARCH AND ENLIGHTENMENT.]

Feraferia

U.S. witchcraft group founded in 1967 in Los Angeles. It was devoted to the "Magic Maiden of the Aquarian Age" and to the worship of the processes of nature.

Filipino Assemblies of the First Born

U.S. PENTECOSTAL group founded by Julian Barnabe in 1933 in California. Membership consists of Filipino immigrants in California and Hawaii.

Filipino Christian Church

Philippine nationalist group created as a result of a schism in the PHILIPPINE INDEPENDENT CHURCH.

Findhorn Foundation

British Christian-ANTHROPOSOPHICAL-ROSICRUCIAN group founded in 1963 in northern Scotland by Eileen Caddy, Peter Caddy, Alexis Edwards, and Roger Benson. The founders claim to receive direct and detailed messages from the Christian God dealing with every aspect of life. They also report communications from devas, elves, fairies, and gnomes, as well as the nature god Pan. Describing itself as a "theocratic democracy," the group has the stated aim "to usher in the New Age; to raise the vibrations by

the awareness of the Christ Consciousness within each one." The Foundation operates the Onearth Network of Resource People, also known as the Network of Light.

Fire-Baptized Holiness Association

U.S. PENTECOSTAL organization started in Iowa in 1895 and officially founded in 1898 in Anderson, South Carolina, under the leadership of Benjamin Hardin Irwin. Later the name was changed to the Fire-Baptized Holiness Church. In 1911 the group merged with the PENTECOSTAL HOLINESS CHURCH.

Fire-Baptized Holiness Church of God of the Americas

Based in Atlanta, Georgia, this U.S. African American PENTECOSTAL group was founded by W. E. Fuller (1875–1958) in 1908. He withdrew from the mostly white FIRE-BAPTIZED HOLINESS ASSOCIATION because of discrimination.

First Born Church of Christ

U.S. Native American syncretistic movement founded by Jonathan Koshiway, a former MORMON missionary, in 1914. The group's central ritual incorporated the use of peyote to achieve a psychedelic state. It was absorbed by the NATIVE AMERICAN CHURCH in the 1920s.

First Born Church of the Living God, The

U.K. PENTECOSTAL movement founded

in the 1960s with a membership of West Indian origin.

First Century Church

U.S. Christian-occultist group founded by David N. Bubar in Memphis, Tennesee, in 1969. Bubar tried to make a name for himself as a prophet, and in 1975 he predicted a disaster at the Sponge Rubber Plant in Shelton, Connecticut. He was sent to prison following his conviction for arson.

First Church of Divine Immanence

U.S. NEW THOUGHT group founded in 1952 by Henry Milton Ellis (?–1970) as a "mail order denomination" that distributed its teachings by mail.

First Community Church of America

U.S. FUNDAMENTALIST group founded by Robert Taylor in the 1970s.

First Ethiopian Church

African independent Christian group founded in Zimbabwe (then Southern Rhodesia) in 1926.

First Hebrew Presbyterian Christian Church

U.S. HEBREW CHRISTIAN congregation founded by David Bronstein in Chicago in 1934. It later separated from the Presbyterian Church and became nondenominational.

First Interdenominational Christian Association

U.S. PENTECOSTAL group founded in 1946 in Atlanta, Georgia, by Watson Sorrow following a dispute over healing in the Georgia Conference of the PENTECOSTAL HOLINESS CHURCH.

First Spiritualist Church of New York

Part of the INTERNATIONAL GENERAL ASSEMBLY OF SPIRITUALISTS, this U.S. spiritualist congregation was based in New York City and led by Arthur Ford (1897–1971).

First United Church of Jesus Christ (Apostolic)

Jamaican indigenous PENTECOSTAL movement started in the 1960s among Jamaican immigrants in Great Britain. It is connected with the BETHEL APOSTOLIC (SHILO) CHURCH.

First Universal Spiritualist Church of New York City

U.S. spiritualist congregation founded by Clifford Bias in 1959 and led by him until his death in 1987. [See also UNIVERSAL SPIRITUALIST ASSOCIATION.]

Fisherfolk Communities of Celebration

International Christian FUNDAMENTALIST group of communes, with branches located in Colorado, England, and Scotland.

Five Fold Path, Inc.

Also known as Agnihotra—The Purifying Fire, this is an international Western Hindu-oriented group founded in 1973 near Baltimore, Maryland, by Vasant Paranjpe. It is devoted to the Hindu ritual of *agnihotra*, in which cow dung mixed with ghee and brown rice is burned twice a day. This process is believed to purify the atmosphere and the human mind.

Five Percenters

U.S. Islamic group started in the 1970s as a splinter of the NATION OF ISLAM (NOI).

Foi Apostolique Nationale

Haitian independent Christian movement founded around 1950.

Fondation Teilhard de Chardin and Association des Amis de Pierre Teilhard de Chardin

French Christian group founded in 1965 to promote the teachings of the Jesuit Pierre Teilhard de Chardin, who tried to interpret evolution within the framework of Christianity. Affliated with the TEILHARD CENTRE in London. [*See also* AMERICAN TEILHARD ASSOCIATION.]

Forest Gate Church

British offshoot of JEHOVAH'S WITNESSES founded in the 1930s in London by F. G. Goad, Sr. (?–1950).

Formosa Christian Mission

Chinese indigenous FUNDAMENTALIST church founded in Taiwan in 1955.

Fort Wayne Gospel Temple

U.S. MILLENARIAN group founded by B. E. Rediger, a former Mennonite, in Fort Wayne, Indiana, in the 1920s.

Foundation Church of Divine Truth

U.S. Christian-spiritualist group founded in Washington, D.C., in 1985, succeeding the Foundation Church of the New Birth. It disseminates the same teachings as the earlier group.

Foundation Faith of God

Formerly known as Foundation Faith of the Millennium and Foundation Church of the Millennium, this U.S. occultist group was founded in 1974 by Christopher de Peyer and Peter McCormick following a schism in THE PROCESS, OR THE CHURCH OF THE FINAL JUDGMENT PROCESS. Members expect the imminent coming of a messiah, who will lead humanity into a new age. Spiritual healing is practiced.

Sources:

Bainbridge, W. S. *Satan's Power: Ethnography of a Deviant Psychotherapy Cult.* Berkeley: University of California Press, 1978.

Evans, C. *Cults of Unreason.* London: Harrap, 1973.

Foundation for *A Course in Miracles* (FACIM)

Formerly known as the Inner Miracle Partnership, this is a U.S. occultist-Christian group founded around 1980 by

Gloria and Kenneth Wapnick and based in New York state. It is devoted to teaching *A Course in Miracles*, a book published in 1975 by Helen Schucman, who claimed to have been the medium for a divine revelation. [*See also* FOUNDATION FOR INNER PEACE; *and* INTERFAITH FELLOWSHIP.]

Foundation for Biblical Research

U.S. ADVENTIST group formed by Dr. Ernest L. Martin, former chairman of the theology department at Ambassador College. Dissenting from the policies of the WORLDWIDE CHURCH OF GOD, the group rejected the autocratic leadership style characterized by Herbert W. Armstrong, and opposed tithing and baptism.

Foundation for Inner Peace

U.S. occultist-Christian group founded by Judith Skutch in 1975 in New York City, and devoted to the teaching of *A Course in Miracles*.

Foundation for Toward the Light

U.S. Christian esoteric group founded in the 1980s.

Foundation of Human Understanding

U.S. Christian-occultist group founded in 1961 in Los Angeles by Roy Masters (1928–). The founder was born in London to a Jewish family and came to the United States in 1949. In the 1950s he opened an Institute for Hypnosis, but was imprisoned for practicing medicine without a license. Since then he has been teaching meditation, operating mainly through radio broadcasts and literature.

Foundation of I, Inc. (Freedom of the Cosmos)

U.S. occultist group founded in the 1980s and based in New York City. It claims to employ ancient Hawaiian processes to teach its followers "the art of resolving problems and releasing blocks to your Self-identity—the Self or Mind in partnership with the Divine creator."

Foundation of Religious Transition

U.S. Christian-occultist group founded in 1969 by James A. and Diane Pike. Formerly the Episcopal Bishop of California, James Pike (1912–1969) decided to leave his church because of doctrinal disagreements that led to his trial for heresy. Pike did not accept the idea of the Trinity or the inerrancy of the Bible, and became committed to spiritualism. The medium Arthur Ford, who had been involved in several Spiritualist groups (FIRST SPIRITUALIST CHURCH OF NEW YORK), introduced Pike to spiritualism, through seances in which he claimed communication with Pike's dead son. Pike died unexpectedly in September 1969, and the group's name was changed to the Bishop Pike Foundation. In 1972 it merged with the LOVE PROJECT.

Foundation of Revelation

U.S. Hindu-oriented group founded in 1971 in San Francisco. It was devoted to

141

The Very Reverend James Pike, Dean of the Cathedral of St. John the Divine. He later left the Protestant Episcopal Church over doctrinal differences and established the Foundation of Religious Transition.

the mysterious prophecies of an un-named Indian holy man who predicted the coming of the new age of Siva Kalpa in 1966.

Foursquare Gospel, International Church of

Also known as Foursquare Gospel International, this is an international PENTECOSTAL, ADVENTIST group founded in Los Angeles in 1921 as the Angelus Temple by "Sister" Aimee Semple McPherson (1890–1944). The official name was adopted in 1927. The founder was born Aimee Elizabeth Kennedy in Ontario, Canada, and by the age of thir-teen was a celebrated public speaker. By age twenty she was internationally known for her flamboyant preaching style. She died of an apparently acciden-tal overdose of barbiturates following a nervous breakdown.

The name Foursquare refers to the four cornerstones of faith: regeneration, baptism in the spirit, divine healing, and the Second Coming. Another explana-tion the group offers is that "it takes its name from a vision McPherson had while delivering a sermon in Oakland, California. In that vision she saw the complete Gospel of Jesus Christ as the Savior, the Healer, the Baptizer with the Holy Spirit, and as the Soon Coming King."

McPherson once said: "I bring consola-tion to the great middle class, leaving those below to the salvation army, and those above to themselves." The Church practices "healing, tongues, and proph-ecy." It has operated the first church-owned radio station in the United States, KFSG (Kall Foursquare Gospel) and has had an active publication program through the Angelus Bible Institute. [*See also* EMMANUEL.]

Sources:

Epstein, D. M. *Sister Aimee: The Life of Aimee Semple McPherson*. New York: Harcourt Brace Jovanovich, 1993.

Thomas, L. *The Vanishing Evangelist*. New York: Viking, 1959.

Fratellanza Cosmica ("Cosmic Fraternity")

Italian occultist UFO group founded in 1962 in Porto Sant'Elpidio by Eugenio Siragusa, who reported receiving many messages from extraterrestrials. The group was disbanded in 1978, but most of its ideas appeared again in 1979 with the founding of NONSIAMOSOLI.

Fraternitas Rosae Crucis

U.S. ROSICRUCIAN group founded in Bos-ton 1868 by Pascal Beverly Randolph (1825–1875). The founder developed a system of occult sexuality or "sex magick," to be practiced only by married couples. In the early twentieth century, the group was reorganized by R. Swinburne Clymer (?–1966), who be-came Supreme Grand Master. Its doc-trine combines monotheism with Hindu ideas of karma and reincarnation. Aim-ing at better health through positive thinking is a recommended practice, part of "Organic Law." The group operates the Church of Illumination.

Fraternitas Rosicruciana Antiqua

International ROSICRUCIAN group founded by Arnoldo Krumm-Heller in

Germany in the early twentieth century. It is reported to have inspired several modern occultist groups. [*See also* GNOSIS-GNOSTIC ASSOCIATION OF ANTHROPOLOGY AND SCIENCE.]

Fraternité Blanche Universelle (FBU)

Known in English-speaking countries as the Universal White Brotherhood, this is an international occultist-Theosophical-Christian group. It was officially founded in 1947 in Paris by Omraam Mikhael Aivanhov, or Ivanoff (1900–1986), who was born in Bulgaria and arrived in France in 1937. In 1978, the "Fondation Pobeda Ouspech Universelle" was founded in Vaduz, Lichtenstein, to promote worldwide propagation of the group's ideas. The FBU has been reported to have ties to neo-Nazi groups in Europe.

Aivanhov claimed to have been sent by his spiritual master, Peter Duenov, and to have had a secret Tibetan teacher, like Duenov, who is considered the "nineteenth Grand Master of Humanity." Aivanhov was known as "The Solar Guru" because of the importance ascribed to the sun in his teachings. Group doctrine is reminiscent of THEOSOPHY ideas about "hidden wisdom" and "evolved beings," in addition to a melange of astrology, yoga, and Christian traditions. Intoxicants are forbidden, and meals are simple and vegetarian. Special physical exercises are designed to "balance electromagnetic forces in the body." Sexual relations are forbidden. The group claims to prepare the new world order for the "Age of Aquarius." Branches of the FBU have operated in Europe and North America.

Fraternité "Salve Regina" du Fre'chou

French Catholic schismatic group founded in 1977 by Roger Kozic and Michel Fernandez. In 1977 Kozic started reporting the witnessing of apparitions of the Virgin Mary, who announced the coming of global chaos. Many miracles and visions have been reported later at the same site, which has become a pilgrimage spot for many. The pronouncements and activities of the Fraternité have been denounced by the Roman Catholic Church.

Fraternity of St. Pius X

Known informally as the Lefebvrists, this is an international Catholic traditionalist movement founded by Archbishop Marcel Lefebvre (1906–1991) in 1965. Lefebvre, who was made archbishop by Pope Pius XII, started the movement following the Second Vatican Council (1962–1965), which introduced many reforms into Roman Catholic practices and doctrines. He was excommunicated from the Roman Catholic Church in 1988 after consecrating four bishops.

The movement regards itself as the guardian of tradition against what it considers heresies and the deterioration of church authority and faith caused by satanic reforms. It protests the obligatory use of the 1965 revised ritual, known as *Novus Ordo*, in place of the Tridentine Mass formulated by Pope Pius V in 1570. It is also opposed to the ecumenical movement, which encourages contacts with other religions, and espouses strong right-wing political views. The movement has had branches in Europe, North America, South America, and Oceania. Its English-speaking branches have been

Roman Catholic dissident Archbishop Marcel Lefebvre ordains a priest at Econe, Switzerland. Lefebvre was the founder of the Fraternity of St. Pius X.

known collectively as the Catholic Tridentine Church. [*See also* SOCIETY OF ST. PIUS V.]

Frazier Chapel

U.S. B'NAI NOACH congregation started in the 1980s by Jack Saunders, a former Baptist minister.

Free Christian Zion Church of Christ, The

U.S. African American conservative Protestant group founded in Redemption, Arkansas, in 1906 by E. D. Brown.

Free Church of God in Christ

U.S. African American PENTECOSTAL group founded in 1915 by E. J. Morris in Enid, Oklahoma.

Free Daist Avataric Communion

Formerly known as the Free Daist Avabhasan Communion, Free Daist Communion, Crazy Wisdom Fellowship, Johannine Daist Community, the Laughing Man Institute, the Dawn Horse Communion, Free Primitive Church of Divine Communion, Free Communion Church, Dawn Horse Fellowship, Da Free John, or Bubba Free John, this is a loose grouping of followers of Free John (1939–), whose real name is Franklin Albert Jones. He is a native of New York City, a graduate of Stanford University, and a disciple of Rudi (Albert Rudolph or Swami Rudrananda), who started the group in 1972 in California. Free John has also claimed to be a disciple of the gurus Muktananda, Nityananda, and Ramana Maharshi. He says he achieved "spiritual enlightenment" and "a permanent awakening to God-Realization" on September 10, 1970. In 1979 he retired from active leadership of the group.

In 1985, Da Free John became Da Kalki (Heart Master Da Love-Ananda) or Avadhoota Da Love-Ananda Hridayam, and the group became the Free Daist Communion. More recently, Da Kalki changed his name to Da Avabhasa (The "Bright"), known also as the Divine World-Teacher and True Heart Master. In 1995, he became known as the Avatara Adi Da. The various name changes of both the group and its leader are believed to contribute to the followers' well-being. The group offers Hindu-inspired teachings, meditation, and a gurudisciple relationship. Members are promised "Realization" of a "Divine Condition" through "a sacred relationship with Da Kalki." "Bubba Free John elucidates all the philosophical and esoteric matters that must be considered in spiritual or real life. But Bubba is not a mere intellectual or speculative philosopher. His writings, like all his actions, express the elegance and conscious intensity of Divine Ignorance, of God-Realization, which is his constant Enjoyment." In 1994, Da Avabhasa said: "I grant all my own excesses to those who Love me, in exchange for all their doubts and sufferings. Those who bind themselves to Me through love are inherently Free of fear and necessity. They Transcend the causes of experience, and they Dissolve in the Heart of God. What is a Greater Message than This?"

Free Gospel Church, Inc.

U.S. PENTECOSTAL group founded in 1916 by Frank and William Casley and based in Western Pennsylvania.

Free Presbyterian Church (Paisleyite)

Northern Ireland Protestant group founded by Ian Paisley (1926?–) in 1951 in dissent from the established Presbyterian Church. It emphasizes a strong anti-Catholic position and is tied to the Unionist position in Northern Ireland.

Free Protestant Episcopal Church

British Protestant church formed in 1897 through the union of three small dissenting bodies. Doctrine mostly follows that of the Protestant Episcopal Church, but members are conscientious objectors. Branches have developed in the United States and Canada.

Free Will Baptist Church of the Pentecostal Faith

U.S. PENTECOSTAL group formed in the 1950s in South Carolina.

Friday Religion

Syncretistic Melanesian religion started in the Northern Solomon Islands in 1958. It grew out of the Roman Catholic Church. Its practices are PENTECOSTAL, with Catholic liturgy.

Friends of Israel

Canadian HEBREW CHRISTIAN group based in Hamilton, Ontario, which was founded in 1892.

Friends of Israel Gospel Ministry

U.S. HEBREW CHRISTIAN group founded by Elwood McQuaid in the 1980s and based in New Jersey.

Friends of the Holy Spirit (FHS)

Known also as Arata a Roho Mutheru, this is a Kenyan independent Christian PENTECOSTAL group founded in 1946 among the Kikuyu and Kamba people, and inspired by Anglican missionaries.

Fukkatsu No Kirisuto Kyodan (Church of the Resurrected Christ)

Japanese indigenous Christian group founded in Nagano prefecture, northwest of Tokyo, in the 1950s.

Full Gospel Central Church

Also known as the S-Church, and originally known as the Full Gospel Revival Centre, this is a Korean Christian PENTECOSTAL movement. It was founded by Yonggi Cho (1936–), who at age nineteen reported a visit by Jesus Christ that made him a Christian for life. The movement started in 1958, and the present name was adopted in 1962. The doctrine resembles that of the ASSEMBLIES OF GOD. Practices include glossolalia, or speaking in tongues, and faith healing. Followers are promised both physical health and material prosperity. Branches have developed in the United States and Canada.

The Reverend Ian Paisley, founder of the Free Presbyterian Church, protests the British government's Anglo-Irish Agreement in 1987.

Full Gospel Church Association

Also known as the Full Gospel Church of God, this is a U.S. PENTECOSTAL group founded by Dennis W. Thorn in 1952 in Amarillo, Texas. Its doctrine emphasizes healing and tithing.

Full Gospel Church in Australia

Australian indigenous PENTECOSTAL group started in 1962 in a secession from the ASSEMBLIES OF GOD.

Full Gospel Defenders Conference of America

Philadelphia-based U.S. PENTECOSTAL group with doctrinal emphasis on miracles and signs.

Full Gospel Evangelical Association

U.S. PENTECOSTAL group resulting from a schism during the late 1940s in the APOSTOLIC FAITH CHURCH (KANSAS). The dissenting group was first known as the Ministerial and Missionary Alliance of the Original Trinity Apostolic Faith, Inc., and in 1952 formed the Association.

Full Gospel Fellowship of Churches and Ministries, International (FGFCMI)

U.S. PENTECOSTAL group emphasizing healing and mission work overseas. FGFCMI was founded by Gordon Lindsey (1906–1973) in 1949 and officially incorporated in 1962. The UNITED PENTECOSTAL FAITH CHURCH is affiliated with this group.

Full Gospel Minister Association

U.S. PENTECOSTAL group based in East Jordan, Michigan, that issues credentials to both ministers and churches. Members are conscientious objectors.

Full Gospel Tabernacle

U.S. BRITISH-ISRAELIST group founded in the 1930s in Tulsa, Oklahoma, by Jonathan Ellsworth Perkins, former Methodist minister.

Full Salvation Union

U.S. schismatic Christian group founded in Lansing, Michigan, in 1934 by James F. Andrews. The group's doctrine prohibits the observance of ceremonies.

Fundamentalism

U.S. Protestant movement guided by the doctrine of complete faith in five fundamentals: the inerrancy of the Bible, the virgin birth of Jesus, the supernatural atonement, the physical resurrection of Jesus, and the authenticity of the Gospel miracles.

Another version of the "five points" includes: the divine inspiration of the Bible, the depravity of man, redemption through the blood of Christ, the true church as a body composed of all believers, and the coming of Christ to establish his reign.

In 1983, a convention of fundamentalist Baptists in Kansas City, Missouri, affirmed the following five fundamentals: inerrant scripture; Christ is God in the flesh; Christ died for the sins of mankind; Christ rose bodily; Christ will return bodily.

Sources:

Furniss, N. F. *The* FUNDAMENTALIST *Controversy, 1918–1931.* New Haven: Yale University Press, 1954.

Marsden, G. M. *Fundamentalism and American Culture.* Oxford: Oxford University Press, 1980.

Niebuhr, H. R. "Fundamentalism." In *Encyclopedia of the Social Sciences*, VI. New York: 1937.

Sandeen, E. R. *The Roots of Fundamentalism.* Chicago: University of Chicago Press, 1970.

Fundamentalist Army, The

Originally known as the Open Door Community Church. U.S. FUNDAMENTALIST, evangelical, semicommunal group founded by Robert Leslie Hymers, Jr., (1941–), former Southern Baptist minister, in San Fernando Valley, California, in 1975. Faith healing and exorcism are practiced. The group has operated the Open Door Messianic Jewish Congregation since 1977.

Fuso Kyo

Japanese Shinto sect founded in 1873 by Shisdhino Nakaba (?–1884). The doctrine and practice focus on Mt. Fuji, which is known also as Fuso. The group is polytheistic and proclaims a return to original Shinto.

Future Foundation

U.S. occultist group, founded in Stenauer, Nebraska, by Gerald W. Gottula in 1969. Doctrine includes belief in a coming New Age, and practices include astrology, faith healing, and psychic prophecy.

G

Gallican Church (Église Gallicane, Église Catholic Française)

French OLD CATHOLIC group started in 1883 and reorganized in 1907 by Joseph René Vilatte. It practices some Roman Catholic traditions but rejects papal authority and papal infallibility. It follows a THEOSOPHICAL Christianity. There is an emphasis on gnosticism, occultism, and faith healing. The THEOSOPHICAL influence makes it similar in beliefs and practices to the LIBERAL CATHOLIC CHURCH. Gallican Church has had connections with other Old Catholic and traditionalist Catholic groups in Europe and North America.

Ganden Mahayana Center

Also known as Ganden Tekchen Ling, this is a U.S. Tibetan Buddhist group based in Wisconsin and founded by Geshe Lhundup Sopa in the 1970s. It is devoted to spreading Tibetan Buddhism in the West.

Source:
Sopa, G., and Hopkins, J. *Practice and Theory of Tibetan Buddhism.* New York: Grove Press, 1976.

Ganienkah

U.S. Native American religious commune founded by members of the Mohawk people in the Adirondack Mountains in 1974.

Gedatsu Church of America

California-based U.S. branch of the Japanese GEDATSU-KAI movement, brought to the United States in the 1940s and incorporated in 1951.

Gedatsu-Kai (Salvation Society)

Japanese religion founded in 1929 by Okano Eizo (1881–1948). Also known as Seiken, and posthumously known as Gedatsu Kongo, Okano was a former priest in the Shugendo sect of Japanese Buddhism. He is viewed as a deity, known as *Gedatsu Kongo Sonja*. The doctrine combines Christian, Shinto, and Buddhist ideas in attempting to preserve traditional Japanese values of ancestor worship and national loyalty.

Source:
Earhart, H. B. *Gedatsu-Kai and Religion in Contemporary Japan.* Bloomington, IN: Indiana University Press, 1989.

Geistige Loge

Swiss spiritualist-Christian group founded in Zurich in 1948 by Beatrice Brunner (?–1983). After the founder's death, it was split into two groups, Pro Beatrice and the Geistchristliche Gemeinschaft. Both are devoted to the messages reportedly received by the founder from other worlds.

Gelug-Pa ("Yellow Hat")

The largest of the four sects of Tibetan Buddhism, Gelug-Pa is led by the 98th Ganden Tripa, known as Ganden Tri Rinpoche (1921–), who was crowned by the XIV Dalai Lama in 1984. The Dalai Lama is considered a follower of this tradition. [*See also* MANJUSHRI INSTITUTE.]

The XIV Dalai Lama of Tibet (left) greets Archbishop of Canterbury Robert Runcie in London during a visit in 1988. The Dalai Lama is a follower of the Gelug-Pa (Yellow Hat) sect of Tibetan Buddhism.

Gemeinde der Christen Ecclesia

German Christian PENTECOSTAL movement started in 1944.

Gemeinde Jesu Christi in Deutschland

German Christian PENTECOSTAL movement started in 1943.

Gemeinschaft Entschie Christen

German Christian PENTECOSTAL movement started in the 1950s.

General Assembly and Church of the First Born

U.S. PENTECOSTAL group founded in 1907. Their doctrine denies original sin and members practice healing and speaking in tongues. They do not consult medical doctors. In 1976 a child of group members died after medical care was denied by the parents. An Oklahoma court ruled that another child of the same family would be transferred to government care.

General Assembly of Spiritualists

Founded in 1931 when the New York State Association of the NATIONAL SPIRITUALIST ASSOCIATION OF CHURCHES left the NSAC. The immediate cause was a statement condemning belief in reincarnation. The General Assembly follows other NSAC principles, but also espouses reincarnation.

General Church of the New Jerusalem

U.S. Swedenborgian group founded in 1840 due to a schism in the Church of the New Jerusalem. [See also SWEDENBORG FOUNDATION.]

General Conference of the Church of God (Seventh Day)

Popularly known as the Church of God (Seventh Day), this is a U.S. Sabbath-keeping, adventist movement whose members have rejected the teachings of Ellen G. White and the SEVENTH-DAY ADVENTIST CHURCH. While the latter group was being organized in the mid-nineteenth century and became the largest among ADVENTIST groups, smaller congregations kept their independence. In 1906, these groups were incorporated as the Churches of God (Adventist) Unattached Congregations.

The group has a strong Old Testament orientation, and, in addition to keeping the Saturday Sabbath, forbids the use of tobacco, alcohol, and pork. Major Christian festivals, including Christmas and Easter, are ignored as they are considered pagan.

General Conference of the Evangelical Baptist Church

Originally known as the Church of the Full Gospel, Inc., this U.S. PENTECOSTAL group was founded in 1935 in Goldsboro, North Carolina, by R. H. Askew. Doctrine emphasizes healing, speaking in tongues, and tithing. This group had a close affiliation with the Full Gospel Pentecostal Church of Maryland.

General Convention of the New Jerusalem

The first Swedenborgian organization in the United States, founded in 1817, with headquarters in Newton, Massachusetts. [*See also* SWEDENBORG FOUNDATION.]

General Council of the Churches of God

Formed in 1950 as a result of dissent within the GENERAL CONFERENCE OF THE CHURCH OF GOD, this is a U.S. Sabbath-keeping, ADVENTIST group with head-quaters in Meridian, Idaho. [*See also* ADVENTISTS, SECOND; *and* SEVENTH-DAY ADVENTIST CHURCH.]

General Psionics, Church of

U.S. occultist group founded by John L. Douglas and Henry D. Frazier in Redondo Beach, California, in 1968. It has operated mainly by mail.

Georgian Church, The

Neo-pagan U.S. group founded by George Patterson (?–1984) in the mid-1970s, and originally known as the Church of Wicca of Bakersfield. The doctrine and rituals are devoted to the worship of the Mother Goddess. [*See also* COVENANT OF THE GODDESS; *and* WICCA.]

Gereja Pantekosta de Indonesia

Indonesian PENTECOSTAL group started by U.S. missionaries sent by BETHEL TEMPLE in the 1960s.

Ghana Apostolic Church

PENTECOSTAL group founded in the early twentieth century in the then British colony of Gold Coast. This group seceded from the APOSTOLIC CHURCH OF GHANA.

Glad Tidings Missionary Society

North American PENTECOSTAL group that grew out of the Glad Tidings Temple of Vancouver, British Columbia. The LATTER RAIN MOVEMENT inspired the Missionary Society.

Glainn Sidhr Order

International neo-pagan organization founded in the 1970s.

Glanton Brethren

British PLYMOUTH BRETHREN group. A. E. Booth, the founder of the ERIE BIBLE TRUTH DEPOT, was associated with this British group. [*See also* ATHANOR FELLOWSHIP; *and* EARTHSPIRIT COMMUNITY.]

Glastonbury Community

British mystical community founded in the 1960s around a belief in angels and fairies, and contact with them. Glastonbury is the focus of many legendary traditions, including the tomb of King Arthur and the first Christian church in Britain. It was also the site of a great medieval Benedictine monastery destroyed by order of Henry VIII in 1538.

Glenridge Christian Fellowship

South African PENTECOSTAL group started in 1985 in Durban by former members of the INVISIBLE CHURCH.

Glide Memorial Methodist Church

U.S. radical Christian congregation started in San Francisco in the 1960s.

Gnostic Center of Los Angeles

U.S. occultist group based in Los Angeles, devoted to teaching "sexual alchemy, the Kabala, meditation, astral travel, and dream yoga."

Gnosis-Gnostic Association of Anthropology and Science

Also known as Associacion Gnostica de Estudios de Antropologia y Ciencias (AGEAC) or as the Gnostic Association of Cultural and Anthropological Studies, this is an international THEOSOPHICAL, Eastern-oriented, occultist group founded in Mexico in 1952 by Victor Manuel Perralta (?–1977). He adopted the name Samael Aunweur or Samael Aun Weor, which has gnostic meaning. Samael Aun Weor is considered the "venerable teacher" and "avatar." The group's founder was a member of FRATERNITAS ROSICRUCIANA ANTIQUA, and his teachings include "alchemy, Tibetan psychology, and Zen meditation." Group activities include instruction in yoga, meditation, and the Kabala, as well as "theurgy (performance of miracles), astral travel, the laws of karma, alchemy and tantra." Group beliefs include the idea of an astral body and an alchemical birth, contacts with extraterrestrial civilizations, and the future return of the "lost continents" of Atlantis and Lemuria.

The group's center is in Mexico, with branches in Spain and the United States. The California branch is known as the Gnostic Institute of Universal Charity.

Other branches in the United States and Great Britain are known as the Gnostic Institute of Anthropology (GIA).

Gnostic Society

U.S. THEOSOPHICAL group based in Los Angeles that is officially devoted to teaching the original works of H. P. Blavatsky, founder of the Theosophical Society.

Godianism

Nigerian syncretistic group combining Christian elements with traditional African rituals.

God Is Love

Brazilian Protestant evangelical group founded in Rio de Janeiro in the 1960s.

God of the Universe Church

African independent PENTECOSTAL church founded in 1962 among the Luo people in Kenya.

God's House of Prayer for All Nations, Inc.

U.S. PENTECOSTAL group founded in 1964 in Peoria, Illinois, by Tommie Lawrence, formerly of the CHURCH OF GOD IN CHRIST. The group emphasizes faith healing and maintains contact with the MIRACLE REVIVAL FELLOWSHIP.

God's Kingdom Society

Nigerian independent Christian church started in 1934. The society rejects traditional Christian rituals and festivals and asserts that members are the true successors to Biblical Jews. It operates the Holy Village of Salem.

Goshen Fellowship

British offshoot of JEHOVAH'S WITNESSES founded in 1951 in London.

Gospel Assemblies

U.S. PENTECOSTAL group founded by William Sowders (1879–1952) in 1914 in Louisville, Kentucky. Its doctrine is unique among Pentecostal groups in deviating significantly from the FUNDAMENTALIST Trinitarian position. It also follows a belief in DISPENSATIONALISM, *i.e.* dividing history into several periods, and in the notion that 1914 was the beginning of the last dispensation, the end of time. This latter idea was adopted from Charles T. Russell, the founder of JEHOVAH'S WITNESSES. The group emphasizes its lack of formal membership or creed, except for the centrality of the Bible.

Following the death of the founder, the group was divided into several assemblies, each claiming the original name.

Gospel Harvesters Evangelistic Association

Also known as the International Communion of Charismatic Churches, this U.S. PENTECOSTAL group was founded in 1961 in Atlanta by Earl P. Paulk, Jr. It promotes the "Kingdom Church" or "Kingdom Now" doctrine, which is critical of established churches and calls for the Christianization of society.

Gospel Harvesters Evangelistic Association (Buffalo)

North American PENTECOSTAL group founded in 1962 in Buffalo, New York, by Rose Pezzino. Branches operate in Canada and the Southern United States.

Grace and Truth Christian Congregation

Israeli MESSIANIC JUDAISM congregation started in 1976 by Baruch Maoz. It describes itself as "Reformed in doctrine."

Grace Gospel Evangelistic Association International, Inc.

U.S. PENTECOSTAL group started in the mid-1930s. Its doctrine combines PENTECOSTALISM with Calvinism, emphasizing predestination rather than free will in the achievement of grace.

Grace Gospel Fellowship

U.S. FUNDAMENTALIST, DISPENSATIONALIST group founded in 1944 by J. C. O'Hair and Harry Bultema.

Grace Gospel Missions

U.S. FUNDAMENTALIST, DISPENSATIONALIST mission organization that promotes fundamentalist Christianity. It was first formed in January 1939 under the name World Wide Grace Testimony.

Grail Message (Gralsbewegung)

International occultist-syncretist movement founded in 1928 in Austria by Oskar Ernst Bernhardt (1875–1941) of

Bischofswerda, Germany. In 1924 he started publishing his revelations under the name Abd-ru-shin. The Message is a combination of Western and Hindu ideas, but without any Christian notions. Branches have operated in Western Europe, Australia, and the United States.

Greater Refuge Temple

U.S. PENTECOSTAL group started in New York City in the 1950s. Affiliated with the CHURCH OF OUR LORD JESUS CHRIST OF THE APOSTOLIC FAITH OF GREAT BRITAIN.

Greater World Christian Spiritualist League

International spiritualist group founded in London in 1920. It promotes a combination of Christianity and the practice of spirit communication and spiritual healing. Branches operate all over the English-speaking world.

Great School of the Masters

U.S. THEOSOPHIST-occultist group based in California. It was founded in 1883 by John E. Richardson, who said he had received messages from an Indian master named Hoo-Kna-ka. The group has operated the School of Natural Science, which offers correspondence courses.

Guild of Health

British faith healing group started in the early twentieth century. It has attempted to reconcile religious faith with medical views.

Gurdjieff Foundation

U.S. occultist group founded in New York in 1953 by John Pentland (1907–1984). It has served as a center for GURDJIEFF teaching and activities. In existence in New York until the late 1970s, the Foundation then moved to San Francisco, where a branch had existed since 1955.

Gurdjieff Groups

Georgei Ivanovich (G. I.) Gurdjieff (1874?–1949) was the creator of a twentieth-century occult tradition, sometimes known as the Fourth Way School, that has reached a special degree of fame and acceptance. Ideas connected with Gurdjieff appear in a variety of modern occult groups and new religions.

Gurdjieff was reportedly born in Alexandropol, Armenia. According to some of his followers, he received his higher education in Kars, and then "disappeared" for twenty years. Like Madame Blavatsky, who is a famous figure within THEOSOPHICAL circles, Gurdjieff repeatedly said he had spent several years in Central Asia and Tibet, studying with mysterious "masters" of "ancient wisdom" during his travels in the East. However, neither the travels nor the Masters have been substantiated. In 1922 he founded the Institute for the Harmonious Development of Man in Fontainebleau, near Paris. Also known as Le Prieure (the Priory), the Institute existed until 1933.

His teachings were put into writing by Pyotr Demainovitch (P. D.) Ouspensky (1878–1947), his most important disciple and exponent, who continued to teach his ideas after severing personal relations with the Master, Gurdjieff, in 1932.

G. I. Gurdjieff, head of the Institute for the Harmonious Development of Man, arrives on a visit to the United States.

The tradition is sometimes referred to as G-O, for Gurdjieff-Ouspensky, and is also known as the Fourth Way, the Gurdjieff Work, or just the Work.

Gurdjieff taught that while humans possess not one but four brains (instinctive, moving, emotional, and intellectual), these organs are uncoordinated, and so man is "asleep" and has to become conscious through various exercises. There are seven evolutionary levels. The exercises include long silences, meditation, prayer, "cultivating the opposite" by going against one's ingrained habits, and going against one's limits by fasting and sleep deprivation. Infractions of rules and laxness in exercises lead to heavy fines. Followers celebrate Gurdjieff's birthday, January 13, and the day of his death, October 29.

Since there was only one Master and no real organization, and secrecy about special knowledge is of the essence, Gurdjieff followers are rather elusive. They meet privately in small groups, with one teacher and his helpers, and do not normally wish to attract attention. However, several Gurdjieff groups do advertise their existence in an attempt to recruit members. In the United States, one known group is the GURDJIEFF FOUNDATION. Another group, the INSTITUTE FOR RELIGIOUS DEVELOPMENT, includes the disciples of W. A. Nyland, who was once affiliated with the Foundation. [See also CLAYMONT COURT; FELLOWSHIP OF FRIENDS; INSTITUTE FOR THE COMPARATIVE STUDY OF HISTORY, PHILOSOPHY, AND THE SCIENCES; INSTITUTE FOR THE HARMONIOUS DEVELOPMENT OF THE HUMAN BEING; ORAGE GROUP; THE PROSPEROS; SHERBORNE SCHOOL; SHERBORNE STUDIES GROUP; *and* SUBUD.]

Sources:

Ellwood, R. S. *Religious and Spiritual Groups in Modern America*. Englewood Cliffs, NJ: Prentice-Hall, 1973.

Webb, J. *The Harmonious Circle: The Lives and Work of G. I. Gurdjieff, P. D. Ouspensky, and Their Followers*. New York: G. P. Putnam, 1980.

Gurdjieff Studies Group

British occultist group founded in London in the 1980s.

Guru Bawa Fellowship

Also known as the Bawa Muhaiyaddeen Fellowship, this is a North American Islamic-oriented group founded in 1974 around the personality of Muhaiyaddeen M. R. Bawa (?–1986). Bawa described himself as a "contemporary Sufi." Guru Bawa was a Tamil from Sri Lanka reputed to have established a spiritual school there around 1940, teaching the unity of God and human unity in God. In 1971 he arrived in the United States and set up fellowship groups for his students. According to the Fellowship, "Guru Bawa emphasizes the living of Universal Divine Qualities and Characteristics." Bawa's doctrine includes belief in reincarnation, and he claims to carry on the work of twenty-five divine messengers, including Moses, Jesus, and Muhammad.

H

Hahalis Welfare Society

Melanesian syncretistic, communal CARGO CULT movement started in 1957 on Buka Island in the Northern Solomons. It grew out of Roman Catholic traditions. In the 1960s, the group maintained complete communal living, including group marriage. It gradually became a political movement.

Haidakhan Samaj

Western Hindu-inspired group devoted to the teachings of Haidakhan Baba, also known as Babaji Nagaraj (?–1984) of the Himalayas. Several branches have opened in Europe and North America. [*See also* INTERNATIONAL BABAJI KRIYA YOGA SANGAM.]

Hall Deliverance Foundation

U.S. PENTECOSTAL-healing group built around the personality of Franklin Hall, who started a healing ministry in 1946. The group's doctrine recommends prayer and fasting. Hall's book presenting his methods is titled *Atomic Power with God with Fasting and Prayer* (1973). The group is based in Phoenix, Arizona.

Hallelujah Church

Guyanan indigenous church founded by the prophet Abel in the Macushi people around 1870. Later the movement was led by a succession of prophets, with an emphasis on prayer and moral discipline. The movement's center is in the village of Amokokopai ("New Jerusalem").

Halveti-Jerrahi Order of New York

U.S. Sufi group, based in New York City. Founded in the 1970s, it was led by Muzaffer al-Ashki. The group claims to follow the teachings of Pir Nureddin Jerrahi, who founded the Jerrahi order in Istanbul in the seventeenth century. It operates the Massjid al-Farah al Ashki.

Hanafi Madh-Hab Center

U.S. Muslim group started in 1967. Historically, Hanafi is the most liberal of the four legal schools of Sunni Islam. (The three others are Maliki, Shafii, and Hanbali). A group aligning itself with the Hanafi tradition was founded in the United States in 1967 by Hammas Abdul Khalis (formerly Ernest Timothy McGee), who thus broke away from the NATION OF ISLAM. This group, made up of African Americans, is known as the Hanafi Muslims.

The conflict between the Hanafis and the Nation of Islam led to lethal violence. On January 10, 1973, several members of the Nation of Islam broke into the home of Hamaas Abdul Khalis, killed three of his children and paralyzed his wife for life. In 1977, members of the Hanafi Muslims were involved in a takeover of a charitable Jewish organization in Washington, D.C., in order to draw attention to the 1973 incident and their demands for retribution.

Handsome Lake Religion

Also known as Longhouse Religion, this

Hamaas Abdul Khaalis, leader of the Hanafi Muslims.

is a syncretistic Native American movement founded by the Seneca chief Ganiodayo (Handsome Lake) (1735–1815) in 1799. After a long period of decline and demoralization, the Seneca were revitalized by the chief's visions, which called for the adoption of a puritan-like ethic. Handsome Lake was changed by his visions, from an alcoholic to a prophet who saved his people. His new religion banned whiskey, witchcraft, and secret societies, and introduced the confession of sins as its main ritual. Later, the movement spread among the Iroquois. Thirty years after the prophet's death it was codified and named Gaiwiio (the Old Way). It still exists among the Iroquois in northern New York and Canada.

Source:
Wallace, A. F. C. *The Death and Rebirth of the Seneca.* New York: Knopf, 1970.

Hanuman Fellowship

U.S. Hindu group in California founded in the 1970s. It is "based on the study and practice of Ashtanga Yoga as taught by Baba Hari Dass." Fellowship practices include meditation, yoga, and charitable activities.

Hanuman Foundation

U.S. Hindu group founded by Baba Ram Dass in 1974. Hanuman is devoted to promoting the knowledge of Hindu beliefs and practices in the West. Baba Ram Dass was born Richard Alpert in 1931 in Boston. After earning a Ph.D. in psychology from Stanford University in 1967, he first went to India and found his guru, Neem Karoli Baba, who named him Ram Dass.

Source:

Ram Dass. *Be Here Now.* New York: Crown, 1971.

Harris Movement

Also known as the Harrist Church, this is an indigenous Christian movement founded by William Wade Harris (c. 1850–1929) in West Africa. Harris, a Liberian of the Grebo people, took an active part in his group's struggle against foreign domination, supporting an insurrection against the American settlers in Liberia, which demanded British rule. Imprisoned, he gained the nickname of "Old Man Union Jack." In a Christian revelation, he claimed to have seen the Angel Gabriel, who instructed him to preach. His message, which he started preaching in 1913, was one of an African Christianity. It was based on the principles of Christian baptism, opposition to traditional paganism, and opposition to European clothes and customs. Between 1913 and 1915, he led some 120,000 people in the Ivory Coast and Ghana to leave traditional religions and join his movement. French authorities in the Ivory Coast reacted violently to Harris and his movement. Later, some members, with the leader's encouragement, joined Methodist and Roman Catholic churches, but the movement survived and has continued to flourish in West Africa. After the founder's death, John Ahui and Albert Atcho continued

Harris's work in the Ivory Coast, where the church has become officially recognized. There have been many schisms, with various groups claiming the Harris legacy. It has also influenced several independent groups, such as TWELVE APOSTLES.

Sources:

Haliburton, G. M. *The Prophet Harris.* London: Longman, 1971.

Walker, S. S. *The Religious Revolution in the Ivory Coast: The Prophet Harris and the Harrist Church.* Chapel Hill: University of North Carolina Press, 1983.

Healing Order of the Sufi Order

Also known as the Sufi Healing Order, this is a U.S. branch of the SUFI ORDER IN THE WEST devoted to faith healing. Founded by Himayat Inayati in the late 1970s, it is based in Leicester, North Carolina.

Healthy, Happy, Holy Organization (3HO)

Officially known as the Sikh Dharma of the Western Hemisphere, and popularly known as the White Sikhs, this is an orthodox Sikh movement created for Western followers. It was founded in Los Angeles, California, in 1969 by Harbhajan Singh Khalsa Yogiji (1929–), also known as Yogi Bhajan or Siri Singh Sahib. The 3HO is actually the educational arm of the movement.

Sikh doctrine, as developed by Guru Nanak (1439–1538), was inspired by both Islam and Hinduism. Nanak's writings, known as *Siri Guru Granth Sahib*, are the

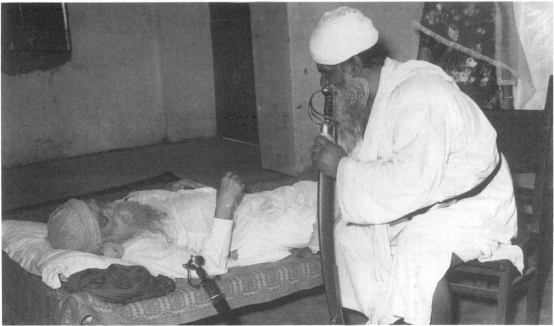

Sikh leader Tara Singh and his wife (top) are shown before he undertakes a "fast unto death" in the Golden Temple at Amritsar, India. Below, he begins his fast. He ended his protest, however, in expectation of government concessions to his demands.

Sikh scripture. The religion is strictly monotheistic and utilizes mantras and meditation, following Hindu traditions. Fish, meat, and drugs are avoided. Members are enjoined to carry out the five k's of Skih tradition: *kesh*, tying the hair under a turban; *kangha*, using a comb; *kachera*, special underwear; *kara*, wearing a steel bracelet; and *kirpan*, wearing a dagger. Wearing the turban at all times has led the Sikhs to have legal trouble with military and police authorities all over the world. Members adopt Punjabi names and practice meditation and "full moon celebrations." 3HO practices go beyond traditional Sikhism in the teaching of Kundalini yoga techniques. The group's doctrine also includes beliefs in "electromagnetic fields," special energy in human hair, and magical mantras providing protection and prosperity. In the 1970s, the group proclaimed the coming of the Aquarian Age. There have been some 3HO communes in the United States.

Sources:

Cole, W. O., and Sambhi, Piara Singh. *The Sikhs*. London: Routledge & Kegan Paul, 1978.

Khushwant Singh. *A History of the Sikhs*. Princeton: Princeton University Press, 1963–1966.

Heart Consciousness Church

U.S. communal group founded in California in 1975. The church is based on "that essence common to the Holistic Health Movement, the Human Potential Movement and Universal Spirituality . . . group sharing of spiritual energy; meditation; chanting; . . . surrendering to the infinite (God, Brahman, Tao, the Void) without and within us all; respect for the wisdom of the great teachers." It operates the Harbin Hot Springs Community in Middletown, California.

Heaven's Gate

Also known as the Higher Source and formerly known as Bo and Peep and Total Overcomers Anonymous, this is a U.S. Christian-UFO group started in 1975 in Los Angeles by a former music professor, Marshall Herff Applewhite (1932–1997), and a registered nurse, Bonnie Lu Trousedale Nettles (1928–1985). The two met in the early 1970s when Applewhite was hospitalized with heart problems and had a near-death experience. Soon after his recovery the two traveled together, preaching their system for enlightenment as they crossed the country. They called themselves Bo and Peep, and at other times were known as Winnie and Pooh, Chip and Dale, "The Him and the Her" and later as Do and Ti.

The group's doctrine, known as Human Individual Metamorphosis (HIM), aims to liberate humans from the endless cycle of reincarnation. Early in their proselytizing, Applewhite and Nettles also called each other "the Two" in reference to a New Testament prophecy about two witnesses. In accordance with the prophecy, Do and Ti said that they would be assassinated and resurrected three days later. Following the resurrection they would be lifted up by a UFO to the divine kingdom in outer space.

Between 1975 and 1992, the group apparently moved frequently, living on campgrounds, in motels, and sometimes in rented houses. Early in this period, the group is reported to have communed for a couple of years on a campground in Laramie, WY. Then, during the 1980s,

Workers from the San Diego Coroner's office remove the bodies of victims of the Heaven's Gate mass suicide.

the group traveled to different cities in the United States recruiting new followers usually by distributing posters inviting people to a "lecture" on UFOs. At these meetings the group presented their belief system and invited interested parties to join them. It has been reported that potential recruitees were allowed to join the group only if members felt certain that the individual was making an informed and autonomous decision and that he or she was absolutely certain that they wanted to join.

When Nettles died of cancer in 1985, the original prophecy that "the Two" would be assassinated, resurrected, and then taken away by UFOs was abandoned. Applewhite began preaching that one's body is merely a container or "vessel" for a transferable soul. In order to reach a higher level, one has to leave behind the physical container of their earth-bound body so that their soul can rendezvous with a new extraterrestrial body. In preparation for the outer space journey, followers agreed to get rid of most material possessions and worldly attachments. Followers quit their jobs and became estranged from their families (unless family members joined the group).

Strict rules and routines were enforced in order to compel members to deny the demands of the body. Members lived highly routine lives, waking early to pray, taking meals communally and at the same time every day, and performing drills so that they would be ready for sudden spacecraft visits. Some former members have reported that at different times they were sent by Do and Ti to beg for food; at other times they were instructed to hold tuning forks to their heads for hours at a time in order to learn telepathy, as well as practice other exercises to develop psychic ability. Members wore identical uniforms and had identical haircuts. Marriage and sexual relationships were forbidden and some male members had themselves castrated in order to be liberate themselves from physical desires.

In October 1996, Applewhite and 38 members of the group rented an estate in Rancho Santa Fe, California. They established a business called Higher Source, which offered graphics services and designed WEB pages.

In late March 1997, everyone at the estate committed suicide, some by ingesting a mixture of alcohol and barbiturates, some by asphyxiation. They were found lying on their backs on bunk beds, cots, and mattresses, wearing cotton pants, black shirts, and identical sneakers. They all had in their possession passports or driver's licenses, a roll of quarters and/or a five dollar bill. Most were also found covered in purple shrouds. It is believed that a group of eight senior members assisted the others with their suicides which were carried out in shifts.

Victims ranged in age from 26 to 72 Twelve of the members were in their forties. There were 21 females and 18 males. Videotaped statements made by members indicated that they were taking this step in preparation for an expected encounter with extraterrestrials arriving in a spaceship trailing in the wake of the Hale-Bopp comet, which was visible from Earth at the time of the suicides. There are reported to be anywhere from 200 to 1000 surviving members of the cult.

Hebrew Christian Alliance

British HEBREW CHRISTIAN organization founded in London in 1866 by A. M. Meyer with the aim of providing fellowship for "Christian Israelites." Its members retained their respective memberships in various Christian churches.

Hebrew Christian Assembly-Jerusalem Congregation

Israeli HEBREW CHRISTIAN group based in Jerusalem, founded around 1970 by Ze'ev Kofsman, Jacob Goren, and Victor Smadja. The group's theology has been that of the PLYMOUTH BRETHREN. [See also MESSIANIC ASSEMBLY OF ISRAEL.]

Hebrew Christianity

International movement that developed out of the efforts of Christian groups to convert Jews in the nineteenth century. The message proclaimed by Hebrew Christianity is the possibility of combining Jewish identity and FUNDAMENTALIST Christian beliefs. The rituals combine Jewish and Protestant elements. While defining themselves as loyal to the Jewish people, member have accepted Jesus as the true Messiah. They proclaim a double loyalty, to Jewish identity and to Christianity, though they reject the use of the term Christian. Often, the use of traditional Christian terms is avoided. Thus, the term Jesus Christ is replaced by Yeshua, and New Testament by Holy Scripture or New Covenant.

While the Hebrew Christian missionary movement was founded in Europe during the nineteenth century, it has existed in the United States since 1915 in various organizational forms. Leaders of the various groups are ordained by Baptist churches, and maintain close contact with Fundamentalist groups. Individual congregations have differed significantly in doctrine and rituals. [*See also* MESSIANIC JUDAISM.]

Sources:

Pruter, K. *Jewish Christians in the United States: A Bibliography.* New York: Garland Publishing, 1986.

Sobel, B. Z. *Hebrew Christianity: The Thirteenth Tribe.* New York: Wiley, 1974.

Hephzibah Faith Missionary Association

U.S. evangelical PENTECOSTAL group founded in Glenwood, Iowa, in 1892.

Hepzebah House

U.S. FUNDAMENTALIST group based in New York City and founded in the 1940s. It was influenced by the ideas of T. Austin Sparks, founder of the HONOR OAK CHRISTIAN FELLOWSHIP CENTRE in London. [*See also* THIS TESTIMONY.]

Heralds of the New Age

New Zealand-based UFO group founded in the 1950s. The Heralds claimed to relay messages from extraterrestrial beings.

Herero Church

Namibian indigenous Christian church established around 1960, with branches around Southern Africa.

Hicksite Friends

U.S. Society of Friends group that seceded from the main body of Quakers in the United States in 1828. It was named after Elias Hicks (1748–1830), who led the movement with his Unitarian tendencies. In 1826 Hicks denied the notion of the divinity of Jesus Christ, declaring that he recognized no other Savior than the Inner Light. This group contrasted with the Conservative Friends, also known as Wilburites, after John Wilbur.

Himalayan Academy

U.S. commune founded in 1962 in Virginia City, Nevada. The Academy followed a combination of Hinduism and Christianity.

Himalayan International Institute of Yoga Science and Philosophy

Also known as the Himalayan Institute, this is an international Hindu-oriented group with headquarters in Honesdale, Pennsylvania. It was founded in 1971 by Sri Swami Rama (1925–), who has been teaching "the system of super-conscious meditation." Rama was born in India, "raised in the cave monasteries of the Himalayas," and became a monk as a young man. He came to the United States in 1969. Group branches operate in Canada, Western Europe, India, and Trinidad.

Hindu American Religious Institute

U.S. Hindu group based in western Pennsylvania. It was founded by Shakaracharya Swami Swanandashram around 1970 with the aim of spreading Hindu beliefs in the United States. The founder's doctrine follows: "That Unchangeable Eternal Consciousness you are, know thyself. We live to know what is the truth behind life. We hear the truth; we meditate upon the truth; and we realize the truth. That is the aim of life."

Hindu Mahasabha

Hindu revival movement formed in 1906 to unite ultra-orthodox Hindus, who oppose any reform, particularly of the caste system, and also object to the marriage of widows. It is also strongly opposed to both Islam and westernization. The movement has played a political role in fighting for Hindu nationalism.

His Name Ministries

U.S. PENTECOSTAL, evangelical group based in California. It was founded around 1970.

His Place

U.S. Christian FUNDAMENTALIST organization that operated in Los Angeles, California, in the early 1970s as part of the JESUS MOVEMENT. Its resident minister was known as Reverend Blessit.

Hoa Hao

Also known as Phat Giao Hoa Hao. Vietnamese MILLENARIAN movement founded in 1939 by Huyen Phu So (1919–1947), who was assassinated in 1947 by the Vietminh. The movement was puritanical, peasant-based, and centered in the western Mekong Delta. Its doctrine was based on a return to traditional Buddhism, with a minimum of theology and no ritual. When Ngo Din Diem came to power in Vietnam in 1954, the Hoa Hao controlled a whole province in South Vietnam. In March 1954, Diem defeated the Hoa Hao militia, but local organizations survived. In July 1956, the most important of the Hoa Hao military leaders, Ba Cut, was executed. [*See also* CAO DAI.]

Hohm

U.S. Hindu-occultist group founded in 1975 in New Jersey by Lee Lozowick. The leader awoke one morning in 1975 to find himself *aware*, *i.e.* able to transmit ultimate truths to his followers through words or through his very presence. He has offered his followers thoughts on gurus, God, existence, and the meaning of life.

"Holiness"

U.S. groups known by this name expect (or require) their members to experience: 1) conversion; 2) sanctification (in a lifestyle emphasizing modesty and simplicity); and 3) being filled with the Holy Spirit. Step 3 may consist of a vision, a dream, healing, or glossolalia (speaking in tongues).

Holistic Community

U.S. ANTHROPOSOPHICAL-occultist commune founded in Mt. Freedom, New Jersey, in the 1970s. Doctrine and practices are based on the teachings of Rudolf Steiner and Edgar Cayce, Prominent Occultist Figures. [*See also* ASSOCIATION FOR RESEARCH AND ENLIGHTENMENT.]

Holy Apostle Mission Church of South Africa

South African independent, indigenous ZIONIST church founded by Lucy S. Mofokeng in 1943. It is one of the few South African independent churches founded by a woman.

Source:
Sundkler, B. G. M. *Bantu Prophets in South Africa*. London: Oxford University Press, 1961.

Holy Catholic Apostolic Church in Zion

South African independent, indigenous ZIONIST church founded around 1920 by J. G. Phillips.

Holy Earth Assembly (THEA), The

U.S. neo-pagan church founded in the 1980s. It was created to perform "legal handfastings" (pagan weddings) and conduct training programs for pagan clergy.

Holy Feedback Church

U.S. group founded in California in the late 1960s. It was devoted to biofeedback.

Holy Ghost Church of East Africa

African independent Christian PENTE-COSTAL group that was formed in 1934 among the Kikuyu of Kenya. It arose out of the liberal wing of the Aroti revival movement, and forms part of the WAKORINO group of churches.

Holy Ghost Repair Service, Inc.

U.S. JESUS MOVEMENT center founded in the early 1970s in Denver, Colorado.

Holy Ground

Native American indigenous-Christian group started in 1921 among the Apache of New Mexico. Its doctrine emphasizes monotheism and combines New Testament figures, such as Jesus Christ, with traditional mythology.

Holy Order of Mans (HOOM)

U.S. Christian-occultist group using meditation techniques as well as "all true spiritual paths and teachers." Headquartered in San Francisco, it was founded in 1961 by Paul W. Blighton (?–1974), a retired electrician and minister, and a former member of AMORC. The Holy Order of Mans was officially incorporated in 1968. The Order presented itself as a way to revitalize Christianity. It claimed that its teachings are derived from ancient Christian mysteries, and offered its own version of the New Testament. In addition, it advocated the use of tarot cards, interpreted in a Christian way. Starting in 1979, the group's orientation changed, and it adopted a more traditional Christian outlook, and then an Eastern Orthodox belief system. In 1988 the group joined a Greek Orthodox organization and changed its name to Christ the Savior Brotherhood. The group had branches, including the Christian

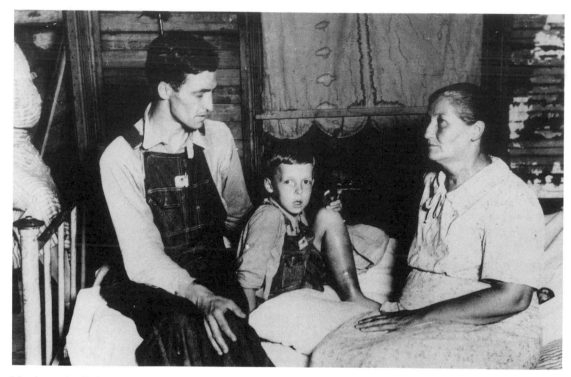

Members of a "holiness" sect pray for their ailing son, refusing medical help.

Community Bureau in Fort Worth, Texas, and centers in Europe and Latin America.

Holy Shankaracharya Order

U.S. Hindu monastic group based in western Pennsylvania, founded in 1968. This group also operates the Shankaracharya Pitham Sadhanalaya Ashram in Virginia. [*See also* YOGIRAJ.]

Holy Spirit Church of Zayun

African independent Christian PENTE-COSTAL group formed in 1962 by the Kikuyu of Kenya out of the Aroti revival movement. The Holy Spirit Church is

known as Maroti, members wear a red 'M' on their robes with red or blue turbans. The color green is forbidden. The church is part of the WAKORINO group of churches.

Holy Spirit Movement

Ugandan syncretistic religious-political movement founded in 1986 by Alice Lakwena ("Messenger," 1960–) of the Acholi people. She is known to her followers as "Mama Alice" and is the daughter of an Anglican Sunday school teacher. She founded the Movement after she reported receiving messages from the Holy Spirit. The group has been fighting the Ugandan government forces, and its members believe they are immune to bullets once annointed in a ritual ceremony. In 1987, the founder fled to Kenya. In 1989, her followers started collaborating with the Uganda's People's Army, led by Milton Obote, but suffered serious defeats. Some of the followers joined the LORD'S RESISTANCE ARMY, led by Alice Lakwena's cousin.

Holy Trinity Healing Church

African independent PENTECOSTAL church founded in Ghana in 1954 in a secession from the Roman Catholic Church.

Holy Zion Apostolic Zululand Church in South Africa

South African independent ZIONIST church founded in the early twentieth century.

Home of the Dharma

U.S. branch of the ARYA MAITREYA MANDALA Tibetan Buddhist order, founded in San Francisco in 1967.

Home of Truth Movement

Initially known as the Christian Science Home, this is a U.S. NEW THOUGHT group founded in 1888 in San Francisco by Annie Rix Militz, a student of Emma Curtis Hopkins. The group's doctrine emphasizes the possibilities of "Christian mind healing" to overcome illness and death. [*See also* HOPKINS ASSOCIATION, EMMA C.]

Source:
Braden, C. S. *Spirits in Rebellion*. Dallas: SMU Press, 1963.

Honbushin

First known as Mirokukai, this is a Japanese religion created following a schism in HONMICHI after the founder's death in 1958. Honmichi formed around the founder's second daughter, Tama, who claimed to be his true successor. Honbushin means True Constitution.

Honmichi-Kyo

First known as Tenri Kenkyukai (Tenri Study Association) and then Tenri Honmichi (Tenri True Way), this is a Japanese Shinto-inspired religion that grew out of the TENRIKYO movement. It was founded in 1925 by a Tenrikyo missionary, Ajijiro Onishi (1881–1958). In 1913 Onishi became convinced that he had received a divine revelation, which led him to claim that he should reign over the Tenrikyo movement. Its doctrine is MILLENARIAN, focusing on the figure of the founder.

Honmonbutsu-Rissho

Japanese Nichiren-inspired group founded in 1857 by Seifu Nagamatsu (1817–1890), who demanded in his teachings that each family recite the Lotus Sutra. [*See also* SOKA GAKKAI SOCIETY.]

Honor Oak Christian Fellowship Centre

British FUNDAMENTALIST Christian group founded in London around 1920 by T. Austin Sparks, a former Baptist. Sparks' writings later inspired THIS TESTIMONY, a U.S. Fundamentalist group. [*See also* HEPZEBAH HOUSE; THE LOCAL CHURCH; *and* WESTMORELAND CHAPEL.]

171

Hopkins Association, Emma C.

U.S. NEW THOUGHT group founded by Emma Curtis Hopkins (?–1925), a former CHRISTIAN SCIENCE leader, in 1886 in Chicago. In 1887, the Illinois Metaphysical College, also known as the Christian Science Theological Seminary, was started. The Association influenced many similar groups, such as the CHURCH OF RELIGIOUS PHILOSOPHY, HOME OF TRUTH MOVEMENT, and the UNITY SCHOOL OF CHRISTIANITY, whose founders were all students of Hopkins. In many ways, she was the mother of the New Thought movement. She also made special efforts to promote and empower women. Her ideas were carried on through JOY FARM and the Ministry of the High Walls.

House of God Which Is the Church of the Living God, the Pillar and Ground of Truth

Originally known as the Church of the Living God, the Pillar and Ground of Truth, this U.S. African American PENTECOSTAL group was founded in 1925 as a result of a schism in the CHURCH OF THE LIVING GOD (CHRISTIAN WORKERS FOR FELLOWSHIP). It ceased to exist in the 1950s.

House of God Which Is the Church of the Living God, the Pillar and Ground of Truth Without Controversy

U.S. African American PENTECOSTAL group founded in the 1930s as a result of a schism in the church of the living god, the pillar and ground of the truth.

House of Israel

Caribbean African American syncretistic group, started in the 1920s. Its members claim to be the heirs to ancient Jews.

House of Israel-Zion

Ghanaian syncretistic group founded in the 1970s by Aaron Ahomtre-Toakyirifah and inspired by the teachings of the UNITED ISRAEL WORLD UNION.

House of Judah

U.S. African American, BLACK HEBREWS group founded by William A. Lewis and based in Allegan County, Michigan. This group received much publicity in 1982 when a child died as a result of beating and its mother was convicted of involuntary manslaughter. In 1986 group leaders were convicted on charges of conspiring to enslave children. The group's doctrine calls for strong discipline and prescribes corporal punishment.

House of Prayer for All People

U.S. ADVENTIST, BRITISH-ISRAELIST group founded by William Lester Blessing (1900–1984) in 1941 in Denver, Colorado. According to Blessing, Yashua, the messiah, is already here and will make himself known before the year 2000 by establishing his kingdom on Earth. Blessing has also promoted ideas about the Great Pyramid, UFOs, and psychic phenomena. In the 1940s he distributed literature that was anti-Semitic, anti-black, and anti-Catholic.

Source:
Roy, J. L. *Apostles of Discord*. Boston: Beacon Press, 1953.

House of the Goddess

British neo-pagan group founded by Shan, a "coven mother," in London in 1985. Its aim is "to provide contact, support, study and celebration for anyone interested in Paganism, and in particular, the Craft." It is led by women, and "respect for the feminine is a priority."

House of the Lord

U.S. African American PENTECOSTAL group founded in 1925 in Detroit by W. H. Johnson. The group advocates a strict conduct code that forbids worldly amusements, fighting in wars, life insurance, and real estate ownership. Glossolalia, or speaking in tongues, is practiced.

House of the Lord

U.S. African American PENTECOSTAL group founded in the 1960s in Brooklyn, New York. Glossolalia (speaking in tongues) and other ecstatic displays are practiced.

Huna Research Associates

U.S. occultist group founded around 1950 by Max Freedom Long (?–1971). It claims to have knowledge of the magical practices of the Hawaiian Huna religion. Members study the teachings of Long, who claimed to have found connections between Huna and Christianity. [See also CHURCH OF BASIC TRUTH.]

I

"I Am"

Known originally as the Great I Am or Mighty I Am, this U.S. THEOSOPHICAL group was founded in the 1930s in Los Angeles by Guy W. Ballard (1878–1939). The founder, who worked as a spiritualist in the 1920s, reported that in 1930 near Mt. Shasta, California, he had a meeting with Master Saint-Germain, who gave him much arcane knowledge about karma and reincarnation. Departing from traditional Theosophical teachings, Ballard taught that the Ascended Masters (and Jesus of the New Testament) do not limit themselves to Central Asia, but visit the western United States. Ballard worked with his wife Edna (?–1971) and his son Donald in propagating these ideas. In the 1940s the group was convicted of mail fraud but won acquittal in the U.S. Supreme Court. The group headquarters are known as the Saint Germain Foundation, located on Mt. Shasta. [See also THEOSOPHY.]

I Am Ashram

North American Hindu group founded in 1970 by Sri Mata Atmananda of Canada.

Ibandla Lika Kristu (Church of Christ)

South African indigenous PENTECOSTAL church founded in 1910. Male members are required to have beards.

Ibandla Loku Kanya (Church of the Light)

South African indigenous church founded by Timothy Cekwane (1873–1950). Cekwane had been a preacher in the Presbyterian Church of Africa until he had a revelation following the appearance of Halley's Comet in 1910. Cekwane had stigmata on his hands; thus, blood is central to the symbolism and practices of the group. He was considered the Son of God by his followers.

Sources:

Sundkler, B. G. M. *Bantu Prophets in South Africa*. London: Oxford University Press, 1961.

———. *Zulu Zion and Some Swazi Zionists*. London: Oxford University Press, 1976.

Ibis Fraternity

U.S. occultist-spiritualist group founded in the 1940s by W. E. Butler. Practices emphasize communications with past lives.

Idapo Mimo Cherubim and Seraphim

African independent PENTECOSTAL group founded in Nigeria in 1954.

Identity Movement

Also known as Christian Identity, Christian Israel, or Covenant Congregations, this is a Christian movement based on a white supremacist interpretation of Biblical Mythology. It is a combination of U.S. Protestant FUNDAMENTALISM and

Guy W. Ballard, founder of the Theosophical group the Great I Am (now known simply as "I Am"), with his wife, Edna.

BRITISH ISRAELISM developed by Wesley Swift (?–1970) in the 1940s. This interpretation claims that the peoples of Northern Europe, referred to as Anglo-Saxons, are the true Children of Israel. According to the group's doctrine, Adam was the first "Israelite," or white man. Before Adam was created, God also created Africans, who the group believes, are without souls. Jews are considered the descendants of Cain, who is regarded as the child of Satan and Eve; and Africans are called pre-Adamic, "beasts of the field" and "mud people." The movement calls Jews "Edomites," who are responsible for historical and mythological catastrophe. They believe that the Jews were behind the French Revolution of 1789, the Russian Revolution of 1917, the two World Wars (1914–1918, 1939–1945), the Korean War (1950–1953), the Vietnam War (1965–1975), and the founding of the United Nations (1945). The group also believes that the U.S. government is part of a Satanic conspiracy aimed at enslaving white Christians, and that taxes and public schooling are part of this plot. The white Christians, they say, are the descendents of Adam, through Abel, and thus the only true children of God. They expect a global apocalypse very soon which will be a final battle between the white Christians and the Jews.

Unlike BRITISH ISRAELISM, which poses Anglo-Saxons as descendants of ancient Jews, Identity claims that ancient Jews were identical with Anglo-Saxons. Biblical references to Israel as the "chosen nation" are regarded as actual references to Anglo-Saxons. Groups associated with Identity theology have been explicitly anti-Semitic, blaming Jews for recent social and economic problems in the United States and promoting the idea of an Aryan nation based on racial purity. Identity groups are also known as Covenant Congregations. [*See also* ASSEMBLY OF CHRISTIAN SOLDIERS; CHRISTIAN CONSERVATIVE CHURCH OF AMERICA; CHRISTIAN DEFENSE LEAGUE; CHRISTIAN PATRIOTS DEFENSE LEAGUE (CPDL); THE CHURCH OF ISRAEL; THE CHURCH OF JESUS CHRIST; CHURCH OF JESUS CHRIST CHRISTIAN-ARYAN NATIONS; THE COVENANT, THE SWORD, THE ARM OF THE LORD (CSA); CRUSADE FOR CHRIST AND COUNTRY; THE MOUNTAIN CHURCH OF JESUS CHRIST THE SAVIOUR; NEW CHRISTIAN CRUSADE CHURCH; NEW HARMONY CHRISTIAN CRUSADE; THE ORDER; PATHFINDER CHURCH; SHEPHERD'S CHAPEL; *and* SWORD OF CHRIST GOOD NEWS MINISTRIES.]

Iesu Fukuin Kyodan (Gospel of Jesus Church)

Japanese indigenous Christian church founded in Tokyo in 1947. It has a branch in Brazil.

Iesu no Mitama Kyokai (Spirit of Jesus Church)

Japanese indigenous Christian church founded in the 1950s, with a branch in Brazil known as Igreja de Spirito Jesus.

Iglesia Apostolica de la Fe en Cristo Jesus (IAFCJ)

Guatemalan independent Christian church founded in 1952.

Iglesia Bando Evangelico Gedeon

Also known in the United States as the Gilgal Evangelistic International Church and as the Soldiers of the Cross of Christ Evangelical International Church. This is a Spanish-speaking PENTECOSTAL group founded as the Gideon Mission in the early 1920s in Havana, Cuba, by Ernest William Sellers, who died in 1953. The group follows Old Testament sabbath and dietary laws, and emphasizes prophecy and revelation in dreams. In the 1950s mission work was started in Latin America and the United States. In 1969, following the Cuban revolution, the group moved its headquarters to Miami, Florida.

Iglesia Catolica Nacional Guatemalteca

Guatemalan independent Catholic church formed in 1978 by secession from the Roman Catholic Church.

Iglesia Cristiana del Norte

Colombian Protestant PENTECOSTAL group founded around 1950 in Bogotà.

Iglesia Cristiana Pentecostes

Colombian Protestant PENTECOSTAL group founded around 1965.

Iglesia de Dios Cristiana Pentecostal

Argentinian Protestant PENTECOSTAL group founded in 1954 in Buenos Aires.

Iglesia de Dios Pentecostal

Also known as the Pentecostal Church of God, this is a Puerto Rican PENTECOSTAL group, founded in the 1930s. Healing and tithing are emphasized. [See also CONCILIO LATINO-AMERICANO DE LA IGLESIA DE DIOS PENTECOSTAL DE NEW YORK, INCORPORADO.]

Iglesia del Principe de Paz

Guatemalan independent PENTECOSTAL church formed in 1945. Its doctrine and practice emphasize possession, exorcism, and healing.

Iglesia Edificada de Jesucristo

Officially known as the Edified Church of Jesus Christ, this is a Philippine indigenous Protestant group founded in 1956.

Iglesia Espirita Veridica del Espiritu Santo

Philippine indigenous Christian spiritualist group founded in 1904.

Iglesia Evangelica del Emanuel

South American indigenous PENTECOSTAL group started in 1945 in Chile.

Iglesia Evangelica Israelita del Nuevo Pacto

Chilean ADVENTIST church founded in 1948.

Iglesia Evangelica Pentecostal de Chile

South American indigenous PENTECOSTAL group started in 1933. Although it was formed in Chile, it now has

177

branches in other South American countries.

Iglesia Filipinista

Officially known as the United Filipino Church, this is a Philippine indigenous Christian group, founded in 1962 by former members of the Roman Catholic Church.

Iglesia ni Jesucristo Bagong Jerusalem

Officially known as the Church of Jesus Christ New Jerusalem, this is an indigenous Philippine PENTECOSTAL church. It was formed in 1918 in Manila.

Iglesia Ng Dios Kay Kristo Jesus

Officially known as the Church of God in Jesus Christ, this independent Protestant group in the Philippines was started in 1922 in Manila.

Iglesia ni Cristo Manalista, Inc.

Officially known as the Church of Christ, this is a MILLENARIAN Christian group in the Philippines. It was founded in 1913 by Felix Manalo (1886–1963), a former Catholic who claimed a divine mission of recreating the original Christian church. It has been nationalistic in emphasis and has developed into a political force by directing members how to vote in national elections. The group has operated missions in North America and Europe since 1968.

Iglesia Sagrada Ng Lahi

Officially known as the Sacred Church of the Race, this is a Philippine indigenous syncretistic church, with a strong nationalist emphasis, combining Christian ritual and folk traditions.

Iglesia Sionista

Chilean ADVENTIST church founded in 1945 by secession from the SEVENTH DAY ADVENTISTS. It follows some Old Testament customs.

Iglesia Watawat Ng Lahi

Officially known as the Banner of the Race Church, this is a Philippine indigenous Christian-spiritualist group, formed in 1936 by former Roman Catholics. It is characterized by a nationalist ideology, and it combines an anti-Roman Catholic doctrine with a structure based on that of the Roman Catholic Church. Part of its doctrine is the belief in the eventual return of José Rizal, the Filipino national martyr.

Igreja Adventista de Promessa

Brazilian PENTECOSTAL group formed in 1958 by secession from the SEVENTH-DAY ADVENTISTS. This group, unlike the SEVENTH-DAY ADVENTISTS, keeps a Sunday Sabbath.

Igreja Brasileira

Brazilian Christian movement formed in 1961 by secession from the Roman Catholic Church.

Igreja Catolica Apostolic Brasileira (ICAB)

Brazilian Catholic movement formed in

1945 by secession from the Roman Catholic Church.

Igreja Expectante

Brazilian ROSICRUCIAN group started in the early twentieth century.

Imisi Jesu

African independent Christian PENTECOSTAL group founded in Nigeria in 1964.

Independent Assemblies of God, International

North American PENTECOSTAL group, developing out of the Scandinavian Assemblies of God in the United States, Canada, and Other Lands, which was formed in 1918, and out of similar groups in Scandinavian communities in the northern United States. The Independent Assemblies of God was formed in 1935, and the current name was adopted in 1948, following a schism over predictions of the coming millennium. The dissenting group became INDEPENDENT ASSEMBLIES OF GOD (UNINCORPORATED).

Independent Assemblies of God (Unincorporated)

North American PENTECOSTAL group founded in 1948 following a schism in the INDEPENDENT ASSEMBLIES OF GOD.

Independent Church of Filipino Christians

Philippine nationalist group created as a result of a schism in the PHILIPPINE INDEPENDENT CHURCH (PIC).

Independent Church of India

Indian indigenous Christian church started in 1930.

Independent Church of Jesus Christ of Latter-Day Saints

European branch of SONS AHMAN ISRAEL, a U.S. polygamist MORMON group.

Independent Fundamental Churches of America (IFCA)

U.S. Christian FUNDAMENTALIST group founded in 1922 by R. Lee Kirkland, under the name of the AMERICAN CONFERENCE OF UNDENOMINATED CHURCHES. This conference was superseded in 1930 by the Independent Fundamental Churches of America, founded in Cicero, Illinois.

Independent Fundamentalist Bible Churches

U.S. FUNDAMENTALIST group formed in 1965 by Marion H. Reynolds, W. E. Standridge, Henry Campbell, and Kenneth L. Barth. Its headquarters are in Los Angeles, California.

Independent Methodist Church of South Africa

South African indigenous church founded in 1904 in Makosini, near Mahamba, southern Swaziland, by Joel Msimang (?–1935), a former pastor in the Methodist mission.

Sources:

Sundkler, B. G. M. *Bantu Prophets in South Africa.* London: Oxford University Press, 1961.

————. *Zulu Zion and Some Swazi Zionists.* London: Oxford University Press, 1976.

Independent Old Catholic Church

U.S. OLD CATHOLIC group founded by Richard Bridges in California in the 1960s.

Independent Pentecostal Christian Church

Mexican indigenous PENTECOSTAL group founded in the early twentieth century.

Independent Spiritualist Association (ISA)

U.S. spiritualist organization founded in 1924 by Amanda Flowers, upon her withdrawal from the NATIONAL SPIRITUALIST ASSOCIATION OF CHURCHES. The ISA allows members to follow a belief in reincarnation. Two leading members, John Bunker and Clifford Bias, left the ISA to form the Spiritualist Episcopal Church.

Source:

Judah. J. S. *The History and Philosophy of the Metaphysical Movements in America.* Philadelphia: Westminster, 1967.

Independent Theosophical Society

THEOSOPHICAL organization founded in 1923 by T. H. Martyn, General Secretary of the Australian branch of the Theosophical Society.

Indian Pentecostal Church of God

Indian indigenous PENTECOSTAL church, begun among the Telugu in 1924.

Indian Shaker Church

Native American indigenous Christian movement started by John Slocum of the Squaxin people in 1881 in Puget Sound. Slocum received a revelation while in a coma, and in 1882 his wife Mary experienced a shaking paroxysm, regarded as a divine manifestation, through which John was cured of his illness. The movement replaced traditional shamanistic healing with shaking and dance rituals— with an overall Christian bent. Over the years it has spread on the U.S. Pacific coast.

Source:

Barnett, H. G. *Indian Shakers.* Carbondale: Southern Illinois University Press, 1957.

Infinite Way Society

North American dissident CHRISTIAN SCIENCE group founded in 1946 by Joel S. Goldsmith (1892–1964). In addition to healing practices, the group advocates contemplative meditation.

Inner Circle Kethra E'da Foundation

U.S. spiritualist group based in California. It was founded in 1945 by Mark

(d. 1969) and Irene Probert. Teachings consist of messages from "ancient masters" long dead, who communicated them to Mark Probert while he was in a trance.

Inner Circle of Enchantment, Inc. (ICE)

U.S. occultist NEW THOUGHT group founded by Sally Stern in New Jersey in the 1980s. It is devoted to psychic development through home study.

Inner Light Foundation

U.S. Christian occultist group founded in 1967 in Novato, California, by the spiritualist medium Betty Bethards. "The principle objective of the Inner Light Foundation is to engage in spiritual, educational, charitable, and scientific activities which foster, develop, and achieve in mankind an awareness of his unity with God, the Universal Consciousness."

Inner Peace Movement (IPM)

International occultist group founded by Francisco Coll, a former member of the SPIRITUAL FRONTIERS FELLOWSHIP, in 1964. The group teaches self-realization.

Source:
Scott, G. G. *Cult and Countercult. A Study of a Spiritual Growth Group and a Witchcraft Order.* Westport, Conn.: Greenwood, 1980.

Inner Powers Society

U.S. NEW THOUGHT group founded by Alfred Pritchard in Yucca Valley, California, in the 1950s. Its doctrine empha-

sized the coming of a "New Age." The group, which operated mainly by correspondence, ceased to exist in the 1970s.

Insight Meditation Society

U.S. Buddhist-inspired group started around 1980 by Joseph Goldstein, Catherine Ingram, and Sharon Salzberg. It is based in Barre, Massachusetts. The main practice is "mindfulness meditation."

Institute for Cultural Research

British occultist group founded in 1965 in Coombe Springs, P.D. Ouspensky's estate in England, as the Society for Understanding Fundamental Ideas (SUFI) by John Godolphin Bennett (1897–1974) and Idries Shah (1924–). Shah, an Indian of Afghan descent, has been one of the most visible promoters of Sufism in the West since the 1950s. The Institute is now based at Langston Green, England. [*See also* GURDJIEFF GROUPS.]

Institute for Planetary Synthesis (IPS)

Swiss occultist group founded in 1981 in Geneva by Rudolf Schneider (1932–). Its doctrines have been strongly influenced by the teachings of Alice Bailey of the LUCIS TRUST, as well as by the ideas of the WORLD TEACHER TRUST. The group proclaims a message of imminent salvation and world change.

Institute for Religious Development

U.S. GURDJIEFF GROUP founded by Wilhelm A. Nyland (?–1975). Nyland was an associate of Gurdjieff from 1924 to 1949 and then went to the United States to spread Gurdjieff's message. Until 1975 Nyland was the leader of the Institute, which is based near New York City.

Institute for Research on the Dissemination of Human Knowledge

U.S. group devoted to promoting the ideas of Idries Shah. It was founded in the late 1960s in Boulder, Colorado. [See also INSTITUTE FOR CULTURAL RESEARCH; and SUFI ORDER IN THE WEST.]

Institute for the Comparative Study of History, Philosophy, and the Sciences

Group founded in 1946 by John Godolphin Bennett (1897–1974) and other disciples of P. D. Ouspensky. It is based in Coombe Springs, Ouspensky's estate in England. Bennett was later involved in SUBUD, but in 1968 he converted to the Roman Catholic Church. [See also CLAYMONT COURT; and GURDJIEFF GROUPS.]

Institute for the Harmonious Development of the Human Being

U.S. GURDJIEFF GROUP founded and directed by E. J. Gold in California. Gold's teachings are eclectic, using ideas and practices from many traditions. The group's core beliefs include reincarnation, spiritual evolution, and a search for "control over the soul's destiny," as well as belief in Atlantis and a spaceship that saved humanity after Atlantis was flooded. Gold claims to be the direct successor to Gurdjieff, and also to be a Sufi. Also, the group has been referred to as Shakti.

Source:
Westley, F. *The Complex Forms of the Religious Life*. Chico, Calif.: Scholars Press, 1983.

Institute of Cosmic Wisdom

U.S. occultist group founded by Clark Wilkerson in the late 1940s in Playa del Ray, California. Its doctrine combines NEW THOUGHT with HUNA magic.

Institute of Mentalphysics

U.S. occultist group founded in 1927 in Los Angeles by Edwin John Dingle (1881–1972), also known as Ding Le Mei, who claimed to have studied the ancient wisdom of the "Aryans" in Tibet. The group is devoted to meditation, yoga, and other spiritual practices, which are supposed to lead "to the highest development of the total person, body, mind, and spirit, one is evolutionarily able to achieve."

Institute of Pyramidology

British offshoot of JEHOVAH'S WITNESSES founded in 1940 in London by Adam Rutherford. Relying on the teachings of Charles Taze Russell, it claims that the Great Pyramid of Egypt is a major source of occult knowledge, or "The Bible in Stone."

Instituto Para el Desarrollo Armonico del Hombre

Argentinian GURDJIEFF GROUP founded in the 1970s in Mar del Palata.

Integral Center of Self-Abidance (ICSA)

Formerly known as the Intercosmic Center of Spiritual Associations and the International Center for Self-Analysis, this is a U.S. Hindu group, founded in 1958 by Shri Brahmananda Sarasvati and Rammurti Sriram Mishra. Based in North Syracuse, New York, it has been directed by Srimati Margaret Coble. ICSA doctrine emphasizes "the One Presence-Power-Reality." It "presents a clear message of the unity and common spirituality of humanity, summed up by the universal statement, I AM."

Integral Yoga Institute (IYI)

International Hindu group, with headquarters in the United States, founded by Sri Swami Satchidananda, also known as Narayan, who was a disciple of Sivananda. Swami Satchidananda came to the United States in 1966 and then founded the Institute in San Francisco, California. The Swami has advocated the use of yoga techniques, which include hatha (physical posture, breathing, and deep relaxation) raja (concentration and meditation), japa (repeating a mantra), karma (selfless actions), bhakti (devotional practices), and jnana (self-inquiry). Branches, sometimes known as Satchidananda Ashram-Yogaville, have operated in Sri Lanka, Australia, Europe, and Africa. [See also DIVINE LIFE SOCIETY; and SIVENANDA YOGA VEDANTA CHURCH.]

Interfaith Fellowship

U.S. occultist Christian group, based in New York State. It was founded in the 1980s by Jon Mundy, a Methodist minister, and Diane Berke. It is devoted to teaching *A Course in Miracles*, published in 1975 by Helen Schucman, who claimed to have been the medium for a divine revelation. The Fellowship offers regular worship services.

Interfaith Ministries for Renewal

U.S. FUNDAMENTALIST group started as part of the JESUS MOVEMENT around 1970 in Des Moines, Iowa. It is active in media and outreach activities.

Interfaith Temple or Interfaith, Inc.

U.S. Jewish syncretistic group based in New York City, founded by Joseph H. Gelberman in the early 1970s. Its doctrine combines Jewish beliefs and practices with Hindu and THEOSOPHICAL concepts. It operates the Institute of Personal Religion, the New Light Temple, and the New Seminary, which trains Interfaith ministers as well as rabbis. The group has worked with NEW THOUGHT organizations. [See also TREE OF LIFE.]

International Association for Liberal Christians and Religious Freedom

International liberal Christian group founded in the United States in 1910 as the International Council of Unitarians and other Liberal Religious Thinkers and Workers. It was renamed the International Congress of Free Christians and other Religious Liberals in 1930. The current name was adopted in the 1950s.

International Babaji Kriya Yoga Sangam

International Hindu group founded in 1952. It is "guided by Yogi S.A.A. Ramaiah, disciple of Master Babaji Nagaraj of the Himalayas. Kriya Yoga involves hatha, kundalini, mantra, dhyana, pranayama, and bhakti yogas." [*See also* HAIDAKHAN SAMAJI.]

International Christian Churches

PENTECOSTAL group with members in Hawaii and the Philippines. It was founded in 1943 by Franco Manuel, former member of the DISCIPLES OF CHRIST CHURCH in Hawaii.

International Christian Ministries

U.S. FUNDAMENTALIST, evangelical group, which was started as part of the JESUS MOVEMENT in 1969 by Duane Peterson. It is based in southern California.

International Churches of Christ

International FUNDAMENTALIST organization founded in Boston in 1980 and developed from the BOSTON CHURCH OF CHRIST. It is the major expression of what has been called the SHEPHERDING MOVEMENT, or "discipleship," which includes the BODY OF CHRIST, CHRISTIAN GROWTH MINISTRIES, and CHRISTIAN RESTORATION MINISTRIES. The Church has operated affiliated groups in the United States, Latin America, and Europe. [*See also* CROSSROADS CHURCHES OF CHRIST; LONDON CHURCH OF CHRIST; *and* NEW YORK CHURCH OF CHRIST.]

International Church of Spiritual Vision, Inc.

Also known as Western Prayer Warriors, this U.S. PENTECOSTAL, ADVENTIST, and occultist group was founded in the 1960s by Dallas Turner, known in his singing career as Nevada Slim. The group keeps in contact with its members mostly by mail.

International Community of Christ

U.S. Christian THEOSOPHIST organization founded by Gene Savoy (1927–) in 1957. It offers correspondence courses and other materials through the mail explaining its message of a New Christianity. The message includes claims about "nuclear energy in the brain," "the mystery of the Essences," and "electromagnetic force fields." The organization also offers a *Decoded New Testament* and the "oral traditions of the Essenes." It operates the Jamilian University of the Ordained in Reno, Nevada.

International Deliverance Churches

U.S. PENTECOSTAL group founded by W. V. Grant and based in Dallas. The group focuses on the practice of faith healing.

International Evangelism Crusades

International PENTECOSTAL group founded in 1959 by Frank E. Stranges. The group's doctrine includes belief in extraterrestrial contacts. It has had branches in North America and Asia.

International General Assembly of Spiritualists

U.S. Christian spiritualist organization founded in New York City in 1931 and incorporated in Buffalo, New York, in 1936 by Arthur Ford (1897–1971). The group's doctrine emphasizes prayer, healing, and spiritual development. Branches have operated in Asia and Africa.

International Hebrew Christian Alliance of America

U.S. HEBREW CHRISTIAN organization founded in 1925.

International Metaphysical Association

International independent CHRISTIAN SCIENCE group founded in 1955. Disputing the authority of the Church of Christ, Scientist, it is officially committed to the original teachings of Mary Baker Eddy.

International Order of St. Luke the Physician

International Christian NEW THOUGHT group founded in 1946 by John Gayner Banks. Members are devoted to spiritual healing.

International Pentecostal Assemblies

U.S. PENTECOSTAL group founded in 1936 through the merger of the National and International Pentecostal Missionary Union and the Association of Pentecostal Assemblies. Members believe in healing and in a personal devil. The doctrine is similar to that of the CHURCH OF GOD (CLEVELAND, TENNESSEE). Doctrine used to include a ban on military service.

International Pentecostal Church of Christ

U.S. PENTECOSTAL group founded by John Stroup in 1917 in Kentucky. Starting in the 1920s and until 1934, it was united with the Full Gospel Pentecostal Church of Maryland and the United Pentecostal Association. Similar in doctrine to the CHURCH OF GOD (CLEVELAND, TENNESSEE). In 1976 it became part of the INTERNATIONAL PENTECOSTAL HOLINESS CHURCH.

International Pentecostal Holiness Church

U.S. PENTECOSTAL organization officially founded in 1900 in Fayetteville, North Carolina, by A. B. Crumpler, a former Methodist preacher. In 1911 the group merged with the FIRE-BAPTIZED HOLINESS ASSOCIATION. Its credo emphasized glossolalia (speaking in tongues) as a major practice and proof of baptism by the Holy Spirit.

International School of Yoga and Vedanta

Also known as the Yoga Research Foundation, this is a U.S. Hindu group founded in 1969 in Miami by Swami Jyotir Maya Nanda (1931–), who studied under Swami Sivananda Saraswati.

A. C. Bhaktivedanta Swami Prabhupada, spiritual leader of the Hare Krishna movement in San Francisco.

International Society for Krishna Consciousness (ISKCON)

Known all over the world by the popular name Hare Krishna, this is a Hindu revival movement that has reached the West and was formally organized in the United States in 1966. It was founded by A. C. Bhaktivedanta Swami Prabhupada, who was born in Calcutta as Abhay Charan De in 1896, arrived in the United States in 1965, and died in 1977 in Vrndavana, India.

ISKCON doctrine is based on the *Bhagavad-Gita*, as interpreted by Bhaktivedanta. This interpretation emphasizes the priority of Krishna, who is defined as the Supreme Personality of the Godhead. ISKCON rituals are classified as *bhakti*, or devotion. Followers believe that "the most perfect action is to serve Krishna." This sentence sums up the *bhakti* spirit. The holy name of Krishna must be pronounced 1,728 times a day. The chant, or *mantra*, for which members of the group have become known, is: *Hare Krishna, Hare Krishna, Krishna, Krishna, Hare, Hare, Hare Rama, Hare Rama, Rama Rama, Hare, Hare.* The group's doctrine reflects the appearance of a revitalization movement that started in the nineteenth century in Bengal within the traditional Caitanya (Gaudiya) Vaisnavism of India. According to this tradition, the last incarnation of Krishna occurred in 1486 in India,

Statement of beliefs from the International Society of Krishna Consciousness:

The International Society for Krishna Consciousness is a denomination of the Guadiya Vaishnava faith, a devotional tradition based on the teachings of *Bhagavad-Gita* and the Bhagavat Purana (Srimad Bhagavatam). The Vedic scriptures state that spiritual life begins when one inquires into the nature of the absolute truth, the Supreme Godhead. Gaudiya Vaishnavas are monotheists and know the personality of Godhead as Krishna, the all-attractive, although it is recognized that the Supreme has unlimited names such as Rama, Buddha, Vishnu, Jehova, Allah, etc. The goal of Gaudiya Vaisnavism is to re-establish our love for the Supreme Godhead.

The Vedas also enjoin that the understanding of the self, as being nonmaterial or spiritual by nature, is the preliminary stage of realization of the absolute truth. One can clearly understand knowledge of self-realization and the Supreme only by accepting the guidance of a genuine spiritual master, just as one learns the essence of any subject from a perfected practitioner.

The congregational chanting of the maha-mantra, Hare Kirshna, Hare Krishna, Krishna Krishna, Hare Hare, Hare Rama, Hare Rama, Rama Rama, Hare Hare as promoted by Shri Chaitanya, is accepted as the most effective means of self-purification in this age. The mantra has been described by saints in the tradition as a prayer to the Lord asking, "Please Lord, engage me in your service." Devotees may accept formal initiation into the chanting of the Holy Name by vowing to abstain from intoxication, gambling, illicit sexual connections, and the eating of meat, fish or eggs. They also vow at that time to chant a prescribed number of mantras each day.

when Caitanya appeared. A succession of disciples then began, down to Sri Srimad Bhakitisiddhanta Sarasvati Gosvami Maharaja in the early twentieth century, the guru who initiated Bhaktivedanta in 1933. ISKCON's vision of the ideal society includes an agrarian economy based on the protection of cows, and the division of society into four castes.

The rules of conduct order disciples to abstain from all intoxicants (tobacco, alcohol, coffee, tea, narcotics, and soft drugs), as well as meat, fish, and eggs. All eating is considered an act of worship. Sex is allowed only for procreation within marriage. Members adopt Sanskrit names that express devotion.

Members are distinguished by their distinctive dress and grooming, which include saffron robes, color marks on their faces, and, for men, shaved heads except for a topknot (by which Krishna will pick them up when the world ends). The group is known for *sankirtan*, or ritual begging, and has often been accused of deceptive practices in its fundraising activities, which can be observed in some of the world's largest cities. The group has sent missionaries to India and has established centers there, but most of its members are Westerners.

In 1972 an ISKCON temple opened in Mayapurand, India. The Krishna Balaram Mandir in Vrndavana, India, which is now the official world center, opened in 1973.

In 1972 Srita Prabhupada formed a Governing Body Commission (GBC) to help manage ISKCON. Beginning with twelve members, the GBC had thirty-four members in 1994. Following the founder's death in 1977, there were a number of schisms and defections, which included members of the GBC. The North American branches of ISKCON established close contacts with immigrant Hindus in the 1980s.

Sources:

Daner, F. *The American Children of Krishna*. New York: Holt, Rinehart & Winston, 1975.

Hubner, J., and Gruson, L. *Monkey on a Stick: Murder, Madness and the Hare Krishnas*. San Diego: Harcourt Brace Jovanmovich, 1988.

Judah, J. S. *Hare Krishna and the Counter-culture*. New York: Wiley, 1974.

Rochford, E. B. Jr. *Hare Krishna in America*. New Brunswick, N.J.: Rutgers University Press, 1985.

Shinn, L. D. *The Dark Lord: Cult Images and the Hare Krishnas in America*. Philadelphia: Westminster Press, 1987.

International Society of Divine Love

International Hindu group founded in 1980 by Prakashanand H. D. Saraswati (1929–), known as "His Divinity."

"Spending most of his lifetime in the isolated retreats of Braj (in India), Shree Swamiji, realizing the need of the souls, has introduced his visual experiences to the world, discriminately explaining all the five sciences of matter, mind, soul, God, and divine love. Thus his teachings hold the authentic originality of the Ancient Indian Scriptures and his method of meditation is unbelievably effective." Branches of this group have operated in the United States, Europe, and New Zealand.

International Society of Divine Revelation

Latin American Hindu-oriented group organized as a monastic order. It was founded in the 1960s by Guru Devananda Mahraj in São Paolo, Brazil.

International Spiritualist Federation

International spiritualist organization based in London, with members in forty nations.

International Yoga Fellowship in America

U.S. Hindu group founded by Eddie Brahmananda Shapiro, who was "empowered by Paramahansa Satyananda" during a trip to India in 1968.

Invisible Church

Also known as Invis, this is a South African FUNDAMENTALIST communal group, founded in Durban in the 1970s by Carel Cronje.

Invitation à la Vie Intense (IVI)

International Christian occultist healing group founded in 1983 in Paris by Yvonne Trubert (1922–). "Pray-Love-Heal" is the group's slogan and goal. Its doctrine combines Roman Catholic elements with Hindu ideas of reincarnation. Group members are said to be reincarnations of early Christians. Healing consists of "harmonizing the three bodies: physical, energetic, and astral," and members claim cures of all known diseases. Group branches have operated in Western Europe.

Ishvara (Lifewave)

British Eastern-inspired group started in the 1970s. It is led by John Herbert Yarr, known as "Divine Master Ishvara" or "the perfect master Yarr." The group's doctrine predicts the imminent coming of the Age of Aquarius.

Islam-Is

Indonesian early-twentieth century syncretistic movement that combined Islamic and Christian ideas. [See also KRISLAM; and KRISLAPI.]

Israeli School of UPK

U.S. "black Israelite" group, based in New York City. Members claim that African Americans are the descendants of the mythological tribe of Judah, and that those known as Jews today have usurped their identity from its rightful owners.

Israelitas del Nuevo Pacto Universal ("Israelites of the New Universal Covenant")

Peruvian independent indigenous church started in the 1950s among the Aymara Indians. In 1989 some members of the group migrated to Israel, where they were granted citizenship after converting to Judaism.

"Israelites"

South African independent, MILLENARIAN separatist group founded in 1918 by Enoch Mgijima (1858–1928), a former member of the CHURCH OF GOD AND SAINTS OF CHRIST, who was excommunicated by the Church for preaching end-of-the-world visions. His followers settled in a colony in Bullhoek, near Queenstown. The doctrine was Old Testament–oriented. Mgijima claimed to have been chosen as prophet by the God of Israel and sent to his people. The New Testament was regarded as a fiction created by the whites. The Israelites were Jehova's elect, fighting for land against the Midianites and the Philistines, and He would deliver them from bondage and let them crush the Europeans. When the South African military approached the colony on May 24, 1921, Mgijima told his followers that they were immune to bullets. The outcome was that 117 Israelites were killed. The movement survived this tragedy as well as the death of its founder.

Source:

Sundkler, B. G. M. *Bantu Prophets in South Africa*. London: Oxford University Press, 1961.

Israel Soodo Won (Israel Monastery)

Korean Christian monastic group founded in the 1940s by Paik Moon Kim, a self-proclaimed messiah. Sun Myung Moon, the founder of the UNIFICATION CHURCH, is reported to have spent six months in this group in 1945.

Israel Universal Divine Spiritual Churches of Christ

U.S. association of African American spiritualist churches in New Orleans, Louisiana, founded by Ernest J. Johnson in the 1960s.

Istituto Mater Boni Consilii

Italian traditionalist Roman Catholic group, which split from the FRATERNITY OF ST. PIUS X in the 1980s.

Italian Pentecostal Assemblies of God

U.S. PENTECOSTAL group founded by John Santamaria and his son Rocco, who started evangelical work among Italian immigrants in 1904. The group was organized in 1907 and later merged with the UNORGANIZED ITALIAN CHRISTIAN CHURCHES OF NORTH AMERICA to form the CHRISTIAN CHURCH OF NORTH AMERICA.

Ittoen ("Garden of Light")

Japanese religion started after World War II by Nishida Tenko. Tenko was elected to the upper chamber of the Japanese Diet in 1947.

Izumo-Taishakyo

Japanese religion started in 1873, growing out of the main Shinto tradition.

J

Jain Meditation International Center

North American Jain-inspired group founded in New York City in 1975 by Gurudev Shree Chitrabhanu (1923–), a former Jain monk who emigrated to the United States in 1971. Devoted to spreading the ancient Jain tradition of India in the West, it is connected with JAIN SAMAJ EUROPE.

Source:
Jaini, P. S. *The Jaina Path of Purification.* Berkeley: University of California Press, 1979.

Jain Samaj Europe

International group dedicated to spreading the Jain tradition in Europe, founded by Natubhai Shah in 1988. It is connected with the JAIN MEDITATION INTERNATIONAL CENTER.

Jala Sangha

U.S. Hindu-oriented group founded in 1970 in Redondo Beach, California, by Yogi Yukteswar Sri Bbajhan.

Jamaa ("Family")

Zairian separatist Catholic movement started in the 1940s in the Katanga province of what was then known as the Belgian Congo. Formed by Placide Tempels, a Belgian Franciscan priest, it became officially independent of the Roman Catholic Church in 1953. Its doctrine emphasizes the importance of the nuclear family.

Source:
Fabian, J. *Jamaa: A Charismatic Movement in Katanga.* Evanston: Northwestern University Press, 1971.

Jappa Tabernacle

U.S. FUNDAMENTALIST, PENTECOSTAL group connected with BRITISH ISRAELISM. It was founded by Otis B. Read in Baltimore in the 1940s.

Jean-Michel et Son Équipe (Jean-Michel and His Team)

International Christian PENTECOSTAL group founded by Jean-Michel Cravanzola (1945–) in Switzerland in 1971. The founder moved to the United States in 1982, after being convicted of fraud in Lausanne in 1979. Group doctrine rejects belief in the Trinity and promotes faith healing. Branches have operated in France, Switzerland, and North America. The Swiss branch has used the name Action et Compassion.

Jehovah Jireh Christ Church

African independent PENTECOSTAL group founded in Nigeria in 1958. Its doctrine prohibits the use of medicine.

Jehovah's Witnesses

Officially known, since 1939, as the Watchtower Bible and Tract Society, the International Bible Students Association, or Jehovah's Christian Witnesses, it was incorporated in 1884 as the Zion's Watch

A soloist lifts her voice in prayer during an annual convention of Jehovah's Witnesses.

192

Tower Tract Society, and is sometimes known as Russellites or as Watch Tower Society (WTS). It is a Christian AD-VENTIST group with worldwide activities, headquartered in Brooklyn, New York, since 1909. The center in Brooklyn is known as Bethel. The Witnesses' governing body has twelve members. Officially, Witnesses regard their group as a world religion separate from all other traditions, but they still claim to be the true Christians. They often refer to themselves as Bible Students.

The history of the Witnesses starts with the work of Charles Taze Russell. Born in 1852 in Pittsburgh, Pennsylvania, to a family of Presbyterian and Congregational background, Russell in 1870 joined an ADVENTIST group that followed the ideas of Jonas Wendell. Wendell predicted that 1874 would be the time of the Second Coming, but Russell believed that the presence of God on Earth began in 1874.

In 1879 Russell published the first issue of *Zion's Watch Tower and Herald of Christ's Presence*, later to become the *Watchtower*, which became the organ of a movement known as "Millenial Dawn Bible Students." In 1881 the Zion's Watch Tower Tract Society was founded, and members were known as Bible Students.

According to Russell's doctrine, history is divided into three periods: from the Biblical Creation to the Biblical Flood; from the Flood to Jesus Christ's death; and from Jesus Christ's death to 1914, the date of salvation for the 144,000 "elect."

In 1886 Russell revealed his timetable for the millennium. According to this plan, the Harvest period or the "millenial dawn period" (1874–1914) would end with the "battle of Armageddon," the establishment of God's direct rule on Earth, and the restoration of mankind to perfection. During the millenial dawn period the Jews would return to Palestine and gentile governments would be overthrown. The coming of World War I in 1914 was considered a confirmation of the prophecies; but as God's direct rule on Earth did not start, the date was revised to 1918. Russell died in 1916. Witnesses claim, however, that in 1914 Jesus Christ did indeed start a period of "invisible rule" on Earth.

Joseph Franklin Rutherford (1869–1941), known as "Judge," succeeded the founder as leader. In 1920 he pronounced what has become a well-known Witness slogan, "Millions now living will never die." He kept annoucing dates for the end of the world, first 1920, then 1925, and then 1940. In 1931 the Watch Tower Bible and Tract Society became officially known as Jehovah's Witnesses. It experienced a significant revival during the Great Depression in the United States. In 1969 Nathan Homer Knorr (1905–1977), Rutherford's successor as spiritual leader of the group, stated that the Millennium of Christ's reign on Earth would start in 1975. Later, the date of October 2, 1984, was proclaimed. Witnesses believed that the End would come before the generation who saw the events of 1914 passed away. Frederick W. Franz (1894–1990) served as President between 1977 and 1990. Since 1990 the President of the Watchtower Society, who is the only Witness allowed to interpret the Bible, has been Milton Henschel. In 1995 specific references to timetables were discouraged for the first time.

The Witnesses' beliefs are based on the following system of chronology:

11,025 B.C. Animals are created.
4025 B.C. (Autumn) Man is created.

2370 B.C.   The entire human race, except for eight individuals, is drowned in the Flood.

607 B.C.   Jerusalem falls and the Time of the Gentiles begins.

455 B.C.   A decree is issued to rebuild Jerusalem's walls and start the seventy weeks of Daniel. (Daniel 9:24 is a proclamation by the Angel Gabriel to the effect that seventy weeks will suffice to restore Jerusalem. In Witness lore, the seventy weeks extend from 455 B.C. through A.D. 36.)

A.D. 29   Baptism of Christ.

A.D. 33   Death of Christ.

A.D. 36   End of the seventy weeks of Daniel.

A.D. 1914   End of the Time of the Gentiles and start of the Time of the End.

A.D. 1918   Christ comes to his temple for judgment.

A.D. 1919   Babylon falls and the new nation of Jehovah's Witnesses is born.

A.D. 1975   The 6,000 years of human existence end.

"It is the belief of Jehovah's Witnesses that they adhere to the oldest religion on earth: the worship of Almighty God as revealed in his Bible as Jehovah. All of Jehovah's Witnesses are considered to be ministers of the gospel and to have no human leader." The Witnesses' doctrine claims to be faithful to the Bible, as shown by the use of the name Jehovah for the deity, and by their belief in a literal Kingdom of God (their temples are known as Kingdom Hall). They celebrate the Lord's evening meal once a year on the date corresponding to the Jewish Nissan 14. Unleavened bread and red wine are passed around "in symbol of Christ's sinless body and sacrificial blood." Witnesses reject the notion of the Christian Trinity and the idea of an immortal soul; they believe in baptism by immersion, do not participate in politics, never vote, and refuse blood transfusions. Numerous legal cases have been brought in various countries over this last refusal, and courts have ordered blood transfusions as part of medical treatment to children of Witnesses. Members describe the Roman Catholic Church as the "Whore of Babylon" and regard the United Nations as especially dangerous and evil.

Witnesses' relations with secular authorities have often been strained, sometimes with serious and tragic consequences. Under the Nazi regime in Germany, Witnesses were subject to imprisonment and extermination. Because of their refusal to bear arms or salute national flags, Witnesses have been subjected to legal actions, persecution, and imprisonment in many countries, including Cyprus, Greece, Malawi, Yugoslavia, China, Poland, Zaire, and Israel. Since the late 1960s, there have been reports of massacres in Malawi, because Witnesses refused to join the ruling party. Only in 1974 were legal restrictions on the distribution of Witness publications removed in Portugal, and only in 1981 in Belgium. In 1986 Jehovah's Witnesses were officially banned in Zaire. In June 1989 Jehovah's Witnesses were officially expelled from Ghana. During 1995 and 1996 Witnesses in Singapore were sentenced and fined for "membership in an illegal organization"; since 1972 Jehovah's Witnesses have been declared an illegal organization there.

Since World War II Jehovah's Witnesses have experienced a significant growth in numbers and activity, and they are now found in most countries of the world. Their best-known publications, *The Watchtower* and *Awake!*, were said in 1987 to have a combined distribution of 23 million. They distribute literature and proselytize by visiting people at their homes.

The British branch of Jehovah's Witnesses, founded 1914, is known as the International Bible Students Association. [*See also* ASSOCIATION FRANCAISE DES LIBRES ÉTUDIANTS DE LA BIBLE; BACK TO THE BIBLE WAY; BEREAN BIBLE STUDENTS CHURCH; BIBLE FELLOWSHIP UNION; INSTITUTE OF PYRAMIDOLOGY; KITAWALA; LAYMEN'S HOME MISSIONARY MOVEMENT; PASTORAL BIBLE INSTITUTE; PROVIDENCE INDUSTRIAL MISSION; WATCHTOWER; *and* WATCH TOWER MOVEMENT.]

Sources:

Beckford, J. *The Trumpet of Prophecy: A Sociological Study of Jehovah's Witnesses.* Oxford: Blackwell, 1975.

Botting, H., and Botting, G. *The Orwellian World of the Jehovah's Witnesses.* Toronto: University of Toronto Press, 1984.

Penton, J. *Apocalypse Delayed.* Toronto: University of Toronto Press, 1985.

Rogerson, A. *Millions Now Living Will Never Die.* London: Constable, 1969.

Sterling, C. W. *The Witnesses.* Chicago: Henry Regnery, 1975.

Stroup, H. H. *The Jehovah's Witnesses.* New York: Columbia University Press, 1945.

Jesu-No-Mitama-Kyokai ("Church of the Spirit of Jesus")

Japanese indigenous sabbatarian and MILLENARIAN Christian group, founded in 1940 by Jun Inai (?–1970). The group rejects belief in the Trinity and practices glossolalia (speaking in tongues).

Jesus Christ Light and Power

U.S. JESUS MOVEMENT organization, in existence in Southern California in the early 1970s.

Jesus Christ the Name above Every Name

Filipino independent evangelical Christian group started in the 1970s.

Jesus Divine Healing Church

African indigenous PENTECOSTAL group founded in Ghana in 1952 by former members of the Roman Catholic Church.

Jesus Family (Ye-su Chia T'ing)

Chinese indigenous Christian communal church founded in 1921 and suppressed by the Communist regime in the early 1950s.

Jesus Family (Ye-su Chia T'ing)

Chinese indigenous Christian church, possibly a revival of the group named above, founded in Shandong province in the 1970s and suppressed by the Communist regime in early 1982. Its thirty-seven members were given prison sentences ranging from two to twelve years.

Jesus Fellowship Church

British PENTECOSTAL, FUNDAMENTALIST group started in 1969 by Noel Stanton.

Many of its members have lived in communal households.

Jesus for Africa

South African interracial FUNDAMENTALIST group started in the 1980s.

Jesus Mobilization Committee

U.S. FUNDAMENTALIST Christian commune, in existence in the early 1970s in Marin County, California, as part of the JESUS MOVEMENT.

Jesus Movement

Also known as Jesus Children, Jesus People, Jesus Revolution, or Jesus Freaks, this was a movement made up of FUNDAMENTALIST Christian groups, many of them communal, that sprang up in the United States and Western Europe between the late 1960s and the late 1970s. At the height of its success, the movement was said to number 200 communes in California alone.

Only a few of the groups started in this period survived past the mid-1970s, among them the Children of God (now THE FAMILY), the CHURCH OF BIBLE UNDERSTANDING, and the NORTHEAST KINGDOM COMMUNITY CHURCH. [See also CHRISTIAN WORLD LIBERATION FRONT; and KOINONIA COMMUNITY.]

Sources:

Ellwood, R. S. *One Way: The Jesus Movement and Its Meaning.* Englewood Cliffs, N.J.: Prentice-Hall, 1973.

Richardson, J. T., Stewart, M. W., and Simmonds, R. B. *Organized Miracles.* New Brunswick, N.J.: Transaction Books, 1979.

Streiker, L. D. *The Jesus Trip.* Nashville, Tenn.: Abingdon Press, 1971.

Jesus People U.S.A.

U.S. JESUS MOVEMENT communal group, founded in 1969 by John and Dawn Herven, which was based in the Grace Tabernacle in Chicago.

Jetsun Sakya Center (JSC)

U.S. Tibetan Buddhist group originating with the Ngor sect of the Tibetan Sakya School. It was founded in 1977 by Dezhung Rinpoche and has been based in New York City. Practices include meditation and yoga. [See also VAJRADHATU.]

Jeungsan

Also known as Jeung-san gyo or U-da gyo, this is an indigenous Korean movement. Founded in the mid-nineteenth century, it has developed into about six branches.

Jewish Science, Society of

Also known as the Society for Applied Judaism, this is a U.S. group developed as a Jewish equivalent of CHRISTIAN SCIENCE. It was founded in 1922 by Morris Lichtenstein (1890–1938) in New York City. The founder was born in Lithuania, came to the United States in 1907, and was ordained as a REFORM JUDAISM rabbi in 1916.

The origins of this group can be traced first to significant numbers of Jewish converts to Christian Science around the turn of the century and to attempts by Jewish leaders to counter that trend. In

1916 Alfred Geiger Moses, a Reform Judaism rabbi, published the book titled *Jewish Science*, which became the foundation of the group's doctrine. Jewish Science states that "The God consciousness in me expresses itself in Health, in Calmness, in Peace, in Power and in Happiness. I am calm and cheerful; I hate no one; I envy no one; there is no worry or fear in me; I trust in God all the time." [*See also* NEW THOUGHT.]

Source:

Meyer, D. *The Positive Thinkers*. New York: Pantheon Books, 1980.

Jews for Jesus

North American Hebrew Christian evangelical organization, dedicated to spreading the message of HEBREW CHRISTIANITY, which is the possibility of combining Jewish identity and Christian beliefs of the FUNDAMENTALIST variety. The rituals combine Jewish and Protestant elements. Jesus Christ of the New Testament is known as Yeshua or Y'shua.

Jews for Jesus was founded in 1970 in northern California by Moishe Rosen. In 1973 it was incorporated under the official name Hineni Ministries. Branches operate in major U.S. and Canadian urban centers.

Source:

Sobel, B. Z. *Hebrew Christianity: The Thirteenth Tribe*. New York: Wiley, 1974.

Jiu-Kyo

Japanese new religion, with shamanistic features, founded by Jikoson in 1952.

John Frum (Jon Frum)

Melanesian syncretistic, MILLENARIAN movement (CARGO CULT) started on Tanna Island, New Hebrides (now Vanuatu) in 1936. Its doctrine combines the return of ancestor worship with native separatism. The basic belief is in the imminent appearance of the savior John Frum (Broom), who is either presented as a traditional deity or as the "king of America," who will deliver the "cargo" (cars, machines, and other modern products) by airplanes and will get rid of the Europeans. According to some reports, a prophecy in 1939 predicted that America would throw out the French and the British and rid Tanna Island of the missionaries. Four years later U.S. forces made it into the largest base in the Pacific. Followers worship before red-painted images of John Frum, red crosses, and red-painted airplanes.

Johrei

Officially known as the Society of Johrei, and sometimes known as Johrei Fellowship, this is a Japanese monotheistic "healing" movement. It was founded in 1971 as a breakaway group from SEKAI KYUSEI KYO (World Messianic Association). It claims to follow the original teachings of Mikichi Okada (1882–1955), the founder of Sekai Kyusei Kyo.

Johrei is "divine light transmitted to heal sickness or affliction . . . channeled through the palm of its administrator and accompanied by prayers." This is the major healing procedure followed by the group. It also promotes theories about "purification" of the body from "alien substances," nutrition, and "nature farming." Affiliated churches include

197

Moishe Rosen, founder of Jews for Jesus (courtesy Jews for Jesus).

Light of Salvation Church (Kyoto), Reimi Church (Kyoto, Tokyo), Mesia Kyokwe (Korea), and Templo Messianic Universal (Brazil).

Jordanites (Jordonites)

Guyanian indigenous PENTECOSTAL group founded in 1917 in Georgetown. It is strongly Old Testament–oriented, claiming to carry on ancient Judaic rituals.

Jotabeche Pentecostal Methodist Church

Chilean PENTECOSTAL movement founded in the 1950s and based in Santiago.

Joya Houses

U.S. Hindu group founded in the 1970s by Joyce Green, former "divine Mother" in the HANUMAN FOUNDATION.

Joy Farm

U.S. NEW THOUGHT healing center founded in Connecticut after the death of New Thought leader Emma Curtis Hopkins in 1925. [*See also* EMMA C. HOPKINS ASSOCIATION.]

Judah Israel Mission

Syncretistic African group founded in 1961 in Kimilili, Kenya, by former members of the Anglican Church. Practices include traditional sacrifices at the group's temple.

K

Kabbalistic Order of Rosa Cruz

International ROSICRUCIAN group active mainly in Latin America.

Kadampa Center for Tibetan Buddhism

U.S. Tibetan Buddhist center founded by Roger Corless in 1980.

Kagyu Droden Kunchab

U.S. Tibetan Buddhist center founded by Kalu Rinpoche and based in San Francisco. It has been associated with KAGYU KUNKHYAB CHULING.

Kagyu E-vam Buddhist Institute

Australian Tibetan Buddhist center founded by Traleg Kyabgon Rinpoche in Melbourne in 1980.

Kagyu Kunkhyab Chuling

North American Tibetan Buddhist group devoted to spreading the doctrines of the Tibetan Kagyu order in the West. It was founded around 1970 by Lama Kalu Rinpoche, a spiritual teacher of the Tibetan Buddhist Kargyudpa order.

Kagyu Ling

Western Tibetan Buddhist group in Europe, with headquarters in France. It was started in the early 1970s by Lama Kalu Rinpoche, a spiritual teacher of the Ti-

betan Buddhist Kargyudpa order. On July 17, 1994, a four-year-old boy, born in Paris to Asian parents, was consecrated by the group as Tulkou Kalou Rinpoche, the reincarnation of Kalu Rinpoche, one of the greatest masters in the history of Tibetan Buddhism.

Kamalashila

Western Tibetan Buddhist group founded in Germany in the 1980s.

Kanda Dia Kinzinga ("People for Eternal Life")

African indigenous Christian group, started in the 1950s in the Belgian Congo (now Zaire). It has since spread to other nations in central Africa.

Kardecism

Modern spiritualist doctrine named for Allan Kardec (1804–1869), French spiritualist, who was born Hyppolyte Leon Denizard Rivail. Following a "conversion" in which he communicated with the dead, he had contacts with the spirits of "Allan" and "Kardec," names which he chose to adopt as his own. During a spiritualist seance, he claimed to have had a revelation by a spirit named "Truth," who gave him the mission of founding one great universal religion, based on spiritualism and belief in reincarnation. He had only a few followers during his lifetime, but his teachings influenced spiritualist movements all over the world; his tomb at the Père-Lachaise Cemetery in Paris is still a place of pilgrimage and worship. In Brazil, Kardecism has been popular since the nineteenth century, and in 1957 the government there issued a postage stamp bearing Kardec's portrait. It has especially influenced the UMBANDA movement of Brazil.

Kargyudpa Order

U.S. Tibetan Buddhist group based in southern California and associated with KAGYU KUNKHYAB CHULING. It was founded around 1979 by Lama Kalu Rinpoche of the Buddhist Kargyudpa Order.

Kargyu Dsamling Kunchab

U.S. Tibetan Buddhist group based in New York City and associated with KAGYU KUNKHYAB CHULING.

Karma Kagyu Institute

International Tibetan Buddhist group devoted to spreading the doctrines of the Tibetan Karma Kagyu lineage in the West. It was founded around 1980 in Woodstock, New York, by Jamgon Kongtrul Rinpoche, who claimed to be the "lineage holder" of Karma Kagyu. In the 1990s, it opened centers in Eastern Europe.

Karma Kagyu Samye-Ling

British Tibetan Buddhist group devoted to spreading the doctrines of the Tibetan Karma Kagyu lineage.

Karma Triyana Dharmachakra

U.S. Tibetan Buddhist group, based in Woodstock, New York, and devoted to the teachings of the Gyalwa Karmapa, the head of the Kagyupa order of Tibetan Buddhism. Founded in 1976, the group is headed by Lama Tenzin Choney, aided by Lama Kathar and Lama Gangha. It operates a monastery in Woodstock and branches around the United States, which are known as Karma Thegsum Choling.

Karm Ling

French Tibetan Buddhist group founded in the 1970s.

Kayavarohan

U.S. Hindu commune, based in St. Helena, California, and founded by Yogeshwar Muni in the 1970s. The group follows Hindu traditions and practices, including "yogic health" and meditation. Kayavarohan has operated the Santana Dharma Foundation, offering meditation training to nonmembers.

Kenya Foundation of the Prophets Church

African independent Christian PENTECOSTAL group, which was formed in 1927 among the Kikuyu. Its custom is to pray facing Mount Kenya. It is part of the WAKORINO group of churches.

Kerista Village

U.S. commune, founded in 1971 in San Francisco, based on the concept of polyfidelity in "multiple marriages." Its religion is based on "a benevolent Divinity that had no gender and wanted human beings to be free, fun-loving, equalitarian, and rational." The group was dissolved in 1994.

Kimbanguist Movement

Known officially as L'Église de Jesus Christ par le Prophete Simon Kimbangu (Church of Jesus Christ on Earth through the Prophet Simon Kimbangu) or EJCSK or EJCK, and otherwise known as ngunzism, SK. This African Christian MILLENARIAN movement was founded in 1921 in the Belgian Congo (now Zaire) by Simon Kimbangu (1889–1951), an oil refinery worker from Bakongo. In 1915 he was baptized and subsequently was trained as a Baptist catechist, but he failed to become a pastor. In April 1921 Kimbangu proclaimed the imminent departure of all whites and offered himself as a healer and savior. He soon became known as a charismatic preacher and healer. Under Belgian colonial rule, Kimbangu was sentenced to death for sedition, but the sentence was commuted to life imprisonment. He died in prison after thirty years.

In addition to healings, the movement promises an imminent golden age which follows the Second Coming. The doctrine and practices combine traditional ancestor worship with Christian rites and prayers. Members pray "in the name of the Father, the Son, and the Holy Ghost descended into Simon Kimbangu." Nkamba, the village where he was born and is now buried, has become known as the "New Jerusalem," a center of pilgrimage. Members believe that Kimbangu was sent to Earth by Jesus Christ, and some expect his imminent return. Before the coming of independence in 1960, the movement was mainly anti-colonialist; since then it has adopted an anti-witchcraft emphasis.

The church has become the largest independent church in central Africa, with branches in Zaire and neighboring countries. The founder's three sons have been its leaders. In 1970 L'Église became a member of the World Council of Churches. In 1971 it was one of only four churches recognized by the government of Zaire. Many other groups claim to carry on Simon Kimbangu's legacy.

Sources:

Balandier, G. *Ambiguous Africa: Cultures in Collision.* New York: Pantheon Books, 1966.

MacGaffey, W. *Modern Kongo Prophets.* Bloomington: Indiana University Press, 1983.

Martin, M. L. *Kimbangu: An African Prophet and His Church.* Oxford: Basil Blackwell, 1975.

King David's Spiritual Temple of Truth Association

U.S. African American PENTECOSTAL church founded in the 1920s. In 1952 it merged with ST. PAUL'S SPIRITUAL CHURCH CONVOCATION and NATIONAL DAVID SPIRITUAL TEMPLE OF CHRIST CHURCH UNION (INC.) U.S.A., to form the UNIVERSAL CHRISTIAN SPIRITUAL FAITH AND CHURCHES FOR ALL NATIONS.

Kingdom Fellowship Church

U.S. BRITISH ISRAELIST group founded in the 1930s by Robertson Orr, a former Presbyterian minister, in Long Beach, California.

Kingdom Message Association

U.S. BRITISH ISRAELIST group based in New York City. It was founded and headed by C. Lewis Fowler. Later Fowler headed the Kingdom Bible Seminary in St. Petersburg, Florida.

Source:
Roy, J. L. *Apostles of Discord*. Boston: Beacon Press, 1953.

Kingdom of Yahweh

U.S. BRITISH ISRAELIST, spiritualist, and ADVENTIST group. It was founded by Joseph Jeffers in Houston after World War II as the successor to KINGDOM TEMPLE, INC. In 1952 it was moved to Sarasota, Florida. In addition to the standard British Israelism beliefs about the descent of the Anglo-Saxons from ancient Israel, this group adopted the keeping of Saturday as the Sabbath, and the use of Yahweh as the name for God. The group claimed that the New Age began in 1900, and it reported messages from the spirit world. It was dissolved in the 1970s.

Source:
Roy, J. L. *Apostles of Discord*. Boston: Beacon Press, 1953.

Kingdom Temple, Inc.

U.S. BRITISH ISRAELIST group founded in 1935 by Joseph Jeffers, former Baptist preacher, in Los Angeles, California. In 1943 Jeffers announced that he was "the Christ." In 1945 he was sentenced to four years in a federal prison for violating a divorce settlement with his second wife. While Jeffers was in prison, his third wife operated the Temple of Yahweh in Cabazon, California. [*See also* KINGDOM OF YAHWEH.]

Source:
Roy, J. L. *Apostles of Discord*. Boston: Beacon Press, 1953.

Kirisuto Dendo-Dan

Japanese indigenous Christian PENTECOSTAL group founded in 1951.

Kirisuto Shinsu-Kyodan (Christ Heart Church)

Japanese indigenous Christian group founded in 1927.

Kirpal Ruhani Satsang

Also known as the Kirpal Light Satsang, this is a Western Sikh-inspired group. It claims to be the authentic successor to the RUHANI SATSANG, which was led by Kirpal Singh (1896–1974). Kirpal Ruhani Satsang was founded by Kirpal Singh's disciple Thakar Singh, known as "the present living Master, Sant Thakar Singh Ji." The group "is devoted to communicating the truth about human existence, its nature and purpose as expressed by the Masters of the Yoga of Inner Light and Sound." Its headquarters are in California, and branches have operated in Western Europe and the United States.

Kitawala (Chitawala)

African syncretistic messianic movement started in the 1920s in Zaire (then the Belgian Congo). It was founded by Nyirenda, who called himself Mwana Lesa ("son of God"), under the influence of JEHOVAH'S WITNESSES, by way of the WATCHTOWER movement. The founder was executed in 1926. The movement's doctrine describes a divine family, in which the eldest son is black, but his birthright is stolen by a white brother. The movement promises a new age, in which whites will be ruined and blacks restored to their divine position of seniority. The movement has become connected with the KIMBANGUIST MOVEMENT. Its branches have operated also among Africans in Western Europe.

Knights Templar New Age Church

U.S. occultist group founded in the late 1980s by Duane Mantley and Charles Hamilton, and based in Phoenix, Arizona. It describes itself as a "New Age/Eclectic Church." Practices include Tarot divination and "rune readings."

Koab

Also known as the Society of the One Almighty God, Bamalaki, or Malakite Church, this is an African independent movement, started in Uganda in 1914 in secession from the Anglican Mission Church.

Kodesh Church of Immanuel

U.S. African American Conservative Protestant group founded in 1929 in Pittsburgh by Frank Russell Killingsworth. Members follow a strict behavior code, forbidding alcohol, tobacco, and "prideful" dress.

Kofuku No Kagaku ("The Institute for Research in Human Happiness")

Japanese religion started in October, 1986, by Ryuho Okawa (1956–), who claims to serve as a medium for well-known historical figures, such as Jesus Christ, Buddha, Confucius, Muhammad, Beethoven, and Picasso. The founder is a law graduate of the University of Tokyo, and he studied international finance at New York University. On March 23, 1981, he had a "revelation and realized his mission of saving all humankind." The founder "is an incarnation of Lord El Cantare, the supreme grand spirit of the terrestrial spirit group. A part of the El Cantare consciousness once incarnated as Shakyamuni Buddha in India and at another time as Hermes in Greece." The group "aims to create a utopia on earth through the practice of 'the love that gives' and the pursuit of 'enlightenment' by everybody in the world." Branches of the group have operated in Japan, the United States, and Great Britain.

Koinonia

U.S. "spiritual and educational community" founded in 1952 near Baltimore, Maryland. In Koinonia "many 'new age' and traditional paths and forms of worship meet and share the energy as the community strives to reverence and to experience the Universal Spirit in its many dancing manifestations."

Koinonia Community

U.S. Christian FUNDAMENTALIST commune, which was in existence in Santa Cruz, California, in the late 1960s–early 1970s as part of the JESUS MOVEMENT. The group was led by Margaret Ravick. It practiced glossolalia (speaking in tongues) and exorcism, and regarded established Christian churches as satanic. [See also CHRISTIAN WORLD LIBERATION FRONT.]

Koinonia Partners

U.S. Christian commune founded in 1942 as Koinonia Farm near Americus, Georgia, by Clarence Jordan. The present name was adopted in 1968. The group adopted radical stances vis-a-vis its environment, preaching, and practices; racial integration; equality; and economic justice, all inspired by a radical interpretation of Christianity.

Konkokyo ("Golden Light Teaching")

Japanese Shinto-inspired religion. It was founded by Bunjiro Kawate (1814–1883), also known as Konko Daijin, following a religious experience at age forty-five (*i.e.*, in 1859). The group's syncretistic doctrine includes the figure *Tenchi Kane no Kami* (*Konjin*), who is believed to be the parent god of heaven and earth. The group leader is a mediator between the believers and God, through whom individual salvation is achieved. Unlike other Japanese new religions, Konkokyo has taken a determined stance against political activities. Branches have operated in North America.

Kosmon Movement

The European branch of the UNIVERSAL FAITHISTS OF KOSMON, founded by George Morley around 1920 in London.

Kosmunity

Canadian religious commune located in British Columbia, which claimed to follow "the Essene tradition of purity in diet, lifestyle, and spiritual learning."

Kripalu Center

U.S. branch of KRIPALU YOGA ASHRAM started in the late 1970s. Since 1983 it has been located in Lenox, Massachusetts.

Kripalu Yoga Ashram

U.S. Hindu commune based in Sumneytown, Pennsylvania. It was established in 1971 by Yogi Amrit Desai, known as Gurudev (1932–), an Indian immigrant who came to the United States in 1960. The commune is devoted to the teaching of Shaktiput Kundalini Yoga and Kripalu Yoga. Desai advocates vegetarianism and occasional fasts.

Krishnamurti Foundation

International organization founded in 1969 and based in Ojai, California. It is dedicated to spreading the teachings of Jiddu Krishnamurti (1895–1986). Krishnamurti was born in Madanapalle, India, to a Brahmin family, and at the age of thirteen he was "discovered" by Charles Webster Leadbeater and Annie Wood Besant, two leaders of the THEOSOPHICAL SOCIETY. Leadbeater saw the boy bathing, and realized that he was the "Vehicle of the next World Teacher," the avatar, "God incarnate."

The Order of the Star in the East was set up to promote the World Teacher, the *jaggathguru*, in 1911, and Krishnamurti and his brother were educated in England. In 1923 Besant announced that Krishnamurti was indeed the new World Teacher. In 1929, however, Krishnamurti rejected the role of avatar and the Order was dissolved. Nevertheless, Krishnamurti's early writings, before 1929, are still used by Theosophical groups around the world. For the rest of

Jiddu Krishnamurti with his foster mother, Annie Wood Besant, leader of the Theosophical Society.

206

his long life, Krishnamurti acted as the non-Guru Guru for thousands, preaching a message of independence and a rejection of leaders, be they religious or secular. Krishnamurti's religious faith was ecumenical and eclectic, combining East and West. He included Jesus Christ, Lao-tzu, and other great mystics on his list of "enlightened beings." There were Krishnamurti-inspired schools and centers in India as well as in the West. The British branch of the Foundation is known as the Krishnamurti Foundation Trust Ltd. [*See also* LIBERAL CATHOLIC CHURCH; *and* THEOSOPHY.]

Source:
Tillett, G. *The Elder Brother: A Biography of Charles Webster Leadbeater*. London: Routledge & Kegan Paul, 1982.

Krislam

Indonesian twentieth-century syncretistic movement, which combined Islamic and Christian beliefs.

Krislapi

Indonesian twentieth-century syncretistic movement, which combined Islamic, Christian, and Buddhist ideas.

Kundalini Research Foundation

U.S. Hindu-oriented group founded in 1970 in New York City by Gene Kieffer and other followers of Gopi Krishna (1903–1984). *Kundalini*, in Hindu lore, means sexual energy supposedly localized in the base of the spine. Kundalini yoga attempts to release this energy for use in the human brain.

Kurozumi Kyo

Japanese new religion founded in 1815 by Munetada Kurozumi (1780–1850), a Shinto priest who had a mystical experience of union with the sun-goddess. Group practices include faith healing, as developed by the founder.

Source:
Hardacre, H. *Kurozumikyo and the New Religions of Japan*. Princeton, N.J.: Princeton University Press, 1986.

Kwang Lim Methodist Church

Korean independent PENTECOSTAL group founded in 1950.

L

Lama Foundation

U.S. syncretistic religious commune located near San Christobal, New Mexico, and founded in 1967 by Steve Durkee. Practices stem from Buddhist, Christian, and Sufi traditions. This commune has hosted teachers of various traditions, and has published their teachings. In the 1970s one of the best-known visitors was Baba Hari Dass, a Hindu monk who practices continual silence and communicates by writing on a chalkboard. Since 1971 he has visited the Lama Foundation several times.

Lamaist Buddhist Monastery of America

U.S. Tibetan Buddhist monastery founded by the Tibetan Lama Geshe Wangyal (1902–1983) in the 1960s. Geshe Wangyal went to the United States in 1955 to serve as Lama to the Kalmuck-Mongolian community there. The monastery, in Howell, New Jersey, was known as Labsum Shedrub Ling. [*See also* TIBETAN BUDDHIST LEARNING CENTER.]

Lama Tzong Khapa

International Tibetan Buddhist group founded in the 1970s in Pomaia, Tuscany. It operates the Foundation for the Preservation of the Mahayana Tradition.

Lama Yeshe Movement

Tibetan Buddhist movement in the West, founded by exiled Tibetan monks. The founder, Lama Yeshe, died in 1984. As of 1987, the group was reported to have thirty-three meditation centers around the world. A two-year-old Spanish boy, Osael Ita Torres, was selected as the reincarnation of Lama Yeshe in March 1987.

Lamb of God

U.S. charismatic, communal group, growing out of the CATHOLIC CHARISMATIC RENEWAL movement, which was founded in the early 1970s in Timonium, Maryland.

Lamb of God Church

U.S. PENTECOSTAL group, founded in 1942 by Rose Soares. Based in Hawaii, it appeals to indigenous Hawaiians.

Laodicean Home Missionary Movement

U.S. ADVENTIST group started in 1955 by John W. Krewson as a result of a schism in the LAYMEN'S HOME MISSIONARY MOVEMENT. Krewson has been in dispute with Raymond Jolly of the Movement, and also with John J. Hoefle of the EPIPHANY BIBLE STUDENTS ASSOCIATION. [*See also* JEHOVAH'S WITNESSES.]

Last Church of Christ

African indigenous Christian church founded in Zambia in the 1950s.

Last Day Messenger Assemblies

U.S. FUNDAMENTALIST, DISPENSATIONA-

LIST group concentrated in the western areas of the United States and Canada. It was founded by Nels Thompson in the 1920s in Oakland, California.

Last Ministry Church

African indigenous MILLENARIAN PENTE-COSTAL group, which was founded in Kenya around 1965.

Latin Rite Catholic Church

International traditionalist Catholic movement, led by Pierre Martin Ngo-Dinh-Thuc, former Archibishop of Hue, Vietnam. Thuc, who rejects the reforms introduced into the Roman Catholic Church after 1965, has ordained, since 1975, many leaders of dissenting Catholic groups in North and South America. [See also FRATERNITY OF ST. PIUS X; SERVANTS OF THE SACRED HEART OF JESUS AND MARY; and UNION CATOLICA TRENTO.]

Latter Rain Movement

North American MILLENARIAN PENTE-COSTAL movement, which started in 1946 in the Sharon Orphanage and School, North Battleford, Saskatchewan, Canada, following a schism in the local branch of the ASSEMBLIES OF GOD. It was led by George Hawtin and Percy Hunt. Faith healing, glossolalia, and prophecies were practiced. Some groups in this movement later developed into the MANIFEST SONS OF GOD, or "overcomers," and into the CHRISTIAN GROWTH MINISTRIES. Several congregations in the United States have been committed to the Latter Rain vision, while keeping their independence. There are no official

congregations, central hierarchy, or canonized theology. Movement branches have operated since the 1960s in Europe.

Source:
Durrand, T. C. & Shupe, A. *Metaphors of Social Control in a Pentecostal Sect.* Lewiston, N.Y.: Edwin Mellen Press, 1983.

Laye

Heterodox Islamic movement founded among the Lebu people of Senegal in 1883 by Seydina Limamu (?–1909). He claimed a divine call to revive and expand traditional Islam, which led him to reject central Islamic practices, such as the pilgrimage to Mecca. In addition to opposition from Orthodox Muslims, the movement endured persecution by French colonial authorities and has survived, being led by the prophet's descendants.

Laymen's Home Missionary Movement (LHMM)

U.S. Christian ADVENTIST group created by a schism in the Watch Tower Bible and Tract Society (JEHOVAH'S WITNESSES) in 1918. Paul S. L. Johnson, in dispute with J. R. Rutherford, left the movement, together with Raymond Jolly, and joined in forming the PASTORAL BIBLE INSTITUTE. Later on Johnson and Jolly withdrew and founded the Laymen's Home Missionary Movement.

The Movement follows the original teachings of Charles Taze Russell, which, for the Witnesses, have been superseded by Rutherford's teachings. Following Johnson's death in 1950, Jolly succeeded to the leadership. Branches of this group have been operating in Europe. [*See also* EPIPHANY BIBLE STUDENTS ASSOCIATION; *and* LAODICEAN HOME MISSIONARY MOVEMENT.]

Laymen's Movement for a Christian World

U.S. spiritualist group based in Rye, New York.

LDS Scripture Researchers

U.S. dissident MORMON group, also known as "Believe God Society" and "Doers of the Word." It was founded by Sherman Russell Lloyd in Salt Lake City, Utah, in the 1950s. Members believe in the second coming of Joseph Smith and study the teachings of Emanuel Swedenborg. [*See also* SWEDENBORG FOUNDATION.]

Lectorium Rosicrucianum

Also known as the Rosicrucian Society, the Spiritual School of the Golden Rosycross, and the International School of the Golden Rosycross, this is an international ROSICRUCIAN group founded in Holland in 1924 by J. Van Rijckenborgh and other former members of the ROSICRUCIAN FELLOWSHIP. The group's doctrine combines Christian and THEOSOPHICAL elements. It proposes that mankind's problems lie in overcoming the endless cycles of reincarnation and the separation from divine order. These will come to an end when humans model themselves after Jesus Christ. The group has had branches in Western Europe, New Zealand, and North America.

Lederer Messianic Ministries

Also known as the Lederer Foundation, this U.S. HEBREW CHRISTIAN group was founded in 1936 by members of the Lederer family in Baltimore, Maryland.

Leroy Jenkins Evangelistic Association

U.S. PENTECOSTAL healing group led by Leroy Jenkins, a disciple of A. A. Allen. In 1979 Jenkins was convicted of conspiracy to commit arson and sentenced to twelve years in prison. Paroled in 1985, he has resumed his activities as a faith healer. [*See also* MIRACLE REVIVAL FELLOWSHIP.]

Source:
Randi, J. *The Faith Healers.* Buffalo: Prometheus Books, 1987.

Source:
Lawrence, P. *Road Belong Cargo.* Manchester: Manchester University Press, 1964.

Liberal Catholic Church (LCC)

International THEOSOPHICAL-Christian group founded in 1916 in London by Charles Webster Leadbeater, a British leader in the early Theosophical movement, and James Ingall Wedgewood, who served as its first presiding bishop. Wedgewood traveled to the United States in 1917 and started the movement there.

The group conducts regular church services and operates branches around the world. Its doctrine includes a belief in reincarnation, and it interprets Christianity along Theosophical lines, viewing

Faith healer Leroy Jenkins, founder of the Leroy Jenkins Evangelistic Association.

Christian mythology as part of a long chain of events tied to the Ascended Masters. "The world is the theatre of an ordered plan, according to which the spirit of man, by repeatedly expressing himself in varying conditions of life and experience, continually unfolds his powers." Special emphasis is placed on faith healing.

Source:
Tillett, G. *The Elder Brother: A Biography of Charles Webster Leadbeater.* London: Routledge & Kegan Paul, 1982.

Liberal Judaism

Official label for many REFORM JUDAISM congregations in Central and Western Europe.

Liberal Judaism

Formally known as the Jewish Religious Union, this is a radical variety of REFORM JUDAISM, established in London in 1902 by Claude Montefiore and Lily Montagu, and known only in Great Britain. Montefiore aimed at a new interpretation of Jewish heritage, through the elevation of "prophetic" or "higher" Judaism over the legalistic, priestly tradition. This meant also recognizing the Jewish legacy in the New Testament. Services eliminated most elements of synagogue traditions, and were marked by mixed seating for men and women, and the elimination of Hebrew and of the Torah-reading rituals. Its center has been the West London Synagogue of British Jews.

Sources:
Kessler, E., ed. *An English Jew: The Life and Writings of Claude Montefiore.* London: Valentine Michell, 1989.

Umansky, E. M. *Lily Montague and the Advancement of Liberal Judaism.* Lewiston, N.Y.: Edwin Mellen, 1983.

Unterman, A. *Jews: Their Religious Beliefs and Practices.* London: Routledge & Kegan Paul, 1981.

Liborismo

Syncretist, Catholic spiritualist movement in the Dominican Republic. Its origins date back to an indigenous movement led by Liborio Mateo, who claimed to be God's messenger in 1910. Mateo was killed in 1922, but his ideas have lived on. Followers go on pilgrimage to the village of Palma Sola.

Lichtcentrum Bethanien

Swiss Christian spiritualist group founded in 1967 by Frieda Maria Lämmle (1907–). The founder claimed to have received messages from Jesus Christ.

Lichtkreis Michael

Swiss occultist group founded in Zurich in 1986, inspired by the BRIDGE TO FREEDOM movement in North America.

Life and Light Fellowship

British Christian PENTECOSTAL group founded in 1966, whose members have been drawn from the black community. Emphasis is on "healing crusades" and missions in the Caribbean.

Life Science Church

U.S. Protestant organization offering ordination as a minister by mail.

Life-Study Fellowship

U.S. NEW THOUGHT group founded in 1939 in Noroton, Connecticut, which operates strictly by mail.

Lighthouse Universal Life Church (Lighthouse ULC)

Also known as the Lighthouse Meditation Group, this is a U.S. Hindu-oriented group, founded in the late 1980s by Cathy Florida in Whitmore Lake, Michigan. It has collaborated with the JAIN MEDITATION INTERNATIONAL CENTER.

Light of the Universe

U.S. occultist-UFO group, founded in the early 1960s in Tiffin, Ohio, and led by a teacher known as Maryona. Its doctrine is based on the notion of the soul's progress through reincarnation. Meditation is practiced.

Light of Truth Church

Also known as the Temple of Truth (TOT), this is a U.S. occultist group that was founded in 1973 by Nelson H. White, a former member of the ORDO TEMPLI ASTRATE.

Light of Yoga Society

U.S. Hindu group, founded by Alice Christensen, "a disciple of Swami Rama," in the 1960s, and based in Cleveland. The group is devoted to the spread-

ing of Hindu teachings and practices, including yoga and meditation.

Linbu

European network of occultist schools that follow the traditions of the GURD-JIEFF GROUPS.

Lindisfarne

U.S. occultist group founded in the 1960s by William Irwin Thompson (1938–) in Southampton, New York (later moved to western Massachusetts) and devoted "to the study and realization of a new planetary culture." It is named after the Lindisfarne Priory, founded in the eleventh century by St. Cuthbert in northern England. The group promotes the teachings of the Russian Orthodox mystic Vladimir Soloviev and publishes his works.

Ling Liang

Chinese indigenous Christian church with headquarters in Hong Kong and missionary activities in Chinese communities worldwide.

Lisu Christian Church

Chinese indigenous Christian church founded early in the twentieth century, with branches and activities in the Chinese communities of Asia.

Live Oak Grove

Neo-pagan U.S. group devoted to the Druid tradition, the religion of the ancient Celts in Gaul and Britain. The

Welsh druids, collecting the sacred mistletoe. (see Live Oak Grove)

214

Druid religion was polytheistic and included human sacrifice. Mistletoe was considered sacred and a remedy for illness.

Living Christ Movement

New Zealand Christian occultist group affiliated with the U.S. group ETHERIAN RELIGIOUS SOCIETY OF UNIVERSAL BROTHERHOOD.

Local Church Movement

Also known as Chu Hui So, the Little Flock, the Assembly Hall Churches, and the Witness Lee Movement, this is a Chinese FUNDAMENTALIST Christian group. It was founded in 1923 by Nee Shu Tsu. After his conversion to Christianity Nee used the name To Shen (Watchman), and he is sometimes referred to as Watchman Nee. He founded about 200 churches in China between 1923 and 1950 in an early version of the JESUS MOVEMENT. In 1952 Nee was imprisoned by the Communist government; he died in prison in 1972, and the movement's center moved to Taiwan.

The Western version of the movement was started in 1962 by Stephen Kuang, who had arrived in the United States in 1954. In 1960 a close associate of Nee, known as Witness Lee (1905–), arrived in the United States and settled in Los Angeles, becoming the group's leader.

Nee was influenced by the PLYMOUTH BRETHREN and adopted DISPENSATIONALISM. The Local Church advocates a special role for women, who have to be veiled during church meetings. The group proclaims all other religious organizations to be satanic. The Local Church operates the Fellowship Tract League.

Logos World University Church

U.S. Christian occultist group, sometimes described as an "interfaith church and meditation center," founded in 1983 by Anne Puryear and Herbert Bruce Puryear, former leaders of the ASSOCIATION FOR RESEARCH AND ENLIGHTENMENT. The group's credo includes "the central place of meditation to one's daily spiritual growth" and asserts the "ability of every person to become their own priest." Much of the group's work and beliefs have been inspired by Edgar Cayce and the Association for Research and Enlightenment. Group headquarters are located in Scottsdale, Arizona, with branches and affiliated groups all over the United States. The Church offers a variety of teachings, including spiritualism, Gurdjieff ideas, meditation, and parapsychology. Its founders perform "life readings" and "psychic counseling." [See also GURDJIEFF GROUPS.]

London Church of Christ

Sometimes known as the Central London Church of Christ, or the London Central Church, this is the London branch of the BOSTON CHURCH OF CHRIST, founded in the 1980s. [See also BODY OF CHRIST; CHRISTIAN GROWTH MINISTRIES; CHRISTIAN RESTORATION MINISTRIES; and CROSSROADS CHURCHES OF CHRIST.]

London Messianic Fellowship

British HEBREW CHRISTIAN group founded in the 1970s.

Lord's Covenant Church

U.S. BRITISH ISRAELIST group, based in Phoenix, Arizona, and founded by

Sheldon Emry, a former vice-president of CHRISTIAN RESEARCH, INC. Emry was the author of many publications promoting the British Israelist viewpoint, and had his own radio program, "America's Promise," which was broadcast all over the United States until his death in 1985. After Emry's death, Ben Williams took over as leader of the group.

Lord's Resistance Army (LRA)

Ugandan Christian messianic movement, growing out of the HOLY SPIRIT MOVEMENT. It was started in 1988 by Joseph Kony (1966–), a former altar boy and traditional healer, who in that year claimed a divine revelation. Kony, husband of thirty-two wives, is a first cousin of Alice Lakwena, founder of the Holy Spirit Movement, and he reportedly took over the leadership of some of her followers. The LRA is alleged to have kidnapped young Ugandans who were then forced to join its armed units. In 1995 members of the group started carrying out terrorist attacks in northern Uganda. Hundreds were reported killed in these attacks.

Lorian Association

U.S. occultist commune founded in the 1970s by David Spangler (1945–) near Madison, Wisconsin. (It has since moved to the State of Washington.) It is devoted to the teaching of ANTHROPOSOPHICAL, ROSICRUCIAN, and Eastern ideas, and is inspired by FINDHORN FOUNDATION beliefs.

Lost Israelites of Kenya

African independent Christian movement founded in Kenya around 1960.

Members wear uniforms and march in military style. Doctrine stresses the Ten Commandments.

Lothlorien

U.S. neo-pagan group started by Paul V. Beyerl, which claims to follow both Western WICCAN tradition and Tibetan Buddhist lore.

Lou Movement

European messianic Christian movement. It is named after its founder, the Dutch fisherman Louwrens Voorthuizen (1898–1968), known as "Lou," who declared himself to be the Christian Messiah. Group branches have operated in Western Europe.

Love Family

Also known as the Church of Armageddon or Church of Jesus Christ at Armageddon, this U.S. Christian commune was founded in 1969 by Love Israel, formerly known as Paul Erdman (1940–), in Seattle, Washington. The founder reportedly had a revelation indicating that only he represented the authentic message of the New Testament. Members considered themselves Christians and the true Israelites, and they adopted both biblical names and holy names representing virtues (such as Integrity and Courage), which became permanent. They were enjoined to follow Old Testament dietary laws. The group adopted a new calendar, with new names for days of the week and months, and a new clock.

The founder considered inhaling vapors of toluene (an industrial solvent) to be a religious ritual. This practice was stopped after two members were asphyxiated by toluene in 1972. The group continued to use hyperventilation, hallucinogens, and marijuana as aids to altering consciousness. Later cocaine was heavily used by Love Israel himself. Most members left the group in 1983, but a minority stayed on with the leader in a ranch in eastern Washington. The Church of Armageddon was officially disbanded in 1985, but the group was still in existence as of 1991.

Source:
Allen, S. *Beloved Son*. Indianapolis: Bobbs-Merrill, 1982.

Love Inn

U.S. JESUS MOVEMENT group founded in 1969 in Freeville, New York, by Scott Ross, a former New York City disc jockey.

Love Project

U.S. Christian occultist group founded in 1971 by Arleen Lorrance and Diana K. Pike. In 1972 it merged with the Bishop Pike Foundation, formerly known as the FOUNDATION OF RELIGIOUS TRANSITION.

Lucis Trust

The umbrella organization that operates the Arcane School and World Goodwill. It is an international occultist THEOSOPHICAL group founded by Alice A. Bailey (1880–1949) in New York City in 1923. She was aided by her husband, Foster Bailey. The Baileys had been Theosophists but left the movement in the 1920s after a dispute with the official leadership. Alice A. Bailey wrote at least twenty-four books, eighteen of which are claimed to be the result of collaboration with a Tibetan sage spirit, Djwal Khul,

known sometimes as D. K. or the Tibetan Master. The information in them was supposedly transmitted through telepathy.

The goal of the Arcane School is to develop "the science of soul contact." This is done through the eclectic use of astrology, a syncretistic interpretation of Christianity with the expectation of an imminent Second Coming, and ideas about faith healing. "The function of the school is to assist those at the end of the probationary path to move forward on the path of discipleship, and to assist those already on that path to move on more quickly and to achieve greater effectiveness in service. The training, which is conducted by correspondence, is based on three fundamental requirements—occult meditation, study, and service to humanity." The School proclaims the imminent coming of the Christ as part of the Aquarian Age: "There is widespread expectation that we approach the 'Age of Maitreya,' as it is known in the East, when the world Teacher and present head of the spiritual Hierarchy, the Christ, will reappear among men to sound the keynote of the new age."

The Arcane School also initiates Goodwill Meditation, "a worldwide group of people who link together in thought each week at noon on Wednesday to meditate upon the energy of goodwill . . . to stimulate and increase the use of goodwill in a troubled world." The spread of goodwill is carried out by Triangles, *i.e.*, groups of three individuals, who daily say the Great Invocation.

The Lucis Trust operates the World Goodwill Information and Research Service, established in 1932; the Triangles, founded in 1937; Radio Lucis, which presents the group's doctrine through radio programs; *The Beacon* magazine; Lucis Trust Library; Lucis Productions; and the "World Service Forum." Branches of these groups have operated around the world, coordinated by three centers in New York, London, and Geneva. [*See also* AQUARIAN EDUCATIONAL FOUNDATION; INSTITUTE FOR PLANETARY SYNTHESIS; SERVERS OF THE GREAT ONES, INC.; *and* THE WORLD TEACHER.]

Source:

Judah, J. S. *The History and Philosophy of the Metaphysical Movements in America.* Philadelphia: Westminster, 1967.

Lumpa Church

Known sometimes as the Visible Salvation Church, this is a MILLENARIAN group founded in 1953 by Alice Mulenga Lubusha (?–1978), of the Bemba people in northern Zambia. Lubusha experienced what she described as death; when she was in heaven God handed her a copy of the true Bible and then sent her back to Earth to preach the true gospel. She then named herself Alice Lenshina ("Queen"), and started a holy village in Kasomo, which is known as Sione or New Zion. The movement became very nationalistic and anti-Catholic, and her visions drew a popular following, espe-

Lyndon Baines Johnson, former President of the United States, namesake of a Melanesian Cargo Cult.

cially in the Chinsali district, which was also the home district of Kenneth Kaunda, who later became the Zambian Prime Minister and whose brother Robert became a Lumpa leader. The Lumpa Church was in conflict with the British colonial authorities and then, after Zambian independence, with the ruling United National Independence Party (UNIP). During the struggle for independence, Alice Lenshina banned political activities by Lumpa Church members, and in November 1963 thirty-seven "holy villages" were established for members. In July 1964 Lumpa members, armed with spears and axes, attacked a police station, and government troops killed 587 of them. Later in 1964 the Kaunda government banned the movement and in 1970 expelled its followers.

Luo Roho Church

African indigenous Christian church founded in 1968 in Kenya by secession from the NOMIYA LUO CHURCH (NLC) over the practices of glossolalia and exorcism.

Lutheran Bapedi Church

South African separatist church, founded in 1889 by J. A. Winter, a German missionary to the Bapedi people. This group was one of only eight churches recognized by the South African government in 1960.

Source:
Sundkler, B. G. M. *Bantu Prophets in South Africa.* London: Oxford University Press, 1961.

Lyndon B. Johnson

Melanesian syncretistic group (CARGO CULT) based in New Hanover, and later spreading to the coast of New Ireland. It was started in 1964 by Bosmailik. Members regarded Lyndon B. Johnson, United States President, as their leader and hoped to induce him to come to the island and bring them cargo, *i.e.,* Western-made products and riches. The founder collected the sum of $83,000 in order to "buy" Lyndon B. Johnson.

M

Madeley Trinity Methodist Church

Known originally as the Church of the Way, this was a small congregation in the Free Methodist Church, in Santa Ana, California. It withdrew from the denomination in 1959 after the pastor was accused of deviations from official doctrine. The independent group kept growing in the 1960s and 1970s. The belief in demonic possession of both humans and animals and the practice of exorcism became central to the Church in the 1970s. In the winter of 1979–1980 the group, with more than 100 members, left California for Springfield, Missouri. In the spring of 1980 the membership went into hiding and has been out of sight since then.

Magnificat

Italian traditionalist Catholic group, which is linked to the RENOVATED CHURCH OF CHRIST THE KING, and is based in Brescia.

Maha-Bodhi Society

Buddhist revival movement, founded in 1891 by D. H. Hewavitarne, also known as Anagarika Dhramapala (1864–1933). The founder was born into a well-off Sinhalese family, became Westernized, joined the THEOSOPHICAL SOCIETY in 1884, and became associated with Colonel Henry Steel Olcott, one of the Theosophical Society's leaders. In 1893 he took part in the World's Parliament of Religions, held in Chicago. The Society, which emphasized practical aspects of Buddhism, conducted missionary activities in Western countries.

Maha Yoga Ashram

U.S. Hindu commune based near Boston. It was founded by Yogiraj Shri T. R. Khanna in the late 1960s. Its doctrine is based on "the principles and practices of the eightfold path of raja yoga."

Mahdi

In the Shiite Muslim tradition, the Mahdi is Muhammad ibn al-Hannifiya, who disappeared (or died) in 880 B.C.E. Shiite belief is that the Mahdi, also known as the Hidden Imam, has been in hiding and will come back one day to restore peace and justice. Between the early nineteenth century and the middle of the twentieth, there were three Mahdist movements, combining messianism and anticolonialism, that rebelled against British colonial rule. There was the Nigerian Mahdi, and a Somalian Mahdi, known as the Mad Mullah. Usually, when the term Mahdi is used today, it refers to the Sudan Mahdi, Mohammed Ahmad Ibn Abdallah (1843–1885), whose regime survived for fourteen years, during which he won major battles against the British, who finally defeated him in Omdurman. The figure of the Sudan Mahdi still serves as an inspiration to Islamic movements around the world.

The Sudanese Mahdiyah movement has survived as a political movement led by the Mahdi's descendants, and still plays a major role in Sudanese politics. [*See also* NUBIAN ISLAMIC HEBREWS.]

Source:

Holt, P. M. *The Mahdist State in the Sudan 1881–1898: A Study of Its Origins, Development and Overthrow.* Oxford: Clarendon Press, 1958.

Mahikari ("True Light")

Also known as Sekai Mahikari Bumei Kyodan, this is a Japanese religion. It was founded in 1959 by Okada Yoshikazu (1901–1974), who took the name Okada Kotama (jewel of light) and is known to his followers as Sukui Nushi Sama (lord savior). The group's doctrine has been borrowed mainly from SEKAI KYUSEI KYO, which in turn followed OMOTOKYO teachings. The doctrine combines Eastern and Christian traditions and proclaims the coming millennium. It contains elements from Shinto (ancestor worship, veneration of the Emperor, and emphasis on purity), Buddhism (karma and reincarnation), and Japanese folk religion (miraculous healing).

The founder claimed to be God's emissary, a successor to Buddha and Jesus Christ. He offered his own version of the story of Jesus Christ, according to which Jesus was trained in Japan and did not die on the cross but of old age in Japan. The true teaching of Jesus is held to be that presented by Mahikari. The Japanese are the chosen people, and their language is divine. Mahikari offers immediate salvation in the form of health, harmony, and wealth. Spirit-possession is seen as the main cause of misfortune. There is a special doctrine on the magical causes and cures of illness. Illness is caused through possession by ancestral spirits, and healing through a special "light" that affects the spirits is practiced. Modern medical practices are rejected. The movement has spread to Western Europe, Africa, and the French Caribbean. A splinter group known as SUKYO MAHIKARI was started in 1978.

Source:

Davis, W. *Do-Jo-: Magic and Exorcism in Modern Japan.* Stanford, Calif.: Stanford University Press, 1980.

Mahon Mission of the Baptist Union of South Africa

South African missionary group, devoted to working with Africans. It was founded in 1902 by Edgar Mahon (1867–1936) as the Christian Catholic Church in Zion. The name was changed to Grace Mission Church in 1920. Practices have included faith healing and fortune-telling.

Mai Chaza Church

Also known as Guta ra Jehovah ("City of Jehovah") after its Holy Village and headquarters, this is an African independent church, founded in 1954 in Zimbabwe (then Southern Rhodesia) by Mai ("Mother") Chaza (?–1960). The founder, a former Methodist, claimed supernatural power after her purported death and rebirth. She then became a popular healer and exorcist, and since her death has been known as Mai Chaza Jesus, or "a black messiah."

Makom Ohr Shalom

U.S. Jewish syncretistic group, founded in the 1980s in southern California by Theodore G. Falcon. "Makom ohr Shalom explores the rich heritage of Jewish

221

mysticism and Kabbalah to meet the growing needs of these seeking the spiritual and meditative foundations of their identity and background."

Makuya (Genshifukuin-Kami-No-Makuya-Kyokai)

Japanese indigenous Christian group, also known as the Tabernacle of God or the Original Gospel (Tabernacle) Movement. It was founded by Abraham Ikuro Teshima, who became a Christian in 1948 following a "divine revelation." The group had its origins in the MUKYOKAI movement. It is PENTECOSTAL in doctrine and practices, with an emphasis on faith healing. In addition it has developed a special attachment to Judaism. It claims to follow authentic Judaic traditions, and its members demonstrate a thorough knowledge of modern Hebrew and contemporary Israeli culture. Group branches have operated in North and South America.

Source:
Caldarola, C. *Christianity: The Japanese Way.* Leiden: E. J. Brill, 1979.

Malagasy Protestant Church

African indigenous Christian church, started in 1894 in Madagascar by secession from European missionary groups.

Malango Church

Also known as the Commandments Church, this is an African indigenous PENTECOSTAL church, started in 1968 among the Bemba of Zambia. Its practices center on traditional medicine.

Mama Chi

Syncretist Christian movement among the Guaymi people of Panama. It was started in 1961 by Mama Chi, a woman who reported visions of Jesus Christ and the Virgin Mary.

Manav Kendra

Western Sikh-inspired group that claims to represent the authentic RUHANI SATSANG, led by Kirpal Singh. Its branches operate in Western Europe and the United States. [*See also* SANT BANI ASHRAM; *and* SAWAN KIRPAL RUHANI MISSION.]

Mandala Buddhist Center

U.S. center founded by Jomyo Tanaka in New York City in the 1980s. It claims to represent the tradition of "Shingon Esoteric Buddhism," as practiced in Japan. Shingon Buddhism is an occult tradition founded in Japan in the ninth century. The Center emphasizes the practice of meditation.

Manifest Sons of God

Sometimes known as "overcomers," this is a U.S. Christian MILLENARIAN group that developed in the 1950s out of the Canadian LATTER RAIN MOVEMENT. It parallels in many ways the movement known as CHRISTIAN GROWTH MINISTRIES.

Manjushri Institute

British branch of the Tibetan Buddhist movement of GELUG-PA.

Mansren

Indigenous syncretistic movement (CARGO CULT) that arose several times in the nineteenth century in Biak, in what is today the Indonesian province of West Irian. Several local prophets appeared and predicted the return of the mythical hero Mansren. This return was believed to involve also the delivery of "cargo" and the beginning of a utopian age.

Mara Christian Church

Indian indigenous Christian church founded in 1907 among the Manipuris.

Mara la Aspara

U.S. UFO group founded by Enid Brady, minister of the spiritualist church in Holly Hills, Florida, who reported contacts with extraterrestrials in the late 1950s. In the late 1960s she started relaying messages from Mara la Aspara of Venus. She was joined by John Langdon Watts in the late 1960s. His teachings are similar to those of Edgar Cayce and the ASSOCIATION FOR RESEARCH AND ENLIGHTENMENT.

Maranatha Campus Ministries (Maranatha Christian Churches)

U.S. PENTECOSTAL group founded in 1972 by Bob Weiner at Murray State University in Paducah, Kentucky. Maranatha has operated as a campus ministry, its branches being attached to colleges and universities. It has also taken a public stand on political issues, emphasizing the dangers of a Soviet invasion of the United States through Central America. Members are forbidden conventional dating of the opposite sex, because marriages are supposed to be arranged in heaven. The group was criticized by parents of members in the 1980s, and several members were kidnapped and "deprogrammed."

Margaret Fuller Corporation

U.S. ANTHROPOSOPHY group, founded in 1987 in New York state by Joel Kobran and Gary Lamb, and devoted to the propagation of Rudolf Steiner's ideas.

Maria Legio (of Africa)

Also known as Legio Maria, or Legio Maria of African Mission Church, this is a separatist African movement of Roman Catholic origins, which grew out of the Legio Maria, the Legion of Mary, a lay Irish Roman Catholic organization. Maria Legio was founded in Kenya in 1963 by two Roman Catholic members of the Luo people, Simeon Ondeto (1910–) and Gaudencia Aoko. In doctrine it combines Catholic and traditional African elements. Practices include speaking in tongues, faith healing, and exorcism. Its structure follows that of the Roman Catholic Church, with a pope and cardinals. The movement experienced impressive growth in its early years but then declined.

Maria Lionza

Syncretistic Afro-Catholic spiritualist movement in Venezuela, which started early in the twentieth century in the Sorte Mountains and spread to the cities after World War I. It is reminiscent of UMBANDA in Brazil but includes a majority of local elements. Popular heroes from the history of Venezuela, especially Indians, including Maria Lionza herself, dominate the pantheon of spirits and saints.

Source:
Simpson, G. E. *Black Religions in the New World*. New York: Columbia University Press, 1978.

Maria Rosa Mystica

European dissident Roman Catholic movement. It started in Brescia, Italy, in 1947, when a nurse claimed to have had apparitions of the Virgin Mary. European headquarters are located in Germany, and branches were reported in the United States in the mid-1980s.

Mark-Age Metacenter

U.S. spiritualist Christian group founded in 1962 by Pauline Sharp (1925–), known as the "prophetess Nada-Yolanda." In her visions, Nada-Yolanda deals with "the relationships and the responsibilities between the angelic and the man kingdoms ..., the actual words of the seven archangels ..., spiritual guidelines for the Latter Days and the Second Coming," and plans for a new age of spiritual evolution. The prophetess is in touch with visitors from outer space. Many of the messages and their terminology follow THEOSOPHICAL teachings.

Martinus Institute of Spiritual Science

International occultist, THEOSOPHICAL, spiritualist movement, founded by Martinus (1890–1981) in Copenhagen, Denmark, in the 1920s. It operates the Kosmos Holiday Centre and has branches in Western Europe and the United States. The group teaches a "Science of the Spirit" based on belief in "immortal energy" and reincarnation.

Maruyamakyo

Japanese MILLENARIAN movement founded in the mid-nineteenth century.

Masa Jehovah

Also known as Gaan Tata, this is a nativist syncretistic group, started in the 1880s among the peoples of Saramaka, Djuka, and Boni, living in the interior of Suriname and French Guiana in South America. The group's doctrine combines strong Christian elements with indigenous traditions. In 1936 a prophet named Wensi led a reform movement in the group, pushing it toward a stronger Christian emphasis. In 1972 another prophet, Akalali, led a similar movement, renewing Christian elements within the belief system.

Masowe Apostles

Originally known as the Vapostori (apostles) of Johannes Masowe, then successively as the Korsten Basketweavers, Hosannas, the Apostolic Sabbath Church of God, the African Gospel Church, and, since 1973, as Gospel of God Church, this is an African syncretistic group, founded by John Masowe of the Shona people of Southern Rhodesia, now Zimbabwe. He was born as Shoniwa in 1915. During the famine of 1932 he is reputed to have died and come back to life. Shoniwa retired to the mountains for a few days and came back as Johannes Masowe, John the Baptist. In 1947 the group, by then known as the Apostolic Sabbath Church of God, followed its leader to Port Elizabeth. Until 1962 they lived there, known as the Korsten Basketweavers, a hard-working community. In 1962 the 1880 followers were deported to Northern Rhodesia by the South African government, and they settled in Lusaka (now Zambia). The founder died in 1973, and several schisms followed.

Johannes Masowe, sometimes referred to as "the secret Messiah," told his followers they would not die and they believed he was the Son of God, Jesus returned. He taught that Shona, his native tongue, was the original language of mankind. The group is Sabbatarian and PENTECOSTAL in ritual. It has branches all over East Africa, with a strong presence in Kenya, Zimbabwe, Zambia, and Tanzania.

Source:
Dillon-Malone, C. *The Korsten Basketmakers: A Study of the Masowe Apostles, an Indigenous African Religious Movement.* Manchester: Manchester University Press, 1978.

Mata Amritanandamayi Mission

International Hindu movement led by Mata Amritanandamayi (1953–), who has been traveling in the West since 1987.

Matagiri

U.S. commune, based in Mt. Tremper, New York, which was founded in 1968 by Sam Spanier. It is devoted to spreading the Integral Yoga of SRI AUROBINDO.

Matsouanism (Matswa)

Initially known as Amicalism, this is a nativist African political-messianic movement in Zaire. It was started in 1926 by Andre Grenard Matswa (1899–1942) of the Sundi-Ladi people. He first founded, in Paris, the "Association amicale des originaires de l'Afrique equatoriale française," (also known as Amicale Balali, or amicalisme), a group designed to protect the rights of Africans under French rule. It then moved in the direction of resistance to French colonialism. Matswa was arrested and exiled in 1930, and after he died in prison in 1942, the movement became messianic. Its doctrine is based on the expectation of the founder's return, and he is known as "Jesus-Matswa." In popular beliefs he is linked to another charismatic leader, Simon Kimbangu. The group has survived as the Église Matsouaniste in Zaire and Congo. [*See also* KIMBANGUISM.]

Source:
Balandier, G. *Ambiguous Africa: Cultures in Collision.* New York: Pantheon Books, 1966.

Mazdaznan

Western Zoroastrian renewal movement founded in 1902 by Otoman Zar-Adhust Hanish (1844–1936) and based in Los Angeles. Practices include a prescribed diet, exercises, special breathing techniques, and chanting. Branches have operated in Europe since 1911.

Meadowlark Healing Center

U.S. occultist commune devoted to "inner spiritual healing process." It founded in the 1970s and is based in California.

Meditation Group for the New Age

Originally known as Meditation Mount, and sometimes as the Group for Creative Meditation, this is an international NEW THOUGHT group in the tradition of Alice A. Bailey, founder of the LUCIS TRUST. It has its headquarters in Ojai, California, and branches in Western Europe and Latin America. It was founded in 1950 by Florence Garrique.

Megiddo Mission

U.S. MILLENARIAN group founded in the late nineteenth century by L. T. Nichols. He operated a mission boat on the Mississippi River, the *Megiddo*, which gave the group its name. In 1903 he started a community in Rochester, New York, which has been the group headquarters since then. Group doctrine is based on the imminence of the battle of Armageddon, which will be followed by the millennium.

Meher Baba, Friends of

U.S. group devoted to the teachings of Meher Baba, who was born Merwan Sheheriarji Irani in 1894 in Poona (Pune), India, of Parsee parents. According to tradition, he was born on February 25, which is now celebrated as a holy day by his followers. Many stories of miracles and of contacts with holy men and women are told about Irani's early years. He started his career as a religious leader in India in 1921, and he became known in the West in the early 1930s. In 1921 a Hindu guru named Upasni Maharaj passed on his disciples to Irani, who then became known as Meher Baba ("compassionate father"—*Meher* means "merci-

ful" in some Indian languages and "sun" in Persian; *Baba* means "father"). He now attracted more disciples, whom he called *mandali*, and claimed to be an avatar, "God incarnated." His slogan was "I came not to teach but to awaken." Several ashrams, known as *masts*, were started around India for his *mandali*. He took a vow of silence in 1925, which lasted for most of his life. In 1956 he visited the United States.

According to some followers, in 1968 he broke his silence to communicate a last message to the world before his death several months later (January 31, 1969). According to others, he never uttered a word. Meher Baba taught that he was "God personified," the last in a chain (the "avataric cycle") that included Zoroaster, Krishna, Rama, Buddha, Jesus, and Muhammad. As the last manifestation, his coming closed the cycle. Followers, who regard him as the "Universal Savior," meditate on Meher Baba or contemplate his picture for hours at a time. Meher Baba spoke of the metaphysical unity of humanity, expressed in the saying "We are all one."

The Meher Baba Ashram is in Poona, India. Another Indian center is the Universal Spiritual Centre in Bangalore. Followers are known as "Baba lovers." There are several U.S. groups devoted to his teachings, such as SUFISM REORIENTED and the BABA LEAGUE. The musician Pete Townshend, of the band The Who, claims that Meher Baba helped him to kick his drug habit. [*See also* MEHER DURBAR; SOCIETY FOR AVATAR MEHER BABA; *and* UNIVERSAL SPIRITUAL LEAGUE OF AMERICA.]

Meher Durbar

Formerly known as the Meher Baba

Avatar Meher Baba.

House, this is a U.S. group, based in New York City, devoted to the teachings of MEHER BABA. It was founded in the late 1980s.

Melech Israel

Canadian HEBREW CHRISTIAN organization based in Toronto.

Memeneda Gyidifo

Known as Saturday Believers, or the Saviour Church of Ghana, this is an indigenous Christian church in Ghana, founded in 1924 by Samuel Brako (?–1946). Its doctrinal origins are Methodist, and it puts much emphasis on the avoidance of alcohol.

Menos

Danish occultist group founded in the 1970s.

Merigar

Tibetan Buddhist community based in Tuscany, Italy. It was founded by Namkhai Norbu in the 1970s.

Message to Israel

Canadian HEBREW CHRISTIAN group based in Halifax, Nova Scotia.

Messianic Assembly of Israel

Israeli HEBREW CHRISTIAN group based in Jerusalem. It was founded in 1948 by Ze'ev Kofsman, who had come to Jerusalem from France. The founder reportedly disputed some traditional Christian teachings, such as the canonical status of St. Paul's writings and the divinity of Jesus Christ. Nevertheless, he had contacts with, and received support from, Christian groups abroad including the ASSEMBLIES OF GOD in the United States. The Messianic Assembly had a PENTECOSTAL emphasis. Around 1970 the group merged with two others to form the HEBREW CHRISTIAN ASSEMBLY—JERUSALEM CONGREGATION.

Messianic Hebrew-Christian Fellowship

U.S. HEBREW CHRISTIAN group, founded in the 1980s and based in Harrisburg, Pennsylvania.

Messianic Jewish Alliance

British MESSIANIC JUDAISM group founded in the 1980s.

Messianic Jewish Alliance of America

International HEBREW CHRISTIAN association, founded in 1915 in Chicago as the Hebrew Christian Alliance of America. The name change in 1975 reflected the appearance of MESSIANIC JUDAISM. It is a loose association of more than one hundred groups and congregations around the world, which maintain their independence in many doctrinal matters.

Messianic Judaism

Messianic Judaism developed out of HEBREW CHRISTIANITY in the 1970s in order to counteract the latter's missionary image, and to change its character from Gentile Christian orientation to a more

Jewish tone. There is more emphasis on Jewish nationalism and Jewish ritual practices. Separate Messianic Judaism congregations are promoted, as opposed to "assimilation" within Christian churches. Significant differences exist among individual congregations in doctrine and rituals.

Source:
Rausch, D. *Messianic Judaism: Its History, Theology, and Polity.* Lewiston, N.Y.: Edwin Mellen Press, 1982.

Messianic Synagogue

British MESSIANIC JUDAISM group founded in the 1980s.

Metanoia

European occultist group founded in the 1970s.

Methodist Society

African indigenous group started in 1862 among the Fanti in the Gold Coast (present-day Ghana) in a schism from the Wesleyan Methodist group.

Metropolitan Church Association

Also known as the Burning Bush, this is a U.S. HOLINESS revivalist group, founded in Chicago in 1894.

Mettanokit

U.S. commune based on native American traditions. It was founded in Greenville, New Hampshire, in the late 1970s by Medicine Story.

Michaelsvereinigung

Swiss Christian spiritualist group founded in 1964 by Paul Kuhn (1920–). Its doctrines and practices combine Roman Catholic traditions with beliefs in reincarnation and medium-transmitted messages.

Midwest Pagan Council (MPC)

U.S. organization founded in 1976 that includes three pagan groups in the greater Chicago area. It is committed to promoting a public perception of paganism as a religion.

Millenarianism

An ideology characterizing religious groups that promise imminent collective salvation for the faithful in an earthly paradise that will rise following an apocalyptic destruction ordained by the gods.

Source:
Cohn, N. *The Pursuit of the Millennium* New York: Oxford University Press, 1970.

Mind and Body Science

U.S. occultist group founded in the late 1960s in Scottsdale, Arizona, by Robert H. Frey. The group combined Western occult ideas with Eastern practices, such as meditation.

Ministry of Universal Wisdom

U.S. UFO-THEOSOPHICAL group based in California and founded by George Van Tassel in 1952. The founder has reported receiving messages from extraterrestrials and having meetings with these aliens.

Miracle Distribution Center (MDC)

U.S. Christian NEW THOUGHT group organized around the A COURSE IN MIRACLES belief system. It was started in Fullerton, California, in 1978 by Beverly Hutchinson McNeff. It offers classes, workshops, books, and other materials. [See also CALIFORNIA MIRACLES CENTER; FOUNDATION FOR "A COURSE IN MIRACLES" (FACIM); FOUNDATION FOR INNER PEACE; and INTERFAITH FELLOWSHIP.]

Miracle Life Revival, Inc.

U.S. PENTECOSTAL healing group founded by Neal Vincent Frisby in 1967. It is based at Capstone Cathedral in Phoenix, Arizona.

Miracle Revival Fellowship

Known until 1970 as A. A. Allen Revivals, Inc., this is a U.S. PENTECOSTAL healing group, founded by Asa Alonzo Allen, and led since his death in 1970 by Don Stewart, who coined the current name. Allen earned a reputation as a healer in the 1940s and was active as a traveling healer all over the United States, especially in the South and the West. The group is now active mainly as a licensing agency for ministers worldwide. [See also LEROY JENKINS EVANGELISTIC ASSOCIATION.]

Missionary Christian and Soul Winning Fellowship

U.S. Protestant evangelical group founded in 1957 in Long Beach, California, by Lee Shelley, former minister of the CHRISTIAN AND MISSIONARY ALLI-

ANCE. It conducts missionary campaigns targeted at Jews in California.

Mission de Dieu du Bougie

Also known as Lassyism or Nzambi ya Bougie (God of the Candle), this is an African indigenous, syncretistic movement. It was started in 1953 by Zephirin Simon Lassy (1908–) of the Vili people in the Congo, by secession from the SALVATION ARMY. After traveling for thirty years in Europe and America, the founder joined the Salvation Army in 1946, but then started his own career as a visionary and healer, claiming amazing success. His doctrines combine Salvation Army notions with traditional ideas about magical healing. The movement has spread to Angola.

Mission for the Coming Days

Korean FUNDAMENTALIST, MILLENARIAN Christian church, founded by Chang Man-Ho and Lee Chang-Rim in the 1980s. The founders predicted the end of the world on October 28, 1992, and the church gained much notoriety. Following the debacle of October 1992, Lee Chang-Rim was imprisoned for two years.

Mission Patriotique Nationale

Haitian independent Christian movement founded in the 1950s.

Mita (Iglesia Mita)

Puerto Rican PENTECOSTAL group founded in 1940 by Juanita Garcia Peraga (?–1970), known as Mita, a former member of the ASSEMBLIES OF GOD. The group has branches in Latin America and in the United States, where the membership is drawn from Puerto Rican communities. The term *Mita* refers to the "Word of Life," which only the believers receive, through visions and dreams. The founder was considered a prophet and a healer as well as the incarnation of the Holy Spirit, a status that was passed on to her successor, Teofile Vargas Sein, known as Aaron.

Molokans

Russian Eastern Orthodox dissident sect, founded in Czarist Russia in the late eighteenth century by Simeon Uklein, which grew out of the DOUKHOBORS. Rejecting Doukhobor mysticism, Uklein preached for a return to earlier traditions in the Russian Orthodox Church. He claimed that the historical church fathers had corrupted and diluted true Christianity by introducing pagan traditions, and he therefore opposed all established church rituals. Members of the group drank milk during Lent, something forbidden in the Russian Orthodox Church, and so acquired the name of Molokans, or milk drinkers. Because of their pacifism and their religious ideas, members of the group have been persecuted. Some Molokan groups migrated to the United States in the early twentieth century.

Source:

Moore, W. B. *Molokan Oral Traditions.* Berkeley: University of California Press, 1973.

Moody Church

U.S. FUNDAMENTALIST group, named after the evangelist Dwight Lyman Moody (1837–1899). This Chicago congregation symbolizes historical continuity with nineteenth-century fundamentalism and Moody's historical role as its leader. Moody was a shoe salesman who organized Sunday schools in his spare time and then became a lay preacher. Between 1856 and 1873 he was active in Chicago. In 1873 he started collaborating with Ira David Sankey (1840–1908), and they began a series of preaching tours in the United States, Ireland, and Great Britain. The results have been described as "spectacular." These activities led to the founding of the Student Christian Movement (SCM), a national network of student collectives engaged in spiritual studies and progressive social justice issues.

On October 1, 1876, Moody started a three-and-a-half-month revival campaign involving many thousands, which has become the prototype for evangelical campaigns ever since. Moody used so-called "businessmen tactics," deemphasizing belief in hell and asking audiences to "buy Jesus." The Moody Church is the successor to the Illinois Street Independent Church, which Moody founded in 1864. The congregation, following Moody's teachings, is DISPENSATIONALIST and evangelical. The Moody Bible Institute, a major fundamentalist teaching center, is also named after Moody.

Sources:

Curtis, R. C. *They Called Him Mr. Moody.* Garden City, N.Y.: Doubleday, 1962.

Findlay, J. F. *Dwight L. Moody, American Evangelist, 1837–1899.* Chicago: University of Chicago Press, 1969.

Robertson, D. M. *The Chicago Revival, 1876: Society and Revivalism in a*

Dwight Lyman Moody, founder of the Fundamentalist Moody Church.

Nineteenth-Century City. Metuchen, N.J.: Scarecrow Press, 1989.

Moorish Science Temple of America

U.S. African American nationalist group founded in 1913 in Newark, New Jersey, by Timothy Drew (1886–1936), who adopted the name Noble Drew Ali. Drew authored the *Holy Koran* (unrelated to the Islamic Koran), and claimed that African Americans should be known as Asiatics, Moorish, or Moors, and that their true nation is Morocco. He denounced the common terms Negro and Ethiopian. Later he claimed that Islam was the religion of the Asiatics and defined his followers as Muslims. By 1926 the group had branches in many U.S. cities. After his death several followers claimed to be reincarnations of Noble Drew Ali. His ideas have influenced numerous groups, especially the NATION OF ISLAM.

Source:

Fauset, A. H. *Black Gods of the Metropolis*. Philadelphia: University of Pennsylvania Press, 1944.

Moral Re-Armament (MRA)

Also known as the Oxford Group or Buchmanites, this is an international Christian revitalization movement. It was founded in 1921 in England by the American Lutheran minister Frank N. D. Buchman (1878–1961). Ordained in 1902, Buchman had a "vision of the Cross" in 1908. In 1918, working in China, he started holding "house parties" to attract those who would never go to church. Aiming at a revival of what he considered first-century Christianity, the group was originally known as the First Century Christian Fellowship. In 1921 the group became known as the Oxford Group, seeking to capitalize on the prestige of Oxford University. In 1929 seven Oxford men carried the group's message to South Africa, and in 1938 the name was formally changed to Moral Re-Armament (MRA). This name change took place as the nations of Europe were energetically arming themselves in preparation for what turned out to be World War II. As MRA, the group focused on political and social issues. From its beginnings the group cultivated contact with affluent and well-known personalities and claimed connections in high places. In the 1930s MRA showed pro-Nazi sympathies. During the Cold War period of the late 1940s and early 1950s the group was highly visible in the United States, with a strong anti-Communist orientation. It has been suggested that the name change of 1938 was an attempt to change the group's image as a pro-Nazi organization. Since the death of its founder the group has been in sharp decline but still has some branches around the world.

Apparently the greatest impact of Buchmanism has been its influence on Alcoholics Anonymous and its Twelve Step program, taken from Buchman's doctrines and practices. Buchman's goals were as follows: "The only sane people in an insane world are those controlled by God. God-controlled personalities make God-controlled nationalities. This is the aim of the Oxford Group." The movement operates through small groups cultivating the "four Absolutes" (honesty, purity, unselfishness, love), leading to conversion or *Soul Surgery*. The main ritual is that of "sharing," a public confession of one's sins before the

Frank N. D. Buchman (second from left), founder of Moral Re-Armament.

group at a house-party. Complete surrender of the human will is demanded, and divine guidance is expected on such occasions.

Sources:

Clark, W. H. *The Oxford Group: Its History and Significance*. New York: Bookman Associates, 1951.

Driberg, T. *The Mystery of Moral Re-Armament*. New York: Knopf, 1965.

Eister, A. W. *Drawing-Room Conversation: A Sociological Account of the Oxford Group Movement*. Durham, N.C.: Duke University Press, 1950.

Lean, G. *Frank Buchman: A Life*. London: Constable, 1985.

Ragge, K. *More Revealed: A Critical Analysis of Alcoholics Anonymous and the Twelve Steps*. Henderson, N.C.: Alert! Publishing, 1991.

Mormons

Officially known as The Church of Jesus Christ of Latter-Day Saints (LDS), and often as simply LDS or the Saints (nonmembers are known as Gentiles), this is a U.S. Christian polytheistic MILLENARIAN group. It was founded in 1830 by Joseph Smith, Jr. (1805–1844) in northern New York State. At age fourteen Smith declared that he had spoken with God. Later he had other visions, during some of which, he said, an ancient book written on four tablets was given to him. He claimed to have transcribed this text, which has become known as *The Book of Mormon* and has given its name to the Church. The Book of Mormon is believed to be an ancient revelation to the inhabitants of America, written in Egyptian.

This book is the movement's main scripture, together with a version of the Bible known as *The Pearl of Great Price* (P. of G.P.) and the *Doctrine and Covenants* (D. & C.). On April 6, 1830, Smith and a group of followers founded the Church of Christ, and the name was later changed to the Church of Jesus Christ of Latter-Day Saints. Smith announced to the world that he was "seer, translator, prophet, apostle of Jesus Christ, and elder of the church." In 1835 twelve apostles were appointed and sent to gain converts in the United States. That same year Smith also prophesied the Second Coming. In 1837 the first Mormon missionaries arrived in Great Britain and met some success, as well as some prejudice.

In its early years the movement encountered much violence because of its unconventional beliefs and its advocacy of polygyny (it was first renounced in 1890 and then rescinded in 1904). Opposition forced the group to move first to Ohio, then to Missouri, and then to Illinois, where the city of Nauvoo was founded in 1840. According to some reports, Smith was crowned as a king in 1844. In that year, however, Smith and his brother were killed by a mob. His followers then embarked on a long journey away from the Eastern United States. Led by Brigham Young (1801–1877), they eventually settled in Salt Lake City. In 1850 Young became the first governor of the territory of Utah, which became a state in 1895.

Mormons reject the traditional Christian doctrines of original sin, the Trinity, and salvation by grace, but they believe in the Devil. Mormon doctrine regards the LDS church as a revival and restoration of the organization of the early Christian church, and it attributes a particular and central role to America in history and eschatology. According to this doctrine, Jesus Christ visited the New World, was revealed to the ancient inhabitants of America, and will reveal himself again in Independence, Missouri, as Zion will be built on American soil. In addition, Mormons believe in the literal gathering of Israel and the "restoration of the Ten Tribes." These "Lost Tribes of Israel," according to the Book of Mormon, are native Americans who are actually "Hebrews."

A central tenet of LDS is the belief in a multiplicity of gods and universes. In each universe there is a god, carrying out a master plan for his offspring. Humans and gods represent different levels of spiritual development, and there is eternal progression in the evolution of gods and humans. An essential LDS tenet is the belief in human deification: "as man is, God once was, and as God is, man may become." The LDS believes that God is a physical man with "body, parts, and passions," the son of an earlier god, who achieved divinity by living a righteous life, a path now open to all humans, men and women. "God himself was once as we are now, and is an exalted man, and sits enthroned in yonder heavens! That is the great secret. . . . I might with boldness proclaim from the house-tops that God never had the power to create the spirit of man at all. God himself could not create himself." (Joseph Smith, April 1844). We will all become gods or goddesses if we follow Mormon teachings. This plan of salvation was announced before man's creation. Man, as a spirit, was begotten and born of heavenly parents prior to the creation of mortal life. Adam, when created, was a prophet or a god. This is known as the doctrine of preexistence.

Mormons believe in a female deity, known as the Mother in Heaven or Heavenly Mother, in addition to the Heavenly Father, but the Mother is less important, and no prayers are addressed to her.

Marriage is considered an eternal covenant. Temple ceremonies such as eternal marriage and baptism for the dead are also LDS tenets. In "proxy baptism" LDS members are baptized as they stand in for the dead. The most extensive collection of genealogical records in the world is maintained by the LDS, so that new members can baptize all their ancestors, going back as far as possible. The "covenant of celestial marriage" is a condition for exaltation in Heaven, *i.e.*, deification, which will occur after many stages of progression. The eternal mar-

The angel Moroni delivering the plates of the Book of Mormon to Joseph Smith.

Joseph Smith's Original Temple of Mormonism, at Nauvoo, Illinois.

riage includes the procreation of spirit children by celestial couples in the afterlife.

All Mormons are believed capable of receiving divine revelations at any time, but only within the limits of their jurisdiction. The First President receives revelations for the whole church; a Bishop receives revelation covering his ward, and an Elder receives revelations about his family. Glossolalia (speaking in tongues) and visions were common among the members in the early years of the group, but these were later discouraged. Members avoid caffeine and tobacco. They do not drink colas, alcoholic beverages, coffee, or tea. They tithe their income. Non-Mormons are excluded from Mormon temples, but according to reports from former members ceremonies include dramatic enactments of Mormon mythological narratives. Each Mormon receives a secret name for the purpose of temple work, and is expected to wear a special undergarment at all times. Temple rites show the influence of Masonic traditions, and it is known that Joseph Smith and other Mormon leaders were members of Masonic groups. In addition, other prevailing occultist and spiritualist ideas affected the development of Mormon doctrines in the nineteenth century. Other major sources of influence were the millenarian movements and ideas that were prevalent in the Eastern United States in the 1830s and 1840s.

Mormons expect upheavals and disasters before the Second Coming, which would leave only Mormons unharmed. This leads to a preoccupation with physical survival and the stocking up of emergency supplies of food and water in every Mormon home. Members are expected to have in storage one year's worth of food, in preparation for the global catastrophe. Most male members are involved in the church hierarchy and have official roles in the priesthood, and Mormons enjoy an active community life. Many young Mormons serve for two years as missionaries around the world. According to longevity data, Mormons, like SEVENTH DAY ADVENTISTS, outlive other Americans, apparently because of their avoidance of alcohol, tobacco, and caffeine.

Historically, Africans were banned from Mormon priesthood, but this doctrine was changed in 1978, in what was officially described as a divine revelation to Spencer Kimball, Mormon president at the time. Since the 1960s Mormons have been very active in African countries, and sometimes they have been the target of legal action on the part of governments there. In June 1989 Mormons were officially expelled from Ghana. [*See also* REORGANIZED CHURCH OF JESUS CHRIST OF LATTER DAY SAINTS; *and* UNITED ORDER EFFORT.]

Sources:

Alexander, T. G. *Mormonism in Transition: A History of the Latter-Day Saints 1890–1930*. Urbana: University of Illinois Press, 1986.

Anderson, N. *Desert Saints*. Chicago: University of Chicago Press, 1966.

Arrington, L. J. *Brigham Young: American Moses*. New York: Knopf, 1985.

———, and Britton, D. *The Mormon Experience*. New York: Knopf, 1979.

Bloom, H. *The American Religion: The Making of a Post-Christian Nation*. New York: Simon & Schuster, 1992.

Bringhurst, N. G. *Saints, Slaves, and Blacks: The Changing Place of Black People within Mormonism*. Westport, Conn.: Greenwood Press, 1981.

Brodie, F. M. *No Man Knows My History*. New York: Knopf, 1945.

Bushman, R. L. *Joseph Smith and the Beginnings of Mormonism*. Urbana: University of Illinois Press, 1984.

Foster, L. *Religion and Sexuality: Three American Communal Experiments of the Nineteenth Century*. New York: Oxford University Press, 1981.

Gottlieb, R., and Wiley, P. *America's Saints: The Rise of Mormon Power*. New York: Putnam, 1985.

Hanson, K. J. *Mormonism and the American Experience*. Chicago: University of Chicago Press, 1981.

Heinerman, J., and Shupe, A. *The Mormon Corporate Empire*. Boston: Beacon Press, 1985.

Hill, D. *Joseph Smith: The First Mormon*. Garden City, N.Y.: Doubleday, 1977.

Kern, L. J. *An Ordered Love: Sex Roles and Sexuality in Victorian Utopias—The Shakers, The Mormons, and the Oneida Community*. Chapel Hill: University of North Carolina Press, 1981.

Leone, M. *Roots of Modern Mormonism*. Cambridge, Mass.: Harvard University Press, 1979.

Mullen, R. *The Latter-Day Saints: The Mormons Yesterday and Today*. Garden City, N.Y.: Doubleday, 1966.

O'Dea, T. *The Mormons*. Chicago: University of Chicago Press, 1957.

Shepherd, G. and G. *A Kingdom Transformed: Themes in the Development of Mormonism*. Salt Lake City: University of Utah Press, 1984.

Shipps, J. *Mormonism: The Story of a New Religious Tradition*. Urbana: University of Illinois Press, 1985.

Shupe, A. *The Darker Side of Virtue: Corruption, Scandal, and the Mormon Empire*. Buffalo: Prometheus Press, 1991.

Taves, E. H. *Trouble Enough: Joseph Smith and the Book of Mormon*. Buffalo: Prometheus Press, 1984.

————. *This Is the Place: Brigham Young and the New Zion*. Buffalo: Prometheus Press, 1990.

Underwood, G. *The Millenarian World of Early Mormonism*. Urbana: University of Illinois Press, 1994.

Morningstar

U.S. syncretistic commune founded in Sonoma County, California, in 1966 by the musician Lou Gotlieb. It moved to Taos, New Mexico, in 1967.

Mother Meera

Hindu-inspired international group devoted to an Indian woman known as Meera, the Divine Mother (1960–), who has been living in Germany since the 1980s. She is considered an avatar by her followers.

Robert E. Miles, founder of the Mountain Church of Jesus Christ the Saviour and former Grand Dragon of the Michigan Ku Klux Klan, arrives at court for arraignment on charges of conspiring to bomb school buses. He was later convicted and served a six-year sentence.

Mountain Brook

U.S. NEW THOUGHT group founded by William Samuel in Mountain Brook, Alabama, in 1968. It operates mainly by correspondence.

Mountain Church of Jesus Christ the Saviour

Also known as The Mountain Church or the Mountain Kirk, this is a U.S. Christian IDENTITY, white suprematist, militarist group, associated with the Ku Klux Klan. It was founded by Robert E. Miles, former head of the Michigan Ku Klux Klan, and is based in Cohoctaw, Michigan. Miles developed his own version of Identity, known as dualism, according to which Aryan history is divided into an early period in the North, in which the Norse gods were worshipped, and a later period in West Asia, which produced Christianity. Humanity is divided into two races, whites of the "astral Plane" and non-whites. Another dualism is found in a battle between God and Lucifer, or Yahweh and Satan, who used to be equals. Yahweh exiled Satan to Earth, and Satan, with the help of his allies the Jews, is trying to trick Caucasians.

In the 1970s Miles served six years in federal prison for bombing school buses used in school integration programs. In

240

1988 he was charged by the U.S. government with seditious conspiracy and convicted. In April 1988 some members of the church were acquitted by a jury in Fort Smith, Arkansas, of plotting to overthrow the U.S. government. [*See also* BRITISH ISRAELISM; CHURCH OF JESUS CHRIST CHRISTIAN — ARYAN NATIONS; *and* THE ORDER.]

Mount Rurun Movement

Sometimes known as the Yangoru movement, this is a Melanesian indigenous syncretistic movement (CARGO CULT), started in 1969 in the Yangoru area in the East Sepik province of Papua New Guinea.

Mouvement Croix-Koma (Nailed to the Cross)

African independent movement, which was started in 1964 in the Congo by Ta Malanda (?–1976), a Roman Catholic layman of the Lari people. At first the founder stated that the movement was still part of the Roman Catholic Church, but all links have been severed. The group's doctrine emphasizes opposition to witchcraft in all its forms, and members are required to give up their magical objects in public ceremonies.

Movement of Spiritual Inner Awareness (MSIA)

Also known as the Church of the Movement of Spiritual Inner Awareness, this is a U.S. NEW THOUGHT group, founded in California in 1963 by John-Roger Hinkins (1934–), known as John-Roger. The founder, a former schoolteacher, was born Roger Delano Hinkins to Mormon parents in Utah. He became possessed by a spirit known as "John the Beloved" in 1963. According to another report, John-Roger, after a nine-day coma, found his body inhabited by "the Mystical Traveller, a consciousness that acts as a 'wayshower' in the quest for spiritual inner awareness." MSIA defines itself as "a group of loving people who come together in their common love for the God in their hearts, for the Mystical Traveler through John-Roger, and for one another." John-Roger is considered "the physical embodiment of the Mystical Traveler Consciousness."

This group operates the Baraka Center for "holistic therapy," the John-Roger Foundation (which offers Insight Transformational Seminars), Koh-E-Nor University (which offers "advanced degrees in Applied Human Relations with specialization in Consciousness Facilitating"), the Integrity Foundation (which awards the International Integrity Awards), NOW productions, and the Heartfelt Foundation. It has offered the Insight Transformational Seminars as management-training courses to major corporations. The group also offers "Prosperity" training and expects its members to tithe. It also provides services such as "aura balancing, inner phasing to stop negative habit patterns, and polarity balancing."

On June 19, 1988, "John-Roger passed the keys to the Mystical Traveler Consciousness to John Morton." John-Roger still holds the titles of Mystical Traveler and Preceptor Consciousness. According to media reports, the various MSIA operations have accumulated a vast fortune, and John-Roger has achieved a unique degree of personal influence. In the mid-1980s MSIA counted scores of U.S. celebrities among its followers. On

August 10, 1988, a resolution was passed by the U.S. Congress declaring September 24, John-Roger's birthday, National Integrity Day. Such a resolution needs at least 218 members of Congress as sponsors, and in this case it was also sponsored by 200 cities and forty-six states.

Movimiento Cristiano y Misionero

Argentinian indigenous Pentecostal group started in 1958 by secession from the ASSEMBLIES OF GOD.

Movimiento Gnostico Cristiano Universal de España

Spanish occultist group claiming to develop "universal gnosticism" following the teachings of Samael Aun Weor. It was started in the late 1970s, inspired by GNOSIS. Activities include teaching yoga, meditation, and Kabala. Beliefs include the idea of an astral body and an alchemical birth.

Muchakata

African independent church founded in Zimbabwe in 1942.

Mu Farm

U.S. syncretist commune founded in 1971 near Yoncalla, Oregon, by Fletcher Fist. Its doctrine is eclectic and combines Christianity, Hinduism, and THEOSOPHY.

Mukyokai

Japanese indigenous Christian movement, known as "nonchurch Christianity." It was started by Kanzo Uchimura (1861–1930), a former Methodist, in the early twentieth century. Uchimura in 1891 rebelled publicly against the official status of Shinto as the Japanese national cult and then rebelled against Protestant foreign missions. The group operates in small Bible study groups, with no buildings or clergy. [See also MAKUYA.]

Source:
Caldarola, C. *Christianity: The Japanse Way*. Leiden: E. J. Brill, 1979.

Musama Disco Christo Church (MDCC)

Known officially as the Army of the Cross of Christ Church, this is a syncretistic movement founded in Ghana in 1922 by Joseph William Egyanka Appiah (1893–1948), known to the group as Prophet Jemisemiham Jehu-Appiah, Akaboha I. Healing is the most important practice of this group, as both Western medicine and folk medicine are avoided. Alcohol, tobacco, pork, and blood are proscribed, and menstruating women are kept apart. In services, the group follows Christian PENTECOSTAL practices.

Mystic Connection/Church of Light

U.S. spiritualist group founded by Shari Sumrall in Florida in the 1980s.

N

Nada Community

U.S. Christian mystical monastic community, founded in the 1960s and led by Tessa Bielecki. The community followed rules of strict solitude and silence.

Nagaland Christian Revival Church

Indian indigenous PENTECOSTAL church founded in 1952.

Nagriamel Church of Christ

Melanesian indigenous independent church started in 1967 by secession from the Churches of Christ on the Island of Santos, Vanuatu.

Namdhari

Also known as Kuka, this is a Sikh revival movement, calling for renewal and reform against what it calls the "Hindu corruptions" of Sikhism. It proclaims a continuing line of living gurus, which puts it in clear opposition to majority Sikh doctrine. It was founded in the mid-nineteenth century by Balak Singh (1797–1862), who was succeeded by Ram Singh (1816–1885). [*See also* NIRANKARI.]

Source:
Singh, Khushwant. *A History of the Sikhs.* Princeton, N.J.: Princeton University Press, 1963–1966.

Namhak

Also known as Nam-hak gyo or Yeon-dam gyo, this is an indigenous Korean movement started in the mid-nineteenth century.

Narayananda Universal Yoga Trust

International Hindu group, led by Pramukh Swami, which has been active in several European countries since the 1970s, especially Great Britain and Denmark.

Source:
Williams, R. B. *A New Face of Hinduism.* Cambridge: Cambridge University Press, 1983.

National Association for the Promotion of Holiness

U.S. Protestant group founded in Vineland, New Jersey, in 1867.

National Church of Madras

Indian indigenous church founded in 1886, in opposition to European missionaries.

National Colored Spiritualist Association of Churches

U.S. spiritualist group founded in 1925, as African American members left the NATIONAL SPIRITUALIST ASSOCIATION OF CHURCHES because of its policy of segregation. Otherwise this group was identical to the NSAC in its doctrines and practices.

National David Spiritual Temple of Christ Church Union (Inc.) U.S.A.

U.S. African American PENTECOSTAL church founded in 1932 in Kansas City by David William Short, a former Baptist minister. In 1952 it merged with ST. PAUL'S SPIRITUAL CHURCH CONVOCATION and KING DAVID'S SPIRITUAL TEMPLE OF TRUTH ASSOCIATION to form the UNIVERSAL CHRISTIAN SPIRITUAL FAITH AND CHURCHES FOR ALL NATIONS.

National Institute for Self-Understanding

U.S. organization related to the SELF-REALIZATION FELLOWSHIP. It offers "spiritual readings and counseling."

National Islamic Assembly

U.S. Islamic group, founded in 1985, which has attempted to form an alliance of all African American Islamic-oriented groups. [See also NATION OF ISLAM.]

National Spiritual Alliance

U.S. spiritualist group started in 1913 by secession from the NATIONAL SPIRITUALIST ASSOCIATION OF CHURCHES over the issue of reincarnation. Belief in reincarnation was not a part of the NSAC Declaration of Principles, and the majority objected to its promotion. So a minority of the church created the National Spiritual Alliance and made reincarnation a part of their doctrine.

National Spiritualist Association of Churches (NSAC)

U.S. spiritualist organization founded in Chicago in 1893 by Harrison D. Barrett and James M. Peebles, former Unitarian ministers. This is the largest and the oldest of U.S. spiritualist organizations. Several other groups were created over the years as a result of schisms within the NSAC. Its Declaration of Principles affirms the belief in "Infinite Intelligence," whose expression is the phenomena of nature, both physical and spiritual. It also affirms belief in the continuity of personal identity after "the change called death" and the belief in communication with "the so-called dead." It does not contain references to reincarnation, the Bible, or to traditional Christian concepts. These issues have led a number of splinter groups to secede from the NSAC. [See also GENERAL ASSEMBLY OF SPIRITUALISTS; NATIONAL COLORED SPIRITUALIST ASSOCIATION OF CHURCHES; and NATIONAL SPIRITUAL ALLIANCE.]

Sources:

Brown, S. *The Heyday of Spiritualism*. New York: Hawthorn Books, 1970.

Nelson, G. L. *Spiritualism and Society*. New York: Schocken Books, 1969.

National Spiritual Science Center

U.S. spiritualist group founded in 1941 in Washington, D.C., by Alice W. Tindall, who had been a member of the SPIRITUAL SCIENCE CHURCH.

National Swazi Native Apostolic Church of Africa

South African ZIONIST church, founded by Richard S. Mhlanga, who planned it as the National Swazi Church. The founder believed in faith healing alone but was ready to tolerate the use of medicine in order to receive national status.

Source:

Sundkler, B. G. M. *Bantu Prophets in South Africa*. London: Oxford University Press, 1961.

Nation of Islam (NOI)

Originally named the Lost-Found Nation of Islam in the West, and popularly known as Black Muslims, this is a revitalization movement active among U.S. African Americans, offering them a (non-orthodox) Islamic religious identity and separating them from the surrounding culture. Naming members X, as was done in the early days of the movement, was a symbol of separation and separatism. Later, members were told to change their European "slave names" and adopt Arabic names.

The movement is supposed to have originated in the teachings of the mysterious W. D. Fard, or Wallace D. Fard Muhammad, or Walli Farrad Muhammad, or Wali Fard, the Honorable Master Fard Muhammad, or Professor Forda, a man who appeared in 1930 in Detroit, preached in the black communities of the U.S. Midwest in the early 1930s, and disappeared in 1934. Reportedly Fard propagated the view that African Americans were in reality Muslims separated from their true identity.

Elijah Muhammad (1897–1975), a former Baptist minister named Elijah Poole, who followed Fard and actually founded the NOI, regarded his teacher as a Mahdi, a divine Messiah and prophet. He led the movement from the 1930s to 1975, during which time it experienced significant growth, especially after World War II.

Elijah Muhammad's *Message to the Blackman in America* (1965), a revision and expansion of his earlier *The Supreme Wisdom*, summarizes NOI beliefs, which were expressed in the weekly paper, *Muhammad Speaks*. According to original NOI doctrine, Fard came from "Arabia" to the United States around 1930 and was an incarnation of Allah who appointed Elijah Muhammad as his prophet. The prophet taught that originally all humans were black, until a evil genius named Yakub created a white race of devils on the island of Patmos.

"The great archdeceivers (the white race) were taught by their father, Yakub, 6,000 years ago, how to teach that God is a spirit (spook) and not a man. In the grafting of his people (the white race), Mr. Yakub taught his people to contend with us over the reality of God by asking us of the whereabouts of that first One (God) who created the heavens and the earth, and that, Yakub said, we cannot do. Well, we all know that there was a God in the beginning that created all these things and do know that He does not exist today. But we know again that from that God the person of God continued until today in His people, and today a Supreme One (God) has appeared among us with the same infinite wisdom to bring about a complete change." Following a world upheaval predicted for 1970, black people would assume control of the planet.

The NOI beliefs deviated from orthodox Islam. Malcolm X (Malcolm Little, 1925–1965), who was second in command to Elijah Muhammad, started a movement toward Sunni Islamic orthodoxy, and changed his name to El Hajj Malik Shabazz. After Malcolm X left the

Malcolm X, an early leader of the Nation of Islam.

movement to found his own mosque, he was assassinated in February 1965 by men who were believed to be members of NOI. The group operated a security force known as the Fruit of Islam (FOI).

From its early years, the NOI was active and successful in raising the living standards of its members and in saving individuals from a life of crime and drug addiction. Followers are taught a lifestyle of puritanism and hard work. Alcohol, tobacco, and other drugs were strictly forbidden, as were gambling and dancing. The self-help doctrine preached by the founder led to self-reliance and pride.

After 1975, when Elijah Muhammad died without a will, the group was hurt by suits and countersuits by his twenty-one children, involving his property and the group's property, which was worth many millions of dollars. This was a continuation of "the Elijah Affair," a scandal that rocked the movement in the early 1960s, following the discovery that the founder had fathered children in liaisons with his secretaries.

The founder's son, Herbert D. Muhammad, took over the leadership in 1975, officially changed the name to Nation of Islam, or Bilalians, and opened the membership to all races. In 1977 leadership passed to another son, Wallace Delaney Muhammad, later known as Waarith Deen Muhammad (1934–), who has moved the Nation toward Orthodox Sunni Islam, and changed its name in 1976 to World Community of Al-Islam in the West. The majority of NOI members have followed Warith Deen Muhammad to Sunni Islam. Later, the name Muslim Community of America was adopted; in 1980 it was changed to American Muslim Mission (AMM), before the organization was completely dissolved in 1985 and Waarith Deen Muhammad resigned as leader. His declared intention was to let independent mosques run their affairs as part of the worldwide Sunni Muslim community. In 1986 W. D. Muhammad established an affiliation with the Council of Rabita, an Islamic group founded in 1978 in Mecca.

Nation of Islam (NOI) now denotes, in most cases, the group headed by Abdul Haleem Farrakhan (see below). [*See also* HANAFI MADH-HAB CENTER.]

Sources:

Breitman, G. *The Last Year of Malcolm X.* New York : Schocken, 1968.

———. Porter, I., and Smith, B. *The Assassination of Malcolm X.* New York: Pathfinder Press, 1976.

Elijah Muhammad, founder of the Nation of Islam.

Organized by Louis Farrakhan, leader of the Nation of Islam, the Million Man March promoted a sense of community and shared purpose among African American men in the United States.

Essien-Udom, E. U. *Black Nationalism*. Chicago: University of Chicago Press, 1962.

Lee, M. F. *The Nation of Islam: An American Millenarian Movement*. New York: Edwin Mellen Press, 1988.

Lincoln, C. E. *The Black Muslims in America*. Boston: Beacon Press, 1961.

Nation of Islam (NOI) (Farrakhan)

Also known as the Nation, this is a U.S. African American Muslim-inspired group, founded in 1977 by Abdul Haleem Farrakhan (Louis Eugene Wolcott, 1933–) as a breakaway group from what was then the World Community of Al-Islam in the West, successor to the NATION OF ISLAM (NOI). The declared aim of the new group was to revive the original Nation of Islam concept, as promoted by Elijah Muhammad. Its doctrine emphasizes moral reawakening of African Americans, economic self-help, and some Islamic beliefs. Its leader, born in New York City and raised in Boston, joined the original Nation of Islam during a visit to Chicago in 1955, where he heard a speech by Elijah Muhammad and had a "dream revelation." He was known as Louis X in the late 1950s and became the minister in the Nation of Islam mosque in Boston in 1957. Then he moved to Harlem, New York, where, in 1964, he succeeded Malcolm X as the minister of NOI Temple 7. In 1977 Farrakhan broke away from Wallace D. Muhammad and the latter's drive toward Sunni Islam. Since the late 1970s he has taken an outspoken separatist stand regarding whites, often expressing anti-Semitic views. Since 1979 the group has published *The Final Call*. The group has operated branches in Great Britain as well since the 1980s.

Farrakhan has kept the core beliefs offered by Elijah Muhammad. Master Fard (or Farrad) is regarded as Allah incarnate, and Elijah Muhammad is considered his apostle. Farrakhan has said that in 1985 he met Elijah Muhammad, dead for a decade, in a spaceship. An apocalypse leading to black rule is still expected any time. In 1985 the Nation of Islam (NOI) (Farrakhan) set up People Organized and Working for Economic Rebirth (POWER), designed to create economic self-sufficiency for African Americans. It also operates the Fruit of Islam (FOI) security force, which supplies bodyguards to the group's leaders and other African American dignitaries. The female counterpart of the FOI is MGT, Muslim Girl Training. In 1995 Farrakhan successfully organized the Million Man March on Washington D.C. The March was called a "Holy Day of Atonement" for black men. Attendees were encouraged to pledge their dedication to improving their communities and nurturing their children. Speeches were given by prominent figures in the black community, encouraging self-discipline and self-reliance.

Nation of Islam (NOI) (Jeremiah Shabazz)

U.S. Islamic group, based in Philadelphia and founded by Jeremiah Shabazz in the late 1970s. It grew out of the NATION OF ISLAM (NOI). Shabazz was minister of the Nation of Islam Philadelphia Temple before 1975.

Nation of Islam (NOI) (Silas Muhammad)

U.S. Islamic group based on the West Coast and founded by Silas Muhammad in the late 1970s. It grew out of the NATION OF ISLAM (NOI).

Nation of Yahweh (Hebrew Israelites)

Also known as the Temple of Love or the Followers of Yahweh, this is a U.S. Black Judaism group, founded in the 1970s in Miami, Florida, by Hulon Mitchell, Jr. (1935–), a former member of a PENTECOSTAL church and later a leader in the NATION OF ISLAM (NOI). In the late 1960s Mitchell reported having died and then risen from the dead to pursue a divine mission. By 1979 he was known as Brother Moses. Later he changed his name to Yahweh ben Yahweh, and declared himself the son of God. African Americans, according to Yahweh ben Yahweh, are the lost tribe of Judah. Members are expected to change their first names when joining the group and to adopt the last name Israel. They wear white robes and turbans. They believe in immortality. The group has achieved a measure of influence in Miami, and October 7, 1990, was declared Yahweh ben Yahweh Day by the mayor. In November

Yahweh ben Yahweh, founder of the Nation of Yahweh, also known as the Hebrew Israelites and the Temple of Love.

1990 Yahweh ben Yahweh was indicted, together with sixteen other members of the group, in connection with fourteen cases of murder and other serious crimes. Prosecutors claimed that in the 1980s Yahweh ben Yahweh and his followers used money from an $8 million empire of hotels to finance a group of killers and arsonists. In May 1992 Yahweh ben Yahweh and some of his followers were convicted of federal racketeering conspiracy charges involving fourteen murders, two attempted murders, and arson. The convictions led to long prison terms for the leader and some followers.

Native American Church (NAC)

U.S. Native American, Protestant nativist revitalization movement, combining Christian elements with native tradition. The movement was started in 1906, and in 1909 the name Union Church was adopted. In 1918 the group was incorporated under its present name. The FIRST BORN CHURCH OF CHRIST was later absorbed by this group. The use of peyote in its central ritual has involved the group in legal battles for generations, but it won the right to use it. Public Law 91-513, the Comprehensive Drug Abuse Prevention and Control Act of 1970, as passed by the U.S. Congress, prohibited the use of peyote but made an exemption for members of the Native American Church. In 1990 a U.S. Supreme Court ruling against this exemption cast doubt on the future of the group. In this decision, *Employment Division* v. *Smith*, the Court ruled that a religion cannot be exempted from criminal law. In response to that decision, the U.S. Congress passed the 1993 Religious Freedom Restoration Act; it did not, however, specifically mention peyote. The American Indian Religious Freedom Act Amendment of 1994 resolved this issue and allows the group to continue with its practices.

Sources:

Aberle, D. F. *The Peyote Religion among the Navaho.* Chicago: Aldine, 1966.

Anderson, E. F. *Peyote: The Divine Cactus.* Tucson: University of Arizona Press, 1980.

La Barre, W. *The Peyote Cult.* Hamden, Conn.: Shoe String Press, 1959.

Slotkin, J. S. *The Peyote Religion: A Study in Indian-White Relations.* Glencoe, Ill.: Free Press, 1956.

Native Baptist Church

African indigenous Christian church formed in 1888 in Lagos, Nigeria, in a secession from the Southern Baptist Mission.

Native Independent Congregational Church

South African separatist church founded in 1885, following a secession from the London Missionary Society in Taung, Bechuanaland. It was supported at the time by the tribal chief Kgantlapane.

Native Primitive Church

South African separatist church founded in 1840 in opposition to official missionary groups.

Emerson Jackson of the Native American Church performs a ceremony outside the Supreme Court Building in Washington, D.C. The Court ruled to exempt the sect from laws against use of peyote.

Nazarene Episcopal Ecclesia

International BRITISH-ISRAELIST Protestant group started in 1873, with headquarters in Great Britain.

Nazaretha (or Shembeites)

Officially known as the Nazarite Baptist Church and as the Ama-Nazaretha or Nazarites, this is a South African syncretistic movement, founded by the Zulu prophet Isaiah Shembe (1870–1935) in 1911. As a young man Shembe had many visions in which he was told to repent and leave his four wives. He started working as a healer and exorcist, and he was baptized in 1906 by Baptist missionaries. In 1916 he established a village named Ekuphakameni, eighteen miles from Durban. Then he had a vision telling him to go to the Nhlangakazi mountain in Natal, which has become the Nazarite Holy Mountain. Nhlangakazi is the location of an annual January festival, and Ekuphakameni is the location of a July festival. After the prophet's death, his mantle was inherited by his son Johannes Galilee Shembe. Group doctrine opposes modern medicine, and until 1944 it opposed all vaccinations for members. Shembe rejected Jesus in favor of Jehovah and chose the Saturday Sabbath to replace Sunday. Shembe is considered the Black Christ, risen from the dead, and the Christian Bible is believed to have been written about him.

Source:

Sundkler, B. G. M. *Bantu Prophets in South Africa*. London: Oxford University Press, 1961.

Necedah Shrine

Sometimes known as the Diamond Star Constellation, this is a U.S. independent Catholic group founded by Mary Ann Van Hoof in Wisconsin in the 1960s. In the 1950s Van Hoof reported apparitions of the Virgin Mary as well as "other celestials." These apparitions led to the publication of various revelations. The group operated the Seven Sorrows of Our Sorrowful Mother Infants Home as a home for unwed mothers.

Neological

Official label for REFORM JUDAISM congregations in Hungary during the late nineteenth and twentieth centuries.

Netivyah

Israeli HEBREW CHRISTIAN group founded in the 1950s in Jerusalem by Daniel Zion, former chief rabbi of Bulgaria. The founder's views are unorthodox by traditional Christian standards. The group is committed to preserving some Jewish rabbinical traditions.

Neverdies

Also known as Church of the Living or the Everlasting Gospel, this is a U.S. PENTECOSTAL group based in West Virginia. Members believe in physical immortality. Among the leaders have been Ted Oiler and Henry Holstine.

New Acropolis (NA)

Also known as Nueva Acropolis, this is an international occultist THEOSOPHICAL group founded in 1956 in Buenos Aires

253

by Jorge Angel Livraga (1930–), known as JAL, and his wife, Ada Albrecht. It has developed branches all over Western Europe and Israel. The group offers many public lectures but operates a parallel, secretive "Theosophical Society." Its doctrine includes belief in the reality of fairies as well as plans for a new political order inspired by Plato's *Republic*. It teaches an array of Western occultist traditions, including alchemy, Tibetan and Egyptian lore, and the "cosmic laws of the microcosm and the macrocosm." Other elements in its teachings include reincarnation, astrology, and the secrets of ancient Greek culture. Followers are being prepared for the "Age of Aquarius" by being trained to become "supermen."

New Age Christianity Without Religion

International Christian group founded by Hugh de Cruz in the 1970s. It has headquarters, known as Temple of Light, in the Canary Islands but now has branches worldwide. The largest are in Spain, New Zealand, and Ghana. Doctrine recognizes various masters; chief among them is Sandana, the Jesus Christ of the Aquarian Age. Some Hindu ideas are also promoted.

New Age Church of Being

U.S. group founded in 1988 in Harbin Hot Springs, California, based on the idea of "being at peace with the natural

Members of the Neverdies, also called the Church of the Living, hold a service expounding their belief in immortality.

Members of the New Age Church of Being perform a ritual at the Giza Pyramids near Cairo, Egypt.

and spiritual energies of the land, with the assistance of Shamans and teachers of Native American traditions." Activities include "Full Moon gatherings, equinox and solstice celebrations."

New Age Church of Truth

U.S. PENTECOSTAL occultist group founded in the 1960s by Gilbert N. Holloway (1915–) in Deming, New Mexico. It operates the Christ Light Community.

New Apostolic Church

Initially known as the General Christian Mission, this European FUNDAMENTALIST group was created through a schism in the German branch of the CATHOLIC APOSTOLIC CHURCH, brought about in 1860 by Heinrich Geyer. The schism involved members who doubted the official 1864 prediction for the Second Coming. H. Niehaus became the leader of the New Apostolic Church in 1863. The church started growing after the turn of the century and spread to Switzerland and Austria. There have been three schisms which created three new groups: the APOSTELMAT JUDA in 1902, the REFORMED APOSTOLIC COMMUNITY in 1921, and the APOSTELMAT JESU CHRISTI in 1923.

The group has followed a policy of strict secrecy in regard to its doctrines, as far as nonmembers are concerned. From the headquarters in Dortmund, Germany, branches operate throughout Western Europe and Africa.

New Beginnings

U.S. white supremacist group, founded by Eldon D. Purvis in the 1960s. It is based in Waynesville, North Carolina. This BRITISH ISRAELIST group believes that Anglo-Saxons are the true descendants of the biblical "Children of Israel." Its doctrine also emphasizes traditional PENTECOSTAL beliefs in healing and prophecy.

New Beginnings (Ex-Christian Scientists for Jesus)

U.S. group started by former members of CHRISTIAN SCIENCE who have become evangelical Christians and oppose their former church. The group was founded in 1980 by D. E. Kind, and is based in Anaheim, California.

New Bethel Church of God in Christ (Pentecostal)

U.S. PENTECOSTAL group founded in 1927 by A. D. Bradley, a former member of the CHURCH OF GOD IN CHRIST. Based in San Francisco.

New Christian Crusade Church

U.S. Christian IDENTITY, white supremacist, militarist group, founded in 1971 in Metairie, Louisiana, by James K. Warner, a former member of the American Nazi Party. The group's doctrine is anti-Semitic and supremacist. It is connected with the CHRISTIAN DEFENSE LEAGUE and with the Sons of Liberty.

New Covenant Apostolic Order

U.S. Christian FUNDAMENTALIST MILLENARIAN group, founded in 1975 by Jack Sparks and other former members of the

CHRISTIAN WORLD LIBERATION FRONT in Berkeley, California. In 1979 the group became the Evangelical Orthodox Church (EOC), becoming part of the Eastern Orthodox tradition of Christianity and espousing the Eastern Orthodox emphasis on ritual and on belief in the Virgin Mary as the Mother of God. In 1987 the group joined the Antiochian Orthodox Christian Archdiocese of North America, an Orthodox body founded in the 1930s.

New Covenant Church

U.S. FUNDAMENTALIST group founded in Orlando, Florida, in 1987 by Jim Bakker to continue the television ministry earlier carried out through his Praise the Lord (PTL) Ministries organization. The founder was later sentenced to prison for mishandling funds contributed to by followers of Praise the Lord.

New Covenant Church of God

British PENTECOSTAL group whose members come from the West Indian immigrant community.

New Covenant Fellowship

Australian offshoot of JEHOVAH'S WITNESSES. It was started around 1920.

New Creation Bible Students

Known officially as the Christian Millenial Fellowship, this is a U.S. MILLENARIAN group created by a schism in the Watch Tower Bible and Tract Society in 1910, which also led to the founding of the CHRISTIAN BELIEVERS CONFERENCE. The group is made up of

Italian Americans and has had contacts with similar groups in Italy.

New Directions thru Meditation, Inc.

U.S. occultist group founded and operated by Michael J. Gramlich in the 1970s. It is devoted to "Relational Meditation (relating to self, to others, to the universe)."

New Faith Gospel Apostolic Church of Jesus Christ

South African independent PENTECOSTAL church founded in 1940.

New Harmony Christian Crusade

U.S. IDENTITY group founded by George Udvary, in Mariposa, California, in the 1970s.

New History Society

U.S. BAHAI splinter group founded in New York City in 1929 by Lewis Stuyvesant Chanler and Mirza Ahmad Sohrab (1891–1958), who was excommunicated by the Bahais in the 1930s.

New House of Israel

British SOUTHCOTTITE group started by the followers of John Wroe, founder of the CHRISTIAN ISRAELITES, after Wroe's death in 1863.

New Jerusalem Fellowship

British offshoot of JEHOVAH'S WITNESSES, founded in 1920 by F. S. Edgell (?–1950).

New Life Evangelistic Center

U.S. JESUS MOVEMENT group founded around 1970 in St. Louis.

New Life Worldwide

U.S. Hindu-inspired group, created by Roy Eugene Davis (1931–) in 1964. Davis was a disciple of Paramahansa Yogananda of the SELF-REALIZATION FELLOWSHIP in Los Angeles in the 1950s. The group practiced Yogananda's technique of kriya yoga and collaborated with RELIGIOUS SCIENCE. In the late 1960s it merged with the CHURCH OF THE CHRISTIAN SPIRITUAL ALLIANCE to form the CENTER FOR SPIRITUAL AWARENESS. [See also ANANDA COOPERATIVE VILLAGE and THE TEMPLE OF KRIYA YOGA.]

New Reformed Orthodox Order of the Golden Dawn

U.S. neo-pagan, witchcraft group, started in the 1970s in the San Francisco Bay area.

New Salem Church (Aladura)

African independent PENTECOSTAL group founded in Nigeria in 1956 by Lucy Adeoti.

New Testament Church of God

U.S. "HOLINESS" group founded in Arkansas in 1942.

New Testament Church of God

British PENTECOSTAL independent church with branches in the Jamaican communities of Great Britain. It was founded in 1953 in Wolverhampton and was for a while affiliated with the CHURCH OF GOD (CLEVELAND, TENNESSEE). Tithing, speaking in tongues, and faith healing are practiced.

New Testament Missionary Fellowship

U.S. FUNDAMENTALIST, PENTECOSTAL group founded in 1964 in New York City by Hannah Lowe, who had served as a Protestant missionary for forty years in South America. The founder was referred to as the Prophetess. She advocated chanting and speaking in tongues. Her followers are reported to be working on her estate outside Bogotá, Colombia.

New Thought

U.S. theistic, "mind healing," "positive thinking" movement, started in the nineteenth century and inspired by the work of Phineas Parkhurst Quimby (1802–1866), who had also inspired Mary Baker Eddy, the founder of CHRISTIAN SCIENCE. Quimby died in 1866, but in the 1880s the movement developed under the leadership of Emma Curtis Hopkins, an associate of Mary Baker Eddy (and a former editor of the *Journal of Christian Science*); Ernest S. Holmes; Charles S. Fillmore; and Myrtle Fillmore. "Free Thought" groups held national conventions in the United States starting in 1894; the International Metaphysical League was started in 1899, the National New Thought Alliance in 1908, and the International New Thought Alliance was founded in 1914. In Great Britain the movement has become known as Higher Thought.

The New Thought doctrine is summed up in the belief in "the infinitude of the

Supreme One, the Divinity of man and his infinite possibilities through the creative power of constructive thinking and obedience to the voice of the Indwelling Presence which is our source of Inspiration, Power, Health, and Prosperity."

The New Thought movement combines the ideas of P. P. Quimby with those of Mary Baker Eddy. Healing through the power of mind and the ultimate sovereignty of the mind over material reality were the cornerstones of its ideology. Disease was "unreal" and so it could be overcome by a right-thinking mind, but the existence of matter was never denied. Later, an emphasis on the attainment of financial prosperity and the elimination of "unreal" poverty through "mind power" were added. [*See also* ACTUALISM; THE CHURCH OF THE HEALING CHRIST (DIVINE SCIENCE); A COURSE IN MIRACLES; CRYSTAL CATHEDRAL; DIVINE SCIENCE CHURCH; HOME OF TRUTH MOVEMENT; HOPKINS ASSOCIATION, EMMA C.; PEOPLE FOREVER INTERNATIONAL; RELIGIOUS SCIENCE INTERNATIONAL; UNITED CHURCH OF RELIGIOUS SCIENCE; SCIENCE OF MIND CHURCH; *and* UNITY SCHOOL OF CHRISTIANITY.]

Sources:

Braden, C. S. *Spirits in Rebellion*. Dallas: SMU Press, 1963.

Judah, J. S. *The History and Philosophy of the Metaphysical Movements in America*. Philadelphia: Westminster Press, 1967.

Meyer, D. *The Positive Thinkers*. New York: Pantheon Books, 1980.

Schneider, L., and Dornbusch, S. *Popular Religion*. Chicago: University of Chicago Press, 1958.

New Thought Synagogue

U.S. Jewish variant of NEW THOUGHT, founded in Los Angeles, California, in 1953 by S. Pereira Mendes.

New Vrindaban

Officially known as the League of Devotees at New Vrindaban and sometimes known as the International Society for Krishna Consciousness of West Virginia, this is a U.S. Hindu group that is an offshoot of the INTERNATIONAL SOCIETY FOR KRISHNA CONSCIOUSNESS (ISKCON). In the late 1970s the group, under the leadership of Kirtanananda Swami Bhaktiphada (born Keith Ham of Peekskill, New York), separated from ISKCON. In 1987 Bhaktiphada was expelled from ISKCON by its governing body because of "dishonesty" and "apparent approval of illegal activity." In May 1986 a former member, Steven Bryant, was found murdered in Los Angeles. Bryant had accused New Vrindaban leaders of many criminal offenses. Since 1986 there have been serious accusations (some of which have led to convictions) of criminal involvement by the group and its leader, including murder of former members and drug smuggling. This group has been strongly and repeatedly criticized by ISKCON.

Source:

Hubner, J., and Gruson, L. *Monkey on a Stick: Murder, Madness, and the Hare Krishnas*. San Diego: Harcourt Brace Jovanovich, 1988.

New Wiccan Church

British neo-pagan group founded in the 1980s. It attempts to unite various neo-pagan traditions. [*See also* WICCA.]

New World of Islam

U.S. African American Muslim organization started in the 1970s. It is an offshoot of the NATION OF ISLAM (NOI).

New York Church of Christ

U.S. FUNDAMENTALIST organization based in New York City and founded in 1982 by Steve Johnson. It is a branch of the CROSSROADS CHURCHES OF CHRIST and is structured according to the SHEPHERDING principle, which provides for an authoritarian leadership style and close supervision of members. This style has been the basis of what has been called the "shepherding movement," which includes the BODY OF CHRIST, CHRISTIAN GROWTH MINISTRIES, and CHRISTIAN RESTORATION MINISTRIES.

New York Metaphysical Society

U.S. NEW THOUGHT group founded by Alexander Demaras in the 1970s.

New York Spiritual Center, Inc.

U.S. spiritualist group founded in the 1960s by Renee and Bill Linn. It operates the Metaphysics and Parapsychology Institute, Inc.

Nihon Kirisuto Kyodan

Japanese Protestant organization started in June 1941 by thirty-four Protestant denominations. It is considered the main Christian group in Japan.

Nirankari

Sikh revival movement, calling for renewal and reform, which was started in

Peshawar in the early nineteenth century by Baba Dayal (1783–1855). The group's doctrine calls for a return to the original teachings of Nanak. In addition, it assumes a continuing line of living gurus, which puts it in direct opposition to mainstream Sikh doctrine. [*See also* NAMDHARI.]

Source:
Singh, Khushwant. *A History of the Sikhs.* Princeton, N.J.: Princeton University Press, 1963–1966.

Nityananda Institute

U.S. Hindu group devoted to the teachings of Swami Rudrananda (1928–1973), popularly known as Rudi. Albert Rudolph (Rudi) was born and raised in Brooklyn and became renowned as a spiritual teacher and as a teacher of meditation in the 1960s. Rudrananda was a disciple of Swami Nityananda (?–1961) and Swami Muktananda (1908–1982) but started his own ashram in India in 1969. He was then killed in a plane crash. This group was started in 1973 by Swami Chetananda in Bloomington, Indiana, and later moved to Boston. [*See also* SHREE GURUDEV RUDRANANDA YOGA ASHRAM.]

Noise, The

Melanesian syncretistic group (CARGO CULT), which was started in the Admiralty Islands in February 1947. The founder, Wapei, reported a visit from Jesus Christ and predicted the imminent arrival of cargo, *i.e.*, manufactured goods and wealth. Wapei described cargo ships piloted by Jesus Christ on their way to the island. His followers stopped work-

Two avatars of the Italian occultist group Nonsiamosoli. (Top) Russian monk Grigori Efimovich Rasputin, favorite of Empress Alexandra at the time of World War I. (Bottom) Comte de Cagliostro, adventurer and charlatan, a figure at the court of Louis XVI of France.

ing, started fasting, and destroyed their property. When the prophecy failed, he was killed at his own request. Many of his followers later joined PALIAU CHURCH, but others continued to claim contact with Wapei's spirit.

Nomiya Luo Church

Sometimes known as Nomeya, this is an African indigenous Christian church, founded in 1914 in Kenya by Johana Owalo by secession from the Church Missionary Society (Anglican Church). The name means "God has given me a revelation" and asserts the group's independence from European authority.

Nomiya Luo Sabbath

African syncretistic group founded in 1957 in Kenya by secession from the NOMIYA LUO CHURCH. Its doctrine and practices combine Christian and Islamic elements.

Non-Digressive Church of God

U.S. PENTECOSTAL group founded in the early twentieth century.

Nonsiamosoli ("We Are Not Alone")

Italian occultist UFO group founded in 1979 in Porto Sant'Elpidio by Giorgio Bongiovanni. Many of the group's ideas came from an earlier group, FRATELLANZA COSMICA, which was disbanded in 1978. This new group's doctrine combined Catholic traditions and Western occultism, together with messages received from "extraterrestrials." Bongiovanni reported apparitions of the

Virgin Mary of Fatima. Eugenio Siragusa (1919–), the founder of Fratellanza Cosmica, is believed by Nonsiamosoli to be the reincarnation of a priest from Atlantis, as well as of Cagliostro and Rasputin.

Noohra Foundation

U.S. Christian NEW THOUGHT group founded in 1970 in California to promote the teachings of George M. Lamsa (1892–1975), who in 1927 founded the Aramaic Bible Society. Lamsa was the originator of the theory that the New Testament had been written in Aramaic and had to be interpreted according to ancient Aramaic language and traditions.

North American Old Roman Catholic Church

U.S. OLD CATHOLIC group founded in 1916 in Chicago by Carmel Henry Carfora (?–1958), who was born in Italy and came to the United States as a Roman Catholic priest. This group displayed doctrinal and ritualistic conservatism. Following Carfora's death there were schisms and the group came to the verge of complete disappearance.

Northeast Kingdom Community Church

Also known as the Church at Island Pond and originally known as the Vine Christian Community, this is a U.S. FUNDAMENTALIST, PENTECOSTAL communal group founded in 1972 by Gene Spriggs and Martha Spriggs in Chattanooga, Tennessee. It grew out of the JESUS MOVEMENT of the early 1970s. Later the group moved to the northeast United States, establishing communities in Vermont and Massachusetts. It has been involved in several controversies and legal disputes since the 1970s, stemming from accusations of authoritarianism and child abuse.

Noul Ierusalem

Romanian Christian ADVENTIST group founded in 1991 by Marian Zidaru.

Nuba Divine Healing Church

African indigenous PENTECOSTAL healing group founded in Ghana in 1957.

Nubian Islamic Hebrews

Also known as the Community of Ansaar Affairs in America, or Ansaaru Islaam, or Ansaru Allah Community, this is a U.S. Islamic African American group founded in the late 1960s in Brooklyn, New York, by the leader known as Al Imaam Issa Al Haadi Al Mahdi. The founder says he is the great-grandson of the nineteenth-century Sudanese Mahdi, Mohammed Ahmad Ibn Abdallah (1843–1885). His brand of Islam proclaims to be the only authentic one, and preaches a conservative interpretation of the Koran. Members live in same-sex dormitories and have a chance to cohabit with spouses only once every three months. Until 1992 polygyny was practiced and women members were veiled. The doctrine includes a prediction of the coming of the apocalypse in the year 2000, after which only group members will survive. The group has operated several economic organizations designed to foster self-reliance and self-respect. [See also MAHDI; and NATION OF ISLAM (NOI).]

A member of the Northeast Kingdom Community Church in custody of police on charges of child abuse.

Nucleo Ubaldiano di Metafisica (Ubaldian Nucleus of Metaphysics)

Popularly known as La Grande Sintesi (after the group's scripture), this is an Italian occultist Christian group. It was founded in the 1930s by Pietro Ubaldi (1886–1972), a former Catholic who was excommunicated in 1932 for his pantheist ideas and his claims of divine revelations. Branches have operated in Latin America.

Nu Yoga

European Hindu-oriented group started in the 1970s by Sanatanananda.

Nyabingi

One of the RASTAFARIAN groups active historically in Jamaica. The name was attached to them because of their use of the Nyabingi or Nyaket drums. They were the most puritanical and separatist, believing that the touch of nonmembers was polluting.

Nyingmapa Center

U.S. Tibetan Buddhist group based in Berkeley, California, which was founded in 1969 by Tarthang Tulku Rinpoche. It represents the Tibetan Nyingmapa tradition and teaches meditation that is believed to enhance health.

O

Odinist Committee

British neo-pagan group, started in the 1980s, which follows Norse mythology and worships its pantheon. It has promoted the idea of the racial superiority of the "Nordic Race."

Odinists

North American neo-pagan group, started in the 1960s, which follows Norse mythology and worships its pantheon. It has been affiliated with extreme right-wing political causes and groups and to ideas of the racial superiority of the "Nordic Race."

Ohio Bible Fellowship

U.S. Christian FUNDAMENTALIST group founded in 1968 by former members of the INDEPENDENT FUNDAMENTAL CHURCHES OF AMERICA (IFCA) who believed that the IFCA was not sufficiently fundamentalist.

Ohtm

Belgian occultist group that follows the ancient "Hermetic Tetramegystus" teachings. It has branches in several European countries.

Old Aglypayans

Philippine nationalist group created as a result of a schism in the PHILIPPINE INDEPENDENT CHURCH (PIC).

Old Apostolic Church

British ADVENTIST group created through a schism in the CATHOLIC APOSTOLIC CHURCH. It has operated branches and missions overseas.

Old Catholics

This term, appearing in the names of numerous churches, signifies groups that have separated from the Roman Catholic Church at various times. The earliest such split was in 1724, creating the Dutch Church of Utrecht. In the nineteenth century, there was a wave of schisms, when German, Austrian, and Swiss groups refused to accept the doctrine of papal infallibility, which was proclaimed in 1870. In some cases, the schismatic movement was related to earlier attempts to gain autonomy from Roman Catholic hierarchy.

Under the leadership of J. J. Dölinger (1799–1890) of Germany, dissenters from Germany, France, Austria, and Switzerland met in a congress in Cologne in 1872. These groups adopted rules allowing priests to marry and to conduct services in the vernacular. In Switzerland, Old Catholics are officially known as the Christian Catholic Church. Later, several East European groups, mainly Polish, refused to accept Roman Catholic authority. Old Catholic churches now operate all over the world. Following the Second Vatican Council of 1962–1965, there was a fourth wave of schisms, creating *traditionalist* Catholic groups, which claim to preserve earlier Catholic rituals and traditions. Some Old Catholic groups have also been traditionalist in this sense, faithful to earlier customary rituals. [*See also* POLISH OLD CATHOLIC CHURCH IN AMERICA; *and* POLISH NATIONAL CATHOLIC CHURCH.]

Sources:

Anson, P. F. *Bishops at Large*. London: Faber and Faber, 1964.

Pruter, K., and Melton, J. G. *The Old Catholic Sourcebook*. New York: Garland, 1983.

Old Catholic Church in America

U.S. OLD CATHOLIC group founded by William Henry Francis Brothers (1887–1979) in 1917. Following the founder's death, there were schisms and decline.

Old Time Faith, Inc.

U.S. FUNDAMENTALIST group founded by

Marjoe Gortner, former minister in the Fundamentalist Old Time Faith sect, who was ordained at the age of four.

Essie Binkley in the 1940s in Los Angeles. In 1949 Binkley ordained Marjoe Gortner (1945–) as a minister. He performed marriages and became a well-known child preacher. In 1973 Gortner produced a film, *Marjoe*, about the life of a child preacher and the world of revival-tent evangelism and faith healing.

Olive Tree Fellowship

Australian HEBREW CHRISTIAN group based in Melbourne.

Olosanto

African indigenous syncretistic movement started in 1953 in Angola under the influence of KIMBANGUISM and MATSOUANISM.

Omotokyo (Omoto or Oomoto)

Japanese MILLENARIAN, Shinto-inspired new religion, whose name is translated as "The Teaching of the Great Origin." It was founded in 1899 by Mrs. Nao Deguchi (1836–1918), a former KONKOKYO teacher. In January 1892, she became convinced of her possession by a divine power. She started acting as a faith healer and then joined Konkokyo, becoming a teacher. Later she began preaching a message of world reformation and the coming of the kingdom of heaven. Her adopted son Onisaburo Deguchi (1870–1948) became the leader after her death. The group, while popular, was subject to government persecution in the 1920s and 1930s. In 1935, 550 policemen attacked the group's headquarters and destroyed the buildings completely. After World War II the group was revived and reorganized.

Omotokyo gave rise to several new movements, including SEKAI KYUSEI KYO and SEICHO-NO-IE.

One World Family

Also known as the Universal Industrial Church of the New World Comforter, or the Messiah's World Crusade, this U.S. communal movement was founded in 1966 in San Francisco by Allen Noonan (1918–), also known as Allen-Michael. The movement's doctrine combines Christian ideas with beliefs about communication with extraterrestrial beings. Noonan says he traveled to outer space in 1947 and since then has been receiving messages from extraterrestrial beings as well as Christian-oriented revelations.

Open Bible Church

U.S. BRITISH ISRAELIST group based in Baltimore and headed by Otis B. Read, Jr.

Open Bible Standard Churches, Inc.

U.S. PENTECOSTAL group founded in 1935 by a merger of two groups, the Open Bible Evangelistic Association and the Bible Standard, Inc. The group's doctrine emphasizes healing and tithing.

Orage Group

New York GURDJIEFF GROUP under the guidance of A. R. Orage (1871–1932). Orage was a noted British literary critic in the 1920s, when he left this work to become a Gurdjieff disciple in France. Then he was sent to the United States as a missionary, where he spent seven years

between 1924 and 1931. Orage was quite successful in his efforts and provided Gurdjieff with vital financial support. However, he was removed by Gurdjieff himself, who told him to stop teaching and disbanded the New York group. Orage returned to his work in literary criticism.

Orden Fiat Lux

Swiss Christian spiritualist group founded in 1975 by Erika Bertschinger (known as Uriella), a former follower of the GEISTIGE LOGE. The founder reports messages from Jesus Christ.

Order, The

Also known as the Silent Brotherhood, this U.S. Christian group was part of the IDENTITY MOVEMENT and was actually the military wing of the CHURCH OF JESUS CHRIST CHRISTIAN—ARYAN NATIONS. It was founded in October 1983 by Robert Jay Mathews (1953–1984). In June, 1984, two group members assassinated Denver radio personality Alan Berg. Later, group members obtained $3.6 million in an armed robbery. The Order's founder, Robert Jay Mathews, was killed in a shootout with FBI and other government agents in December 1984, in Whidbey Island, Washington.

Since 1984, members of The Order have been convicted numerous times of conspiracy against the U.S. government, arson, and murder, following several violent incidents in which they were involved. The two members convicted of the murder of Alan Berg were sentenced in U.S. District Court in Denver, Colorado in 1987 to one hundred and fifty years in prison each. The group ceased to exist after 1984, but their actions continued to inspire acts of violence on the part of Identity followers.

Source:
Martinez, T., and Guinther, J. *Brotherhood of Murder*. New York: McGraw-Hill, 1988.

Order of Ethiopia

South African independent indigenous group founded in 1900 by James M. Dwane (?–1915) after he seceded from the ETHIOPIAN CATHOLIC CHURCH OF SOUTH AFRICA and joined the Order to the Anglican Church. Only a minority of the Ethiopian Church members followed Dwane, and the membership has remained limited to the Xhosa people.

Source:
Sundkler, B. G. M. *Bantu Prophets in South Africa*. London: Oxford University Press, 1961.

Order of Fransisters and Franbrothers

U.S. group, inspired by St. Francis of Assisi, founded in 1963 in Denver, Colorado, by Laurel Elizabeth Keyes. The group is "interreligious, embracing all faiths, East and West. The intentions of Fransisters and Franbrothers is identity with their Ideal, feeling that daily living is an offering of Love. It is important to do one's best and for Life to know that one of Its extensions is coming closer to Its Source. Teaching, healing,

Alan Berg, Denver talk-show host who was murdered by members of The Order, military wing of the Church of Jesus Christ Christian–Aryan Nations.

A painting by Giovanni Bellini of Saint Francis of Assisi, inspiration of the group Fransisters and Franbrothers.

and retreats are main activities." The Order operates the Restorium retreat center.

Order of St. Luke

U.S. group, growing out of the Protestant Episcopalian Church, that was founded in the 1950s. It is devoted to spiritual healing.

Order of the Cross

International Christian THEOSOPHICAL group founded in 1904 in Great Britain by John Todd Ferrier (1858–1942). The founder claimed revelations that helped him recover the "missing" parts of the New Testament. These once-lost teachings include the belief in reincarnation, opposition to the taking of any life, and complete refusal to engage in violent action. Thus, members are vegetarians and pacifists.

Order of the Initiates of Tibet

U.S. THEOSOPHICAL group founded in Washington, D.C., in 1909.

Ordine Dei Maestri Shan

Italian occultist group of THEOSOPHICAL origins founded in the 1970s in Turin by Giancarlo Barbadoro. It teaches "the oldest esoteric doctrine," transmitted in an ancient language known as Shannar.

Ordine Esoterico Del Loto Bianco

Italian occultist group of THEOSOPHICAL origins founded in 1980 by Giuseppe Filipponio.

Ordo Templi Astrate (OTA)

U.S. occultist group founded in 1970 in Pasadena, California. It claims to continue the traditions of the ORDO TEMPLI ORIENTIS (OTO).

Ordo Templi Orientis (OTO)

Also known as the Order of the Temple of the Orient, this is an international occultist, neo-pagan group founded in Germany in 1895 by Karl Kellner. The group believes in the existence of a "witch cult," comprised of enlightened pagan women who worship a horned goatlike figure; it has survived in Europe since ancient times. Members of Ordo Templi Orientis use the image of the Baphomet, a winged, goat-headed figure. In 1912 Aleister Crowley (1875–1947) became the head of its British branch. The group still exists, in two segments, one following Crowley and the other keeping the original German tradition. There have been branches of both factions in the United States and Western Europe.

(Original) Church of God, Inc.

U.S. PENTECOSTAL group founded in 1917 by Joseph L. Scott, following a schism in the CHURCH OF GOD (CLEVELAND, TENNESSEE). Tithing is practiced.

Original Pentecostal Church of God

U.S. PENTECOSTAL group, noted for the occasional handling of snakes by members, who are popularly known as "snake handlers." It was founded in the early twentieth century in rural Kentucky. [*See also* CHURCH OF ALL NATIONS; *and* DOLLY POND CHURCH OF GOD WITH SIGNS FOLLOWING.]

Orthodox Presbyterian Church

Originally known as the Presbyterian Church in America, this U.S. FUNDAMENTALIST group was founded by J. Gresham Machen in 1937, in dissent from the Presbyterian Church in the U.S.A. [*See also* BIBLE PRESBYTERIAN CHURCH; *and* WESTMINSTER BIBLICAL FELLOWSHIP.]

Osirian Temple Assembly

U.S. occultist group based in New Jersey. It claims to follow ancient Egyptian teachings and temple services.

Our Lady of the Roses

Also known as the Virgin of Bayside Shrine, or the Mary Help of Mothers Shrine, this is a U.S. traditionalist Roman Catholic group founded in 1970 by Veronica Lueken (1923–) in New York City. The founder claimed to have had visions since 1967 and to receive regular messages from the Holy Virgin, at her home in 1970 and also near the Vatican Pavilion at the 1964 World's Fair site in

Flushing Meadows, New York. The messages reported by Lueken call for a return to the pre-Vatican II church rituals and rules, and contain denunciations of modern "permissiveness," homosexuality, and "Satanic" groups that she claimed were involved in cannibalistic child sacrifice. In addition, the messages report on the alleged murder of Pope John Paul I and announce an imminent apocalypse, the destruction of the world monetary system, and the deaths of world leaders. Her followers testify to numerous miracles that have occurred at the site of the Vatican Pavillion, referred to as "The Lourdes of America."

P

Source:

Mead, M. *New Lives for Old: Cultural Transformation, Manus, 1928–1953.* New York: William Morrow, 1956.

Pacific Institute of Science and Humanities

U.S. GURDJIEFF GROUP founded by George and Mary Cornelius around 1975; it is based in Oregon.

Padanaram

U.S. Christian commune founded in 1966 in Indiana by Daniel Wright, who had a divine revelation on the spot where the settlement was founded. The group aims at reviving "the primitive lifestyle in the Book of Acts" of the New Testament. Its economic operations have been extremely successful.

Paliau Church

Syncretistic movement (CARGO CULT) on Manus of the Great Admiralty Islands in Melanesia. It was started by the prophet Paliau, a former policeman, in December 1946. In 1954 it developed into a political movement and a Christian church. The group's doctrine was based on messianic Christianity, and it also called for rejection of polygyny and native rituals. Moreover, Paliau criticized the "cargo" movements as well as traditional rank, clan, and tribe divisions, and advocated economic planning and cooperation. This group, the first indigenous church in Melanesia, grew out of the Roman Catholic Church and later developed close relations with Protestant churches, advocating national unity and modern agriculture. [*See also* THE NOISE.]

Palmarian Catholic Church

Sometimes known as the Holy Palmarian Church, this is an international Roman Catholic traditionalist group. It was founded in 1968 in Palmar de Troya, Spain, by Ferdinand Clemente Dominguez y Gomez (1946–), who had failed in his bid to become a Catholic priest. The founder claimed many apocalyptic visions and predictions resulting from contacts with the Virgin Mary. These included predictions of a Communist takeover in Spain and of major schisms in the Roman Catholic Church. Members consider the late dictator of Spain, Generalissimo Francisco Franco, a saint, and they reject the authority of the Roman Catholic Church, while keeping most of its traditions. In September 1976 Dominguez and his followers were officially excommunicated from the Roman Catholic Church, and in 1978 he declared himself to be Pope Gregory XVII. The group operates the Order of the Holy Visage. It has collaborated with the RENOVATED CHURCH OF CHRIST THE KING and with the APOSTLES OF INFINITE LOVE.

Pan African Orthodox Christian Church

Formerly known as The Shrine of the Black Madonna, this is a U.S. Christian African American nationalist group founded by Albert B. Cleage (who has changed his name to Jaramogi Abebe Agyeman) in Detroit, Michigan, in the 1960s. The group's doctrine claims that

Generalissimo Francisco Franco of Spain, considered a saint by members of the Palmarian Catholic Church.

events described in the Bible and biblical figures relate to black history. The ancient Israelites were black, and all major religions, including Islam, Buddhism, and Christianity, were developed by black people. Whites have created only paganism. Christianity, in its black version, is designed to liberate black people in the United States.

Pansophic Institute

U.S. group devoted to spreading the ideas of Tibetan Buddhism. It was founded in 1973 by Simon Grimes in Reno, Nevada. It has operated the School of Universal Wisdom.

Pastoral Bible Institute (PBI)

International ADVENTIST group founded in the early 1920s in the United States. Following the death of Charles Taze Russell in 1916, there was a dispute about his successor in the Watch Tower Tract and Bible Society. Joseph R. Rutherford was opposed by R. H. Hirsh, I. F. Hoskins, A. I. Ritchie, and J. D. Wright. After Rutherford gained the leadership position in 1918, these opponents left and started the PBI.

Doctrinally, they follow the original writings of Charles Taze Russell, which have been superseded by Joseph R. Rutherford's writings in the official JEHOVAH'S WITNESSES movement.

Pathfinder Church

U.S. Christian church founded by Karl Schott in Spokane, Washington, in the 1980s. It is part of the IDENTITY MOVEMENT.

Pathwork, The

U.S. occultist group started in 1957 by Eva Broch (also known as Eva Pierrakos, ?–1979) in New York State. The group's teachings are claimed to have been delivered to Pierrakos by "a spirit being of Light known as the Guide" through "the spiritual channel" between 1957 and 1979, and these 258 teaching are known as the Guide Lectures. The group offers the public "channelled spiritual teachings which outline a powerful and expansive process for observing and transforming our shadow side, while simultaneously cultivating our divinity." This belief system "is inspired by attunement to the Living Force (Inner Godself, Christ Consciousness) within each of us." In addition, meditation and faith healing are practiced. The group has operated the Institute for Core Energetics in New York City, the Phoenicia Pathwork Center in New York State, and the SEVENOAKS COMMUNITY in Virginia. Its branches have been active throughout the United States.

Peculiar People

British Protestant group founded in England in 1828 and focused around faith healing. Treatment in cases of illness consisted of being anointed by the elders.

Peniel

Israeli MESSIANIC JUDAISM group founded in the mid-1970s in Tiberias, Israel. Its doctrine and practices are PENTECOSTAL.

Peniel Missions

U.S. evangelical Protestant group

founded by T. P. Ferguson in Los Angeles in the 1880s. It operated in major cities on the West Coast of the United States until the 1970s.

Pentecostal

Denotes Christian groups that stress personal religious experience rather than doctrine and involve glossolalia (or speaking in tongues), faith healing, and prophecy, all seen as a "baptism of the spirit." Glossolalia is considered the first sign of "the power of the Holy Ghost." The term Pentecostal has been used interchangeably with CHARISMATIC. The term Classical Pentecostals refers to Christians who are followers of officially Pentecostal groups that were started in the early twentieth century. The term Neo-Pentecostals refers to Christians committed to Charismatic practices while keeping their membership in mainstream Protestant groups. Catholic Pentecostals are those who follow Charismatic practices while keeping their membership in the Roman Catholic Church.

Pentecostalism in the United States grew out of earlier developments, which included the healing and "HOLINESS" movements between 1880 and 1900. Modern, twentieth-century Pentecostalism is said to have started in the winter of 1900–1901 in the Bethel Bible College in Topeka, Kansas, and then in the Azusa Street Mission in Los Angeles in 1906. On January 1, 1901, Charles Parham led his Bible School of Holiness group in Baptism in the Holy Ghost. One woman, Agnes Ozman, was said to have spoken Chinese for three days. Others are thought to have spoken different tongues. Parham thought he spoke Swedish. William J. Seymour, a former African American Baptist preacher, was recruited by Parham in 1906 in Houston. He carried the Pentecostal vision to California.

Throughout the century there have been waves of Pentecostal renewal. In the 1990s the "Toronto Blessing," an ecstatic style of worship that started in the chapel at the Toronto International Airport, spread in North America and Great Britain. [*See also* APOSTOLIC FAITH CHURCH (KANSAS); *and* CATHOLIC CHARISMATIC RENEWAL.]

Sources:

Anderson, R. M. *Vision of the Disinherited: The Making of American Pentecostalism.* New York: Oxford University Press, 1979.

Bradfield, C. D. *Neo-Pentecostalism: A Sociological Assessment.* Washington, D.C.: University Press of America, 1979.

Goodman, F. D. *Speaking in Tongues: A Cross-Cultural Study of Glossolalia.* Chicago: University of Chicago Press, 1972.

Hollenweger, W. J. *The Pentecostals.* London: SCM Press, 1972.

Kelsey, M. T. *Tongue Speaking.* Garden City, N.Y.: Doubleday, 1968.

Kildahl, J. P. *The Psychology of Speaking in Tongues.* New York: Harper & Row, 1972.

Sneck, W. J. *Charismatic Spiritual Gifts.* Washington, D.C.: University Press of America, 1981.

Pentecostal Assemblies of the World

U.S. African American PENTECOSTAL group founded by G. T. Haywood in 1919. Originally it was an integrated church; most of its white members left in 1924 to found the Pentecostal Church, Inc. Strict dress and conduct codes are emphasized, and healing is practiced. It is based in Indianapolis. [*See also* APOSTOLIC CHURCH OF JESUS CHRIST.]

Pentecostal Churches of the World

British PENTECOSTAL church whose membership comes from the West Indian immigrant community.

Pentecostal Church of God

Indian indigenous PENTECOSTAL group based in the region of Andhra Pradesh.

Pentecostal Church of God

First known as the Pentecostal Assemblies of the U.S.A., this U.S. PENTECOSTAL group was started in 1919 in Chicago by John C. Sinclair and George Brinkman. The current name was adopted in 1979. It is based in Joplin, Missouri.

Pentecostal Church of Zion

U.S. PENTECOSTAL group operating in the Midwest. It was founded by Luther S. Howard in 1954. Howard was a minister of the Holy Bible Mission, which was dissolved around 1950, following the death of its founder. Some of its former ministers followed Howard into the Pentecostal Church of Zion. The group keeps many Old Testament commandments, including the avoidance of unclean meats, and believes in continuing revelation.

Pentecostal Evangelical Church

U.S. PENTECOSTAL group founded in 1936. It is identical in doctrine and practices to the PENTECOSTAL CHURCH OF GOD, which was started in 1919 in Chicago by John C. Sinclair and George Brinkman.

Pentecostal Fellowship of North America

U.S. PENTECOSTAL organization that incorporates several independent small churches in the United States.

Pentecostal Fire-Baptized Holiness Church

U.S. PENTECOSTAL group formed in 1918 as a result of a schism in the PENTECOSTAL HOLINESS CHURCH. Doctrine is stricter, compared to the parent body, in regard to attire and entertainment. Neither jewelry for women nor neckties for men is allowed, nor are visits to fairs or theaters. Disputes over dress standards led to a schism and the founding of EMMANUEL HOLINESS CHURCH.

Pentecostal Holiness Church, International

U.S. PENTECOSTAL group formed early in the twentieth century, following the late nineteenth-century "HOLINESS" revival in the South. Doctrine emphasizes plain dress and glossolalia, or speaking in tongues.

People Forever International (PFI, People Forever)

Formerly known as The Eternal Flame Foundation, and known also as the Arizona Immortals or the Forever People, this is a U.S. NEW THOUGHT group "dedicated to building a deathless world." It was founded in Scottsdale, Arizona, in the late 1960s by Charles Paul Brown (1935–), a former Presbyterian minister and nightclub singer. In the spring of 1960 Brown had a vision of Jesus Christ together with a "cellular awakening," or the revelation of physical immortality as a reality. He was joined in leading the group by BernaDeane Brown (1937–) and James R. Strole (1949–). Doctrine is connected to Christian theology, but it claims that "death is actually a fabrication or lie imposed on our minds and bodies by a ruling death consciousness in order to control the species of man and keep him in eternal bondage. . . . [T]here will never be lasting peace on earth until the Last Enemy of Man, Which Is Death is abolished. . . . [M]ost religions believe that physical immortality will eventually take place in the bodies of mankind upon the earth. However, it is always projected into some future dispensation due to misconceptions and religious dogmas. We feel the time IS NOW for an immortal species of mankind to be birthed upon the planet."

People of Praise (POP)

U.S. charismatic ecumenical group, growing out of the CATHOLIC CHARISMATIC RENEWAL movement. It was founded in 1971 in South Bend, Indiana, by Paul Decelles and Kevin Ranaghan. It has operated twenty-five branches in North America and the Caribbean.

People of the Living God

U.S. Christian PENTECOSTAL commune based in Tennessee. It was founded in 1932 by Harry Miller. Members practice economic equality and follow a simple lifestyle, saving most of their income for missionary work. The group's doctrine attacks all established churches as sectarian.

People's Christian Church

Founded in 1916 in New York City by Elmer E. Franke (1861–1946), it is an offshoot of the SEVENTH-DAY ADVENTIST CHURCH. Church beliefs resemble closely those of the SDA, but the status of Ellen G. White as prophetess is denied.

People Searching Inside (PSI)

Also known as the Kundalini Research Institute, this is an international Hindu-oriented group, founded in 1976 in Canada by Joseph F. Dippong, a follower of Gopi Krishna (1903–1984). Kundalini, in Hindu lore, means sexual energy supposedly localized in the base of the spine. Kundalini yoga attempts to release this energy for use in the human brain. PSI branches have operated in Canada and Great Britain. [*See also* KUNDALINI RESEARCH FOUNDATION.]

People's Temple Christian (Disciples) Church

Popularly known as the People's Temple, this U.S. Christian group was one of the most notorious religious movements of recent history, becoming the subject of worldwide horror when 913 of its members committed suicide on November 18, 1978, in Jonestown, Guyana. Founded in

Members of Jim Jones's People's Temple lie dead in Jonestown, Guyana, after their leader joined them in a mass suicide.

1956 in Indiana as the Community National Church, its membership was comprised of individuals of lower socio-economic standing. Its founder, James Warren (Jim) Jones, was born near Lyon, Indiana, on May 13, 1931. From early childhood he imitated preachers. According to some reports, he claimed to be able to perform miracles soon after becoming a minister in Indianapolis.

Jones also practiced faith healing, and his followers attributed various miracles to him. He was active in integration when the idea was still quite unpopular, and he had a significant African American following. In the late 1950s Jones started developing an integrated church.

He became an ordained minister of the DISCIPLES OF CHRIST in 1965 and then moved to California with 150 followers, first to Ukiah and then to San Francisco. Most members were poor African Americans, but Jones was able to establish ties with political leaders in the San Francisco area. Throughout its existence in San Francisco, the People's Temple was actually a mainstream Protestant congregation, belonging to the Christian Church (Disciples of Christ). Based in the Fillmore district of San Francisco, it was a community of activists fighting racism and poverty. It operated drug rehabilitation programs, soup kitchens, and day-care centers. According to some reports,

Jones was influenced by the FATHER DI-VINE MOVEMENT and by Father Divine himself, who died in 1965, the year Jones was first ordained. He was addressed later on as "Daddy" Jones.

In 1974 the group started gradually moving its members to the communal settlement of Jonestown, in Guyana, South America, and in 1977 Jones himself and several hundred followers moved there. This departure from California was caused by growing frictions with ex-members and critical media reports. During the 1970s people reported that Jones was becoming increasingly abusive, dictatorial, and paranoid. Members were subjected to beatings, sexual abuse, and constant humiliation. When U.S. Congressman Leo Ryan traveled to Guyana to investigate claims of abuse in the group in November, 1978, he was received by Jones and shown around the settlement. After leaving the site, Ryan and members of his party were shot and killed by Jones's guards. Back at the commune, the scene also turned deadly. On November 18, 1978, 913 members died in a mass suicide on orders from Jones, who was among them. Among the dead, 199 were over sixty-five, 300 were under sixteen, and 137 were under eleven. It should be noted that most of the members who died with Jones were African American females, a fact that reflects the demographics of its membership.

Sources:

Hall, J. R. *Gone from the Promised Land: Jonestown in American Cultural History.* New Brunswick, N.J.: Transaction Books, 1987.

Kilduff, M., and Javers, R. *The Suicide Cult.* New York: Bantam, 1978.

Klineman, G., Butler, S., and Conn, D. *The Cult that Died: The Tragedy of Jim Jones and the People's Temple.* New York: Putnam, 1980.

Levi, K. *Violence and Religious Commitment: Implications of Jim Jones's People's Temple Movement.* University Park: Pennsylvania State University Press, 1982.

Moore, R., and McGehee, F. *New Religious Movements, Mass Suicide, and People's Temple.* Lewiston, N.Y.: Edwin Mellen Press, 1989.

Naipaul, S. *Journey to Nowhere: A New World Tragedy.* New York: Simon & Schuster, 1981.

Wrightsman, J. M. *Making Sense of the Jonestown Suicides: A Sociological History of People's Temple.* Lewiston, N.Y.: Edwin Mellen Press, 1983.

Perfect Liberty Kyodan (PL Kyodan)

Japanese Shinto-inspired religion founded in 1946 by Tokuchika Miki (1900–). It grew out of the Hitonomichi (Way of Mankind) branch of the SHINTO-TOKUMITSU-LYO movement, which was founded in 1912 by Tokumitsu Kanada (1863–1924). Hitonomichi was suppressed by the government in 1937 and was revived as P L Kyodan. The group is committed to monotheism, faith healing, and expectations of an upcoming total salvation. Illness is viewed as a divine message, indicating violation of sacred law. Such divine warnings have been collected and analyzed by computer to produce prescriptions of correct behavior. Members aim to achieve *makato* (heart, truth, and sincerity) so that their behavior may be free from egotistical influences. "Once the ego is suppressed, every action becomes an expression of the divine within." Activities include classes in traditional arts, such as poetry, dance, and calligraphy. U.S. branches, known by the name Perfect Liberty, have operated since 1960 on the West Coast.

Sources:

Bach, M. *The Power of Perfect Liberty.* Englewood Cliffs, N.J.: Prentice-Hall, 1971.

Ellwood, R. S. *The Eagle and the Rising Sun.* Philadelphia: Westminster, 1974.

Petite Église (Vendeenne)

French Catholic group founded in 1801 by thirty-eight bishops who rejected the concordat of July 15, 1801, reached by the Roman Catholic Church under Pope Pius VII and Napoleon's French government. According the agreement, known as "le concordat de l'an IX," the head of the secular government appointed French bishops, who then took an oath of loyalty to the government.

Philadelphia-Verein

German Christian PENTECOSTAL group started in Württemberg in 1946. Practices include prophecies and faith healing.

Philippine Independent Church (PIC)

Also known as the Aglipayan Church and as the *Iglesia Filipina Independiente,* this is a schismatic Catholic movement operating in the Philippines and among Filipino communities overseas. It was started in 1890 and officially founded in 1902 by Isabelo de los Reyes, Sr. (1864–1938) and Gregorio Aglipay (1860–1940). Aglipay was a Roman Catholic priest who initiated a secession from the Catholic Church, taking 45 percent of its members. Since 1948 the PIC has had close relations with the Protestant Episcopal Church, which has consecrated its bishops. The PIC has played an important part in the struggle for Filipino independence from Spanish and U.S. colonialism. The PIC has emphasized vernacular liturgy and has canonized Filipino nationalist heroes. Clergy are allowed to marry. Many schisms in the PIC over the years have led to an estimated 120 new Philippine independent churches.

Philippine Unitarian Church

Philippine nationalist group created as a result of a schism in the PHILIPPINE INDEPENDENT CHURCH (PIC).

Philosophical Research Society

U.S. THEOSOPHICAL, ROSICRUCIAN group founded by Manly Palmer Hall (1901–) in 1934 and devoted to the teaching of all Western occult traditions. Hall's system is a eclectic combination of Theosophy with other occult traditions.

Pilgrim Wesleyan Holiness Church

British PENTECOSTAL church whose membership is made up of West Indian immigrants.

Pillar of Fire

U.S. conservative Protestant, FUNDAMENTALIST, and PENTECOSTAL group founded in 1901 in Denver, Colorado. Originated as the Pentecostal Union by Alma White (1862–1946), it adopted the present name in 1917. In the 1920s the group supported the Ku Klux Klan, but throughout its existence it supported women's rights. Missions have operated in Europe, Asia, and Africa.

Pitenamu Society

Papua, New Guinea, syncretistic movement that started in the 1970s. It has been active also as a political pressure group.

P L Kyodan Association International

This is the international affiliate of PERFECT LIBERTY KYODAN.

Plymouth Brethren

Informally known as the Church of God, this is a Protestant MILLENARIAN movement founded in 1830 by John Nelson Darby (1800–1882) in Plymouth, England. Darby was a curate in the Episcopalian Church of Ireland until 1827, when he felt obliged to leave it because he could no longer accept its doctrines. Darby declared that the essence of Christianity was the expectation of Christ's imminent return. He set himself the task of reformulating the one true church of Jesus Christ of New Testament tradition.

In Dublin Darby had followers who became known as Brethren. The Brethren are strongly opposed to any formalism or organization along church or denominational lines. They accept the Bible as divinely inspired, absolutely and completely. Teachings are influenced by Calvinism and millenarianism. There is no formal clergy. Their emphasis on the complete autonomy of local churches has tended to encourage schisms. They believe in seven dispensations, or ages (Innocence, Conscience, Government, Promise, Law, Grace, and the Personal Reign of Christ). The Plymouth Brethren have been divided into several small factions, as the result of many schisms since the mid-nineteenth century.

Sources:

Coad, F. R. *A History of the Brethren Movement.* London: Paternoster Press, 1968.

Ehlert, A. D. *A Bibliographic History of Dispensationalism.* Grand Rapids, Mich.: Baker Book House, 1965.

Noel, N. *A History of the Brethren.* Denver: William F. Knapp, 1936.

Plymouth Brethren (Exclusive: Booth-Continental)

International faction of the PLYMOUTH BRETHREN movement, characterized by strict FUNDAMENTALISM, DISPENSATIONALISM, and an ascetic lifestyle. The group opposes modern amenities such as television, newspapers, and computers. Contacts with nonmembers are actively discouraged. Members never vote, hold public office, or join other organizations.

Polish Mariavite Church

The Mariavite movement started in

Members of the international faction of the Plymouth Brethren, who call themselves the Exclusive Brethren, arrive for a mass meeting in Surrey, England.

Poland in 1893, when a member of the Third Order of St. Francis, a Roman Catholic order, Sister Felicia (Maria Franciska Kozlowska) claimed to have been visited by the Virgin Mary, who told her to establish a new order, made up of both men and women and dedicated to the Virgin. The official Polish Catholic hierarchy excommunicated this new order in 1906. Nevertheless, it developed into a large church, which at one point had more than half a million members. Now, however, it is quite small. Its innovations included the ordination of women to all levels of the church hierarchy.

Polish National Catholic Church (PNCC)

U.S. Catholic group which had its beginnings in March 1897. It was officially formed in 1904 in Scranton, Pennsylvania, with founder Francis Hodur as leader. It represents a movement for cultural autonomy among Polish immigrants in the United States, who resented being led by non-Polish priests. The dissent took the form of aligning with the OLD CATHOLIC movement, which rejects the authority of Rome while remaining loyal to Catholic liturgy and dogma. This is one of the few U.S. churches connected with the Old Catholic movement in Europe. In 1985 its priests were recognized by the Roman Catholic Church. It is the only immigrant-based U.S. church to form a mission in the immigrants' homeland. This mission, in turn, created the Polish Catholic Church.

Positive Thinking Ministry

U.S. occultist group based in New York City. It was founded in the early 1980s by Kenneth G. Dickkerson. Practices included Kirlian photography, psychic readings, and past life revelations.

Power of Jesus Around the World Church

African independendent PENTECOSTAL group started among the Luo of Kenya in 1955.

Prarthana Samaj

Also referred to as the "Prayer Society," founded in 1867 in Bombay by Atmaram Pandurang (1823–1898). Prarthana Samaj is a Hindu renewal group, which is any group that attempts to renew Hinduism by changes in doctrine or by reviving earlier forms. Like the BRAHMA SAMAJ and the ARYA SAMAJ, it preached social reform and monotheism. It was especially influenced by the former. At the same time, members kept the caste rules and traditional Hindu worship practices.

Source:
Farquhar, J. N. *Modern Religious Movements In India*. New York: Macmillan, 1919.

Prasure Institute

Western Hindu group based in Europe. It was started in the 1970s.

Prema Dharmasala and Fellowship Association; Prema World Community

Also known as World Community, this is a U.S. syncretistic communal group founded in 1970 by Sri Vasudevadas, who has combined the teachings of the Sufi Orders with those of Paramahansa Yogananda, founder of the SELF-REALIZATION FELLOWSHIP. The group, based near Virginia Beach, Virginia, also operates the Temple of Cosmic Religion.

Primitive Advent Christian Church

U.S. ADVENTIST group started in central West Virginia as a result of a schism in the ADVENT CHRISTIAN CHURCH.

Primitive Christian Church (Église Christique Primitive)

Western European Christian occultist group, founded in Paris in 1935 by Nicolas Strati by secession from the Roman Catholic Church in France. Its doctrine and practices focus on faith healing. Its branches have operated in Switzerland and Germany.

Primitive Church of Antioch

Western European Catholic group begun in 1961 by secession from the Roman Catholic Church in Austria.

Primitive Church of Christ, Scientist

Independent CHRISTIAN SCIENCE group founded by Leon Greenbaum in St. Louis, following the death of Christian Science founder Mary Baker Eddy in 1910.

Process, or the Church of the Final Judgment Process, The

Known officially as The Church of the Final Judgment, and popularly known as The Process, this is an occultist Christian group founded in 1963 in London by two members of SCIENTOLOGY, Robert Moore, also known as Robert de Grimston, and Mary Anne de Grimston. The group was an offshoot of Scientology practices and first known as Compulsions Analysis, or "The Family." By 1966 it had become The Process, designed to bring about unlimited personal development. Then a group of two dozen followers moved to Yucatan, Mexico, turning in a more religious, and less psychotherapeutic, direction, drawing on the ROSICRUCIAN tradition. It developed a pantheon of four gods: Lucifer, Jehovah, Christ, and Satan. Group doctrine stated that the world would end around the year 2000 but that members of the group would be saved. Then the leader Robert de Grimston was expelled because of his overemphasis on Satanic themes and with him three of the four gods of the pantheon. Only Jehovah was left. By 1972 the group was based in Toronto, Canada. In 1973 the group renamed itself THE FOUNDATION FAITH OF GOD; it later moved to New York City, and then to Arizona. Since then the group has been hard to trace.

Sources:

Bainbridge, W. S. *Satan's Power: Ethnography of a Deviant Psychotherapy Cult.* Berkeley: University of California Press, 1978.

Evans, C. *Cults of Unreason.* London: Harrap, 1973.

Progressive Judaism

In Great Britain, this is a subgroup of REFORM JUDAISM. The term "progressive" is sometimes used in other countries, especially in Europe, to denote Reform Judaism.

Prosperos, The

U.S. GURDJIEFF GROUP founded by Thane Walker and Phez Khalil in Florida in 1956. It refers to itself as a Fourth Way School, and is based on a master-disciple relationship leading to "personal liberation."

Providence Industrial Mission

An independent African Christian movement founded by John Chilembwe in 1898 in Malawi (then Nyasaland). The founder was educated in the United States, became a JEHOVAH'S WITNESSES preacher, and then established the church as a part of a move for independence from British rule. He died leading a rebellion in 1915. His main church was destroyed and the movement banned by the British, but it was revived in 1925. Since then it has undergone a schism but still exists in Malawi.

Source:

Shepperson, G., and Price, T. *Independent African: John Chilembwe and the Origins, Setting and Significance of the Nyasaland Native Rising of 1915.* Edinburgh: Edinburgh University Press, 1958.

Punjaji

An Indian "holy man," a follower of RAMANA MAHARSHI, who has established a Western following.

Purgatorial Society, The

U.S. MILLENARIAN group started in 1931 in Brooklyn, New York, by Luci Mayer Barrow, who predicted the imminent coming of a new world order.

Q

Quimby Center

U.S. NEW THOUGHT group founded in 1966 by Neva Dell Hunter (?–1978) in Alamagordo, New Mexico. Doctrine is Hindu-inspired, and includes belief in reincarnation. Practices include spiritual healing through aura balancing, karmic life readings, and psychic counseling.

R

Radhasoami Satsang

Sikh revival group founded in 1861 in Agra, northern India by Tulsi Ram, better known as Siva Dayal Saheb or Soamiji Maharaj (1818–1878). He left behind two books of scriptures, both titled *Sar Bachan*, one in prose and the other in poetry. After the death of the founder there has been a succession of gurus, with some dispute.

The movement claims to be a continuation of the Sant Mat tradition of northern India and appears to combine Hindu and Sikh elements. The name Radha Soami means the Supreme Being, and it is also the name of the founder, who it was believed was the perfect incarnation of God. The guru, known as the Sant Satguru, occupies a central position in the group's doctrine. He is the source of all revelation and salvation, as well as the source of secret meditation techniques taught to disciples. Pictures of the gurus are worshiped. Membership is kept secret and may overlap with adherence to other religious faiths. All religions are held to be equally true, but the group's faith is supreme. Special meditation techniques are the core of the secret practices.

Since the nineteenth century the movement has developed into independent branches, including the small RADHASOAMI SATSANG SOAMIBAGH and RADHASOAMI SATSANG DAYALBAGH, and the large RADHASOAMI SATSANG BEAS. In turn, these groups have inspired new movements. Branches of all these groups can be found in Western Europe and the United States.

Sources:

Farquhar, J. N. *Modern Religious Movements In India*. New York: Macmillan, 1919.

Lane, D. C. *The Radhasoami Tradition: A Critical History of Guru Successorship*. New York: Garland, 1992.

Radhasoami Satsang Beas

The largest and most influential of the Radhasoami Satsang branches. Its leader, Baba Sawan Singh (1858–1948), was the master of both Charan Singh, who succeeded him, and Kirpal Singh, who started his own movement. He developed contacts with North American followers as early as 1911. The group's center is in Beas, Punjab, India. Western branches have operated in Europe and North America.

Radhasoami Satsang Dayalbagh

One of the successor groups to RADHASOAMI SATSANG, based in Agra, India. The group has inspired and influenced new movements, especially in Western countries. [*see also* RADHASOAMI SATSANG; *and* RADHASOAMI SATSANG BEAS.]

Sources:

Farquhar, J. N. *Modern Religious Movements in India*. New York: MacMillan, 1919.

Lane, D. C. *The Radhasoami Tradition: A Critical History of Guru Successorship*. New York: Garland, 1992.

Radhasoami Satsang Soamibagh

Sikh revival group, a branch of the RADHASOAMI SATSANG. It was started in 1907.

Raëlians

Originally known as the Mouvement pour l'Accueil des Elohim Créateurs de l'Humanité (MADECH), this is an international occultist group. It was founded in 1973 in France by Claude Vorilhon (1946–) a journalist now known to group members as Räel. The founder has claimed contacts with extraterrestrials who relayed messages about humankind's being in great danger, which might be averted by group activities. These include Sensual Meditation and telepathic communication with extraterrestrials. The group believes that humans were created as the result of DNA experiments in a "space-laboratory," and that Jews are the chosen people, being directly descended from extraterrestrials. The group's doctrine calls for the establishment of a "Geniocracy" on Earth, led by the superior white race. The countdown to the "golden age," beginning when the extraterrestrial "Elohim" would land on Earth, started in 1973. The group has expressed the wish to obtain land in Israel for the landing site, but the Israeli government has not responded to its repeated requests.

Members are expected to tithe and deed their property to the group. Drug use is forbidden, and sexual freedom is advocated as the way to achieve "spiritual liberation." Sexuality is treated as pleasure-giving, divorced from procreation, which is viewed as superfluous, as extraterrestrials will take it over soon. Homosexual and bisexual contacts are encouraged. In 1992 there were claims in the French media about sexual abuse of children in this group. Raëlians operate the Mouvement pour la Géniocratie Mondiale, based in Geneva. The membership is mainly French-speaking, based in Europe, with the Swiss and Canadian branches being the most active. There is also a branch in Japan.

Rainbow Family of Living Light

U.S. pantheistic-occultist communal movement founded by Barry Adams in the late 1960s. Its doctrine combines Christian ideas with pantheism, THEOSOPHY, and Hindu ideas. There are no formal rituals, but meditation and chanting are practiced. Marijuana is regarded as sacramental.

Rajneesh Foundation International (RFI)

Now known as Osho Meditation or Osho Friends International, initially known as Paras Rajneesh Meditation or the Neo-Sannyas International Movement, and also known by such popular nicknames as the Orange people, Neo-Sannyasin Movement, Sannyasins, and Rajneesh Meditation. This Westernized Hindu group is the reflection and the creature of its founder. Bhagwan (Sanskrit meaning "Lord God" or "The Blessed One") Shree Rajneesh was born on December 11, 1931, as Chandra Mohan in a small town in central India, of Jain background. Raj or Rajneesh was his nickname. He experienced "enlightenment" on March 2l, 1953, while sitting under a maulshree tree. Between 1957 and 1967 he taught at the Raipur Sanskrit College and at the University of Jabalpur. In 1967 he re-

Annual assembly of the Rainbow Family of Living Light, occultist communal movement that regards marijuana as sacramental.

signed from his academic position to devote his life to the "spiritual regeneration of humanity." In 1970 he started the Neo-Sannyas International Movement in Manali, India. In 1971 he took the name Bhagwan Shree Rajneesh and revealed the story of his 1953 enlightenment and of his previous incarnation as a great sage 700 years earlier. According to this account, in the thirteenth century Rajneesh was three days away from enlightenment when he decided to leave his body and return in the twentieth century to proclaim his message. By 1972 he had about fifty Western followers, who donned ochre robes, changed their names upon initiation, and carried his picture with them at all times. In 1974 Rajneesh and seven disciples established the Shree Rajneesh Ashram and the Rajneesh Foundation at Koregaon Park in Poona, about 100 miles southeast of Bombay. Rajneesh Meditation Centers were established in the West during the 1970s. In 1979 the Ashram had about 200 residents, most of them foreigners. By the end of 1980 it had 1,500 residents and was prosperous and self-sufficient. Tensions with the surrounding Indian community and the Indian government's decision to cancel the tax-exempt status of the group led to a decision to move.

In 1981 Rajneesh took a vow of silence and moved to the United States. He first settled in Montclair, New Jersey, and then, together with 280 of his followers, he settled in Antelope, Wasco County, Oregon, founding the Rajneesh Neo-Sannyas International Commune or Rajneeshpuram.

By that time the movement had 200 branches worldwide. The development of the Oregon commune, which housed hundreds of active followers and covered 64,229 acres, led to increasing fric-

tion with its neighbors. The movement took over the neighboring city of Antelope. This was done in 1984, when it imported 4,000 homeless people from sixteen metropolitan areas in the United States to become local voters and thus stack the polls in its favor in the November elections.

In 1983 Rajneesh predicted an earthquake that would devastate much of the West Coast. In 1984 he announced that AIDS was the scourge predicted by Nostradamus and that billions would die from it within the next decade. In 1985 RFI publications predicted floods, earthquakes, and nuclear war within the next decade.

In Europe the RFI opened schools, communes, business corporations, discoteques, and restaurants, many of which enjoyed success at their initial stage (1981–1983), but collapsed after 1986.

On October 27, 1985, Rajneesh was arrested by U.S. government agents in Charlotte, North Carolina, as he was trying to leave the United States. He was accused of several offenses, mainly immigration fraud. On November 14, 1985, Rajneesh in a plea bargain pleaded guilty to two felonies (arranging false marriage of foreign disciples to Americans), paid a heavy fine ($400,000 in cash), and left the United States forever. Several of his associates later pleaded guilty to attempted murder charges. Two weeks later followers were told to leave Rajneeshpuram, and by January 1987 the commune was empty. A fleet of ninety-three luxury cars used by the leader for daily drives in front of his admiring followers was sold.

Several attempts by Rajneesh to enter countries in Europe (Greece, Ireland) and elsewhere (Uruguay, Jamaica,

Bhagwan Shree Rajneesh in custody on charges of immigration fraud. After confessing and paying a fine, he left the United States in 1985.

Nepal) failed, as Rajneesh became an international *persona non grata*. After being refused entry to twenty-one countries, he returned to India. In late 1989 he changed his name to Osho ("on whom the heavens shower flowers"), and on January 19, 1990, he died. Before his death he created the Inner Circle, a committee of twenty-one sannyasins charged with the administration of the movement. His chosen successor, known as Amrito, has been the acting head of the Inner Circle.

The movement's doctrine reflects its founder's personality and leadership. Disciples follow four guidelines: they wear the colors of sunrise, meditate daily, adopt a new Sanskrit name, and wear a *mala* (a necklace with a picture of Rajneesh) at all times. Rajneesh is held to be the messiah figure prophesied by both Eastern and Western traditions, and believers fiercely attack established religions. Rajneeshism is apparently an unsystematic combination of "religious attitudes and methods for work on the self, eastern and western—from Krishna to Gurdjieff, from Pantajali to Wilhelm Reich." The movement's combination of Western material wealth and the spirituality of the East is expected to create a "New Man," also known as "Zorbah the Buddha." The Rajneesh doctrine includes belief in reincarnation and *karma* (destiny determined by behavior in past lives). Thus, beggars should not be helped, because they are working out their past sins. There is an emphasis on free sexual expression and the valuing of sexuality, which is described as following the "tantric-oriented" tradition. At the same time, no marriage or children are allowed to members.

Rajneesh's followers expect a cataclysm that will end life on Earth. Only Rajneesh followers may survive, and even that is not certain.

The main Rajneesh ritual is the White Robe Brotherhood meditation, during which followers express their devotion to Osho and his teachings. During his life Osho would perform, speak, and dance on stage in front of them as they meditated. Since Osho's death the ceremony is practiced with the help of videotapes, with followers sitting in front of the screen. This is recommended as daily practice. The anniversary of Osho's death is the major event of the year.

Sources:

Belfrage, S. *Flowers of Emptiness.* New York: Dial, 1981.

Carter, L. F. *Charisma and Control in Rajneeshpuram: The Role of Shared Values in the Creation of a Community.* New York: Cambridge University Press, 1990.

Gordon, J. S. *The Golden Guru: The Strange Journey of Bhagwan Shree Rajneesh.* Lexington, Mass.: Stephen Green Press, 1987.

Mangalwadi, V. *The World of Gurus.* New Delhi: Vikas Publishing House, 1977.

Mehta, G. *Karma Cola.* New York: Simon & Schuster, 1979.

Menen, A. *The Mystics.* New York: Dial Press, 1974.

Milne, H. *Bhagwan: The God that Failed.* New York: St. Martin's Press, 1988.

Palmer, S. J. *Moon Sisters, Krishna Mothers, Rajneesh Lovers.* Syracuse, N.Y.: Syracuse University Press, 1994.

Raj-Yoga Math and Retreat

U.S. Hindu monastic group, based in the State of Washington, which was founded by Satchakrananda in the 1960s. It is devoted to the practice of various yoga techniques.

Ramabahi Mukti Mission

Indian independent Christian group founded in 1905 in Mukti by Pandita Ramabai.

Ramakrishna Math and Mission

Also known as the Ramakrishna Movement, this is a Hindu revival group devoted to spreading the teachings of Sri Ramakrishna Paramahamsa (1836–1886), born Gadadhar Chatterji to poor Brahmin parents in the village of Karmarpukar in Bengal, India. The group's namesake spent his life studying Christianity and Islam, while remaining a devout Hindu, in an attempt to develop a syncretistic system. He is reported to have had visions of Hindu gods, as well as of Muhammad and Jesus Christ. He was devoted to the goddess Kali and to the gods Rama and Krishna, and so in 1864 he adopted the name Ramakrishna. In 1874 he started to explore Christianity and had visions of Jesus Christ. During the last six years of his life Ramakrishna formed a group of followers; among them was Vivekananda, who was entrusted with the task of continuing the master's work.

The movement's actual founder, and best known figure, aside from Ramakrishna himself, is Vivekananda (1863–1902), born as Narendranath Datta to a high-caste Calcutta family. Vivekananda was first a follower of BRAHMA SAMAJ but then became a disciple of Ramakrishna. After Ramakrishna's death Vivekananda renounced secular life and devoted himself to the master's teachings. In 1893 Vivekananda traveled to the Parliament of Religions, which was held together with the World's Fair in Chicago. He became the focus of much publicity and interest, and he gave lecture tours in the United States and Great Britain. This was the beginning of the movement's overseas missionary work. Vivekananda took another trip to the United States and Europe in 1899–1900, taking part in the Congress of Religions in Paris in 1900. His best-known Western convert was Nivedita (Margaret E. Noble, 1867–1911), a British woman, converted in 1896, who devoted her post-conversion life to charity and writing. She founded the Nivedita Girls' School, became Vivekananda's biographer, and edited his published teachings.

The Ramakrishna Mission was formally started by Vivekananda in 1897, and both the Math and the Mission have been based since that time in Belur, India. The movement's doctrine, based on Ramakrishna's reflections on major world religions, expresses the idea of the basic unity of all religions, tolerance toward different faiths and practices, and the value of the meditative life. Practices include monastic living and selfless service to the poor and sick. The Mission, which is devoted to social service, is attached to every Math (monastery).

Many groups all over the world claim to follow the teachings of Sri Ramakrishna. These teachings have also influenced many Western writers and artists, such as Romain Rolland (1866–1944).

A depiction of the Hindu deity Rama, worshiped as the seventh incarnation of Vishnu. This deity is claimed by various religious sects.

Sources:

Bassuk, D. E. *Incarnation in Hinduism and Christianity: The Myth of the Godman.* Atlantic Highlands, N.J.: Humanities Press, 1986.

Isherwood, C. *Ramakrishna and His Disciples.* New York: Simon & Schuster, 1965.

Ramakrishna Vedanta Centre

British branch of the international VEDANTA SOCIETY, founded in London in 1948.

Ramakrishna Vedanta Society

U.S. Hindu group founded in Boston in 1926 by Swami Akhilananda (1894–1962), who served as its leader until his death. The Society is dedicated to spreading the Hindu message in the United States.

Ramakrishna—Vivekananda Center

The New York City branch of the U.S. VEDANTA SOCIETY. It was founded in 1933.

Ramana Maharshi

Ramana Maharshi (1879–1950) was a Hindu holy man who at age seventeen renounced the world and moved to the Arunachala hill. Four years later he moved into nearby Virupaska Deva cave, where he lived for sixteen years. By 1903, at age twenty-four, Ramana became known as Maharshi and his fame spread throughout India and the West. He was noted for his asceticism and de-votion to spiritual matters. He believed in the value of silence, and he practiced it, granting only brief interviews to his disciples. He preached a search for perfection and self-knowledge. Although Ramana Maharshi never started a movement, his followers carry on activities devoted to the propagation of his teachings, which are represented by the following: "Divine Grace is essential for realization. It leads one to God-realization, but such Grace is vouchsafed only to him who is a true devotee or a yogin, who has striven hard on the path toward freedom." Since the 1980s Poonjaji of Lucknow is considered by some the successor to Ramana Maharshi.

Ramana Maharshi Foundation

British group of RAMANA MAHARSHI followers founded in the 1990s.

Rama Rajya Parisha

Hindu revitalization movement started in the early twentieth century. It has led a struggle against Westernization and is considered the most conservative of the revival groups.

Rama Seminars

Formerly known as Lakshmi Meditation, this is a U.S. Hindu-oriented meditation group based in Malibu, California, and founded in 1979 by Rama, or Zen Master Rama (formerly Frederick Lenz, 1950–). It promotes Eastern meditation techniques and traditions. Rama had been a disciple of SRI CHIMNOY but decided to found his own group after realizing that he was "one of the twelve truly enlightened beings on the planet."

Ranson Pentecostal African Methodist Episcopalian Zion

British PENTECOSTAL group founded in the 1970s in London by Black Caribbean immigrants.

Rapana Church

Maori syncretistic separatist movement with a mostly Christian doctrine.

Rashtriya Swayamasevak Sangh (RSS)

Hindu revitalization movement founded in 1925 by Kashavrao Baliram Hedgewar (1889–1940). It is one of the main conservative Hindu groups and operates the Jana Sangh political party. It was implicated in the assassination of Mahatma Gandhi in 1948 and was declared illegal by the Indian government in 1992, following major interreligious rioting in India.

Source:

Baxter, C. *The Jana Sangh: A Biography of an Indian Political Party*. Philadelphia: University of Pennsylvania Press, 1969.

Rastafarians (Ras Tafari, Rasta)

An overall name for a loosely defined messianic movement among poor Jamaicans which spread to Great Britain and the United States. It began in 1930 under the influence of Marcus Garvey's (1887–1940) "Back to Africa" movement and inspired by the coronation of Ras Tafari Makonnen (later known as Haile Selassie) as Emperor of Ethiopia. Haile Selassie (1892–1975) has been regarded not only as the black Messiah, coming to liberate all black people (who are believed to be the true Jews) but as Jah the living God. Haile Selassie paid a visit to Jamaica in 1966, but he never commented publicly on the Rastafarian beliefs. However, several hundred Rastas journeyed to Ethiopia following the visit. They have stayed there but experienced legal trouble in 1996 because of their use of cannabis. Selassie died in 1975, but some followers claim he is still alive.

Many legends relate wonders attributed to Haile Selassie and the colors of the Ethiopian flag. Green (for the land of Africa), yellow (for African gold), and red (for the Church Triumphant) are the colors adopted by the Rastafarians. Members wear these colors in scarves or hats. Members are often distinguished by their "dreadlocks," long, plaited, matted hair.

In the 1930s the movement was led by Leonard Howell, a follower of Marcus Garvey who created a commune of Rastafarians in which marijuana was raised, among other crops. In 1941 police raided the commune and arrested seventy members. During the 1930s, there were several Rasta riots in Jamaica, as poor believers sold their belongings and went to ports and airports, waiting to be taken to Africa. Christianity is rejected by the movement, but the Christian Bible is used and quoted, and biblical symbols are used as inspiration. The Bible is regarded as black history, usurped and distorted by whites. April 1 is celebrated as the beginning of the year, and Ras Tafari's Coronation Day is another holiday.

Rastafarians have no houses of worship, but gatherings often take place. Saturday is the Sabbath. Taboos on food prepared by nonmembers and on pork

Haile Selassie, at the time of his coronation as Emperor of Ethiopia. He was the inspiration of the Rastafarian movement.

are observed. Menstrual taboos are strictly observed, and women are segregated during menstruation. All medical treatments, especially surgical operations and blood transfusions, are avoided. Funerals and cemeteries are also taboo. Followers smoke marijuana (known as ganja) as a sacrament, and this has led to difficulties with police in Britain and the United States. Reggae music has also been associated with Rastafarians. In the 1970s the movement gained international visibility thanks to its promotion by the Reggae singer Robert Nesta (Bob) Marley (1945–1981). Since the 1970s the movement has penetrated Native American peoples in the southwestern United States, such as the Hopi, as well as sub-Saharan Africa. Reggae music is said to have played a major role in this growth. Recognized groups that have developed out of the movement include the African Cultural League, AFRICAN METHODIST EPISCOPAL CHURCH, the Ethiopian Coptic Faith, the Ethiopian National Congress, the Ethiopian Orthodox Church (EOC), the ETHIOPIAN ZION COPTIC CHURCH, the United Ethiopian Body, the Ethiopian Youth Cosmic Faith, the Fraternal Solidarity of United Ethiopians, the NYABINGI, the TWELVE TRIBES OF ISRAEL, the United Afro-West Indian Brotherhood, and the Universal Black Improvement Organization. Membership is often informal and group divisions far from strict. [See also AFRICAN REFORM COPTIC CHURCH OF GOD IN CHRIST; THE FIRST FRUIT OF PRAYER, GOD'S ARMY CAMP RASTAFARIAN.]

Sources:

Barrett, L. E. *Soul Force: African Heritage in Afro-American Religion*. New York: Doubleday, 1974.

———. *The Rastafarians: Sounds of Cultural Dissonance*. Boston: Beacon Press, 1977.

Chevannes, B. *Rastafari*. Syracuse, N.Y.: Syracuse University Press, 1994.

Cronon, E. D. *Black Moses: The Story of Marcus Garvey and the Universal Negro Improvement Association*. Madison: University of Wisconsin Press, 1955.

Cashmore, E. *Rastaman : The Rastafarian Movement in England*. London: Allen & Unwin, 1985.

Simpson, G. E. *Black Religions in the New World*. New York: Columbia University Press, 1978.

Williams, K. M. *The Rastafarians*. London: Ward, Lock Educational, 1981.

Ras Tafari Melchizedek Orthodox Church

Jamaican indigenous Christian PENTECOSTAL church founded in Kingston in the 1940s. Branches have operated since 1960 in London, attracting some Europeans.

Ratana Church

Maori syncretistic religious-political movement, founded in 1925 by Tahupotiki Wiremu Ratana (1873–1939). In 1918, acting as a healer during the flu epidemic, he started having visions and promised his followers that angels from heaven would come to protect them. The sources of the Church's doctrine are mostly Christian, but it regards Ratana as the main intermediary in its members' relations with the supernatural world.

The movement has been represented in the New Zealand parliament as a political party, and it is the strongest Maori group there. [*See also* RINGATU.]

Reba Place Fellowship

U.S. Mennonite communal movement which, starting in 1957, created several communes in the Midwest. Communes included the Reba Place Fellowship in Evanston, Illinois; Plow Creek in Bureau County, Illinois; New Creation in Newton, Kansas; and Fellowship of Hope in Elkhart, Indiana.

Reconstructionism

U.S. Jewish radical renewal and reform movement developed out of CONSERVATIVE JUDAISM by Mordecai M. Kaplan (1881–1983), officially separating from the parent movement in 1922. Kaplan's view, captured in the title of his best-known book, *Judaism as a Civilization: Towards a Reconstruction of American-Jewish Life*, is that Judaism is a civilization and not just a religion.

This is today the smallest Jewish denomination in the United States, having one theological seminary in Philadelphia. [*See also* REFORM JUDAISM.]

Source:
Kaplan, M. M. *Judaism as a Civilization: Towards a Reconstruction of American-Jewish Life.* New York: Yoseloff, 1957.

Reformed Apostolic Community (Refomiert-Apostolische Gemeindebund)

An offshoot of the NEW APOSTOLIC CHURCH in Germany. It was formed in 1921 and is based in Dresden. [*See also* CATHOLIC APOSTOLIC CHURCH.]

Reformed Congregation of the Goddess

U.S. neo-pagan group founded by Samantha River (known as Jade) in the 1970s in Madison, Wisconsin. It celebrates Halloween as New Year's Eve, follows a calendar that adds 8,000 years to any CE year, and admits only women.

Reformed Druids of North America

U.S. neo-pagan group based in California. It was started in the 1960s.

Reformed Ogboni Fraternity

Nigerian syncretistic group that combines traditional African ideas with Christian rituals.

Reformed Presbyterian Church, Evangelical Synod

U.S. FUNDAMENTALIST group founded in 1965 through the merger of the Reformed Presbyterian Church in North America, General Synod (formed in 1833) and the Evangelical Presbyterian Church (formed in 1956 out of the BIBLE PRESBYTERIAN CHURCH). This group opposed the separation of church and state in the United States, and it aspired to have the United States proclaimed a "Christian nation." In 1982 it became part of a larger conservative group, the Presbyterian Church in America. [*See also* ORTHODOX PRESBYTERIAN CHURCH.]

Reformed Zion Union Apostolic Church

U.S. African American "HOLINESS" Protestant group founded in Virginia in 1869.

Reform Judaism

International Jewish renewal movement that rejects historical Jewish practices in favor of adjustments to modern life. The earliest ideas of reforming Orthodox Judaism appeared in the late eighteenth century in Germany. In the 1840s conferences of modernist rabbis in Germany started formalizing changes in liturgy and beliefs. The main thrust of these changes was directed against traditional rituals and practices, which appeared antiquated. Jewish identity was to be preserved through an emphasis on ethical beliefs rather than on obedience to revealed truth.

In the United States the development of a strong Reform Judaism took place in the nineteenth century under the leadership of I. M. Wise (1819–1900). In the 1820s the Reformed Society of Israelites was formed, but it did not not survive for long.

The formal founding of Reform Judaism in the United States can be dated to 1885, when the Pittsburgh Platform was adopted by a conference of rabbis. The Platform rejected the Jewish Oral Tradition and ritual traditions. In 1935, in its Columbus Platform, the movement expressed a partial return to ritual and tradition. [*See also* CONSERVATIVE JUDAISM; LIBERAL JUDAISM; *and* RECONSTRUCTIONISM.]

Isaac Mayer Wise, leader of Reform Judaism (courtesy of the UAHC Press).

Sources:

Blau, J. L., ed. *Reform Judaism: A Historical Perspective.* New York: Ktav, 1973.

Meyer, M. A. *Response to Modernity: A History of the Reform Movement in Judaism.* New York: Oxford University Press, 1988.

Rudavsky, D. *Modern Jewish Religious Movements: A History of Emancipation and Adjustment.* New York: Behrman, 1967.

Reiha-No-Hikari

Japanese new religion started in the 1950s. It is devoted to the salvation of mankind and world peace, through the mantra of *Goshugojin-sama, Nidai-sama.* It is based on the claim that "Goshugojin-sama (the guardian God of humanity) who is now one with Nidai-sama (the Second) will lead you by Reiha (the divine power of God) to endless happiness." Branches have operated in the United States and Great Britain.

Reiyu-Kai Kyodan (Spiritual Friends Association)

Japanese Buddhist revival movement derived from out of the Nichiren Shu Buddhist tradition. It was founded in Tokyo in 1922 by Kimi Kotani (1901–1971) and Kabutaro Kubo (1892–1944). Doctrine emphasizes faith healing, the Lotus Sutra, ancestor worship, and patriarchal morality. It is believed that the daily recitation of the Lotus Sutra "can create awareness and appreciation of the vertical line of 'past-time' interconnection extending from one's ancestors through one's parents to oneself." The RISSHO KOSEI KAI group grew out of this movement. Branches of Reiyu-Kai Kyodan have operated in Europe, Asia, and the Americas. The U.S. branch is known as Reiyukai America Association. [*See also* RISSHO KOSEI KAI; *and* SOKA GAKKAI SOCIETY.]

Source:

Hardacre, H. *Lay Buddhism in Contemporary Japan: Reiyukai Kyodan.* Princeton, N.J.: Princeton University Press, 1984.

Religious Science International

Formerly known as the International Association of Religious Science Churches, this U.S. NEW THOUGHT group was founded in 1948 by Ernest Holmes (1887–1960) in Los Angeles as part of the Religious Science movement. Later this organization became a dissenting group from the UNITED CHURCH OF RELIGIOUS SCIENCE. In its credo the group states: "We believe that the Universal Spirit, which is God, operates through a Universal Mind, which is the Law of God; and that we are surrounded by the Creative Mind, which receives the direct impress of our thought and acts upon it. . . . We believe in the healing of the sick through the power of this Mind." In addition to ministers, this group ordains "licensed practitioners" who provide "personal spiritual mind treatment work" based on the "Science of Mind." [*See also* CHRISTIAN SCIENCE.]

Sources:

Braden, C. S. *Spirits in Rebellion.* Dallas: SMU Press, 1963.

Judah, J. S. *The History and Philosophy of the Metaphysical Movements in*

America. Philadelphia: Westminster Press, 1967.

Remnant Church

Indigenous independent PENTECOSTAL group. It was started among the Kwara'ae-speaking people on Malaita in the Solomon Islands in 1954 by secession from the South Sea Evangelical mission.

Remnant Church

Australian Hebrew-Christian group started in the 1950s. The group follows strict observation of the Sabbath.

Remnant Churches of God

Caribbean African American PENTE-COSTAL group started in the 1920s.

Renaissance Church-Community

Earlier known as the Brotherhood of the Spirit, and also known as the Renaissance Movement, this is a U.S. communal revitalization movement. It was started by Michael J. Metelica (1951–), who is also called Michael Rapunzel. The group was established in western Massachusetts and officially incorporated in 1974. The doctrine combines traditional MILLENARIAN ideas with notions of the "Aquarian Age." The *Aquarian Gospel*, a nineteenth-century book, is the basis of the group's religious beliefs, among which reincarnation is central. The founder is considered a reincarnation of Christ. Members consider themselves the pioneers of the New Age, which, they believe, will start following a series of ecological disasters, earthquakes and civil disorders. The movement has oper-ated successful musical groups to spread its message.

Source:
Borowski, K. *Attempting an Alternative Society*. Norwood, Penn.: Norwood Editions, 1984.

Renovated Church of Christ the King (Église du Christ-Roi Renovée)

Also known as the Renewed Church of Christ the King. This Western European dissenting Roman Catholic group was founded by Michel Collin (1905–1974), a Catholic priest from Dijon, France. Collin was ordained in 1933. However, he was defrocked by the Church in 1951 following his claims of apparitions, revelations, and divine consecrations.

In 1961 Collin named himself pope under the name of Clement XV. During the 1960s he collaborated with other dissenting OLD CATHOLIC and Roman Catholic groups, especially the APOSTLES OF INFI-NITE LOVE. The group challenged the authority of the Roman Catholic Church and the papacy, accusing the Church of becoming too modern. Collin (or Clement XV) died after fasting for 100 days, as an act of devotion. Since his death his followers have been active in Western Europe, sometimes collaborating with other dissenting Catholic groups. [*See also* MAGNIFICAT.]

Source:
Delestre, A. *Clement XV*. Nancy: Presses Universitaires, 1985.

Reorganized Church of Jesus Christ of Latter-Day Saints

Originally known as the New Organiza-

The assassination of Joseph Smith, founder of Mormonism.

tion. This is a MORMON splinter group created after the murder of Joseph Smith, Jr., the founder and Prophet of Mormonism, in 1844. Following Smith's death the movement split into several groups, each claiming Smith's legacy. It is estimated that twenty-five such groups are in existence today, and the largest is the Reorganized Church.

When, following Smith's death, Brigham Young led a group of the Prophet's followers west to Utah, the Prophet's wife Emma refused to join. With her sons and a remnant of her husband's followers she moved to Independence, Missouri, where the Reorganized Church was officially founded on April 6, 1860. Joseph Smith III became Prophet, Seer, and Revelator, and descendants of the Prophet have presided ever since.

Unlike the faction established by Brigham Young, the Reorganized Church has always opposed polygyny. It has also never accepted such mainstream Mormon tenets as the anthropomorphic view of the Godhead, celestial (eternal) marriages, a plurality of gods, humans becoming gods, or baptism for the dead. It holds that salvation can be achieved only through Jesus Christ.

The Church has grown considerably since its inception. Its base of strength is the U.S. Midwest. It has failed in its efforts to acquire the temple lot at Independence, Missouri (designated by Joseph Smith, Jr. as the location of the Second Coming), but church headquarters are across the street from the lot, which is owned by THE CHURCH OF CHRIST (TEMPLE LOT). Branches of this group also operate in Western Europe. [*See also*

CHURCH OF THE FIRST BORN OF THE FULLNESS OF TIMES; *and* UNITED ORDER EFFORT.]

Restoration Movement

North American PENTECOSTAL movement started in the early 1980s. It was inspired by the LATTER RAIN MOVEMENT of the late 1940s. Restorationists believe that the period of the last 450 years has seen the restoration of the ancient Christian Church—evidenced by the Pentecostal revival of the twentieth century.

Resurrected Church of God

U.S. PENTECOSTAL African American group started in Philadelphia in the 1950s. Branches exist in the West Indian community in Great Britain.

Revelation Apostolic Church in Zion

South African independent indigenous ZIONIST church founded in the 1940s.

Revival Zion

Sometimes known as Revival or Pocomania. This is a Jamaican syncrestistic African Christian movement. It originated during the nineteenth-century Protestant evangelical revivals, especially the Great Revival of 1861, and took many forms. Followers believe in possession by a great number of supernatural beings. There is a general emphasis on dreams, visions, and trances. Faith healing is also practiced. Starting in the 1930s, many of the followers of Revival Zion became Rastas. [*See also* RASTAFARIANS.]

Rhema

Formerly known as École de Vie Abondante, this is a French FUNDAMENTALIST healing group. It was founded in 1972 in Clichy by J. L. Jayet.

Rhema Bible Church

International Christian charismatic church founded in the United States in the 1960s. Branches exist in southern Africa.

Rigpa

International network of Tibetan Buddhism centers founded by Sogyal Rinpoche in the 1980s.

Ringatu

Known as the Church of the Upraised Hand, this syncretistic Maori movement was started by Te Kooti Rikirangi of the Rongowhakota people in 1868. It was influenced by HAU HAU, and represented a combination of traditional Maori and Christian ideas. The group adopted beliefs and imagery from Christian mythology, such as the "lost tribes of Israel," while emphasizing that only the Maori were the chosen people. Faith healing and Saturday worship are practiced, and its liturgy is based on the Hebrew Bible. Among Maori syncretistic groups, it is considered the closest to traditional Christianity. [*See also* CHURCH OF TE KOOTI RIKIRANGI; *and* RATANA CHURCH.]

Rissho Kosei-Kai (Integrative Becoming, or The Society for the Establishment of Righteousness and Friendly Relations)

Japanese new religion, emerging from the Nichiren Buddhist tradition. It was founded in 1938 by two former members of REIYU-KAI KYODAN, Nikkyo Niwano (1906–) and Myoko Naganuma (1899–1957). Worship practices focus on the Lotus Sutra, group counseling, and divination. The group counseling process is carried out through the *hosa*, where about twelve members sit in a circle around a leader (*kambu*). The leader responds to questions according to the *shitai no homon*, the law explaining the causes of anxiety. The session is devoted to teaching how to develop immunity to pain according to traditional Buddhist doctrines. Group branches have operated in the United States, South America, and Asia since the 1960s. In the 1990s its growing political power in Japan has been a source of controversy. [*See also* SOKA GAKKAI SOCIETY.]

Sources:
McFarland, H. N. *The Rush Hour of the Gods.* New York: Macmillan, 1967.

Guthrie, S. *A Japanese New Religion: Rissho Kosei-Kai in a Mountain Hamlet.* Ann Arbor: Center for Japanese Studies, University of Michigan, 1988.

"Rizalist"

Popular name for numerous Filipino groups whose doctrines include the belief in the return of José Rizal, the Filipino national hero and martyr. [*See also* IGLESIA WATAWAT NG LAHI.]

Roho Church of the God of Israel

Originally the World Spiritual Israel Church, this is an African independent PENTECOSTAL group. It was created in Kenya in 1960.

Roho Musalaba (Spirit Cross Church)

Officially known as the Cross Church of East Africa. This is an African independent Protestant group created around 1940 by secession from the Anglican mission church.

Ron's Organization and Network for Standard Tech

European SCIENTOLOGY splinter group. It was founded around 1980 in Frankfurt, Germany, by Bill Robertson (known as "Captain Bill").

Roosevelt Spiritual Memorial Benevolent Association

U.S. spiritualist group founded in 1949.

Root of David Ministries

U.S. evangelical group founded in the late 1980s by Roger Abergal in Encino, California.

Rose-Croix D'or

European ROSICRUCIAN organization based in Lausanne, Switzerland.

Rosh Pina Congregation

U.S. HEBREW CHRISTIAN group founded

by Marvin Morrison in the 1970s and based in Baltimore.

Rosicrucian Anthroposophic League

U.S. occultist group formed in an attempt to combine ANTHROPOSOPHY and the ROSICRUCIAN tradition. It was founded in San Francisco by Samuel Richard Parchment in 1932 as an offshoot of the ROSICRUCIAN FELLOWSHIP.

Rosicrucian Fellowship

U.S. occultist group founded in 1908 in Columbus, Ohio. The founder, Carl Louis van Grasshoff, also known as Max Heindel (1865–1919), served as the head of the Los Angeles Theosophical Lodge in 1904–1905. Heindel claimed to be "an authorized messenger of the Elder Brothers of the Rose Cross, who are working to disseminate throughout the Western world the deeper Spiritual meanings which are both concealed and revealed within the Christian religion." Within two years after its start, the group had branches in Los Angeles, Seattle, Portland, and North Yakima, Washington. For many years group headquarters have been located in Mount Ecclesia, Oceanside, California. The group lists the International Association of Christian Mystics among its affiliations. [*See also* THEOSOPHY.]

Rosicrucians

Also known as the Order of the Rosy Cross, or the Brotherhood of the Rosy Cross, this is a legendary medieval brotherhood devoted to magic and alchemy. According to legend, the founder was Christian Rosenkreutz (1378–1484), who had brought his scientific and esoteric knowledge with him from the East. Since the early seventeenth century, when this legend was first published in Germany (in the form of three books purporting to have been written by Rosenkreutz himself), various esoteric groups have claimed the mantle of medieval Rosicrucian origins.

The Rosicrucian ideals are said to be the "unity of opposites" and the quest for earthly immortality. Their teachings include alleged ancient traditions, Christian ideas and symbols, and an amalgam of Western occult beliefs, including alchemy and various divination practices.

The Rosicrucian tradition and ideas have affected hundreds of modern religious movements, some of which do not always acknowledge such influence (e.g. THEOSOPHY and the EMIN SOCIETY). They also had an influence on poets and writers such as the poet Percy Bysshe Shelley (1792–1822) and his wife Mary Wollstonecraft Shelley (1797–1851). [*See also* AMORC ROSICRUCIAN ORDER; ANCIENT MAYANS, ORDER OF; AUSAR AUSET SOCIETY; FRATERNITAS ROSAE CRUCIS; LECTORIUM ROSICRUCIANUM; ORDO TEMPLI ORIENTIS; ROSICRUCIAN ANTHROPOSOPHIC LEAGUE; ROSICRUCIAN FELLOWSHIP; SOCIETAS ROSICRUCIANA IN AMERICA; *and* SOCIETAS ROSICRUCIANA IN ANGLIA.]

Source:

Yates, F. A. *The Rosicrucian Enlightenment*. London: Routledge & Kegan Paul, 1972.

Ruhani Satsang

Also known in the West as the Fellowship of the Spirit, this is a branch of the

RADHASOAMI SATSANG movement. It was started in 1951 following a dispute over the succession to leadership in the RADHASOAMI SATSANG BEAS. Kirpal Singh (1896–1974), who lost the leadership in the Beas group to Jagat Singh, started the new movement, which in turn gave rise to other groups. [*See also* ECKANKAR; KIRPAL RUHANI SATSANG; SANT BANI ASHRAM; *and* SAWAN KIRPAL RUHANI MISSION.]

Ruponiso Rwa Jesu

African independent Christian church. It was started in Zimbabwe in the 1950s by secession from the Roman Catholic Church.

S

Sabbath Jerusalem Church

African independent church founded by Philemon Butelezi among the Zulu of South Africa in the 1940s. The founder claimed to be Jesus Christ and practiced faith healing.

Sabian Assembly

U.S. occultist group founded in 1923 by Marc Edmund Jones in Los Angeles. Jones drew his ideas from THEOSOPHY, NEW THOUGHT, spiritualism, and Eastern traditions. He also claimed to follow the Kabbalah. Group practices have included Tarot readings and astrology.

Sacred Name Movement

U.S. Protestant movement that advocates the use of Hebrew names for Christian deities, such as using only the name Yahweh for the biblical God, and the name Yehoshua for Jesus of the New Testament. [*See also* ASSEMBLIES OF YAHWEH; ASSEMBLIES OF YAHWEH (MICHIGAN); *and* ASSEMBLY OF YAHVAH.]

Sacred Order of Cherubim and Seraphim Society

African independent Christian PENTE-COSTAL group founded in Nigeria around 1950 by Christiana Emmanuel Abiodun (1908–). It is one of the many groups claiming the CHERUBIM AND SERAPHIM heritage.

Sacred Order of the Silent Brotherhood

African independent Christian PENTE-COSTAL group founded in Ghana in 1961.

Sage Community

U.S. faith healing group founded by Gay Luce in the late 1970s.

Sahaja Yoga

Hindu-inspired Western group devoted to the teachings of Shri Mataji Nirmala Devi (Mrs. C. P. Shrivastava; 1923–). It was started in 1970 and has branches in numerous European countries. Members are promised complete "self-realization" through devotion to the founder, who was born completely self-realized. Nirmala Devi was raised in a Christian family, and she teaches that "every true Religion in its purest form has no boundaries but belongs to us all for our spiritual emancipation."

"Sahaja means 'born within' and 'spontaneous'; Yoga [means] 'union with the Divine.' Self-realization is a physiological process and a spiritual transformation where the Kundalini or Holy Spirit is awakened within and travels up the spinal cord to enlighten the subtle centres of the central nervous system. This subtle system is built within every human being and therefore Self-Realization is available to anyone who sincerely wants it."

Sai Baba

Sai Baba of Shirdi (1856–1918), a famous Indian holy man, was considered an avatar, an incarnation of God. He was so admired that both Muslims and Hindus claimed him as their own. His ancestry is unclear, however, as thousands of miracle stories have grown up around him. At age twenty-three he settled in Shirdi, which became a place of pilgrimage. His disciple Sri Upasani Baba set up an ashram in Sakori, near Nasik in northern India.

Followers of Sai Baba abstain from meat and drugs of any kind. His Indian devotees have built shrines in his name all over the country, and there have been Western groups of his admirers outside India. [*See also* SATHYA SAI BABA.]

St. John's Apostolic Faith Mission of South Africa

South African indigenous PENTECOSTAL and ZIONIST church. It was started in 1924 by Christina Mokutudu Nku (Ma Nku, 1894–), a Sotho-speaking Ndebele prophetess in Evaton, near Johannesburg. It was formally founded in 1944 by secession from the Anglican Church. The founder reportedly started having visions and hearing voices at age twelve. According to her followers, she had healing powers and could create curative powers in water by praying over it.

Source:
Sundkler, B. G. M. *Bantu Prophets in South Africa*. London: Oxford University Press, 1961.

St. Paul's Apostolic Faith Mission

South African indigenous PENTECOSTAL healing church started in 1959.

St. Paul's Spiritual Church Convocation

U.S. African American PENTECOSTAL group. In 1952 it merged with the NATIONAL DAVID SPIRITUAL TEMPLE OF CHRIST CHURCH UNION (INC.) U.S.A. and KING DAVID'S SPIRITUAL TEMPLE OF TRUTH ASSOCIATION to form the UNIVERSAL CHRISTIAN SPIRITUAL FAITH AND CHURCHES FOR ALL NATIONS.

St. Peter's Healing Church

African independent Protestant church founded in 1973 in Freetown, Sierra Leone. It has operated several branches around Freetown.

Saiva Siddhanta Church

Also known as the Wailua University of the Contemplative Arts, and as Subramuniya Yoga Order. This is a U.S. Hindu group founded in 1957 in Hawaii by Subramuniya (1927–), a North American student of Hinduism. Meditation and yoga are practiced, and an ascetic lifestyle is advocated.

Sakya Tagchen Choling Center

Also known as the Monastery of Tibetan Buddhism. This is a U.S. Tibetan Buddhist group based in the State of Washington and founded in the 1970s by Jigdal Dagchen Sakya Rinpoche. It is committed to the Sakya sect of Vajrayana Buddhism.

Salem Acres

U.S. Christian commune founded by Lester B. Anderson in the late 1960s near

Rock City, Illinois. Group doctrine emphasizes both PENTECOSTALISM (speaking in tongues and faith healing) and the keeping of Old Testament commandments regarding the Sabbath and diet.

Salvation Army, The

International Christian FUNDAMENTALIST movement. It was founded in 1878 in London by William Booth (1829–1912), a Methodist minister who left his church in 1865 to organize the Christian Mission, which was devoted to social service. In 1878 the Mission was organized along "military" lines, and became the Salvation Army. Its style of operation was influenced by U.S. revivalists who were active in Great Britain in the middle

General William Booth, founder of the Salvation Army.

of the nineteenth century, but the emphasis on social welfare was its own. In 1890 Booth published *In Darkest England and the Way Out*, which called not only for welfare but for farm colonies and emigration to solve the problem of widespread poverty in Britain.

In the United States the Army was founded in Philadelphia in 1879 by Eliza Shirley, a British immigrant. Shortly afterward an official delegation was sent from London, and George Railton became the first National Commander. Members of the Booth family, including Catherine Booth (1829–1890) and the founder's son, William Bramwell Booth (1856–1929), have been active in leading the movement. William Bramwell Booth was the leader between 1912 and 1929. He was followed by Edward Higgins (1929–1934), Evangeline Booth (1934–1939), G. L. Carpenter (1939–1946), Albert Osborn, and Eva Burrows.

The movement's doctrine is based on "personal justification," the personal experience of becoming "born again" through the acceptance of Jesus Christ. There are no sacraments, but Founder's Day (July 2) is a memorial day for all dead Army members. The commitment to social service is based on the assumption that the satisfaction of basic needs must precede any religious awakening.

The Army has maintained social service programs that have become widely admired. These include the largest rehabilitation program for alcoholics in the United States, thrift shops, and halfway houses, organized in more than 3,000 local centers around the world. At the end of the nineteenth century it initiated an unsuccessful homesteading program for the urban poor in the United States. It also operates the largest program in the world for locating

Evangeline Booth, daughter of the founder of the Salvation Army and commander from 1934 to 1939.

missing persons. [*See also* AMERICAN RESCUE WORKERS; *and* VOLUNTEERS OF AMERICA.]

Sources:

Collier, R. *The General Next to God.* New York: Dutton, 1965.

Coutts, J. *The Salvationists.* London: Mowbrays, 1977.

McKinley, E. H. *Marching to Glory.* New York: Harper & Row, 1980.

Murdoch, N. H. *The Origins of the Salvation Army.* Knoxville: University of Tennessee Press, 1995.

Sandall, R. *The History of the Salvation Army.* London: T. Nelson, 1947–1973.

Spence, C. C. *The Salvation Army Farm Colonies.* Tucson: University of Arizona Press, 1985.

Samhan Ng Amang Ka-Amahan at Inang Ka-Inainahan

Officially known as the Church of Father of Fathers and Mother of Mothers, this is an indigenous Philippine Protestant group with a nationalist ideology. It was started in 1951.

Samoan Full Gospel Church

Samoan indigenous PENTECOSTAL group founded around 1965.

Samye Ling

Western Tibetan Buddhist monastery founded in Scotland in the 1960s by Akong Rinpoche.

Sanby Kyodan

Japanese indigenous Christian church based in Hiroshima.

Santa Anita Church

U.S. NEW THOUGHT group based in California. It was founded in the 1970s by Margaret Stevens.

Sant Bani Ashram

North American Sikh organization founded in the 1970s in New Hampshire by Russell Perkins. It is devoted to the teachings of Ajaib Singh, a disciple of Kirpal Singh (1896–1974). The organization offers "initiation into the path of Surat Shabd Yoga [translated as the yoga of the celestial sound], a path of love and discipline that embraces the essence of the teachings of all True Masters." [*See also* KIRPAL RUHANI SATSANG; RADHASOAMI SATSANG; *and* SAWAN KIRPAL RUHANI MISSION.]

Santiniketan

Known as The House of Peace, this is an Indian religious academy founded by Rabindranath Tagore (1861–1941), poet, musician, and Nobel laureate in literature who attempted to develop a universal religion based on the notion of unity among all world faiths. [*See also* ARYA SAMAJ; *and* BRAHMA SAMAJ.]

Sarva Dharma Sambhava Kendra

Sometimes known as the Chandra Group after its leader, Nemi Chand Ghandi (1949–), known as Chandra

Swami. This is an international Hindu revival movement founded in the 1970s in India. The group opened branches in Western Europe in the 1980s, and Chandra Swami attracted much attention. In 1986 his name was tied in the media to financial scandals in Great Britian and India, which threw the movement into a serious crisis.

Sathya Sai Baba

Sathya Sai Baba (1926–) is one of India's leading gurus of the twentieth century. He claims to be a reincarnation of SAI BABA of Shirdi. He was born Sathya Narayana Raju in South India, and at age fourteen he claimed to be the incarnation of Sai Baba. In 1963 he claimed to be an incarnation of the god Shiva.

Sathya Sai Baba has predicted that his own death will take place in 2022. He is believed to have the largest following of any Hindu holy man in modern times. Groups of his followers operate in India and in many Western countries.

Source:
Bassuk, D. E. *Incarnation in Hinduism and Christianity: The Myth of the Godman.* Atlantic Highlands, N.J.: Humanities Press, 1986.

Sathya Sai Baba Central Committee of America

U.S. Hindu group based in California. It is devoted to the teachings of SATHYA SAI BABA.

Sathya Sai Baba National Headquarters of America

U.S. Hindu-inspired group based in Cali-fornia. It is devoted to the teachings of SATHYA SAI BABA. Its doctrine is expressed as follows: "The message of the 'Fatherhood of God and the Brotherhood of Man,' which Jesus Christ proclaimed two thousand years ago, should become a living faith for the achievement of real peace and the unity of mankind."

Sathya Sai Baba Society

U.S. Hindu group founded in 1961 and based in California. Devoted to spreading the message of SATHYA SAI BABA, the Society has published at least thirty volumes of his teachings.

Satyananda Ashram

International Hindu movement devoted to the teachings of Swami Satyananda of Bihar, and to the practice of Tantric yoga.

Saviour's Apostolic Church of Nigeria

African indigenous PENTECOSTAL church founded in Nigeria in 1941.

Savitria

U.S. occultist commune founded in 1969 in North Baltimore, Maryland, by Robert Hieronimus. Its aim is to prepare for the coming Aquarian Age, and its practices include meditation. A strict conduct code is followed.

Sawan Kirpal Ruhani Mission

International RADHASOAMI SATSANG group that recognizes Sant Darshan Singh (1921–), the son of Kirpal Singh

(1896–1974), as his father's true heir. The group claims that Sant Darshan Singh had been trained by Hazur Baba Sawan Singh (1858–1948). The group's name combines the names of Hazur Baba Sawan Singh and of Sant Kirpal Singh. Its doctrine is based on the Radhasoami Satsang traditions and the teachings of Kirpal Singh. "We can attain self-knowledge and God-realization through mystic experiences on the path of the Masters." [*See also* RUHANI SATSANG; *and* SANT BANI ASHRAM.]

School of Economic Science (SES)

British occultist group started in the 1920s and officially founded in London in 1937. It follows the GURDJIEFF GROUP tradition as well as some Platonic and Hindu ideas. It is connected to the SCHOOL OF PRACTICAL PHILOSOPHY in New York.

School of Esoteric Studies

U.S. occultist group, a splinter group formed by members of the Arcane School in 1956, after the death of its founder. [*See also* LUCIS TRUST.]

School of Light and Realization (SOLAR)

U.S. occultist group inspired by the teachings of Alice Bailey and THEOSOPHY. It was founded in 1969 by Norman Craemer near Traverse City, Michigan. The School is engaged in preparing its students for the coming of the Christ and the beginning of the Aquarian Age.

School of Practical Philosophy

U.S. occultist, syncretistic group. It was founded in the 1960s and is based in New York City. It combines a GURDJIEFF GROUP approach with Hindu teachings. The School claims to be guided by Shankara Charya, an Indian teacher.

School of the Prophets, The

U.S. PENTECOSTAL group founded in the early twentieth century in Louisville, Kentucky.

School of Truth

South African NEW THOUGHT group, originally known as the School of Practical Christianity. It was founded by Nicol C. Campbell in 1937 in Johannesburg. Its doctrine emphasizes adherence to Christianity, and members are expected to tithe. Branches have operated in Zimbabwe and the United States.

School of Universal Philosophy and Healing

British spiritualist group founded by Gladys Spearman-Cook in London in the 1950s.

Science of Mind Church

U.S. NEW THOUGHT group based in Los Angeles. It was founded by Frederick Bailes in the 1950s.

Science of Spirituality

North American branch of the RADHASOAMI SATSANG movement. It was started in 1990 by Sant Rajinder Singh, who claims to be the successor to Sant Darshan Singh. The group teaches "how to meditate through the process of inversion. Spirituality then becomes a science verifiable within ourselves." [*See also* ECKANKAR; KIRPAL RUHANI SATSANG; SANT BANI ASHRAM; *and* SAWAN KIRPAL RUHANI MISSION.]

Scientology, Church of

Earlier known as the Hubbard Association of Scientologists International, and often advertised as Dianetics, this is an international organization that professes to be a religion, though such claims are doubted by some. It has been criticized for charging its followers for services and products, and as critics believe, should therefore be classified as a profit-making institution rather than a religious one. Its description here implies no recognition as a religion.

It was founded by Lafayette Ronald (L. Ron) Hubbard (1911–1986) in the 1950s. May 9, 1950, the day when *Dianetics: The Modern Science of Mental Health* was published, is considered by many as Scientology's birthdate, though the Church of Scientology was founded four years later. The day is celebrated by Scientologists, together with March 13, Hubbard's birthday.

Dianetics has been a best-selling book ever since it first came on the market in 1950. As late as 1988 it appeared on the *New York Times* paperback best-sellers list (classified under "Advice, How-to and Miscellaneous") for sixty-two consecutive weeks (critics have charged that books have been purchased by the group to inflate sales figures). Dianetics began as a secular psychotherapy movement but it soon developed into a "religion," organized through local churches that are tightly run by the group's headquarters.

The Church of Scientology has inspired probably more social science research and more media attention than any other similar group, and its activities all over the world have been studied and reported widely.

Scientology seems to have been involved in an unusual amount of litigation and criminal cases. In 1958 the U.S. Internal Revenue Service revoked its tax-exempt status, and in 1963 the U.S. Food and Drug Administration seized materials used in the Scientology "auditing," including books and E-meters. Scientology has failed in its attempts to regain its tax-exempt status in the United States. In Great Britain, Minister of Health Kenneth Robinson replied on December 5, 1966, to a question in Parliament: "I do not think that any further enquiry is necessary to establish that the activities of this organisation [the Church of Scientology] are potentially harmful. I have no doubt that Scientology is totally valueless in promoting health and, in particular, that people seeking help with problems of mental health can gain nothing from the attentions of this organisation." Lord Windlesham, in an official letter from the Home Office, declared Scientology "to be harmful and contrary to the public interest," though Hubbard was the only Scientologist ever precluded (on August 13, 1970) from entering the United Kingdom. The investigation into Scientology in Britain led to possibly the best study of its nature ever published, *Enquiry into the Practice and Effects of Scientology*.

In 1965 the group's activities were banned in Australia (leading the group to change its name to the Church of the New Faith), but in 1983 this act was re-

L. Ron Hubbard, founder of Scientology, saying good-bye to his staff after having been ordered out of the country by the government of Rhodesia.

versed by the Australian High Court. In 1984 an Australian court ruled that Scientology was a religion and therefore entitled to tax-exempt status.

On February 14, 1978, L. Ron Hubbard (*in absentia*) and two associates were sentenced to prison terms and heavy fines by a French court in Paris. Hubbard himself received a sentence of four years and a fine of 35,000 francs. The sentences were upheld by an appellate court on February 29, 1980. The tax-exempt status of the group in France was revoked in 1985, after it had been determined that its aim was profit-making. In the United States, Scientology has been sued by former members because of its practices, and in some cases the former members have won damage rulings. In July 1985 a court of appeals in Copenhagen decided that the Church of Scientology is a profit-making venture and so must pay taxes on its income. In April 1986 the Danish Justice Minister announced a decision to deport forty Scientologists who were running the European and African Headquarters for the Church in Copenhagen.

In 1988 Scientology was charged by the Canadian government with the theft of government documents, and it expressed readiness to donate $1 million to charity if charges were dropped. In November 1988 court proceedings were initiated in Spain against Heber Jentsch, the leader of the Church at the time.

In November, 1996, Jean-Jaques Mazier, a French Scientology leader, was convicted of manslaughter following the death by suicide of a member.

The official goal of Scientology, as stated by its founder in *What Is Scientology*, is to lead humankind "to total freedom and truth." In the same volume Scientology is defined as "the study of knowing how to know and deal with Man as a spirit separate from his mind and body. . . . Scientology is used to increase spiritual freedom, intelligence, ability, to produce immortality."

Hubbard claimed that in the course of his research, he "came across incontrovertible scientifically validated evidence of the existence of the human soul." According to Scientology doctrine, the universe is populated by *thetans*, a large group of omnipotent, eternal beings. The *thetans* created the world as we know it. Later on, the thetans gave up most of their powers and became human beings. All humans can return to the state of *thetan* if they follow Scientology and its procedures. The first step on the road is that of *clear*. One becomes *clear* through *auditing* or *processing* and then is totally free of psychoses, neuroses, compulsions, or inhibitions and does not suffer from any psychosomatic diseases. His or her intelligence, as measured by IQ tests, is superior to normal. Scientology believes in reincarnation, and one who has become *clear* in this life will carry his excellence to the next one. Hubbard reported in 1963 a visit to Heaven, where the grounds looked "like the Busch Gardens in Pasadena."

Scientology operates numerous organizations, such as the Alliance for the Preservation of Religious Liberty, Narconon, the Citizens Commission on Human Rights, the Committee on Public Health and Safety, American Citizens for Honesty in Government, the Committee for a Safe Environment, and the National Commission on Law Enforcement and Social Justice. In April 1977 Scientology in the United States joined with the UNIFICATION CHURCH and the Children of God (now called THE FAMILY) to form the Alliance for the Preservation of Religious Liberty. In addition to these U.S. organizations, which are best known, Scientology has established scores of similar organizations in other countries.

The Religious Research Foundation was a front organization to which revenues were channeled to avoid taxes. Another front organization, created to operate within U.S. government institutions, and so claiming to be specifically nonreligious, is the Concerned Businessmen's Association of America, which also operates The Way to Happiness Foundation. Scientology has reportedly offered "corporate innovation" programs to several U.S. corporations. [*See also* DIANOLOGY AND EDUCTIVISM; *and* DUGA (ABILITY).]

Sources:

Croydon, B., and Hubbard, L. R. , Jr. *L. Ron Hubbard: Messiah or Madman?* Secaucus, N.J.: Lyle Stuart, 1987.

Evans, C. *Cults of Unreason.* London: Harrap, 1973.

Lord Foster. *Enquiry into the Practice and Effects of Scientology.* London: Her Majesty's Stationery Office, 1971.

Malko, G. *Scientology: The New Religion.* New York: Dell, 1970.

Miller, R. *Barefaced Messiah: The True Story of L. Ron Hubbard.* New York: Holt, 1987.

Wallis, R. *The Road to Total Freedom: A Sociological Analysis of Scientology.* New York: Columbia University Press, 1976.

Seax-Wica Seminary

U.S. neo-pagan group founded by Raymond Buckland in the early 1970s and based in Charlottesville, Virginia. It is devoted to what Buckland has called Saxon Witchcraft, which is the worship of the old Saxon deities Woden and Freya, representing the male and female principles. [*See also* COVENANT OF THE GODDESS.]

Seeker's Quest

U.S. esoteric Christianity group founded in the 1950s in California by Woods Mattingly. In 1970 the group merged with the CHRIST MINISTRY FOUNDATION, and Mattingly became the leader, but the two groups separated again in 1972. Healing through "spiritual work" is a major practice.

Seibo no Mikuni

Japanese indigenous Christian conservative group. It was founded in the 1970s and has operated missions in Europe.

Seicho-no-Ie

Known sometimes as the Truth of Life, this is a Japanese Shinto-inspired new religion whose name means the House of Growth. Founded in 1930 by Masaharu Taniguchi (1893–1987), it grew out of the OMOTOKYO (OMOTO) movement, and it combines Shinto, Buddhist, and Christian concepts. It was influenced by U.S. NEW THOUGHT ideas and, especially, by RELIGIOUS SCIENCE. Teachings emphasize positive thinking and meditation. At the same time Seicho-no-Ie is tied to the historical tradition of Japanese particularism.

"The practice of shinsokan, a form of meditation, is the method by which members strive to realize the Truth, the Truth that one is a child of God, pure and sinless." Group branches have opened in the United States as well as in Europe. The group has been involved in politics and promotes a right-wing ideology for Japan.

Sources:

Judah, J. S. *The History and Philosophy of the Metaphysical Movements in America.* Philadelphia: Westminster Press, 1967.

McFarland, H. N. *The Rush Hour of the Gods.* New York: Macmillan, 1967.

Thomsen, H. *The New Religions of Japan.* Rutland, Ver.: Charles E. Tuttle, 1963.

Sei Iesu Kai ("Holy Jesus Society")

Japanese indigenous Christian PENTE-COSTAL group founded in the 1960s in Tokyo.

Sekai Kyusei Kyo (SKK-World Messianic Association)

Japanese Shinto-inspired new religion that grew out of the OMOTOKYO movement. It was founded in 1950 as Sekai Meshiakyo (Church of World Messianity, or C.W.M.) by Mikichi Okada (1882–1955), known by his followers as Meishu-sama. Okada became a member of Omotokyo in 1923 and a leader after 1926. He left that group in 1935 to found the Dai Nippon Kannon Kai. In 1948 he founded the Nippon Miroku Kyokai. Sekai Kyusei started as a healing movement with Buddhist orientation but has moved closer to Christian-

ity. It now teaches the coming of the Messianic age and the practice of faith healing. Branches operate in the United States, Latin America, and East Asia. [*See also* ANANAIKYO; JOHREI; SEICHO-NO-IE; *and* WORLD MESSIANITY.]

Self-Realization Fellowship

U.S. Hindu group founded in 1935 in Los Angeles by Paramahansa Yogananda (1893–1952), who was born in India and studied under Swami Sri Yukteswar. In 1918 Yogananda founded the YOGODA SATSANGA SOCIETY in India and in 1920 came to the United States and started teaching yoga in Los Angeles. The group offers "direct personal experience of

Paramahansa Yogananda, founder of the Self-Realization Fellowship.

God" through the practice of kriya yoga, a technique of "deep meditation affecting energy centers in the body." It also operates the Church of All Religions as well as branches in Western Europe. [*See also* SELF-REVELATION CHURCH OF ABSOLUTE MONISM.]

Self-Revelation Church of Absolute Monism

U.S. Hindu group started by Paramahansa Yogananda in 1927 and later led by Swami Premananda. In addition to Yogananda teachings, the group emphasizes the teachings of Gandhi. The group operates the Swami Order of Absolute Monism for those members who want to commit themselves to the monastic life. It also operates one mission in India. [*See also* SELF-REALIZATION FELLOWSHIP.]

Seng Khasi

Revitalization and reform movement of the traditional Khasi tribal religion of northeastern India. It was started in 1899 by U Jeebon Roy. In response to the encroachment of Christian missionaries, its founders worked with the BRAHMA SAMAJ and the Unitarian Church to create a monotheistic religion with a personal god (known as *U Blei*) and with no priesthood. This religion was designed to replace the traditional animistic religion, which was based on ancestor worship.

Servants of the Light

British THEOSOPHICAL group whose members claim to follow "the mystery schools of the ancient Mediterranean world" and the "Bardic traditions of the West." Hindu ideas are also followed as well as psychic messages.

Servants of the Light

U.S. ecumenical community founded in Minneapolis, Minnesota, in the 1970s. It developed out of the CATHOLIC CHARISMATIC RENEWAL movement.

Servants of the Sacred Heart of Jesus and Mary

U.S. traditionalist Catholic group started in 1981 in Friendwood, Texas, by George J. Musey. It has been tied to several other traditionalist groups in the United States.

Servers of the Great Ones, Inc.

U.S. occultist group founded in the 1960s and based in Boston. The group's doctrine is described as follows: "Eastern and Western techniques are used to develop receptivity to soul contact and the ability to channel spiritual energies toward those areas of the planet most in need; for example, to the United Nations, to any nations in conflict, to bring about racial harmony, and to humanity in general." Classes offered include meditation and "Qabbalah, tarot, I Ching, and the Path of Discipleship." "At the time of the full moon, we link up with meditation groups around the world by using the Great Invocation." Another activity is "the sponsoring of public gatherings annually on World Goodwill Day, the full moon of Gemini." [*See also* LUCIS TRUST.]

Seva Foundation

U.S. Hindu group devoted to the propagation of traditional Hindu teachings in the West. It was founded by Ram Dass in the 1970s. [*See also* HANUMAN FOUNDATION.]

Sevenoaks Community

U.S. commune founded in 1972 by Donovan Thesenga. The group is committed to the PATHWORK "spiritual growth" philosophy.

Seventh-Day Adventist Church (SDA)

International ADVENTIST movement started in the United States in the mid-nineteenth century. Its founder, Ellen Gould White (née Harmon; 1827–1915), was, as an adolescent, a follower of William Miller, who predicted the Second Advent in 1844. Two months after the great disappointment of October 22, 1844, White started having visions, which continued for thirty-three years.

White suggested that Miller was right in his calculations but wrong in his definition of the predicted event. What actually occurred in 1844, she said, was the cleansing of the divine sanctuary, instead of the earthly one, which Miller had predicted. On October 22, 1844, she stated, Jesus Christ entered the Holy of Holies in heaven. This was revealed to her in one of her visions. Very early on, White and her followers adopted the idea of keeping a Saturday Sabbath as part of their strong Old Testament orientation. The name Seventh-Day Adventist Church was adopted in 1860.

The SDA theology is based on the doctrine of "present truth," which means an urgent message of apocalypse and redemption ("Day of Armageddon") in the immediate future. White's apocalyptic prophecies also include visions of the persecution of the faithful, Sabbath-keeping elect ("God's Remnant people") preceding the Advent. Roman Catholics as well as the U.S. government are viewed as future persecutors. Other Christian traditions are considered "churches of Babylon." SDA practices include baptism by immersion, a ban on the use of alcohol or tobacco, and tithing. Members are vegetarians who put much effort into health and diet (tea and coffee are avoided). There are strong prohibitions against theater, dancing, gambling, card playing, reading fiction, and the wearing of jewelry and makeup. SDA members used to be conscientious objectors to war but served and died as medics, unarmed, on the battlefield. Since 1973, as the SDA changed its position, members have served in the armed forces. Out of concern for the status of minority religions, The Church operates the International Religious Liberty Association.

The group's concern with health has led worldwide medical crusades that have helped millions in the Third World. According to studies, SDA members outlive all other Americans by five years because of their vegetarian diet and avoidance of tobacco, alcohol, coffee, and tea. An early SDA member was John Harvey Kellogg, inventor of corn flakes. [*See also* ADVENTISTS, SECOND; SEVENTH-DAY CHRISTIAN CONFERENCE; SEVENTH DAY CHURCH OF GOD; *and* TWENTIETH CENTURY CHURCH OF GOD.]

Sources:

Bull, M., & Lockhart, K. *Seeking a Sanctuary: Seventh-Day Adventism and the American Dream.* San Francisco: Harper and Row, 1989.

Numbers, R. L. *Prophetess of Health: A Study of Ellen G. White*. New York: Harper & Row, 1976.

Seventh-Day Adventist Reform Movement

International ADVENTIST movement created in 1923 by German SEVENTH-DAY ADVENTISTS who felt that conscientious objection to military service should be a formal requirement of fellowship in the SDA movement. When their demand was not met, they left the organization and established the Reform Movement. Its members were persecuted and murdered in Nazi Germany, while members of the SEVENTH-DAY ADVENTIST CHURCH were tolerated. The Reform Movement has had branches in Europe, North America, and Oceania.

Seventh-Day Christian Conference

U.S. Sabbath-keeping ADVENTIST church with congregations in the United States and overseas missions in the Caribbean. It was founded in 1934 in New York City.

Seventh Day Church of God

U.S. ADVENTIST group formed in the early 1950s. It is an offshoot of the GENERAL CONFERENCE OF THE CHURCH OF GOD, with which it is identical in matters of doctrine.

Seventh Day Pentecostal Church of the Living God

U.S. PENTECOSTAL group founded by Charles Gamble, a former Roman Catholic and Baptist layman. Its doctrine adopts some Old Testament rules, including keeping Saturday as the Sabbath.

Shakers

Officially named the United Society of Believers in Christ's Second Appearing, or the United Society of Believers. This U.S. MILLENARIAN Christian communal group is popularly known as Shakers (or "Shaking Quakers") because of their custom of "shaking off the flesh." This shaking started as ecstatic spasms during meetings and then developed into dances accompanied by speaking in tongues. It was founded in 1774 in England by Ann Lee Standerin (1736–1787), known to her followers as "Mother Ann Lee" and "Mother of the New Creation." She formulated the group's ascetic, antisexual ideals, which included complete celibacy. Standerin lost four children in infancy and almost died herself giving birth to the last one. She then experienced a series of visions in which sexual contacts between Adam and Eve were seen as the source of all evil and suffering. In 1758 Standerin joined the British group then known as the French Prophets, which was made up of British Quakers inspired by the French Camisards. Standerin and her followers left England, and around 1780 the group started communal settlements around the United States. At the height of their success they had fifty-nine communes with almost 4,000 members. But there were frequent internal conflicts and economic difficulties as well as high defection rates.

Shaker teachings included a belief in the duality of God, who was viewed as being both male and female. Mother Ann represented the female principle, while Jesus Christ represented maleness. She was also known as the Word, or Christ in His Second Coming. The group believed in converting the dead and thus claimed famous historical personages among its members, such as George Washington, Napoleon, and Queen Elizabeth I. Prescribed celibacy was one step in a program designed to bring about the Millennium. Despite the female-oriented nature of Shaker theology, it was the male leaders who were in control until a decline in male membership forced a change.

Sources:

Andrews, E. D. *The People Called Shakers.* New York: Oxford University Press, 1953.

Desroche, H. *The American Shakers.* Amherst: University of Massachusetts Press, 1971.

Faber, D. *The Perfect Life.* New York: Farrar, Straus and Giroux, 1974.

Foster, L. *Religion and Sexuality: Three American Communal Experiments of the Nineteenth Century.* New York: Oxford University Press, 1981.

Kern, L. J. *An Ordered Love: Sex Roles and Sexuality in Victorian Utopias—The Shakers, the Mormons, and the Oneida Community.* Chapel Hill: University of North Carolina Press, 1981.

Melcher, M. F. *The Shaker Adventure.* Princeton, N.J.: Princeton University Press, 1941.

Morse, F. *The Shakers and the World's People.* New York: Dodd, Mead, 1980.

Promey, S. M. *Spiritual Spectacles: Vision and Image in Mid-Nineteenth-Century Shakerism.* Bloomington: Indiana University Press, 1993.

Stein, S. J. *The Shaker Experience in America: A History of the United Society of Believers.* New Haven, Conn.: Yale University Press, 1992.

Whitworth, J. *God's Blueprints: A Sociological Study of Three Utopian Sects.* London: Routledge & Kegan Paul, 1975.

Shakers

Syncretistic African Christian movement based in St. Vincent, West Indies. Members often enter possession trances. The British authorities issued a prohibition against the group in 1912, which was repealed in 1965. [*See also* SHOUTERS (SPIRITUAL BAPTISTS).]

Shalom Center

U.S. JESUS MOVEMENT group founded in the early 1970s in Colorado Springs, Colorado.

Shankaracharya

Hindu intellectual reform movement started in the early twentieth century. It called for a return to Vedanta Hinduism. [*See also* ARYA SAMAJ; *and* RAMAKRISHNA MATH AND MISSION.]

Shanti Mandir Temple of Peace

U.S. Hindu group founded in 1987 by Nityananda (1962–), a native of Bombay. In 1981 Nityananda was appointed

Sister Mildred Barker, head of the Shaker colony at Sabbathday Lake, Maine, looks over items to be sold at an auction in 1972.

with his sister Chidvilasananda (1958–) as co-successor to Baba Muktananda Paramahansa (1908–1982), the founder of the SYDA FOUNDATION. This succession was announced by Muktananda Paramahansa a few months before his death. Nityananda left the Syda movement in 1985 and founded his own group.

Shanti Mandir practices include chanting and meditation. "There is only one thing I would like to achieve: I want people to have the *experience* of God and *know* that they are God. With no doubt to have the full conviction, 'Yes, I am that Truth. I am that consciousness.'" The group is associated with the Mahamandaleshwar ashram in India.

Shanti Nilaya

U.S. spiritualist group founded in 1979 in California by Elisabeth Kübler-Ross. Group doctrine includes the notion of out-of-body travel and the etheral body.

Source:
Gill, D. *Quest: The Life of Elisabeth Kübler-Ross.* San Francisco: Harper & Row, 1980.

Shanti Yogi Institute

U.S. Hindu group founded by Shanti Desai, known as Shanti Yoga, in 1973 in New Jersey. It is devoted to teaching "hatha yoga, raja yoga, and meditation following the path of surrender."

Shema Yisroel Synagogue

British MESSIANIC JUDAISM group founded in Brighton in 1994 by Phil Sharp (1960–).

Shepherding

Organizational style in several U.S. FUNDAMENTALIST organizations which is marked by authoritarian leadership and close supervision of members. New members are assigned a "discipler" who supervises their behavior. This style has been the basis of what has been called the "shepherding movement," or "discipleship" as well as the House Church Movement, Total Commitment Movement, or "multiplying churches." Groups employing shepherding include the BODY OF CHRIST, CHRISTIAN GROWTH MINISTRIES, and CHRISTIAN RESTORATION MINISTRIES.

Shepherd's Chapel

U.S. IDENTITY group founded by Arnold Murray in the 1970s and based in Gravette, Arkansas.

Sherborne School

The British school of the GURDJIEFF GROUP founded and directed by John G. Bennett (?–1975), who elaborated his version of Gurdjieff's work. It was named after Bennett's residence, Sherborne House, in Sherborne near Cheltenham, Gloucestershire. Also known as the Coombe Springs group. [*See also* CLAYMONT COURT; *and* INSTITUTE FOR THE COMPARATIVE STUDY OF HISTORY, PHILOSOPHY, AND THE SCIENCES.]

Sherborne Studies Group

U.S. GURDJIEFF GROUP based in Beverly Hills, California, and associated with CLAYMONT COURT. Members follow the teachings of John G. Bennett.

Shilohites

British MILLENARIAN group comprised of the followers of Zion Ward (assumed name of John Ward [1781–1837]). Born in Ireland, Ward was a Methodist, then a Baptist, and then a member of the SOUTHCOTTITES. In 1825 he announced various divine revelations and in 1828 proclaimed that he was "Zion" or "Shiloh," the true son of Joanna Southcott. For the last ten years of his life he preached to a small group of followers and published his prophecies.

Shilo Pentecostal Fellowship

British multiracial PENTECOSTAL group founded in 1965 in the West Indian community of London.

Shiloh True Light Church of Christ

U.S. ADVENTIST group founded in 1870 by Cunningham Boyle (1831–1884), a Methodist layman. Based on his reading of the Bible, Boyle proclaimed the generation of 100 years to end in 1970 with the coming of Jesus Christ. The group is based in North Carolina.

An austere lifestyle is followed by members, only plain attire is allowed, and television or movies are avoided. The group is fiercely opposed to any government control, and in 1971 it won the legal right to educate its children. In 1986 it experienced legal difficulties for breaking child-labor laws, because male children were employed as bricklayers as part of its educational program. The group has been under government scrutiny since then.

Shiloh Trust

U.S. PENTECOSTAL commune founded in the 1930s by Eugene Crosby Monroe (1880–1961) and based in Sulphur Springs, Arkansas.

Shilo United Church of Christ (Apostolic)

British PENTECOSTAL group founded in 1958 in the West Indian community of London.

Shinreikyo

Japanese new religion founded by Kanichi Otsuka after World War II. Doctrine focuses on faith healing. Its branches have operated in the United States since the 1960s.

Shinto-Shin-Kyo (Shinto New Religion)

Japanese new religion, representing shamanistic traditions, founded after World War II by Itoko Unigame.

Shinto-Tokumitsu-Kyo

Shinto revival movement founded in 1912 by Tokumitsu Kanada (1863–1924). Its Hitonomichi branch, suppressed by the Japanese government in 1937, was revived in 1946 as PERFECT LIBERTY KYODAN.

Shinyo-En (Shinnyoen)

Japanese new religious movement, of Buddhist origins, founded by Shinjo Ito in 1936. Doctrine is based on the worship of the ground god and the sky god in order to control the evil influences of lost souls, and members are promised supernatural powers. Overseas branches have opened in the United States, Europe, and Asia since the 1960s.

Shion Kirisuto Kyokai (Zion Christian Church)

Japanese indigenous Christian movement founded in the 1950s.

Shoresh Yishai

U.S. HEBREW CHRISTIAN group founded in the 1970s as the Church of Jesus the Messiah and based in Long Island, New York. It developed out of a Lutheran congregation whose leaders came to believe that in order to practice true Christianity and to follow Jesus Christ of the New Testament, they had to practice traditional Judaism. Members have started following the complete Orthodox Jewish rules of conduct and ritual.

Shouters (Spiritual Baptists)

Also known as Shango Baptists or Jordanites. This is a Caribbean syncretistic African Christian movement started in the late nineteenth century and based in Trinidad, Grenada, and other Caribbean islands. Followers practice "possession by spirits" and speaking in tongues. The British authorities tried to suppress the group, issuing a total prohibition in 1917, which was repealed in 1961. [*See also* BEDWARDISM.]

Sources:
Glazier, S. D. *Marchin' the Pilgrims Home: Leadership and Decision-Making in an Afro-Caribbean Faith.* Westport, Conn.: Greenwood Press, 1983.

Simpson, G. E. *Black Religions in the New World.* New York: Columbia University Press, 1978.

Shree Gurudev Ashram California

U.S. Siddha meditation center associated with the SYDA FOUNDATION.

Shree Gurudev Rudrananda Yoga Ashram

U.S. Hindu group devoted to the teachings of Swami Rudrananda (1928–1973), popularly known as Rudi (Albert Rudolph). Rudrananda was an American renowned as a spiritual teacher and teacher of meditation in the 1960s; he was killed in a plane crash. He had been a disciple of Swami Nityananda (?–1961) and Swami Muktananda (1908–1982) but started his own ashram in India in 1969. The U.S. group started in the early 1970s. Rudrananda's faith is often summed up as "[t]he total person must be consumed to support life in its depth—to allow for creative interchange between a human being and God."

Shri Ram Chandra Mission (Sahaj Marg)

International Hindu movement named after its founder, Shri Ram Chandraji Maharaj (1899–1983). The group has branches in Europe.

Shri Vishva Seva Ashram

U.S. Hindu group founded by Swami Vishva Hitesehiji in 1980; it is based in New York City.

Siddha Yoga

Hindu religious movement started in the 1950s in India. It has been connected with, and has inspired, several Western groups.

"Sign Followers"

U.S. "HOLINESS" groups that follow the five signs of Christian faith, as listed in Mark, 16:17–18: "And these signs shall follow them that believe; In my name shall they cast out devils; they shall speak with new tongues; They shall take up serpents; and if they drink any deadly thing, it shall not hurt them; they shall lay hands on the sick, and they shall recover." This is considered the source of such practices as exorcism, glossolalia, and faith healing, which are relatively common, and also of snake handling and the drinking of poison, which are somewhat uncommon.

Sinai Church of East Africa

African indigenous PENTECOSTAL movement started in 1965 in the Luhya people of Kenya.

Sin-Gye Gyo

Korean syncretistic indigenous movement started in the early twentieth century.

Sirius Community

U.S. occultist commune started in 1978 by Gordon Davidson and Corinne McLaughlin, former members of the FINDHORN FOUNDATION, near Amherst, Masssachusetts. It is guided by "a vision to attain the highest good in all levels of God's creation—field and forest, plants and animals, humans and angels, earth and stars. The spiritual understandings we strive to embody have been lived by visionaries in all cultures down through the ages: faith in God, love, truth, cooperation, honoring the oneness of all life, detachment from desire, meditation, and service to the world. . . . [W]e serve the world through our meditation. We work to create positive thought-forms of peace and healing for the world, as we know that energy follows thought." Members follow the traditions of Findhorn, Yogananda (see SELF-REALIZATION FELLOWSHIP), Alice Bailey (see LUCIS TRUST), and others.

The group believes in living with attunement to the "devas" (nature spirits) and also in overcoming financial difficulties through positive attitudes. It operates the Sirius School of Spiritual Science.

Sisters of Gaia

British feminist, neo-pagan "goddess group" started in the 1980s and based in Cambridge. Membership is limited to women.

Sivananda Yoga Vedanta Centers International

International Hindu-inspired group with branches in several Western countries, including France, Germany, United States, and Canada. It was founded in 1957 by Swami Vishnu Devananda (1927–). It is devoted to the teachings of Swami Sivananda Saraswati (1887–1963), a renowned Hindu holy man. In 1924 Sivananda opened a small

Swami Sivananda Saraswati, Indian holy man who was the inspiration for numerous groups.

Sivananda Yoga Vedanta Church

U.S. Hindu-oriented group founded in the 1960s by Victoria Coanda in South Milwaukee, Wisconsin. It is devoted to the teachings of Swami Sivananda Saraswati (1887–1963), a noted twentieth-century Hindu guru who was the teacher of Swami Satchidananda and Swami Vishnu Devananda. [*See also* DIVINE LIFE SOCIETY; INTEGRAL YOGA INSTITUTE; *and* SIVANANDA YOGA VEDANTA CENTERS INTERNATIONAL.]

Smith Venner

Scandinavian Christian group founded in Norway in the early twentieth century by Johann Oskar Smith (1871–1943). The group has branches in Western Europe and the United States.

free dispensary, which later became a hospital, and he preached selfless service to humanity as the highest calling. In 1969 Vishnu Devananda founded True World Order (TWO) to foster international peace and brotherhood.

The group's doctrine is based on combining and teaching all yoga techniques. Headquarters are at the Sivananda Ashram Yoga Camp in Val Morin, near Montreal. It operates the Sivananda Ashram Yoga Ranch in New York State and the Sivananda Dhanwantari Ashram in Neyyar Dam, India, among other centers. [*See also* DIVINE LIFE SOCIETY; *and* INTEGRAL YOGA INSTITUTE.]

Swami Vishnu-devananda, founder of the Sivananda Yoga Vedanta Centers.

Societas Rosicruciana in America

U.S. occultist group started in 1907 in Boston by Sylvester C. Gould. After Gould died in 1909 the leadership of the group passed on to George Winslow Plummer (1876–1944).

Societas Rosicruciana in Anglia

British nineteenth-century occultist group founded in 1865. It contributed to the development of other groups in Great Britain and the United States, such as the Hermetic Order of the Golden Dawn.

Society for Avatar Meher Baba

U.S. group devoted to the teachings of Meher Baba. [*See also* MEHER BABA, FRIENDS OF; SUFISM REORIENTED, INC.; *and* THE UNIVERSAL SPIRITUAL LEAGUE OF AMERICA.]

Society for Proclaiming Britain Is Israel

BRITISH ISRAELIST group started in the nineteenth century in London. Its aim was identifying Celto-Anglo-Saxon peoples with the Israel of the Old Testament.

Society of Christ, Inc.

U.S. spiritualist Christian group founded in Los Angeles in the 1970s.

Society of Pragmatic Mysticism

U.S. NEW THOUGHT group founded in the 1940s by Mildred Mann (?–1971) in New York City. Its doctrine is summed up as follows: "Pragmatic Mysticism is a truth teaching based on the Bible and the eternal laws of God. It is the practice of the presence of God in every-day life with conscious effort and direction."

Society of St. Pius V

Traditionalist Catholic group in the United States. It was created as an offshoot of the FRATERNITY OF ST. PIUS X and was led by Clarence Kelly. Members of the Society believe that Cardinal Lefebvre and the Fraternity were too liberal in their approach. They oppose all recent reforms in the Roman Catholic Church and conduct services in Latin. The Society of St. Pius V operates a convent, St. Joseph's Novitiate, which follows the traditional monastic rules that dominated such institutions before the Roman Catholic reforms of the 1960s.

Soja We Mwari

Also known as Soldiers of God, this is an African independent Christian FUNDAMENTALIST group founded in 1938 by secession from the SALVATION ARMY.

Soka Gakkai International

An organization of national SOKA GAKKAI SOCIETY groups founded in 1975. It professes to have members in 115 nations. It supports the United Nations and has a non-governmental organization status (NGO) there. Since 1993 it has operated the Boston Research Center for the 21st Century. [*see also* SOKA GAKKAI OF AMERICA.]

American members of Nichiren Shoshu of America chant during a meeting.

Sources:

Anesaki, M. *Nichiren the Buddhist Prophet.* Cambridge, Mass.: Harvard University Press, 1916.

Brannen, N. S. *Soka Gakkai.* Richmond, Va.: John Knox Press, 1968.

Dator, J. A. *Soka Gakkai: Builders of the Third Civilization.* Seattle: University of Washington Press, 1969.

Metraux, D. *The History and Theology of Soka Gakkai.* Lewiston, N.Y.: Edwin Mellen Press, 1988.

Murata, K. *Japan's New Buddhism.* New York: Walker/Weatherhill, 1969.

White, J. W. *The Sokkagakkai and Mass Society.* Stanford, Calif.: Stanford University Press, 1970.

Soka Gakkai of America (SKUSA)

Formerly known as Nichiren Shoshu Soka Gakkai of America. This is the U.S. branch of SOKA GAKKAI SOCIETY, a Japanese new religion that reached the United States in 1957. The first Soka Gakkai emissary in the United States, Masayasua Sadanaga, started to recruit members in Los Angeles. In 1972 he changed his name to George M. Williams and the group's name to Nichiren Shoshu.

"The object of worship in Nichiren Shoshu Buddhism is the Dai-Gohonzon, inscribed by the founder, Nichiren Daishonin, on October 12, 1279, with the aim of enabling all people to attain absolute happiness and bring about world peace. The Gohonzon literally means the most fundamental and respectable entity. It contains the life-force and the fundamental law inherent in the whole universe which is Nam-myoho-renge-kyo." By following the "fundamental law," the individual can achieve enlightenment and happiness.

Following the excommunication of SOKA GAKKAI SOCIETY by Nichiren Shoshu in 1991, the name Nichiren Shoshu Soka Gakkai of America was changed to Soka Gakkai of America.

Soka Gakkai Society ("Value Creation Society")

Buddhist religious-political movement based in Japan. It was founded in 1930 by Tsunesaburo Makiguchi (1871–1944) and Josei Toda (1900–1958), principal and teacher, respectively, at an elementary school in Tokyo. Its religious origins are in the Nichiren Shoshu Buddhist Movement. Soon after its founding the group suffered government persecution. Makiguchi was arrested and died in prison. In 1960 Daisaku Ikeda (1928–) was elected as the third president of the movement. It was once represented in politics through the Komeito (Clean Government) Party. Komeito was organized in 1964 and in 1970 formally separated itself from Soka Gakkai. Despite the formal separation, Soka Gakkai's role in Japanese politics and its nationalism have been a permanent source of much controversy over the years. Soka Gakkai has become a true mass movement, and

it has been accused by critics of being neo-fascist and of acting for the restoration of Shintoism as the state religion of Japan. Media reports point to its ability to mobilize its members as a unified voting bloc. Its declared aim is to achieve "Buddhist democracy," which is defined as a parliamentary democracy in which every individual "has been awakened to the principles of Buddhism." Komeito has been quite active in fighting against environmental pollution in Japan.

Soka Gakkai is one of forty groups today that claim to follow the teachings of Nichiren Daishonin (1222–1282), who was in 1253 the founder of Japan's first Buddhist native sect, known as *Hokke-Shu* (Lotus sect). The group offers its members happiness, which is defined as "the attainment of enlightenment through perfection and the realization of all desires." This is achieved through the chanting of the *gongyo*, the Lotus Mantra Chant—*Nam Yoho Rengay Kyo* ("Adoration to the Lotus of the Wonderful Law"), formulated by Nichiren in 1253. Chanting the *gongyo* twice a day in front of the *Gohonzon*, the sacred scroll, is believed to bring about material prosperity and happiness. While chanting the *gongyo* is supposed to bring about success and happiness, all difficulties and misfortunes are explained as the result of *Sansho Shima*, three obstacles and four devils.

The *Dai-Gohonzon*, inscribed by Nichiren Daishonin himself, is kept at the main temple in Japan. "The object of worship in Nichiren Shoshu Buddhism is the Dai-Gohonzon, inscribed by the founder, Nichiren Daishonin, on October 12, 1279, with the aim of enabling all people to attain absolute happiness and bring about world peace. The Gohonzon literally means the most fundamental and respectable entity. It contains the life-force and the fundamental law inherent in the whole universe which is Nam-myoho-renge-kyo." There is also an expectation of a global apocalypse, which would bring about the victory of "True Buddhism."

Group members gather at the *Zadankai*, a discussion meeting which is central to the group's activities, and they are organized into *kumi*, units of ten families, and the *han*, composed of five to ten *kumi*. Soka Gakkai was considered a lay organization affiliated with Nichiren Shoshu, but in 1991 Soka Gakkai was excommunicated by Nichiren Shoshu because of disputes over authority. [*See also* SOKA GAKKAI INTERNATIONAL; *and* SOKA GAKKAI OF AMERICA.]

Solar Cross Fellowship

U.S. UFO-THEOSOPHICAL group based in Auburn, California. It was founded in the 1950s by Rudolph H. Pestalozzi and was focused on communicating with "space brothers." This group merged with the SOLAR LIGHT CENTER in the 1960s.

Solar Light Center

U.S. UFO-THEOSOPHICAL group founded by Marianne Francis, also known as Aleuti Francesca. It began in the mid-1960s in Central Point, Oregon. Members believe in the Great White Brotherhood and reincarnation, and they expect the second coming of Jesus Christ soon. They communicate with various "spiritual masters" and "outer-space intelligence." [*See also* SOLAR CROSS FELLOWSHIP.]

Solar Temple, Order of (Ordre du Temple Solaire)

International ROSICRUCIAN-Christian group. It was started in the 1980s by Luc Jouret (1948–1994), a Belgian practitioner of homeopathy, and Joseph di Mambro (1924–1994), a Canadian. The group has been active in France and in French-speaking areas of Canada, Switzerland, and Belgium. Solar Temple members sign over their assets to the group, and according to some reports it had amassed over $90 million. Jouret preached a coming apocalypse, for which members had to prepare by arming themselves. At the same time, there were promises of a "transition to the future," an afterlife for members on another planet near Sirius, the brightest star. On October 4, 1994, forty-six members and four children were found dead in two locations in Granges-sur-Salvan, and in Cheiry, near Geneva, Switzerland, and in Morin, Québec. The victims were shot and then set on fire; the leaders, who did the shootings, committed suicide. Five days earlier two former members and their infant son were slaughtered in Québec. On December 16, 1995, in a repetition of the same apparent ceremony, thirteen more members and three children met their death, laid out in a star pattern in the Vercors region of eastern France. The ceremonial killings were explained on the basis of the group's belief in a new life on another planet after death. "We leave this earth to rediscover a Plane of Absolute Truth, far from the hypocrisy and oppression of this world," said a collective suicide note. The killings in Québec were explained as the result of the victims' disobedience to the leaders in having a baby without permission.

Workers in Switzerland sift through the remains of the scene of a mass suicide committed by members of the Order of Solar Temple.

Sons Ahman Israel

U.S. polygamist, MORMON syncretistic group started in 1981 by David Israel in Utah. Its doctrine combines traditional Mormon elements with ideas about Kabbalah, gnosticism, and claims of recent revelations. The group has a European branch, known as INDEPENDENT CHURCH OF JESUS CHRIST OF LATTER-DAY SAINTS.

Sons of Freedom

Officially known as the Christian Community of Universal Brotherhood and later as the Union of Spiritual Communities; popularly known as Freedomites or "svobodniki." This group was created by a split in the DOUKHOBORS, an anarchist religious group based in Canada. Its doctrine calls for the rejection of materialism, extreme vegetarianism, and opposition to all goverment regulations and government-sponsored education. The group has been involved in 130 violent incidents, including bombings and arson, directed at other Doukhobor groups and the Canadian government, between 1960 and 1985.

Source:
Holt, S. *Terror in the Name of God.* New York: Crown, 1965.

Southcottites

Followers of Joanna Southcott (1750–1814) who started an Adventist movement in the early 19th century in Great Britain. Southcott predicted the imminent coming of Christ, but also ascribed a special role to a woman who would be the Bride of the lamb as well as his Mother. Southcott then claimed to be that special woman. She started proclaiming prophecies in 1792. In 1801 she started publishing her prophesies and gathering followers. Her followers received official documents which declared them to be "Sealed of the Lord." Thousands joined the movement and received these "seals." In 1814, when Southcott was 64, she announced that she was pregnant with the special divine child, but the birth failed to materialize and Southcott died on December 27 of that year. Her followers were demoralized, but some regrouped and formed several churches. [*See also* CHRISTIAN ISRAELITES; *and* NEW HOUSE OF ISRAEL.]

Source:
Balleine, G. R. *Past Finding Out: The Tragic Story of Joanna Southcott and Her Successors.* New York: Macmillan, 1956.

Sovereign Universal Order of the Holy Trinity

International Christian movement founded in Brazil in the 1950s. Its founder is known as the messiah "Inri Cristo," a new incarnation of the Christian Jesus Christ. Its branches have operated mostly in Western Europe.

Spirit of Jesus Christ

Japanese indigenous Christian church formed in 1937 by secession from the ASSEMBLIES OF GOD. It operates missions in North and South America.

Spiritual Fellowship of America

U.S. NEW THOUGHT group founded by Pat Fenske in the 1970s in Philadelphia.

Spiritual Frontiers Fellowship

U.S. spiritualist group whose membership has consisted of Protestant ministers and laymen affiliated with established churches, together with members of THEOSOPHICAL and spiritualist groups. It was founded in March 1956 by Albin Bro, Paul Higgins, and Arthur Ford, the famous medium and former minister of the FIRST SPIRITUALIST CHURCH OF NEW YORK. It publishes journals that promote the combined Christian-spiritualist-Eastern point of view. Members attend weekly meetings in which the "pure white light of Jesus" and "the laser beam of God's love" are used to search "the God within," through the use of "spiritual healing, astral travel, psychometry, and aura readings." Meditation is also practiced. Membership and activities have been mostly concentrated in the U.S. Midwest. [*See also* INNER PEACE MOVEMENT.]

Source:

Wagner, M. B. *Metaphysics in Midwestern America.* Columbus: Ohio State University Press, 1983.

Spiritual Life Institute

North American Christian mystical group founded by Teresa Bielecki around 1980. The group maintains monastic retreats in Colorado and Nova Scotia, and teaches "concrete mystical practices."

Spiritual Science Church

Also known as Spiritual Science Mother Church. This is a U.S. spiritualist Christian group founded in 1923 by "Mother" Julia O. Forrest, who had been a CHRISTIAN SCIENCE practitioner. The Church combines some Christian traditions with THEOSOPHY and Christian Science. There is an emphasis on healing, and less attention is paid to spirit communication, compared to other spiritualist groups. [*See also* THE AQUARIAN BROTHERHOOD OF CHRIST; ASSOCIATED SPIRITUALISTS; *and* NATIONAL SPIRITUAL SCIENCE CENTER.]

Spiritual Science Fellowship

North American spiritualist-NEW THOUGHT group based in Montreal and founded by John Rossnner.

Spiritual Science of Mind Center

NEW THOUGHT, occultist group based in New York City. It was founded in 1990 by Steve Bernat, and offers "scientific prayer technology" leading to "spiritual empowerment."

Spiritual Unity of Nations

British occultist group founded in the 1970s by Joseph Busby. It is devoted to uniting the "spiritual power" of world nations.

Spring Grove

U.S. spiritualist community founded in the 1980s in Marin County, California, by Bruce Davis. Its doctrine is based on combining Christian mysticism with "psychical healing" and shamanism. The founder claims to have started his "spiritual training . . . in the company of psychic healers in the Philippines" and "has studied with an Eskimo shaman in Alaska, trained in the Christian-based mysticism of 'A Course in Miracles'."

Springhill Community

U.S. spiritual community founded in the late 1970s in Asby, Massachusetts. Practices emphasize silent meditation and prayer.

Sri Aurobindo

International Hindu group inspired by Aravinda Ackroyd Ghose (1872–1950), Indian philosopher and mystic, who became known as Sri Aurobindo after devoting himself completely to a life of contemplation. After receiving both a traditional and a Western education, Ghose became an extreme nationalist and pursued a political career in the Indian independence movement. His move toward religion started in 1903, with an experience of the "vacant infinite." In 1908 he met a yogi who taught him how to experience "the Absolute." Then in 1909, while in prison, he had a vision of Krishna, which convinced him to leave politics. The following year he renounced all political and worldly pursuits and founded an ashram in Pondicherry, India, which was then a French colony.

On November 24, 1926, he was reported to have experienced "The Day of Siddhi," the point of contact with the "Supermind." His ashram attracted both Indian and Western followers. His best-known convert was the Frenchwoman Mira Richard (née Alfassa; 1878–1973), who first visited the ashram in 1914 and settled there permanently in 1920. She became known as The Mother, and became a full partner of Aurobindo, whom she believed to be God descended to Earth. He in turn saw her as "Divine Consciousness." She became the administrative leader of the ashram and led it to growth and material wealth. On February 29, 1956, she announced her avatarhood, *i.e.*, her divinity, and became regarded as the "Divine Mother" by her followers. In the 1960s she founded the New Age Association, and in 1968 she established the city of Auroville. Since then Aurobindo disciples have been building Auroville, the "City of Human Unity." Groups of Sri Aurobindo followers have operated in the West. Aurobindo's teachings constitute an attempt to adapt Hinduism to modern life, influenced by ramakrishna and Vivekananda. He advocated the use of yoga techniques and founded what he called Integral Yoga. Aurobindo is known for his conception of supraconsciousness, the final stage of human evolution, which will overcome material life and individual consciousness. This level will be achieved only by a small elite, the kernel of a new human race. [*See also* ATMANIKETAN ASHRAM; MATAGIRI; *and* RAMAKRISHNA-VIVEKANARDA.]

Sources:

Bassuk, D. E. *Incarnation in Hinduism and Christianity: The Myth of the Godman.* Atlantic Highlands, N.J.: Humanities Press, 1986.

McDermott, R., ed. *The Essential Aurobindo.* New York: Schocken Books, 1963.

Sri Aurobindo International Center Foundation

U.S. group devoted to the teachings of SRI AUROBINDO. It was founded in

Mira Alfassa, partner of Sri Aurobindo and founder of the city of Auroville.

Conceived in 1967, this was the initial approach to the design of Auroville, the first international city devoted to human unity and world peace. (See Sri Aurobindo)

Sri Chimnoy, leader of a Hindu sect bearing his name, prepares for a marathon race held in New York City in honor of his forty-eighth birthday in 1979.

1953 in New York by Mrs. Moore Montgomery.

Sri Chimnoy

Known officially as Aspiration-Body-Temple-Service. This is an international group devoted to the teachings of Sri Chimnoy (Chimnoy Kumar Ghose), a Bengali author and former postal clerk in the United States, born in 1931. He has been based in New York City since the 1960s, teaching a form of Hinduism described as the "path of grace" and inspired by SRI AUROBINDO. The group states that, "Through Divine Love, one-pointed devotion, and unconditional surrender to the highest, the disciple comes to the realization of his eternal oneness with the Supreme." The group practices "nondenominational meditation." Followers celebrate the birthday of Sri Chimnoy's mother, Yogamaya Ghose, who was born on April 3, 1894. Group branches have been active in Western Europe. The group operates the Committee for Spiritual Poetry, which has awarded the Sri Chimnoy Poetry Awards.

Sri Ma Anandamayi Ashrams

Twentieth-century Hindu movement focused on the personality of Sri Ma Anandamayi. The first ashram was founded in 1932 in Dehra Dun, India.

Western branches have existed since the 1960s. [*See also* ANANDAMAYEE CHARITABLE SOCIETY; *and* SRI MA ANANDAMAYI MONASTERY.]

Sri Ma Anandamayi Monastery

U.S. Hindu monastic group founded in 1967 by Swami Nirmalananda Giri in Oklahoma City, Oklahoma. It is devoted to keeping the memory and teachings of Sri Ma Anandamayi (or Anandamayee), a famous Hindu woman saint (1896–1960). Members practice mantra meditation.

Sri Rama Foundation

North American Hindu group devoted to the teachings of Baba Hari Dass; it was founded in 1971 in California. Practice focuses on yoga.

Sri Ram Ashrama

U.S. Hindu commune founded in 1967 as the Ananda Ashrama by Swami Abhayananda. Group practices focus on meditation and yoga.

Sserulanda Spiritual Planetary Community

Also known as the Sserulanda Nsulo Y'obulamu Spiritual Foundation. This is a Ugandan syncretistic group founded in the 1970s by J. K. Mugonza (1937–), a former Roman Catholic trained in India by a RADHASOAMI master. To his disciples Mugonza is known as Bambi Baaba, "Redeemer of the New Age." His doctrines combine Hindu and Sikh ideas with the vocabulary of THEOSOPHY and UFO lore. He also promotes the notion of Uganda as the chosen nation, destined to lead the world in "spiritual splendour."

Standard Church of America

North American conservative Protestant group founded in 1919 in Watertown, New York, by Ralph G. Horner. Headquarters are in Borchville, Ontario, Canada.

Starcross Monastic Community

U.S. mystical retreat community founded by Tolbert McCarroll in the late 1960s. The overall orientation is Christian, with special reference to medieval Christian masters, but Eastern traditions are also used, including meditation. Starcross operates the Humanist Institute, which offers meditation classes.

Stelle Community

U.S. THEOSOPHICAL occultist group founded by Richard Kieninger (1927–) in Chicago in 1953. Doctrine predicts a series of world catastrophes, starting in 1976–1977, leading to a nuclear war in 1999, and culminating in a major catastrophe on May 5, 2000, in which 90 percent of humanity will be destroyed. Members of the community will be among the 10 percent saved.

Stonegate Christian Community

U.S. evangelical commune based in West Virginia; founded in the 1980s.

Story, The

Papua New Guinea syncretistic movement (CARGO CULT) started among the

341

Kaliai people of New Britain in the 1970s. Followers of this movement abandoned their villages on the coast and moved to the interior. The group believed that certain mountains were filled with "cargo" that had been prepared by the "ancestors." Moving inland and going back to the traditional way of life was the means to obtaining it. Confessions and singing were considered essential to purification in preparation for the cargo.

Stromen Van Kracht (Streams of Power; Courants de Puissance)

International PENTECOSTAL, FUNDAMENTALIST Christian movement started in Holland in 1952. Since 1960 it has spread to the Caribbean, South America, Africa, and across Europe. Speaking in tongues and faith healing are practiced.

Subba Rao

Syncretist Christian-Hindu movement started among the Telugu in Andhra Pradesh, India. It is opposed to all hierarchies and organizations, and holds massive "healing" campaigns.

Subud

Western movement of Islamic-Hindu origins. It was started by Pak Muhammad Subuh (1901–1985), known as Bapak ("father"). Bapak had a divine revelation in 1925 and started teaching Subud on the Indonesian island of Java in 1933. The movement appeared in the West for the first time in England in 1957 through the efforts of John G. Bennet, a British follower of GURDJIEFF GROUPS, after he met a disciple of Subud. The name Subud comes from a combina-

tion of the Sanskrit terms *Susila, Buddhi,* and *Dharma,* and is unrelated to the founder's name. The central practice of Subud is known as *latihan,* an ecstatic exercise done in groups varying in size from a few to hundreds, segregated by sex, and leading to the experience of bliss. Disciples describe it as an inner awakening during which "the life force" enters the soul of the believer. The experience may also be used to help reach personal decisions through sensing true inner feelings. The *latihan* is practiced twice a week. There is also the ritual of *salamatan,* which is a feast for the membership. Subud members change their names, not only for internal group occasions, but also in official documents. [*See also* SUFI ORDER IN THE WEST.]

Source:
Needleman, J. *The New Religions.* Garden City, N.Y.: Doubleday, 1970.

Sufi Islamia Ruhaniat Society

U.S. Sufi group. This California-based group was founded in 1968 by Samuel L. Lewis (1896–1971), known as Murshid Sam or "Sufi Sam." He was reputedly a member of the Chisti Order of Sufis. He has been succeeded by Murshid Moineddin Jablonski and Masheikh Wali Ali Meyer. The group practices and teaches Sufi meditation and dancing.

Sufi Order in the West

Also known as the International Sufi Order and, in German-speaking countries, as Zenith Institute. This is an international Islamic-inspired Western group devoted to teaching the tradition of

Pir Vilayat Inayat Khan, leader and son of the founder of the Sufi Order in the West.

Sufism (*i.e.*, Islamic mysticism) together with Universal Worship, which pays respects to all major world religions and adopts Christian, Buddhist, and yogic traditions. Actually, it combines Hindu and Islamic elements in its teachings and follows practices that include meditation, recitation, rhythmic chanting, and dancing.

The group was founded in England in 1914 by Hazrat Inayat Khan (1881–1927), who was born in India to a family of Muslim musicians. Between 1903 and 1907 he was a disciple of a Sufi master, and then he traveled as a pilgrim throughout India, Burma, and Ceylon, while performing as a musician. In 1910 he visited the United States and Europe, performing and lecturing. Between 1914 and 1920 he was in London, building up the Sufi Movement. He then traveled in the West, founding Sufi centers wherever he went, until 1926, when he returned to India. Hazrat Inayat Khan, known as "Pir-o-Murshid," was succeeded as the group's leader by his son Pir Vilayat Inayat Khan (1916–). The new leader founded the ABODE OF THE MESSAGE in upstate New York; it now serves as headquarters.

Sufism Reoriented, Inc.

U.S. group devoted to the teaching of MEHER BABA; it is based in San Francisco. Originally started as a Sufi group early in the twentieth century, the group changed its orientation in 1952 when its leader, Ivy Oneita Duce (1895–1980), known as Murshida (teacher), first met Meher Baba. It has published English versions of Meher Baba's collections of messages. [*See also* BABA LEAGUE; *and* MEHER DURBAR.]

Sukyo Mahikari

Splinter group that grew out of MAHIKARI ("True Light") following the death of its founder. It was started in 1978 by Sekiguchi Sakae. Its doctrine is identical to that of Mahikari, but it claims to be more loyal to the founder's teachings.

Summum Church

U.S. occultist group founded in 1975 by Claude Rex Nowell in Salt Lake City, Utah. Its practices include meditation, pyramid building, and mummification.

Sunergos Institute, Inc.

U.S. religious commune located in Jasper, Arkansas, and founded around 1970. Its doctrine is based on a combination of Western and Eastern ideas.

Sung Rak Baptist Church

Korean independent PENTECOSTAL group that emphasizes faith healing and exorcism.

Sunray Meditation Society

U.S. occultist group, based in New York City, which promotes Native American traditions. Founded in the 1970s in Huntington, Vermont, it is led by "planetary teacher" Dhyani Ywahoo, "the 27th holder of the Ywahoo lineage and a member of the traditional Etawa Band of the eastern Tsalagi (Cherokee) Nation." The group operates the Sunray School of Sacred Studies.

Suttangam Sabhi

Officially known as the Pure Church, this

is an Indian independent Christian group. It was founded in 1925 in Tinnevelly by secession from the Anglican Church of India.

Swaminarayana

Hindu group founded in the late eighteenth century. In 1802 the founder, Swami Ramananda (1781–1830), known also as Sri Swaminarayan, who claimed to be God himself, ceded his place to twenty-one-year-old Swami Sahajanand. The latter reformed the group and created a body of five hundred monks. In his book *Shikshapatri* (1826) he specifies the rules of conduct for followers, which prohibit murder, theft, suicide, meat, wine, self-mutilation, adultery, gambling, tobacco, and the breaking of Hindu caste laws. Monks are forbidden to have any contacts with women or even talk about them. *Shikshapatri* is read daily by all members of the group. Branches of this group have opened among Hindus living in the West since the 1950s.

Sources:

Brent, P. *Godmen of India*. Chicago: Quadrangle Books, 1972.

Williams, R. B. *A New Face of Hinduism: The Swaminarayan Religion*. New York: Cambridge University Press, 1984.

Swami Shantiananda Center

U.S. Hindu group based in Tennessee. It was founded by Swami Shantiananda around 1970 and is devoted to the teaching of Hindu beliefs and practices, including meditation and yoga.

Swatow Christian Church

Chinese indigenous church founded in 1909. After 1949 it moved to Hong Kong.

Swazi Christian Church in Zion of South Africa

African indigenous "ZIONIST" church founded in South Africa in 1937 by B. P. Mncina. Branches exist all over southern Africa.

Swedenborg Foundation

One of several organizations that together represent a worldwide movement of those who follow the teachings of the Swedish mystic Emanuel Swedenborg (1688–1772). Swedenborg was the son of a bishop and professor of theology at Uppsala. He was trained as a mining engineer, and as an inventor made significant contributions to the technology of mining and metallurgy. In 1743, at age fifty-five, he started having visions of angels, heaven, and hell. He declared that for thirty years he was in daily contact with the spiritual world. According to these visions, the world is divided into three regions: the heavens, the hells, and the world of spirits. These visions were contained in his many books, which were first published anonymously in Great Britain.

Swedenborg's visions are cast within a Christian framework and proclaim a spiritual Second Coming of Jesus Christ, instead of a physical one. The Writings, as the visions are called, claim that Jesus Christ is both the redeemer and the creator. However, according to the Writings the Church founded by Jesus Christ came to its end in 1587, and Swedenborg is the divinely inspired messenger of the

Emanuel Swedenborg.

nity Construction. Westport, Conn.: Greenwood Press, 1983.

Toksvig, S. *Emanuel Swedenborg, Scientist and Mystic.* New Haven, Conn.: Yale University Press, 1948.

Sword of Christ Good News Ministries

U.S. Christian IDENTITY group founded in the 1970s in Arkansas by Ralph P. Forbes, a former leader in the American Nazi Party.

Syda Foundation (Siddha Yoga Dham Associates)

International Hindu group founded in 1975 to promote Siddha Meditation in

new one. The full name of the new group is the New Church Signified by the New Jerusalem in the Revelation.

Organizations promoting Swedenborg's ideas started soon after his death. The best known among them are the Church of the New Jerusalem ("New Church"), founded in 1782, and the Swedenborg Society of London, founded in 1810, which is the world center of the movement. Swedenborgian groups now exist in Sweden, throughout the English-speaking world, and in southern Africa. John Chapman (1774–1845), known as "Johnny Appleseed," was instrumental in spreading the message in the United States.

Sources:
Meyers, M. A. *New World Jerusalem: The Swedenborgian Experience in Commu-*

The grave of John Chapman, who as "Johnny Appleseed" spent much of his life planting apple trees and spreading the message of Emanuel Swedenborg in the United States.

the West. Siddha Meditation is a technique taught by followers of Swami Muktananda Paramahansa (1908–1982). Muktananda, whose home ashram, Sri Gurudev Siddha Peeth, is in Ganeshpuri, near Bombay, followed the devotional tradition that he had learned from Swami Nityananda. He was born on May 16, 1908, and at age fifteen started wandering after first meeting Swami Nityananda. He became Swami Nityananda's disciple only at age thirty-nine; he then settled down in Ganeshpuri in 1956, and in 1961, when Swami Nityananda died, he inherited his mantle. In the 1970s he spent two years in the United States. In 1981, a few months before his death, Muktananda appointed Nityananda (1962–) and his sister Chidvilasananda (1958–) as his co-successors. Nityananda left the Syda movement in 1985 and then founded his own group, the SHANTI MANDIR TEMPLE OF PEACE. Since 1985 the movement has been led by Swami Chidvilasananda, who is known to her followers as Gurumayi.

The underlying traditions of Syda are Vedanta and Kashmir Shaivism, and the practices are of kundalini yoga. Siddha yoga offers a process of quick enlightenment known as *shaktipat*. "Shaktipat is a subtle spiritual process by which the Guru transmits his divine power into the aspirant either by touch, word, look or thought." "Through chanting, meditation, and adherence to spiritual discipline a seeker can cut through 'the dramas of the mind' and experience the joy and divinity of the Self that lies within." Branches of this group in the United States are known as Siddha Yoga Dham.

Source:

Brent, P. *Godmen of India*. Chicago: Quadrangle Books, 1972.

Sylla Movement

Heterodox Islamic movement founded by Yakouba Sylla in the Ivory Coast in the 1930s. He claimed to have received revelations from Fatima, the daughter of Muhammad, and he rejected most Islamic traditions.

T

Tagarab

Melanesian indigenous movement (CARGO CULT), started along the Rai coast of New Guinea in the 1930s and named after its leader. During World War II members believed that the Japanese troops were ancestor spirits and would help them obtain "cargo," or manufactured goods.

Source:
Lawrence, P. *Road Belong Cargo.* Manchester: Manchester University Press, 1964.

Taishakyo

Japanese Shinto-oriented new religion. It was founded in 1873 by Sonfuku Senge.

"Taro Cult"

New Guinea syncretistic movement (CARGO CULT) started in 1914 by Buninia, a member of the Orokaiva people. Following a vision of his father's spirit, Buninia developed magical practices for improving the taro crops. Believers worship taro spirits, which are expected to provide European goods ("cargo") or massive crops. Rituals include ecstatic dancing and "spirit possession."

Source:
Williams, F. E. *Orokaiva Magic.* London: Oxford University Press, 1928.

Tayu Fellowship

U.S. neo-pagan homosexual group founded in the 1970s in California by Daniel Inesse. Its doctrine refers to the ancient Greek gods as guides.

Teaching of the Inner Christ, Inc.

Formerly known as the Society for the Teaching of the Inner Christ, Inc., and also known as the Brotherhood of Followers of the Present Jesus. This U.S. Christian-Hindu-occultist group was founded in 1965 in San Diego by Ann Potter Meyer and Peter Victor Meyer. Its inspiration is drawn from the "master teachers Jesus and Babaji," and its practices include meditation and "spiritual healing." [*See also* INTERNATIONAL BABAJI KRIYA YOGA SANGAM.]

Te Atua Wera

Maori nativist syncretistic prophet who in 1833 claimed that the Maoris were the Jews talked about in the Old Testament, an idea that influenced other Maori movements. [*See also* CHURCH OF TE KOOTI RIKIRANGI; RATANA CHURCH; *and* RINGATU.]

Teilhard Centre, The

British Christian group founded in 1965 in London to promote the teachings of the Jesuit Pierre Teilhard de Chardin, who tried to interpret evolution within the framework of Christianity. It is affliated with the FONDATION TEILHARD DE CHARDIN and ASSOCIATION DES AMIS DE PIERRE TEILHARD DE CHARDIN in Paris. [*See also* AMERICAN TEILHARD ASSOCIATION.]

Temoins du Christ Revenu (Christ's Witnesses)

Known sometimes as l'Église Universelle du Christ de Montfavet. This is a French Christian "healing" group founded in 1950 by Georges Roux, a mailman (born in 1903) in Montfavet, in the French province of Var. Roux, who claimed to be a reincarnation of Jesus Christ, became known as "Christ de Montfavet" and offered healing services through the laying on of hands. The group's dietary rules forbid coffee, tobacco, tea, canned foods, and deep frying; members are promised a life span of 120 years if they avoid these "five poisons." Another rule forbids members the use of normal medicine instead advocating faith healing and the power of prayer. This ban led, in 1954, to charges that three children of members had died of neglect due to the withholding of medical attention. Legal proceedings were initiated, and an outcry arose against the group.

Roux predicted the disappearance of all "forces of evil" from Earth on January 1, 1982, but he died on December 26, 1981. In the late 1980s the group adopted the name Alliance Universelle, with active branches in Western Europe.

Temple de L'arc-en-Ciel (Rainbow Temple)

Swiss PENTECOSTAL, BRITISH ISRAELIST group founded in 1947 in Lausanne by Elie Bussy. Members are required to follow Old Testament traditions regarding food and personal appearance.

Temple of Cosmic Religion

International Hindu movement devoted to spreading Hindu teachings in the West. Founded in 1967 by Satguru Sant Keshavadas as the Dasashram International Center, the movement emphasizes yoga and meditation in its doctrine.

Temple of Kriya Yoga

U.S. Hindu group founded in the 1950s by Melvin Higgins, also known as Sri Goswami Kriyananda. Kriyananda was a student of Paramahansa Yoganada of the SELF-REALIZATION FELLOWSHIP and started the Temple after Yogananda's death in 1952. The Temple also operates the College of Occult Sciences. Activities include "Classes, counseling, and individual instruction in yoga, meditation, mystical philosophy, the spiritual sciences, and sane, joyous living."

Pierre Teilhard de Chardin during World War I.

349

Temple of the Eternal Light, Inc.

U.S. Christian occultist pagan group. Described as "an Omni-Denominational religious fellowship," the Temple was founded by Jerome Peartree and Karen DePolito in 1985 in New York City. It offers "self-improvement through Magick," teaching "Caballa, Tarot, Crystals, WICCA." WICCAN festivals are celebrated as is a "Gnostic Mass."

Temple of the Goddess Within

U.S. neo-pagan, feminist association of covens. It was founded by Ann Forfreedom and is based in Sacramento, California. [*See also* COVENANT OF THE GODDESS.]

Temple of Thelema

U.S. occultist group that grew out of ORDO TEMPLI ORIENTIS (OTO); it is based in Los Angeles, California. It is described as "an Initiatory and Training Order working on the 'Golden Dawn' system revised to conform to the Thelemic principle of the *Book of the Law* and the works of Aleister Crowley."

Temple of Universal Judaism

Also known as Congregation Daat Elohim (Knowledge of God). This is a U.S. Jewish Reform group with an ecumenical emphasis. It was founded in New York City in 1975 by Roy A. Rosenberg. Its doctrine emphasizes the

---

Statement of Principles of the Temple of Universal Judaism:

1. We believe that humanity and the universe, in all their complexity and contradiction, manifest the One Living God.
2. We believe that the truths of Universal Judaism are appropriate for all people. Participation is open to all who desire it, and there is no barrier to the marriage of a Jew to a non-Jew, since both share equally in the divine image of Man male and female.
3. We hold that the insights of the great religious teachers of the world should become part of our spiritual life.
4. We believe that mankind's quest for truth yields the revelation of God, from the dawn of human consciousness to the present.
5. We believe that we have the obligation to modify teaching and practices handed down from the past as our knowledge and appreciation of truth change and grow. What we do and teach must reflect the basic ideal linking humanity with God—You shall love your neighbor as yourself.
6. We feel a kinship with the people of the land of Israel and rejoice in their prosperity, and seek a lasting peace with justice for all the peoples of the Middle East in which the people of Israel will share.
7. We believe that redemption is a state of mind in which we mingle a concern for others with a quest for our own happiness. As we seek a way of life fulfilling for both others and ourselves, we help establish the Kingdom of God on earth.

commonality of world religions and universalism in moral concerns. [*See also* REFORM JUDAISM.]

Temple of Universal Law

U.S. spiritualist THEOSOPHIST group founded in 1936 in Chicago by Charlotte Bright.

Temple of Universal Peace

Hindu revival group founded in Madras, India, in 1935 by Swami Paranjothi. It is devoted to the practice of kundalini yoga, which strives to unleash an energy believed to rest at the base of the spine. [*See also* WORLD COMMUNITY SERVICE.]

Temple of Wicca

U.S. neo-pagan group based in Los Angeles. Founded in the 1980s, it is devoted to the promotion of "positive energy." "Through ritual magic, Wiccans believe, the powerful energy contained in all of us can be strengthened and channeled in useful directions. Rooted in ancient traditions, witches (both male and female) practice only positive magic in ceremonies that center on the earth, the universe, and regeneration. Believing in the principle of karma, witches encircle themselves with positive energy to tap the forces of universal goodness. This, witches feel, enables them to lead successful and spiritually balanced lives." [*See also* WICCA.]

Templegesellschaft

Also known as Templars, Friends of the Temple, or Jerusalem Friends. This is a German MILLENARIAN group founded in 1854 in Württemberg by Christopher Hoffmann (1815–1885), whose brother, Wilhelm Hoffmann (1806–1873) was personal chaplain to King Friedrich Wilhelm IV (1795–1861) of Prussia. Members started settling in Palestine around 1868 and established colonies in Haifa, in the Galilee, and near Jaffa, which were in existence until April 1948. Its members did play a role in introducing modern technology to nineteenth-century Palestine. The founder called for the immediate construction of the ancient temple in Jerusalem, in anticipation of the imminent Second Coming of Jesus Christ. This would create a new Christian people. The group's doctrine was Old Testament–oriented, rejecting belief in the Trinity and the divinity of Jesus Christ, and calling for a theocratic state. During World War II Temple Society members were interned and expelled from Palestine by the British as enemy aliens. Later, group members settled in the United States, Russia, Sweden, and Switzerland.

Tenrikyo ("Heavenly Reason Teaching")

Japanese messianic syncretistic movement, originating in the Shinto tradition but including also Buddhist and Christian elements. It was started by Mrs. Omiki Nakayama (1798–1887). The founder came from a prosperous farming family belonging to the Jodo Buddhist sect. She was married at age twelve to Zenbei Nakayama, a farmer, and she had six children while in her early twenties. At age forty she had her first revelation, namely that she was possessed by the god Tenri, and so the movement regards 1838 as the date of its founding. In 1862 a group was formed, and forty years later it was officially recognized by the Japanese government. The group scripture is known as Ofudesaki. Nakayama is considered the Messiah, and many stories of miracles performed by her are told by members in support of their beliefs. Doctrine holds that God has chosen to manifest himself through her in order to save humankind. Nakayama is considered the Temple of God and His mediator on Earth. Tenrikyo doctrine also promises the imminent coming of the heavenly kingdom, which is its eventual goal.

The movement is sometimes referred to as the Japanese CHRISTIAN SCIENCE because of the beliefs it shares with the group founded in the nineteenth century in the United States. A pertinent connection is that the root of suffering and sickness is in the mind. Those who manage to overcome anger, selfishness, and other negative feelings may live to age 115, free from sickness and worry. After World War II Tenrikyo started to take an active part in Japanese politics. Branches have operated among Japanese in North America and in Brazil. [*See also* HONMICHI-KYO.]

Tensho Kotai Jingu Kyo

Also known as Mioshi or Odoru-Shukyo ("Dancing Religion"). This is a Japanese syncretistic movement of Shinto origins. It was founded in 1945 by Kitamura Sayo (1900–1967), known to her followers as "Ogamisama" (the goddess). In 1943 she started having experiences of being possessed by the Shinto god Tensho Kotai Jungu. Later she claimed to be Jesus Christ and Buddha. Group practices include "healing" and ecstatic dancing.

Group doctrine calls for getting rid of the root evils, which are considered the human weaknesses of regret, desire, love, and hatred. Branches have operated on all continents.

Tharpa Choeling

Swiss Tibetan Buddhist group founded in 1977 in the Canton of Vaud.

Theocentric Foundation

U.S. occultist THEOSOPHICAL group founded in 1959 in Phoenix, Arizona. It is the successor to the Shangrila Missions, the Eden Foundation, the Manhattan Philosophical Center, and the THEOCENTRIC TEMPLE. The group teaches "Hermetic theology."

Theocentric Temple

U.S. occultist THEOSOPHICAL group which was succeeded by the THEOCENTRIC FOUNDATION.

Theocratic Commune Natural Health Service

U.S. Christian healing commune founded in Detroit in the 1970s by Raymond Allen Archer (1940–). Archer advocated a strict diet of raw fruits and vegetables. In 1978 he was charged with manslaughter after his two children died of malnutrition.

Theosophical Order of Service, The

British THEOSOPHICAL charity organization founded in London in 1908 by Annie Besant.

Theosophical Society in America

U.S. THEOSOPHICAL group founded in 1895 by William Q. Judge following a dispute with Annie Besant, the leader of the Theosophical Society. Most American Theosophists followed Judge and joined the new group.

Theosophical Society in England

British THEOSOPHICAL group affiliated with the THEOSOPHICAL SOCIETY IN AMERICA. It operates the Foundation for Theosophical Studies and the Blavatsky Trust.

Theosophy

Theosophy has been in many ways the prototype for the Western new religion. It combines Western occult traditions, Eastern ideas, and ideals of self-improvement, leading the way to hundreds of similar and subsidiary groups.

The Theosophical Society was founded in 1875 in New York City. It was formed by Helena Petrovna Blavatsky (1831–1891), who first attracted public attention in the 1870s as a medium, aided by Colonel Henry Steel Olcott (1832–1907), William Quan Judge (1851–1896), Gerry Brown, and twelve other followers. Madame Blavatsky claimed to have spent about forty years traveling in the East, especially Tibet, and meeting the Masters of Ancient Wisdom, or the Adepts, as well as taking part in the Italian wars of independence on the side of Garibaldi. Actually, she was born in Russia (née Hahn), married General Blavatsky at seventeen, and ran away a year later. She founded a spiritualist group in Cairo around 1870. In 1874 she came to the United States and gained some attention as a defender of spiritualism.

Theosophy first started as a spiritualist group and drew its adherents from among the many spiritualists in New York at the time, but it later developed a distinct doctrine. The Theosophical Society sought contact with Indian groups and in 1878 established an alliance with the ARYA SAMAJ. It became known for four years as the Theosophical Society of the Arya Samaj. Blavatsky's claims of supernatural powers and contacts were investigated in India in 1884 by Richard Hodgson of the London Society for Psychical Research, who denounced them as fraudulent trickery.

Theosophy became an important force in the life of the intellectual elite in Great Britain and in India through the activities of Annie Wood Besant (1847–1933), who founded in 1898 the Benares Central Hindu College as a missionary Theosophical institution. Besant was also influential in the development of Indian nationalism. Colonel Olcott was instrumental in starting a Buddhist revival movement in Ceylon (now Sri Lanka).

Besant was chosen by Blavatsky to succeed her as the head of the Theosophical Society. In 1911 Besant proclaimed Jiddo KRISHNAMURTI (1895–1986) to be the coming "World Teacher," the avatar. Krishnamurti rejected this assignment in 1929. The Theosophical Society has maintained its world headquarters in Adyar, India, since 1877. It maintains educational centers and publishing outlets in many countries, such as the Krotona Institute of Theosophy in Ojai, California.

The beliefs of the Theosophical Society are expounded in Blavatsky's books *Isis Unveiled* (1877) and *The Secret Doctrine: The Synthesis of Science, Religion, and Philosophy* (1888). Blavatsky claimed that

Helen a Petrovna Blavatsky, famous mystic and founder of the Theosophical Society.

she was in touch with adepts known as the Brotherhood of Luxor, a branch of the Great White Brotherhood, a group of people that believe they have attained a superior spiritual knowledge and understanding. She stated that she had been chosen by a Buddha incarnation named Tsong-kha-pa to save the world. She would be guided in this endeavor by two secret masters known as the Mahatma Morya and the Mahatma Koot Hoomi.

"Theosophy, meaning 'wisdom-religion,' asserts the unity of everything in the universe and the existence of a knowledge at once scientific, philosophical and religious." Theosophical doctrine claims to be based on esoteric knowledge and to embody the eternal truths supposedly basic to all world religions. It proclaims a synthesis of religion, philosophy, and science, and conducts an investigation of the laws of nature and powers latent in human beings. It is a syncretistic collection of occultist beliefs, ideas supposedly derived from ancient Egypt, and some ideas derived from Hinduism. Western occult traditions, such as astrology, are revered and upheld. To this day there is still an Astrological Lodge of the Theosophical Society.

There is a belief in a Universal Spirit and a hierarchy of perfected beings (the White Brotherhood, the Adepts, the Masters, the Mahatmas), who supervise the evolution of the world. There is a belief in both reincarnation as part of evolution and communication with the dead. Spiritual evolution is possible as souls transmigrate, or pass from one state of existence to another. The number seven is considered the key to understanding the universe, as there are seven basic forces in nature, seven planes of reality (Divine, Spiritual, Intuitional, Mental, Emotional, Etheric, Physical), and seven human races in evolutionary order, of which the Aryans are held to be the fifth. In the future, the sixth and seventh races will appear. Each "root race" has seven "sub-races" and each sub-race has seven "branch-races." For example, the "lemurians" were the third root race. They were ape-like giants who gradually evolved into something like modern man, but Lemuria was engulfed in a great convulsion shortly after a sub-race had migrated to Atlantis, where they began the fourth root race.

There have been many schisms in the Theosophical movement, starting with the establishment of the Theosophical Organization by W. Q. Judge in 1895. A schism in European Theosophy led in 1912 to the founding of the ANTHROPOSOPHICAL SOCIETY by Rudolf Steiner. [*See also* LIBERAL CATHOLIC CHURCH; THE THEOSOPHICAL ORDER OF SERVICE; UNITED LODGE OF THEOSOPHISTS; *and* UNIVERSAL BROTHERHOOD.]

Sources:

Campbell, B. F. *Ancient Wisdom Revived: A History of the Theosophical Movement.* Berkeley: University of California Press, 1980.

Meade, M. *Madame Blavatsky: The Woman Behind the Myth.* New York: Putnam, 1980.

Nethercot, A. H. *The First Five Lives of Annie Besant.* Chicago: University of Chicago Press, 1960.

———. *The Last Four Lives of Annie Besant.* Chicago: University of Chicago Press, 1963.

Williams, G. M. *Priestess of the Occult.* New York: Knopf, 1946.

Third Civilization

Japanese new religion founded by Koji Ogasawara. It is based on a new interpretation of the Shinto scriptures together with the idea of the Kototama Principle, which is the origin and end of all human life. This principle will lead the world to the Third Civilization and the coming of the messiah. The movement's branches have operated in Europe and the United States.

This Testimony

Also known as Testimony Book Ministry. This is a U.S. FUNDAMENTALIST group that is the U.S. branch of the British HONOR OAK CHRISTIAN FELLOW-SHIP CENTRE, an organization founded around 1920 by T. Austin Sparks. In doctrine it is closely related to the LOCAL CHURCH MOVEMENT, with one exception. This Testimony follows the teachings of local Church founder Watchman Nee but not those of Witness Lee, his successor.

Thomas Merton Center

Canadian syncretistic group founded around 1970 by Linda Sabbath. It has a combined Eastern-Western doctrine that follows "the basic system of Patanjali's yoga, adapted for contemporary Western consciousness, and . . . the spiritual traditions of St. John of the Cross and St. Theresa of Avila." Practices focused on contemplative prayer.

Tibetan Buddhist Learning Center

U.S. center for the teaching of Tibetan Buddhism. It was founded in 1958 in Washington, New Jersey, by Leshe Wangyal (1902–1983). Its aim is to develop "a Buddhism that is culturally American," and it has engaged in many activities in connection with the XIV Dalai Lama (1935–), designed to make Tibetan Buddhism better known. It is connected with the LAMAIST BUDDHIST MONASTERY OF AMERICA.

Timely Messenger Fellowship

U.S. informal association of FUNDAMEN-TALIST, DISPENSATIONALIST Christians. It was founded by Ike T. Sidebottom in 1939 and is based in Fort Worth, Texas. It publishes *The Timely Messenger* and broadcasts radio programs. [*See also* GRACE GOSPEL FELLOWSHIP.]

Tipan Ng Panginoon

Philippine indigenous Protestant group founded in 1907.

Today Church

Originally known as the Academy of Mind Dynamics, this is a U.S. NEW THOUGHT group. It was founded by Bud and Carmen Moshier in Dallas, Texas, in 1969.

Towards the Light

European occultist movement founded in the 1950s.

Traditional Christian Catholic Church

International traditionalist Catholic movement with its world center in

Québec and missions in the United States, Europe, and Hong Kong. Its ideology is based on religious and political conservatism, and it opposes all innovations in the Roman Catholic Church since the Second Vatican Council. The church was founded by Thomas Fehervary and a group of Hungarian immigrants who came to Québec after the Hungarian revolt of 1956.

Traleg Tulku

Western Tibetan Buddhist group based in Melbourne, Australia. It is led by Traleg Rinpoche, who claimed to be the ninth Traleg Tulku meditation master. The group is devoted to promoting Tibetan Buddhist teachings in the West. It was founded around 1980.

Transcendental Meditation

Officially known today as the World Plan Executive Council, this is a Western Hindu movement dedicated to promoting both Hindu doctrines and traditional Hindu meditation techniques. The movement and its various affiliated organizations were founded by a native of India known as the Maharishi Mahesh Yogi, whose birth name is reported to be either J. N. Srivastava or Mahesh Prasad Varma (born on October 18 in either 1911 or 1918). A former Hindu monk, the Maharishi is reputed to have studied with a famous teacher named Brahmanda Sarasurati, or Swami Krishanand Saraswati, or Guru Dev. It was Guru Dev who was taught the special meditation technique that became known as Transcendental Meditation (TM). In 1958 the Maharishi left India on a mission to the West and arrived in the United States in 1959. The Spiritual Re-generation Movement Foundation, the early organizational form of TM, was incorporated by the Maharishi and others in Los Angeles in 1959. In the late 1960s and early 1970s many affiliated organizations were created to spread the teaching of TM, including universities and international students' movements, such as the Spiritual Regeneration movement.

The religious nature of TM instruction has been a matter of legal dispute in the United States since the early 1970s. The matter was brought to court before Federal Judge H. Curtis Meanor, at the U.S. District Court for the District of New Jersey. Judge Meanor's ruling on October 19, 1977, stated that "The [TM] and the teaching thereof, the concepts of the field of pure Creative Intelligence, Creative Intelligence, and Bliss-Consciousness . . . and the puja ceremony, are all religious in nature within the context of the establishment clause of the First Amendment of the United States Constitution." On February 2, 1979, this ruling was upheld by the U.S. Court of Appeals. The TM organization never appealed that ruling. Thus, the view that TM activities are religious in nature has stood rather rigorous legal tests. In order to analyze the religious nature of TM, it seems beneficial to divide TM into two very different activities. The first is of the daily meditation technique, which does not usually mean a real religious involvement. Graduates of the daily meditation TM training are often unaware of the religious nature of the puja (graduation) ceremony and are unconcerned about the religious background of the technique. The second activity is that of advanced meditation techniques and more esoteric beliefs, and individuals committed to those are clearly disciples of a reli-

Maharishi Mahesh Yogi, founder of Transcendental Meditation.

358

gion. In 1976 TM initiated its Siddhi Program, which promises its participants such abilities as levitation and invisibility.

The advanced meditators, or "Governors of the Age of Enlightenment," are reportedly capable of creating amazing effects. TM doctrine speaks of a "unified field" of nature that is affected by advanced meditation by advanced meditators (known as Sidhas or Sidhi). According to TM precepts, simultaneous meditation by the square root of 1 percent of the world population (about 9,000 people) would lead to cosmic changes, resolving political conflicts, lowering crime rates and boosting stock market prices.

In late 1970, the TM organization began referring to itself as the World Government. This World Government announced in January 1979 that its governors had restored peace to the five most troubled areas of the world: Central America, southern Africa, the Middle East, Iran, and Southeast Asia. In 1983 the World Government announced that it had in its possession an "Invincible defense" that would "neutralize the destructive capabilities of all those who possess the power of destruction found at the electronic and nuclear levels." This was followed by an invitation to the governments of several countries to purchase their protection: "to contract on the basis of the Age of Enlightenment to solve their problems on the basis of cost reimbursement after the target is reached . . . every government already knows what must be achieved, and the World Government has already developed techniques to fulfill any requirement." TM has also offered "Immortality . . . through this unified field-based approach to health."

The historical origins of the Maharishi's teachings are said to be in the tradition founded by Sankaracharya, a Hindu reformer of the Middle Ages who led a movement that revived Hinduism.

In 1980 TM opened a center in India, and later that decade started promoting Ayurveda medicine, which is an Indian ancient medical tradition based on the use of herbs, fruits, and prayers. Also in the 1980s the movement started operating the Maharishi University of Natural Law (MUNL) in Great Britain. In 1995 TM bought the former Bentwaters airbase, 80 miles northeast of London, for $12 million, to be made into the Maharishi International University. It was predicted by TM that the meditation by 2,000 students would influence positively the consciousness of the whole country.

In the late 1980s TM started marketing the "Maharishi Ayur-Ved" system, a "complete system of natural care." Under that brand name TM began selling various herbal medicines. Later on TM started offering jyotish, its own astrological belief system. In the 1990s TM founded the Natural Law Party (NLP), which took part in several national election campaigns in Great Britain, Denmark, Israel, and other countries. The NLP obtained 60,000 votes during the general elections in Britain in 1992 and 1,737 votes in the Israeli general election of the same year.

Sources:

Chopra, D. *Return of the Rishi*. Boston: Houghton Mifflin, 1987.

White, J. *Everything You Wanted to Know About TM—Including How to Do It*. New York: Berkeley Publishing, 1976.

A view of the 7,000 practitioners of Transcendental Meditation gathered at the Maharishi International University in Iowa in 1983. It is their belief that simultaneous meditation by the square root of 1 percent of the world population (about 7,000 people) would bring about cosmic changes.

Tree of Life

Formerly known as the NEW SYNAGOGUE and as the Little Synagogue, this is a U.S. Jewish NEW THOUGHT group founded by Joseph H. Gelberman in New York City in the 1960s. Its doctrine is eclectic and combines Eastern meditation with traditional Jewish prayers and psychological counseling. The name Tree of Life was adopted in the late 1980s, when Gelberman was joined by Burt Aaron Siegel in leading the group. [*See also* INTERFAITH TEMPLE.]

Triumph the Church and Kingdom of God in Christ (International)

Known commonly as the Triumph Church. This is a U.S. evangelical Protestant group with African American membership based in the southern United States. It was founded by E. D. Smith in 1902. Members are forbidden tobacco, tea, coffee, and alcohol, and are enjoined to follow a strict behavior code. [*See also* CHURCH OF UNIVERSAL TRIUMPH/THE DOMINION OF GOD.]

Trois Saints Coeurs (Three Holy Hearts)

European Protestant sect founded in the 1960s by Roger Melchior and his three brothers. Established in Belgium, it later moved to France. It has been involved in several legal difficulties and scandals.

Source:

Lecerf, Y. *Les Marchands de Dieu.* Bruxelles: Complexe, 1975.

True Church of Christ, International

U.S. Christian occultist group founded by Christian Weyand in Buffalo, New York, in the 1960s. The group claims to provide the only authentic texts of the Bible and other ancient lost works. It advocates the use of psychic powers.

True Church of Christ (New Bethlehem)

African independent PENTECOSTAL church founded in 1957 among the Ashanti of Ghana by Lucy Kudjo. Its practices emphasize healing through magical objects.

True Faith Church

African indigenous PENTECOSTAL group founded in 1921 in Ghana by former members of the Methodist Church.

True Fellowship Pentecostal Church of God of America

U.S. African American PENTECOSTAL group founded by Charles E. Waters, Sr.

It began in 1964 in Baltimore, following a schism in the ALPHA AND OMEGA PENTECOSTAL CHURCH OF GOD OF AMERICA, INC.

True Followers of Christ

U.S. FUNDAMENTALIST group that forbids the use of medical care in favor of faith healing. Members have served prison terms for failing to provide their children with medical treatment.

True Grace Memorial House of Prayer

U.S. African American PENTECOSTAL group based in Washington, D.C. It was founded in 1960 by Thomas O. Johnson, as a result of a schism in the UNITED HOUSE OF PRAYER FOR ALL PEOPLE.

True Jesus Church (Chen Ye-Su Chiao Hui)

Chinese indigenous Christian church started in 1917 by secession from European missionary groups. Since the early 1950s it has maintained headquarters in Taichung, Taiwan, with branches in Chinese communities around the world.

True Light Church of Christ

Formerly known as Shiloh True Light Church of Christ (Braswell). This U.S. MILLENARIAN group was started in 1969 as a result of dissent within the SHILOH TRUE LIGHT CHURCH OF CHRIST. Two members, Herman Flake Braswell and Clyde M. Huntley, led the dissenting faction. This group took the prophecy of the

361

Second Coming in 1970 quite literally, leaving jobs and businesses. Huntley committed suicide in May 1970, following the disconfirmation. The group has declined ever since.

Truth Consciousness

International Hindu group founded in 1960 in India by Amar Joyti and devoted to his teachings. Its branches have operated in North America, New Zealand, and India.

Truth for Today

International FUNDAMENTALIST, DISPENSATIONALIST movement formed around the Church of the Open Book in London. There are also congregations in North America, which publish *Truth for Today* magazine.

Truth Station, The

U.S. FUNDAMENTALIST Christian group founded in the 1970s and based in southern California. Members are asked to reject medicine and rely on faith healing. One death has been reported as a result.

Tuka

Fijian messianic syncretistic movement started in 1863 when the prophet Ndugumoi started predicting a cosmic upheaval. This convulsion would bring about the disappearance of religion. Jehovah, the European god, would be subordinated to local deities; subsequently, all Europeans would disappear from the earth. After 1882 Ndugumoi held court surrounded by armed guards. He prom-ised his followers immortality (*Tuka*) and permanent youth, while he declared himself immortal and invulnerable. He also promised the return of dead ancestors. Despite the prophet's expulsion and his later death in 1897, the movement prospered until 1920, as followers continued to believe that Ndugumoi was still alive. There was a resurgence of the movement in the mid-1930s, and another one in March, 1984.

Twelve Apostles

Known commonly as Nackabah and officially as the Church of the Twelve Apostles. This is a Christian syncretistic movement in Ghana founded by Grace Tani, John Nackabah, and John Hackman in 1914, as a result of a revival movement led by William Wade Harris. Leadership has passed to the sons of John Nackabah. Doctrine is officially tied to the Methodist Church, but in reality there is an overwhelming emphasis on healing and prophecy. Pork and tobacco are prohibited, and fasts are recommended. [*See also* HARRIS MOVEMENT.]

Source:
Bäeta, C. G. *Prophetism in Ghana*. London: SCM Press, 1962.

Twelve Tribes of Israel

International RASTAFARIAN group, considered the most important outside of Jamaica. It is also one of the few Rasta groups that accept whites as members. In terms of beliefs, members of the Twelve Tribes of Israel do not necessarily believe in the divinity of Haile Selassie.

Twentieth Century Church of God

U.S. ADVENTIST group founded in dissent from the WORLDWIDE CHURCH OF GOD by Al Carrozzo in 1974. The group has its headquarters in Vacaville, California, and circulates several publications.

Twer Nyame Church

Known officially as the Divine Fellowship. This is an African indigenous PENTECOSTAL group founded in Ghana in 1962 by secession from the CHURCH OF THE LORD (ALADURA). Practices emphasize healing through prayer and magical oils.

Two-By-Two's, The

Also known as the Christian Fellowship, People on the Way, Disciples of Jesus, Friends, "go-preachers," or "Cooneyites." This FUNDAMENTALIST Evangelical group grew out of the British nineteenth-century FAITH MISSION movement. It was founded in Ireland in 1900 by William Irvine (1863–1947) and in 1903 reached the United States. Edward Cooney was one of the most active early members, giving his name to the group. Members become wandering preachers, living off the proceeds of collection plates. Group doctrine advocates a life-style of extreme simplicity and poverty.

U

Umbanda

Syncretistic spiritualist movement in Brazil that combines strong African and Catholic elements together with indigenous Indian rituals and components of the spiritualist KARDECISM school. The first Umbanda group was founded in 1907, and since then thousands more have been started. Umbanda is loosely organized, but formal organization began to emerge in the 1920s in Rio de Janeiro and São Paolo. According to Umbanda doctrine, spirits form armies known as "phalanxes" headed by African gods or Roman Catholic saints. The supreme God is surrounded by lesser deities, each of whom commands a phalanx. Spirits are also divided by social class and race. A more successful reincarnation is promised to believers who obey their personal deities.

Source:
Simpson, G. E. *Black Religions in the New World*. New York: Columbia University Press, 1978.

Unarius Educational Foundation (UNARIUS—Science of Life)

U.S. UFO-THEOSOPHICAL group founded in 1954 by Ernest L. Norman in El Cajon, California. Its name is an acronym of UNiversal ARticulate Interdimensional Understanding of Science. Its doctrine is eclectic, combining ideas from all Western occult traditions of modern times. The founder is presented as "Ernest L.

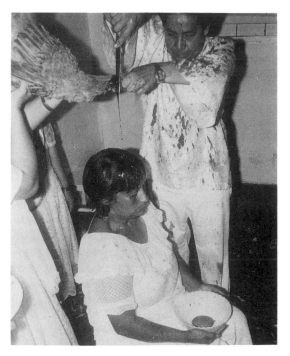

Priest José Paiva performing an ancient African Brazilian ritual believed to cure illness.

Norman, the Archangel Raphael, incarnated 2,000 years ago as Jesus of Nazareth. He also lived the life of the Pharaoh Akhenaton 3,500 years ago. He was the historically famous teacher Anaxagoras, [who lived] about 500 B.C."

Group doctrine predicts that by 2001, "an interstellar Starship carrying 1,000 space scientists from the Planet Myton, in the Starcluster of the Pleiades—the Constellation Taurus—will arrive on Earth and land on the raised portion of Atlantis in the Caribbean Sea!" In the meantime, group members are aided by "Space Brothers—Advanced Beings who live on the higher Spiritual Worlds."

The group, which has been headed by Ruth Norman (known as URIEL—Universal Radiant Infinite Eternal Light) since her husband's death, has operated the Academy of Parapsychology, Healing and Psychic Sciences. "Past life therapy—the new science of Reincarnation physics" is also provided.

Undenominational Church of the Lord

U.S. "HOLINESS" group founded in 1918 in southern California by Jesse N. Blakeley. It operates overseas missions in India and Africa.

Understanding, Inc.

U.S. UFO-THEOSOPHICAL group founded in 1955 by Daniel Fry. Based in Tonapah, Arizona, it merged in the early 1970s with the UNIVERSAL FAITH AND WISDOM ASSOCIATION.

Unification Association of Christian Sabbath Keepers

U.S. organization of African American Sabbath-keeping ADVENTISTS. Founded in 1956 in New York City by Thomas I. C. Hughes, it incorporated several existing congregations in the greater New York area. The organization has maintained missionary outposts in Africa and the Caribbean. Over the years it has developed a much larger membership base overseas as the number of U.S. members has decreased.

Unification Church

Most commonly known as "Moonies" or the Unification Movement (UM), officially called the Holy Spirit Association for the Unification of World Christianity (HSA-UWC), and sometimes known as Pioneers of the New Age, the Unified Family, Tongil Kyohoe (in Korea), Tongil Family (in Europe), and by the names of its many front organizations. This is a Christian MILLENARIAN group, founded on May 1, 1954, in Seoul, South Korea.

Its founder, Sun Myung Moon, was born as Yong Myung Moon on January 6, 1920, in Korea to Presbyterian parents. He changed his name later. In his early years he was influenced by various PENTECOSTAL and millenarian groups, and at age sixteen he had a "divine revelation" in the form of a visit by Jesus Christ on Easter morning, 1936, which changed the course of his life. According to Moon, he was trained in Japan as an electrical engineer; later, he was arrested in 1946 in Pyongyang by the Communist regime of North Korea. Many of the claims regarding his imprisonment and trials are very much in dispute. It is contended by nonchurch sources that most of Moon's legal entanglements have stemmed from morals charges.

The Unification Church first appeared as a religious group in Korea between 1951 and 1954 among Presbyterian missionaries. It was officially founded in 1954. Its scripture, the *Divine Principle*, was first published in 1956. In 1959 the first missionary, Miss Young Oon Kim, went to the United States, and in 1965 Moon held his first global tour, traveling to forty countries. The movement's goal is to prepare for the coming of "the Lord of the Second Advent" by unifying world Christianity. Unification Church theology, summarized in the *Divine Principle*, combines Christianity with Eastern, especially Buddhist, ideas. Moon divides human history (which he claims means only 6,000 years—since the creation of Adam) into four periods: from Adam to

The Reverend Sun Myung Moon and his wife, Hak Ja Han, officiate at a mass wedding in Madison Square Garden, New York.

Unification Church founder Sun Myung Moon and his wife sprinkle newlyweds with water during a mass wedding in Seoul, South Korea.

Abraham, 2,000 years of night; from Abraham to Jesus, 2,000 years of education; from Jesus to the twentieth century, 2,000 years of development. This period, according to Moon, is leading to the fourth era, that of Perfection, about to start soon, with the establishment, or restoration, of the Kingdom of Heaven on earth under the new Messiah. The doctrine holds that mankind will be redeemed by a perfect man, married to a perfect woman, and having perfect children. God gave mankind a first chance to achieve that with the creation of Adam and Eve, and a second chance in Jesus, but in both cases the Perfect Family was not created. The fall of humanity first occurred because Eve had an illicit sexual relationship with Satan. Jesus Christ failed in his mission because he did not marry and because he was not accepted by the Jews. In the twentieth century came another chance, with the perfect man appearing on Earth, and the Kingdom of God within reach. This man, according to Moon's calculations, should have been born between 1917 and 1930.

Moon once predicted the coming of the Christian millennium in 1967. According to another Unification Church calculation, 1981 was to be the year of "final victory," twenty-one years after the Marriage of the Lamb, that is the marriage of Sun Myung Moon to Hak Ja Han, the "New Eve," in 1960. Moon came to be considered the expected perfect man, and he and his wife Hak Ja Han (second or fourth wife, according to differing counts) are known as the True Parents. Members refer to Moon as "Father" or "Master." While Moon has not clearly proclaimed himself the Messiah, it is apparent that Unification Church members consider him just that, and refer to him

as the "Lord of the Second Advent." The present time is described as the Last Days before the Second Advent.

According to Unification Church theology, Korea is the "New Israel" (while Japan is the "Eve nation"), and the Korean language will be the language of the divine kingdom on Earth in the future.

One version of the Church doctrine is presented as "Godism," a set of ideas consisting of the belief in God, life after death, and the "sanctity of the individual." Outsiders are thought to be under the control of Satan.

This Church is among the best-known of the new religions, possibly because of the amount of controversy surrounding it and the amount of research done on it. The Unification Church has been involved in a number of lawsuits. It has sued several newspapers, including the *New York Times*, for libel, but it has lost in every case. In 1982 Moon was sentenced by a U.S. District Judge in New York City to eighteen months in prison and a $25,000 fine for income tax evasion, after the prosecution had proved misuse of funds and forging of documents. Following the failure of his appeals, he was incarcerated during 1984 and 1985.

Since 1961, Moon has officiated at mass weddings in which thousands have been married—some before ever meeting their mates—following the leader's instructions. Not all participants are Unification Church members, and there is a considerable fee involved. On August 24, 1995, 35,000 couples were reported to have been married in one such ceremony in Seoul. Unification Church marriages are not supposed to be consummated immediately, and annulment is possible during the first three years of the marriage. The marriage is performed through a sequence of rites: the Matching

Ceremony, during which Moon matches partners; the secret Wine Ceremony, when the partners join Moon's family; the public mass Blessing Ceremony; and the Three-Day Rite when the marriage is consummated.

The Unification Church has operated scores of profitable business corporations in Korea, Japan, the United States, and Latin America. These have included Dong Wha Titanium (Korea), Hankook Titanium (Korea), Ill Hwa Pharmaceuticals (Korea and Japan), Sekai Nippo (Japan), and Toitsu Sangyo (Japan). The Church also owns New World Communications, which operates several newspapers, including the *Washington Times*, and several publishing houses. It has also owned newspapers in Latin America.

In Austria the Church founded a political party known as Neue Mitte. Among the leaders of the movement is Bo Hi Pak, who was a military attache at the Korean Embassy in Washington, D.C., between 1961 and 1964.

The Unification Church has been associated with right-wing political groups and causes all over the world. In Bolivia it was involved in the overthrow of the elected government in 1980 by General Garcia Mesa, and in Honduras it was involved in supporting General Gustavo Alvarez in 1983. Neither leader stayed in power for long. Despite the Unification Church's anti-Communist ideology and activities, it was reported in 1995 that it was establishing ties with the regime in North Korea. Since 1989 the Church has established branches all over Eastern Europe and the former Soviet Union.

The Church has, since its beginnings, operated scores of front organizations, which sometimes hide their religious connections and present themselves behind a variety of titles and acronyms. These have included the American Freedom Coalition (AFC), the Assembly of World Religions (AWR), CARP (Collegiate Association for the Research of Principles), CAUSA (Confederation of Associations for the Unification of American Societies), Freedom Leadership Foundation, Global Congress of the World's Religions (1993), Home Church Program, International Conference on the Unity of the Sciences (ICUS), International Cultural Foundation (ICF), International Federation for Victory over Communism (Victory over Communism or V.O.C), International Middle East Alliance, International Security Council, International Religious Foundation, National Council for the Church and Social Action, New Ecumenical Research Association (New ERA), New Educational Development Systems, Inc. (NEDS), New Hope Singers International, One World Crusade, Professors World Peace Academy, Project Unity, Project Volunteer, the Washington Institute for Values in Public Policy, World Festival of Culture, and the Youth Seminar of World Religions (YSWR).

Sources:

Barker, E. *The Making of a Moonie.* Oxford: Basil Blackwell, 1984.

Boettcher, R. *Gifts of Deceit.* New York: Holt, Rinehart & Winston, 1980.

Bromley, D. A., and Shupe, A. D., Jr. *"Moonies" in America: Cult, Church, and Crusade.* Beverly Hills, Calif.: Sage, 1979.

Grace, J. H. *Sex and Marriage in the Unification Church.* Lewiston, N.Y.: Edwin Mellen Press, 1985.

Horowitz, I. L. *Science, Sin, and Scholarship: The Politics of Reverend Moon and the Unification Church.* Cambridge, Mass.: MIT Press, 1979.

Kim, C. S. *Rev. Sun Myung Moon.* Washington, D.C.: University Press of America, 1978.

Lewis, W. *Moon.* Boston: Beacon Press, 1985.

Lofland, J. *Doomsday Cult.* New York: Irvington Publishers, 1978.

Union Catolica Trento

Mexican traditionalist Catholic movement, founded in 1981 by Moises Carmona and Adolfo Zamora, who were consecrated by Pierre Martin Ngo-Dinh-Thuc, of the LATIN-RITE CATHOLIC CHURCH. The movement rejects all reforms introduced into the Roman Catholic Church after 1965. [*See also* SERVANTS OF THE SACRED HEART OF JESUS AND MARY.]

Union of Apostolic Christians

International Christian group founded in 1954 by secession from the NEW APOSTOLIC CHURCH.

Union of Messianic Jewish Congregations

International HEBREW CHRISTIAN organization founded in 1979. It loosely draws together numerous groups from all over the world. It has headquarters at BETH MESSIAH CONGREGATION in Gaithersburg, Maryland. [*See also* MESSIANIC JEWISH ALLIANCE OF AMERICA; *and* MESSIANIC JUDAISM.]

Union Spiritista Cristina de Filipinas, Inc.

Syncretistic, indigenous church founded in the Philippines in 1900. Doctrine combines Christianity, spiritualism, and some Hindu concepts. Faith healing is practiced.

Unis

U.S. GURDJIEFF GROUP founded in the 1960s and based in New Jersey.

United Apostolic Faith Church

British PENTECOSTAL, BRITISH ISRAELIST group. Founded in London around 1910, it now has branches in South Africa.

United Christian Church and Ministerial Association

U.S. PENTECOSTAL group founded by H. Richard Hall in 1956 in Cleveland, Tennessee. Its main activity is the ordination of Pentecostal ministers by mail.

United Christian Scientists

U.S. offshoot of CHRISTIAN SCIENCE founded in 1975 and based in San Jose, California. Its members have criticized the Christian Science leadership for its authoritarian rule. In 1987 the group won its legal battle to publish its own version of *Science and Health with Key to the Scriptures* by Mary Baker Eddy.

United Christians Church

Ghanian independent Christian PENTECOSTAL church founded in 1940 by

369

Reverend Ike (right), founder of the United Church and Science of Living, talks with members of his group.

Salome Mamle Odum (c. 1900–), a former member of the Presbyterian Church of Ghana.

United Church and Science of Living Institute

U.S. NEW THOUGHT group founded in 1966 by Frederick Eikerekoetter II, a former Baptist minister also known as Reverend Ike. Most members are African Americans. The doctrine, known as "Science of Living," emphasizes not only healing, but also material prosperity. Reverend Ike speaks to followers through radio and television shows and reaches wide audiences.

United Church of Religious Science

Also known as the United Churches of Religious Science, this is a U.S. NEW THOUGHT group founded by Ernest Holmes (1887–1960) in 1952 in Los Angeles. It grew out of the Southern California Metaphysical Institute (started in 1916) and the Institute of Religious Science and Philosophy (started in 1927). This group's credo is very similar to that of RELIGIOUS SCIENCE INTERNATIONAL. "Religious Science is a fusion of Eastern and Western philosophies designed to help individuals realize that they are special emanations from God." Religious Science proclaims the ability of the subjective mind to "heal" and teaches a method of prayer known as "spiritual mind treatment." The basic belief is that "nothing needs to be healed, just God to be revealed."

Source:
Judah, J. S. *The History and Philosophy of the Metaphysical Movements in America.* Philadelphia: Westminster Press, 1967.

United Evangelical Churches

U.S. PENTECOSTAL group based in California. It was founded in 1960 by members of mainstream Protestant churches in the United States who joined the neo-Pentecostal revival.

United Holy Church of America

U.S. African American PENTECOSTAL group originating in Method, North Carolina, in 1886. After many organizational changes and name changes (Big Kahara Holiness Association, the Holy Church of North Carolina and Virginia), it moved north and is currently based on the East Coast.

United House of Prayer for All People

Originally known as the House of Prayer for All the People. This is a U.S. African American PENTECOSTAL group founded in 1925 by Marcelino Manoel de Graca (1884–1960), popularly known as "Sweet Daddy Grace." The group was built on and functioned around the leader's flamboyant personality. De Graca referred to himself as God and promised "salvation by Grace only." Members do-

nated as much as they could for the leader's benefit and then bought Daddy Grace products that included soap, toothpaste, and shoe polish. A strict conduct code was enforced. Following the founder's death, there were leadership disputes, and the group suffered a schism, leading to the formation of the TRUE GRACE MEMORIAL HOUSE OF PRAYER.

Source:
Fauset, A. H. *Black Gods of the Metropolis.* Philadelphia: University of Pennsylvania Press, 1944.

United Israel World Fellowship

U.S. BRITISH ISRAELIST group founded by James A. Lovell (1908–) in 1946 and based in Fort Worth, Texas. Before founding the group, Lovell, who was born in Texas and served as a Baptist minister, had founded two British Israelist churches in California.

Source:
Roy, R. L. *Apostles of Discord.* Boston: Beacon Press, 1953.

United Israel World Union

U.S. Jewish group with some features of BRITISH ISRAELISM, founded by David Horowitz in 1943. It believes that the "message of the Hebrew Bible" is meant for all nations and that some gentiles are descendants of the "ten lost tribes of Israel." Horowitz claims to have received instructions from Moshe Ghibbory, a divine messenger. Ghibbory reportedly lived in a cave in Jerusalem in the 1920s, when Horowitz met him. The group has been active in missionary work among non-Jews in Latin America and Africa. [*See also* HOUSE OF ISRAEL-ZION.]

United Leadership Council of Hebrew Israelites

U.S. federation founded in Chicago in 1967 by Robert Devine, James Hodge, and Richard Nolen. Group is based on the "Black Jews" settlement of 1896, which was a U.S. African American group that practiced a combination of Christianity, Judaism, and black nationalism.

United Lodge of Theosophists

International THEOSOPHICAL group with headquarters in the United States. It was founded in 1909 by Robert Crosbie, when he was ejected from the UNIVERSAL BROTHERHOOD AND THEOSOPHICAL SOCIETY by Katherine Tingley, founder of the U.S. Theosophical organization. Branches operate in North America, India, and Western Europe.

Source:

Campbell, B. F. *Ancient Wisdom Revived: A History of the Theosophical Movement*. Berkeley: University of California Press, 1980.

United Missionary Church

U.S. Christian evangelical group founded in Potsdam, Ohio, in 1947.

A Mormon family of the 1870s: two wives and nine children. Polygyny is still practiced by at least one Mormon group in Utah, the United Order Effort.

United Native African Church

Nigerian independent African church founded in Lagos in 1891 in dissent from the European-led Church Missionary Society.

United Order Effort

U.S. group of conservative MORMONS who believe in and practice polygyny as it was practiced in nineteenth-century Mormonism. Despite many efforts to suppress polygyny, the practice still exists in this group and in several others. The doctrine also forbids sexual relations during pregnancy, lactation, and menstruation. The group was started in the early 1930s in Utah. Members, living in communes, are concentrated in the Utah-Arizona border area in the Western United States, with their center in Colorado City, Arizona. There is also a commune in British Columbia, Canada.

Source:
Bradlee, B. Jr., and Van Atta, D. *Prophet of Blood*. New York: Putnam, 1981.

United Pentecostal Church

U.S. PENTECOSTAL group formed in 1945 through a merger of the Pentecostal Assemblies of Jesus Christ and the Pentecostal Church, Inc. Its doctrine is that of "oneness," rejecting Christian trinitarianism. There is a strict dress code and emphasis on modesty and the avoidance of worldly amusements.

United Pentecostal Faith Church

Canadian PENTECOSTAL group emphasizing healing and mission work overseas. It is affiliated with the FULL GOSPEL FELLOWSHIP OF CHURCHES AND MINISTRIES, INTERNATIONAL.

United Seventh-Day Brethren

U.S. ADVENTIST Sabbatarian group founded in 1947 in Oklahoma. Its doctrine emphasizes an Old Testament orientation and a denial of the immortality of the soul. [*See also* ADVENT CHRISTIAN CHURCH; *and* SEVENTH-DAY ADVENTIST CHURCH.]

Unity School of Christianity

Originally known as the Unity Society of Practical Christianity. This is a U.S. NEW THOUGHT-Christian group founded in 1903 by Charles Fillmore (1854–1948), who was influenced by Emma Curtis Hopkins, considered the mother of the NEW THOUGHT movement and spiritualism. The group teaches "practical Christianity," which means that it follows some Christian tenets, such as biblical authority and the divinity of Jesus Christ, but also espouses reincarnation as a step toward immortality. All individuals are considered to be potentially divine. [*See also* CHRISTIAN SCIENCE; DIVINE SCIENCE CHURCH; HOPKINS ASSOCIATION, EMMA C.; *and* RELIGIOUS SCIENCE.]

Sources:
Braden, C. S. *Spirits in Rebellion*. Dallas: SMU Press, 1963.

D'Andrade, H. *Charles Fillmore: Herald of the New Age*. New York: Harper & Row, 1974.

Universal Apostolic Church of Life

North American OLD CATHOLIC group started in 1955.

Universal Brotherhood

New Zealand MILLENARIAN commune founded by Fred Robinson in the 1960s.

Universal Brotherhood

U.S. THEOSOPHICAL group founded by Ureal Vercilli Charles, who heads the First Church of Spiritual Vision in New York City. The group claims to be guided by the Great White Brotherhood, considered to be an elite group that has attained a higher level of spiritual enlightenment.

Universal Brotherhood and Theosophical Society

U.S. THEOSOPHICAL organization, founded by Katherine Tingley (1847–1927) in 1898, after a dispute with Ernest Hargrove, the president of the Theosophical Society in America. In 1897 Mrs. Tingley organized the International Brotherhood League, a group that was active in charity and welfare work and gained much publicity during the Spanish-American War. Mrs. Tingley also founded the Point Loma community and school in San Diego, California, which was in existence from 1897 to 1942, graduating 2500 students. Gottfried de Purucker was Tingley's successor as head of the organization from 1929 until his death in 1942. He changed the organization's name to the Theosophical Society. After 1942 the organization headquarters were moved to Covina, near Los Angeles, and then in 1951 to Altadena, near Pasadena, California. THE UNITED LODGE OF THEOSOPHISTS was founded in 1909 by Robert Crosbie, who was rejected from the Brotherhood by Mrs. Tingley. [See also THEOSOPHY.]

Sources:

Campbell, B. F. *Ancient Wisdom Revived: A History of the Theosophical Movement.* Berkeley: University of California Press, 1980.

Greenwalt, E. A. *The Point Loma Community in California, 1897–1942: A Theosophical Experiment.* Berkeley: University of California Press, 1955.

Universal Christ Church

U.S. spiritualist group founded in 1970 in Los Angeles by Anthony Benik.

Universal Christian Spiritual Faith and Churches for All Nations

U.S. African American PENTECOSTAL church founded in 1952 through a merger of the NATIONAL DAVID SPIRITUAL TEMPLE OF CHRIST CHURCH UNION (INC.) U.S.A. with ST. PAUL'S SPIRITUAL CHURCH CONVOCATION, and with the KING DAVID'S SPIRITUAL TEMPLE OF TRUTH ASSOCIATION.

David William Short, who founded the National David Spiritual Temple of Christ Church Union (Inc.) U.S.A. in 1932, became leader of the new body. The group emphasizes faith healing and to a lesser extent speaking in tongues.

Universal Church

Brooklyn, N.Y., "New Age" group started in 1992. It is dedicated to the simulation of exorcism as a self-liberation process.

Universal Church of Aquaria

U.S. UFO-THEOSOPHICAL group founded in 1954 by Ernest L. Norman. The Universal Church of Aquaria started in New England and then expanded to branches in Detroit, Chicago, Toledo, Spokane, Los Angeles, Milwaukee, and several overseas locations. Astrology was central to the doctrine and practices of this group, which included a College of Astrology in southern California.

Universal Church of Scientific Truth

U.S. NEW THOUGHT group founded by Joseph T. Ferguson in Birmingham, Alabama, in the 1950s. It is affiliated with the Institute of Metaphysics and offers "metaphysical healing" and the attainment of a "superconscious mind."

Universal Church of the Kingdom of God

International PENTECOSTAL evangelical group founded in Rio de Janeiro, Brazil, in 1977 by Edir Macedo (1945–). The group practices faith healing and exorcisms for individuals "possessed by malignant spirits" and the Devil. North American branches were opened in 1986, when Macedo moved to the United States. Group headquarters are based in São Paolo, Brazil, and the group owns numerous business corporations and a television network in Brazil.

Universal Church of the Master

U.S. spiritualist group founded in Los Angeles, California, in 1908 by Robert Fitzgerald. [See also GENERAL ASSEMBLY OF SPIRITUALISTS; NATIONAL COLORED SPIRITUALIST ASSOCIATION OF CHURCHES; NATIONAL SPIRITUAL ALLIANCE; and NATIONAL SPIRITUALIST ASSOCIATION OF CHURCHES (NSAC).]

Universal Church, the Mystical Body of Christ

U.S. PENTECOSTAL, MILLENARIAN group founded in the 1970s by R. O. Frazier of Saginaw, Michigan. The doctrine calls for the creation of a Christian government to prepare for the end of times. A strict conduct code is followed, and faith healing is practiced.

Universal Faith and Wisdom Association

U.S. THEOSOPHICAL group founded by Enid Smith in Tonapah, Arizona. In the early 1970s it merged with UNDERSTANDING, INC.

Universal Faithists of Kosmon

Also known as Universal Brotherhood of Faithists or just Faithists. This is a messianic communal U.S. movement founded in 1883 in New York City by John Ballou Newbrough (1828–1891), dentist and spiritualist. Newbrough published in 1882 OAHSPE: A New Bible, which he said was dictated to him by angels. It contained a 78,000-year history of the earth, as well as "occurrences in the spiritual world" during the same time. During the Kosmon Era, which started in the

An exorcism is performed in a service of the Universal Church of the Kingdom of God, a Brazilian movement with branches in the United States.

nineteenth century, the world will be transformed into a heavenly kingdom. "The OAHSPE Bible is not a destroyer of old systems or religions, but reveals a new one adapted to this age wherein all mortals can be brothers and sisters. It speaks of the life and destiny of mankind, and unfolds the Character and Person of the Creator, along with those called Sons and Daughters of GOD." Followers study this scripture and have attempted to establish communes in the United States, Canada, and Great Britain. They are vegetarian and believe in nonviolence and "extrasensory vision." Subsidiary organizations have included the Kosmon Library, the Essenes of Kosmon, and the Faithist Farm. [*See also* ELOHISTS; *and* KOSMON MOVEMENT.]

Source:
Goodspeed, E. J. *Modern Apocrypha*. Boston: Beacon Press, 1956.

Universal Fellowship of Metropolitan Community Churches

U.S. Christian homosexual group founded in 1968 in Los Angeles by Troy D. Perry, a former minister of the CHURCH OF GOD OF PROPHECY. Branches have operated in Latin America, Europe, Africa, and Australia.

Universal Great Brotherhood AUM Solar Line

International THEOSOPHICAL group with headquarters in Mexico City. It was founded in 1948 by Serge Raynaud de la Ferriere (1916–1962). "Its goal is the re-education of humanity toward world peace through a synthesis of science and religion, emphasizing the techniques of yoga, meditation, cosmobiology, t'ai chi, I-Ching, karate, Qabbalah, psychology, and art." Branches have operated in the United States and Mexico.

Universal Hagar Spiritual Church

U.S. African American spiritualist group founded in 1923 by George Willie Hurley (1884–1942). Hurley's teachings combined Christianity, spiritualism, astrology, and other aspects of occultism. He claimed to be God incarnate. He also claimed that African Americans (referred to as "Ethiopians") were the true Jews, descendants of the Biblical Israelites.

Source:
Baer, H. A. *The Black Spiritual Movement: A Religious Response to Racism*. Knoxville: University of Tennessee Press, 1984.

Universal Harmony Foundation

U.S. spiritualist group founded in 1942 by J. Bertran and Helene Gerling. It was first known as the Universal Psychic Science Association. It is based in Seminole, Florida, where it operates a seminary. [*See also* GENERAL ASSEMBLY OF SPIRITUALISTS; NATIONAL COLORED SPIRITUALIST ASSOCIATION OF CHURCHES; NATIONAL SPIRITUAL ALLIANCE; *and* NATIONAL SPIRITUALIST ASSOCIATION OF CHURCHES (NSAC).]

Universal Life (Universelles Leben)

Also known as the Homebringing Mission of Jesus Christ (Heimholungs-werk Jesu Christi). This is an international Christian group founded in 1975 (and officially incorporated in 1984) by Gabrielle Wittek, known as the teaching prophetess of the Lord. She was born in Germany in 1931 to a Catholic family. Following her mother's death in 1970, she began having visions and hearing voices; starting in 1975 she reported messages from God and his angels, as well as from Jesus Christ. In addition to Christianity, Hindu ideas such as karma have been adopted. Universal Life teaches holistic medicine and operates its own treatment center, Haus der Gesundheit, a *Naturklinik* offering revitalization treatment.

Members practice meditation and spiritual healing. The group operates the Inner Spirit-of-Christ Churches (ISOCC). Branches have opened in South Africa, Australia, the United States, Israel, Italy, and Spain.

Universal Life Church

U.S. "mail-order" church, founded in the 1960s by Kirby J. Hensley, and offering ordination to all interested individuals.

Universal Link

British Christian spiritualist group started in April 1961 as the result of a revelation experienced by Richard Grave of Worthing, England. In this experience Grave saw a "Christlike figure." A series of messages proclaiming the Second Coming followed. At one point, an exact date of Christmas 1967 was given. Followers study these revelations and expect the Millennium soon.

Universal Peace Institute

U.S. NEW THOUGHT group founded in Mount Rose, Pennsylvania, in 1934 by Lillian K. Daniel.

Universal Prayer Fellowship

British PENTECOSTAL group with membership of West African immigrants. Its practices emphasize faith healing and fasting.

Universal Shrine of Divine Guidance

U.S. Christian-occultist group founded by Mark Karras in 1966.

Universal Spiritualist Association

U.S. spiritualist group founded in 1956 by Clifford Bias and others after a schism in the Spiritualist Episcopal Church. In doctrine the new group was similar to the old one, namely Christian spiritualism.

Universal Spiritual League of America

Informally known as "Meher Baba Lovers," this U.S. group, devoted to the personality and teaching of Meher Baba, had its beginnings in the 1930s, when North Americans first came in contact with the Indian Meher Baba movement. The group has been active in publishing Meher Baba literature. [*See also* THE BABA LEAGUE; MEHER BABA, FRIENDS OF; MEHER DURBAR; *and* SUFISM REORIENTED.]

Universal Spiritual Temple of the New Era—Temple of Celestial Light

Also known as Luz Celestial, Inc., this is a U.S. Christian-occultist group founded in the 1980s by Tanja Nahoum in Queens, New York. Practices include "channeling" and receiving messages from "Master Jesus, Master Saint Germain, Master El Morya and others."

Universal Truth Foundation

U.S. syncretistic group based in Phoenix, Arizona. It was founded in the early 1970s and combines Western and Hindu traditions. Practice focuses on Hindu meditation.

Universal World Church

U.S. PENTECOSTAL group based in Los Angeles. It was founded in 1952 by O. L. Jaggars. The group has operated the University of the World Church.

Universariun Foundation

U.S. UFO-THEOSOPHICAL group founded in 1958 in Portland, Oregon, by Zelrun Karsleigh. Messages are reported from the spirit world and from "ascended masters." Group doctrine is similar to that of "I AM."

University Bible Fellowship

U.S. FUNDAMENTALIST group started in the 1970s. It has been accused of isolating members from friends and family.

University of Life Church

U.S. occultist group based in Phoenix, Arizona, and founded in the early 1960s by Richard Ireland. The founder first claimed to be able to communicate with souls of the dead and gave public demonstrations of telepathy. In the 1970s the group started offering meditation classes.

University of Metaphysics

U.S. NEW THOUGHT group founded by Mary Pendergast and based in Portland, Oregon. This group is a continuation of the activities of Albert C. Grier, the founder of the CHURCH OF THE TRUTH.

University of the Science of Spirit

U.S. dissident CHRISTIAN SCIENCE group started around 1890 in Chicago by Edward J. Arens.

University of the Trees

U.S. mystical group founded by Christopher Hills and based in Boulder Creek, California. Beliefs and practices were a combination of Christian, Hindu, and Tibetan Buddhist traditions.

Unorganized Italian Christian Churches of North America

U.S. PENTECOSTAL group started by Louis Francescon, who conducted evangelical work among Italian immigrants in Chicago in 1904. The group was organized in 1927, incorporated in 1948, and later merged with the ITALIAN PENTECOSTAL ASSEMBLIES OF GOD to form the CHRISTIAN CHURCH OF NORTH AMERICA.

Urantia Foundation

Also known as the Urantia Brotherhood. This is a U.S. Christian-occultist group headquartered in Chicago. Its teachings are contained in the 2,097-page *Urantia Book*, published in 1955 by Bill Sadler, Jr. The book is said to complete the Christian New Testament. It describes the history of the Earth (Urantia), the galaxy around it, and the life of Jesus Christ. It suggests a universe of seven levels, headed by a Trinity of Trinities. The center of the universe is the Isle of Paradise. All celestial and terrestrial beings are in a process of evolving into a universal consciousness. Members of this group usually keep their membership in established Christian churches. Related organizations include the Second Society Foundation and the Jesusonian Foundation. Some branches of this group have operated in Europe.

Urersa Reflective Center

California branch of the URANTIA FOUNDATION founded by A. D. Thorington in Encino in the 1960s.

V

Vajradhatu

Sometimes known as the Vajradhatu International Buddhist Church. This is a North American Tibetan Buddhist group, officially descended from the Tibetan Kargyupa, Kagyu, and Nyingma sects of Vajrayana Buddhism. It was founded by Chogyam Trungpa Rinpoche (1939–1986), also known as Vidyadhara. After leaving Tibet in 1959 Trungpa settled in the United Kingdom. In 1967 he became the head of a monastery in Scotland, and in 1970 he moved to the United States. Vajradhatu was officially formed in 1973, and in 1974 Trungpa founded the Naropa Institute, (named after the medieval Buddhist holy man Naropa), a teaching center for disciples and the general public operated by the Nalanda Foundation (named after the legendary medieval Buddhist University of Nalanda). The Naropa Institute granted B.A. and M.A. degrees for the first time in 1977. In 1976 Trungpa named a successor, Thomas Rich, who took the name Osel Tendzin. Tendzin became the leader, or "dharma heir of Vidyadhara," upon Trungpa's death in 1986. In March, 1989, Osel Tendzin was accused of having sexual relations with disciples and of knowingly transmitting the AIDS virus among them. He was asked to resign from his position; he died in 1990. Since 1993 the group's leader has been Osel Mukpo, son of Chogyam Trungpa.

Vajradhatu has offered an eclectic, Westernized version of Tibetan Buddhism created by its founder. Contrary to the widely held image of the Buddhist monk, Trungpa was visibly noncelibate, drank alcohol quite heavily, enjoyed meat, and smoked tobacco. For spiritual reasons he objected to the use of marijuana. Trungpa is believed by followers to have been an incarnation of Trungpa Tulku, an old Tibetan master.

Vajradhatu headquarters are known as Karma Dzong, and regional centers are known as Dharmadhatus or Dharma Study Groups (DSG). The group's retreat center in Vermont is known as Karme-Choling (formerly Tail of the Tiger). Vajradhatu has operated the Maitri Center for Psychology, which used Tibetan meditation techniques, known as Maitri, for the treatment of psychological disorders. In the 1970s the group operated more than 150 business enterprises, including law firms, medical clinics, and investment corporations.

Sources:

Clark, T. *The Great Naropa Poetry Wars.* Santa Barbara, Calif.: Cadmus Editions, 1980.

Cox, H. *Turning East: The Promises and Peril of the New Orientalism.* New York: Simon & Schuster, 1977.

Vajrapani Institute for Wisdom Culture

International Tibetan Buddhist group "under the guidance of Lama Thubten Yeshe and Lama Thubten Zopa Rinpoche" with branches in Europe and the United States.

Vedanta Society

Known in the United States as the American Vedanta Society and internationally as the Ramakrishna Mission in the West, this is an international Hindu revival movement. The name Vedanta literally means the concluding portions of the ancient Hindu Veda scriptures; more broadly it applies to all literature and tradition derived from the Vedas. This group is made up of Western followers of ancient Hindu traditions.

The Vedanta Society was founded in the United States by Swami Vivekananda, who arrived in the country for the World Congress of Religions, held in Chicago in 1893. The Society was formally started in 1894 in New York City by Vivekananda and Francis (later Lord) Leggett. It is actually the Western branch of the RAMAKRISHNA MATH AND MISSION, founded in India in the nineteenth century, and its strongest base is in California. Its best-known Hindu leader was Swami Prabhavananda, and its best-known Western members were Aldous Huxley and Christopher Isherwood.

"The fundamental truths of Vedanta are that the Godhead, the underlying reality, is omnipresent within each of us, within every creature and object, so man in his true nature is God; it is the purpose of man's life on earth to unfold and manifest this Godhead, which is eternally existent within him, but hidden; and truth is universal in that men seek the Godhead in various ways, but what they all seek is the same." Followers practice "a combination of jnana, karma and raja yoga." The Vedanta Society in the United States is officially under the guidance of the Ramakrishna Order of India. Other branches operate in Argentina, Canada, France, the Netherlands, Russia, Switzerland, and Great Britain. [*See also* ANANDA ASHRAMA; *and* RAMAKRISHNA VEDANTA CENTRE.]

Sources:

Damrell, J. *Seeking Spiritual Meaning: The World of Vedanta*. Beverly Hills, Calif.: Sage, 1977.

Isherwood, C. *Ramakrishna and His Disciples*. New York: Simon & Schuster, 1965.

Jackson, C. T. *Vedanta for the West: The Ramakrishna Movement in the United States*. Bloomington: Indiana University Press, 1994.

Vedic Church of East Africa

Hindu movement that represents the African branch of ARYA SAMAJ; it operates in Indian communities.

Vedic Cultural Center

Sometimes known as the Vedantic Cul-

Aldous Huxley, noted English writer, who was a member of the Hindu Vedanta Society.

Swami Prabhavananda, leader of the California-based Vedanta Society.

tural Society, this is a Hindu group incorporating the former INTERNATIONAL SOCIETY FOR KRISHNA CONSCIOUSNESS (ISKCON) temple in Berkeley, California. It was founded by Srila Hansadutta Swami, formerly Hans Kary, after his excommunication from ISKCON in 1983. The reason for his exclusion from ISKCON was his advocacy of the use of weapons and his continuing possession of weapons, which led to his arrest in 1980. Hansadutta was arrested again in 1983 after being involved in a shooting incident.

Venturism

U.S. belief system created by members of the American Cryonics Society, Inc. in the 1980s. Cryonics refers to the practice of freezing a dead body in order to preserve it for revival at some future date. Venturism is committed to the elimination of death.

Vimala Prakashan Trust

Also known as the Friends of Vimala Thakar or the Vimala Thakar Foundation. This is an international, Western-oriented, Hindu group founded in the 1960s by Vimala Thakar and dedicated to spreading her teachings. Thakar has been close to KRISHNAMURTI, and her beliefs are similar to his. Branches have operated in the United States and Europe.

Vineyard Christian Fellowship

U.S. evangelical, charismatic group started in 1982 in Anaheim, California, by John Wimber. It is an outgrowth of CALVARY CHAPEL and several JESUS MOVEMENT groups and has branches (known as "vineyards") in North and South America.

Vishwa Hindu Parishad (VHP)

Known also as Hindu Visva Parisad, this is a Hindu revival organization founded in 1964 and serving as an umbrella organization for many religious groups. Its aim is a united Hindu India, and it operates also in Indian communities abroad. In December 1992 it was declared illegal by the Indian government, following inter-religious rioting that killed thousands.

Voice of Calvary

U.S. Christian FUNDAMENTALIST commune located in Mississippi. It was founded in the 1970s.

Voice of Daniel

Known as Silon Daniel, this is a syncretistic Melanesian group. It was started in 1932 on Raga and Pentecost islands of the New Hebrides by Daniel Tambe, a former Anglican lay reader who followed instructions received in a vision.

Voice of Elijah, Inc.

U.S. evangelical, MILLENARIAN group. It was founded in 1970 in Spokane, Washington, by Carl and Sandra Parks, who were inspired by the contemporary JESUS MOVEMENT.

Voice of Prophecy Church

African indigenous PENTECOSTAL Sabbatarian church started in 1960 by

Susanna Nyabulwa in the Luo group of Kenya.

Voice of Salvation and Healing Church

African indigenous PENTECOSTAL church started in 1954 in the Luo group of Kenya. Faith healing and glossolalia are emphasized.

Volunteers of America

U.S. Christian FUNDAMENTALIST group founded in 1896 by Marshall Ballington Booth and Maud Booth, the son and daughter-in-law of William Booth, the founder of the SALVATION ARMY. The younger Booth had served as National Commander of the Salvation Army in the United States but resigned in 1891 after a disagreement with his father. The group follows the doctrine and practices of the Salvation Army and provides social service programs throughout the United States.

Vrai Église Catholique

French schismatic Catholic group started in 1964. It has established branches in Belgium.

Wakorino

A group of African independent Christian PENTECOSTAL churches formed among the Kikuyu of Kenya between the 1920s and the 1960s. In most churches, members wear white turbans, but in the HOLY SPIRIT CHURCH OF ZAYUN they wear red or blue turbans. These churches developed out of the Watu wa Mungu and the Aroti movements. The Wakorino group of churches includes the AFRICAN MISSION OF HOLY GHOST CHURCH; CHOSEN CHURCH OF THE HOLY SPIRIT OF KENYA; CHRISTIAN HOLY GHOST CHURCH OF EAST AFRICA; HOLY GHOST CHURCH OF EAST AFRICA; and the KENYA FOUNDATION OF THE PROPHETS CHURCH.

Waldorf Institute

U.S. ANTHROPOSOPHY group based in Spring Valley, New York, with branches in California. It operates the Threefold Educational Foundation and the Fellowship Community, as well as Anthroposophy study courses and teacher training programs, known as Sunbridge College.

Walk (Church of the Living Word), The

U.S. FUNDAMENTALIST, occultist, "New Testament Church" based in California. It was founded in 1954 by John Robert Stevens (1919–1983). The founder, known as the Apostle, was raised in Washington, Iowa, by a FOURSQUARE GOSPEL CHURCH family. The group has regularly published revelations received by the Apostle, which deal with psychic experiences, auras, astrology, and spiritualism. The group's doctrine emphasizes the imminence of the Second Coming.

Watchman Healing Mission

Also known as Church of the Watchtower, People of the Watchman (Bamulonda), and the People of Jehovah and Michael. Started in 1937, this is a Zambian independent Christian communal movement inspired by the WATCH TOWER MOVEMENT of Elliot Kamwana in Malawi. Its members live in communal villages.

Watchtower

Sometimes known as the Independent Watchtower. This is an African MILLENARIAN movement founded by Jeremiah Gondwe, leader of a "holy village" in Northern Rhodesia (now Zambia) around 1940. Since then, the movement has spread to the Congo (now Zaire) and Rhodesia (now Zimbabwe). The movement caused rebellions in what were then the European colonies of Northern Rhodesia, Nyasaland, and Belgian Congo.

Watch Tower Movement

Also known as the Kamwana Movement. This is an African MILLENARIAN movement inspired by JEHOVAH'S WITNESSES. It was started in 1907 in Nyasaland (now Malawi) by Elliot Kamwana. The leader was exposed to the Witnesses' ideas in South Africa, and he brought to Nyasaland a message of an impending New Age in which Africans would take over from Europeans and taxes would be abolished. Enthusiasm for the "American" message of the Witnesses was possibly nourished by the belief that all Americans were African Americans, who would arrive in airplanes to deliver native Africans from oppression. The founder was deported by British authorities in 1909, and the movement ended. Nevertheless, Kamwana's movement served as the direct or indirect inspiration for other movements, such as Kitawala.

Source:

Kaufmann, R. *Millenarisme et Acculturation.* Bruxelles: Universite Libre de Bruxelles, 1963.

Watchtower Movement

Sometimes known as the Church of the Watch Tower. This is an African indigenous movement that started as a branch of the Watchtower Bible and Tract Society (JEHOVAH'S WITNESSES) and then became independent. The movement's leaders were Hanoc Sindano, Leviticus Kanjele, and Shadrach Sinkala, and the movement's center was in Tukamulozya. Sindano preached the coming End and called on his listeners to be saved and baptized, so that they would enjoy peace and prosperity when the End came. Then the unbaptized would die, and the whites would be defeated. A major practice was glossolalia (speaking in tongues), known locally as *chongo*. Between 1917–1919 members of the Watchtower started a rebellion in Northern Rhodesia (now Zambia). More than one hundred activists were sentenced following the end of this rebellion.

Way International, Inc., The

Sometimes known as the Way Bible Research Institute. This is a U.S. FUNDAMENTALIST group founded in 1953 by Victor Paul Wierwille (1918–1985) when he started teaching a course called Power for Abundant Living, based on his reinterpretation of the New Testament. Officially, the group dates its existence from 1942, when Wierwille claimed he had a divine revelation. In 1951 he spoke in tongues for the first time. In the early 1950s he started to practice faith healing and led speaking in tongues sessions. In the late 1960s Wierwille was active in California and gained followers there. In October 1982 L. Craig Martindale, born in 1950, became the second president of the organization, and Wierwille retired. Defined as a "Biblical research and teaching ministry," the group has its headquarters in New Knoxville, Ohio, and branches all over the world. It is especially active in Latin America, Great Britain, and Western Europe.

The group's doctrines differ from Orthodox Christianity in many details, including in their interpretation of the text of the New Testament. Wierwille, who did not believe in the divinity of Jesus Christ, stated that Jesus Christ, "the Promised Seed," was born on Wednesday, September 11, 3 B.C.E., between the hours of 6:15 and 7:45 p.m. He also expressed strong anti-Communist, anti-Catholic, and anti-Semitic views, resulting in several public controversies. Members are encouraged to live communally, and are charged fees for participating in the thirty-six-hour Power for Abundant Living courses. The course contents include materials and ideas taken from Dale Carnegie as well as aerobic exercises.

In 1979 The Way International was listed by Dun & Bradstreet as a "well-established business." In 1980 it was reported to have assets in excess of $12 million, including a corporate jet used in worldwide travel.

Way of the Cross Church

U.S. African American PENTECOSTAL group founded in 1927 by Henry C. Brooks and based in Washington, D.C.

Weg Der Mitte

European Buddhist group based in Berlin and founded by Daya Mullins in the 1970s.

Welt-Spirale

European THEOSOPHICAL group founded by Leopold Brandstätter (1915–1968) and inspired by the AGNI YOGA SOCIETY.

Weni Mwanguvu

Also known as the Miracle Revival Fellowship Pente Church, this is an African Independent Pentecostal group founded in 1948 by secession from the Anglican Church.

Wesleyan Methodist Church of Brazil

Brazilian PENTECOSTAL organization founded in the 1940s. In 1983 it became affiliated with the INTERNATIONAL PENTECOSTAL HOLINESS CHURCH.

Wesleyan Pentecostal Church

PENTECOSTAL group in Chile. It was founded in 1970 by Victor Manuel Mora, who was also active in the Socialist Party of Chile.

Western Bible Students Association

This group, based in Seattle, Washington, is the West Coast branch of the CHRISTIAN BELIEVERS CONFERENCE.

Western Buddhist Order

Western Buddhist group active in Europe. It was founded in the 1970s.

Westminster Biblical Fellowship

U.S. FUNDAMENTALIST group founded in 1969 when a group of members left the BIBLE PRESBYTERIAN CHURCH in protest against the leadership of Carl McIntire.

Westmoreland Chapel

U.S. FUNDAMENTALIST congregation based in Los Angeles. It constitutes one U.S. branch of the HONOR OAK CHRISTIAN FELLOWSHIP CENTRE. Its founder, Carl B. Harrison, served earlier with the Honor Oak Centre. [*See also* THIS TESTIMONY.]

White Eagle Lodge

Sometimes known as the Church of the White Eagle Lodge, this is an international spiritualist, occultist-Christian group based in England. It was founded in 1934 by Grace Cooke (?–1979). The leader served as a medium for the messages from the spirit world; her contact was White Eagle, a "Red Indian" and a member of the "White Brotherhood," a group that teaches five cosmic laws: reincarnation, cause and effect, opportunity, correspondence, and equilibrium. Published in several books since the 1950s, messages are also received from the "Interplanetary Brotherhood." Members practice astrology and faith healing. Branches have operated in Europe, North America, and Africa.

White Star

U.S. UFO group based in Joshua Tree, California, and founded in 1957 by Doris C. LaVesque. Messages from the spirit world and from UFO "command centers" are reported.

Wicca

General term for the belief system of neo-paganism and witchcraft.

Wisdom Institute of Spiritual Education

U.S. NEW THOUGHT group founded by Frank and Martha Baker in Dallas, Texas, in the 1950s. It offers "perfection of the spirit, mind, and body."

Wisdom's Goldenrod Center for Philosophic Studies

U.S. THEOSOPHICAL syncretistic group founded in 1972 by Anthony Damiani (1922–1984) in upstate New York. It is devoted to the teachings of Paul Brunton. [See also BRUNTON (PAUL) PHILOSOPHIC FOUNDATION.]

Wokofu African Church

East African independent FUNDAMEN-

TALIST church. It was started in 1966 by secession from the SALVATION ARMY.

Won Buddhism

Korean syncretistic movement. Started in 1924 as a Buddhist renewal attempt, it then developed to combine Buddhist and Christian elements. Its monks are allowed to marry, and women are allowed active roles in the ritual, which is Western in syle.

Word Foundation

U.S. occultist group founded in 1950. It is devoted to distributing the revelations (which started in 1893) of Harold M. Percival (1868–1953), an early THEOSO-PHIST.

Word of Faith Ministries

U.S. Christian NEW THOUGHT group founded by Jim Kaseman in the 1970s. The group promotes "Positive Thinking," which is supposed to counter the effects of "Satan's work" in this world. It is connected with the WORD OF LIFE CHURCH in Sweden. Its branches have appeared since 1990 in the Baltic countries of Lithuania and Latvia.

Word of God

U.S. FUNDAMENTALIST, charismatic group that grew out of the CATHOLIC CHARISMATIC RENEWAL movement. It was founded by Steve Clark and Ralph Martin, former Catholic activists, in Ann Arbor, Michigan, in 1967. It started as an organization of Roman Catholic charismatic households, in which married couples, singles, nuns, and priests lived communally. The group today practices what is known as SHEPHERDING or "discipleship," which provides an authoritarian leadership style and close supervision of members. This style has been the basis of the "shepherding movement," which includes the BODY OF CHRIST, CHRISTIAN GROWTH MINISTRIES, and CHRISTIAN RESTORATION MINISTRIES. In the early 1970s, Word of God became connected with the Christian Growth Ministries.

Members of the Word of God, who mostly come from a Roman Catholic background, are required to tithe. Exorcisms known as "deliverances" are often practiced. Members are also told to prepare for a coming apocalypse, and some of them have committed themselves to celibacy. Word of God operates the Sword of the Spirit, an international subsidiary; it was formed in 1983 and has branches around the world. Through its own subsidiaries, the Sword of the Spirit is said to support various right-wing political causes around the world. [See also NEW YORK CHURCH OF CHRIST.]

Word of Life Church (Livets Ord)

Swedish Christian NEW THOUGHT group founded in 1983 by Ulf Ekman, a former Church of Sweden minister. The group emphasizes "Positive Thinking" and believes in faith healing and exorcism. There is also a strong emphasis on material prosperity through faith. The group's inspiration comes from Norman Vincent Peale, Robert H. Schuller, Yongi Cho, and Kenneth Hagin. It has engaged in missionary work in Eastern Europe. [See also "FAITH" MOVEMENT; and WORD OF FAITH MINISTRIES.]

Workers Together with Elohim

Established in 1975 by Charles Andy Dugger, son of A. N. Dugger, founder of the CHURCH OF GOD (JERUSALEM). Following the elder Dugger's death, the son was accused of both doctrinal deviation and adultery and was removed from his father's church.

Work of Christ

U.S. charismatic communal group that grew out of the CATHOLIC CHARISMATIC RENEWAL movement. It was founded in the early 1970s in Lansing, Michigan. It is connected to the WORD OF GOD group.

World Catalyst Church

U.S. occultist group founded in 1967 in Butte, Montana. Its practices focus on meditation.

World Christian Soldiers Church

African indigenous Christian movement started in 1966 in the Luo people of Kenya.

World Community Service

Hindu revival group founded in Madras, India, in 1958 by Vethathiri Maharaj. The group is devoted to the practice of kundalini yoga, which strives to unleash the energy that rests at the base of the spine. The founder has developed new techniques known as Simplified Kundalini Yoga. Branches have operated in North America. [See also TEMPLE OF UNIVERSAL PEACE.]

World Congress of Faiths

British ecumenical group founded in 1936 by Francis Younghusband. It "brings together the committed followers of the great religions, as well as those who are 'seekers,' in an international movement of all who cherish spiritual values." The group is active in organizing and sponsoring numerous interreligious events in Great Britain and elsewhere.

World Insight

Founded by Kenneth Storey and Gary Arvidson in 1974, this group was created as a result of the schisms in the WORLDWIDE CHURCH OF GOD.

World Institute of Avasthology

U.S. THEOSOPHICAL group founded by Benito F. Reyes in Ojai, California, in the 1980s.

World Messianity

U.S. branch of SEKAI KYUSEI KYO (SKK—WORLD MESSIANIC ASSOCIATION), a Japanese new religion. Its doctrine is monotheistic, and members expect imminent world salvation. Faith healing is practiced.

World Renewal, Incorporated

Initially known as the Berean Fellowship International, this U.S. PENTECOSTAL group was founded in 1963 by Warren Litzman in Dallas, Texas. Mission centers are operated overseas. The group doctrine emphasizes speaking in tongues.

World Teacher, The

Also known as the Tara Center and informally as Christ Maitreya. This British occultist group was started in 1980 by Benjamin Creme (1922–), a follower of the Arcane School since the 1950s. According to Creme, Maitreya or "The Christ" (or "the Messiah, Krishna, the Imam Mahdi, the 5th Buddha") appeared in this world on July 19, 1977, and has been living in Great Britain "as an apparently ordinary man in the Asian community of London." The Maitreya had formed his intention to return to the world in June 1945, and was supposed to reveal himself in 1982. [*See also* LUCIS TRUST.]

World Teacher Trust

International Hindu-oriented movement founded in India in 1971 by Ekkirala Krishnamacharya (1926–1984). It proclaims the imminent coming of the World Teacher.

Worldwide Church of God

U.S. Christian FUNDAMENTALIST group founded by Herbert W. Armstrong (1893–1986). Armstrong had been ordained in the Oregon Conference of the Church of God (Seventh-Day) in 1931. Three years later, he formed his own organization, the Radio Church of God, in Eugene, Oregon. He also started publishing *The Plain Truth* magazine, which is distributed free of charge and known by now to tens of millions around the world. His radio broadcast "The World Tomorrow" has been among the first in the emerging field of electronic media preaching. In 1947 the church founded

Members of the Worldwide Church of God stage a sit-in demonstration in California during legal disputes over financial contributions.

Ambassador College, located at church headquarters in Pasadena, California.

In doctrine, the Worldwide Church of God emphasizes Old Testament law and rejects major Christian holidays (Christmas and Easter) as pagan. The Christian idea of the Trinity is also rejected. Moreover, the church also celebrates the seven Old Testament feasts of Passover, Pentecost, Trumpets, Atonement, Tabernacles, the Last Great Day, and the First Day of the Sacred Year. The founder referred to himself as "God's Chosen Apostle." Quite early, Armstrong also adopted BRITISH ISRAELISM, the belief that the "ten lost tribes" mentioned in the Old Testament were the ancestors of "Anglo-Saxon peoples." Members are told to

avoid modern medicine, considered "pagan worship," and to offer tithes to the Church. Until 1976 Armstrong taught that remarried members of the Church should divorce their second spouse and remarry the first. After this teaching was repealed, he married a divorced woman.

In the early 1970s the church was torn by schisms, and at least seven splinter groups were formed. Garner Ted Armstrong, the founder's son and righthand man, was accused of sexual immorality, and Armstrong himself was accused of financial corruption. In 1978 Garner Ted Armstrong was excommunicated, and he founded CHURCH OF GOD, INTERNATIONAL. In 1978 the Worldwide Church was the subject of government investigations and a lawsuit by the State of California, after dissidents complained about the handling of financial contributions. After the Church went into receivership in 1979, the charges were dropped. [*See also* ASSOCIATED CHURCHES OF GOD; CHURCH OF GOD (CLEVELAND, TENNESSEE); CHURCH OF GOD, THE ETERNAL; CHURCH OF GOD SEVENTH ERA; FOUNDATION FOR BIBLICAL RESEARCH; GENERAL CONFERENCE OF THE CHURCH OF GOD (SEVENTH DAY); TWENTIETH CENTURY CHURCH OF GOD; *and* WORLD INSIGHT.

Wrekin Trust, The

British group founded by George Trevelyan in 1971 "to meet the needs of the growing number of people who are now searching for a deeper understanding of the spiritual worldview."

X

Xat American Indian Medicine Society

U.S. group devoted to the preservation and propagation of Native American religious traditions. It operates the CENTER OF FIRST LIGHT.

Y

Yahweh's Temple

Known until 1981 as the Jesus Church. This is a U.S. PENTECOSTAL group founded in 1947 in Cleveland, Tennessee, by Samuel E. Officer, a former member of the CHURCH OF GOD (CLEVELAND, TENNESSEE). Its doctrine combines ADVENTIST, Sabbatarian, and SACRED NAME MOVEMENT elements.

Yaliwan's Movement

New Guinea indigenous movement (CARGO CULT) started by Matthias Yaliwan, or Yeliwan (1930–) in the Wewak region, near Sepik, in Papua New Guinea. In 1971 Yaliwan led 60,000 followers to a mountaintop in the expectation of finding a buried cargo. In March 1972, he was elected to the Papua New Guinea House of Assembly by a majority of 7,200 to 435 votes. The leader since then has disavowed any Cargo beliefs.

Yasodhara Ashram Society

North American Western Hindu group. It was founded in 1956 by Sylvia Hellman (1911–), also known as Swami Sivananda Radha, who was a disciple of Swami Sivananda Saraswati in the Sivananda Ashram in Rishikesh, India. The group's doctrine centers around various yoga traditions. It is based in British Columbia and is built around a core of disciples committed to the monastic life. Branches, known as Shambalah Houses, have operated in North America and England.

Yeshe Nyingpo

U.S. Tibetan Buddhist group founded in 1976. It is devoted to the teachings of its founder, known as His Holiness Dudjom, Rinpoche, "head of the Nyingmapa order of Tibetan Buddhism." It is based in New York City.

Yeshe Nyingpo Argyen Cho Dhing

West Coast center of YESHE NYINGPO ORGYEN CHO DZONG.

Yeshe Nyingpo Orgyen Cho Dzong

U. S. Tibetan Buddhist group, founded in 1976, and devoted to the teachings of its founder, known as His Holiness Dudjom, Rinpoche, "head of the Nyingmapa order of Tibetan Buddhism." It has been based in New York City.

Yoga House

U.S. Hindu group founded by Dadaji Vimalananda (1942–) in the 1970s. Practices include meditation and chanting.

Yoga Institute of Consciousness

U.S. Tibetan Buddhist-oriented group founded in the 1960s by Jessica Lynott (1930–), known also as Swami Savitri Priza.

Yogi Gupta Ashram, Inc.

U.S. Hindu group founded in 1954 and based in New York City. It is devoted to spreading the teachings of Yogi Gupta (also known as Swami Kailashnanada), the founder of the Kailashnanada Mission in Rishikesh, India. Doctrine stresses the practice of yoga exercises and vegetarianism.

Yogiraj

U.S. Hindu group, devoted to the teachings of Swami Swanandashram (1921–), which focus on the practice of yoga exercises. This group became a part of the HOLY SHANKACHARYA ORDER in the late 1970s.

Yogoda Satsanga Society

Hindu group founded in 1918 in India by Paramahansa Yogananda (1893–1952); it is based on the Yogoda yoga technique developed by him. Yogananda later founded the SELF-REALIZATION FELLOWSHIP in the United States.

Yoido Full Gospel (Pentecostal) Church

Korean PENTECOSTAL group founded in the 1960s and based in Seoul.

Yoruba Lacumi

U.S. group founded by Luisa Teish in the 1970s. It claims to maintain African traditions of Yoruba magic and religion.

Young Nak Presbyterian Church

Korean independent PENTECOSTAL group founded in the 1950s.

Your Heritage

U.S. BRITISH ISRAELIST, white supremacist group founded by Bertrand L. Comparet and based in San Diego, California.

Z

Zion Apostolic Church of South Africa

South African independent indigenous "ZIONIST" church founded around 1914 in Johannesburg by Elias Mahlangu (1881–1960).

Zion Apostolic Faith Mission

South African indigenous "ZIONIST" church. Founded in 1917 by Edward Lion in Basutoland, it has spread to other countries in Southern Africa.

Source:
Sundkler, B. G. M. *Zulu Zion and Some Swazi Zionists.* London: Oxford University Press, 1976.

Zion Apostolic in Jerusalem Church

South African indigenous "ZIONIST" church founded in 1925. Membership is of the Zulu, and its main emphasis is on healing practices. Branches operate in the nations of southern Africa.

Zion Apostolic Swazi Church of South Africa

South African independent indigenous "ZIONIST" church. It was founded in 1918 in Johannesburg by Josiah Mlangeni and Mzimela, two Swazi preachers in dissent from the ZION APOSTOLIC CHURCH OF SOUTH AFRICA.

Zion Christian Church (ZCC)

South African indigenous "ZIONIST" church founded in 1925 by Ingatius Lekganyane (?–1948) near Pietersburg, Northern Transvaal. The founder, who named his first son Jesus, was known as a miraculous healer and respected as a god.

ZCC has become the leading organization among independent South African churches, and its festivals at Zion City Moriah are occasions for visits by government leaders. Church branches have operated in other southern Africa nations.

Sources:
Sundkler, B. G. M. *Bantu Prophets in South Africa.* London: Oxford University Press, 1961.

———. *Zulu Zion and Some Swazi Zionists.* London: Oxford University Press, 1976.

Zion Free Church Impumalanga Gospel of South Africa

South African indigenous "ZIONIST" church. It was founded by Job S. Mtanti in 1910 in response to the passing of Halley's Comet. He reported then that the Holy Spirit had descended on him.

"Zionists"

Collective name denoting numerous (2,500 by some estimates) syncretistic movements in South Africa that are noted for their practices of faith healing, speaking in tongues, and traditional African purification rites, as well as for the central role of their founders-prophets. Many use the terms "Zion," "Apostolic,"

"Pentecostal," and "Faith" in their names. These churches are all tied to the influence of the CHRISTIAN CATHOLIC APOSTOLIC CHURCH, of Zion City, Illinois, which carried out mission work in South Africa around the turn of the century. Historically, they were separatists within their own communities and were described as antiwhite. [*See also* "ETHIOPIANS".]

Zion Messianic Fellowship

Canadian HEBREW CHRISTIAN group started in the 1960s and based in Vancouver.

Zion's Order of the Sons of Levi

U.S. dissident MORMON group. It was founded in 1951 by Marl Kilgore, a former member of the AARONIC ORDER, in Bicknell, Utah, and later based near Mansfield, Missouri. Doctrine is based on standard Mormon teachings and additional revelations through Kilgore.

Zion Prophets Church

Zambian independent Christian church that approves of traditional polygyny and enjoys much political influence.

Ziwezano Church

African independent Christian church started around 1960 among the Manyika of Zimbabwe.

ALTERNATE GROUP NAMES INDEX

The Alternate Group Names Index includes former and alternate names, as well as acronyms and nicknames. If you are wondering which group is associated with the acronym 3HO, or where you can find information on the Freedomites within this encyclopedia, you would find the answers in this index.

A

A/G, *see* Assemblies of God

A.A. Allen Revivals, Inc., *see* Miracle Revival Fellowship

AAC, *see* Advanced Ability Center

AACJM, *see* African Apostolic Church of Johane Maranke

AAIII, *see* Ahmadiyya Anjuman Isha'at Islam Lahore

ABC, *see* African Brotherhood Church

Abeita Culture Center, *see* Black Hebrews

Abibipim, *see* African Universal Church

Ability, *see* Duga

Abode Community, *see* Abode of the Message, The

ACAC, *see* Bible Presbyterian Church

Academy of Mind Dynamics, *see* Today Church

ACCC, *see* Bible Presbyterian Church

ACIM, *see* A Course in Miracles

Action et Compassion, *see* Jean-Michel et Son Équipe

ACV, *see* Ananda Cooperative Village

Adi Brahma Samaj, *see* Brahma Samaj

AFA, *see* Church of Apostolic Faith of Africa

AFM, *see* Apostolic Faith Mission

African Apostles, *see* African Apostolic Church of Johane Maranke

African Congregational Church, *see* Chibarirwe

African Cultural League, *see* Rastafarians

African God Worshippers Fellowship Society, *see* Apostolic Hierarchy Church

African Gospel Church, *see* Masowe Apostles

Afro-American Imani Temple, *see* African American Catholic Congregation

Agape Lodge, *see* Church of Thelema

AGEAC, *see* Gnosis-Gnostic Association of Anthropology and Science

Aglipayan Church, *see* Philippine Independent Church

Agnihotra, *see* Five Fold Path, The

AGUC, *see* Africa Gospel Unity Church

Agudat Keren B'nai No'ach, *see* B'nai Noach

Ahmadis, *see* Ahmadiyya Movement

Ahmadiyya Society for the Propagation of Islam, *see* Ahmadiyya Anjuman Isha'at Islam Lahore

AICN, *see* African Israel Church Ninevah

AIPC, *see* African Independent Pentecostal Church

AJC, *see* Apostelmat Jesu Christi

Alamo Christian Church, *see* Alamo Christian Foundation

Alamo Foundation/Music Square Church, *see* Alamo Christian Foundation

Alcoholics Anonymous, *see* Moral Re-Armament

Aleuti Francesca, *see* Solar Light Center

Alliance for the Preservation of Religious Liberty, *see* Scientology

Alliance Universelle, *see* Temoins du Christ Revenu

Alpha and Omega Church of God Tabernacles, *see* Alpha and Omega Pentecostal Church of God of America, Inc.

Ama-Nazaretha, *see* Nazaretha

AmahlokoHloko, *see* Christian Apostolic Faith Church in Zion

Amana (Faithfulness) Church Society, *see* Amana Church Society

AME, *see* African Methodist Episcopal Church

American Christian Action Council, *see* Bible Presbyterian Church

Chip and Dale, *see* Heaven's Gate

Chitawala, *see* Kitawala

Chondogwan, *see* Chondokwon

Christ Heart Church, *see* Kirisuto Shinsu-Kyodan

Christ Maitreya, *see* World Teacher, The

Christengemeinschaft, *see* Christian Community Church

Christian Apostolic Church, *see* Christian Catholic Apostolic Church in Zion

Christian Believers Assembly, *see* Christian Believers Conference

Christian Catholic Church in Zion, *see* Mahon Mission of the Baptist Union of South Africa

Christian Community, *see* Christian Community Church

Christian Community Bureau, *see* Holy Order of Mans

Christian Community of Universal Brotherhood
  see Doukhobors
  see Sons of Freedom

Christian Defense League, *see* Church of Christian Liberty, The

Christian Echoes Ministry, *see* Church of the Christian Crusade

Christian Faith Band, *see* Church of God (Apostolic)

Christian Fellowship, *see* Two-By-Two's, The

Christian Fellowship Church, *see* Etoism

Christian Identity, *see* Identity Movement

Christian Israel, *see* Identity Movement

Christian Millenial Fellowship, *see* New Creation Bible Students

Christian Ministries, *see* Body of Christ, The

Christian Science Home, *see* Home of Truth Movement

Christian Science Theological Seminary, *see* Hopkins Association, Emma C.

Christian Union, *see* Church of God (Cleveland, Tennessee)

Christ's Witnesses, *see* Temoins du Christ Revenu

Chu Hui So, *see* Local Church Movement

Church of Armageddon, *see* Love Family

Church at Island Pond, *see* Northeast Kingdom Community Church

Church of the Canaanites, *see* Church of the Holy Ghost/Spirit, The

Church of Christ
  see Ibandla Lika Kristu
  see Iglesia ni Christo Manalista, Inc.

Church of Christ, Scientist, *see* Christian Science

Church of Christ for the Union of the Bantu and Protection of Bantu Customs, *see* Church of Christ for the Union of Bantu

Church of Christ-Consciousness, *see* Center of Light Community, The

Church of Christian Heritage, *see* Church of Israel, The

Church of Circle Wicca, *see* Circle Sanctuary

Church of Eductivism, *see* Dianology and Eductivism

Church of the Eminent Way, *see* Emin Society, The

Church of the Family of God and of Jesus Christ, *see* Divine Prayer Society 1944

Church of Father of Fathers and Mother of Mothers, *see* Samhan Ng Amang Ka-Amahan at Inang Ka-Inainahan

Church of the Final Judgement, The, *see* Process, The

Church of the Full Gospel, Inc., *see* General Conference of the Evangelical Baptist Church

Church of the Gentiles, *see* Church of the Holy Ghost/Spirit, The

Church of God, *see* Plymouth Brethren

Church of God in Jesus Christ, *see* Iglesia Ng Dios Kay Kristo Jesus

Church of God (Seventh Day), *see* General Conference of the Church of God (Seventh Day)

Church of the Great Shepherd, *see* Christian Restoration Ministries

Church of Jesus Christ at Armageddon, *see* Love Family

Church of Jesus Christ of Latter-Day Saints, *see* Mormons

Church of Jesus Christ New Jerusalem, *see* Iglesia ni Jesucristo Bagong Jerusalem

Church of Jesus Christ in Solemn Assembly, The, *see* Confederate Nations of Israel

Church of Jesus the Messiah, *see* Shoresh Yishai

Church of the Jews, *see* Church of the Holy Ghost/Spirit, The

Church of John Maranke, *see* African Apostolic Church of Johane Maranke

Church of Light, *see* Brotherhood of Light

Church of the Living, *see* Neverdies

Church of the Living God
   see Church of the Living God, General Assembly
   see House of God Which Is the Church of the Living God, the Pillar and Ground of Truth

Church Missionary Society, *see* Nomiya Luo Church

Church of the Movement of Spiritual Inner Awareness, *see* Movement of Spiritual Inner Awareness

Church of the New Civilization, *see* Advanced Ability Center

Church of the Open Book, *see* Truth for Today

Church of the Redeemed, *see* Beekmanites

Church of the Resurrected Christ, *see* Fukkatsu No Kirisuto Kyodan

Church of the Spirit, *see* Church of the Holy Ghost/Spirit, The

"Church of the Spirit of Jesus", *see* Jesu-No-Mitama-Kyokai

Church Triumphant, *see* Beekmanites

Church of True Inspiration, *see* Amana Church Society

Church of the Twelve Apostles, *see* Twelve Apostles

Church of the Upraised Hand, *see* Ringatu

Church of the Watch Tower, *see* Watchtower Movement

Church of the Watchtower, *see* Watchman Healing Mission

Church of the Way, *see* Madeley Trinity Methodist Church

Church of the White Eagle Lodge, *see* White Eagle Lodge

Church of Wicca of Bakersfield, *see* Georgian Church, The

Church of World Messianity, *see* Sekai Kyusei Kyo

"City of Jehovah", *see* Mai Chaza Church

CLA, *see* Church of the Lord (Aladura)

Classics Expositor, *see* Bible Churches

Claymont Society for Continuous Education, Inc., *see* Claymont Court

CMA, *see* Christian and Missionary Alliance

COBU, *see* Church of Bible Understanding

COG, *see* Family, The

COGIC, *see* Church of God in Christ

College of Occult Sciences, *see* Temple of Kriya Yoga

Collegiate Association for the Research of Principles, *see* Unification Church

Colored Methodist Episcopal Church, *see* Christian Methodist Episcopal Church

Commandments Church, *see* Malango Church

Committee for Spiritual Poetry, *see* Sri Chimnoy

Commune de Nazareth, *see* Famile de Nazareth

Community of Ansaar Affairs in America, *see* Nubian Islamic Hebrews

Community National Church, *see* People's Temple Christian (Disciples) Church

Community of True Inspiration, *see* Amana Church Society

Compulsions Analysis, *see* Process, The

Concerned Businessmen's Association of America, *see* Scientology

Congregation Daat Elohim, *see* Temple of Universal Judaism

Congregation of Elohim, *see* Church of God (Jerusalem)

Conservative Friends, *see* Hicksite Friends

"Cooneyites", *see* Two-By-Two's, The

"Cosmic Fraternity", *see* Fratellanza Cosmica

COTC, *see* Church of the Creator

Courants de Puissance, *see* Stromen Van Kracht

Covenant Congregations, *see* Identity Movement

CPDL, *see* Christian Patriots Defense League

Crazy Wisdom Fellowship, *see* Free Daist Avataric Communion

Cross Church of East Africa, *see* Roho Musalaba

Equality-Fraternity-Liberty Church, *see* Equifrilibricum World Religion

Eternal Flame Foundation, *see* People Forever International

Eternal Sacred Order of Cherubim and Seraphim, *see* Cherubim and Seraphim

Ethiopian Church, *see* Ethiopian Catholic Church of South Africa

Ethiopian Coptic Faith, *see* Rastafarians

Ethiopian National Congress, *see* Rastafarians

Ethiopian Orthodox Church, *see* Rastafarians

Ethiopian Overcoming Holy Church of God, *see* Apostolic Overcoming Holy Church of God

Evangelical Adventists, *see* Adventists, Second

Evangelical Orthodox Church, *see* New Covenant Apostolic Order

Evangelical Presbyterian Church, *see* Bible Presbyterian Church

Evangelistic Missionary Alliance, *see* Bethel Ministerial Association

Everlasting Gospel, *see* Neverdies

Ex-Christian Scientists for Jesus, *see* New Beginnings

Exclusive Brethren, *see* Plymouth Brethren (Exclusive)

F

FACIM, *see* Foundation for *A Course in Miracles*

Faculty of Color, *see* Emin Society, The

Faith Assembly, *see* Faith Assembly World Wide Church of Christ

Faith Tabernacle, *see* Christ Apostolic Church

Faithists, *see* Universal Faithists of Kosmon

"Family", *see* Jamaa

Family of Elohim, *see* Church of God (Jerusalem)

Family of Love, *see* Family, The

FBU, *see* Fraternité Blanche Universelle

FEB, *see* Federacao Espirita Brasileira

Federatio Universalis Dirigens Ordines Societaesque Initiationis

Fellowship Community, *see* Waldorf Institute

Fellowship of the Spirit, *see* Ruhani Satsang

Fellowship Tract League, *see* Local Church Movement

FGFCMI, *see* Full Gospel Fellowship of Churches and Ministries, International

FHS, *see* Friends of the Holy Spirit

Finger of God, The *see* Etzba Elohim

Fire-Baptized Holiness Church, *see* Fire-Baptized Holiness Association

First Century Christian Fellowship, *see* Moral Re-Armament

First Church of Christ, Scientist, *see* Christian Science

First Fruit of Prayer, *see* African Reform Coptic Church of God in Christ

FOF, *see* Fellowship of Friends

FOI, *see* Fellowship of Isis

Followers of Emilyo, *see* Bana Ba Mutimu

Followers of Yahweh, *see* Nation of Yahweh

"Fondation Pobeda Ouspech Universelle", *see* Fraternité Blanche Universelle

Forever Family, *see* Church of Bible Understanding

Forever People, *see* People Forever International

Foundation Church of the Millenium, *see* Foundation Faith of God

Foundation Church of the New Birth, *see* Foundation Church of Divine Truth

Foundation Faith of the Millenium, *see* Foundation Faith of God

Foundation for the Preservation of the Mahayana Tradition, *see* Lama Tzong Khapa

Foundation for Theosophical Studies, *see* Theosophical Society in America

Foundation of Universal Unity, *see* Emissaries of Divine Light

Foursquare Gospel International, *see* Foursquare Gospel, International Church of

Fourth Way School, *see* Gurdjieff Groups

Free Communion Church, *see* Free Daist Avataric Communion

Free Daist Avabhasan Communion, *see* Free Daist Avataric Communion

Free Daist Communion, see Free Daist
Avataric Communion
Free John, see Free Daist Avataric
Communion
Free Primitive Church of Divine
Communion, see Free Daist Avataric
Communion
Freedom of the Cosmos, see Foundation of
I, Inc.
Freedomites, see Sons of Freedom
Friends, see Two-By-Two's, The
Friends of the Temple, see
Templegesellschaft
Friends of Vimala Thakar, see Vimala
Prakashan Trust
Fruit of Islam, see Nation of Islam
(Farrakhan)
FUDOSI, see Federation Universelle des
Ordres et Sociétés Initiatiques
Full Gospel Church of God
  see African Gospel Church
  see Full Gospel Church Association
Full Gospel Revival Centre, see Full Gospel
Central Church

G
Gaan Tata, see Masa Jehovah
Gaiwiio, see Handsome Lake Religion
Ganden Tekchen Ling, see Ganden
Mahayana Center
"Garden of Light", see Ittoen
GBG, see Choronzon Club
General Christian Mission, see New
Apostolic Church
Genshifukuin-Kami-No-Makuya-Kyokai, see
Makuya
GIA, see Gnosis-Gnostic Association of
Anthropology and Science
Gidan Bishara, see Chad Brothers
Gilgal Evangelistic International Church, see
Iglesia Bando Evangelico Gedeon
Giurisdavidici, see Chiesa Guirisdavica
Glory Barn Faith Assembly, see Faith
Assembly World Wide Church of
Christ
Gnostic Association of Cultural and
Anthropological Studies, see Gnosis-
Gnostic Association of Anthropology

and Science
Gnostic Institute of Anthropology, see
Gnosis-Gnostic Association of
Anthropology and Science
"go-preachers," see Two-By-Two's, The
God of the Candle, see Mission de Dieu du
Bougie
God's Army Camp, see African Reform
Coptic Church of God in Christ
"Golden Light Teaching", see Konkokyo
Gospel of God Church, see Masowe
Apostles
Gospel of Jesus Christ, see Iesu Fukuin
Kyodan
Grace Mission Church, see Mahon Mission
of the Baptist Union of South Africa
Gralsbewegung, see Grail Message
Grande Sintesi, La, see Nucleo Ubaldiano di
Metafisica
Great I Am, see "I Am"
Great Brotherhood of God, see Choronzon
Club
Great Sun Teaching, see Dai-Hizen-Kyo
Great White Brotherhood
  see Aquarian Foundation
  see Solar Light Center
  see Theosophy
  see Universal Brotherhood
Greater Grace World Outreach, see Bible
Speaks
Group for Creative Meditation, see
Meditation Group for the New Age
Guérisseur, le, see Antoinisme
Guta ra Jehovah, see Mai Chaza Church

H
HaMa'ayan, see Beit Immanuel
Hare Krishna Movement, see International
Society for Krishna Consciousness
Harrist Church, see Harris Movement
Heartfelt Foundation, see Movement of
Spiritual Inner Awareness
"Heavenly Reason Teaching", see Tenrikyo
Hebrew Christian Alliance of America, see
Messianic Jewish Alliance of America
Hebrew Israelites
  see Black Hebrews
  see Nation of Yahweh

Hermetic Order of the Golden Dawn
  see Builders of the Adytum
  see Societas Rosicruciana in Anglia
Hidden Iman, *see* Mahdi
Higher Source, *see* Heaven's Gate
Higher Thought, *see* New Thought
HIM, *see* Heaven's Gate
The Him and the Her, *see* Heaven's Gate
Himalayan Institute, *see* Himalayan
  International Institute of Yoga Science
  and Philosophy
Hindu Visva Parisad, *see* Vishwa Hindu
  Parishad
Hineni Ministries, *see* Jews for Jesus
"His Divinity", *see* International Society of
  Divine Love
Holiness Church, *see* Church of God
  (Cleveland, Tennessee)
Holy Alamo Christian Churches,
  Consecrated, *see* Alamo Christian
  Foundation
Holy Apostles Community, *see* Brotherhood
  of the Cross and Star
Holy Catholic Apostolic Church, *see*
  Catholic Apostolic Church
Holy Church of North Carolina, *see* United
  Holy Church of America
"Holy Jesus Society", *see* Sei Iesu Kai
Holy Palmarian Church, *see* Palmarian
  Catholic Church
Holy Spirit Association for the Unification
  of World Christianity, *see* Unification
  Church
Holy Spirit Church of East Africa, *see* Dini
  Ya Roho
Homebringing Mission of Jesus Christ, *see*
  Univeral Life
HOOM, *see* Holy Order of Mans
Hosannas, *see* Masowe Apostles
House Church Movement
  see Christian Restoration Ministries
  see Shepherding
House of Peace, The, *see* Santiniketan
House of Prayer of All the People, *see*
  United House of Prayer for All People
Hubbard Association of Scientologists
  International, *see* Scientology
Human Individual Metamorphosis, *see*
  Heaven's Gate

Humanist Institute, *see* Starcross Monastic
  Community
Hutterian Brethren, *see* Bruderhof
Hutterian Society of Brothers, *see* Bruderhof

I
IAFCJ, *see* Iglesia Apostolica de la Fe en
  Cristo Jesus
ICAB, *see* Igreja Catolica Apostolic
  Brasileira
ICCC, *see* Bible Presbyterian Church
ICE, *see* Inner Circle of Enchantment, Inc.
ICSA, *see* Integral Center of Self-Abidance
Identified Flying Objects, *see* Arising Sun
  IFO
IFCA, *see* Independent Fundamental
  Churches of America
Iglesia Defensores de la Fe, *see* Defenders of
  the Faith
Iglesia Filipina Independente, *see* Philippine
  Independent Church
Iglesia Mita, *see* Mita
Igreja de Spirito Jesus, *see* Iesu no Mitama
  Kyokai
Igreja Evangelica Pente O Brasil Para
  Christo, *see* Brazil for Christ
ILC, *see* Fellowship of the Inner Light
Illinois Metaphysical College, *see* Hopkins
  Association, Emma C.
Illinois Street Independent Church, *see*
  Moody Church
Imani Temple, *see* African American
  Catholic Congregation
Independent Episcopal Church, *see* African
  Orthodox Church
Independent Watchtower, *see* Watchtower
Inner Light Consciousness, *see* Fellowship
  of the Inner Light
Inner Miracle Partnership, see Foundation
  for *A Course in Miracles*
Inner Spirit-of-Christ Churches, *see*
  Universal Life
Institute of Ability, *see* Abilitism
Institute for Core Energetics, *see* Pathwork,
  The
Institute for the Harmonious Development
  of Man, *see* Gurdjieff Groups
Institute of Personal Religion, *see* Interfaith
  Temple

Institute of Religious Science and Philosophy, *see* United Church of Religious Science

Institute for Research in Human Happiness, The, *see* Kofuku No Kagaku

Integrative Becoming, *see* Rissho Kosei-Kai

Integrity Foundation, *see* Movement of Spiritual Inner Awareness

Integrity Society, *see* Emissaries of Divine Light

Intercosmic Center of Spiritual Associations, *see* Integral Center of Self-Abidance

Interfaith, Inc., *see* Interfaith Temple

International Association of Christian Mystics,
 see Rosicrucian Fellowship

International Association of Religious Science Churches, *see* Religious Science International

International Bible Students Association, *see* Jehovah's Witnesses

International Brotherhood League, *see* Universal Brotherhood and Theosophical Society

International Center for Self-Analysis, *see* Integral Center of Self-Abidance

International Communion of Charismatic Churches, *see* Gospel Harvesters Evangelistic Association

International Congress of Free Christians, *see* International Association for Liberal Christians

International Council of Christian Churches, *see* Bible Presbyterian Church

International Council of Unitarians and Other Liberal Religious Thinkers and Workers, *see* International Association for Liberal Christians

International Metaphysical League, *see* New Thought

International Society of Krishna Consciousness of West Virginia, *see* New Vrindaban

International Sufi Order, *see* Sufi Order in the West

IPM, *see* Inner Peace Movement

IPS, *see* Institute for Planetary Synthesis

Irvingites, *see* Catholic Apostolic Church

ISA, *see* Independent Spiritualist Association

ISKCON, *see* International Society of Krishna Consciousness

ISOCC, *see* Universal Life

Israel Anglican Church, *see* Dini Ya Msambwa

"Israelites of the New Universal Covenant", *see* Israelitas del Nuevo Pacto Universal

IVI, *see* Invitation à la Vie Intense

IYI, *see* Integral Yoga Institute

J

Jamaica Native Baptist Free Church, *see* Bedwardism

Jana Sangh Party, *see* Rashtriya Swayamasevak Sangh

Jean-Michel and His Team, *see* Jean-Michel et Son Équipe

Jehova Shammah, *see* Assemblies

Jehovah's Christian Witnesses, *see* Jehovah's Witnesses

Jerusalem Friends, *see* Templegesellschaft

Jesus Children, *see* Jesus Movement

Jesus Church, *see* Yahweh's Temple

Jesus Freaks, *see* Jesus Movement

Jesus People, *see* Jesus Movement

Jesusonian Foundation, *see* Urantia Foundation

Jeung-san gyo, *see* Jeungsan

Johannine Daist Community, *see* Free Daist Avataric Communion

Johera, *see* Church of Christ in Africa

John-Roger Foundation, *see* Movement of Spiritual Inner Awareness

Jon Frum, *see* John Frum

Jordonites, *see* Jordanites

JSC, *see* Jetsun Sakya Center

K

Kamwana Movement, *see* Watch Tower Movement

Kanitos, *see* Église Sanito

Karma Thegsum Choling, *see* Karma Triyana Dharmachakra

Karme-Choling, *see* Vajradhatu

Khakism, *see* Église des Noirs en Afrique Centrale

Kingdom Bible Seminary, *see* Kingdom Message Association

Kingdom of God Nation, The, *see* Black Hebrews

Kirpal Light Satsang, *see* Kirpal Ruhani Satsang

Koh-E-Nor University, *see* Movement of Spiritual Inner Awareness

Komeito Party, *see* Soka Gakkai Society

Korean Christian Revival Society, *see* Chondokwon

Korsten Basketweavers, *see* Masowe Apostles

Kosmos Holiday Centre, *see* Martinus Institute of Spiritual Science

Ku Klux Klan
  see Assembly of Christian Soldiers
  see Church of Jesus Christ

Kuka, *see* Namdhari

Kundalini Research Institute, *see* People Searching Inside

L

La Phalange, *see* Communion Phalangiste

Labsum Shedrub Ling, *see* Lamaist Buddhist Monastery of America

Lake City Group, *see* Association of Sananda and Sanat Kumara

Lakshmi Meditation, *see* Rama Seminars

Lassyism, *see* Mission de Dieu du Bougie

Last Church of God and His Christ, *see* Bangemela

Latin American Council of the Pentecostal Church of God, New York, *see* Concilio Latino-Americano de la Iglesia de Dios Pentecostal de New York

Laughing Man Institute, *see* Free Daist Avataric Communion

LCC, *see* Liberal Catholic Church

LDS, *see* Mormons

League of Devotees at New Vrindaban, *see* New Vrindaban

Lederer Foundation, *see* Lederer Messianic Ministries

Lefebvrists, *see* Fraternity of St. Pius X

Legio Maria, *see* Maria Legio (of Africa)

L'Église de Jesus Christ par le Prophete Simon Kimbangu, *see* Kimbanguist Movement

Levites, *see* Aaronic Order

Lexington Church of Christ, *see* Boston Church of Christ

LHMM, *see* Laymen's Home Missionary Movement

Lifewave, *see* Ishvara

Light of Salvation Church, *see* Johrei

Lighthouse Meditation Group, *see* Lighthouse Universal Life Church

Lighthouse Ranch Commune, *see* Church of the Complete Word

Lighthouse ULC, *see* Lighthouse Universal Life Church

Ligue de la Contre Réforme Catholic, *see* Communion Phalangiste

Little Flock, *see* Local Church Movement

Little Synagogue, *see* Tree of Life

Livets Ord, *see* Word of Life Church

London Central Church, *see* London Church of Christ

London Missionary Society, *see* Native Independent Congregational Church

Longhouse Religion, *see* Handsome Lake Religion

Lord Is There Temple, *see* Divine Healer's Church

Lost-Found Nation of Islam in the West, *see* Nation of Islam

Lotu ni Gauna, *see* Church of Time

LRA, *see* Lord's Resistance Army

Luz Celestial, Inc., *see* Universal Spiritual Temple of New Era

M

Mabilitsa's Zion, *see* Christian Apostolic Church in Zion

MADECH, *see* Raëlians

Maharishi International University, *see* Transcendental Meditation

Maitri Center for Psychology, *see* Vajradhatu

Malakite Church, *see* Koab

Marantha Christian Churches, *see* Marantha Campus Ministries

Maroti, *see* Holy Spirit Church of Zayun

Pillar and Ground of Truth, *see* Church of
the Living God, General Assembly

Pioneers of the New Age, *see* Unification
Church

Pisgah Grande, *see* Christ Faith Mission

PL Kyodan, *see* Perfect Liberty Kyodan

P'nai, *see* Aleph: Alliance for Jewish
Renewal

PNCC, *see* Polish National Catholic
Church

Pocomania, *see* Revival Zion

POP, *see* People of Praise

Power for Abundant Living, *see* Way
International, Inc., The

Praise the Lord Ministries, *see* New
Covenant Church

"Prayer Society", *see* Prarthana Samaj

Preaching Tabernacle, *see* Chondokwon

Presbyterian Church in America, *see*
Orthodox Presbyterian Church

Prieure, Le, *see* Gurdjieff Groups

PSI, *see* People Searching Inside

PTL, *see* New Covenant Church

Pyramid Church, *see* Christian Restoration
Ministries

Q

Quadianis, *see* Ahmadiyya Movement

R

Ra Un Nefer Amen, *see* Ausar Auset Society

Radio Church of God, *see* Worldwide
Church of God

Radio Lucis, *see* Lucis Trust

Rainbow Temple, *see* Temple de L'arc-en-
Ciel

Raja Yoga, *see* Brahma Kumaris

Ramakrishna Mission, *see* Vedanta Society

Ramakrishna Movement, *see* Ramakrishna
Math and Mission

Ras Tafari, *see* Rastafarians

Rassemblement des Amis, *see* Fellowship of
Friends

Reimi Church, *see* Johrei

Reiyukai America Association, *see* Reiyu-
Kai Kyodan

Religion d'Eboga, *see* Bwiti

Religion of the Ancestral Spirits, *see* Dini Ya
Msambwa

Religion du Cocotier, *see* Coconut Palm
Movement

Religious Fellowship, *see* Aleph: Alliance
for Jewish Renewal

Religious Research Foundation, *see*
Scientology

Remeyites, *see* Bahais Under the Hereditary
Guardianship

Renaissance Movement, *see* Renaissance
Church-Community

Renewed Church of Christ the King, *see*
Renovated Church of Christ the King

Restoration Movement, *see* Disciples of
Christ

Revival, *see* Revival Zion

RFI, *see* Rajneesh Foundation International

Rosicrucian Society, *see* Lectorium
Rosicrucianum

RSS, *see* Rashtriya Swayamasevak Sangh

Russellites, *see* Jehovah's Witnesses

S

S-Church, *see* Full Gospel Central Church

Sacred Church of the Race, *see* Iglesia
Sagrada Ng Lahi

Sahaj Marg, *see* Shri Ram Chandra Mission

St. Joseph's Novitiate, *see* Society of St.
Pius V

Saints
  see Église Sanito
  see Mormons

Salvation Society, *see* Gedatsu-Kai

Sanitos, *see* Église Sanito

Sannyasins, *see* Rajneesh Foundation
International

Santana Dharma Foundations
  see Abilitism
  see Kayavarohan

Saturday Believers, *see* Memeneda Gyidifo

"The Saved Ones", *see* Balokole

Saviour Church of Ghana, *see* Memeneda
Gyidifo

School of Natural Science, *see* Great School
of the Masters

School of Practical Christianity, *see* School
of Truth

SCM, *see* Moody Church

SDA, *see* Seventh-Day Adventist Church

Second Adventists, *see* Adventists

Universelles Leben, *see* Universal Life

Urantia Brotherhood, *see* Urantia Foundation

Utah Levites, *see* Aaronic Order

V

Vajradhatu International Buddhist Church, *see* Vajradhatu

"Value Creation Society", *see* Soka Gakkai Society

VaPostori, *see* African Apostolic Church of Johane Maranke

Vapostori of Johannes Masowe, *see* Masowe Apostles

Vedantic Cultural Society, *see* Vedic Cultural Center

Vendeenne, *see* Petite Église

VHP, *see* Vishwa Hindu Parishad

Vimala Thakar Foundation, *see* Vimala Prakashan Trust

Vine Christian Community, *see* Northeast Kingdom Community Church

Virgin of Bayside Shrine, *see* Our Lady of the Roses

Visible Salvation Church, *see* Lumpa Church

W

Wailua University of the Contemplative Arts, *see* Saiva Siddhanta Church

Walters, James Donald, *see* Ananda Cooperative Village

Washington Times, *see* Unification Church

Watch Tower Society, *see* Jehovah's Witnesses

Watchtower Bible and Tract Society, *see* Jehovah's Witnesses

Watu wa Mungos
  see African Mission of Holy Ghost Church
  see Wakorino

Way Bible Research Institute, *see* Way International, Inc., The

"We Are Not Alone", *see* Nonsiamosoli

We People, *see* Church of Bible Understanding

Western Prayer Warriors, *see* International Church of Spiritual Vision, Inc.

White Cross Society, *see* Atitso Gaxie Habobo

White Light Society, *see* Byakko Shinkokai

White Sikhs, *see* Healthy, Happy, Holy Organization

Wiccan Church, *see* Circle Sanctuary

Wilburites, *see* Hicksite Friends

Winnie and Pooh, *see* Heaven's Gate

Witness Lee Movement, *see* Local Church Movement

Word Church, *see* Church of the Complete Word

Word Mission, *see* Body of Christ, The

World Community, *see* Prema Dharmasala and Fellowship Association

World Community of Al-Islam in the West, *see* Nation of Islam

World Goodwill, *see* Lucis Trust

World Goodwill Information and Research Service, *see* Lucis Trust

World Plan Executive Council, *see* Transcendental Meditation

World Spiritual Israel Church, *see* Roho Church of the God of Israel

World Spiritual University, *see* Brahma Kumaris

World Union of Universal Religion and Universal Peace, *see* Bahai World Union

World Wide Grace Testimony, *see* Grace Gospel Missions

WTS, *see* Jehovah's Witnesses

Y

Yangoru Movement, *see* Mount Rurun Movement

Ye-su Chia T'ing, *see* Jesus Family

"Yellow Hat", *see* Gelug-Pa

Yeon-dam gyo, *see* Namhak

Yoga Research Foundation, *see* International School of Yoga and Vedanta

Z

ZCC, *see* Zion Christian Church

Zenith Institute, *see* Sufi Order in the West

Zion Christian Church, *see* Shion Kirisuto Kyokai

Zion's Watch Tower Tract Society, *see* Jehovah's Witnesses

CATEGORICAL INDEX

The Categorical Index groups entries by common attributes. Thus, if you are looking for information about communal groups, or about organizations connected to Tibetan Buddhism, you will find them arranged under these headings.

Beth Bnai Abraham (BBA)
Bible Way Church of our Lord Jesus Christ
    World Wide
Christian Methodist Episcopal Church
Christ's Sanctified Holy Church
Churches of God, Holiness
Church of Christ (Holiness) USA, The
Church of God and Saints of Christ, The
    ("Black Jews")
Church of God (Black Jews)
Church of God in Christ
Church of God in Christ, Congregational
Church of God in Christ, International, The
Church of Holy Christ
Church of Our Lord Jesus Christ of the
    Apostolic Faith
Church of the Living God
Church of the Living God, Christian
    Workers for Fellowship
Church of the Living God, General
    Assembly
Church of Universal Triumph, The/The
    Dominion of God
Commandment Keepers Congregation of
    the Living God
Embassy of the Gheez-Americans
Ethiopian Hebrews
Father Divine Movement
Father Jehovah (Father Jehovia)
Fire Baptized Holiness Church of God of
    the Americas
Free Christian Zion Church of Christ, The
Free Church of God in Christ
Hanafi Madh-Hab Center
House of God Which is the Church of the
    Living God, the Pillar and Ground of
    Truth, The
House of God Which is the Church
    of the Living God, the Pillar and
    Ground of Truth Without
    Controversy, The
House of Israel
House of Judah
House of the Lord
Imani Temple
Israeli School of UPK, The
Israel Universal Divine Spiritual Churches
    of Christ
King David's Spiritual Temple of Truth
    Association
Kodesh Church of Immanuel

Moorish Science Temple of America
National Colored Spiritualist Association of
    Churches
National David Spiritual Temple of Christ
    Church Union (Inc.) USA
Nation of Islam (NOI)
Nation of Islam (NOI) (Farrakhan)
Nation of Islam (NOI) (Silas Muhammad)
Nation of Islam (NOI) (Jeremiah
    Shabazz)
Nation of Yahweh (Hebrew Israelites)
Nubian Islamic Hebrews
Pentecostal Assemblies of the World
Reformed Zion Union Apostolic Church,
    The
Resurrected Church of God
Revival Zion
St. Paul's Spiritual Church Convocation
Triumph the Church and Kingdom of God
    in Christ, International
True Fellowship Pentecostal Church of God
    of America.
True Grace Memorial House of Prayer
Unification Association of Christian
    Sabbath Keepers, The
United Holy Church of America
United House of Prayer for all People
United Leadership Council of Hebrew
    Israelites (ULCHI)
Universal Christian Spiritual Faith and
    Churches for all Nations
Universal Hagar's Spiritual Church
Way of the Cross Church
Yoruba Lacumi

"BLACK JEWS":

Apostolic Overcoming Holy Church of God
    (AOH Church Of God)
Beth Bnai Abraham (BBA)
Black Hebrews, The (The Kingdom of God
    Nation)
Church of God and Saints of Christ, The
    ("Black Jews")
Church of God (Black Jews)
Commandment Keepers Congregation of
    the Living God
Ethiopian Hebrews
House of Judah
Israeli School of UPK, The
Moorish Zionist Temple

United Leadership Council of Hebrew
  Israelites (ULCHI)

BRITISH-ISRAELISM:

Anglo-Saxon Federation of America
Association of Covenant People, The
Beacon Light Ministry
Bible Pattern Church Fellowship
British Israel World Federation
Calvary Fellowship, Inc.
Christian Conservative Church of America
Christian Nationalist Crusade
Christian Research, Inc.
Christ's Gospel Fellowship
Church of Israel, The
Church of Jesus Christ-Christian
Church of the Covenants
Destiny of America Foundation
Full Gospel Tabernacle
Gospel Temple
House of Prayer for all People, The
Jappa Tabernacle
Kingdom Fellowship Church
Kingdom Message Association
Kingdom of Yahweh
Kingdom Temple, Inc.
Lord's Covenant Church, The
Nazarene Episcopal Ecclesia
New Beginnings
New Christian Crusade Church
Open Bible Church
Society for Proclaiming Britain Is Israel
Temple de L'arc-En-Ciel (Rainbow Temple)
Truth and Liberty Temple
United Apostolic Faith Church
United Israel World Fellowship
United Israel World Union (UIWU)
Worldwide Church of God
Your Heritage

BUDDHISM:

Insight Meditation Society
Maha-Bodhi Society
Mandala Buddhist Center
Soka Gakkai
Weg Der Mitte
Western Buddhist Order

World Teacher, The
  See Tibetan Buddhism

"CARGO CULTS":

Black Kings Movement
Coming of Jesus
Doliasi Custom
Etoism
Hahalis Welfare Society
John Frum (Jon Frum)
Lyndon B. Johnson
Mansren
Mount Rurun Movement
Noise, The
Paliau Church
Story, The
Tagarab
"Taro Cult"
Yaliwan's Movement

CHRISTIAN IDENTITY *see* IDENTITY
  MOVEMENT

COMMUNAL GROUPS, 19TH CENTURY:

Amana Church Society
House of Israel
Shakers
Universal Faithists of Kosmon (UFK)

COMMUNAL GROUPS, 20TH CENTURY:

Ammal's Garden
Aum Center for Self-Realization
Bear Tribe, The
Bruderhof
Builders, The
Center of Light Community, The
Chinook Community
Christ Brotherhood
Christian Community
Christian Community of Boston
Church of the Redeemer Community
Church of the Saviour
Circle of Angels, The
Colony, The

Covenant, the Sword, the Arm of the Lord
Damanhur
Dawn Horse Communion
Deva Community
Earth People
Farm, The
Fisherfolk Communities of Celebration
Ganienkah
Heart Consciousness Church
Himalayan Academy
Holistic Community
Invisible Church
Jesus Mobilization Committee
Jesus People USA
Kayavarohan
Kerista Village
Koinonia
Koinonia Community
Koinonia Partners
Kosmunity
Kripalu Yoga Ashram
Lama Foundation
Lamb of God
Lorian Association
Love Family
Maha Yoga Ashram
Matagiri
Meadowlark Healing Center
Mettanokit
Morningstar
Mu Farm
Nada Community
Northeast Kingdom Community Church
One World Family
Padanaram
People of the Living God
Prema Dharmasala and Fellowship
    Association; Prema World Community
Rainbow Family of Living Light
Raj-Yoga Math and Retreat
Reba Place Fellowship
Renaissance Church-Community
Salem Acres
Savitria
Sevenoaks Community
Shiloh Trust
Sirius Community
Springhill Community
Spring Grove
Sri Ram Ashrama
Stelle Community

Stonegate Christian Community
Sunergos Institute, Inc.
Theocratic Commune Natural Health
    Service
Universal Brotherhood
Universal Faithists of Kosmon (UFK)
Vision Mound Community
Voice of Calvary
Work of Christ

FUNDAMENTALIST:

Alamo Christian Foundation
American Conference of Undenominated
    Churches
American Evangelical Christian Churches
American Rescue Workers
Associated Gospel Churches
Association for Research and
    Enlightenment, Inc., The
Astrological, Metaphysical, Occult,
    Revelatory, Enlightenment Church
Berean Bible Fellowship
Berean Bible Fellowship (Chicago)
Berean Fundamental Churches
Bethany Bible Church and Related
    Independent Bible Churches
Bible Churches
Bible Pattern Church Fellowship
Bible Presbyterian Church
Bible Speaks
Bible Temple
Body of Christ
Boston Church of Christ
Bread of Life Ministries
Brethren in Christ
Calvary Chapel
Calvary Fellowship Inc.
Camp Farthest Out
Cathedral of Tomorrow
Christian Revolutionary Brotherhood
Christian Union
Christian World Liberation Front
Christ's Gospel Fellowship
Churches of Christ in Christian Union of
    Ohio, The
Churches of God in the British Isles and
    Overseas
Church of Bible Understanding
Church of Christian Liberty, The

Church of God (Cleveland, Ohio)
Church of the Christian Crusade
Church of the Complete Word
Church of the Covenants
Church of the Kingdom of God,
    Philanthropic Assembly, The
"Church Which is Christ's Body," The
Communtity Chapel and Bible Training
    Center
Concordant Publishing Concern
Covenant Community Fellowship
Cross Roads Churches of Christ
Defenders of the Christian Faith, Inc.
Defenders of the Faith
Eben Hazer
Ecclesia
Elim Foursquare Gospel
Elim Pentecostal Church
Evangelical Methodist Church, The
Evangelical Ministers and Churches,
    International, Inc.
Faith Bible Church
Faith Movement
Family, The
Fellowship of Independent Evangelical
    Churches
First Community Church of America
Fisherfolk Communities of Celebration
Formosa Christian Mission
Fundamentalist Army, The
Grace Gospel Fellowship
Grace Gospel Missions
Hepzebah House
His Place
Honor Oak Christian Fellowship Centre
Independent Fundamental Churches of
    America
Independent Fundamentalist Bible
    Churches
Interfaith Ministries for Renewal
International Christian Ministries
International Churches of Christ
Invisible Church
Jappa Tabernacle
Jesus Fellowship Church
Jesus for Africa
Jesus Mobilization Committee
Koinonia Community
Last Day Messenger Assemblies

Local Church Movement
Mission for the Coming Days
Moody Church
New Apostolic Church
New Covenant Apostolic Order
New Covenant Church
New Testament Missionary Fellowship
New York Church of Christ
Northeast Kingdom Community Church
Ohio Bible Fellowship
Old Time Faith, Inc.
Orthodox Presbyterian Church
Pillar of Fire
Reformed Presbyterian Church, Evangelical
    Synod
Rhema
Salvation Army, The
Shepherding
Soja We Mwari
Stromen Van Kracht
This Testimony
Timely Messenger Fellowship
True Followers of Christ
Truth for Today
Truth Station, The
Two-by-Two's
University Bible Fellowship
Voice of Calvary
Volunteers of America
Walk (Church of the Living Word), The
Way International, Inc., The
Westminster Biblical Fellowship
Westmoreland Chapel
Wokofu African Church
Word of God
Worldwide Church of God

GURDJIEFF GROUPS:

Cafh Spiritual Culture Society
Circle of Angels, The
Claymount Court
Fellowship of Friends (FOF)
Gurdjieff Foundation
Gurdjieff Groups
Gurdjieff Studies Group
Institute for Cultural Research
Institute for Religious Development

Institute for the Comparative Study of
    History, Philosophy, and the Sciences
Institute for the Harmonious Development
    of the Human Being
Instituto Para El Desarrollo Armonico Del
    Hombre
Orage Group
Pacific Institute of Science and Humanities
Prosperos, The
School of Economic Science
School of Practical Philosophy
Sherborne School
Sherborne Studies Group
Subud
Unis

HEBREW-CHRISTIAN GROUPS:

American Messianic Fellowship
Ariel Ministries Hebrew Christian
Bethesda
Beth Yeshua
B'nai Yeshua
B'nei Avraham
Chosen People Ministries
Christian Messianic Fellowship
Christian Witness to Israel
Emmanuel Messianic Congregation
First Hebrew Presbyterian Christian Church
Friends of Israel (FOI)
Friends of Israel Gospel Ministry
Grace and Truth Christian Congregation
Hebrew Christian Alliance
Hebrew Christian Assembly—Jerusalem
    Congregation
International Hebrew Christian Alliance of
    America
Jews for Jesus
Lederer Messianic Ministries
London Messianic Fellowship
Melech Israel
Message to Israel
Messianic Assembly of Israel
Messianic Jewish Alliance
Messianic Jewish Alliance of America
    (MJA)
Messianic Synagogue
Netivyah
Olive Tree Fellowship

Peniel
Remnant Church
Rosh Pina Congregation
Shema Yisroel Synagogue
Shoresh Yishai
Zion Messianic Fellowship
See also Messianic Judaism

HINDU, HINDU-ORIENTED, AND
HINDU-INSPIRED INTERNATIONAL
AND WESTERN GROUPS:

Ahimsa Community
Akhanananda Saraswati, Swami
Ananda Ashrama
Ananda Cooperative Village
Ananda Marga
Anandamayee Charitable Society
Arunachala Ashrama Bhagavan Sri Ramana
    Maharshi Center, Inc.
Atmaniketan Ashram
Brahma Kumaris (Raja Yoga)
Center for Spiritual Awareness (CSA)
Chiltern Yoga Foundation
Chinmaya Mission
Church of the Christian Spiritual Alliance
    (CSA)
Community of the Many Names of God
Cultural Integration Fellowship
Deva Foundation
Divine Life Society
Divine Light Centrum
Divine Light Mission (DLM)
East-West Cultural Center
Five Fold Path, Inc.
Foundation of Revelation
Haidakhan Samaj
Hanuman Fellowship, The
Hanuman Foundation
Himalayan Academy
Himalayan International Institute of Yoga
    Science and Philosophy
The Hindu American Religious Institute
Hohm
Holy Order of Ezekiel
Holy Shankaracharya Order, The
I Am Ashram
Integral Center of Self-Abidance (ICSA)
Integral Yoga Institute (IYI)

HINDU REFORM AND REVIVAL
GROUPS:

Brahma Samaj
Chinmaya Mission
Church of the New Dispensation, The
Deva Samaj
Hindu Mahasabha
Pranthana Samaj
Ramakrishna Math and Mission
Ramana Maharshi
Rama Rajya Parisha
Rashtriya Swayamasevak Sangh (BSS)
Sai Baba
Santiniketan
Sarva Dharma Sambhava Kendra
Shankaracharya
Siddha Yoga
Sri Aurobindo
Subba Rao
Swaminarayana
Temple of Universal Peace
Vedic Church of East Africa
Vishwa Hindu Parishad (VHP)
World Community Service
Yogoda Satsanga Society

IDENTITY MOVEMENT (CHRISTIAN IDENTITY):

Assembly of Christian Soldiers
Christian Conservative Church of America
Christian Defense League
Christian Patriots Defense League (CPDL)
Church of Israel, The
Church of Jesus Christ, The
Church of Jesus Christ Christian—Aryan
    Nations
Church of the Creator (COTC)
Covenant, the Sword, the Arm of the Lord,
    The (CSA)
Crusade for Christ and Country
Elohim City
Mountain Church of Jesus Christ the
    Saviour, The
New Christian Crusade Church
New Harmony Christian Crusade
Order, The
Pathfinder Church
Shepherd's Chapel
Sword of Christ Good News Ministries

ISLAM:

Ahmadiyya Anjuman Isha'at Islam
Ahmadiyya Movement
Al-Arqam
Babism
Bahais
Daheshism
Death Angels
Five Percenters
Guru Bawa Fellowship
Halveti-Jerrahi Order of New York
Hanafi Madh-Hab Center
Islam-Is
Krislam
Laye
National Islamic Assembly
New World of Islam
Nubian Islamic Hebrews
Subud
Sylla Movement

JEHOVAH'S WITNESSES (AND RELATED GROUPS):

Association Francaise Des Libres Etudiants
    De La Bible
Back to the Bible Way
Berean Bible Institute
Berean Bible Students Church
Bible Fellowship Union
Bible Student Examiner, The
Chiesa Cristiana Millenarista
Christian Millenial Church
Christian Truth Institute
Eben Haezer
Forest Gate Church
Goshen Fellowship
The Institute of Pyramidology
Kitawala
Laodicean Home Missionary Movement
Laymen's Home Missionary Movement
    (LHMM)
New Covenant Fellowship
New Creation Bible Students
New Jerusalem Fellowship
Pastoral Bible Institute (PBI)
Providence Industrial Mission

Watchman Healing Mission
Watchtower
Watch Tower Movement
Watchtower Movement
Western Bible Students Association

JESUS MOVEMENT:

Christian World Liberation Front (CWLF)
Church of Bible Understanding (COBU)
Family, The
Fellowship of Christian Pilgrims
His Place
Holy Ghost Repair Service, Inc.
International Christian Ministries
Jesus Christ Light and Power
Jesus Mobilization Committee
Jesus People U.S.A.
Koinonia Community
Love Inn
New Life Evangelistic Center
Shalom Center
Zion's Inn

JUDAISM (AND RELATED GROUPS):

Aleph: Alliance for Jewish Renewal
Aquarian Minyan of Berkeley
B'nai Noach ("Children Of Noach")
Congregation Beit Shechinah
Conservative Judaism
Dor Hashalom
Emmanuel
Frazier Chapel
Interfaith Temple or Interfaith, Inc.
Jewish Science, Society of
Liberal Judaism
Makom Ohr Shalom
Neological
New Thought Synagogue
Progressive Judaism
Reconstructionism
Temple of Universal Judaism
Tree of Life

MESSIANIC JUDAISM:

Beit Assaph

Beit Immanuel
Beth Messiah
Beth Messiah
Beth Messiah
Beth Messiah Congregation
Christian Witness to Israel
Congregation of the Messiah
Grace and Truth Christian Congregation
Jews for Jesus
Messianic Hebrew-Christian Fellowship
Messianic Jewish Alliance of America
Peniel
Union of Messianic Jewish Congregations
See also Hebrew Christian Groups

MILLENARIAN:

Amis de L'Homme
Ananaikyo
Babism
Cao Dai
Catholic Apostolic Church
Chiesa Guirisdavidica
Chiesa Universale Guirisdavidica
Ch'ondogyo
Christadelphians
Christian Believers Conference
Christian Catholic Apostolic Church in
    Zion
Christian Israelites
Christian World Liberation Front
Christohanon
Church of the Kingdom of God,
    Philanthropic Assembly, The
Church of Time
Church of Universal Triumph
Coconut Palm Movement
Colorum
Disciples of Christ
Dispensationalism
Fort Wayne Gospel Temple
Hoa Hao
Honmichi-Kyo
Iglesia ni Cristo Manalista, Inc.
"Israelites"
Jesu-No Mitama-Kyokai
John Frum
Kimbanguist Movement
Last Ministry Church

Latter Rain Movement
Lumpa Church
Manifest Sons of God
Maruyamakyo
Megiddo Mission
Millenarianism
Mission for the Coming Days
Mormons
New Covenant Apostolic Order
New Creation Bible Students
Omotokyo
Plymouth Brethren
Purgatorical Society, The
Renaissance Church-Community
Shakers
Shilohites
Templegesellschaft
True Light Church of Christ
Unification Church
Universal Brotherhood
Universal Church, the Mystical Body of
    Christ
Voice of Elijah, Inc.
Watchtower
Watch Tower Movement

MORMONS:

Aaronic Order
Apostolic United Order
Church of Christ (Bible and Book of
    Mormon Teaching)
Church of Christ (Fettingite)
Church of Christ (Temple Lot)
Church of Christ at Halley's Bluff, The
Church of Christ with the Elijah
    Message
Church of Jesus Christ, The
    (Bickertonites)
Church of the First Born of the Fullness of
    Times
Church of the Lamb of God
Confederate Nations of Israel
LDS Scripture Researchers
Reorganized Church of Jesus Christ of
    Latter-Day Saints (RLDS)
Sons Ahman Israel (SAI)
United Order Effort
Zion Order of the Sons of Levi

NATIVE AMERICAN:

American Indian Evangelical Church
Bear Tribe, The
Center of the First Light, The
First Born Church of Christ
Ganienkah
Handsome Lake Religion
Holy Ground
Indian Shaker Church
Mettanokit
Native American Church (NAC)
Sunray Meditation Society
Xat American Indian Medicine Society

NEO-PAGAN GROUPS:

Ancient Order of Druids
Asatru
Athanor Fellowship
Calumet Pagan Temple
Church of All Worlds
Church of the Eternal Source
Circle Sanctuary
Coven of Arianhu
Covenant of the Goddess
Denver Area Wiccan Network (DAWN)
Dianic Wicca
Earthspirit Community
Fanscifiaroan Church of Wicca
Fellowship of Isis (FOI)
Fereferia
The Georgian Church
Glainn Sidhr Order
Glastonbury Community
Holy Earth Assemby (THEA)
House of the Goddess
Live Oak Grove
Lothlorien
Midwest Pagan Council (MPC)
New Age Church of Being
New Reformed Orthodox Order of the
    Golden Dawn
New Wiccan Church
Odinist Committee
Odinists
Reformed Congregation of the Goddess
Reformed Druids of North America
Seax-Wica Seminary

Raëlians
Rainbow Family of Living Light
Rosicrucian Anthroposophic League
Rosicrucian Fellowship
Sabian Assembly
Savitra
School of Economic Studies (SES)
School of Esoteric Studies
School of Light and Realization (SOLAR)
School of Practical Philosophy
Servers of the Great Ones, Inc.
Sirius Community
Societas Rosicruciana in America
Societas Rosicruciana in Anglia
Spiritual Science of Mind Center
Spiritual Unity of Nations
Stelle Community
Summum Church
Sunray Meditation Society
Teaching of the Inner Christ, Inc.
Temple of the Eternal Light, Inc.
Temple of Thelema
Theocentric Foundation
Theocentric Temple
Towards the Light
True Church of Christ, International
Universal Shrine of Divine Guidance
Universal Spiritual Temple of the New Era-
    Temple of Celestial Light
University of Life Church
Urantia Foundation
Walk (Church of the Living Word), The
White Eagle Lodge
Word Foundation
World Catalyst Church
World Teacher, The

OLD CATHOLIC GROUPS:

American Catholic Church
American Catholic Church (Syro-
    Antiochean)
American Orthodox Catholic Church
Archdiocese of the Old Catholic Church in
    America
Chiesa Cattolica Riformata D'italia
Christ Catholic Church (Diocese of
    Boston)

Chriszekial Elias
Church of Mary Mystical Rose of Perpetual
    Help
Église Catholique Gallicane Autocephale
Evangelical Catholic Church of New York
Gallican Church
Independent Old Catholic Church
North American Old Roman Catholic
    Church (NAORCC)
Old Catholic Church in America
Polish Mariavite Church
Polish National Catholic Church
Universal Apostolic Church of Life

PAGANISM see NEO-PAGAN

PENTECOSTAL:

Acts of Apostles Christ's Church, Nigeria
African Apostolic Church St. Simon and St.
    Johan
African Assemblies of God
African Divine Church
African Independent Pentecostal Church
African Israel Church Nineveh
African Mission of Holy Ghost Church
African Universal Church
Aladura
Aladura International Church
Alpha and Omega Christian Church
Alpha and Omega Pentecostal Church of
    God of America, Inc.
American Evangelical Association, The
American Indian Evangelical Church
Anchor Bay Evangelistic Association
Antioch Church
Apostles in Zion Church
Apostolic Church
Apostolic Church of Ghana
Apostolic Church of God
Apostolic Church of God Christians
Apostolic Church of Great Britian
Apostolic Church of Jesus
Apostolic Church of Jesus Christ
Apostolic Church of Jesus Christ
Apostolic Divine Church of Ghana
Apostolic Door of Faith
Apostolic Faith
Apostolic Faith (Born Again) Church

Apostolic Faith and Acts Church
Apostolic Faith Church
Apostolic Faith Church (Kansas)
Apostolic Faith Holy Gospel Church
Apostolic Faith Mission
Apostolic Faith Mission of Portland,
    Oregon, U.S.A.
Apostolic Faith of Africa
Apostolic Faith Star Church
Apostolic Fellowship Tabernacle
Apostolic Gospel Faith of Jesus Christ, The
Apostolic Holy Zion Mission of South
    Africa
Apostolic Overcoming Holy Church of God
Apostolic Reformed Church of Ghana
Apostolowo fe Dedefia Habobo
Assemblies of God
Assemblies of God in Great Britain and
    Ireland
Assemblies of the First-Born
Assemblies of the Lord Jesus Christ
Assembly of Christian Churches, Inc., The
Associated Brotherhood of Christians
Association of International Gospel
    Assemblies, Inc.
Association of Seventh Day Pentecostal
    Assemblies
Atitso Gaxie Habobo
Balokole
Bantu Bethlehem Church of Zion in South
    Africa
Baptist Church of God
Beit Assaph
Bethany Church Mission
Bethel Apostolic (Shiloh) Church
Bethel Christian Temple
Bethel Ministerial Association
Bethel Temple
Bethesda Church Mission
Bible Pattern Church Fellowship
Bible Temple
Bible Way Church of Our Lord Jesus Christ
    World Wide
Body of Christ, The
Branham Tabernacle
Brazil for Christ
Calvary Fellowship Inc.
Clavary Pentecostal Church
Carolina Evangelistic Association

Celestial Church of Christ
Cherubim and Seraphim Church of Zion in
    Nigeria
Chosen Church of the Holy Spirit of Kenya
Christ Apostolic Mission Church
Christ Apostolic Universal Church
Christ Faith Mission
Christian Church of North America, The
Christian Growth Ministries
Christian Holy Ghost Church of East Africa
Christianisme Prophetique en Afrique
Christian Restoration Ministries
Christian Zion Church
Christ's Army Church
Christ's Gospel Fellowship
Christ's Sanctified Holy Catholic Church
Churches of God, Holiness
Church of All Nations
Church of Apostolic Faith of Africa
Church of God (Apostolic)
Church of God (Cleveland, Tennessee)
Church of God (Jerusalem Acres), The
Church of God (U.K.)
Church of God (World Headquarters)
Church of God by Faith
Church of God in Christ
Church of God in Christ (COGIC)
Church of God in Christ, Congregation
Church of God in Christ, International, The
Church of God in Christ, Pentecostal, The
Church of God of Prophecy
Church of God of the Apostolic Faith
Church of God of the Mountain Assembly,
    The
Church of God of the Original Mountain
    Assembly
Church of the God of the Union Assembly
Church of God, the House of Prayer
Church of Grace
Church of Holy Christ
Church of Messiah
Church of Our Lord Jesus Christ of the
    Apostolic Faith
Church of Our Lord Jesus Christ of the
    Apostolic Faith
Church of the Covenants
Church of the First-Born
Church of the Little Children
Church of the Living God, Christian

Workers Fellowship
Church of the Living God, General Assembly
Church of the Lord Jesus Christ of the Apostolic Faith
Church of the New Life
Community Chapel and Bible Training Center
Concilio Latino Americano de la Iglesia de Dios Pentecostal de New York, Inc.
Concilio Olazabal de Iglesias Latino Americano
Congregacao Crista
Congregational Holiness Church
Damascus Christian Church
Deliverance Church
Dini Ya Roho
Divine Healers Church
Divine Healing Church of Christ
Divine Healing Church of Israel
Divine Prayer Society 1944
Dolly Pond Church of God with Signs Following
Door of Faith Churches of Hawaii
Eglise Apostolique Unie en Afrique
Eglise Protestante Evangelique
El Bethel Church
Elim Foursquare Gospel
Elim Missionary Assemblies
Elim Pentecostal Church
Emmanuel Church of Christ Oneness Pentecostal
Emmanuel Holiness Church
"Envoy of the Messiah"
Epis Holy Temple and Tabernacle Mission
Ethiopian National Church, Nigeria
Etoism
Evangelical Bible Church
Evangelical Church of Pentecost
Faith Assembly World Wide Church of Christ
Faith Movement
Faith Tabernacle
F'eden Church
Fellowship of Christian Believers
Fellowship of Christian Pilgrims
Filipino Assemblies of the First Born
Fire-Baptized Holiness Associaion
Fire-Baptized Holiness Church of God of the Americas
First Born Church of the Living God, The

First Interdenominational Christian Association
First United Church of Jesus Christ
Free Church of God in Christ
Free Gospel Church, Inc.
Free Will Baptist Church of the Pentecostal Faith
Friends of the Holy Spirit
Full Gospel Central Church
Full Gospel Church Association
Full Gospel Church of Australia
Full Gospel Defenders Conference of America
Full Gospel Evangelical Association
Full Gospel Fellowship of Churches and Ministries, International
Full Gospel Ministry Association
Gemeinde der Christin Ecclesia
Gemeinde Jesu Christi in Deutschland
Gemeindeschafte Entschie Christien
General Assembly and Church of the First Born
Gereja Pantekosta de Indonesia
Ghana Apostolic Church
Glad Tidings Missionary Society
Glen Ridge Christian Fellowship
God of the Universe Church
God's House of Prayer for All Nations, Inc.
Gospel Assemblies
Gospel Harvesters Evangelistic Association (Buffalo)
Grace Gospel Evangelistic Association International, Inc.
Greater Refuge Temple
Hephzibah Faith Missionary Association
Holy Ghost Church of East Africa
Holy Spirit Church of Zayun
Holy Trinity Healing Church
House of God Which is the Church of the Living God, the Pillar and Ground of Truth
House of God Which is the Church of the Living God, the Pillar and Ground of Truth Without Controversy
House of the Lord
House of the Lord
Ibandla Lika Christu
Idapo Mimo Cherubim and Seraphim
Iglesia Bando Evangelico Gedeon
Iglesia Cristiana del Norte
Iglesia Cristiana Pentecostes

Iglesia de Dios Cristiana Pentecostal
Iglesia de Dios Pentecostal
Iglesia del Principe de Paz
Iglesia Evangelica del Emanuel
Iglesia Evangelica Pentecostal de Chili
Iglesia ni Jesu Cristo Bagong Jerusalem
Igreja Adventista de Promessa
Imisi Jesu
Independent Assemblies of God,
    International
Independent Assemblies of God
    (Unincorporated)
Independent Pentecostal Christian Church
Indian Pentecostal Church of God
International Christian Churches
International Deliverance Churches
International Evangelism Crusades
International Pentecostal Assemblies
International Pentecostal Church of Christ
International Pentecostal Holiness Church
Italian Pentecostal Assemblies of God
Jappa Tabernacle
Jehovah Jireh Christ Church
Jesus Divine Healing Church
Jordanites
Jotabeche Pentecostal Methodist Church
Kenya Foundation of the Prophets Church
King David's Spiritual Temple of Truth
    Association
Kirisuto Dendo-Dan
Kwang Lim Methodist Church
Lamb of God Church
Last Ministry Church
Latter Rain Movement
Leroy Jenkins Evangelistic Association
Life and Light Fellowship
Malango Church
Maranatha Campus Ministries
Miracle Life Revival Inc.
Miracle Revival Fellowship
Mita
Movimiento Cristiano y Misionero
Nagaland Christian Revival Church
National David Spiritual Temple of Christ
    Church Union (Inc.) U.S.A.
Neverdies
New Age Church of Truth
New Bethel Church of God in Christ
    (Pentecostal)

New Covenant Church of God
New Faith Gospel Apostolic Church of
    Jesus Christ
New Salem Church (Aladura)
New Testament Church of God
New Testament Missionary Fellowship
Nondigressive Church of God
Northeast Kingdom Community Church
Nuba Divine Healing Church
Open Bible Standard Churches Inc.
(Original) Church of God, Inc.
Original Pentecostal Church of God
Pentecostal Assemblies of the World
Pentecostal Churches of the World
Pentecostal Church of God
Pentecostal Church of God
Pentecostal Church of Zion
Pentecostal Evangelical Church
Pentecostal Fellowship of North America
Pentecostal Fire Baptized Holiness Church
Pentecostal Holiness Church, International
People of the Living God
Philadelphia-Verein
Pilgrim Wesleyan Holiness Church
Pillar of Fire
Power of Jesus Around the World Church
Ranson Pentecostal African Methodist
    Episcopalian Zion
Ras Tafari Melchizedek Orthodox Church
Remnant Church, The
Remnant Churches of God
Restoration Movement
Resurrected Church of God
Roho Church of the God of Israel
Sacred Order of Cherubim and Seraphim
    Society
Sacred Order of the Silent Brotherhood
Saint John's Apostolic Faith Mission of
    South Africa
Saint Paul's Apostolic Faith Mission
Saint Paul's Spiritual Church Convocation
Samoan Full Gospel Church
Saviour's Apostolic Church of Nigeria
School of the Prophets, The
Sei Iesu Kai
Seventh Day Pentecostal Church of the
    Living God
Shilo Pentecostal Fellowship
Shiloh Trust

Shilo United Church of Christ (Apostolic)
Sinai Church of East Africa
Sung Rak Baptist Church
True Church of Christ New Bethlehem
True Faith Church
Truth Fellowship Pentecostal Church of
    God of America
True Grace Memorial House of Prayer
Twer Nyame Church
United Christian Church and Ministerial
    Association
United Christians Church
United Evangelical Churches
United Holy Church of America
United House of Prayer for All People
United Pentecostal Church
United Pentecostal Faith Church
Universal Christian Spiritual Faith and
    Churches of All Nations
Universal Church of the Kingdom of God
Universal Prayer Fellowship
Universal World Church
Unorganized Italian Christian Churches of
    North America
Voice of Prophecy Church
Voice of Salvation and Healing Church
Wakorino
Way of the Cross Church
Weni Mwanguvu
Wesleyan Methodist Church of Brazil
Wesleyan Pentecostal Church
World Renewal, Inc.
Yahweh's Temple
Yoido Full Gosple (Pentecostal) Church
Young Nak Presbyterian Church

PROTESTANT:

African Brotherhood Church
African Church Mission
African Church of the Holy Spirit
African Divine Church
African Independent Church of Kenya
African Independent Pentecostal Church
Amana Church Society
American Rescue Workers
Antioch Baptist Church
Apostelmat Jesu Christi

Apostelmat Juda
Apostolic Christian Church (Nazarean), The
Apostolic Christian Church of America
Ayie Remb Yesu
Bakole
Basic Bible Churches of America
Bible Holiness Mission
Bible Missionary Church
Body of Christ
Brazil for Christ
Catholic Charismatic Renewal
Christian Brotherhood Church
Christian Community Church
Christian Fellowship International
Christian Nation Church, USA
Christian Restoration Ministries
Christian Theocratic Holy Church of God
Crystal Cathedral
Disciples of Christ
Dispensationalism
Duck River (and Kindred) Association of
    Baptists
Emmanuel Association
Equifrilibricum World Religion
Ethiopians
Free Christian Zion Church of Christ, The
Free Presbyterian Church (Paisleyite)
Free Protestant Episcopal Church
Fundamentalism
God is Love
Identity Movement
Iglesia Cristiana del Norte
Iglesia Cristiana Pentecostes
Iglesia de Dios Cristiana Pentecostal
Iglesia Edifica de Jesucristo
Iglesia Ng Dios Kay Kristo Jesus
Kodesh Church of Immanuel
Life Science Church
Malagasy Protestant Church
Missionary Christian and Soul Winning
    Fellowship
National Association for the Promotion of
    Holiness
Native America Church
Nazarene Episcopal Ecclesia
Nihon Kirisuto Kyodan
Order of St. Luke
Peculiar People
Peniel Missions

Pillar of Fire
Plymouth Brethren
Reformed Zion Union Apostolic Church
Roho Musalaba
Sacred Name Movement
St. Peter's Healing Church
Samhan Ng Amang Ka-Amahamat Inang
    Ka-Inainahan
Standard Church of America
Tipan Ng Panginoon
Triumph of the Church and Kingdom
    (International)
Trois Saints Coeurs
United Evangelical Churches

RASTAFARIAN:

African Reform Coptic Church of God in
    Christ, the First Fruit of Prayer, God's
    Army Camp
Dreads, The
Ethiopian Zion Coptic Church
Nyabingi
Rastafarians
Revival Zion
Twelve Tribes of Israel

ROMAN CATHOLICS, TRADITIONALIST
    see TRADITIONALIST ROMAN
    CATHOLICS

ROSICRUCIANS:

AMORC Rosicrucian Order
Ancient Mayans, Order of
Ausar Auset Society
Fraternitas Rosae Crucis
Lectorium Rosicrucianum
Ordo Templi Orienti
Rosicrucian Anthroposophic League
Rosicrucian Fellowship
Societas Rosicruciana in America (SRIA)
Societas Rosicruciana in Anglia

SABBATH-KEEPING GROUPS:

Advent Sabbath Church
Apostolic Church of God
Assemblies of Yahweh (Michigan)
Church of God, Body of Christ
Church of God (Sabbatarian)
Church of God (Seventh-Day, Salem, West
    Virginia)
General Conference of the Church of God
    (Seventh Day)
General Council of the Churches of God
People's Christian Church
Seventh-Day Adventist Church (SDA)
Seventh-Day Adventist Reform
    Movement
Seventh-Day Christian Conference
Seventh Day Church of God
Seventh Day Pentecostal Church of the
    Living God
Unification Association of Christian
    Sabbath Keepers, The
United Seventh-Day Brethren
Voice of Prophecy Church

SCIENTOLOGY:

Abilitism
Advanced Ability Center (AAC)
Dianology and Eductivism
Duga (Ability)
Process, or the Church of the Final
    Judgment Process, The
Ron's Organization and Network for
    Standard Tech
Scientology, Church of

SIKHISM:

Eckankar
Healthy, Happy, Holy, Organization (3HO)
Kirpal Ruhani Satsang
Manav Kendra
Namdhari
Nirankari
Radhasoami Satsang

Radhasoami Satsang Beas
Radhasoami Satsang Soamibagh
Ruhani Satsang
Sant Bani Ashram
Sawan Kirpal Ruhani Mission

"SNAKE HANDLERS":

Church of All Nations
Dolly Pond Church of God with Signs
    Following
Original Pentecostal Church of God, The

SPIRITUALISTS:

Agasha Temple of Wisdom
"Ange Albert"
Apres
Aquarian Brotherhood of Christ, The
Aquarian Foundation
Associated Spiritualists
Association for the Understanding of Man,
    The
Astara Foundation
Atlanteans
Baptist Movement of Divine Healing-
    Meditation, The
Basilio Scientific School
Batuque
Escuela Cientifica Basilio
Fellowship of the Inner Light
First Spiritualist Church of New York
First Universal Spiritualist Church of New
    York City
Foundation Church of Divine Truth
Geistige Loge
General Assembly of Spiritualists (GAS)
Greater World Christian Spiritualist
    League, The
Ibis Fraternity
Independent Spiritualist Association (ISA)
Inner Circle Kethra E'da Foundation
International General Assembly of
    Spiritualists (IGAS)
International Spiritualist Federation
Israel Universal Divine Spiritual Churches
    of Christ

Kardecism
Kingdom of Yahweh
Lichtcentrum Bethanien
Mark-Age Metacenter
Martinus Institute of Spiritual Science
Michaelsvereinigung
Mystic Connection/Church Of Light
National Colored Spiritualist Association of
    Churches
National David Spiritual Temple of Christ
    Church Union (Inc.) U.S.A.
National Spiritual Alliance
National Spiritualist Association of
    Churches (NSAC)
National Spiritual Science Center
New York Spiritual Center, Inc.
Orden Fiat Lux
Progressive Spiritual Church
Roosevelt Spiritual Memorial Benevolent
    Association
School of Universal Philosophy and
    Healing
Shanti Nilaya
Society of Christ, Inc.
Spiritual Frontiers Fellowship (SFF)
Spiritual Science Church
Spiritual Science Fellowship
Star Light Fellowship
Temple of Universal Law
Umbanda
Universal Christ Church
Universal Church of the Master (UCM)
Universal Hagar's Spiritual Church
Universal Harmony Foundation
Universal Link
Universal Spiritualist Association
Universal Spiritual Temple of the New
    Era—Temple of Celestial Light
White Eagle Lodge

SUFISM:

The Abode of the Message
Arica Institute
Baba League, The
Beshara Trust
Halveti-Jerrahi Order of New York
Healing Order of the Sufi Order

Institute for Cultural Research
Institute for Research on the Dissemination
    of Human Knowledge
Meher Baba, Friends of
Meher Durbar
Prema Dharmasala and Fellowship
    Association; Prema World Community
The Sufi Islamia Ruhaniat Society
Sufi Order of the West
Sufism Reoriented, Inc.
The Universal Spiritual League of America

THEOSOPHY GROUPS:

Agni Yoga Society
American Universalist Temple of Divine
    Wisdom
Anthroposophy Society
Aquarian Educational Foundation
Aquarian Foundation
Astara Foundation
The Bridge Center for Spiritual Studies
Chirothesian Church of Faith
Church of Religious Philosophy
Concept-Therapy Institute
Deva Community
Fellowship of Crotona
Gnostic Society
Great School of the Masters
"I Am"
Independent Theosophical Society
Interfaith Temple or Interfaith, Inc.
International Community of Christ
Krishnamurti
Liberal Catholic Church (LCC)
Mark-Age Metacenter
Martinus Institute
Ministry of Universal Wisdom
New Acropolis (NA)
New Age Christianity Without Religion
Order of the Cross
Order of the Initiates of Tibet
Ordine Dei Maestri Shan
Pansophic Institute
Philosophical Research Society
School of Light and Realization (SOLAR)
Servants of the Light (SOL)

Solar Cross Fellowship
Solar Light Center
Stelle Community
Temple of Universal Law
Theocentric Foundation
Theosophical Order of Service, The (TOS)
Theosophical Society in America
Theosophy
Unarius Educational Foundation (Unarius-
    Science Of Life)
Understanding, Inc.
United Lodge of Theosophists (ULT)
Universal Brotherhood
Universal Brotherhood and Theosophical
    Society
Universal Faith and Wisdom Association
The Universal Great Brotherhood AUM
    Solar Line
Universarium Foundation
University of the Trees
Welt-Spirale
Wisdom's Goldenrod Center for
    Philosophic Studies

TIBETAN BUDDHISM:

Arya Maitreya Mandala
Dorje Khyung Dzong
Ewam Choden Tibetan Buddhist Center
Ganden Mahayana Center
Gelug-Pa ("Yellow Hat")
Home of the Dharma
Jetsun Sakya Center (JSC)
Kadampa Center for Tibetan Buddhism
Kagyu Droden Kunchab
Kagyu E-Vam Buddhist Institute
Kagyu Kunkhyab Chuling
Kagyu Ling
Kamalashila
Kargyudpa Order
Kargyu Dsamling Kunchab
Karma Kagyu Institute
Karma Kagyu Samye-Ling
Karma Triyana Dharmachakra (KTD)
Karm Ling
Lamaist Buddhist Monastery of America
Lama Tzong Khapa

GEOGRAPHICAL INDEX

The Geographical Index groups entries by geographical location or region. Thus, if you are looking for information about new religious movements in Korea, or the names of organizations that originated in Italy, you will find them grouped under these headings. In some cases, when a group's activities are spread throughout a region, or are not narrowed to a specific country, we have listed these under a broader heading such as African Groups or North American Groups.

ANGOLA:
Mission de Dieu du Bougie
Olosanto
Vrai Èglise Catholique

AFRICAN GROUPS:
African Greek Orthodox Church
Apostles in Zion Church
Christianisme Prophetique En Afrique
Church of Cherubim and Seraphim
Church of the Ancestors
Église Adaiste
Église Akeiste
Église Deimatiste
Église du Christianisme Celeste du Benin
Evangelical Church of Pentecost
Harris Movement
Herero Church
Kanda Dia Kinzinga ("People for Eternal Life")
Kimbanguist Movement
Kitawala
Lumpa Church
Malagasy Protestant Church
Maria Legio (of Africa)
Masowe Apostles
Matsouanism (Matswa)
Musama Disco Christo Church (MDCC)
Roho Musalaba (Spirit Cross Church)
Sacred Order of Cherubim and Seraphim Society
St. Peter's Healing Church
Sinai Church of East Africa (SCEA)
Soja We Mwari
Watch Tower Movement
Watchtower Movement
Weni Mwanguvu

Wokofu African Church (WAC)
 see ANGOLA, BENIN, CONGO (Democratic Republic of Congo, Formerly Zaire), CONGO REPUBLIC (People's Republic of the Congo), GABON, GHANA, IVORY COAST, KENYA, MADAGASCAR, MALAWI, NIGERIA, RUANDA-URUNDI, SENEGAL, SIERRA LEONE, SOMALIA, SOUTH AFRICA, SUDAN, TANZANIA, UGANDA, ZAIRE, ZAMBIA, ZIMBABWE

ARGENTINA:
Basilio Scientific School
Body of Christ
Christian Brotherhood Church (CBC)
Christian Holy Ghost Church of East Africa (CHGC)
Cafh Spiritual Culture Society
Escuela Cientifica Basilio
Iglesia de Dios Cristiana Pentecostal
Instituto Para el Desarrollo Armonico del Hombre
Movimiento Christiano y Misionero
New Acropolis (NA)

ASIAN GROUPS:
Al-Arqam
American Evangelistic Association, The

AUSTRALIA:
Berean Bible Institute
Chiltern Yoga Foundation
Christian Israelites
Christian Truth Institute
Church of the Mystic Christ
Full Gospel Church in Australia

Independent Theosophical Society
Kagyu E-vam Buddhist Institute
New Covenant Fellowship
Olive Tree Fellowship
Remnant Church
Traleg Tulag

AUSTRIA:
Grail Message (Gralsbewegung)
New Apostolic Church
Primitive Church of Antioch
Unification Church

BELGIUM:
Antoinisme
Ohtm
Solar Temple, Order of (Ordre du Temple
    Solaire)

BENIN:
Èglise du Christianisme Celeste du Benin

BRAZIL:
Batuque
Brazil for Christ (OBPC)
Candomblé
Church of the New Life
Congregacao Crista
Discipulos de Santissima Trinidade, Sede
    (DSTS)
"Envoy of the Messiah"
Federacao Espirita Brasileira (FEB)
God Is Love
Igreja Adventista de Promessa
Igreja Brasileira
Igreja Catolica Apostolic Brasileira (ICAB)
Igreja Expectante
International Society of Divine Revelation
    (SIRD)
Sovereign Universal Order of the Holy
    Trinity (SOUST)
Umbanda
Universal Church of the Kingdom of God
Wesleyan Methodist Church of Brazil
    (WMC)

CANADA:
Apostles of Infinite Love
Association of Covenant People
Association of Seventh-Day Pentecostal
    Assemblies
Bible Holiness Movement
Christian Fellowship International
Christian Messianic Fellowship
Dawn of Truth
Doukhobors
Friends of Israel
Glad Tidings Missionary Society
Gospel Harvesters Evangelistic Association
    (Buffalo)
Handsome Lake Religion
I Am Ashram
Independent Assemblies of God,
    International
Kosmunity
Latter Rain Movement
Melech Isreal
Message to Israel
People Searching Inside (PSI)
Raëlians
Solar Temple, Order of (Ordre du Temple
    Solaire)
Sons of Freedom
Sivananda Yoga Vedanta Centers
    International
Thomas Merton Center
Traditional Christian Catholic Church
United Pentecostal Faith Church
Yasodhara Ashram Society
Zion Messianic Fellowship

CARRIBEAN GROUPS:
Antioch Baptist Church
Remnant Churches of God
Shouters (Spiritual Baptists)

CHILI:
Arica Institute
Iglesia Evangelica Israelita del Nuevo Pacto
Iglesia Sionista
Jotabeche Pentecostal Methodist Church
Wesleyan Pentecostal Church

Jesus Fellowship Church
Karma Kagyu Samye-Ling
Life and Light Fellowship
Odinist Committee
Old Apostolic Church
Order of the Cross
Pentecostal Churches of the World
Pilgrim Wesleyan Holiness Church
Progressive Judaism
Ramana Maharshi Foundation
Rastafarians World Congress of Faiths
Seventh-Day Adventist Reform Movement
Sivananda Yoga Vedanta Centers
    International
Templegesellschaft
Universal Life (Universelles Leben)
Wrekin Trust, The
Xat American Indian Medicine Society
Yahweh's Temple

GUATEMALA:
Iglesia Apostolica de la Fe en Cristo Jesus
Iglesia Cristo Jesus (IAFCJ)
Iglesia Catolica Nacional Guatemalteca
Iglesia del Principe de Paz

GUYANA:
Hallelujah Church
Jordanites (Jordonites)

HAITI:
Foi Apostolique Nationale
Mission Patriotique Nationale

HOLLAND:
Eben Haezer
Lectorium Rosicrucianum
Stromen Van Kracht (Streams of Power;
    Courants de Puissance)

HONG KONG:
Traditional Christian Catholic Church

INDIA:
Ahmadiyya Movement

Akhanananda Saraswati, Swami
Ananda Marga
Apostolic Fellowship Tabernacle
Arya Maitreya Mandala
Arya Samaj
Assemblies (Jehova Shammah)
Assemblies of Jesus Christ
Brahma Kumaris (Raja Yoga)
Brahma Samaj
Chinmaya Mission
Church of the New Dispensation, The
Divine Life Society (Divine Life
    Consciousness)
Divine Life Mission (DLM)
Fellowship of the Followers of Jesus
Hindu Church of the Lord Jesus
Hindu Mahasabha
Independent Church of India
Indian Pentecostal Church of God
Mara Christian Church
Nagaland Christian Revival Church
    (NCRC)
National Church of Madras
Pentecostal Church of God
Prarthana Samaj
Punjaji
Radhasoami Satsang
Radhasoami Satsang Beas
Radhasoami Satsang Dayalbagh
Radhasoami Satsang Soamibagh
Ramabahi Mukti Mission
Ramakrishna Math and Mission
Ramana Maharshi
Rama Rajya Parisha
Rashtriya Swayamasevak Sangh (RSS)
Ruhani Satsang
Sai Baba
Santiniketan
Sarva Dharma Sambhava Kendra
Sathya Sai Baba
Seng Khasi
Siddha Yoga
Sri Aurobindo
Sri Ma Anandamayi Ashrams
Subba Rao
Suttangam Sabhi
Swaminarayana
Temple of Universal Peace
Truth Consciousness
Vishwa Hindu Parishad (VHP)
World Community Service

World Teacher Trust
Yogoda Satsanga Society

INDONESIA:
Agama Islam Desjati
Agama Jawa
Agama Jawa-Sunda
Bungan
Gereja Pantekosta de Indonesia
Islam-Is
Krislam
Krislapi
Mansren
Nimboran
Subud

IRAN:
Babism

IRELAND:
Assemblies of God in Great Britain and
    Ireland
Two-By-Two's

ISRAEL:
Bahais
Bahai World Federation
Beit Assaph
Beit Immanuel
Bethesda
Black Hebrews
Cafh Spiritual Society
Da'at
Emin Society, The
Etzba Elohim (The Finger of God)
Grace and Truth Christian Congregation
Hebrew Christian Assembly-Jerusalem
    Congregation
Messianic Assembly of Israel
Netivyah
Peniel

ITALY:
Associazione Pitagorica
Chiesa Cattolica Riformata d'Italia

Chiesa Cristiana Millenarista
Chiesa Guirisdavidica
Chiesa Universale Guiris-Davidica
Damanhur
Fratellanza Cosmica
Istituto Mater Boni Consilii
Lama Tzong Khapa
Magnificat
Maria Rosa Mystica
Merigar
Nonsiamosoli ("We Are Not Alone")
Nucleo Ubaldiano di Metafisica (Ubaldian
    Nucleus of Metaphysics)
Ordine Dei Maestri Shan
Ordine Esoterico Del Loto Bianco

IVORY COAST:
Sylla Movement

JAMAICA:
African Reform Coptic Church of God in
    Christ, the First Fruit of Prayer, God's
    Army Camp
Assemblies of the First-Born
Bedwardism
Bethel Apostolic (Shilo) Church
Black Israelites
Church of the First-Born
Ethiopian Zion Coptic Church
First United Church of Jesus Christ
    (Apostolic)
Nyabingi
Rastafarians
Ras Tafari Melchizedek Orthodox
    Church
Revival Zion

JAPAN:
Agon Kyo
Amen Church
Ananaikyo
Aum Shinrikyo (Aum Supreme Truth)
Bussho Gohnen Kai
Byakko Shinkokai
Dai-Hizen-Kyo
Fukkatsu No Kirisuto Kyodan

447

Assemblies of the Lord Jesus Christ, Inc.
Assemblies of Yahweh
Assemblies of Yahweh (Michigan)
Assembly, The
Assembly of Christian Churches, Inc., The
Assembly of Christian Soldiers
Assembly of Yahvah
Associated Brotherhood of Christians
Associated Gospel Churches
Associated Spiritualists
Association for Research and
    Enlightenment, Inc., The (ARE)
Association for the Understanding of Man,
    The
Association of International Gospel
    Assemblies, Inc.
Association of Sananda and Sanat Kumara
Association of Seventh-Day Pentecostal
    Assemblies
Astara Foundation
Astrological, Metaphysical, Occult,
    Revelatory, Enlightenment Church
    (AMORE)
Athanor Fellowship
Atmaniketan Ashram
Atom Foundation
Aum Center for Self-Realization
Aum Shinrikyo (Aum Supreme Truth)
Ausar Auset Society
Baba League, The
Back to the Bible Way
Bahais Under the Hereditary Guardianship
Bahais Under the Provisions of the
    Covenant (BUPC)
Baptist Movement of Divine Healing-
    Mediation, The
Basic Bible Churches of America
Beacon Light Ministry
Bear Tribe, The
Berean Bible Fellowship
Berean Bible Fellowship (Chicago)
Berean Bible Students Church
Berean Fundamental Churches
Bethany Bible Church and Related
    Independent Bible Churches
Beth Bnai Abraham (BBA)
Bethel Christian Temple
Bethel Ministerial Association
Bethel Temple
Beth Messiah
Beth Messiah

Beth Messiah
Beth Messiah Congregation
Beth Yeshua
Bible Churches (Classics Expositor)
Bible Missionary Church
Bible Presbyterian Church
Bible Speaks
Bible Student Examiner, The
Bible Temple
Bible Way Church of Our Lord Jesus Christ
    World Wide
Biosophical Institute (Biosophy)
Black Hebrews (The Kingdom of God
    Nation)
Blue Rose Ministry
B'nai Noach ("Children of Noach")
B'nai Yeshua
Body of Christ, The
Boston Church of Christ (BCC)
Bovar (Oric) Group
Branch Seventh Day Adventists (Branch
    SDA)
Branham Tabernacle
Bridge Center for Spiritual Studies, The
Bridge Meditation Center, The
Bridge to Freedom, The
Brotherhood of Light
Brother Julius
Brunton (Paul) Philosophic Foundation
Builders, The
Builders of the Adytum (BOTA)
California Miracles Center
Calumet Pagan Temple
Calvary Chapel
Calvary Fellowship, Inc.
Calvary Pentecostal Church
Camp Farthest Out
Carolina Evangelistic Association
Cathedral of Tomorrow
Catholic Charismatic Renewal (CCR)
Center for Consciousness
Center for Spiritual Awareness (CSA)
Center of First Light, The
Center of Light Community, The
Chinook Community
Chirothesian Church of Faith
Chosen People Ministries
Christanada Yoga Ashram
Christ Brotherhood
Christ Brotherhood, Inc.
Christ Catholic Church (Diocese of Boston)

Shanti Yogi Institute
Shepherding
Shepherd's Chapel
Sherborne Studies Group
Shiloh True Light Church of Christ
Shiloh Trust
Shoresh Yishai
Shree Gurudev Ashram California
Shree Gurudev Rudrananda Yoga Ashram
Shri Vishva Seva Ashram
"Sign Followers"
Sirius Community
Sivananda Yoga Vedanta Centers International
Sivananda Yoga Vedanta Church
Societas Rosicruciana in America
Society for Avatar Meher Baba
Society of Christ, Inc.
Society of Pragmatic Mysticism
Society of Pius V.
Soka Gakkai of America
Solar Cross Fellowship
Solar Light Center
Sons Ahman Israel
Spiritual Fellowship of America
Spiritual Frontiers Fellowship
Spiritual Science of Mind Center
Spring Grove
Springhill Community
Sri Aurobindo International Center Foundation
Sri Chimnoy
Sri Ma Anandamayi Monastery
Sri Ram Ashrama
Starcross Monastic Community
Stelle Community
Stonegate Christian Community
Sufi Islamia Ruhaniat Society
Sufism Reoriented, Inc.
Summum Church
Sunergos Institute, Inc.
Sunray Meditation Society
Swami Shantiananda Center
Swedenborg Foundation
Sword of Christ Good News Ministries
Tayu Fellowship
Teaching of the Inner Christ, Inc.
Temple of Kriya Yoga
Temple of the Eternal Light, Inc.
Temple of the Goddess Within
Temple of Thelema

Temple of Universal Judaism
Temple of Universal Law
Temple of Wicca
Theocentric Foundation
Theocentric Temple
Theocentric Commune Natural Health Service
Theosophical Society in America
This Testimony
Tibetan Buddhist Learning Center
Timely Messenger Fellowship
Today Church
Traditional Christian Catholic Church
Tree of Life
Triumph the Church and Kingdom of God in Christ (International)
True Church of Christ, International
True Followers of Christ
True Grace Memorial House of Prayer
True Light Church of Christ
Truth Station, The
Twentieth Century Church of God
Unarius Educational Foundation (UNARIUS—Science of Life)
Undenominational Church of the Lord
Understanding, Inc.
Unification Association of Christian Sabbath Keepers
Unification Church
Union of Messianic Jewish Congregations
Unis
United Christian Scientists
United Church and Science of Living Institute
United Church of Living Science
United Evangelical Churches
United Holy Church of America
United House of Prayer for All People
United Israel World Fellowship
United Israel World Union
United Leadership Council of Hebrew Israelites
United Lodge of Theosophists
United Missionary Church
United Order Effort
United Pentecostal Church
United Seventh-Day Brethren
Unity School of Christianity
Universal Brotherhood
Universal Brotherhood and Theosophical Society

Universal Christ Church
Universal Christian Spiritual Faith and
    Churches for All Nations
Universal Church
Universal Church of Aquaria
Universal Church of Scientific Truth
Universal Church of the Master
Universal Church, the Mystical Body of
    Christ
Universal Faith and Wisdom Association
Universal Faithists of Kosmon
Universal Fellowship of Metropolitan
    Community Churches
Universal Hagar Spiritual Church
Universal Harmony Foundation
Universal Peace Association
Universal Shrine of Divine Guidance
Universal Spiritualist Association
Universal Spiritual League of America
Universal Spiritual Temple of the New
    Era—Temple of Celestial Light
Universal Truth Foundation
Universal World Church
Universariun Foundation
University of Life Church
University of Metaphysics
University of the Science of Spirit
University of the Trees
Unorganized Italian Christian Churches of
    North America
Urantia Foundation
Uresa Reflective Center
Vajradhatu
Vajrapani Institute for Wisdom Culture
Vedanta Society
Vedic Church of East Africa
Vedic Cultural Center
Venturism
Vimala Prakashan Trust
Vineyard Christian Fellowship
Voice of Calvary
Voice of Elijah, Inc.
Volunteers of America
Waldorf Institute
Walk (Church of the Living Word), The
Way International, Inc., The
Way of the Cross Church
Western Bible Students Association
Westminster Biblical Fellowship
Westmoreland Chapel
White Star

Wisdom Institute of Spiritual Education
Wisdom's Goldenrod Center for
    Philosophical Studies
Word Foundation
Word of Faith Ministries
Word of God
Work of Christ
World Catalyst Church
World Institute of Avasthology
World Messianity
World Renewal, Incorporated
Worldwide Church of God
Yeshe Nyingpo
Yeshe Nyingpo Argyen Cho Dhing
Yeshe Nyingpo Orgyen Cho Dzong
Yoga House
Yoga Institute of Consciousness
Yogi Gupta Ashram, Inc.
Yogiraj
Yoruba Lacumi
Your Heritage
Zion's Order of the Sons of Levi

VENEZUELA:
Maria Lionza

VIETNAM:
Cao Dai
Coconut Palm Movement
Hoa Hao
Latin Rite Catholic Church

WALES:
Apostolic Church
Apostolic Church of Great Britain
Community of the Many Names of God

WEST INDIES:
Shakers

ZAIRE see CONGO (DEMOCRATIC
    REPUBLIC OF CONGO)

ZAMBIA:
African Apostolic Church of Johane
    Maranke (AACJM)

PERSONAL NAMES INDEX

The Personal Names Index consists of leaders, founders, and important figures affiliated with particular religious groups included in this encyclopedia. For instance, if you wanted to learn with what groups Austin T. Sparks is associated, or to see in how many entries Annie Besant is mentioned, you would find that information below.

C

Caddy, Eileen and Peter, *see* Findhorn
Foundation

Caillaux, *see* Evadisme

Cameron, W.J., *see* Anglo-Saxon Federation
of America

Campbell, Alexander, *see* Disciples of Christ

Campbell, Henry, *see* Independent
Fundamentalist Bible Churches

Campbell, Nicol C., *see* School of Truth

Canavese, Baldissero, *see* Damanhur

Carfora, Carmel Henry, *see* North American
Old Roman Catholic Church

Carmona, Moise, *see* Union Catolica Trento

Carpenter, G.L., *see* Salvation Army, The

Carrozzo, Al, *see* Twentieth Century Church
of God

Carter, Ben-Ami, *see* Black Hebrews

Case, Paul, *see* Builders of the Adytum

Casely, Frank and William, *see* Free Gospel
Church, Inc.

Cayce, Charles Thomas, *see* Association for
Research and Enlightenment, Inc., The

Cayce, Edgar
see Association for Research and
Enlightenment, Inc., The
see Holistic Community

Cayce, Hugh Lynn, *see* Association for
Research and Enlightenment, Inc., The

Cecil, Martin, *see* Emissaries of Divine Light

Cekwane, Timothy, *see* Ibandla Loku Kanya

Chaney, Robert and Earlyne, *see* Astara
Foundation

Chang-Rim, Lee, *see* Mission for the
Coming Days

Chanler, Lewis Stuyvesant, *see* New History
Society

Chapman, John, *see* Swedenborg Foundation

Charan, Kali, *see* Bornhos

Charles, Ureal Vercilli, *see* Universal
Brotherhood

Charya, Shankara, *see* School of Practical
Philosophy

Chatterji, Gadadhar, see Ramakrishna Math
and Mission

Chaudhuri, Haridas, *see* Cultural
Integration Fellowship

Chaza, Mai "Mother", *see* Mai Chaza
Church

Chelpan, Chot, *see* Burkhanism

Chernoff, Martin, *see* Beth Messiah

Cherry, F.S., *see* Church of God (Black Jews)

Chetananda, Swami, *see* Nityananda
Institute

Chetti, Kandiswamy, *see* Fellowship of the
Followers of Jesus

Chi, Mama, *see* Mama Chi
see Shanti Mandir Temple of Peace
see Syda Foundation

Chieu, Nguyen Van, *see* Cao Dai

Chilembwe, John, *see* Providence Industrial
Mission

Chiliza, Job, *see* African Gospel Church

Chinmayananda, Swami, *see* Chinmaya
Mission

Chitrabhanu, Gurudev Shree, *see* Jain
Meditation International Center

Cho, Yongi
see Full Gospel Central Church
see Word of Life Church

Christensen, Alice, *see* Light of Yoga Society

Christian, William, *see* Church of the Living
God, Christian Workers for Fellowship

Christopher, Daniel, *see* Holy Order of
Ezekiel

Clark, Glenn, *see* Camp Farthest Out

Clark, Steve, *see* Word of God

Clarke, Richard, *see* Calumet Pagan Temple

Cleague, Albert B., *see* Pan African
Orthodox Christian Church

Clement, Robert, *see* Eucharistic Catholic
Church

"Clubs Archedia", *see* Association
Internationale des Clubs Archedia
Sciences et Traditions

Clymer, R. Swinburne, *see* Fraternitas Rosae
Crucis

Coanda, Victoria, *see* Sivananda Yoga
Vedanta Church

Cobb, C.E. ("Buddy"), *see* Body of Christ,
The

Coble, Srimati Margaret, *see* Integral Center
of Self-Abidance

Cohen, Raymond, *see* Beth Yeshua

Cohn, Leopold, *see* Chosen People
Ministries

Cole, Raymond C., *see* Church of God, the
Eternal

Deguchi, Mrs. Nao, *see* Omotokyo

Delbauche, Albert, *see* Amis de la Croix Glorieuse de Dozule

Demaras, Alexander, *see* New York Metaphysical Society

DePolito, Karen, *see* Temple of the Eternal Light, Inc.

Desai, Shanti, *see* Shanti Yogi Institute

Desai, Yogi Amrit, *see* Kripalu Yoga Ashram

Devananda, Swami Vishnu, *see* Sivananda Yoga Vedanta Centers International

Devi, Shri Mataji Nirmala, *see* Sahaja Yoga

Devi, Srimata Gayati, *see* Ananda Ashrama

Devine, Major Morgan J., *see* Father Divine Movement

Devine, Robert, *see* United Leadership Council of Hebrew Israelites

di Mambro, Joseph, *see* Solar Temple, Order of

Dickkerson, Kenneth G., *see* Positive Thinking Ministry

Dingle, Edwin John, *see* Institute of Mentalphysics

Dippong, Joseph F., *see* People Searching Inside

Divine, Father Major Jealous, *see* Father Divine Movement

"Divine Master Ishvara", *see* Ishvara

Dölinger, J.J., *see* Old Catholics

Dominguezy Gomez, Ferdinand Clemente, *see* Palmarian Catholic Church

Dooling, James A., III, *see* Church of the Gift of God

Douglas, John E., *see* American Evangelistic Association, The

Douglas, John L., *see* General Psionics, Church of

Dowie, John Alexander, *see* Christian Catholic Apostolic Church in Zion

Draves, W.A., *see* Church of Christ with the Elijah Message

Drew, Timothy, *see* Moorish Science Temple of America

Drummond, Henry, *see* Catholic Apostolic Church

Duce, Ivy Oneita, *see* Sufism Reoriented, Inc.

Duenov, Peter, *see* Fraternité Blanche Universelle

Dugger, A.N.
  see Church of God (Jerusalem)
  see Workers Together with Elohim

Dugger, Charles Andy
  see Church of God (Jerusalem)
  see Workers Together with Elohim

Duke, Caroline,
  see Aquarian Brotherhood of Christ, The

Dunlap, Shirlee, *see* Circle of Light

Durdin-Robertson, Lawrence, Pamela, and Olivia, *see* Fellowship of Isis

Durkee, Steve, *see* Lama Foundation

Durkin, Jim, *see* Church of the Complete Word

Dwane, James M.
  see Ethiopian Catholic Church of South Africa
  see Order of Ethiopia

Dyson, Fred, *see* Christian World Liberation Front

E

Ebongo, Offu, *see* Brotherhood of the Cross and Star

Eddy, Asa Gilbert, *see* Christian Science

Eddy, Mary Baker
  see Christian Science
  see Church Triumphant
  see Evangelical Christian Science Church
  see International Metaphysical Association
  see New Thought
  see Primitive Church of Christ, Scientist

Edgell, F.S., *see* New Jerusalem Fellowship

Edminster, Clyde, *see* Calvary Fellowship, Inc.

Edwards, Alexis, *see* Findhorn Foundation

Effendi, Abbas, *see* Babism

Effendi, Amin, *see* Bahai World Federation

Effendi, Shogi, *see* Babism

Eikerekoetter, Frederick, II, *see* United Church and Science of Living Institute

Eizo, Okano, *see* Gedatsu-Kai

Ekman, Ulf, *see* Word of Life Church

El-Legion, Michael, *see* Extra Terrestrial Communications Network

el-Qadiani, *see* Ahmadiyya Movement

Fruchtenbaum, Arnold, *see* Ariel Ministries

Fry, Daniel, *see* Understanding, Inc.

Fuller, W.E., *see* Fire-Baptized Holiness Church of God in the Americas

G

Gaard, Conrad, *see* Destiny of America Foundation

Gaillard, "Soeur", *see* Église Protestante Evangelique

Gale, William (Bill) Potter
  see Christian Defense League
  see Church of Jesus Christ-Christian

Gamble, Charles, *see* Seventh Day Pentecostal Church of the Living God

Gandhi, Mahatma, *see* Rashtriya Swayamasevak Sangh

Ganiodayo, *see* Handsome Lake Religion

Ganneau, *see* Evadisme

Garman, W.O.H., *see* Associated Gospel Churches

Garr, A.G., *see* Carolina Evangelistic Association

Garrique, Florence, *see* Meditation Group for the New Age

Garvey, Marcus
  see Afro-Athlican Constructive Gaathly
  see Rastafarians

Gaskin, Stephen, *see* Farm, The

Gayman, Daniel, *see* Church of Israel, The

Gelberman, Joseph H.
  see Interfaith Temple
  see Tree of Life

Gerling, Helene, *see* Universal Harmony Foundation

Geyer, Heinrich, *see* New Apostolic Church

Ghandi, Nemi Chand, *see* Sarva Dharma Sambhava Kendra

Ghibbory, Moshe, *see* United Israel World Union

Ghose, Aravinda Ackroyd, *see* Sri Aurobindo

Ghose, Chimnoy Kumar, *see* Sri Chimnoy

Ghose, Yogamaya, *see* Sri Chimnoy

Gibson, Joan, *see* Church of Inner Wisdom

Gilbert, Viola, *see* Cosmic Star Temple

Giri, Swami Nirmalananda, *see* Sri Ma Anandamayi Monastery

Giro, Elvira, *see* Chiesa Universale Guirisdavidica

Glendenning, Maurice Lerrie, *see* Aaronic Order

Glover, F.R.A., *see* British Israelism

Goad, F.G., Sr., *see* Forest Gate Church

Goduka, Jonas, *see* African Native Mission Church

Goi, Masahisa, *see* Byakko Shinkokai

Goldsmith, Joel S., *see* Infinite Way Society

Goldstein, Joseph, *see* Insight Meditation Society

Gondwe, Jeremiah, *see* Watchtower

Goodrich, Roy D., *see* Back to the Bible Way

Gordon, Charles Robert, *see* Astrological, Metaphysical, Occult, Revelatory, Enlightenment Church

Gordon, Keith, *see* Ethiopian Zion Coptic Church

Goren, Jacob, *see* Hebrew Christian Assembly-Jerusalem Congregation

Gortner, Marjoe, *see* Old Time Faith, Inc.

Gotlieb, Lou, *see* Morningstar

Gottula, Gerald W., *see* Future Foundation

Gould, Sylvester C., *see* Societas Rosicruciana in America

Govan, John George, *see* Faith Mission

Govinda, Lama Angarika, *see* Arya Maitreya Mandala

Grace, Sweet Daddy, *see* United House of Prayer for All People

Graf, Gene and Eva, *see* Center of Light Community, The

Gramlich, Michael J., *see* New Directions thru Meditation, Inc.

Grant, W.V., *see* International Deliverance Churches

Grave, Richard, *see* Universal Link

Gray, John Harvey, *see* Church of the Loving Servant

Green, Joyce, *see* Joya Houses

Greenbaum, Leon, *see* Primitive Church of Christ, Scientist

Greene, H.M., *see* Anglo-Saxon Christian Association

Greider, Melvin, *see* Faith Assembly World Wide Church of Christ

Grier, Albert C.

see Church of the Healing Christ (Divine Science), The
see Church of the Truth
see University of Metaphysics
Griffith, Glenn, *see* Bible Missionary Church
Grimes, Simon, *see* Pan African Orthodox Christian Church
Gupta, Yogi, *see* Yogi Gupta Ashram, Inc.
Gurdjieff, Georgei Ivanovich
  see Claymont Court
  see Gurdjieff Groups
Guru Ma, *see* Church Universal and Triumphant
Gurudev, *see* Kripalu Yoga Ashram
Gustafson, George, *see* Assembly, The
G'Zell, Otter, *see* Church of All Worlds

H
Hackman, John, *see* Twelve Apostles
Hagen, Walter, *see* Essene Center
Hagin, Kenneth
  see Faith Movement
  see Word of Life Church
Hall, Franklin, *see* Hall Deliverance Foundation
Hall, H. Richard, *see* United Christian Church and Ministerial Association
Hall, Manly Palmer, *see* Philosophical Research Society
Halsey, Wallace C., *see* Christ Brotherhood, Inc.
Ham, Keith, *see* New Vrindaban
Hamilton, Charles, *see* Knights Templar New Age Church
Hamilton, Ellen Gould, *see* Seventh-Day Adventist Church
Hancock, Pauline, *see* Church of Christ
Hanish, Otoman Zar-Adhust, *see* Mazdaznan
Hannifiya, Muhammad ibn al-, *see* Mahdi
Hanson, Minnie, *see* Apostolic Faith Mission
Harden, Thomas, *see* Dolly Pond Church of God with Signs Following
Hargis, Billy James, *see* Church of the Christian Crusade
Hargrove, Ernest, *see* Universal Brotherhood and Theosophical Society
Harrell, John

see Christian Conservative Church of America
see Christian Patriots Defense League
Harris, William Wade
  see Église Deimatiste
  see Harris Movement
  see Twelve Apostles
Harrison, Carl B., *see* Westmoreland Chapel
Hawtin, George, *see* Latter Rain Movement
Haywood, G.T., *see* Pentecostal Assemblies of the World
Hedgecock, Franklin, *see* Fanscifiaroan Church of Wicca
Hedgewar, Kashavrao Baliram, *see* Rashtriya Swayamasevak Sangh
Heindel, Max, *see* Rosicrucian Fellowship
Hellman, Sylvia, *see* Yasodhara Ashram Society
Hennings, H.C., *see* Christian Believers Conference
Henry, Claudius, *see* African Reform Coptic Church of God in Christ
Henry, Romiche, *see* Apocalypse Society, Inc., The
Henschel, Milton, *see* Jehovah's Witnesses
Hensley, Kirby J., *see* Universal Life
Hepetika, Rua Kenana, *see* Church of Te Kooti Rikirangi
Hepker, George H., *see* Church of Apostolic Faith of Africa
Herrigel, Wilhelm, *see* Bahai World Union
Herven, John and Dawn, *see* Jesus People U.S.A.
Hewavitarne, D.H., *see* Maha-Bodhi Society
Hickerson, John, *see* Church of the Living God
Hicks, Elias, *see* Hicksite Friends
Hieronimus, Robert, *see* Savitria
Higgins, Edward, *see* Salvation Army, The
Higgins, Melvin, *see* Temple of Kriya Yoga
Higgins, Paul, *see* Spiritual Frontiers Fellowship
Hills, Christopher, *see* University of the Trees
Hine, Edward, *see* British Israelism
Hinkins, John-Roger, *see* Movement of Spiritual Inner Awareness
Hinkins, Roger Delano, *see* Movement of Spiritual Inner Awareness

471

Hinsch, Coraly, *see* Église Evangelique
  Hinchiste
Hirsh, R.H., *see* Pastoral Bible Institute
Hitesehiji, Swami Vishva, *see* Shri Ràm
  Chandra Mission
Hlongwane, J. Mdelwa, *see* Bantu Methodist
  Church
Hodge, James, *see* United Leadership
  Council of Hebrew Israelites
Hodgson, Richard, *see* Theosophy
Hodur, Francis, *see* Polish National Catholic
  Church
Hoefle, John J.
  see Epiphany Bible Students Association
  see Laodicean Home Missionary
    Movement
Hoffman, Bernard Lazar, *see* Alamo
  Christian Foundation
Hoffman, Christopher, *see*
  Templegesellschaft
Hoffman, Wilhelm, *see* Templegesellschaft
Holloway, Gilbert N., *see* New Age Church
  of Truth
Holly, Bob, *see* Faith Bible Chapel
Holmes, Ernest
  see New Thought
  see Religious Science International
  see United Church of Religious Science
Holstine, Henry, *see* Neverdies
Hopkins, Emma Curtis
  see Home of Truth Movement
  see Hopkins Association, Emma C.
  see Joy Farm
  see New Thought
  see Unity School of Christianity
Horn, Edith Opal, *see* Alamo Christian
  Foundation
Horner, Jack, *see* Dianlogy and Eductivism
Horner, Ralph G., *see* Standard Church of
  America
Horowitz, David, *see* United Israel World
  Union
Hoskins, I.F., *see* Pastoral Bible Institute
Houston, Jean, *see* Dromenon
Houteff, Florence
  see Branch Seventh Day Adventists
  see Davidian Seventh-Day Adventist
    Association
Houteff, Victor T.

  see Branch Seventh Day Adventists
  see Davidian Seventh-Day Adventist
    Association
Howard, Luther S., *see* Pentecostal Church
  of Zion
Howell, Leonard, *see* Rastafarians
Howell, Rachel, *see* Branch Seventh Day
  Adventists
Howell, Vernon Wayne, *see* Branch Seventh
  Day Adventists
Hubbard, L. Ron
  see Dianlogy and Eductivism
  see Scientology
Hudson, A.D., *see* Bible Fellowship Union
Hughes, Thomas I.C.
  see Advent Sabbath Church
  see Unification Association of Christian
    Sabbath Keepers
Hull, Fritz and Vivian, *see* Chinook
  Community
Humbard, Rex, Jr., *see* Cathedral of
  Tomorrow
Hunt, Perry, *see* Latter Rain Movement
Hunter, Neva Dell, *see* Quimby Center
Huntley, Clyde M., *see* True Light Church
  of Christ
Hurley, George Willie, *see* Universal Hagar
  Spiritual Church
Hurtienne, E.A., *see* Etherian Religious
  Society of Universal Brotherhood
Hutchinson, W.O., *see* Apostolic Faith
  Church
Huxley, Aldous, *see* Vedanta Society
Hyman, Barry I., *see* Christian
  Revolutionary Brotherhood
Hymers, Robert Leslie, *see* Fundamentalist
  Army, The

I

Ichazo, Oscar, *see* Arica Institute
Ike, Reverend, *see* United Church and
  Science of Living Institute
Ikeda, Daisaku, *see* Soka Gakkai Society
Inai, Jun, *see* Jesu-No-Mitama-Kyokai
Inayati, Himayat, *see* Healing Order of the
  Sufi Order
Inesse, Daniel, *see* Tayu Fellowship
Ingram, Catherine, *see* Insight Meditation
  Society

K

Kago, Willy "Nganga", *see* Church of Apostolic Faith of Africa

Kailashnananda, Swami, *see* Yogi Gupta Ashram, Inc.

Kalo, Sclomo, *see* Da'at

Kalzang, Tulku Lama Geshe Ngawang, *see* Arya Maitreya Mandala

Kamwana, Elliot
  see Watch Tower Movement
  see Watchman Healing Mission

Kanada, Tokumitsu
  see Perfect Liberty Kyodan
  see Shinto-Tokumitsu-Kyo

Kanjele, Leviticus, *see* Watchtower Movement

Kaplan, Mordecai M., *see* Reconstructionism

Kapoustin, Sergei, *see* Doukhobors

Kardec, Allan, *see* Kardecism

Karmapa, Gyalwa, *see* Karma Triyana Dharmachakra

Karras, Mark, *see* Universal Shrine of Divine Guidance

Karsleigh, Zelrun, *see* Universarium Foundation

Kary, Hans, *see* Vedic Cultural Center

Kaseman, Jim, *see* Word of Faith Ministries

Kaunda, Kenneth, *see* Lumpa Church

Kawate, Bunjiro, *see* Konkokyo

Keech, Marian, *see* Association of Sananda and Sanat Kumara

Kess, Amy, *see* Church of Tzaddi

Kellner, Karl, *see* Ordo Templi Orientis

Kellogg, John Harvey, *see* Seventh-Day Adventist Church

Kelly, Clarence, *see* Society of St. Pius V

Kennedy, Aimee Elizabeth, *see* Foursquare Gospel, International Church of

Kent, Grady R., *see* Church of God (Jerusalem Acres), The

Keshavadas, Satguru Sant, *see* Temple of Cosmic Religion

Kettner, Frederick, *see* Biosophical Institute

Keyes, Laurel Elizabeth, *see* Order of Fransisters and Franbrothers

Kgantlapane, *see* Native Independent Congregational Church

Khalil, Phez, *see* Prosperos, The

Khalis, Hammas Abdul, *see* Hanafi Madh-Hab Center

Khambule, George, *see* Church of Christ, the Congregation of All Saints of South Africa

Khan, Hazrat Inayat, *see* Sufi Order in the West

Khan, Pir Vilayat Inayat
  see Abode of the Message, The
  see Sufi Order in the West

Khanna, Yogiraj Shri T.R., *see* Maha Yoga Ashram

Kieffer, Gene, *see* Kundalini Research Foundation

Kieninger, Richard, *see* Stelle Community

Kilgore, Marl, *see* Zion's Order of Sons of Levi

Killingsworth, Frank Russell, *see* Kodesh Church of Immanuel

Kim, Paik Moon, *see* Israel Soodo Won

Kimball, Spencer, *see* Mormons

Kimbangu, Simon, *see* Kimbanguist Movement

Kind, D.E., *see* New Beginnings

King, George, *see* Aetherius Society

King, His Emminence Sir George, *see* Aetherius Society

Kirkland, R. Lee
  see American Conference of Undenominated Churches
  see Independent Fundamental Churches of America

Klassen, Bernard "Ben", *see* Church of the Creator

Knight, Henry, *see* Beit Immanuel

Knoch, Adolph Ernst, *see* Concordant Publishing Concern

Knorr, Nathan Homer, *see* Jehovah's Witnesses

Kobran, Joel, *see* Margaret Fuller Corporation

Koch, Gerka, *see* Christian Research, Inc.

Kofsman, Ze'ev
  see Hebrew Christian Assembly-Jerusalem Congregation
  see Messianic Assembly of Israel

Kongo, Gedatsu, *see* Gedatsu-Kai

König, Karl, *see* Camphill Movement

Kony, Joseph, *see* Lord's Resistance Army

Linn, Bill, *see* New York Spiritual Center, Inc.

Linn, Renee, *see* New York Spiritual Center, Inc.

Lion, Edward, *see* Zion Apostolic Faith Mission

Lionza, Maria, *see* Maria Lionza

Little, Malcolm, *see* Nation of Islam

Litzman, Warren, *see* World Renewal, Inc.

Livraga, Jorge Angel, *see* New Acropolis

Lloyd, Sherman Russell, *see* LDS Scripture Researchers

Lochbaum, Ada, *see* Apostolic Faith

Lochbaum, Charles, *see* Apostolic Faith

Loden, David, *see* Beit Assaph

Loncontirth, Sadhu, *see* Atmaniketan Ashram

Long, Max Freedom, *see* Huna Research Associates

Lorrance, Arleen, *see* Love Project

Lovell, James A., *see* United Israel World Fellowship

Lowe, Hannah, *see* New Testament Missionary Fellowship

Lozowick, Lee, *see* Hohm

Lubusha, Alice Mulenga, *see* Lumpa Church

Lucas, Chuck, *see* Crossroads Churches of Christ

Luce, Gay, *see* Sage Community

Lueken, Veronica, *see* Our Lady of the Roses

Lynott, Jessica, *see* Yoga Institute of Consciousness

M

Mabilitsa, Paul, *see* Christian Apostolic Church in Zion

McAlister, Robert, *see* Church of the New Life

McCarroll, Tolbert, *see* Starcross Monastic Community

McClain, John, *see* Christ Center for Postive Living

McComb, Samuel, *see* Emmanuel Movement

McCormick, Peter, *see* Foundation Faith of God

Macedo, Edir, *see* Universal Church of the Kingdom of God

MacEwen, Anne, *see* Essene Network International

McGee, Ernest Timothy, *see* Hanafi Madh-Hab Center

McGuire, George Alexander, *see* African Orthodox Church

Machen, J. Gresham, *see* Orthodox Presbyterian Church

McIntire, Carl
  see Bible Presbyterian Church
  see Westminster Biblical Fellowship

McKean, Kip, *see* Boston Church of Christ

McLain, C.E., *see* Bible Churches

McLaughlin, Corinne, *see* Sirius Community

McNeff, Beverly Hutchinson, *see* Miracle Distribution Center

McPhail, M.L., *see* Christian Believers Conference

McPherson, "Sister" Aimee Semple, *see* Foursquare Gospel, International Church of

McQuaid, Elwook, *see* Friends of Israel Gospel Ministry

Maharaj, Deva, *see* Deva Foundation

Maharaj, Shri Ram Chandraji, *see* Shri Ram Chandra Mission

Maharaj, Soamiji, *see* Radhasoami Satsang

Maharaj, Vethathiri, *see* World Community Service

Maharaj Ji, Guru, *see* Divine Light Mission

Maharshi, Ramana, *see* Ramana Maharshi

Maharshi, Sri Bhagavan Ramana, *see* Arunachala Ashrama Bhagavan Sir Ramana Maharshi Center, Inc.

Mahdi, AI Imaam Issa AI Haadi AI, *see* Nubian Islamic Hebrews

Mahlangu, Elias, *see* Zion Apostolic Church of South Africa

Mahon, Edgar, *see* Mahon Mission of the Baptist Union of South Africa

Mahraj, Guru Devananda, *see* International Society of Divine Revelation

Makiguchi, Tsunesaburo, *see* Soka Gakkai Society

Makonnen, Ras Tafari, *see* Rastafarians

Malanda, Ta, *see* Mouvement Croix-Koma

Malicdan, Philip S., *see* Cultural Minorities Spiritual Fraternization Church of the Philippines

"Mama Alice", *see* Holy Spirit Movement

Man-Ho, Chang, *see* Mission for the Coming Days

Manalo, Felix, *see* Iglesia ni Christo Manalista, Inc.

Mann, Mildred, *see* Society of Pragmatic Mysticism

Mantley, Duane, *see* Knights Templar New Age Church

Manuel, Franco, *see* International Christian Churches

Maoz, Baruch, *see* Grace and Truth Christian Congregation

Mapah, Le, *see* Evadisme

Maranke, Johane, *see* African Apostolic Church of Johane Maranke

Marine, Frederick B., *see* Evangelical Bible Church

Marley, Robert Nesta, *see* Rastafarians

Marrs, R.F., *see* Church of God (Sabbatarian)

Marrs, Roy, *see* Church of God (Sabbatarian)

Martin, Dorothy, *see* Association of Sananda and Sanat Kumara

Martin, Dr. Ernest L., *see* Foundation for Biblical Research

Martin, Ralph, *see* Word of God

Martindale, L. Craig, *see* Way International, Inc., The

Martinus, *see* Martinus Institute of Spiritual Science

Martyn, T.H., *see* Independent Theosophical Society

Maryona, *see* Light of the Universe

Mason, C.H., *see* Church of Christ (Holiness) U.S.A.

Mason, Charles H., *see* Church of God in Christ

Masowe, Johannes, *see* Masowe Apostles

Masters, Robert, *see* Dromenon

Masters, Roy, *see* Foundation of Human Understanding

Mateo, Liborio, *see* Liborismo

Mathews, Robert Jay, *see* Order, The

Matrisciana, Pat, *see* Christian World Liberation Front

Matswa, Andre Grenard, *see* Matsouanism

Matthew, Wentworth Arthur, *see* Commandment Keepers Congregation of the Living God

Mattingly, Woods, *see* Seeker's Quest

Mayo, David
  see Advanced Ability Center; Adventists, Second
  see Duga

Meeker, Lloyd Arthur, *see* Emissaries of Divine Light

Meera, *see* Mother Meera

Meishu-sama, *see* Sekai Kyusei Kyo

Melchior, Roger, *see* Trois Saints Coeurs

Mendes, S. Pereira, *see* New Thought Synagogue

Meshiakyo, Sekai, *see* Sekai Kyusei Kyo

Metelica, Michael J., *see* Renaissance Church-Community

Meyer, A.M., *see* Hebrew Christian Alliance

Meyer, Ann Potter, *see* Teaching of the Inner Christ, Inc.

Meyer, Peter Victor, *see* Teaching of the Inner Christ, Inc.

Meyer, Jacob O., *see* Assemblies of Yahweh

Meyer, Masheikh Wali Ali, *see* Sufi Islamia Ruhaniat Society

Mgijima, Enoch, *see* "Israelites"

Mhlanga, Richard S., *see* National Swazi Native Apostolic Chruch of Africa

Miki, Tokuchika, *see* Perfect Liberty Kyodan

Miles, Robert E., *see* Mountain Church of Jesus Christ the Saviour

Militz, Annie Rix, *see* Home of Truth Movement

Millar, Robert G.
  see Covenant, the Sword, the Arm of the Lord, The
  see Elohim City

Miller, Harry, *see* People of the Living God

Miller, William
  see Advent Christian Church
  see Seventh-Day Adventist Church

Miranda, David Martins de, *see* "Envoy of the Messiah"

Mishra, Ramanurti, M.D., *see* Ananda Ashrama

Mishra, Rammurti Sriram, *see* Integral Center of Self-Abidance

Mitchell, Hulon, Jr., *see* Nation of Yahweh

Mlangeni, Josiah, *see* Zion Apostolic Swazi Church of South Africa

Mncina, B.P., *see* Swazi Christian Church in Zion of South Africa

"Mo", *see* Family, The

Mofokeng, Lucy S., *see* Holy Apostle Mission Church of South Africa

Mohan, Chandra, *see* Rajneesh Foundation International

Mohr, Gordon "Jack", *see* Crusade for Christ and Country

Mokone, Mangena M., *see* Ethiopian Catholic Church of South Africa

Momberume, Muchabaya, *see* African Apostolic Church of Johane Maranke

Monroe, Eugene Crosby, *see* Shiloh Trust

Montagu, Lily, *see* Liberal Judaism

Montandon, James A., *see* Church of Mercavah

Montefiore, Claude, *see* Liberal Judaism

Montgomery, G.H., *see* Defenders of the Christian Faith, Inc.

Montgomery, Mrs. Moore, *see* Sir Aurobindo International Center Foundation

Montt, Efrain Rios, *see* Church of the Complete Word

Moody, Dwight Lyman, *see* Moody Church

Moon, Sun Myung
    see Broad Sea Church
    see Israel Soodo Won
    see Unification Church

Moore, Robert, *see* Process, The Mora Victor Manuel, *see* Wesleyan Pentecostal Church

Morley, George, *see* Kosmon Movement

Morris, E.J., *see* Free Church of God in Christ

Morris, Samuel, *see* Father Jehovah

Morrison, Marvin, *see* Rosh Pina Congregation

Morton, John, *see* Movement of Spiritual Inner Awareness

Moses, Alfred Geiger, *see* Jewish Science, Society of

Moses, Brother, *see* Nation of Yahweh

Moshier, Bud and Carmen, *see* Today Church

Mother, *see* Church Universal and Triumphant

Mother Earth, *see* Earth People

Moyle, Olin, *see* Bible Student Examiner, The

Msibi, Titus M., *see* Congregational Catholic Apostolic Church in Zion of South Africa

Msimang, Joel, *see* Independent Methodist Church of South Africa

Mtanti, Job S., *see* Zion Free Church Impumalanga Gospel of South Africa

Mugonza, J.K., *see* Sserulanda Spiritual Planetary Community

Muhammad, Ali-, *see* Babism

Muhammad, Ashaari, *see* Al-Arqam

Muhammad, Elijah, *see* Nation of Islam

Muhammad, Herbert D., *see* Nation of Islam

Muhammad, Silas, *see* Nation of Islam (Silas Muhammad)

Muhammad, Waarith Deen, *see* Nation of Islam

Muhammad, Wallace Delaney, *see* Nation of Islam

Muhammad, Walli Farrad, *see* Nation of Islam

Mukpo, Osel, *see* Vajradhatu

Muktananda, Swami, *see* Shree Gurudev Rudrananda Yoga Ashram

Mull, Gregory, *see* Church Universal and Triumphant

Mullins, Daya, *see* Weg Der Mitte

Mulvin, Jerry, *see* Divine Science of Light and Sound, The

Mumford, Bob, *see* Christian Growth Ministries

Mundy, Jon, *see* Interfaith Fellowship

Muni, Yogeshwar, *see* Kayavarohan

Murai, Hideo, *see* Aum Shinrikyo

Murray, Arnold, *see* Shepherd's Chapel

Murray, Jacqueline, *see* Atlanteans

Murshida, *see* Sufism Reoriented, Inc.

Musey, George J.
    see Congregation of Mary the Immaculate Queen
    see Servants of the Sacred Heart of Jesus and Mary

Musser, Joseph, *see* Apostolic United Order

Mvuyana, Gardiner, *see* African Congregational Chruch

Mwana Lesa, *see* Kitawala

Odum, Salome Mamle, *see* United
  Christians Church
Officer, Samuel E., *see* Yahweh's Temple
"Ogamisama", *see* Tensho Kotai Jingu Kyo
Ogasawara, Koji, *see* Third Civilization
O'Hair, J.C., *see* Grace Gospel Fellowship
Oiler, Ted, *see* Neverdies
Okada, Mikichi
  see Johrei
  see Sekai Kyusei Kyo
Okawa, Ryuho, *see* Kofuku No Kagaku
Oke, Adeniran, *see* Ethiopian National
  Church, Nigeria
Olazabal, Francisco
  see Bethel Christian Temple
  see Concilio Olazabel de Iglesias Latino
  Americano
Olcott, Colonel Henry Steel
  see Maha-Bodhi Society
  see Theosophy
Olsen, Ivan E., *see* Berean Fundamental
  Churches
Olszewaski, Chester, *see* Chriszekial Elias
Ondeto, Simeon, *see* Maria Legio (of Africa)
O'Neil, H. Edwin and Lois, *see* Church of
  the Christian Spiritual Alliance
Onishi, Ajijiro, *see* Honmichi-Kyo
Orage, A.R., *see* Orage Group
Orimo, Nami, *see* Dai-Hizen-Kyo
Orr, Robertson, *see* Kingdom Fellowship
Ortiz, Juan Carlos, *see* Body of Christ
Osborn, Albert, *see* Salvation Army, The
Oschoffa, S.B.J., *see* Celestial Church of
  Christ
Oshitelu, Josiah O., *see* Aladura
Osho, *see* Rajneesh Foundation International
Otsuka, Kanichi, *see* Shinreikyo
Otto, A. Stuart, *see* Church of the Trinity
  (Invisible Ministry)
Ouspensky, Pyotr Demainovitch, *see*
  Gurdjieff Groups
Owalo, Johana, *see* Nomiya Luo Church
Ozman, Agnes, *see* Pentecostal

P
Paisley, Ian, *see* Free Presbyterian Church
  (Paisleyite)
Pak, Bo Hi, *see* Unification Church
Paliau, *see* Paliau Church

Pandurang, Atmaram, *see* Prarthana Samaj
Paramahamsa, Sivanarayana, *see* Bornhos
Paramahamsa, Sri Ramakrishna, *see*
  Ramakrishna Math and Mission
Paramahansa, Baba Muktananda, *see* Shanti
  Mandir Temple of Peace
Paramahansa, Swami Muktananda, *see* Syda
  Foundation
Paramahansa, Swami, *see* Ananda
  Ashrama
Paranjothi, Swami, *see* Temple of Universal
  Law
Paranjpe, Vasant, *see* Five Fold Path, The
Parchment, Samuel Richard, *see* Rosicrucian
  Anthroposophic League
Parham, Charles
  see Apostolic Faith Church (Kansas)
  see Pentecostal
Parker, Gerson, *see* Black Hebrews
Parker, Merle E., *see* American School of
  Mental Vivology
Parks, Carl and Sandra, *see* Voice of Elijah,
  Inc.
Parsons, Jack, *see* Church of Thelema
"Paterson", *see* Christ Brotherhood
Patterson, George, *see* Georgian Church,
  The
Paulk, Earl P., Jr., *see* Gospel Harvesters
  Evangelistic Association
Paulsen, Norman, *see* Builders, The
Peale, Norman Vincent, *see* Word of Life
  Church
Peartree, Jerome, *see* Temple of the Eternal
  Light, Inc.
Peebles, James M., *see* National Spiritualist
  Association of Churches
Pendergast, Mary, *see* University of
  Metaphysics
Pentland, John, *see* Gurdjieff Foundation
Penton, M. James, *see* Christian Fellowship
  International
Peraga, Juanita Garcia, *see* Mita
Percival, Harold M., *see* Word Foundation
Perkins, Jonathan Ellsworth, *see* Full Gospel
  Tabernacle
Perkins, Russell, *see* Saint Bani Ashram
Perralta, Victor Manuel, *see* Gnosis-Gnostic
  Association of Anthropology and
  Science

Perry, Troy D., *see* Universal Fellowship of Metropolitan Community Churches

Pestalozzi, Rudolph H., *see* Solar Cross Fellowship

Peterson, Duane, *see* International Christian Ministries

Pezzino, Rose, *see* Gospel Harvesters Evangelistic Association (Buffalo)

Phillips, J.G., *see* Holy Catholic Apostolic Church in Zion

Phillips, Magdalen Mabel, *see* Alpha and Omega Pentecostal Church of God of America, Inc.

Phillips, William Thomas, *see* Apostolic Overcoming Holy Church of God

Pierrakos, Eva, *see* Pathwork, The

Pike, Diana K., *see* Love Project

Pike, James A. and Diane, *see* Foundation of Religious Transition

Piller, Ken and Mona, *see* Aum Center for Self-Realization

Plummer, George Winslow, *see* Societas Rosicruciana in America

Ponticello, Tony, *see* California Miracles Center

Poole, Elijah, *see* Nation of Islam

Poonjaji, *see* Ramana Maharshi

Portal, Eugenio, *see* Basilio Scientific School

Poteat, Harrison W., *see* Church of God, the House of Prayer

Poulain, Pierre, *see* Église de la Sainte Famille

Prabhupada, A.C. Bhaktivedanta Swami, *see* International Society for Krishna Consciousness

Premananda, Swami, *see* Self-Revelation Church of Absolute Monism

Prince, Derek, *see* Christian Growth Ministries

Pritchard, Alfred, *see* Inner Powers Society

Priza, Jessica Lynott, *see* Yoga Institute of Consciousness

Probert, Mark and Irene, *see* Inner Circle Kethra E'da Foundation

Prophet, Elizabeth Clare (Wolf), *see* Church Universal and Triumphant

Prophet, Mark, *see* Church Universal and Triumphant

Prophet Cherry, *see* Church of God (Black Jews)

Prophet Jones, *see* Church of Universal Triumph/The Dominion of God

Pruter, Karl, *see* Christ Catholic Church

Pulkingham, W. Graham, *see* Church of the Redeemer Community

Purvis, Eldon D., *see* New Beginnings

Puryear, Anne and Herbert Bruce, *see* Logos World University Church

Q

Quimby, Phineas Parkhurst
  see Christian Science
  see New Thought

R

Radha, Swami Sivananda, *see* Yasodhara Ashram Society

Raël, *see* Raëlians

Railton, George, *see* Salvation Army, The

Rain Shine, *see* Etzba Elohim

Raj, Dada Lekh, *see* Brahma Kumaris

Rajneesh, Bhagwan Shree, *see* Rajneesh Foundation International

Ram, Tulsi, *see* Radhasoami Satsang

Rama, *see* Rama Seminars

Rama, Sri Swami, *see* Himalayan International Institute of Yoga Science and Philosophy

Rama, Swami, *see* Light of Yoga Society

Ramabai, Pandita, *see* Ramabahi Mukti Mission

Ramaiah, Yogi S.A.A., *see* International Babaji Kriya Yoga Sangam

Ramananda, Swami, *see* Swaminarayana

Rami, Chet, *see* Cherubim and Seraphim

Ramushus, T.M., *see* Bantu Methodist Church

Ranaghan, Kevin, *see* People of Praise

Rand, Howard B., *see* Anglo-Saxon Federation of America

Randolph, Pascal Beverly, *see* Fraternitas Rosae Crucis

Rapunzel, Michael, *see* Renaissance Church-Community

Ratana, Tahupotiki Wiremu, *see* Ratana Church

Rauf, Bulent, *see* Beshara Trust

Ravick, Margaret, *see* Koinonia Community

Rawat-Balyogeshwar, Pratap Singh, *see* Divine Light Mission

Read, Otis B.
  see Jappa Tabernacle
  see Open Bible Church

Rediger, B.E., *see* Fort Wayne Gospel Temple

Reghini, Arturo, *see* Associazione Pitagorica

Remey, Charles Mason, *see* Bahais Under the Hereditary Guardianship

Resch, Francis X., *see* Archdiocese of the Old Catholic Church in America

Reuben, Abihu, *see* Ethiopian Hebrews

Reyes, Benito F., *see* World Institute of Avasthology

Reynolds, Marion, *see* Independent Fundamentalist Bible Churches

Rhinehart, Keith Milton, *see* Aquarian Foundation

Rich, Thomas, *see* Vajradhatu

Richard, Mira, *see* Sri Aurobindo

Richard Brothers, *see* British Israelism

Richardson, John E., *see* Great School of the Masters

Rijckenborgh, J. Van, *see* Lectorium Rosicrucianum

Rikirangi, Te Kooti
  see Church of Te Kooti Rikirangi
  see Ringatu

Rinpoche, Akong, *see* Samye Ling

Rinpoche, Chogyam Trungpa, *see* Vajradhatu

Rinpoche, Dezhung, *see* Jetsun Sakya Center

Rinpoche, Ganden Tri, *see* Gelug-Pa

Rinpoche, His Holiness Dudjom, *see* Yeshe Nyingpo

Rinpoche, Jamgon Kongtrul, *see* Karma Kagyu Institute

Rinpoche, Jigdal Dagchen Sakya, *see* Sakya Tagchen Choling Center

Rinpoche, Kalu, *see* Kagyu Droden Kunchab

Rinpoche, Lama Kalu
  see Kagyu Kunkhyab Chuling
  see Kargyudpa Order

Rinpoche, Lama Thubtez Zopa, *see* Vajrapani Institute for Wisdom Culture

Rinpoche, Sogyal, *see* Rigpa

Rinpoche, Tarthang Tulku, *see* Nyingmapa Center

Rinpoche, Traleg, *see* Traleg Tulku

Rinpoche, Traleg Kyabgon, *see* Kagyu E-vam Buddhist Institute

Rinpoche, Tulku Kalou, *see* Kagyu Ling

Ritchie, A.I., *see* Pastoral Bible Institute

Ritchings, Edna Rose, *see* Father Divine Movement

Rittelmeyer, Friedrich, *see* Christian Community Church

Rivail, Hyppolyte Leon Denizard, *see* Kardecism

River, Samantha, *see* Reformed Congregation of the Goddess

Rizal, José
  see Iglesia Watawat Ng Lahi
  see "Rizalist"

Robb, Thomas Arthur, *see* Church of Jesus Christ, The

Robertson, Bill, *see* Ron's Organization

Roden, Ben, *see* Branch Seventh Day Adventists

Roden, George, *see* Branch Seventh Day Adventists

Roden, Lois, *see* Branch Seventh Day Adventists

Roerich, Nicholas, *see* Agni Yoga Society

Rolland, Romain, *see* Ramakrishna Math and Mission

Rosen, Moishe, *see* Jews for Jesus

Rosenberg, Roy A., *see* Temple of Universal Judaism

Rosenblum, Arthur, *see* Aquarian Research Foundation

Rosenfarb, Joseph, *see* Beth Messiah

Rosenkreutz, Christian, *see* Rosicrucians

Ross, Scott, *see* Love Inn

Rossner, John, *see* Spiritual Science Fellowship

Roux, Georges, *see* Temoins du Christ Revenu

Roy, Ram Mohan, *see* Brahma Samai

Roy, U Jeebon, *see* Seng Khasi

Rudolph, Albert (Rudi)
  see Nityananda Institute
  see Shree Gurudev Rudrananda Yoga Ashram

Rudrananda, Swami

White, Ellen G., *see* People's Christian
    Church
White, Ellen Gould, *see* Seventh-Day
    Adventist Church
White, Nelson H., *see* Light of Truth Church
White, Ruth, *see* Bahai World Union
Wierwille, Victor Paul, *see* Way
    International, Inc., The
Wilbur, John, *see* Hicksite Friends
Wilkerson, Clark, *see* Institue of Cosmic
    Wisdom
Wilkie, Herbert F., *see* American Catholic
    Church
Williams, Ben, *see* Lord's Covenant Church
Williams, Daniel Powell, *see* Apostolic
    Church
Williams, George M., *see* Soka Gakkai of
    America
Williams, Smallwood E., *see* Bible Way
    Church of Our Lord Jesus Christ
    World Wide
Williamson, A.E., *see* Christian Believers
    Conference
Williamson, Bernese, *see* Church of the
    Fuller Concept
Wilson, John, *see* British Israelism
Wimber, John, *see* Vineyard Christian
    Fellowship
Winkler, E. Arthur, *see* Congregational
    Church of Practical Theology
Winrod, Gerald B.
    see Church of Israel, The
    see Defenders of the Christian Faith, Inc.
    see Defenders of the Faith
Winrod, Gordon, *see* Church of Israel, The
Winter, J.A., *see* Lutheran Bapedi Church
Wise, Isaac Mayer, *see* Reform Judaism
Wittek, Gabrielle, *see* Universal Life
Wolcott, Louis Eugene, *see* Nation of Islam
    (Farrakhan)
Worcester, Elwood, *see* Emmanuel
    Movement
Wovenu, Charles Kobla Nutonuti, *see*
    Apostolowo fe Dedefia Habobo
Wright, Daniel, *see* Padanaram
Wright, J.D., *see* Pastoral Bible Institute
Wroe, John
    see Christian Israelites
    see New House of Israel

X
X, Malcolm, *see* Nation of Islam

Y
Yahweh, Yahweh ben, *see* Nation of
    Yahweh
Yaliwan, Matthias, *see* Yaliwan's Movement
Yarr, John Herbert, *see* Ishvara
Yeliwan, Matthias, *see* Yaliwan's Movement
Yeshe, Lama, *see* Lama Yeshe Movement
Yeshe, Lama Thubten, *see* Vajrapani
    Institute for Wisdom Culture
Yoakum, Finis E., *see* Christ Faith Mission
Yogananda, Paramahansa
    see Self-Realization Fellowship
    see Self-Revelation Church of Absolute
        Monism
    see Yogoda Satsanga Society
Yogi, Maharishi Mahesh, *see* Transcendental
    Meditation
Yogiji, Harbhajan Singh Khalsa, *see* Healthy,
    Happy, Holy Organization
Yoshikazu, Okada, *see* Mahikari
Young, Brigham
    see Mormons
    see Reorganized Church of Jesus Christ of
        Latter-Day Saints
Young, June, *see* Arising Sun IFO
Younghusband, Francis, *see* World
    Congress of Faiths
Yukteswar, Swami Sri, *see* Self-Realization
    Fellowship
Ywahoo, Dhyani, *see* Sunray Meditation
    Society

Z
Zain, C.C.
    see Brotherhood of Light
    see Church of Light
Zamora, Adolfo, *see* Union Catolica Trento
Zeiger, Robert S., *see* American Orthodox
    Catholic Church
Zell, Tim, *see* Church of All Worlds
Zenor, Richard, *see* Agasha Temple of
    Wisdom
Zidaru, Marian, *see* Noul Ierusalem
Zimmer, Hermann, *see* Bahai World Union
Zion, Daniel, *see* Netivyah